UPTON PARK
Memories

Edited by TONY McDONALD

First Published in December 2015 by

Football World

Tel: 01708 744 333

www.footballworld.co.uk

www.ex-hammers.com

©Copyright Football World

All rights reserved.

Without limiting the rights under copyright reserved above, no part of this publication may be reproduced, stored in or introduced into retrieval system, or transmitted, in any form or by any means (electronic, mechanical, photocopying, recording or otherwise) without the prior written permission of the copyright owner of this book.

Designed by William Clayton

Printed by Henry Ling Ltd

Distributed by Football World
103 Douglas Road, Hornchurch, Essex, RM11 1AW, England

Distribution email: susie@footballworld.co.uk

ISBN 978-0-9559340-9-4

CONTENTS

Acknowledgements 4	5 GREAT GOALS 202
Introduction 5	6 HIGHS & LOWS 216
History & Timeline 6	Programmes - Helliar Family History 230
Main Entrance 10	Programme illustrations 232
North 14	Home From Home - unusual programmes 250
South 22	Official Publications 251
East 30	Handbooks...256
West 38	Other Publications 258
Boleyn Ground From The Air 46	General Books 260
Inside Story 52	Fanzines 263
Training 58	7 FAVOURITE PLAYERS 264
Upton Park Firsts 66	Autographs 286
1 WHY WEST HAM UNITED? 70	8 CULT HEROES 292
2 ROUTINES & RITUALS 114	Collectables 304
It's Snow Time...132	Tickets 311
Some People Are On The Pitch 135	9 KITS 314
3 MEMORABLE MATCHES & MOMENTS 136	Home Kit illustrations 324
Special Guests 168	Talking Shop 336
Dancing In The Streets 170	10 MOVING ON 338
4 CHARACTERS 178	Forever Moore...360
Darkest Days 188	Ron & John 366
Winter Of Discontent 194	1904-2016: Boleyn Ground Poem.......................368
Banners 199	Final Words 370
Songs & Chants 200	Contributors 372

ACKNOWLEDGEMENTS

The first people to thank are the 200-plus supporters who have made this book possible. Your contributions and the magical memories they evoke are what makes West Ham United supporters so special.

I would also like to thank the following for giving up their time and being helpful. I've leaned heavily on several people who have always answered the call and given such huge practical support, especially Dan Francis, Steve Marsh (www.theyflysohigh.co.uk) and my wife Susie.

Tony Hogg and Terry Roper, two veteran Hammers authors in their own right, demonstrated their vast knowledge and proof-reading skills.

Special thanks and credit must go to Terry Connelly, who visited the Boleyn Ground on an almost daily basis throughout the redevelopment processes to photograph the ever changing Upton Park landscape. His impressive scrapbook collection has also been an invaluable resource.

Where would any of us scribblers be without the photos and images to illuminate the pages. 'A picture is worth a thousand words', right? So we must salute Steve Bacon, Arfa Griffiths (who took the front cover photo), Rob Newell (Digital South), Tony Furby, Richard Austin, Peter Marshall, Jack McDonald and Hilton Teper, plus others who supplied photographs, including Andy Halford, Dave Alexander, Darren Kenny, Gregg Robson, Paul Ford, Ric Kasta, and the contributors who sent in pictures with their copy. Sorry if we have been unable to use them all, for whatever reason, or have missed anybody out.

A big thank you also to Tim Crane, Steve Blowers and Roger Hillier for their input and help with images. Tim's poem at the end of the book encapsulates what the past 112 years have largely been about and is guaranteed to bring a lump to your throat.

INTRODUCTION

THIS book has been coming together for the past 10 years. Or, to be more accurate, 112 years in the making. It was during 2004-05, West Ham's 100th season at Upton Park, that we first circulated a questionnaire to supporters via the pages of our retro *EX* magazine. We received many replies but, for whatever reason, the proposed book, *West Ham United: 100 Years at The Boleyn*, never materialised.

But the great news is that we kept all the entries in a safe place and now, a decade on, they form part of this book, along with all the others who responded much more recently.

One of our original contributors, Gloucestershire-based George Hibbins, was 100-years-old when he sent in his handwritten entry by post. This proud centurion had attended his first game at Upton Park with his father in 1910 at the age of six, when the family ran a dairy in High Street North, East Ham.

George sadly passed away, aged 101, in 2005, but we are delighted that his family gave permission for his contribution to be included here. I was upset that my good friend, Ted Pardoe, died at 82, just before the book went to press. I know he would have been proud to see his name appear alongside all the many others, and so it does.

It is the legacies of George, Ted and countless others that we must preserve and the prime intention of *Upton Park Memories* is to do just that.

This is not a book on the definitive history of West Ham United – I didn't want to go heavy on facts and figures and get bogged down in the minutia offered by other books who specialise in such things and which are already out there. I want *UPM* to be a collection of human emotions, about the experiences of real people.

As you go through the evocative imagery and read the thoughts of ordinary folk and what supporting West Ham means to them, there will doubtless be moments when you laugh out loud and other times when sadness descends. Just like following our team, reading this book is an emotional rollercoaster, too.

Throughout these 372 pages you will hopefully learn a few things that you didn't know from others who have shared their personal anecdotes, opinions and memories with us.

Players who have an affinity with the club have reflected on their special moments as well. In most cases, their comments are taken from previous interviews given to me and my colleagues who write for *EX* and, for easy reference, they appear throughout the book in sky blue panels.

Authors who have written innumerable words about our club, including several of the most respected Hammers historians, also have a say. Their comments all appear in yellow panels.

Above all, whether you agree with what you read or not – and there are plenty of strong opinions voiced, especially when we get on to the emotive subject of the move to the Olympic Stadium, I want you to be entertained and absorbed by *UPM*.

It speaks volumes for Hammers' worldwide appeal that our 200-plus contributors come from far and wide. Not just east London, Essex and the length and breadth of Britain, but four different continents – Europe, Australia, USA and South Africa. From Canning Town to California, Barking to Bulawayo, Hornchurch to Hamburg, Aveley to Antwerp, Old Ford to Oslo, Forest Gate to the Falkland Islands, and way beyond.

But wherever we are from, no matter where we are heading, our cherished claret-and-blue heritage will stay with us, as if part of our DNA.

They can – and will – knock down the Boleyn Ground. But they cannot destroy our Upton Park memories.

I hope this books helps all of us to hang on to them.

Tony McDonald
Hornchurch, Essex
November, 2015

BOLEYN GROUND
History & Timeline

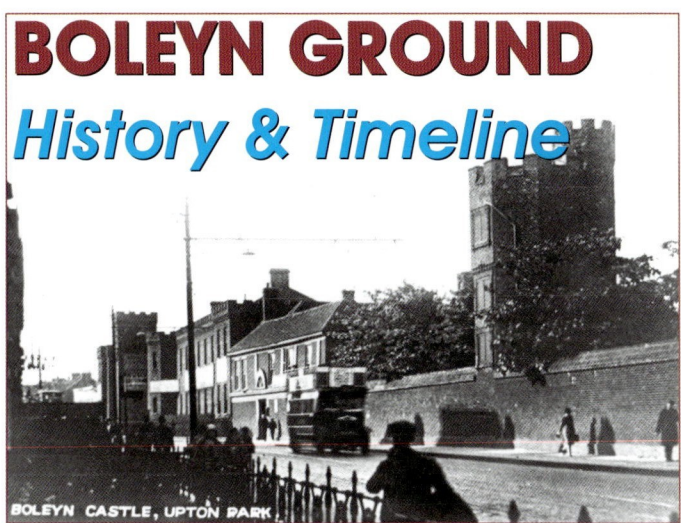

Boleyn Castle and Green Street in the early 1900s.

1904

SO how did West Ham United end up at the Boleyn Ground?

To cut a long story short, the 'Hammers' began life in 1895 as a local shipbuilding company's works team called Thames Ironworks who played their home matches at a ground in Hermit Road, Canning Town.

After being evicted from there in the autumn of 1896, they found a temporary base in Browning Road, East Ham in March 1897 but within a few months they relocated to a smart, new home at the multi-purpose Memorial Grounds in West Ham which had been funded by TIW's owner and football club chairman Arnold Hills. After keeping the club going for five years, philanthropist Hills cut his ties with the football club in 1900, at which point a limited company was formed and the club renamed West Ham United FC on July 5.

Some four years later, and with no sign of securing a lease to remain at the Memorial Grounds, where relations with the owners had soured, club secretary Syd King contacted one of the Brothers from the Roman Catholic reformatory school and an offer was made to the Catholic ecclesiastical authorities to move the football club to this location in Green Street, Upton Park.

Despite initial opposition from the Home Office, a deputation of football club directors arranged to meet influential MP Sir Ernest Gray, and thanks to his assistance and the acceptance of certain conditions, the deal went through.

In August 1904, Southern League Hammers secured their new home for the next 112 years!

The actual stadium was built on a plot of land next to, and in the grounds of, Green Street House, also known as 'The Castle', although talk that King Henry VIII entertained Anne Boleyn there before her execution in May 1536 is speculation not based on fact.

The field in which the pitch was to be laid was originally used to grow potatoes and cabbages and, as such, the pitch was often referred to by the locals as 'The Potato Field' or 'The Cabbage Patch', while the ground itself was originally named 'The Castle' during its initial 1904-05 season.

Pictures of the ground at that time show a two-tier seating accommodation along the west side with a standing area in front, plus covered banking on the opposite side backing onto Priory Road. A directors' box with press facilities was situated in the south-west corner and in the north-west corner were the changing rooms.

When it was first completed the Boleyn Ground had a capacity of 20,000, including 2,000 seats.

The first official pitch measurement was recorded as 112 yards (approx 102 metres) x 72 yards (approx 66m).

1913

The oldest and most dominating feature of the ground, the West Stand, was improved and at this point also incorporated the dressing rooms, with terracing in front.

1919

During 1919 £4,000 was spent on alterations and further stadium improvements. Most of the money went on moving the East Stand back to allow standing room for nine more rows of spectators.

The North Bank, originally an earthen mound with rough terracing, was also extended and raised following the addition of concrete steps in the early 20s. These developments boosted capacity to around 30,000.

1925

Profits from gaining promotion to the first division and reaching the FA Cup Final in 1923 enabled the club to rebuild the West Stand in 1925. The upper tier seats were split into blocks B (990 seats), C (1,210), D (880) and E (1,420, the latter being at the north end of the stand). Strangely, there was no A Block . . . but we'll come to that later!

At the same time, a new West Enclosure below the seats, comprising concrete steps, held 8,000 all standing. It was subsequently reduced to 7,000 when the front wall was set back prior to the start of the 1972-73 season.

The enlarged West Stand measured 352 feet (approx 321m) in length and, from the ground to the roof, stood 81 feet (approx 74m) high.

Another significant change this year saw the old roof from the West Stand transferred to the South Bank, where terracing held 9,400 – slightly less than the other end.

In later years, when segregation was introduced, away fans were housed in the south-west corner of the ground, overlooked by the police control box.

1944

In August 1944 a German V1 flying bomb landed on the south-west corner

UPTON PARK MEMORIES 7

How a WW2 bomb damaged the south-west corner (left) and blew the roof off the main stand.

of the pitch, destroying a large part of the South Bank terrace. The roof was blown off at that end of the ground as well as the main West Stand.

The resulting fire also gutted the club's offices and destroyed historical records and documents.

West Ham were forced to play 10 war-time matches away from home while repairs were carried out, before returning to Upton Park in December 1944.

But it was not until the 50s that West Ham was granted a licence to rebuild the damaged section of the ground.

1961

The North Bank terrace became the last part of the ground to have a roof. Before new safety guidelines were introduced following Lord Justice Taylor's report into the 1989 Hillsborough Stadium disaster, the standing capacity at this end of the Boleyn Ground was 11,070.

1965

Prior to the 1965-66 season, the club finally got around to adding an extra section – A Block, with 750 seats – to the south end of the West Stand, increasing seating capacity on that side of the ground to 5,250.

1968

Summer 1968 marked the end of an era. The popular single-tier covered terrace stand on the east side of the ground, made of timber and corrugated iron and affectionately known as the Chicken Run, where around 4,000 of the most vocal fans stood, was demolished to make way for a new two-tiered East Stand.

With its cantilever roof and costing £170,000, it measures 350 feet in length (approx 320m) and its roof is 50 feet (approx 45m) from ground level.

The East Terrace, with room for 3,300 standing on steps as high as eight inches, opened for the first division London derby v Queens Park Rangers (2/11/68). The action from Hammers' thrilling 4-3 victory was captured by ITV's *The Big Match* cameras perched on the new television gantry at the back of the then unfinished upper tier. The TV gantry was previously positioned in the centre of the West Stand, above the players' tunnel and between the upper and lower levels.

1969

Two months after the East Terrace opened, a maximum of 3,490 tip-up seats spread over 71 rows in the upper tier of the East Stand were used for the first time when Bristol City visited in the FA Cup 3rd round (4/1/69).

The overall capacity of the completed new stand, with family areas at each end, was now extended to 6,786.

1970

Prior to the 1970-71 season the club installed a completely new floodlighting system suitable for colour TV coverage. It would next be upgraded in the summer of 1988.

The crowd of 42,322 that saw West Ham draw 2-2 with Tottenham Hotspur (17/10/70) is accepted as the official record attendance for the Boleyn Ground.

However, a reported 43,528 attended the match v Charlton Athletic (18/4/36), although this cannot be officially confirmed due to the fact that club records were lost when the ground suffered severe damage during German air raids in World War Two.

1974

The north-east corner was rebuilt with a new refreshment bar added. There were already similar small sections of raised terracing in the north-west and south-east corners of the ground, although the closure of the north-west 'cage' in 1977 cut the overall North Bank capacity to 11,070.

1977

To comply with the Safety of Sports Ground Act 1975, capacity on the North Bank had to be cut from 11,070 to 8,580, while the South Bank limit came down from 9,400 to 7,000 as the ground readjusted to a new overall capacity of around 39,500 by the end of 1977-78.

1980

The lowest gate recorded for a competitive first team home match was for the European Cup Winners' Cup tie v Castilla of Spain (1/10/80). No supporters were allowed inside the stadium after UEFA decreed that, if played at Upton Park, the first round, 2nd leg had to be played behind closed doors, Hammers having rejected the option to switch the tie to Sunderland.

The European football federation's ruling followed crowd trouble that marred the 1st leg at the Bernabeu Stadium in Madrid, where one young West Ham fan died after being mown down by a coach and numerous others were injured, sparking banner tabloid headlines such as "You Scum", "Animals" and "Night of Shame".

Travelling Irons fans pointed the finger at the heavy-handed tactics of the Spanish riot police.

An eerie silence greeted the teams onto the field in E13 and there was barely a ripple of polite applause when David Cross scored a hat-trick and Geoff Pike and Paul Goddard added one each in a 5-1 home win that sealed a 6-4 aggregate success.

West Ham and some national newspapers declared the official attendance as 262.

But one national journalist contacted the club on the eve of the game and was told by club secretary Eddie Chapman that the gate would be restricted to the following 253 people:

70 West Ham representatives (11 players, five subs, training staff, club doctor and physio, official interpreter, four in charge of match arrangements and officials, two commercial office staff, directors, wives and guests, first team squad players).

3 FA observers, including secretary Ted Croker.
3 Spanish FA observers.
2 UEFA representatives.
1 standby linesman.
70 Castilla representatives.
16 ball-boys (the club provided six extra match balls to speed up the retrieval process).
50 reporters.
6 TV news cameramen.
2 radio commentators.
20 photographers. (including Tony Furby, who took these pictures).
10 policemen inside the ground.

One scribe who was in the press box to cover the game, Kevin Moseley, reckoned that about 1,000 Hammers fans waited patiently and peacefully outside the ground.

It was reported that West Ham produced 3,000 programmes to be distributed free on the night, with the rest going on sale to Supporters' Club members the next day.

1981

In the summer of 1981 the West Enclosure terrace, which accommodated around 7,000, was replaced by lower tier seating for 2,841.

1989

Embracing football's commercial age, the first executive seating area was introduced in the West Stand upper tier for members of the new 'Academy' lounge and restaurant facility.

1990

October: Disabled enclosure opens in the West Stand.

1993

For those who stood on the South Bank for the last time before its closure, it was a triumphant farewell. Clive Allen scored the goal at that end which clinched a 2-0 victory v Cambridge United (8/5/93) and promotion back to the top flight

1994

Named after the club's greatest ever player, who died of bowel cancer on the morning of February 24, 1993, the 4,000 lower tier seating section of the £5m Bobby Moore Stand opened at the southern end for the 3-3 draw v Norwich City (24/1/94). The two-tier stand was fully operational for the first time at the next home game, when Hammers drew 2-2 with Manchester United (26/2/94).

On March 7, 20,311 saw West Ham meet a Premiership XI in the Bobby Moore Memorial Match that marked the official opening of the stand. In a private ceremony earlier that evening, Stephanie Moore unveiled the bronze bust of her late husband – sculpted by Neale Andrew – in the stand's main reception area.

Once complete, the stand held 7,600 of the most passionate and vocal Hammers fans, as well as the club's administrative offices.

A crowd of 6,844 came to Upton Park to see a live 'beam-back' of the 1-0 FA Cup 5th round replay win at non-league Kidderminster Harriers on large TV screens. West Ham also sold more than 3,000 Kidderminster programmes.

The final league game of the 1993-94 season, v Southampton (7/5/94), carried huge historic significance in that it was the last time a competitive first team match was seen by standing spectators (Tony Gale's testimonial was played the next day). The 11,000 fans who entered the North Bank (8,500) and Chicken Run (2,500) terraces, in a sell-out crowd of 27,000, were offered the chance of free certificates to mark the special occasion.

1995

The £11.5m process of transforming Upton Park into an all-seater stadium was complete with the opening of the Centenary Stand – so named to mark 100 years since Thames Ironworks FC was formed – to replace the North Bank. Only the lower tier was in use for the visit of Ipswich Town on Boxing Day (26/12/94), before the official opening of the whole two-tier stand was performed by deputy leader of the Labour party, John Prescott, before the evening v Everton (13/2/95).

1998

During the summer of 1998 the club installed a new sound system and hot-air undersoil heating for the first time and at a cost of more than £1m.

2000

On Sunday, November 5 a plaque to honour the memory of Bobby Moore was unveiled outside Executive Box 6 in the Bobby Moore Stand by his widow, Stephanie. The special event marked the launch of a new scheme by the Heritage Foundation dedicated to commemorating the achievements of Britain's sporting heroes.

2001

End of an era . . . the visit of Southampton (5/5/01) for the final game of the 2000-01 season was the last to be played in front of the old West Stand before it is demolished that summer.

At the start of the 2001-02 season, the 7,000-capacity upper tier of the new Dr Martens Stand (formerly West Stand) was open for the visit of Leeds United (25/8/01). The lower tier seats were used for the first time when Spurs visited (24/11/01).

The giant, new 15,500-seater stand, including club offices, ticket office, shop and 74 executive boxes on two levels (prices ranging from £26,000 to £35k a season), completed the £35m redevelopment of the Boleyn Ground, increasing capacity from 26,000 to just over 35,000.

The Champions Collection area of the museum.

A break with tradition. From the start of season 2001-02, the West Ham manager (Glenn Roeder), his subs and physio, etc, occupied the dug-out to the right of the halfway line – the same side as the new home team dressing room.

The new-look main stand also includes the West Ham United Quality Hotel, featuring 72 rooms that converted from executive boxes to offer three-star facilities. The club was also granted a wedding licence, enabling couples to tie the knot in the home team dressing room (on non-match days), before celebrating their nuptials in one of the corporate lounges. A theme pub, The Ironworks Bar, was situated on the ground floor, adjacent to the main entrance.

2002

The Doc Marten's Stand was fully operational for the visit of Middlesbrough (23/2/02) and attracted a crowd of 35,420 – a new all-seater record for the club. It was officially opened by HM The Queen on Thursday, May 9.

Although it was a relatively quiet summer at the stadium after two years of construction work, a major change saw the pitch moved 15m towards the Dr Marten's Stand, and widened to make it 66.75m wide by 100.5m long. The playing surface was also raised to comply with the Football Licensing Authority's legislation on sightlines. As it happened, some seats had to be removed from the Bobby Moore lower tier to comply with FLA rules.

The TV gantry also moved from the East Stand to the West Stand from the start of the 2002-03 season.

After huge outlay towards the purchase of unique football memorabilia, the West Ham United Museum – part of the West Stand redevelopment – opened its doors for the first time on August 24. Chairman Terence Brown said the project cost around £4m, with around £2m spent on 72 lots from the Bobby Moore collection auctioned by Christie's.

The focal point of the museum was the 'Champions Collection' of medals, caps, jerseys and other memorabilia won by three of Hammers' all-time greats, Moore, Geoff Hurst and Martin Peters, including the three World Cup winners' medals.

Sadly, the museum closed when Brown sold out to the Icelandics in 2006, although the club has all the items secured in storage with one of the main auction houses and it is to be hoped that at least some of these great items will one day go on display at the Olympic Stadium for future generations of supporters to enjoy.

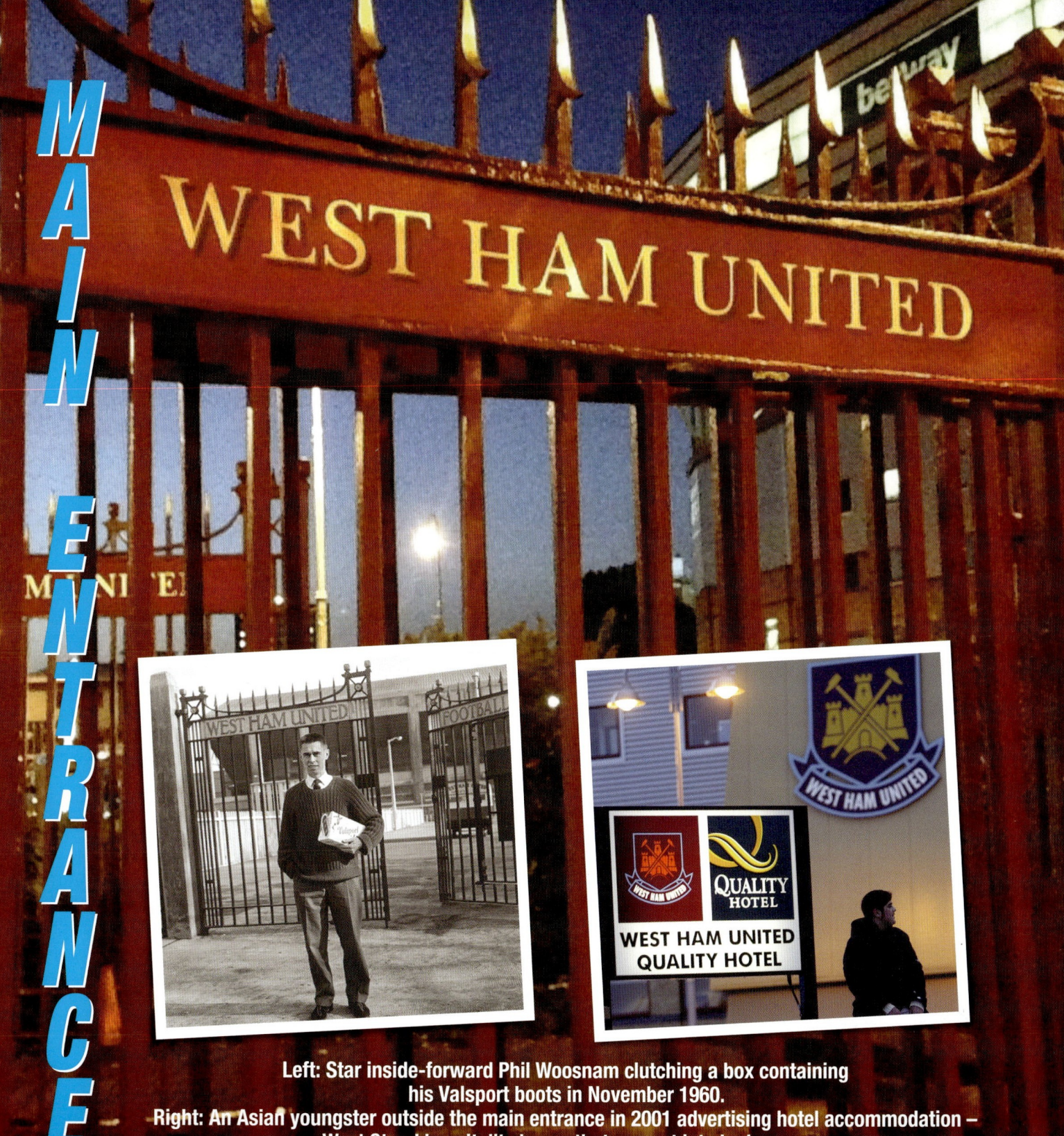

MAIN ENTRANCE

Left: Star inside-forward Phil Woosnam clutching a box containing his Valsport boots in November 1960.
Right: An Asian youngster outside the main entrance in 2001 advertising hotel accommodation – West Stand hospitality boxes that convert into bedrooms.

UPTON PARK MEMORIES 11

An early view of the main gates and West Stand turnstiles.
Below left: Early arrivals wait for the gates to open.
Below right: Is that 'Billy', the famous white horse of 1923, on crowd control duty again?

Top left: Closed circuit TV cameras in operation in March 1969.
Right: Queuing for tickets before the Manchester United game in January 1972, when the top-priced seat in the centre 'C' Block of the main West Stand cost 90p.

UPTON PARK MEMORIES 13

Fans queue to buy tickets for the 1976 European Cup Winners' Cup final v Anderlecht.

Sunshine greets fans strolling to a game in 1980.

Just a smattering of snow on the ground near the main gates but the game v Wolves in January 2010 was still cancelled for safety reasons.

The main entrance has turned into a car park on the eve of a 1982 game.

The illuminated main entrance and gates in 2015.

NORTH

A lone fan watches Ted Hufton minding the North Bank goal in 1921. The advertising hoardings were used after games to flatten the pitch.

The North Bank scoreboard in 1956.

Framework in place for the new roof in 1961.

Calm before the match day storm . . .

The original North Bank terrace was replaced by the two-tiered Centenary Stand when the ground was redeveloped in 1995. Re-named the Sir Trevor Brooking Stand in July 2009.

Terry McDonald: I stood on what was then the open North Bank to see my first game at Upton Park. My dad, Jim, took me when I was about seven or eight to see West Ham v Arsenal in around 1946. In those days you didn't see young supporters wearing hats, scarves or badges, just holding their claret-and-blue rattles.

When I left Harold Road school, which was just the other side of Upton Park station, and joined West Ham in the mid-50s, I saw at first-hand how the groundstaff looking after the pitch would take down some of the advertising hoardings at the back of the North Bank – the Bovril sign, for instance – and then drag the tin sheets across the pitch to smooth out the playing surface, which used to get very muddy in winter.

Sometimes even the players would help out. During the close season, a Leicester-based company laid a red ochre 'track' around all four edges of the pitch which was used for training. But before that happened, us boys had to dig an 18-inch trench where the foundations were laid.

Lo and behold, during one summer I saw Johnny Dick rolling the red ochre on the side of the pitch – he was getting paid by the lot from Leicester to do it. Imagine that happening today . . . the team's leading goalscorer working at the ground to make up the shortfall in his basic wage that was capped at £20 per week in the season.

Ted Pardoe: Although I stood on the North Bank as a kid with my dad, George, they didn't used to call it the North Bank or South Bank back then. It was always "This End" (nearest to Upton Park station), "That End" (South Bank), "Main Stand" or "Chicken Run". The only seats sold had to be pre-booked – you couldn't just queue up for one at the ground.

UPTON PARK MEMORIES 15

When the 'Gates Closed' sign went up before the Monday afternoon FA Cup tie v Hereford United in 1972, a group of fans found a high vantage point on the roof of the flats in Priory Court, at the North Bank end. Inset: Final steps... the North Bank empties for the last time, after the final home game of 1993-94.

The humour was unique and there were so many funny characters over there that every home game was like attending a Royal Variety Performance at the London Palladium. And the crowd never went quiet for even a minute, they would keep each other entertained for two or three hours.

Winters were always freezing in those days and though most of us wore jackets that didn't zip up, you never felt cold because everyone was packed in so tightly. Dad used to lean on the railings at the back and put me on his shoulders so that I could see but most young lads were passed over men's heads down towards the front.

All the men wore cloth caps and smoked cigarettes – Woodbines or Player's Weights. You would be engulfed by clouds of smoke. But for the games played on Christmas Day, men would dress up in their new check Sammy scarves and woollen Astrakhan gloves and smoke Wills Whiffs or Manikin cigars.

You rarely saw any women at football in the 40s and 50s but I recall one particular incident involving a pretty teenage girl. As she was passed down, some bloke grabbed her breast and I heard someone shout: "The dirty bastard grabbed her tit!" We all killed ourselves laughing!

Outside the ground, the two main peanut sellers, Bill Larkin and Percy Dalton, would compete for business. There were no hot dog or burger stands, just sellers with trays of peanuts. You'd eat three bags before you even reached the turnstiles.

Terry Connelly: I saw my first game from the North Bank on August 28, 1954 and continued to stand on that terrace until 1976, when I took a seat in the East Stand. When we played Wolves for the first home game back in the top flight in August 1958, I arrived at the ground at 12.30pm for the 7.30 kick-off and was the first boy onto the North Bank from the east side. I stood dead centre of goal, on the first step.

As the game drew nearer and the crowd grew, there was the incredible sight of boys being passed over people's heads down to the front and I

16 UPTON PARK MEMORIES

North Bank terrace from the West Stand lower in 1994, just before it was demolished to make way for the Centenary Stand.
Below: Sign of the times . . . in the wake of Hillsborough, clubs sent out more warning messages.

eventually ended up about 10 yards from the West Side corner flag. It was a fantastic experience.

My abiding memory between the age of eight and 30, will be the tremendous humour and goodwill that existed there. The cloth cap era was unique and I will never forget it.

In those days Bubbles was sung properly, with two verses, and everybody finished at the same time. We would watch the Chicken Run sway in time to the music and try to imitate them.

Great days. We will never see their like again.

Pete Tydeman: As with most of the youth in those days, I stood on the terraces of the North Bank. The choice being slightly dictated by the price. From memory, the earliest amount I remember paying was 1s 6d. (7.5 pence) – a lot to a young lad in those days.

We would enter the ground through the main gates, walk the short distance towards the old West Stand, turn left and wait in a long, curving queue until the turnstiles opened. I remember the anticipation. It was as though you were entering a temple. I was in awe. For some unknown reason I always felt privileged to be there. A feeling that I thought was not shared by supporters of other larger, more fashionable, London clubs when entering their own domains. We were a family.

Once inside, you were immediately faced with the steps taking you up to the entrance to that famous arena. The feeling of seeing the inside of the stadium and the Upton Park pitch as you reached the top of the stairs was fantastic. The North Bank seemed immense to me at that age.

The hooligan troubles aside, the era did throw up some very interesting characters and fashions. Very shiny Doc Marten's, Cherry Red

Viewed from the South Bank in May 1994.

The shelf in the north-west corner, which was closed for safety reasons in 1977.

Fans on the shelf, or 'Cage', in the north-east corner.

External view of the North Bank and East Stand from Priory Road in 1994.

Harringtons, Green Commando jackets with bright orange lining, jungle green trousers, Ben Sherman and Brutus check shirts, Levi jeans turned up to the top of your boots, with a very small turn-up showing, and braces.

On the smarter side, Lacoste cardigans, Fred Perry polo shirts, Bunter check trousers with tassel loafers, and the introduction of silk scarves that we initially tied round our wrists.

The North Bank was where 'the boys' met every other Saturday. Even if you were not with your mates, there was always someone to chew over the previous week's events, the happenings from our trip to last week's away game or the current strengths or weaknesses of the team.

As is always the case, at the time we never realised the greatness we were witnessing with players such as Hurst, Moore, Peters and the like.

Coming from Wembley (I got my allegiance from a family uncle who came from Ilford), the lads were invariably from the East End or Essex and, as such, were real London characters and had a humour to match. Some, because of their reputation as hard men, I was very wary of at first. But as you got to know them and they recognised you from away games, gradually they let you in. The feeling of belonging became stronger, which in turn cemented your own relationship as a fan of one of the greatest followings in the history of the game.

Your blood became claret-and-blue.

Gary Bush: I stood at the back of the North Bank terrace and the noise

Demolition of the North Bank terrace underway in May 1994, although the two exits into Priory Road are still intact, along with the 'Snack Attack' refreshment bar and shelf terracing in the north-east corner.

generated was terrific, absolutely deafening at times. The humour was also good and you could have a pint while watching the game. The bloke selling the peanuts should have been playing – I'd never seen such nifty footwork as he darted in and out through the crowd. Obviously the best part would come when the lads scored – everybody jumping up and down as one. Just brilliant.

Jack Fawbert: The North Bank with its special atmosphere – give me the 'ends' any time. They are always special places where the working-class (none of this middle-class neutrality from the grandstands) push and pull the game. And the North Bank had a 'magical' feel about it. I still go in the Centenary Stand lower. Can't break the habit of a lifetime.

Richard Bull: In the early 70s I watched from the caged area high up in the corner of the North Bank, next to the West Stand. I spent my early teens growing up with some real characters who regularly stood in the same area. In the 80s I moved to the centre of the North Bank, halfway up, where I could enjoy the atmosphere.

Ian Haywood: The humour and chanting in the North Bank had to be heard to be believed.

R. Austen: When a goal went in at the North Bank end the celebrations were mental, especially after a Ray Stewart penalty.

Mr P. Morgan: After seeing my first match from the West Enclosure I couldn't wait to be part of the vocal support of the North Bank and join in the occasional 'ole knees up'.

Gary Price: The corner of the North Bank (Chicken Run side), where loyal supporters always congregated. We were less critical than the intimidating Chicken Run!

Stuart Allen: My favourite part of the ground was always the North Bank. As I'm over six-foot tall, I never had a problem seeing – the atmosphere under that roof was magical. For some years I was a steward on the North Bank gates but I hated missing part of the game whenever

UPTON PARK MEMORIES

The main load-bearing upright supports for the Centenary Stand are in place.
Right: The north-east corner from Priory Road showing the floodlights still on the ground before being sited on the roof of the new stand.

Centenary Stand and East Stand from Priory Gardens in 2000.
Right: Newly-completed Centenary Stand turnstiles from the Green Street car park in 1995.

Right: View of the West Stand upper tier from the grounds of Priory Court after demolition of the North Bank. A small section of the north-west shelf remains.
Below: A longer-range view from Priory Gardens.

20 UPTON PARK MEMORIES

Above left: Centenary Stand lower tier seating in 1995.
Above right: The north-west corner in 1995. This pic shows temporary floodlights in position.

someone banged on the door and moved to the upper West.

Liam Collins: In the period between 1987-93, the old North Bank is where me and my friend, the late Tim Hall (who sadly died, aged 40, in 2003), always stood. We'd be about midway across, two thirds of the way up, just in front of the hardcore fans (the real hardcore were always up the other end in the South Stand). The banter and songs were great, evoking an atmosphere that was lost when the ground was redeveloped from the early 90s. They were great days, despite getting relegated twice, which did not seem to matter as much in those days.

Robert Wells: I would get to the ground as early as possible, sometimes before the gates opened, to get to the front of the North Bank and as close to the goal as possible, and drape my scarf over the wall.

I later switched to the South Bank, right in the centre at the back, where I could thump the corrugated wall in time to the chants being led by my foghorn-voiced mate Mickey Carmody.

I then moved to the West Enclosure, where there was the most atmosphere in the early 80s, graduating to the Chicken Run a few years later.

My first season ticket was in the old West Stand where, no matter where you sat, your view was somehow obscured by the support posts.

John Burton: In my early years, when I was young and not very tall, I stood in what used to be called the boys' pen, in the raised corner of the North Bank. The steps were large and you could get a great view of the whole pitch. The highlight was at ten-to-three, when you looked down to the left and saw the middle of the Chicken Run getting excited – they were the first people in the ground to see Paddy emerge from the tunnel with his arms raised, leading out the team.

John Reynolds: When I started going to games as a youngster, we always used to stand in the North Bank balcony above the corner flag. Being small, it was a great view. It was from there that I saw Geoff Hurst score six goals v Sunderland (19/10/68) and Pop Robson net on his debut v Forest (24/2/71)..

Siobhan Hattersley: I'm a season ticket holder in the front row of the Centenary Upper Stand. There's a great view but also it's the banter that goes on between the away supporters and West Ham fans in the corner of the East Stand.

UPTON PARK MEMORIES 21

Above left: North-west corner, 1996.
This shows how the Sir Trevor Brooking Stand, large screen and East Stand looked in the final season at Upton Park.

SOUTH

Castle Street circa 1905, a year after West Ham United move to the Boleyn Ground.

A young fan is carried to safety, away from the crush in 1955.

Testing the strength of the crush barriers in 1972.

The original South Bank terrace, accessed from Castle Street and Priory Road, was replaced by the two-tiered, all-seater Bobby Moore South Stand in early 1993.

From the North Bank looking towards the south-west corner.

John Pocklington: I used to line up at 12.00 noon and wait for the gates of the South Bank to open. I was always one of the first in. I'd go on my own from the age of 10, straight behind the goal.

John Goff: Throughout childhood and my early teens I was always the first person in the South Bank and climbed on to the wall in the middle behind the goal net. What a view for so many wonderful goals! I then spent many years at the very back of the North Bank, dead centre of the goal, being part of the wonderful choir and always going home totally hoarse.

John Walsh: It was May 1968, in the days of non-segregation, and we stood in the South Bank near a group of Everton supporters. It was a week before the FA Cup final when Everton played West Brom. I had two Cup final tickets that I wasn't going to use and asked if any of the Everton supporters were interested in buying them. I've never been so near to being kissed by

UPTON PARK MEMORIES 23

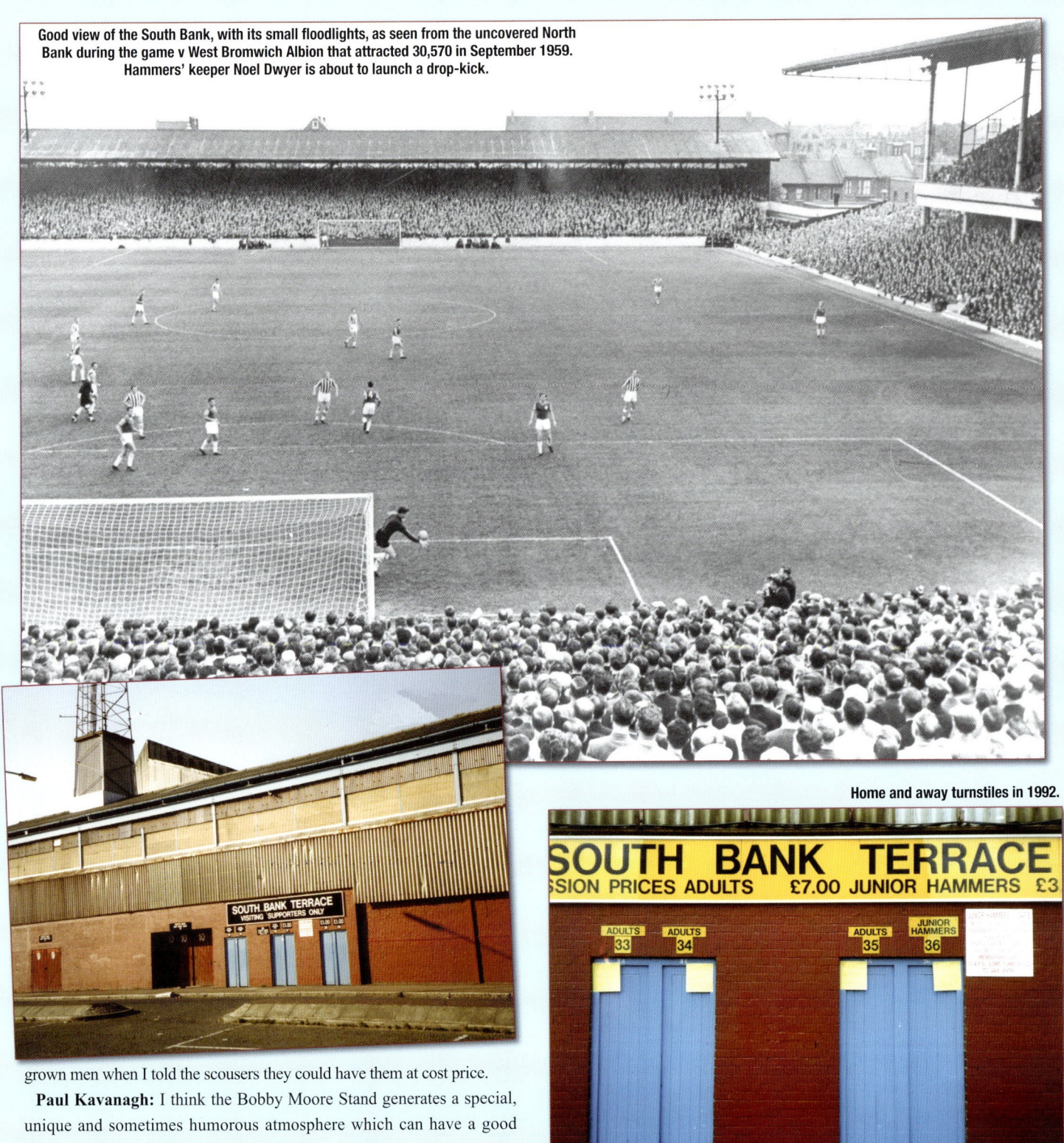

Good view of the South Bank, with its small floodlights, as seen from the uncovered North Bank during the game v West Bromwich Albion that attracted 30,570 in September 1959. Hammers' keeper Noel Dwyer is about to launch a drop-kick.

Home and away turnstiles in 1992.

grown men when I told the scousers they could have them at cost price.

Paul Kavanagh: I think the Bobby Moore Stand generates a special, unique and sometimes humorous atmosphere which can have a good effect on the rest of the stadium and also the players.

24 UPTON PARK MEMORIES

Tony McDonald: When I started going to games on my own from the age of about 11, you really had to be quick off the mark once you went through the turnstiles to secure a place on the big steps or, better still, pressed up against the barrier on one of the four 'ledges' located in each corner of the ground, about 10ft above the terracing. It was from the elevated north-west corner that I saw Pop Robson score a hat-trick in our 5-0 slaughter of Sheffield United in 1971. Health & Safety wouldn't allow it today but the view from up there was always special for us little 'uns.

In the late 60s and 70s, when very few games were all-ticket and you had the freedom to stand where you liked, I tried different parts of the ground. I leant on the front wall at both sides and ends of Upton Park but the South Bank was my favourite place.

You would look around and see smaller kids stood on six-inch high wooden boxes. And because you had secured your position down by the front soon after the turnstiles opened at 12.30-1.00pm, it meant a wait of up to two-and-half hours for kick-off. Luckily, the top of the wall surrounding the pitch at Upton Park used to be flat (painted claret) and wide enough to sit on. So you'd hoist yourself up onto the wall, with your legs dangling on the side of the terracing, and face the crowd, read the pocket-size programme and watch the gaps on the terraces fill up as 3.00pm approached.

You were so close to the players that you could

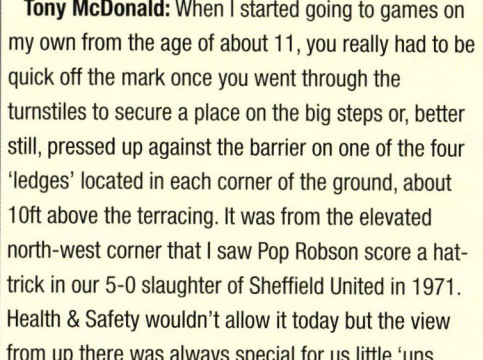

actually reach out and touch the goalkeeper whenever he went behind his goal to retrieve the ball, treading carefully to avoid tripping up on the bottom of the goal netting.

I liked the goal frames, with their unusual smaller arced stanchions, that West Ham used from season 1967-68 (QPR had a similar design). Because the distance between the goal-line and the net was barely more than one yard, followed by a further gap of just another yard to the perimeter wall, those standing at the front and right behind the goal had a great view. There was no finer sight than seeing that net bulging from a Hurst or Peters header.

Netting aficionados and historians out there (they must exist!) will recall the big gaps between the joins in the netting itself, which meant that bottles and other missiles could easily be thrown through the holes and endanger Bobby Ferguson (left) or the visiting No.1. In 1971-72, the club introduced much tighter netting in an attempt to foil the missile-throwers.

White netting was the colour of choice for most clubs in the 60s and 70s, before it became fashionable to adopt the club's main colours and then all kinds of horrible-looking stripy combinations were unleashed.

Call me old fashioned, but a Hurst humdinger always looked better than a Hartson header nestling against claret-and-blue netting, with no stanchion.

UPTON PARK MEMORIES 25

The main picture, taken in 1992, shows the three fences that were used to segregate rival fans on the terraces. The heavily sanded areas in front of the main stand and in the penalty area were par for the course before modern pitch technology.

Left: South-west corner from Castle Street.
Below: Almost ready to begin building the new stand in July 1993.
Right: A few defiant crush barriers await demolition.

26 UPTON PARK MEMORIES

View from Castle Street in 1996, with the Bobby Moore Stand towering above the Supporters' Club (right) and St. Edward's School (left). Inset: Viewed from a similar position pre-1993.

Left: Lower tier seating entrance in Priory Road.
Below: The Bobby Moore South Stand in 1996.

UPTON PARK MEMORIES 27

South-east corner viewed from Executive Box No.6, which was leased by Hammers News Magazine from the new stand's opening in 1994. Notice how much closer the East Stand was to the pitch in those days.

Rear view of the Bobby Moore South Stand and (right) the turnstile entrances in Priory Road in 2000.

28 UPTON PARK MEMORIES

View from Priory Road, with closed retail outlets in the foreground.

Staircase leading to lower tier seats.

Temporary dug-outs are in place for the home game v Leeds United in August 2001 before the new Dr Marten's West Stand was built.

Looking north from the lower tier during the Boxing Day game v Nottingham Forest in 2004.

The Bobby Moore lower in 2009.

The great man's name and number used to promote club merchandise.

UPTON PARK MEMORIES 29

The Bobby Moore bust awaits visitors to the South Stand reception.

EAST

Syd Puddefoot challenges the Crystal Palace keeper in January 1914.

Bomb damage wrecked part of the Chicken Run roof.

Action from the game v Arsenal in 1919.

Spurs' Ted Ditchburn punches clear in 1946.

The East Stand is the oldest section of the Boleyn Ground. The cantilever stand, initially with only one tier of seating above terracing, was built in the summer of 1968, although of course before then that side of the ground was famously known as the Chicken Run.

This small, wooden structure accommodated the most vocal and critical home supporters who were never slow to offer their opinions to players and officials within earshot on that side of the field.

It was the 4,000 or so cockney denizens of the Chicken Run who adopted the Hammers' theme tune and would sway in sync to the words as the strains of Bubbles floated across the air.

How great is it that this sentimental, old tradition has survived modern musical trends and is still sung with great gusto today by Hammers' fans of all ages.

William Lloyd: In the 50s, most supporters in the Chicken Run were mainly dock workers who were always cracking jokes and looking after us youngsters.

Terry McDonald: When I think of the old Chicken Run it brings back memories of my time as a youth team player in the late 50s, when our duties included sweeping out the stands. Johnny Smith and I would rake out endless peanut shells beneath the wooden terracing and find many half crowns and other coins buried among all the rubbish, even the occasional wristwatch that had fallen between the steps. We put all the money we found in a tin and divided it up between the young lads on the groundstaff at the end of the day.

The worst job was on Fridays, when we had to get out bottles of Jeyes fluid and clean out the toilets, which ran the length of the stand.

Many people smoked in those days and when you think that 'The Run' was virtually made of wood with a corrugated iron roof, it's amazing it never caught fire with all those discarded cigarette butts.

Ted Pardoe: After starting on the North Bank, I switched to the Chicken Run in the 50s. The steps – more like wooden sleepers – were a bit higher than those behind the goals, so it was a good place to watch from and the atmosphere was always terrific, too.

Danny Waller: You can't, and never will, beat watching games from the

Unusual view of the Chicken Run (left) in the late 50s and the old houses that ran along Priory Road.

back of the Chicken Run on the halfway line. Not just because 10 of us used to gather there and spend over an hour before the game putting the world to rights. You were close enough to hear players shouting at each other and they were close enough to hear the abuse being hurled at them!

Once the seats went in it took away the atmosphere. Now I sit in the Bobby Moore Stand and take my seat five minutes before kick-off – but it's not the same; no atmosphere.

Kevin Courtney: I used to love standing in the Chicken Run. I'd arrive there early and get as near as possible to the halfway line and lean on the wall. It was great - you were so close to the action and the banter between players and fans was comical.

Mark Sandell: It was the first place I went to and you felt you could trip players up when they came past. I remember a referee having a word with Bobby Moore and, amid much laughter around us, someone shouting out to the ref: "Do you realise who you're talking to?"

Heikki Silvennoinen: Before the all-seater stadium I used to stand in the East Terrace – good view and close to the players and playing surface.

Close-up of the Chicken Run shortly before it was knocked down in the summer of 1968.

UPTON PARK MEMORIES 33

East Stand under construction in the summer of 1968. By the time Hammers played Southampton on October 5 (Martin Peters and the grounded Trevor Brooking are in shot, right), the terracing was finished but seats had still to be installed on the upper tier.

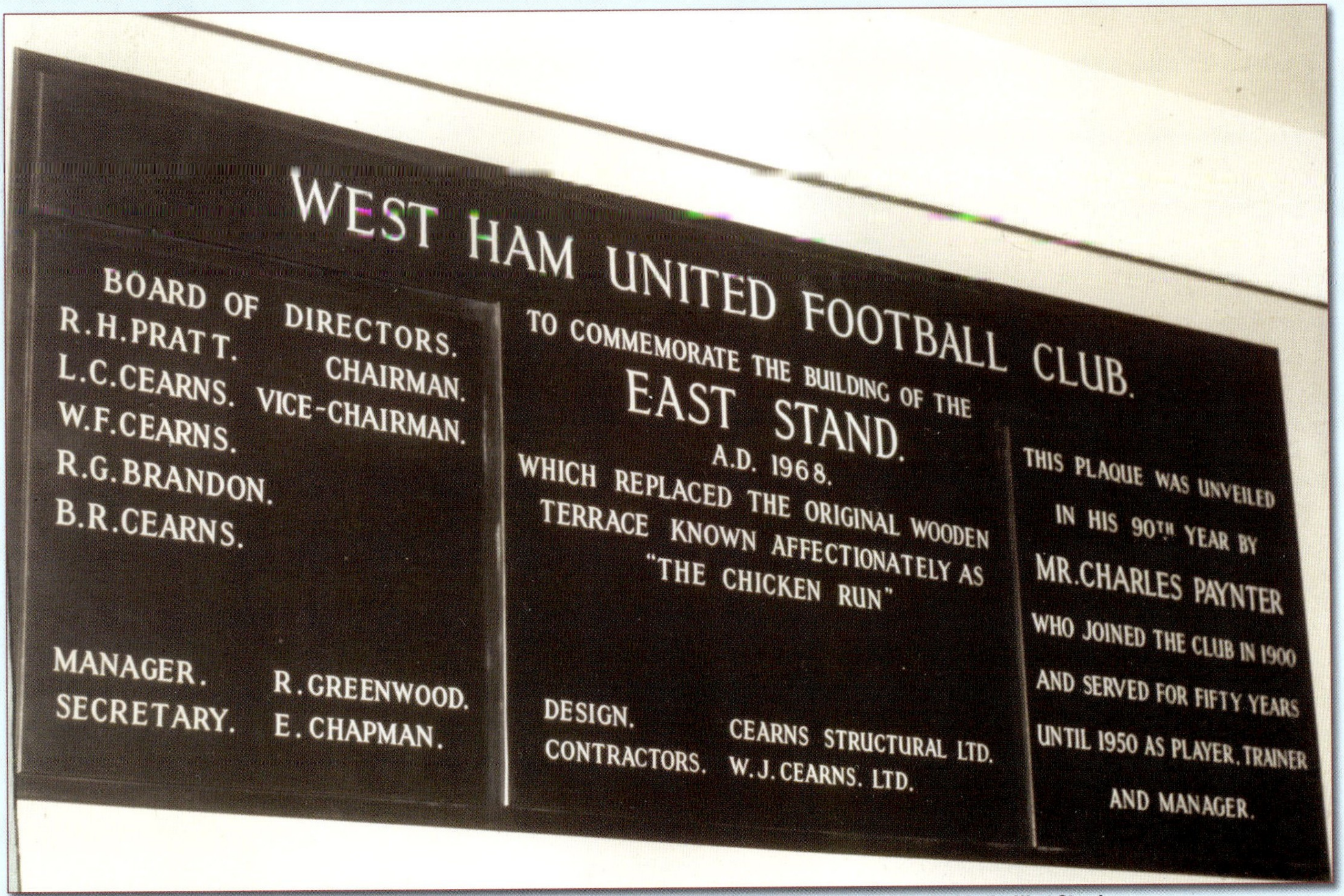

This large plaque to mark the opening of the East Stand by Charlie Paynter was actually sited in the West Stand.

All eyes on Harry Redknapp, a Chicken Run favourite, taking a corner in 1970. Some fans are shielding their eyes from the bright sunlight – a slight drawback of watching from that side of the ground.

UPTON PARK MEMORIES 35

In 1993 before the terracing was replaced by seats in the lower tier section. Although not part of the original design, crush barriers were installed following the Taylor Report into the 1989 Hillsborough disaster. The picture (below left) highlights how close the perimeter wall was to the original playing area.

East Stand and Centenary Stand turnstiles from Priory Road in 1996.

The stand showing the words 'DAGENHAM MOTORS' emblazoned across the bottom tier seats. The name of the club's main sponsor remained there until the 2006-07 season, despite the sponsorship from the Ford car company having ended in 1997. This stand is also the only one left at Upton Park to still have a small minority of wooden seats, in the middle of the upper tier. There were plans to build a new East Stand soon after the Dr. Marten's Stand was completed in 2001, which would have seen stadium capacity rise from 35,345 to around 40,500, but they were put on hold after a combination of resistance from the local residents in Priory Road and the club's relegation from the Premier League in 2003, which plunged the club into debt at the time.

From the south-west corner in 1996.

UPTON PARK MEMORIES 37

The big gap between the East Stand and playing area is evident in this shot taken from the back row of the Bobby Moore Stand at the opening game of the final 2015-16 season. Below: Big screen in the north-east corner confirming victory v Chelsea in October 2015.

The 'cut through' approach between flats in Seymour Road leading to Priory Road and the East Stand.

Coaches for away fans parked in Priory Road.

Cards – not tickets – are the way in these days.

WEST

A group of 50s players larking around in front of the West Enclosure before A block was added at the southern end of the stand in 1965.

Near completion of the roof above A Block.

The southern end of the West Stand, including the players' and directors' entrance, in the late 50s/early 60s.

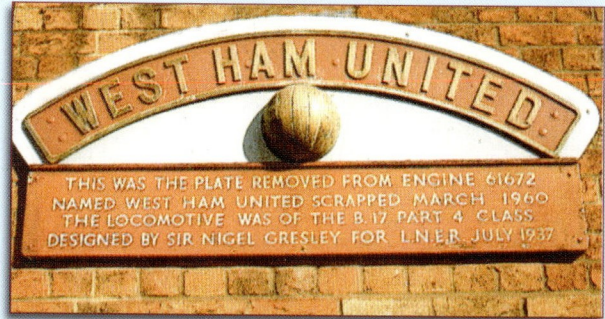

The inscription on this engine plate (which used to be displayed next to the main entrance), read: 'This was the plate removed from Engine 61672 West Ham United scrapped March 1960. The locomotive was of the B.17 Part 4 Class designed by Sir Nigel Gresley for L.N.E.R. July 1937'.

For many years before the term 'naming rights' was introduced by football clubs to further boost their profits, the original West Stand at Upton Park was simply known as the main stand – by far the biggest of the four structures and the only place where you could sit and watch games until the East Stand was built in 1968.

The last of the stands to be redeveloped, it was known as the Dr Marten's Stand – after the club's main sponsor – when it reopened in 2001. After that deal ended in 2009, it reverted to being the West Stand, before becoming the Alpari Stand in 2011 and, finally, the Betway Stand.

It includes two tiers for home supporters, separated by two tiers of executive boxes. The stand also hosts the club's offices, boardroom, corporate lounges, dressing rooms, Stadium Store and the West Ham United Hotel.

The stand's main feature is seen from the exterior of the stadium, either side of the glass-fronted main entrance, where two large turrets were built onto the stand with the club crest embedded on both.

Main turnstile entrance for the upper tier in the late 90s.

UPTON PARK MEMORIES 39

Young Sam Blowers in main reception.

Rear of turnstiles and steps leading to concourse at south-west end.

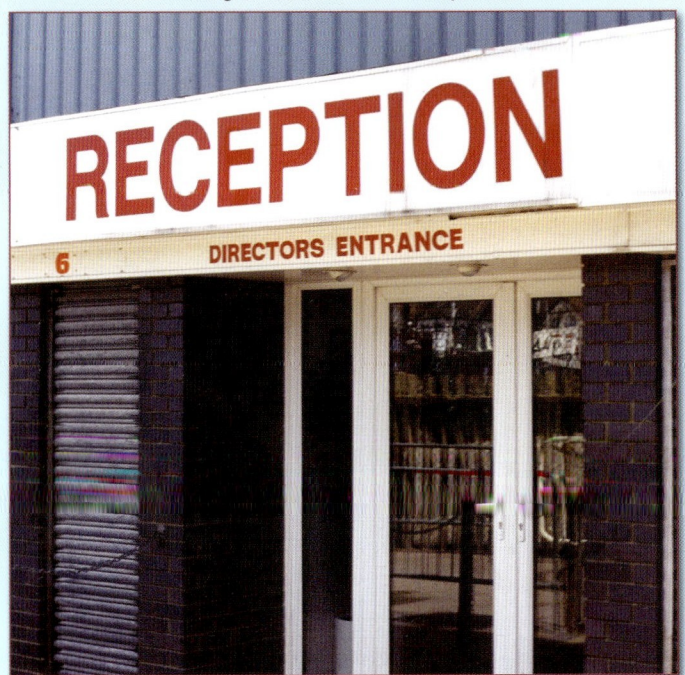

View from the Bobby Moore lower, with the disabled section bottom left.

Steps leading to the West Stand concourse at the north-west end.

View of the lower West seating, with police control room in the foreground and North Bank in the distance.

40 UPTON PARK MEMORIES

Disabled area.

The original wooden seats before they were replaced by plastic.

Players' tunnel in 1993.

Two legends had refreshment bars named after them.

From the back of the press box in 1993.

UPTON PARK MEMORIES 41

Fall and rise of the millennium new-look. An orange crane signals the imminent demise of the portakabin souvenir shop.

The new West Stand was constructed behind the old one.

With all seats removed, the top of the new roof emerges above the old stand.

As if a bomb had hit it, the old stand is on the brink of demolition.

A staircase still visible amid the crumbling debris.

42 UPTON PARK MEMORIES

Alan Shearer leads out Newcastle United across a building site before the start of the second half of the game on September 23, 2001.

Out with the old, in with the new . . .

Only the corners of the Dr Marten's Stand had yet to be completed.

Almost a claret-and-blue sky as Fulham attack during the game on November 3, 2001.

Directors' suite and lounges overlooking the main entrance.

WEST HAM UNITED
betway
official technical kit supplier
DIUM STORE

Final frontier . . . how the entrance to the main stand looked during the final season. Inset: This was also the way in to the Ironworks Bar and hotel.

46 UPTON PARK MEMORIES

BOLEYN GROUND BY AIR

The two photos on this page show two different views of the Boleyn Ground before and during construction of the additional 'A' Block at the southern end of the main West Stand in the summer of 1965.

A match scene from the 1965-66 season, taken from above the corrugated iron roof of the Chicken Run, with the new section of roofing in place above the upper tier seating in 'A' Block of the West Stand and the extended West Enclosure terrace.

On top of the world: Bobby Moore photographed from one of the blocks of flats that flank Priory Road, overlooking the East Stand.

48 UPTON PARK MEMORIES

UPTON PARK MEMORIES   49

50 UPTON PARK MEMORIES

End game: How Hammers' spiritual home looks in 2015-16.

INSIDE STORY
Going behind the scenes . . .

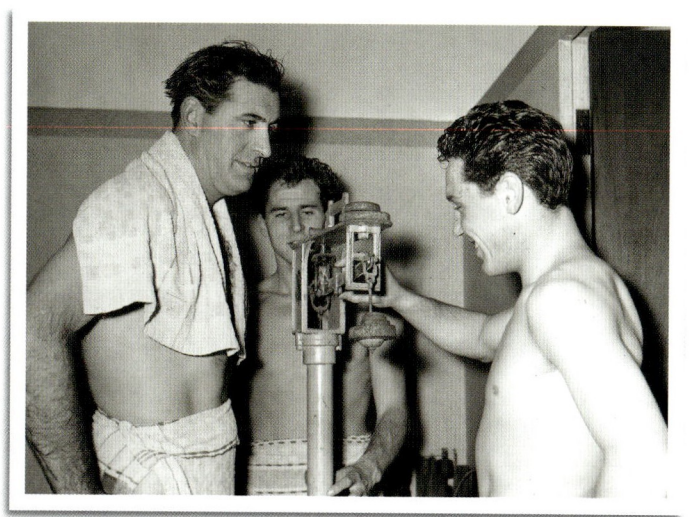

A warm moment between manager Charlie Paynter and skipper Dickie Walker.

Ernie Gregory (lerft) on the weighing scales watched by Bill Lansdowne and Eddie Lewis (right).

With promotion secured in 1981, Paul Brush, Ray Stewart, David Cross and Frank Lampard begin the bath-time celebrations.

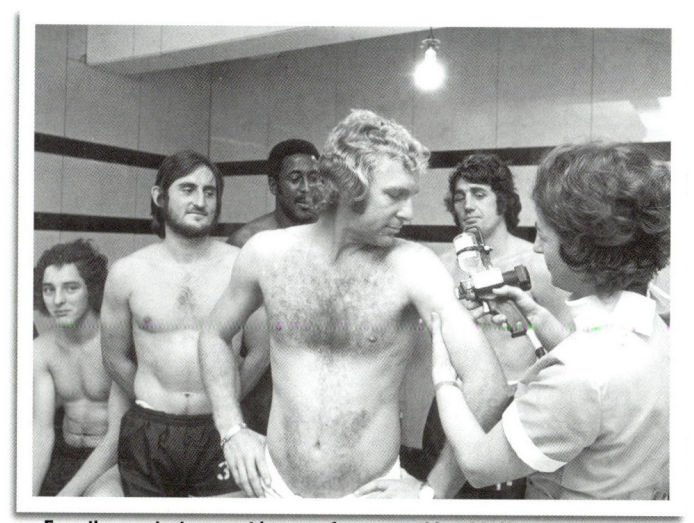

George Sales hard at work in the Upton Park bootroom.

Even the greatest was not immune from everything. It's November 1972 as Bobby Moore receives a flu-jab from nurse Jeanette Welanyk, while John McDowell, Frank Lampard, Clyde Best and Bobby Ferguson look on in trepidation.

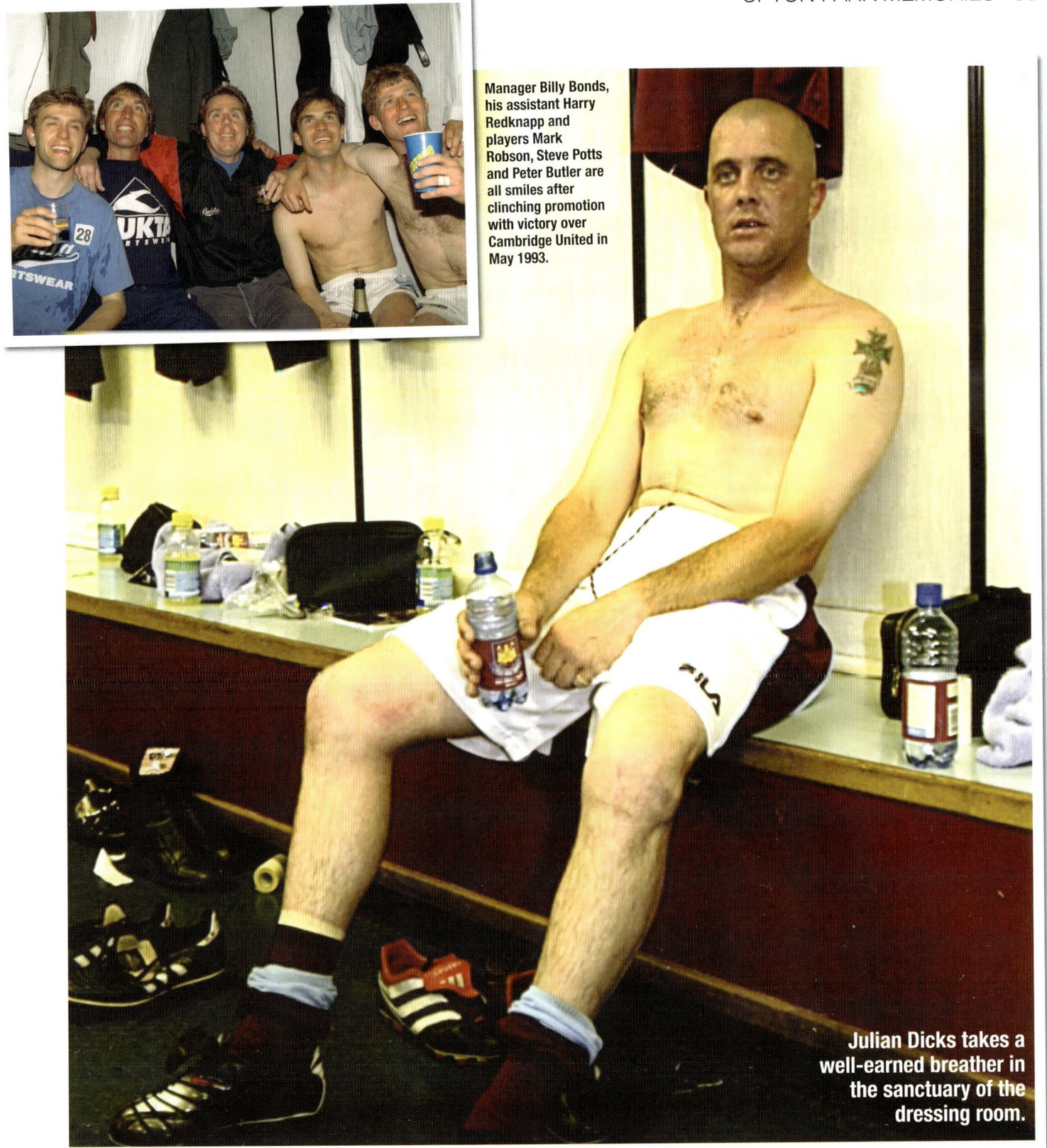

UPTON PARK MEMORIES 53

Manager Billy Bonds, his assistant Harry Redknapp and players Mark Robson, Steve Potts and Peter Butler are all smiles after clinching promotion with victory over Cambridge United in May 1993.

Julian Dicks takes a well-earned breather in the sanctuary of the dressing room.

54 UPTON PARK MEMORIES

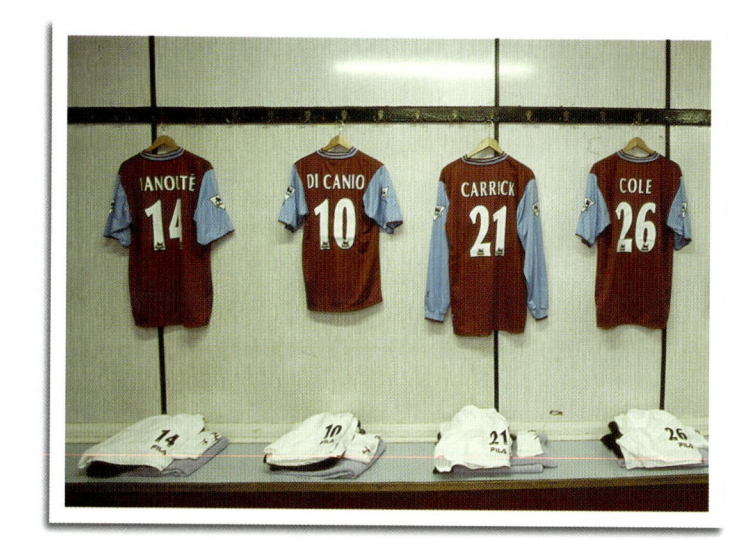

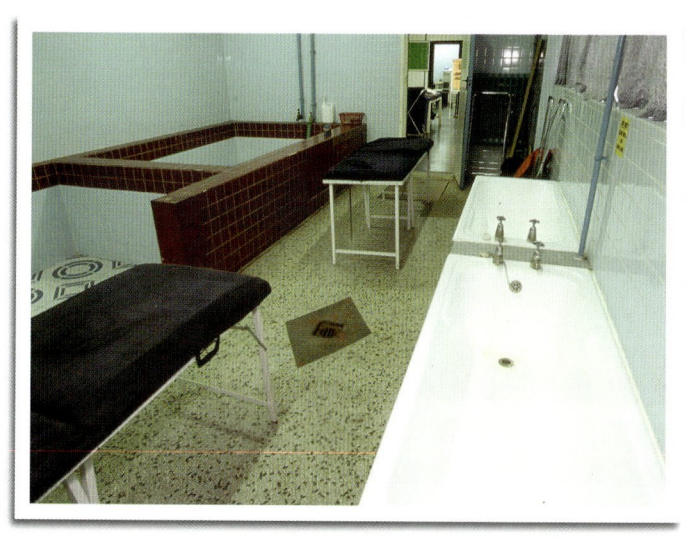

All quiet in the original home dressing room before a game during the 2001-02 season.

UPTON PARK MEMORIES 55

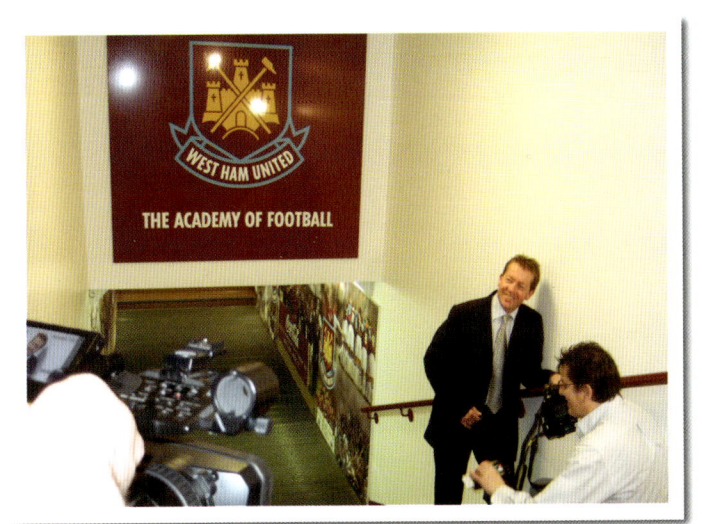

Alan Curbishley obliges photographers after being appointed manager in December 2006.

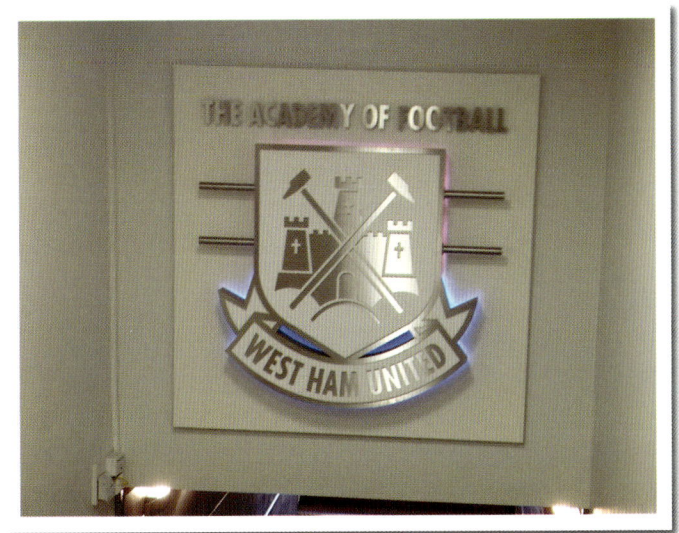

How the players' tunnel area looked in April 2015.

56 UPTON PARK MEMORIES

How the home team dressing room looked at the start of the last season at the Boleyn Ground.

WINNING ITS WHAT WE ARE HERE FOR

UPTON PARK MEMORIES 57

TRAINING

FOR most of the club's 112 years at Upton Park, West Ham's players trained away from the main ground – at Grange Farm, Chigwell and, since the mid-60s, at Chadwell Heath, where the building of an indoor gymnasium and ball court in the early 80s has provided adequate, if not state-of-the-art, facilities. But from time to time, the team also trained at the Boleyn Ground . . .

Enjoying a cuppa during a break in training on the old field in front of the Boleyn Ground are Vic Watson, Walter Pollard, Tommy Yews and Jimmy Ruffell. We reckon this was probably taken during the 1929-30 season.

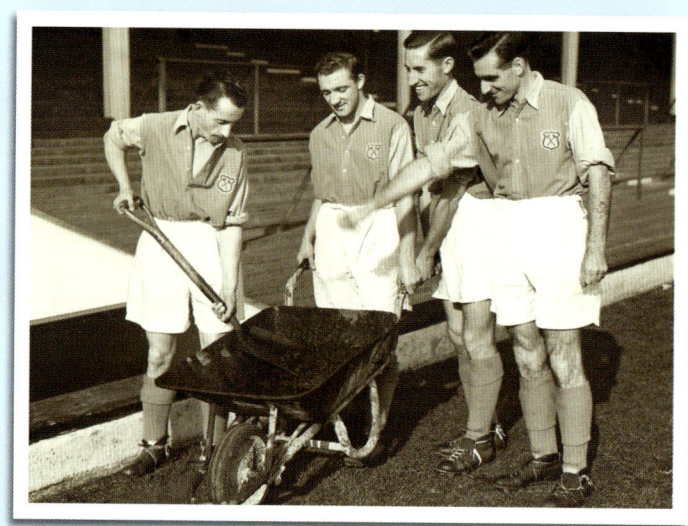

These two pictures from 1910-11, with Robert Fairman and Tommy Randall prominent, were clearly taken before the North Bank terraces were built.

Although players didn't earn much in the early 50s, Tommy Southren surely wasn't on a bonus to lay red ochre around the pitch! At least Jim Barrett jnr, Frank O'Farrell and Fred Kearns seem willing to lend a hand.

UPTON PARK MEMORIES 59

Pre-season sprints didn't get any easier at the Boleyn Ground. Left to right: Eric Armstrong, Bill Nelson, Noel Cantwell, Jimmy Andrews and Dave Sexton.

Trainer Bill Robinson demonstrating the art of ball control to young pro's of the late 50s George Fenn, John Lyall, Terry McDonald, Malcolm Pyke and John Smith.

Tommy Southren, Jimmy Andrews, Jim Barrett jnr, Harry Kinsell and George Wright.

More stars of the early 50s, Left to right: Harry Hooper, Dave Sexton, Tommy Dixon, Johnny Dick and Ken Tucker.

Never a 'tracksuit manager', Ted Fenton still makes his point to (left to right) Mike Grice, Malcolm Musgrove, Ernie Gregory, Ken Brown, Harry Obeney, Andy Malcolm and skipper Noel Cantwell.

Years before the modern indoor gym at Chadwell Heath was built, players used the gym beneath the West Stand for various physical activities. Here Billy Dare and John Bond are having fun on a trampoline, watched by manager Ted Fenton and his players, including Ken Brown, Malcolm Musgrove and Phil Woosnam. Fenton believed the trampoline helped his players to build leg muscle strength and improve balance.

UPTON PARK MEMORIES 61

Pumping Iron: Diminutive 50s striker Billy Dare building himself up with the use of weights – one of the innovative additions to the West Ham training regime in the 50s.

Ted Fenton brought in weightlifting champion Bill Watson (far right) to oversee weight training. Here he keeps a watchful eye on Phil Woosnam and Harry Obeney, with Brian Rhodes and Ken Brown behind them.

Flying Budgie: Johnny Byrne vaults a couple of wooden chairs, while Martin Peters, Joe Kirkup, Alan Sealey, Ron Boyce and Tony Scott wait their turn.

62 UPTON PARK MEMORIES

A snow-covered pitch in the freezing winter of 1962-63 couldn't prevent Hammers from jogging round the perimeter. Bobby Moore (wearing Bill Landowne's top) leads the way from Johnny Byrne, Alan Sealey and Tony Scott.

Jumpers for goalposts, or should that be main gates? A couple of spectators in Green Street get an unexpected close-up view of Jim Standen clinging on to a shot during training in February 1964.

With the English league season finished, Bobby Moore trains alone at a deserted Upton Park in May 1962, just before flying out with England to the World Cup finals in Chile. In this shot we get a good view of the North Bank and West Enclosure terracing.

Como rain or shine: A couple of weeks before the 1964 FA Cup Final, the stadium forecourt became the scene for a dress rehearsal for victory against Preston North End. A few bedraggled onlookers gathered by the main gates and Ron Greenwood (far left) watch as Ronnie Boyce shoots. We can also see Jim Standen, Joe Kirkup and Peter Brabrook in plimsolls trying to avoid the puddles.

64   UPTON PARK MEMORIES

It's December 1966 and injured duo Johnny Byrne and Eddie Bovington sit out this session but get a front row view from the dug-out as Ron Boyce, John Charles and John Sissons go by.

Leather-coated Bobby Moore missed training ahead of the FA Cup tie at Huddersfield in January 1969 but took up a good position at the front of the then new East Terrace to watch Martin Peters go through his paces. Later, Mooro watched from the East Stand corridor as trainer Ernie Gregory (far right) barked his orders during a session of 'doggies'.

UPTON PARK MEMORIES 65

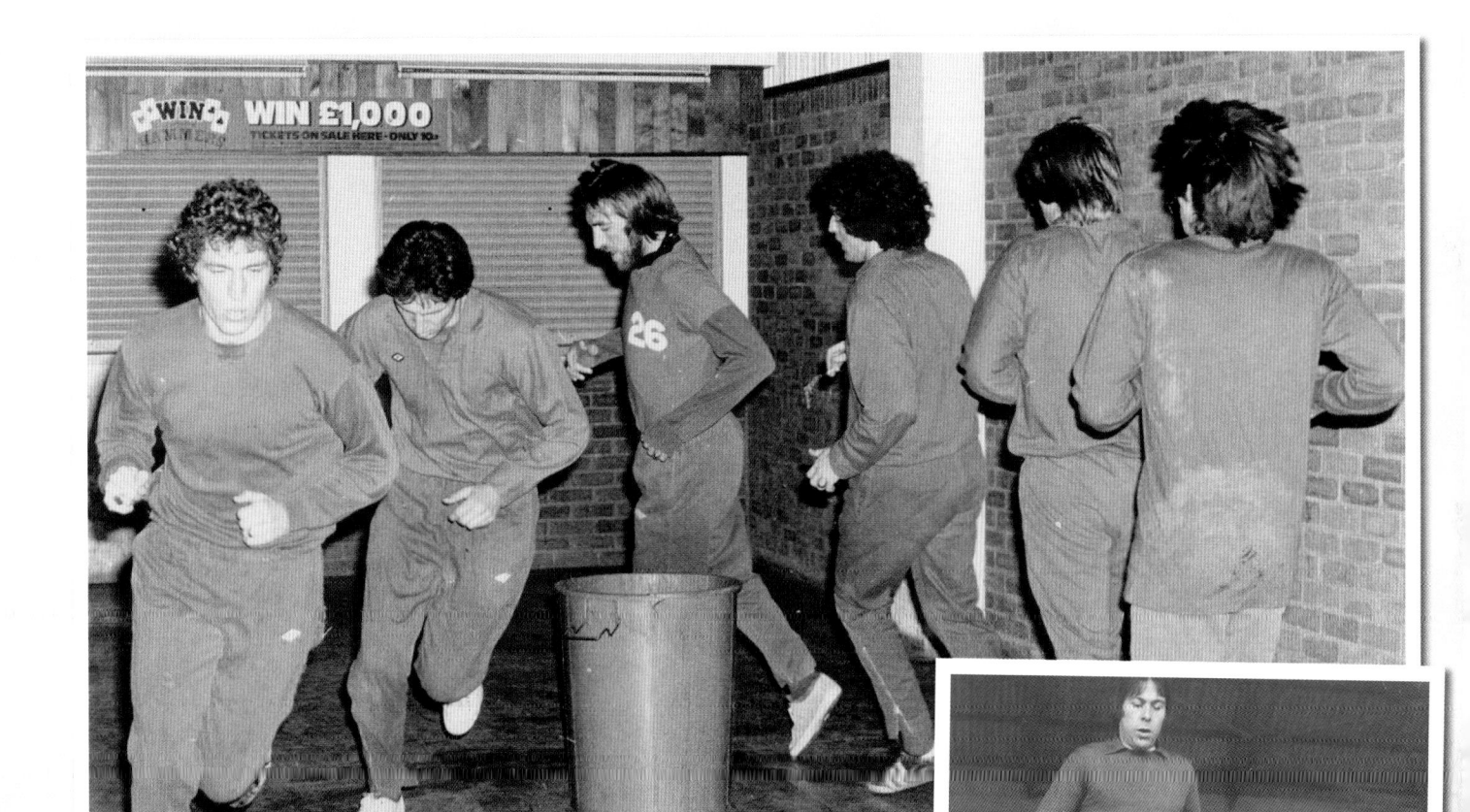

In the late 70s, the East Stand concourse was again the venue for a stint of running. Above: Pat Holland leads the way from Alvin Martin, Billy Bonds, John McDowell and Alan Devonshire. Below: McDowell pictured ahead of Curbishley, David Cross and Devonshire.

Many players have pounded up and down the steps of the stands and terraces during long, punishing spells of rehab. Here's Stuart Pearson in the West Stand in the early 80s.

UPTON PARK FIRSTS

WHILE this book is not intended to be a historical reference, it's important to recognise the most significant landmark moments of the past 112 years . . .

MATCH
The first official match West Ham United played at the Boleyn Ground was the Southern League game v Millwall (1/9/1904). Hammers' team on that historic day: Kingsley, Bamlett, Gardner, Allison, Piercey, Russell, McCartney, Fletcher, Bridgeman, Simmons, Flynn. The side remained unchanged for the first six league games.

GOAL, HAT-TRICK & WIN
Billy Bridgeman, a local lad born at Bromley-by-Bow, wrote his name in the history books by scoring all three goals in that inaugural 3-0 win over deadly rivals Millwall. Contemporary newspaper reports credited Jack Flynn with one of the goals but whatever the truth of it, Bridgeman definitely scored the first official goal at the Boleyn Ground.

With doubt surrounding Bridgeman's hat-trick, we should mention that the next Hammer to score three times in one game was Jack Fletcher, in a 4-0 win v Wellingborough Town (22/10/1904).

DEFEAT
It's fair to say that Upton Park has never exactly been a fortress – our winning 'sequence' at our new home lasted just one game and nine days. Queens Park Rangers became the first team to win in the league at the Boleyn Ground, when they triumphed 3-1 (10/9/1904) in Hammers' second home match of their initial season in E13.

FA CUP TIE
v Brighton & Hove Albion (10/12/1904), a 2-1 defeat . . . and this time Jack Flynn certainly was Irons' undisputed first FA Cup goalscorer. Team: Kingsley, Bamlett, Fair, Allison, Piercey, Russell, McCartney, Fletcher, Bridgeman, Simmons, Flynn.

SENDING-OFF
Hard-tackling centre-half Frank Piercy, nicknamed 'The Old War Horse', was the first Hammer to be given his marching orders in front of his home crowd, during a typically thunderous 2-0 defeat by Millwall (22/2/1908). The previous season Piercy had been banned for a month following an incident in a game v Swindon.

FA CUP HAT-TRICK
A year after George Webb had notched an FA Cup hat-trick at Wolves, he became the first Hammer to do so in the premier cup competition at Upton Park, v Preston North End (4/2/1911).

FOUR-GOAL HAUL
In his first spell with Hammers before his record-breaking £2,000 move to Blackburn Rovers in 1913, Wapping-born Danny Shea became the first Hammer to score four times in a game when he got the lot in a 4-0 win v Plymouth Argyle (28/12/1908).

Geoff Hurst was the first to score four times in a League Cup tie by netting all the goals in a 4-0 battering of Bolton Wanderers (11/10/67).

Billy Bridgeman was the first to make the net bulge.

Hat-trick hero George Webb was always 'up for the Cup'.

Danny Shea plundered four goals v Plymouth.

UPTON PARK MEMORIES

Syd Puddefoot gave a five star performance v Chesterfield.

FIVE-GOAL HAUL
Syd Puddefoot was the first Hammer to score five goals in one game, in the FA Cup 1st round v Chesterfield (10/1/1914) – an 8-1 win.

But Brian Dear scored the fastest five goals in any English Football League game, v West Bromwich Albion (16/4/65), either side of half-time, in a 6-1 victory.

FOOTBALL LEAGUE GAME & GOAL
After being elected to The Football League (Second Division) in 1919, Hammers' opponents in their first league fixture were Lincoln City (30/8/19). James Moyes scored on his debut in a 1-1 draw in front of around 20,000 – but played only one more game for the club.

LEAGUE EVER-PRESENT
Percy Allen played all 42 second division games in 1921-22.

SIX-GOAL HAUL
Hammers' greatest-ever goalscorer, Vic Watson, v Leeds United (9/2/29). Just less than a year later (25/1/30), Watson also recorded Irons' first four-goal haul in the FA Cup against the same opponents.

Watson's staggering club record haul of 326 league and cup goals in 505 matches between 1921 and 1935 will surely never be eclipsed.

As few reading this will have had the privilege of seeing Watson achieve his incredible feats, we must also mention that Geoff Hurst emulated Victor's record a little less than 40 years later by scoring six goals v Sunderland (19/10/68) in an 8-0 slaughter of the Rokermen.

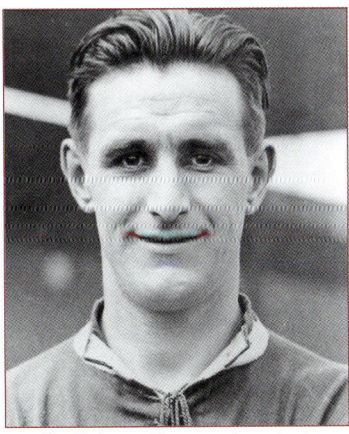

Vic Watson – Hammers' greatest goalscorer.

TESTIMONIAL
Frank Piercy, the first West Ham player to be sent-off at The Boleyn, was also the first to be honoured with a testimonial match, when Hammers beat an Isthmian League XI 5-0 (1/10/31). After he quit playing in 1912, Frank became assistant trainer under Charlie Paynter and continued to serve the club well until his death through illness before the start of the 1931-32 season, so his testimonial was awarded posthumously.

The next testimonial was awarded some 19 years later (22/9/50) to Paynter himself, when Arsenal were beaten 3-1.

HAT-TRICK DEBUTANT
Left-winger Ken Tucker, 22, scored a hat-trick on his debut in a 4-0 home win v Chesterfield (4/7/47). It was an incredible achievement and, even to this day, Tucker remains the only player in Hammers' post-war history to achieve such a feat. Despite his sensational debut, Tucker's opportunities in Hammers' first team were somewhat limited for a number of seasons and it would be a further four years before he scored another goal in league football.

ABANDONED GAME
18,300 left the ground early when the second division game v Grimsby Town (27/11/48) was called off. Hammers were losing 2-1 (George Wright) when fog caused a premature halt in the 50th minute.

FLOODLIGHT GAME
Of all the memorable games played under the fabled Upton Park lights, the first was v Tottenham Hotspur (16/4/53). Back then Spurs were riding high in Division One and had just lost in the FA Cup semi-final. For Hammers, 14th place in Division Two and a 4-1 FA Cup exit in their first round at the hands of West Bromwich Albion did not make 1952-53 a memorable season, so the introduction of floodlights provided a bright distraction from the gloom of mid-table, second tier football.

To prepare his team for playing under the bright lights of east London, manager Ted Fenton held a floodlit practice match between the first XI and the reserves behind closed doors. It must have helped, for Hammers – wearing specially made fluorescent shirts – won 2-1 thanks to first-half goals by Tommy Dixon and Jim Barrett.

Team: Ernie Gregory, George Wright, Harry Kinsell, Derek Parker,

Moments before kick-off in the first floodlight game between West Ham and Spurs in 1953.

68 UPTON PARK MEMORIES

Action from the first live TV game v Holland Sports in 1955.

Malcolm Allison, Doug Bing, Tommy Southren, Jim Barrett, Tommy Dixon, Jimmy Andrews, Harry Hooper.

An attendance of around 25,000 was impressive compared to the average home league gate of 19,800 for that season.

The lighting Installation cost £5,000 and to help recoup this outlay the club arranged a series of friendly floodlit fixtures.

Hammers beat Bury 3-2 (Hooper, Dare, Dick) in the the first home league game played under lights (19/3/56).

LIVE TELEVISED GAME

In co-operation with the BBC, West Ham arranged a friendly v Holland Sports Club of Rotterdam (22/3/55), who were leaders of the Dutch league at the time and one of the pioneers of pro football in the Netherlands. A crowd of 10,600 in the stadium saw a goal-less first-half and the viewers at home who saw the concluding 45 minutes fared no luckier as the game ended 0-0.

Team: George Taylor, George Wright, Noel Cantwell, Andy Malcolm, Malcolm Allison, Frank O'Farrell, Albert Foan, Les Bennett, Dave Sexton, Brian Moore, Malcolm Musgrove.

John Dick netted Hammers' first League Cup goal.

LEAGUE CUP TIE

The Football League Cup, as it was originally known, was introduced in season 1960-61 and Hammers' first opponents were London rivals Charlton Athletic (26/9/60). But the new knockout competition was slow to capture fans' imagination – only 12, 496 paid to see John Dick score our first (equalising) goal, before Malcolm Musgrove and Bobby Moore put the seal on a 3-1 victory.

Team: Brian Rhodes, John Bond, John Lyall, Andy Malcolm, Ken Brown, Bobby Moore, Derek Woodley, John Cartwright, Dave Dunmore, John Dick, Malcolm Musgrove.

LEAGUE CUP HAT-TRICK

After Martin Peters put West Ham in front v Plymouth Argyle (26/9/62), Johnny Byrne stole the limelight with a 20-minute first-half hat-trick – two headers and a penalty – in a 6-0 defeat of the West Country side in front of 9,714.

FIRST BLACK PLAYER

West Ham were trailblazers in giving black players the chance to prove themselves in senior football, at a time when the game was riddled with institutionalised racism and abuse from the terraces was horrendous. John Charles made his debut at left-back in the 1-0 defeat by Blackburn Rovers (4/5/63), just a few weeks before captaining Hammers to victory in the FA Youth Cup Final v Liverpool, and went

Trailblazing full-back John Charles with Leeds United's Mick Jones.

on to play 142 senior league and cup games between then and 1970. By breaking through into the first team, the Canning Town-born defender paved the way for many other black players.

Having handed 'Charlo' his first team debut, manager Ron Greenwood made history again when he selected John's younger brother, Clive, at left-back, plus forwards, Bermudan Clyde Best and Nigerian Ade Coker (scorer of the second goal), for the 2-0 victory v Spurs (1/4/72). This was the first time three black players appeared together in the same top flight team for a Football League match.

EUROPEAN GAME & GOAL

Foreign teams had visited east London in the 50s but the first game in European cup competition was played v La Gantoise of Belgium in the European Cup Winners Cup, 1st round, 2nd leg (7/10/64). With Ron Boyce having scored the only goal of the first leg, Hammers gifted the

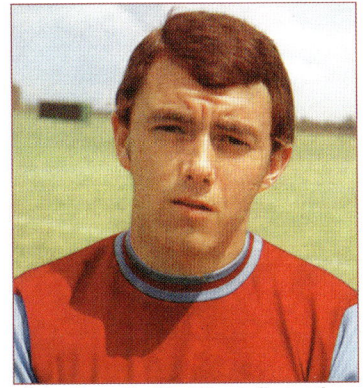

Peter Bennett – West Ham's first active substitute in 1965.

Martin Peters, Eddie Bovington, Ken Brown, Bobby Moore, Peter Brabrook, Ron Boyce, Johnny Byrne, Geoff Hurst, John Sissons.

Ron Greenwood's side recorded their first home European win thanks to a 2-0 (John Bond, Alan Sealey) second round success v Sparta Prague (25/11/64).

SUBSTITUTE

Subs were introduced by the Football League at the start of the 1965-66 season. The first to be called into action from the bench at Upton Park was Peter Bennett, who replaced Jack Burkett in the 53rd minute of the game v Leeds United (28/8/65).

EUROPEAN DEFEAT

Germans Borussia Dortmund became the first visitors to win a competitive European tie at Upton Park, with their decisive 2-1 success in the ECWC semi-final, 1st leg (5/4/66).

ALL-TICKET GAME

On the instructions of The Football League, the visit of Manchester United (16/5/77) was the first all-ticket league match at Upton Park since pre-WW2.

EUROPEAN HAT-TRICK

It was recorded by David Cross v Castilla (1/10/80) on the night of the infamous behind-closed doors ECWC 1st round, 2nd leg which Hammers won 5-1.

SHIRT SPONSOR

The name of West Ham's first major commercial sponsor, Avco Trust, appeared on the front of Hammers' shirt for the visit of Norwich City (22/10/83).

England and Australia line up before the start of the 2003 friendly.

INTERNATIONAL

Upton Park hosted numerous youth internationals and representative games down the years before the first senior international was played there. Unfortunately, it was no spectacle and holds few good memories for those who witnessed England's embarrassing 3-1 friendly defeat by part-timers from Ghent a lifeline when Martin Peters put through his own goal in the return clash. But a 43rd minute strike by Johnny Byrne was enough to send Hammers through, 2-1 on aggregate, in front of a disgruntled 24,000 crowd that paid record gate receipts.

Team: Alan Dickie, John Bond, Australia (12/2/2003). The Aussies were 2-0 ahead with goals from Tony Popovic and Harry Kewell, against a strong red-shirted England side before manager Eriksson completely changed his team for the second-half, leaving most of the near capacity 34,590 crowd wondering why they had bothered.

Francis Jeffers netted England's only goal in the 68th minute before Brett Emerton capped a well deserved win by Frank Farina's side. West Ham were represented on the night by England keeper David James and Socceroo's left-winger Stan Lazaridis, whose free-kick set up their first goal.

England first-half: James; G. Neville, Ferdinand, Campbell, A. Cole; Beckham, Scholes, Lampard, Dyer; Beattie, Owen.

England second-half: Robinson; Mills, Brown, King, Konchesky; Vassell, Hargreaves, Murphy, Jenas; Rooney, Jeffers.

Australia: Schwarzer; Neill, Moore, Popovic (Vidmar, 72), Lazaridis; Emerton, Okon, Skoko (Bresciano, 46), Chipperfield (Grella, 76); Viduka, Kewell (Aloisi, 56).

One slice of history that probably didn't resonate until years later was that in the second-half of this match, Wayne Rooney, at 17 years and 111 days, became the youngest England debutant. In October 2015 Rooney broke Bobby Charlton's record to become England's all-time leading scorer.

The only other full international played at the Boleyn Ground before its closure in 2016 was the friendly between Argentina and Croatia (12/11/2014). Most of the neutral 12,000 crowd coughed up a minimum £25 per ticket and braved the chilly East End night just to see in the flesh the blue-shirted No.10, Lionel Messi, Barcelona's 27-year-old megastar and arguably the world's greatest player at the time, who stroked home a 57th minute penalty at the Bobby Moore Stand end to seal his team's 2-1 win.

Former Hammer Javier Mascherano also played the full 90 minutes for Argentina, while his ex-Upton Park team-mate, Carlos Tevez, was given a hero's reception when he came on to replace Sergio Aguero in the 62nd minute.

Lionel Messi on his only appearance at Upton Park.

Sign of the times . . . a fan gets a 'selfie' on his iPhone with Carlos Tevez on the night the Argentine was accorded a hero's welcome back to Upton Park.

WEST HAM UNITED

1 WHY WEST HAM UNITED?
Your first-ever visit to the Boleyn Ground

JUST why do we support West Ham? It's a question that the majority of us have had cause to ask ourselves on plenty of occasions over the years, and behind every single fan's personal story is a unique answer.

For most, following the club was never a conscious decision or a deliberately chosen path. It is simply in the blood, passed down from previous generations with inextricable links to the east end of London, many dating back to the formation of the Thames Ironworks in 1985 and the subsequent move to our spiritual home, the Boleyn Ground, in 1904.

For others, a quirk of fate or a random event may have led them to discover the claret-and-blue. Our contributors span all 11 decades of football at Upton Park, from the early years of the 20th century right up to the present day, and follow the club from as far afield as Scandinavia, the USA and South Africa.

One thing all have in common, though, is a lifelong affinity with the club that not even some of the darkest footballing days have been able to shake. Fortunes may always be hiding but, once you are West Ham, it seems there is no going back . . .

Q: What, and who was it, that led you to support West Ham United and what do you recall from your first visit to Upton Park

George Hibbins: I first went in 1910 with my father, Ron, when I was six-years-old. This was before West Ham were even in the Football League. Big crowds and a great atmosphere walking to the ground from High Street North, East Ham, where we ran the dairy.

Jim Wilder: My father, Fred Wilder, took me to a reserves' match in 1934 when I was just two. My sister had just been born and Mum wanted me out of the house in Katherine Road, East Ham.

Roy Thomas: A war-time Southern League match (I think it was v Coventry City). My father took me in the Chicken Run, where the old railway sleepers were deep and gave you a better view.

Alec Huett: My dad took me when I was 10, in 1944. I cannot recall who was playing but remember holes in the stand roof after the war. After that there was no other team for me as a young lad and I couldn't wait for each Saturday, to be lifted over the top of the crowd from the back of the stand to the front without touching the ground.

Eric Brown: v Aldershot (23/1/43), won 6-3. I was about 13 and it was near the end of WWII. I was born in Aldershot but Hammers were my team. Aldershot had England's half-back line of Cliff Briton, Stan Cullis and Joe Mercer and to crown it all, there was my football idol Tommy Lawton. Hammers players I recall that day were PC Charlie Bicknell, Sam Small, who scored twice, and George Foreman.

William Lloyd: It was in 1944, when I was aged 11, and Dad took me. All I can remember is that Hammers had a lot of guest players who were in the armed forces at that time.

Patrick John Perry: I started going to West Ham in 1945 as a boy of 13. A friend and I would catch the train from Grays in Essex and visit his aunt and uncle – who had a barber shop opposite the entrance to Upton Park – for a cup of tea before going into the ground. We would go to the corner flag near the North Bank and sit on the wall, and buy a programme – which was just a blue sheet of paper then. On the sheet there were names like A. N. Other for players who were in the armed forces and didn't know whether they would be able to get leave for the game.

Keith Martin: My father, Cyril Martin (who died between the semi-final and the final of our FA Cup triumph in 1964, and was at Wembley for the final against Bolton Wanderers in 1923 and the War Cup final against Blackburn Rovers in 1940) took me and my elder brother Ian on our first visit to Upton Park, v Manchester City (5/10/46). I still have the programme, a single sheet printed by Helliar and Sons on blue paper. Price

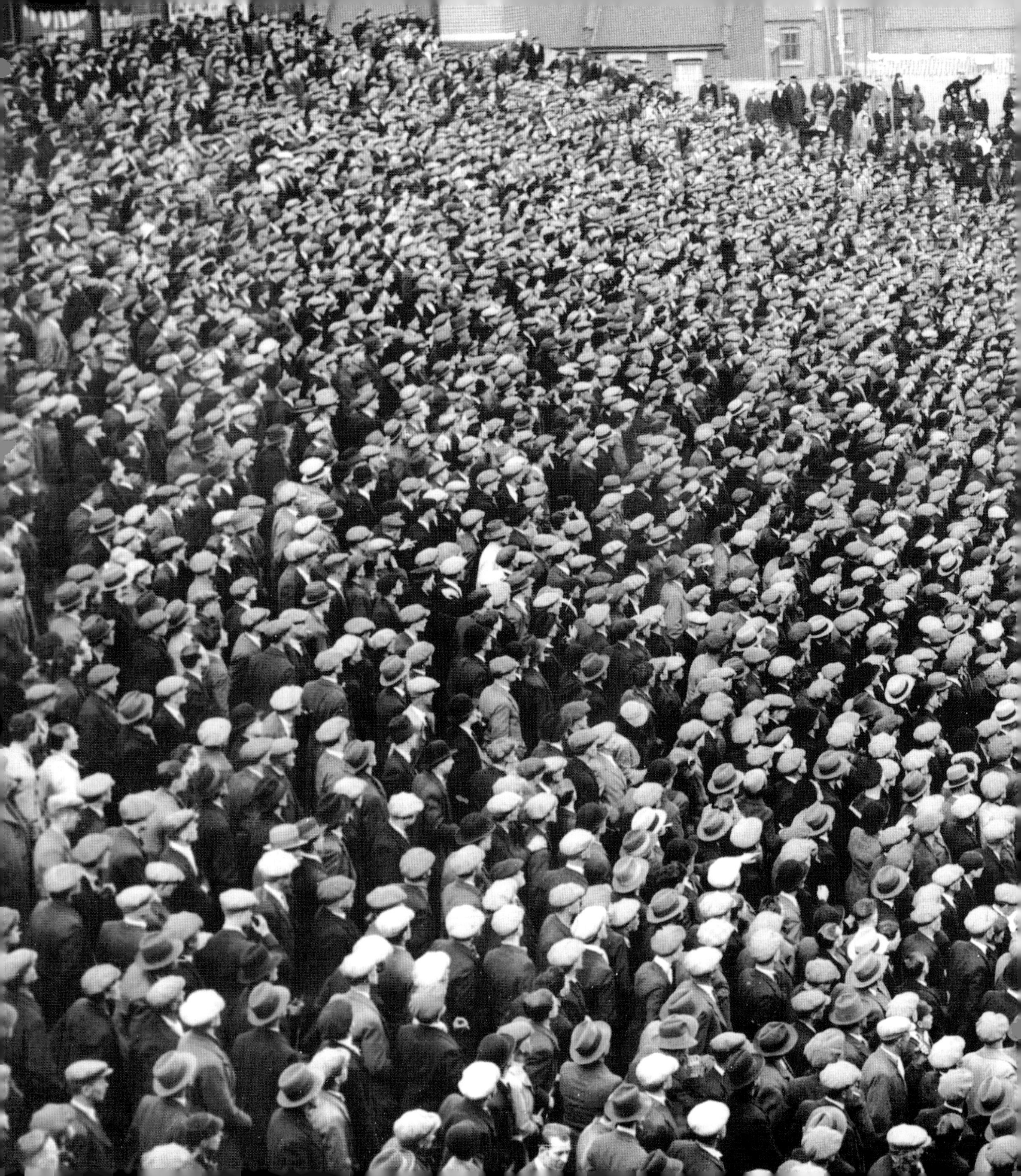

A glimpse into the wonderful world of flat caps, as viewed from the west corner of the uncovered North Bank. West Ham appear to be attacking the Chesterfield goal in April 1933. 11,000 were there to see a 1-0 home defeat.

one penny. We won 1-0 with a header from Archie Macaulay.

Mr G. E. Hill: v Luton Town (25/12/46), 2-1 (Joe Payne, Terry Woodgate). I attended the Christmas Day match with friends from Staffordshire.

Martin Cearns: There was always little doubt that I would spend much of my life watching West Ham United at Upton Park. I was the fourth generation of my family to do so and last season I was delighted when my granddaughters became the sixth. My earliest visits were in the early 50s, when my father, Len, took me to watch the reserves, who used to play on Saturday afternoons at Upton Park when the first team were playing away.

John Pocklington: v Barnsley. It was the early 50s and the pitch was so wet that goalkeeper Ernie Gregory made a save and skidded out of his penalty area.

Ed Gillis: v Southampton (23/8/52). My father, Bill, took me to the opening fixture. I recall climbing the stairs in the main stand, seemingly on the way to heaven. The pitch, from our high vantage point, was gloriously green, the white markings crisply clear. The players looked to be enacting a game of Subbuteo, so far away did they seem, but Ernie Gregory looked reassuringly bigger than most. I had difficulty distinguishing between the ball and Terry Woodgate's bald head at times but the game was won 1-0 (Jimmy Barrett).

Bobby George: I was born and raised in West Ham in the 40s. We lived in Harold Road, Upton Park and a few houses along lived my aunts, uncles, cousins and gran. My dad, Charlie, was a Tottenham supporter and Uncle Jim and cousin Terry McDonald supported West Ham. Jim would tell me about such great players as Vic Watson and Len Goulden, while Dad took me to see Spurs, who had the likes of Alf Ramsey and Eddie Baily.

The earliest recollection I have of Upton Park was the first floodlit game at the ground, a friendly v Spurs (16/4/53). Dad took me along with Jim and Terry. What I particularly remember were the vivid fluorescent shirts of West Ham and, with the bright lights, it was an explosion of colour. I can visualise, still, Malcolm Allison leading the team onto the pitch. His shorts seemed tighter than everybody else's, and he certainly looked the part. West Ham won 2-1 against a good Spurs side that included Baily, Ted Ditchburn and Les Medley.

Reuben Gane: My first match was a second division fixture v Everton

Keith Martin with his aunt and three daughters, Laurie, Heather and Frances, at the club's open day to celebrate the 1980 FA Cup success.

AUTHOR

JOHN POWLES

Books: *Iron in the Blood; Seeing Red For the Claret and Blue; Irons of the South*

IT was 1942 and I was eight when we moved from the Custom House area where I was born to get away from the bombing of the dock area, to Boundary Road, Plaistow which was not a lot safer anyway, but it appeared to be at the time. I had never been to a football match before and knew absolutely nothing about it, but an older boy living a few doors away asked me to go and so began a 72-year journey (to date).

I can remember it well, the game being v Arsenal (11/9/43). Records show that the match resulted in a 2-2 draw with a crowd of 15,000 and I recall being surprised at so many people in one place. I also noticed how so many shouted encouragement to one side in particular, and it was noticeable that a certain player named Sam Small was getting some stick for his performance. Overall, I enjoyed the experience and went a couple more times that season.

It was my intention (if Mum would give me the entrance money) to go again as the new season of 1944-45 got underway but Adolf Hitler put a stop to that when one of his doodlebugs (flying bombs) paid a visit in August, just before the start of the new season. I often think, when I'm among a near 35,000 crowd, how many people were close to the Boleyn Ground on that particular day – I was never evacuated like some of my friends and most grown-ups to the age of 40 were in the army at the time. Most of the kids I knew were not interested in football and I was with one of those when the doodlebug exploded on to the south-west corner of the Upton Park pitch.

We were used to doodlebugs – they had been coming over for some weeks at that time – but on this particular occasion it came a lot lower and cut-out what seemed to be just over our heads. By this time we had literally dived into my mate's Anderson shelter. After an engine 'cut-out' there was usually a deathly silence that created seven to eight seconds of fear but on this occasion, because of its proximity, there followed a long, loud whooshing sound before it hit the ground and exploded.

Knowing it was quite near, we clambered from the dug-out and saw the smoke rising about a five-minute run from us. Taking time to decide what to do, we ran northwards up the road to The Boleyn and Green Street. But Priory Road had already been quickly cordoned off and all we could see was twisted metal and a column of smoke. Thankfully, nobody was killed as the doodlebug exploded on the pitch.

This meant that the Irons had to play all their away matches for the season in one sequence from the start. When the ground was repaired, home fixtures began, and one of those games that I attended resulted in a 5-4 victory v Brighton – after being 4-1 down.

(21/11/53), which ended in a 1-1 draw (Dave Sexton). Aged 12, I went to the match with my school-mate, Johnny Carder, and his dad, Dick. We went to the game in Dick's pick-up truck, parked off the Barking Road and entered into the South Bank through the turnstiles in Castle Street. Although we paid to get in, I soon noticed some other kids were getting in without charge, having been lifted over the turnstiles, while some tiny tots crawled underneath. Most of the little chaps watched the game sitting on the shoulders of their fathers or big brothers. Lads made their way to the front, with adults making way for them, while other youngsters from the back were passed down overhead.

The thing that hit me straight away was the atmosphere in the ground. Coming from Barking, I had only ever watched Barking Town (as they were then), LESSA FC down at River Road or William Warne's factory football team on the Barking bypass. My mates and myself had never actually paid to see a match before – we used to 'bunk in' at Barking by either shinning up a lamp-post in Peto's Alley or climbing over the Vicarage garden wall.

As kids, we also played a lot of parks football on Saturday afternoons, after playing for our school teams in the morning. Sometimes we went to the Electric cinema in Barking (lovingly known as 'The Bug'ole') if Superman or Roy Rogers were featured.

I do not recall seeing any women or girls at the game and lots of the kids had claret-and-blue knitted woollen hats, rosettes and rattles.

The brass band – was it the Leyton Silver Band? – that had played on the field had now retreated to an area beside the players' tunnel, leaving a French-horn soloist to switch to the post horn and blast out *The Post Horn Gallop* as everybody cheered. For me, that piece of music became just as synonymous with West Ham United as *Bubbles*.

Not a lot of people know that *Bubbles* only survived thanks to a few loyal fans in the Chicken Run who kept singing it in the 50s. It then became popular again after our promotion in 1958 and on into the early 60s, and then with our getting to, and winning, the 1964 FA Cup final.

Incidentally, glad to see that your book is based on 'Upton Park' memories and not 'Boleyn Ground' memories. In all my years supporting the club, me and my West Ham mates have always referred to Upton Park as the place

During the war all factories and institutions had their own roof spotters, usually members of staff who did an extra shift. The roof spotter's job was to act as an early warning to those inside the building of the approach of a raid. Here the roof spotter works on while West Ham play Chelsea in December 1940, at the height of The Blitz. The gate was less than 2,000.

AUTHOR
TERRY ROPER

Books: *West Ham in the Sixties: The Jack Burkett Story; West Ham: In My Day (Vol. 1 & 2)*

I MUST have claret-and-blue blood in my veins because my grandad, Oliver Roper, started supporting West Ham in the early 1900s when they were a Southern League club and attended the first ever FA Cup final at Wembley in 1923. The official attendance was given as 126,047 but Grandad always maintained there were many more thousands there that day. He ended up sitting on the touchline with thousands of others as the game got underway. He said it was a miracle there was not a serious loss of life. He admitted to being really scared and feared for his safety.

My dad, Bob, first went to Upton Park in the early 30s, aged 10. My grandparents and dad lived in a small terraced house in Vicarage Lane, just a couple of miles from Upton Park. Their next door neighbour was Syd Puddefoot, one of West Ham's most famous players at the time who had been capped by England. Dad's clearest childhood memory was seeing Puddefoot's claret-and-blue shirt hanging on the washing line after each match. In those far off days, the players, or their wives, were responsible for looking after their own kit. I wonder what the modern-day WAGs would make of such an arrangement.

Unfortunately, I cannot remember my first visit to Upton Park because I was only four at the time. Dad told me it was a second division game v Swansea Town (as they were called then) which ended in a 1-1 draw thanks to a goal from Harry Hooper (23/3/51). The first game that I can actually remember was a 3-3 draw v Bury in December 1954 on a mud-heap of a pitch when I was seven. Malcolm Musgrove (2) and John Dick scored West Ham's goals.

A crowd of 13,400, many in uniform, watched the last league game at Upton Park before World War Two. Hammers were beaten 2-0 by Leicester City on September 2, 1939.

where The Hammers played, not The Boleyn, as appears to be in vogue over the past few years. The Boleyn is the pub on the corner of Green Street and Barking Road that we use for a pint before or after a game. Some of the 50s and 60s players also sometimes used the pub both BEFORE and after games!

Peter Gurr: v Nottingham Forest in around 1953. I was six and watched it from the South Bank with my dad and uncle. Ernie Gregory missed the game through injury, so George Taylor went in goal for us, while Harry Walker was the Forest keeper. I particularly remember those two playing because, at the time, many pubs in the east London area were owned by the well-known London brewery, Taylor Walker!

When I reached the age of 11, I started to go to games on my own and stood in the Chicken Run. You'd throw sixpence down to the peanut seller, who would walk around the edge of the pitch selling, and he'd throw a packet of nuts back in return.

I graduated to the East Stand, then the West Stand (plus a parking space courtesy of then West Ham United director Jack Petchey, until Karren Brady took it off me) and, later, I became a Hammers bond-holder, which has entitled me to big discounts on match tickets to this day.

Terry Connelly: My father, Joe, was an ardent supporter and used to take me to reserve and youth team matches when I was very young. My first visit to Upton Park for a first team fixture was at the age of eight, v Notts County (23/8/54). We won 3-0 (Jimmy Andrews, John Dick, Harry Hooper) and the attendance was 19,000. I remember it was a sunny day, we were in the North Bank on the Chicken Run side and I was a little scared of the number of people – I had never seen that many before. Dad was not in an optimistic mood, as West Ham had lost 5-2 in both of their first two games, away at Swansea and Blackburn. It made no difference to me, though. I had witnessed a 3-0 win and the die was cast for the rest of my life.

Kevin Mansell: I was first taken to West Ham when I was seven by my grandfather, Richard (Dick) Speight, with whom I lived in an extended family household on Canvey Island. He was 67, the same age as me at the time of writing this. In earlier years, I remember him taking me to watch West Ham Boys on Saturday mornings at Clapton's Spotted Dog ground.

The first game I saw at Upton Park was v Middlesbrough (19/3/55), which we won 2-1 (Billy Dare, Malcolm Musgrove). They had a famous player called Charlie Wayman and a black player, Lindy Delapenha, who was the first Jamaican to play in English pro football. Grandad had supported West Ham from its beginnings as Thames Ironworks, when they played at the Memorial Grounds in Canning Town. He was at the 1923 FA Cup final and used to recite the players of his era to me: Ted Hufton, Danny Shea, Jack Tresadern, Vic Watson, Syd Puddefoot and 'Big' Jim Barrett. Three years before he died my Uncle Dick took him to Wembley again, to see West Ham win the FA Cup for the first time.

Crispin Derby: Both sides of my family were East Enders, so supporting West Ham was what we all did – some with more enthusiasm than others, it has to be said. The routine was to visit my grandma and grandad in East Ham before a game and, if possible, my Uncle Joe, Aunt Lil and cousin Steve. Later, from the age of 11 to 15, I would travel from our home in Guildford alone to see West Ham as often as I could afford.

My first game was on Guy Fawkes Day, 1955, aged seven. It was incredibly exciting feeling part of this noisy crowd with their strange shouts and songs. We lost 3-2 to Blackburn (Billy Dare, Harry Hooper). We were in the Chicken Run, so my biggest memory is the huge encouragement for Hooper every time he set off from the halfway line towards the Blackburn goal. I remember being mortified when I read in the *Daily Mirror* that he had been sold to Wolves.

Graham White: v Blackburn Rovers (5/11/55). My friend, John, who lived next door to me in Barking, and I were taken by his dad. We went in the main West Stand and the first thing that struck me was the vivid colours of the two teams, claret-and-blue against Rovers' blue-and-white quarters. I had only seen 'black and white' football on TV before. At the age of 10, I don't suppose I cared that much about the 3-2 defeat – the whole experience was wonderful and I had fireworks to look forward to that evening.

Doug Barrett: My Upton Park initiation came in 1955, aged six. I was taken along by my grandfather, Albert Barrett, and his two sons, my father, Roy, and his brother, my Uncle Dennis. Albert was born in Canning Town in 1896, played for West Ham Boys and was among the 126,000 (give or take tens of thousands!) who watched the 1923 FA Cup final.

We were definitely in the Chicken Run but I don't know who the opponents were that day or the result. All I remember is watching players wearing strange pinkish/red coloured shirts!

When I first started going to The Boleyn at the end of 1955 my favourite place to stand was on the right-hand side of the tunnel wall, far enough down to be able to pass programme and pen over the wall to the players for signatures while they were waiting to go out onto the pitch. I collected quite a few autographs that way. I also remember the smells . . .

Goalkeeping great Ernie Gregory, one of many local lads who came through the ranks. He virtually devoted his life to the club he served for more than 50 years as player, manager (reserves and colts) and coach.

PLAYER
RONNIE BOYCE
Born: 6/1/43, East Ham, east London
WHU career: 1960-72
Position: Central midfielder
Apps: 339, **Goals:** 29

MY family were all West Ham fans and my grandfather, Amos, was actually a turnstile operator at the first-ever FA Cup final at Wembley in 1923. He always used to tell me the story about how he had one of those old market pouches stuffed full of money, but he couldn't get into the ground because there were just too many people already inside – so he didn't see the game.

My grandfather was a West Ham fan through and through. In fact he worked for Thames Ironworks and purchased two shares in West Ham United back in the 20s. They were handed down to my dad and now I've got them.

My dad, Bill, was also invited to a trial at West Ham but it was back in the days when it was much more important to get a trade or a steady job first.

Harry and Margaret Hooper at their wedding . . . a few hours before Harry was dazzling for Hammers on the wing.

embrocation drifting out from the changing rooms and the vanilla-scented tobacco frequently smoked by a guy who used to stand behind me.

David Hughes: I was nine and it was 1955. As usual, I was in the street outside our prefab in Ferns Road, Stratford when I heard my dad, George, call my name. In those days when your dad called out to you, you ran to him. "Want to come with me to West Ham?" he asked – and off we went in his little black Austin (all cars were black then), parking in Walton Road, where a grubby kid offered to 'Look after yer car, mista' (I remember Dad handing a silver 6d to him). The ground looked huge and we settled in E block of the upper tier of the West Stand, fairly adjacent to the edge of the penalty area at the North Bank end. We won the match v Leeds United (5/3/55) 2-1 and I can only recall the Leeds goal, scored in front of us by a huge chap named John Charles.

Richard Miller: v Leeds United (5/3/55). We won 2-1 with goals scored by Albert Foan and Les Bennett. Harry Hooper was actually married in the morning before the game and West Ham made him captain for the day. My uncle, George Clark, had supported West Ham since the 20s and went to the 1923 Cup final. He was a West Ham season ticket holder and took both my father, Lionel, and myself to our first match. George's house at 123 Dereham Road, Barking backed onto Charlie Paynter's garden in Oulton Crescent. For several years my uncle would spend many hours engaged in conversation about football with the West Ham manager over the garden fence on a Sunday morning.

PLAYER
BRIAN DEAR

Born: 18/9/43, West Ham, east London
WHU career: 1962-70
Position: Striker
Apps: 85, **Goals:** 39

I REMEMBER bunking off school to see Johnny Dick score a hat-trick in the FA Cup v Spurs in 1956.

My dad used to stand on the North Bank and I'd climb up the ladder at the back of the open terrace to help the old boy put up the half-time scores on the board.

Then, at half-time, us kids would distract the copper down by the corner of the Chicken Run, hop over the fence, run along underneath the stand and hop over the fence at the other end, to get a better view of the goal we were attacking in the second-half.

I used to get a tanner, a shilling or two bob for 'looking after' people's cars while they watched the matches – even though I'd go in to watch the games myself and only nipped out to stand by their cars 10 minutes from the end! Those who rode to the ground on bicycles would park them in people's front gardens in Priory Road.

I collected the players' autographs on the back of fag wrappers. They wore those big overcoats and, although they were only young men, they looked so old to me.

Vic Keeble had back trouble and walked with a bit of a stoop. No wonder – he drove a little sports car, an Austin Healey Sprite, if I remember rightly!'

I bumped into Ken Tucker, who asked me if I used to nick sweets from his mum's shop around the corner. I said: "Of course I did – we all did!"

Andy Malcolm was my favourite person, though. Hard as nails, he'd run past you in training and rip a hole in your shorts – and we only had one pair a season. But what a lovely fella.

We enjoyed our visit so much that we went to three further West Ham home games that season (against Middlesbrough, Ipswich Town and Rotherham United). We then supported Hammers regularly from 1954-55 onwards and became season ticket holders in 1957-58 – Block D, Row H3, Seats 3 and 4, which cost £4.50 each. Dad remained a ST holder until his death in February 1979. I have now seen more than 1,250 West Ham games at Upton Park.

Steve Derby: Back in 1956, the thought of venturing over to the Boleyn Ground was the furthest thought from my mind. I didn't 'do' football. My overwhelming passion was for steam engines and Saturdays were committed to tripping around London stations collecting numbers. My dad, Joe, had always been on about going to see a football match – I think he had a feeling that no good could ever come from trainspotting – so, more to appease him than anything, I went over to witness Hammers record a 5-2 victory v Preston North End (7/1/56). The significance passed about three feet over my head and on the next available Saturday, I was back being entertained at Euston and Kings Cross once more.

Dave Philpott (a close neighbour to Ron Boyce) was in my class at East

Ham Grammar School and football-barmy. Quite how he managed it, I can't recall, but the pair of us attended a match v Grimsby Town (27/10/56). Little did I know, as we took our places behind the goal on the South Bank, that my life was about to change and one incident crystallised my conversion to the game and West Ham. About halfway through the first-half, Malcolm Musgrove took up the baton. Cutting in from his left-wing position, he reached the penalty area to unleash a thunderous missile that would surely hit the back of the net. And so it would have done but for Grimsby goalkeeper Clarrie Williams. Taking off to his left, horizontal and seemingly five feet off the ground with no visible means of support, he fisted the ball out to safety. Even I could tell that we had witnessed something truly remarkable and the whole crowd roared its approval.

It so happened that we went down 1-0 that day but it didn't really matter to me. A spell had been cast by Clarrie Williams and Malcolm Musgrove and the magic had begun. In the twinkling of an eye, the pair of them had brought me into the joyous realms of West Ham's world. Trainspotting would have to wait.

Mr P. Cappaert: My dad, Charles William Cappaert, took me and my twin brother, Tony, to see us play Bolton Wanderers. We stood on the North Bank and when Nat Lofthouse slammed a header against the metal board that used to display the half-time scores, the sound of it frightened the life out of us.

Tony Clement: v Spurs (8/3/56) for the FA Cup 6th round replay. I was eight. My Uncle Roy had taken me to see my first ever senior game at White Hart Lane five days earlier, when, in front of 69,111, the same

Albert Foan, Frank O'Farrell, Noel Cantwell and John Dick training in the 50s at West Ham speedway and greyhound stadium in Custom House.

teams had drawn 3-3 (John Dick hat-trick).

We lost the replay 2-1 (Billy Dare) – again, in front of a full house of 36,000-plus. Although it was only just over half the attendance of that at Tottenham, there was twice the noise. My uncle and I watched from the 'ledge' in the South Bank, adjacent to the Chicken Run, where I stood on a wooden milk crate.

When we came out at the end of the match, there were so many people we could not catch the trolley bus back to Ilford, so we walked from the ground to home in Windsor Road, off Ilford Lane. It's a long walk even now. But from those two games I was hooked – every penny I got went towards going to watching West Ham again. I would cycle from home and leave my push-bike in the front room of someone's house opposite the ground for tuppence. The 'parking fee' later went up to sixpence – but the bike was still there when I went to pick it up.

My family's support of West Ham goes back to my grandfather and spans some 96 years. I am as sad as they get. I've attended well over 2,500 games, home and away, in my 58 years of following The 'Ammers.

Howard Dawson: FA Cup 3rd round v Grimsby Town (5/1/57), we won 5-3 (so the history books say but I remember nothing about the game or the goals scored by John Dick, Mal Musgrove, Eddie Lewis and a double by Johnny Smith). I then attended reserve matches in 1958-59 and finally became a regular in 1959-60. The first match that season was v Leicester City and we won 3-0. I used to attend with a classmate, John Fisher and his father.

Jeff MacMahon: My grandad, Edmund, took me to see West Ham v Doncaster Rovers (16/3/57), as our family came from Doncaster. I had been pestering him for a while, because we lived in Katherine Road and could hear the roars every match day. That day, he relented, as he wanted to see the Doncaster star Alick Jeffrey, who, unfortunately, turned out to be injured. We went into the North Bank and soon parted company while I was passed over the heads of the crowd, until I reached the front, where I was just tall enough to see over the wall. Other kids around me had brought boxes and kitchen steps to stand on. Even though I was supposed to support Doncaster, I was hooked on West Ham and couldn't wait to go again.

Dave Satchell: I first went with some school friends and one of their dads in 1957. I was 10 and the game was played under floodlights against a team from Holland, which I think was Sparta of Rotterdam. West Ham won 5-0 and to this day I can still see Ernie Gregory, Noel Cantwell and John Bond playing.

Syd Porter: I started supporting West Ham simply because they were my local club. I used to watch Barking but in 1957 my uncle, Len Frost, took me to my first West Ham game and Malcom Musgrove scored two great goals. West Ham were promoted that season and I went with my friend, Tom Ellingford, from then on.

Malcolm Downing: I went to my first game with my friend, Barry Anderton. We both lived in Front Lane, Cranham and his father was the publican of The Plough pub. Barry was 14 and I was 10. My mother said he had to look after me and make sure I didn't get lost. The opponents were Cardiff City (30/11/57). Once in the ground we pushed to the front of the crowd but I couldn't see over the wall until somebody gave me a small crate. The brass band was playing and I could smell the liniment oils.

The bell went for the teams to come out on the pitch. The band struck up *The Post Horn Gallop* and Ken Brown, who was last out, sprinted across to the Chicken Run. I was hooked. The most vivid memory from that game was Vic Keeble heading a ball from the edge of the penalty area and the goalkeeper tipping it over the bar. Vic headed the ball as hard as some people could kick it.

Don Hanley: A 1-1 draw v Liverpool (19/4/58). I was 10 and recall their winger Billy Liddell tearing the home defence apart and giving John Bond a day to forget. My dad said: "We won't win promotion now." Seven days later, we were promoted!

PLAYER
TREVOR BROOKING
Born: 2/10/48, Barking, Essex
WHU career: 1967-84
Position: Central midfield
Apps: 635, **Goals:** 102

ALL my family supported West Ham and I was first taken to Upton Park by my elder brother, Tony, in the late 50s.

I remember watching Andy Malcolm, who was known as 'The Shadow', Phil Woosnam ('The Professor'), Ernie Gregory ('Uncle Ern'), Malcolm Musgrove ('Mad Muzzie') and Vic Keeble and John Dick up front, with the great defensive duo of John Bond and Noel Cantwell. Both John Smith and Mike Grice also made a significant contribution to that team.

The atmosphere was tremendous and I had a really good feel from the club and the people who worked there at that time.

AUTHOR
BRIAN BELTON
Books: *Founded on Iron; Bubbles, Hammers and Dreams; Days of Iron, Johnnie the One; Burn Budgie Byrne; Black Hammers; Men of '64, West Ham United Miscellany*

I WAS taken by my cousin, Steve, and a few of his mates. Aged four, I was not really supposed to be in the ground and my 'carers' were more than twice my age. However, the dad of one of Steve's pals worked on the turnstiles and got us in about an hour before the game. We were squeezed up on the 'shelf' of the North Bank for the visit of Wolves clad in their famous old gold (25/8/58) – West Ham's first Division One match since 1932.

UPTON PARK MEMORIES

Bill Robinson was another great servant of the club. After amassing 61 goals in 105 games as a centre-forward between 1949 and 1952, he became an influential youth coach and then manager Ted Fenton's assistant. In this shot typist Bill is receiving help from another prolific No.9, Vic Keeble.

Malcolm Allison on the lonely road to recovery in 1958 after being cruelly struck down by tuberculosis.

Rob Robinson: My father, Bill Robinson, was undoubtedly instrumental in me becoming a lifelong Hammers fan – along with my mother, Bessie, who used to take me to all the games at Upton Park from the age of three. That was in 1950.

But my first major recollection is, at the age of 11, going to the Manchester United game (8/9/58) under the lights. This was the team managed by Ted Fenton, with Dad as assistant manager. We won 3-2 with goals from John Smith, Johnny Dick and Malcolm Musgrove but it turned out to be more monumental for the debut of a 17-year-old Bobby Moore. I still have the programme from that night, containing the changes to the West Ham line up with Bobby replacing Bill Lansdowne – written by Dad, who actually spelt the name Moore wrong!

Richard Ross: v Manchester Utd (8/9/58). I was eight and sat in the West Stand with my dad, Charles, and brother, John. I can still feel the excitement and, in my memory, the stadium was huge. West Ham, newly-promoted to the first division, won 3-2 but, historically, the importance of the match was that it was, Booby Moore's debut and the end of Malcolm Allison's playing career. Allison, one of the people most responsible for West Ham's promotion, had lost a lung as a result of TB. Fighting back to fitness, he just wanted one game in the first division but Moore was picked instead. Allison, as he said in his autobiography, walked out and went horse racing for two years.

Paul Walker: As with most West Ham fans, it's an east London family thing. My dad, Ron, and his brothers, Ernie and Sid, all born off the Roman Road in Bow and then moving to Caledon Road, East Ham, were all big fans, so there was no other club for me. I recall being picked up from a school pal's party by Dad on the day West Ham won promotion from the second division in 1958, away at Middlesbrough. My old fella was overjoyed, he'd lived through all the bad times after relegation in 1932, the war years, and now Hammers were finally back in the

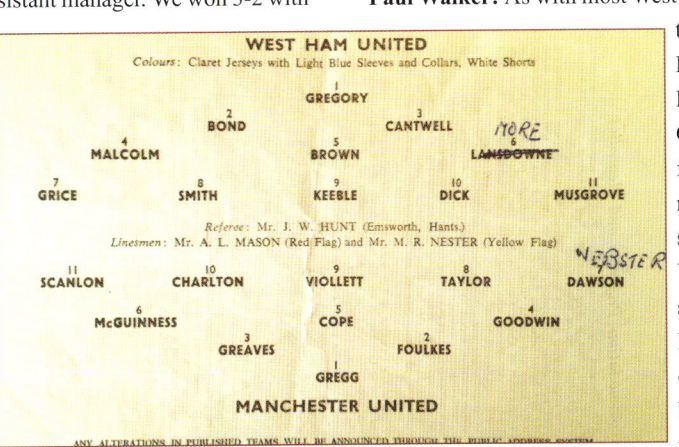

Unfortunately, Bill's spelling was nowhere near as accurate as his goal-scoring prowess (see his son Rob Robinson's entry).

UPTON PARK MEMORIES

AUTHOR

JOHN NORTHCUTT

Books: *West Ham United: The Complete Record*; *West Ham United: On This Day*; *The Claret and Blue Book of West Ham United*; *West Ham United in the League Cup*, *The Definitive West Ham United*; *The Pinnace Collection*

v West Bromwich Albion (26/9/59). Having previously watched games at Millwall and Charlton, where we mainly went to collect autographs, my friend and I took a bus to the other side of Blackwall Tunnel and then another one to the ground, where we went into the South Bank to see first division football for a change.

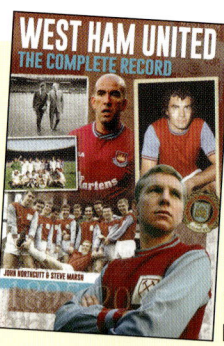

The attendance was just under 30,000 that day, far bigger than the 13,000 or so crowds that I was used to. I really enjoyed the game, the atmosphere and the swaying of the crowd in the Chicken Run as they sang Bubbles.

On the pitch, inside-forward Phil Woosnam ran the show, while wingers Mike Grice and Malcolm Musgrove were also on top form.

---

top flight.

After a lot of badgering, I was finally allowed to go to The Boleyn when I was nine to see us play Nottingham Forest (31/1/59). Dad and Sid put me up on the back tier of the old Chicken Run, a little boy among all those big men. The smoke, the smell . . . there's nothing like it today. We won 5-3 (John Dick and Vic Keeble both scored twice, Phil Woosnam got the other). That team included Ernie Gregory, Noel Cantwell, Andy Malcolm, John Smith, Mike Grice and Malcolm Musgrove – my boyhood heroes.

Terry Foster: v Blackpool, a Monday night floodlit match (16/2/59). I was 14 and it was the first time I had been to a match on my own. West Ham won 1-0 (Johnny Dick). The atmosphere inside the ground is my outstanding memory.

Steve Brackley: v West Bromwich Albion (26/9/59), won 4-1, with goals from Malcolm Musgrove (2), Phil Woosnam and Mike Grice. I was seven and my father took me. We lived at Leytonstone and caught the 686 trolley bus to the ground. We stood in the West Enclosure, near the front towards the North Bank end. Dad put me on a crash barrier so I could get a better view. I believe the barriers were painted green at that time, before the claret-and-blue scheme came in a few years later.

I vividly recall Hammers scoring very early on at the South Bank end and being impressed by the sheer size of the crowd – prior to then Dad had taken me to Clapton's matches at The Spotted Dog and there really was no comparison.

I still have the programme for the match – which, incidentally, includes a letter of apology from a supporter who had thrown a bottle during the game v Leeds United three weeks earlier – and I also have *The Star* sports edition which contains a preview of the game and photos of both teams. It's a bit tatty now but one of my prized possessions.

Dad first started watching Hammers in 1923. Before that his father attended home games at The Memorial Grounds and, on September 1, 1904, saw the first-ever West Ham game at The Boleyn.

Norman Roberts: My dad, Frank, and grandad, Fred, took me to my first game in the early 60s when I was 10. They used to talk about Dick Walker, Ernie Gregory and Lenny Goulden, which gave me the sense that the club was old. I don't recall the opposition for my first game but the noise of the crowd has always stayed with me. People carried rattles to the games in those days and there was such a buzz of excitement that I was hooked immediately.

During my teenage years I started to go to games by myself. I would usually arrive at 10.30am – two hours before the gates opened – so that I could secure my favourite spot on the halfway line in the Chicken Run. I didn't know it at the time but I was watching the greatest era in West Ham's history and those FA Cup and European Cup Winners' Cup runs of the mid-60s were magnificent. I was just a kid, full of dreams and they all seemed to be coming a reality. In the late 60s, I think it was 1967-68,

---

PLAYER

FRANK LAMPARD

Born: 20/9/48, Canning Town, east London
WHU career: 1967-85
Position: Left-back
Apps: 660, Goals: 22

IT was a struggle when I was young. Because I lost my dad when I was five, I lived with my nan and grandad at 142 Liverpool Road, Canning Town. I went to Star Lane primary and then Pretoria Road secondary school.

Uncle George would take me over to Hackney Marshes every Sunday and that's when I caught the football habit. We used to play in the streets all day long. If you were born in Canning Town you only really had three options: work in the docks, play football or become a bank robber. Everyone supported West Ham – there was no other team to follow.

I went to West Ham in the late 50s and early 60s, when people like Harry Obeney, Vic Keeble, Billy Dare, John Bond and Dave Dunmore were playing. Ernie Gregory and Noel Dwyer were the keepers at the time. Johnny Smith used to play tennis over at Hermit Road park in the afternoons.

Upton Park was buzzing back then. Adults would pay to get in but the kids were lifted over the turnstile and got in for free. I used to stand on the South Bank.

I replaced Bonzo at right-back on my debut v Manchester City (18/11/67), who were a frightening team to play back then. I had a fair game and was happy with my performance. Ron (Greenwood) did leave me out for a few games after that but when I returned he played me at left-back for pretty much the rest of the season – until I broke my leg up at Sheffield United. I felt much more comfortable on the left.

I bought my first season ticket for £14.50. I remained a season ticket holder until 1984, when Trevor Brooking retired.

Jack Fawbert: I was 11, in my first year at Dagenham County High School. I had made friends with Steve, who asked if I wanted to go to Upton Park one Saturday with him and another classmate Graham. The opposition was Everton (11/2/61).

We got there early and stood down the front behind the goal on the North Bank. West Ham won 4-0 (Harry Obeney 2, John Dick, Mal Musgrove) and the roar of the North Bank was something I'll never forget – and there wasn't a roof on it in those days to keep the noise in.

Bobby Moore played but I particularly remember Tony Scott on the wing. I recall marvelling at how high Obeney jumped to score his headed goal.

Danny Cooper: To be honest, I can't remember much about my first game at Upton Park. A terrible admission, I know. It would have been 1961 and I think it may have been v Fulham but I do remember we lost. Most of our early football matches were in the company of my Uncle Jim who, like the rest of the family, was an Arsenal fan. Highbury was therefore where I saw my first 'proper' football match. In the enlightened tradition of the times, when your team were away and you were not a fanatic supporter, you went to another London game – except Millwall, which was considered too dangerous for a 10-year-old even then. It took a while to get around to Upton Park, as Jim insisted we would need to learn to swear first!

My support began in 1958 following their promotion to the first division. I'm still not sure why any right-minded seven-year-old would choose West Ham as their team but, somehow, they fitted the role which my wilful act of rebellion demanded. Little did I realise how they would go on to repay me over the years. As an all-grown-up 13-year-old, regular attendance under my own steam was permitted, provided I didn't go in the North Bank. It was another couple of years before I felt brave enough to go in with the big boys, floating between the Chicken Run or behind the goal in the South Bank in the interim, usually with like-minded school mates in tow.

John Burton: My first visit was to watch the reserves in the early 60s. My father had banned me from watching the 'Stiffs', with the promise that I could see the first team when I was older. I was still at primary school and a trip from Seven Kings to Upton Park was an adventure in itself for me and my friend. In those days the reserves played at home on Saturday afternoon while the first team played away. All I can remember about that day is that the reserves won, and the first team lost.

Father must have known where I had been, because when I got home he told me that West Ham Reserves had won (in those days the reserves' results came over on the BBC teleprinter), expecting me to reply: "I know". But I was alert enough to respond with: "Good". As he never even mentioned how the first team had got on, he must have known where I had been!

Alan Porter: My father and his brothers were avid supporters since the 20s. My first game was v Arsenal (21/4/62). I was nine and still a little on the small side to watch from the terraces, so Dad had saved up and got us two seats in Block B of the West Stand. It was years later that an extension was built and Block A arrived, which makes you wonder how the management managed to mix up the alphabet!

For years I was convinced that we lost 4-1 but looking back through the records I see that it was a 3-3 draw (Tony Scott, John Dick, Bill Lansdowne).

Gary Casson: v Sheffield United (29/9/62). Tony Scott scored in a 1-1 draw. I was 10 and I'd nagged my father silly to take me. He had never been to Upton Park either at that point. We lived in north London but my aunt (father's sister) lived just off Green Street in Oakdale Road. I had become passionate about football and with most of my friends supporting either Arsenal or Tottenham, I just decided to be different and chose West Ham. In those days Tottenham were the best team in the country but there was something about the Hammers and Bobby Moore, in particular, that led me to the East End.

My memories of the first game are a little faint but, for some reason, I can still see Phil Woosnam strutting his stuff with his silky skills in the

---

AUTHOR
TONY HOGG
Books: *West Ham United Who's Who* (editions 1, 2 & 3); *West Ham United Quiz Book; Hammers. 100 Years of Football; The Essential History of West Ham United*

v Burnley (29/4/61). I was taken by my father George, who was born in Stratford and worked in the railway yard there for many years. Hammers had played away the previous Saturday, which was my 13th birthday, so this was my belated birthday treat.

Ron Greenwood had just been appointed as West Ham's manager, so a new era was about to begin.

As I took my place on the North Bank with Dad among the 25,385 crowd, that end of the ground had yet to be covered and the new tall floodlight pylons had still to be installed. In fact, Upton Park bore absolutely no resemblance to how it looks today.

Phil Woosnam, who would become one of my all-time favourite players, scored a cracking goal from 20 yards out to spark my first ever celebration of a Hammers goal and my undying support for the team. Although we lost 2-1, I was well and truly hooked on Hammers and I particularly remember a young Alan Sealey, who would become another favourite, playing at centre-forward.

Ernie Gregory, the legendary West Ham goalkeeper who played for many years, including the famous 1958 promotion team. My first West Ham memories are of the 1964 FA Cup run. Although some kids from Aveley, Essex, where we lived, were Spurs fans, mainly due to the famous double winners, more were West Ham, mostly for the same reasons as me. I pestered my parents for a West Ham shirt, eventually bought from East Ham market, and for Dad to take me to Upton Park.

My first games were in the 1964-65 European Cup Winners' Cup-winning campaign, so I've just completed my 50th season. I cannot honestly name the first game but the Good Friday fixture v West Brom in 1965 was the most notable for Brian Dear's five goals in 20 minutes.

Andrew Smith: It was my grandfather, Thomas Barton, who introduced me to supporting the club. He was born in West Ham and had been a regular visitor to Upton Park since the 20s, when his heroes included Syd Puddefoot, Jimmy Ruffell and Vic Watson.

I saw my first match, a goal-less draw v Leicester City (5/12/64), aged nine and was very excited.

Steve Wilks: Born in Plashet Grove, East Ham, I had to be a Hammers fan. My first memories of West Ham were at the age of seven, watching the 1964 FA Cup final. My first visit to Upton Park was in February 1965.

Steve Burton: My father, William George Burton, and grandfather, Joseph Turner, took me to my first home game and now my son also attends. My memories of my first match, v Leeds United in 1965, were standing on the North Bank on the wooden stool Dad made for me.

Steve Mortlock: v West Bromwich Albion on Good Friday (16/4/65). I was five and attended with my dad. We won 6-1 with Brian Dear scoring five goals in 20 minutes either side of half-time. I am not sure I remember much about it but it was certainly a great 'sales pitch' to reel in a new supporter (if only I had known it wasn't always going to be like this!).

Alan Deadman: I was 10 and staying at my aunt Elsie's home in West Ham during the school holidays, as I much preferred East London to my home town of Slough. West Ham were playing their last league game of the season v Blackpool (23/4/65) and my cousin Billy offered to take me to Upton Park. I remember us being a goal down at half-time but soon after Ken Brown headed us level. The noise was deafening when we equalised and I soon learned the words to *Bubbles* and joined in the singing. When Brian Dear hit the winner with 10 minutes to go I was lifted off my feet by the crowd and parted from my cousin for a short while.

I have the programme cover of that first game, enlarged and signed by Brian Dear, framed on my wall at home.

As I got older I used to visit Upton Park as much as I could and stood mostly in the West Enclosure, towards the edge of the North Bank. If I couldn't afford two home games in a week I would even cycle the 70-mile round trip from Slough. When I broke my leg in 1971 I still managed to get to home games – members of the St John's Ambulance Brigade let me sit on the bench pitch-side in front of the North Bank. The only problem was my leg was in the way of players taking corner-kicks, so I had to stand up while they were taken – my endeavours even led to my picture being published in the programme v Newcastle (18/12/71) as 'Fan of the Day'.

Mark Sandell: v Sunderland (23/8/65). I was four and my dad brought a wooden beer crate for me to stand on in the Chicken Run. The noise was unbelievable and when Martin Peters scored (1-1), the bloke next to me clapped so hard he accidentally elbowed me in the eye. When the noise died down, Dad saw that I was crying. He has long since said that I might as well cry at my first game, because I was going to shed many more tears in the name of West Ham over the years. He was right.

Steven Mitchell: Aged eight, I saw West Ham beat Sheffield Wednesday 4-2 (16/10/65), with Martin Britt (2), Martin Peters and Ken Brown scoring. I was enchanted by the vibrant colours of our wonderful claret-and-blue jerseys, which seemed to be dark grey and light grey in my football annuals and on TV in the old black and white world of 50 years ago, and the sheer blondness of skipper Bobby Moore's hair. The smell of Woodbines, pale ale, fried onions and damp gabardine raincoats sticks with me to this day.

John Lawrence: One of our neighbours, Ernie, popped round to our house one Friday evening to ask if I wanted to go to West Ham the following day. I went as company for his son Terry, who was three years older than me. It was a goal-less draw v Stoke City (30/10/65) and at the impressionable age of eight I was amazed by the colours and the noise of the crowd. I remember very little apart from a truckload of back passes and the fact that I stood in the cage in the North Bank – the one that

A recent pic of Brian Dear with the programme for the game, in 1965, that marked his record-breaking five-star performance in front of goal.

Manager Ted Fenton, always proud of his strong Hammers links, cared about his players.

overlooked the main grandstand. The steps were huge and the bit next to the stand had wobbly railings. If you looked down and through them there was a massive drop. Very scary!

Mick Melbourne: My father used to take me to see Spurs and Arsenal in the late 50s, because they were our two nearest teams. I especially enjoyed Spurs (gulp!) but didn't fancy supporting them or anyone else. Arsenal were just dull. In 1958 he took me to see Spurs play newly-promoted West Ham, a midweek game under the floodlights. The combination of a 4-1 win, the claret-and-blue colours and the style had me instantly hooked. I told Dad as we left: "That's my team." Turned out that was his team, too, but he wasn't going to tell me, because, knowing me, I would have supported someone else. West Ham provided the glue in our relationship during an adolescence where we could not agree on much else.

My first visit to Upton Park was v Chelsea (13/11/65). I went with a schoolmate, who deserted me when we got in and joined the away support. We won 2-1 (Peter Brabrook, Martin Peters). Two memories: Racist abuse of John Charles by the Chelsea fans and getting thumped by the same people after cheering our winner.

Ian Haywood: v Olympiakos of Greece, ECWC, 2nd round (24/11/65), won 4-0 with two from Martin Peters and once each from Johnny Byrne and Peter Brabrook. A fantastic game of attacking football from Hammers and, at 15, I was hooked. The games under lights at The Boleyn always had a special atmosphere and that night was just great.

Jeff Garner: My dad, Alf, took me to see my first West Ham match v Everton (27/11/65), when I was seven. It was a 3-0 win (John Sissons 2, Peter Brabrook) and Moore, Hurst and Peters were in the team. I stood with Dad, on my box, in the West Enclosure. Memories of the game are very vague but what I know is that I was hooked even before we got in the ground. I recollect the guys outside selling rosettes and my brother, Keith, still has his one with Bobby Moore's name on.

Dad, grandad Ernest and great-grandad Alfred Ernest all lived locally and did some general duties at the ground in the period during and just after the war, to earn a few bob. Dad told me that one of the duties was to nail the studs onto the players' boots using a cobbler's last. Another great story he told me was that, sometime after the war, his grandad's sight began to fail and he was no longer able to work at the ground. West Ham's manager at that time was Ted Fenton and, knowing of their plight, reserved seats so that Dad could take him along to matches and tell him what was going on. I wish Dad was here now, what stories he could have told.

Alan Chapman: I grew up in Wood Green, north London and, logically, should probably have been a Spurs supporter. My uncle supported them and I was seven when they won the double in 1961. However, my dad had a soft spot for West Ham. He was a ticket collector at King's Cross station and on duty that memorable night in 1958 when Hammers returned from Middlesbrough having clinched the second division championship. He was really impressed with the thousands of West Ham fans who turned up at the station in the early hours of that Sunday morning to welcome the team home. Also, in the days when all teams travelled to away games by train, he said that West Ham players were among the friendliest, with particular mention for Ken Brown who would always stop for a chat.

I think it was in the 1962-63 season that I became a confirmed Hammer and Bobby Moore certainly had an influence on this decision. He was such an iconic figure and rapidly became my boyhood hero.

My first visit to Upton Park was v Blackburn Rovers (12/2/66) in the FA Cup 4th round. I went with two schoolmates, Keith and Dave. We were the only West Ham supporters in our year, in a school full of Spurs and Arsenal fans. Having no idea how long it would take us to get to Upton Park, which seemed miles away on the tube map, we met at Wood Green station at 11.00am . . . and found ourselves strolling along Green Street at midday! We stood in the West Enclosure, towards the North Bank end, so had a good view when Jimmy Bloomfield scored Hammers' first goal – and his only one for the club – with a close-range header. John Byrom scored a hat-trick for Rovers, three times putting them ahead, as the game ended 3-3. My main memory is of our wingers, Peter Brabrook and John Sissons, sending over a stream of crosses, most of which were headed clear by Rovers' centre-half Mike England.

Chris Ball: My dad, Geoff, was a Hammers fan. Although born near the Caledonian Road, he moved to East Ham (Mafeking Avenue) with his parents and two sisters after the war. After marrying my mum we lived in Shelley Avenue, then Katherine Road for 30-odd years.

Dad took me to my first game around Christmas/New Year in season 1966-67 and we stood in the old Chicken Run. I can't remember the score but it was absolutely freezing and I wanted him to take me home at half-time. Needless to say, he didn't.

Phil Garner: My dad, Alf, took me to my first game when I was four, in 1966, but I don't know who we were playing. We stood (or rather I was on his shoulders) where the West Enclosure met the North Bank. My older brothers, Jeff and Keith, would have been in the pen in that corner of the ground with many other kids. I only found out in recent years that, at the age of 10, Dad had worked for the club with his grandad and used to nail the players' studs on in the changing room. We still have the cobbler's anvil they used.

Steven Duhig: My first West Ham-related experience came one summer in the 60s. As usual I was with my friend, Ian Davey. Occasionally we would go out to the park and on one such occasion we noticed, some distance away, a striking, young couple with a baby sprawled across the grass. Ian said: "That's Bobby Moore!" I knew who Bobby was but would not then have recognised him on my own. I suggested: "Why don't you get his autograph then, Ian?" but he was very reluctant and so dared me to do it. I am quite sure that Bobby already knew exactly what was coming, and probably chuckled to himself at our shy indecision.

Bobby was wonderful, even though we were disturbing his private family moments, and I promptly brought back his autograph to Ian. That was my first and closest encounter with the great man. Little did I know how much enjoyment he was to give us all in the coming years.

David Bernstein: My friend, Barry, and I lived in Lea Bridge Road, Leyton and as young boys used to walk to Leyton Orient on a Saturday, until he moved to Forest Gate. We then went to games at Upton Park. We queued at the schoolboys' entrance and paid 1/- admission and 6d for a programme. My first game was v Liverpool (3/9/66) and we drew 1-1 (Geoff Hurst).

Paul Cockerell: My first game at The Boleyn was in August 1967, when I was six. My brother, Pete, who is 15 months younger than me, was my sole companion. It was the first match of the season, we lost 3-2 to Sheffield Wednesday (19/8/67). Hurst and Peters scored but it is best remembered for being the great Billy Bonds' debut.

My nan and aunt lived just up from the ground, in Balaam Street, by The Abbey Arms. It was my Aunt Vera's treat for Pete and I to go to our first match. We caught a bus direct to Balaam Street from our then family home in Dirleton Road, off The Portway opposite West Ham Park. I remember arriving at Nan's maisonette around midday and we soon set off along the Barking Road towards the ground, accompanied by Aunt

Vera. I recall the mixture of excitement and apprehension as the crowds seemed to grow the nearer we got to The Boleyn pub.

Once we arrived in Castle Street everything suddenly seemed to intensify. The mass of different noises and smells suddenly hit me, along with all usual match day hustle and bustle, and I got butterflies in my stomach.

We made our way along the road to what I think was then called the 'Boys Entrance' at the corner of the old South Bank and the end of the Chicken Run. We joined the relatively short queue as Aunty Vera pulled out a bag full of food and drink, which could have fed six adults. After telling me to look after my little brother, she then stuffed a ten bob (50p) note deep into my pocket. She said she'd meet us outside the supporters' club after the game and set off for home – no doubt via the bookies!

We probably had a fair wait before we were let into the ground but it seemed to pass quickly as I was entranced by the thrill of my first match day experience. I'm pretty sure the entrance fee was 2/6 (two shillings and sixpence) each.

I don't recall much of the actual game itself but I remember that we lost and also the brass band playing before the game and during half-time. During the interval we quickly scoffed the mass of Shippams fish paste sarnies (urgh!) we'd been given and I remember being fascinated to see groundstaff hanging up those square black boards with white numbers on, giving out the 'half-times' at either end of the ground.

What I remember most from those far off days are the smells of beer and cigar smoke wafting around the ground – a memory which leaves me longing for simpler, happier and more secure times.

We duly met Aunt Vera (ecstatic due to a tanner each-way win!) and then walked back to Balaam Street for another treat of saveloy and chips before being escorted onto the bus home, where, no doubt, we settled down to watch *Dr. Who* and *The Val Doonican Show*.

Paul Morgan: v Burnley (21/8/67). At 13, I attended the game with an older neighbour and his father. We won 4-2 (Geoff Hurst 2, Martin Peters, Harry Redknapp) and Trevor Brooking made his debut.

Peter Lush: I started supporting West Ham, aged nine, in 1964 because I liked the name and they had just won the FA Cup. Every boy in my class supported a team and once you chose one you couldn't change. The rest of the family were Chelsea supporters because of my uncle Sid, who was a lifelong Blues fan. (I went with Sid to the game at Stamford Bridge in 1986 when we won 4–0. He had a spare ticket. I was among the Chelsea season-ticket holders, so I kept very quiet!)

My first visit to Upton Park was for a London Challenge Cup game in 1967 to see West Ham play against my 'other' team, Hendon – in fact, I travelled to the game on the Hendon supporters' coach. Professional clubs usually fielded a reserve side in that competition, and West Ham won 1–0 with a team that included Trevor Brooking and Frank Lampard, who both made their first team debuts that year.

Gary Price: v Manchester City (18/11/67), we lost 3-2 (Hurst, Peters). Sat in the West Stand upper, I was 10 and the whole place seemed so vast. Frank Lampard made his debut.

Michael Oliver: At the age of nine in December 1967, my dad, Alan, was thinking about taking me to West Ham v Tottenham. We didn't go for some reason but I looked out for the result on *Grandstand*. A week later I was allowed to watch them on *Match of the Day* (won 4-2 at Leicester) and I was hooked. We eventually got to Upton Park to see them lose 1-0 v Chelsea (23/3/68). As well as me and Dad, there was my brother Ed, two school friends, Jonathan and Stephen, and a student who was lodging with us at the time, also called Alan. Dad had never been to Upton Park before either, although his uncles had taken him to see Ilford FC when he was a boy and amateur football attracted large crowds. One of those uncles, Eddie, took me to my second West Ham match a couple of weeks later (6/4/68), a happier result this time as we beat Newcastle United 5-0 with a young Trevor Brooking scoring a hat-trick (plus two from John Sissons).

The main memories of that first match were the size of the crowd (over 36,000), the noise and the chanting. We were as close to the front of the North Bank as we could get, although I couldn't see much of the goal at our end. The match was on TV the next day, although I didn't get to see it as I had to go to Sunday school! I guess ITV wiped the tape, as I've never seen it repeated or turn up on YouTube.

Stuart Allen: v Coventry City (4/5/68). I went with my girlfriend (now wife) and my brother. Ann's family had always supported Hammers, whereas I had no real allegiance to any team but at that time did tend to go and watch Coventry when they were in London. I remember very little of the game (0-0) but the old Chicken Run was being replaced at the end of that season. We must have enjoyed it, because we were back for the Everton game the next week and we've hardly been away since.

Mark Harknett: My dad, Bernie, and grandad, Bert, were both supporters. However, Grandad only went to games sporadically and Dad went to a few in the 50s. He didn't go again until the late 60s and that was only to take me. To be honest, my main influences were the area in which I lived (Stratford/Forest Gate) and my peer group; pretty much everyone at Park Primary School in Stratford supported West Ham. I was six when we won the FA Cup in '64 and I remember our teacher talking about it to the whole class and saying that it was the first time we had ever won it. Dad also took me to see the team parading the cup on the coach as it drove past Plaistow station.

I started badgering him to take me in 1968, aged 10, and my first game was the last one of the 1967-68 season, v Everton (11/5/68). I can't say it was a wonderful experience and I'm amazed I ever wanted to go back! For many years I was convinced that we'd stood on the Chicken Run but I've since learned that it was closed that day, in readiness for the summer

AUTHOR

TONY McDONALD

Books: *West Ham United Who's Who (2nd edition with Tony Hogg); Hammers: 100 Years of Football; Boys of '86: The Untold Story of West Ham United's Greatest-Ever Season (with Dan Francis); West Ham United: The Managers; West Ham: In My Day (Vol 1 & 2 with Terry Roper); Upton Park Memories*

WE beat Burnley (26/8/68) 5-2 under the lights with goals from Geoff Hurst (2), Trevor Brooking (2) and Martin Peters. I watched with my dad, Terry, from our seats quite close to the front of A Block in the upper West Stand, but remember nothing of the game. I was eight and should have realised then that it was typical West Ham to whack Burnley for five just seven days after slumping 4-1 at home to Everton. It was all downhill from there.

That is the short answer. If you don't wish to indulge me, I advise you to turn the page now!

So why did I eventually support West Ham? Eventually? I'll explain . . .

Although our family's love of football is rooted in West Ham, my dad always encouraged me to take a much broader interest in the game, to watch as many teams as possible both live and on TV. By the age of nine I'd gone with friends and their dads to Highbury, White Hart Lane, Craven Cottage and Brisbane Road and just a few months before my first visit to Upton Park I was impressed by Manchester United's 4-1 victory over Benfica in the European Cup final at Wembley – the first game I recall seeing on TV, although I must have watched many others.

In the playground at Chadwell Heath Juniors, in my delusional mind, I was George Best running rings round my hapless class-mates. I had a pair of Best slippers and he was the first player I wanted to find popping out of a packet of the Soccer Stars stickers. He was my boyhood idol. I didn't want to be Bobby Moore. What, a defender? No fun in stopping others from scoring goals, is there?

I had the classic 60s Man U shirt – but then I accumulated numerous other replica tops: Leeds (who were a mighty force back then), Spurs (honest), West Ham (naturally), Arsenal and QPR. And when my Aunt Lucy took me to visit her best friend in the East End one day, the woman's two sons gave me a few more kits that they had out-grown. These included Celtic and Chelsea (including the white stripe and number on the shorts). So if I wasn't pretending to be Bestie, I might be Jimmy Greaves, Geoff Hurst, Rodney Marsh or Charlie George – I've always loved a maverick. Entranced by the 1970 World Cup (the final between Brazil and Italy was the first I saw in colour on TV), I owned that iconic yellow Brazil shirt, resplendent with the badge already woven on to it, well before an England top. I saw myself more as Jairzinho than Jeff Astle.

But you rarely saw kids – and certainly never grown men – wearing replica football tops to games in the 60s. Kits were for wearing to the park, 'jumpers for goal-posts' and all that. You'd kick a ball around with your mates until it got dark and mum was nagging you to come in for your tea, re-enacting great goals and games you had seen on *Match of the Day* or *The Big Match* (does anyone remember its Sunday afternoon predecessor, Star Soccer, hosted by Peter Lorenzo?), not fritter away the best years of your life camped in a bedroom playing computer games or staring gormlessly at your mobile phone.

It seems unbelievable now, but West Ham didn't even sell their own replica shirts when I started going. I got mine from Bobby Moore's sports shop opposite the ground, while most of the others were bought from Bootings in Goodmayes. Kits were very basic but a virtue of their simplicity was that you could mix and match to some extent. For instance, white shorts and socks would do you for West Ham, Celtic and QPR.

You slept a lot easier if the team didn't sport the club crest on its shirt, because the badges came separate to the shirts and were a bugger to sew on. They were invariably square and cutting neatly round the edges, never mind the sewing process, must have caused many mums who lacked the silken touch of a brain surgeon great angst. But then some didn't help themselves by sewing the badge on the right side of the shirt instead of the left – a cardinal sin if ever there was one.

Numbers, too, were awkward. No clubs and few independent retailers sold them until well into the 70s, so, once again, it was left to mum to weave her magic with the sewing machine. A No.7 or No.11 wasn't too testing to create but a No.6 (the one most of us Hammers wanted on our backs) or No.8 was a challenge too far for many. I was fortunate that my mum, Jean, was brilliant on a sewing machine – as you'd expect being the daughter of a professional dressmaker.

However, there were some horrific botch jobs to be seen around the parks of Essex and east London. Some kids, whose mothers were not adept at sewing, took some stick for displaying embarrassingly shoddy handiwork. If Esther Rantzen's Childline had existed then, she wouldn't have had a minute's rest from dealing with poor boys abused by their peers for the shambolic appearance of wonky club crests and numbers. There was a bit of liberty-taking in some cases, too. Some kids thought they could get away with turning up in, say, a No.4 that didn't join up at the top and neither they nor their parents took the business of kit presentation seriously enough.

Repeating my father's free-thinking absorption of football in the widest context, I brought up my two boys to understand that the game didn't begin and end at West Ham. Yes, they had plenty of by now

Terry McDonald proudly wears the shirt we've all dreamed of pulling on at least once in our life. He caught the eye of reporters on his one and only first team appearance against Sparta of Prague.

ever-changing claret-and-blue kits, but I made sure their wardrobes and drawers were also laden with colourful combinations I'd brought back from countries such as Spain and Italy. The colours of Juventus, Inter, AC Milan, Barcelona and, wait for it, Legia Warsaw were all seen hanging from a Romford washing line at various stages of their childhood.

Getting back to Dad's influence but combining it with the wearing of replica kits. One day, aged about nine, I was playing keepy-uppy on our front lawn in Fauna Close, Chadwell Heath, when a large tanker pulled up to deliver oil for our central heating system. I was wearing my amber shirt, black shorts and amber socks with a perfect black '11' on the back of the top. As the tanker driver approached our house, he said knowingly: "Support the Wolves do you, son?" It was a lesson never to assume anything in this life. "No, it's Folkestone Town's kit," I replied, much to his bewilderment. What he couldn't possibly have known was that, for about half an hour that day, in my dream world, I thought I was my dad!

Years later, Dad told me that the tanker driver was Irishman Danny McGowan, who was playing in West Ham's first team in the early 50s when Dad joined the club from school.

I'm proud of the fact that my Old Man, who grew up in Harold Road, Upton Park and starred for West Ham Boys, started his professional playing career with the club he supported as a boy. OK, he played just the one first team game – a friendly 3-3 draw v Sparta Prague (21/3/57) in which he set up one goal and caught the eye of the press, if not Ted Fenton – but he was a key member of their strong Colts team that was beaten by Manchester United in the 1957 FA Youth Cup final and played many times for the reserves, too. An untimely stint of National Service in 1958, just when Hammers were on the rise after gaining promotion, hampered his long-term hopes of breaking through into the first team but he offers no excuses. He happily admits that his prospects of displacing Malcolm Musgrove on the left-wing were remote, so in the autumn of 1959 he took

The author's father, Terry, playing for West Ham Boys v Chelmsford Boys at Upton Park in 1954.

the opportunity to move up the road for regular first team action with Leyton Orient (171 games, 27 goals), where he played his part in O's historic and barely believable elevation to Division One – glory days that are unlikely to ever be dreamed of, let alone repeated, in E10.

Brief spells with third division Reading and in the upper echelons of non-league football with Wimbledon and Folkestone (ah, those unmistakable Kent giants in amber) followed in the late 60s before Dad finished playing and began his 'second life' managing betting shops, which he did right up to his retirement, Saturday being the busiest punting day, he could only take me to midweek matches – hence my Monday night Upton Park bow – but his cousin, Dennis Farrow, who lived just round the corner from the ground in Barking Road, took me to most games throughout that 1968-69 season. Den would make sure I got a place on the wall at the front of the South Bank and then he'd go and watch the game from nearer the back of the terracing, in the days when they used to herd the away fans in the south-west corner.

How lucky was I to begin my claret-and-blue education watching Moore, Hurst and Peters on a regular basis, plus the emergence of Brooking, Bonds and Lampard – six genuine Hammers legends right there playing together in one season, not forgetting steady Ron Boyce. Spoilt rotten. No wonder I find the modern game, riven with greed, cheats, cynicism and celebrity, unpalatable at times. And to think, we only finished eighth that season, which shows how generally high the standard was 'in them days'.

As many contributors to this book will testify, supporting West Ham basically comes down to the family you are born into. Although Dad never put any pressure on me to support his team, it was inevitable that I would. His father, Jim, had been a fan and his mum, Lily, would watch him play in schoolboy and youth games at the Boleyn Ground – I'm told that on one occasion she thumped one particularly critical fan, who had been having a go at her son, over the head with her umbrella! In my parent's early courting days as teenagers, Mum would wait for Dad at the players' entrance after home games.

In the second half of the 90s, it was the turn of my two young sons, George and Jack, to pledge their allegiance to the claret-and-blue cause. I don't suppose they will ever thank me for it!

The team Tony McDonald saw when he started going to Upton Park early in the 1968-69 season. Standing, left to right: Alan Stephenson, Martin Peters, Bobby Ferguson, John Charles, Bobby Moore, Billy Bonds. Front: Harry Redknapp, Ron Boyce, Trevor Brooking, Geoff Hurst, John Sissons.

redevelopment, so we must have stood on the West Side. Bizarrely, I have no memory of there being no supporters in the opposite stand!

My first disappointment was that Geoff Hurst wasn't playing due to injury. My second was the view – it was abysmal, as Dad had neglected to take anything for me to stand on. I moaned about it and he instructed me to go down the front. Off I trekked with no clue as to where I was going. Efforts to get to the front were futile – who in their right minds would give up their perfect view? – so I headed back to Dad. Like being lost in woods, finding my way back was virtually impossible, so I returned to the front and was allowed through only because I wanted to climb over the wall. I was now pitchside and turning right, I headed towards a policeman sitting in front of what must have been the South Bank. My innocent schoolboy brain must have assumed that PC Plod would be a kindly soul who would take pity on me, look after me, ensure that I could see the game and then help me locate Dad at the end. Or at least get an announcement read out over the tannoy. No chance. He just told me to go back and look for my dad!

I made my way back to where I'd climbed over, wandered through the crowd a bit and, being unable to find Dad, ended up standing as near to the front as I could. I could only see one half of the pitch and had a perfect view of the opening goal scored for Everton by Jimmy Husband. I had no view whatsoever of our goal scored by Martin Peters.

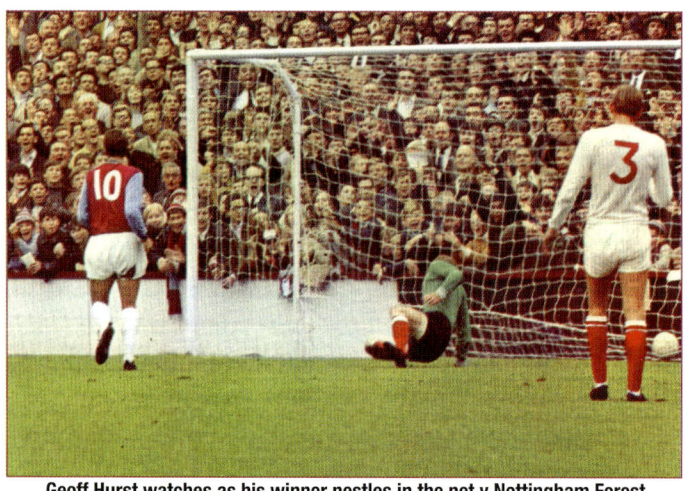

The enormity of my situation then hit me – alone in a huge crowd, Dad nowhere to be seen, Hurst not playing, can't see West Ham attacking – and I started crying! A kind, old lady took pity on me and looked after me until the end of the game. She got me to stand on the wall at the front and look for Dad, who I saw almost straight away.

Apart from Everton's goal, my abiding memory of the actual football was seeing Bobby Moore control a long ball hoofed upfield by an Everton defender by letting it bounce a few times between the ground and his chest. Fantastic skill.

Tony Cullen: I'm one of 12 brothers and sisters and, with the exception of one, all are massive Hammers fans. The family love of West Ham was started by me but thanks go to my late good friend, Raymond Keen, for taking me to my first match, a 1-0 win (Geoff Hurst) v Nottingham Forest (17/8/68). I was due to go to Stamford Bridge that day with another friend but, thankfully, Ray intervened and took me to Upton Park instead.

Richard Bull: v Everton (19/8/68), a Monday night game that we lost 4-1. Accompanied by Dad, I watched it from the back of the North Bank, perched up on one of the metal girders. Martin Peters scored our goal with Harvey, Ball, Husband and Royle netting for Everton.

Ian Puxley: Dad took me, aged nine, to see us play Bolton Wanderers in the League Cup (4/9/68). We stood on the South Bank and saw Geoff Hurst get three in a 7-2 win. Can't remember anything about the game

Geoff Hurst watches as his winner nestles in the net v Nottingham Forest in 1968. It was the first match attended by Tony Cullen, pictured below with his hero in 1999.

PLAYER
JOE DURRELL
Born: 15/3/53, Stepney, east London
WHU career: 1971-72
Position: Winger
Apps: 6, **Goals:** 0

WHEN I arrived at the ground to sign schoolboy forms in the summer of 1968, there was nobody there. Eventually, Ernie Gregory turned up and told me to go and buy 20 fags at the local shop, so the first task I had as a West Ham boy was to go and buy Ernie Gregory a packet of Batchelors cigarettes!

My family were regulars at Upton Park and when I think back I remember going, with Mickey Durrell, to the FA Cup semi v Manchester United as well as the final. To then later play with those same guys is simply unbelievable. As a kid you just can't absorb the full magnitude of that.

On the day of my first team debut v Stoke City (25/9/71), I remember getting on the train at Mile End to go to the ground about an-hour and-half before kick-off. I would be sitting there with the fans.

Gordon Banks was in goal for Stoke and I got injured early on. Before taking the free-kick Bobby Moore came over to me and said: "Try and keep it away from the big man in green," which was a brilliant thing for me to hear at the time. It really settled me down and was just the instruction I needed.

I think I did all right. I wasn't fantastic but I was good enough and we won the game 2-1 (Clyde Best, Bobby Moore). I didn't have any chances but I did put in a few crosses.

but Dad and I became regulars on the South Bank, where I would stand on a fold-up stool he had made me.

Mr G. Pope: v Tottenham (14/9/68), 2-2. I was eight and stood with my dad in the North Bank, not too far behind a young Pat Jennings in goal for Spurs. Torrential rain left us drenched right through. It was the first time I'd seen proper football in colour, as opposed to black and white TV footage, and was overwhelmed to see Moore, Hurst, Peters, Greaves, Gilzean (the latter four scoring the goals), etc, in the flesh. Despite Dad's efforts to lift me up, I was so small that I didn't see much of the action. This, and the fact that I was shivering with the cold and wet, meant that we left at half-time with the game still goal-less. Dad made up for it two weeks later by getting us seats in the West Stand for the visit of Sheffield Wednesday.

John Reynolds: My dad, Terry, first went to Upton Park as a 12-year-old with his Uncle Ted in September 1946 to see West Ham beat Fulham 3-2. Dad took my elder brother, Terry Jnr (aged 10), and myself (seven) to our first game, an entertaining 2-2 draw v Spurs (14/9/68). The attendance was 35,802, yet only three sides of the Boleyn Ground were used that day. The new East Stand was due to open in January, 1969 and I couldn't understand why the crowd was so congested and yet there was an open empty terrace.

I asked Dad where the players' tunnel was and stared at it until he appeared . . . blond hair, white No.6 on the back of his claret-and-blue shirt. Seeing the great Bobby Moore play for the first time . . . it didn't get any better than that.

Roger Hillier: My first visit was one of the most memorable matches in Hammers' history – the 8-0 thrashing of Sunderland (19/10/68), notable for Geoff Hurst's six goals. I briefly met Geoff at one of his book signings and mentioned the display he kindly put on for my 'debut'. He modestly deflected attention away from his scoring feat by asking if I remembered who got the other two goals. And like most supporters, I had forgotten that they were scored by a couple of other West Ham legends, Bobby Moore and Trevor Brooking.

I was 12 at the time and attended with a school mate and his uncle. Sitting in one of the front rows in the West Stand, I had a superb view looking down on the pitch from what seemed a great height. I still treasure the pink match ticket and what has become of my dog-eared programme.

Peter Morris: There was never any real doubt as to my ending up a Hammer. My dad, also Peter, was a supporter, my grandad likewise (he walked all the way from Poplar to Wembley to climb over the wall to see the 1923 FA Cup final). We moved to Forest Gate – within walking distance of the ground – in 1966 and, of course, we had the glamour of Moore, Hurst and Peters.

I did have a brief flirtation with Manchester United – my first footballing memory, aged seven, is watching the 1968 European Cup final and I briefly fancied myself as a Red. But, thankfully, this only lasted for about a fortnight.

My first visit to the Boleyn Ground was in October 1968, to see a reserve match v Reading. I went with Dad, my uncle Greg Gallagher and his son Steve. We stood on the West Enclosure (North Bank end) and watched Hammers win 7-1, with future first team coach Roger Cross scoring twice. The team was captained by Eddie Bovington, in his last season as a pro.

As we were leaving the ground, a wag said that it wasn't always that good, and not to expect big wins every week. It has sometimes felt over the years that it has been downhill all the way!

One other memory of the day is the scaffolding surrounding the near-completed new East Stand, so I missed seeing the old Chicken Run by only a few months.

Steve Perry: It was my dad, Patrick (Paddy), who led me to support West Ham. He has been a fan all of his life (now 82 years). Although he never owned a season ticket, he went to many home games and took great pride in introducing me to the club, instilling in me what it meant to support your local team. I cannot remember the first game that I attended at Upton Park but one that sticks in the memory was a win v QPR (2/11/68) when I was eight. West Ham won 4-3 (a long-range screamer from Bobby Moore, plus goals from Martin Peters, Geoff Hurst and Harry Redknapp) and we watched it from the West Stand upper tier.

I recently saw this game on a recording of *The Big Match*, which used

You don't get much for pound these days but in October 1968 it bought you a grandstand seat to see Hurstie hit Sunderland for six.

PLAYER
ALAN CURBISHLEY
Born: 8/11/54, Forest Gate, east London
WHU career: 1975-79
Position: Midfielder
Apps: 96, **Goals:** 5

IT was great to finally step out onto the field as a West Ham first team player, having been with the club since I was 12.

As a fan I used to watch from the North Bank and I was sat up on the rafters when Geoff Hurst scored his six goals v Sunderland in 1968 – or was it five? Didn't he punch one in? Later, after I became a schoolboy apprentice, I stood and watched games from behind the dugouts in the West Stand lower.

Playing football in the playground, I guess I pretended to be Bobby Moore. He was my biggest favourite.

I recall watching the Wembley cup final triumphs of 1964 and '65 on television at home in Canning Town.

to go out on ITV on a Sunday afternoon. I was surprised how parts of that match still came back to me after all this time and to see the muddy Upton Park pitch again was wonderful. It was surprising how any quality football was played but it made for great excitement.

After the game Dad took me to the West Ham United shop and bought me the club crest for Mum to sow on to my blue tracksuit.

Gary White: My love affair with Hammers dates back to 1966 – I was seven on July 30, the same day West Ham won the World Cup – but my first-ever game at Upton Park was a goalless draw v Chelsea (12/4/69), which I watched from the East Stand with my brother Steve and our dad, John. Although West Ham had the golden trio playing that day, my eye was taken by a rampaging young right-back who was overlapping and putting in some great tackles. It was, of course, 'Bonzo' who remains my favourite all-time Hammer.

Being born in Barking and going to the same infants school that Bobby Moore had previously attended (Westbury), it was a no-brainer that I would be a Hammer. We moved to Hornchurch in 1966 and there were some really strange kids in our class there – Spurs fans.

It was then that I had my first experience as a fan on the receiving end of banter. I remember walking to school one day in 1968 and our milkman, a big Hammers fan, said to me: "Wasn't that terrible about West Ham last night?" I asked what he meant by it and he said we'd lost 3-0 to Mansfield in the FA Cup. I thought it was a joke – he was always kidding around with my parents – and it wasn't until I got to school that, to my horror, I found out it was true. That's when the Spurs-supporting kids slaughtered me in the playground.

It happened again a year or so later, when Martin Peters was sold to Tottenham and we got Jimmy Greaves plus cash in exchange. Jim was great at first but his off-field drink problems soon ended his illustrious playing career.

For me, the mid-70s were an exciting time. Reaching teenage years and then discovering girls was great. Who can forget the hordes of females congregating around the North Bank goal for a close-up view of the good-looking young goalkeeper Mervyn Day, who broke into the first team after Bobby Ferguson was dropped for slagging off the team to the press? We used to stand there chatting up the birds and were able to combine our two main interests, which was great for a 15-year-old with high testosterone levels!

Marco Taviani: My dad, Marcello, told me he had me on his shoulders when West Ham paraded the FA Cup in 1964 but I didn't go to a match with him until the Anglo-Italian Cup tie v Fiorentina in 1975-76. My first visit to Upton Park was in 1969, aged six, and I was taken by my sister, Lorena, and her friend. I remember the opposing team wearing black and white stripes and subsequently found out that it was the first league game of the season, v Newcastle United (9/8/69), which West Ham won 1-0 (Geoff Hurst). I spent a lot of the game in the St. John's Ambulance room, having cut my knee when I fell off the South Bank perimeter wall.

I can't remember a specific incident or occasion that made me want to follow the club, other than being given a West Ham top when I was five or six. Being young and growing up in East Ham, you just supported your local team. At St. John's RC Comprehensive, which was right next door to the ground, all my mates were West Ham too, so there really was no other team to support.

Danny Waller: v Chelsea (11/8/69). I finally got to see West Ham at the age of nine. I had been waiting to see my team live for more than three years – since my older friends in the street where I lived told me that West Ham had won the World Cup. At the age of four my family moved out of my birthplace in Barking to a new village in Essex called Stanford-Le-Hope. Our council estate was built by Newham Council and the street names were from areas of east London: Plaistow Crescent, Stratford Gardens, etc. We lived in Upton Close, so there was only one team to support.

I attended the Chelsea game with my father. After what seemed like an eternity driving along the A13 during rush hour, we finally arrived – and the only initial reaction I can recall is how high the floodlights were. We joined the queue in the forecourt for the nine shilling (45p) seats and began to get increasingly nervous as the 7.30pm kick-off approached and we still weren't in the ground. At about 7.15 the gates closed and the sign went up: 'Seats Sold Out'.

There then ensued a mad dash to the North Bank, where we gained admittance after kick-off. What a crush! Dad stood right at the back and I had no chance of getting through the crowd to see anything, so I got

AUTHOR
PETER THORNE (aka Billy Blagg)
Book: *Nightmare on Green Street*

v Liverpool (22/2/69). I used to have the programme but I left it in a plastic bag outside the gates of the Boleyn Ground when the great man died and I hope it is now buried in the Bobby Moore shrine when the BM Stand was erected.

The match ended 1-1 (John Sissons scoring a cracker). The thing that amazed me then, and I still remember vividly today, was the smell of the grass and how big the players looked, together with the fantastic atmosphere on the North Bank. I wasn't a massive football fan at the time but my best friend had persuaded me that I should go to at least one match to see what it was like. I fell in love with the game that day.

At the end of the match I was looking forward to the next game and talking about travelling away. For many years after I never missed a match.

AUTHOR
STEVE BLOWERS
Book: *Nearly Reached The Sky*

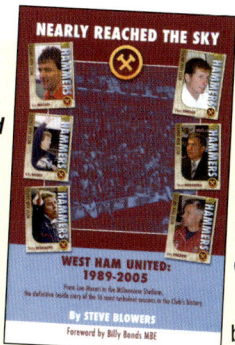

"WE support our local team" is a modern-day Hammers chant but, back then, it really was the only option. My long-awaited Boleyn Ground bow finally arrived on November 28, 1970, when my fellow nine-year-old schoolmate, Ken Main, and his dad, Robert, a staunch Glasgow Rangers supporter who had developed a soft-spot for the Hammers since moving south, invited me to see Ron Greenwood's West Ham United take on Coventry City.

Perched on the edge of my seat, high in the heavens of the West Stand, at long last I found myself watching my heroes, Geoff Hurst and Bobby Moore, through clouds of Mr Main's pipe smoke. I can still vividly recall Clyde Best's bazooka rocking the right-hand angle of the North Bank goal with such force that it rebounded back to him on the edge of the area.

Sadly, the claret-and-blue scarves knotted around our wrists were only brought into play once, when the bear-like Bermudian later found the net, but it was not enough as my crumpled match-day programme tells me that John O'Rourke and David Clements gave Sky Blues a 2-1 win.

Today, some 45 years on and nearly 1,000 visits to Upton Park later, I guess that debut defeat set the tone . . . if only I had known then what I know now. The late Robert Main certainly has a lot to answer for.

lifted on to the bar in the old north-west corner from where I could just about see play between the heads and the roof. Not much of a view but seeing the numbers six and 10 made it all worthwhile. I didn't see the goals from Hurst and Peters go in to give Hammers the 2-0 victory but, some 45 years later, I still remember everything else about it as though it was yesterday.

Ian McMaster: I became a fan around the time of the '66 World Cup. My family lived in Bath, so we had no decent football there, but we had a friend of a friend who lived in Romford and was a West Ham season ticket holder for years. And twice a season, he would send me packages of West Ham programmes.

My first visit to Upton Park was for a night game v Chelsea (11/8/69). Overriding memories of the evening were (a) how exciting it was to see a game under floodlights; and (b) the crush to get into Upton Park station after the game, with police horses trying to control the queue. In fact, Dad was so anxious we would be crushed that we left the queue and walked to Plaistow, something that I often did in later years.

Eamonn McManus: It being a passage of rite after discarding my Georgie Best shirt, having decided at six I did not want to be a 'Cockney Red', I was taken by my brothers, Mick and Patrick, for my first game at

AUTHOR
PETE MAY
Books: *Irons in the Soul; Hammers in the Heart; Flying So High: West Ham's Cup Finals*

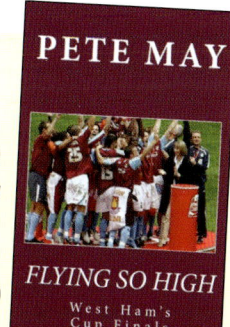

WHEN I was about 10 I became aware that all the other kids at school were really into football. My dad, Dennis, wasn't a fan but I asked him to take me to a match and we tried all the London clubs, visiting Arsenal, Chelsea and Spurs. But there was something special about West Ham, and we were only 10 minutes drive from Upminster tube.

My first game was v Blackpool (31/10/70) and we won 2-1 (Jimmy Greaves, Peter Eustace). Dad became a convert too and used to enjoy the band before matches and, as the players ran out, watching the ball come out of the tunnel followed by the great Bobby Moore.

The Boleyn v Sheffield Wednesday (20/9/69). I stood in the South Bank, down by the wall behind the goal, thinking this is really great and from that moment my life changed. We won 3-0 (Geoff Hurst, Harry Redknapp, O.G.), so onwards and upwards. It has been a long road involving many twists and turns and hopefully will go on for a few more years.

Peter Tydeman: I have been going to West Ham since 1969 but cannot remember the first game I attended. Both my sons are West Ham supporters and, being unable to remember my own first visit, I have made sure they will by mounting the programmes from their first games in a frame.

Pete Gumbrell: v Ipswich Town (14/3/70). The goal-less game was awful, although I didn't think so at the time. As I remember, it was marked by two things: a 30-yard shot from Frank Lampard that missed the goal by inches, and the fact that it was Martin Peters' last appearance before his move to Spurs. My late father took me to the match. We caught the train from Hove to Victoria, then took the tube 18 stops to Upton Park. When we arrived at Upton Park station, Dad asked a fellow supporter the way to the ground. The reply was: "Just follow the crowd." That was 45 years ago and I have been following them ever since.

Kevin Courtney: v Coventry City (28/11/70). Dad took me as a ninth birthday present. We sat up in the 'grandstand' – I'm sure it cost 12 shillings (60p). At half-time three boys climbed over the South Bank wall and ran the length of the pitch. They almost managed to disappear into the North Bank but were apprehended as they tried to climb the wall. Alas, we lost 2-1 (Clyde Best).

Alan Byrne: Being a south Londoner (then living in Tooting, SW17), I didn't want to copy the local lads in supporting either Chelsea, Crystal Palace or even Tottenham. Hammers had a reputation for attacking, entertaining football, so I chose them and have now been a loyal supporter for 45 years. First visit was on a typically cold and damp Saturday in December and I was there with my cousin for the match against his team, Arsenal (4/12/71). Although the game ended 0-0, I was impressed by a nippy right-winger by the name of Harry Redknapp, who managed to get in quite a few dangerous crosses.

Richard Goldby: v Crystal Palace (19/2/72) was memorable to me for the long, convoluted, multi-route bus journey from Bromley, Kent via Bromley-by Bow. By the end of the season I had perfected my thereafter (until I got my own wheels) habitual route by No.47 from Bromley bus garage to London Bridge, walking from Monument along Fenchurch Street to Aldgate East, and then taking the 5, 15 or 23 (whichever came first) to The Boleyn.

It was six weeks or so before my 15th birthday and I travelled alone, as I usually did for the next nine-and-a-half seasons (all my local friends supported other London clubs but none of them got to see their team at Wembley five times in six years, though!) before I moved to Jersey, which restricted my visits.

The game itself (1-1 – Clyde Best scored) wasn't at all memorable but the record books show that Palace, my local team, equalised through David Payne in the 89th minute, while Paul Heffer made his only appearance of the season – and his last-ever for West Ham – as substitute for John McDowell.

Billy Green: Saw us beat Chelsea 3-1 (27/1/73), with goals from Pop Robson (2) and Tommy Taylor. It was an early sixth birthday present for me and the thing that sticks in my mind was the atmosphere of a big 35,336 crowd. Watching your heroes on *The Big Match* just didn't prepare me at all for what it was actually like to be inside Upton Park. I remember Dad telling me to keep an eye on Bobby Moore, as he was the player every schoolboy should try to be like. I don't remember too much of the game but I do recall looking in awe at this tall No.6 who made everything look so easy. I was hooked and poor Dad had to fork out 50p to take me along at every opportunity he could from then on.

Paul Clayden: I went to school in Grays, Essex, where the majority of kids supported Hammers. Saying that, everyone was wearing Leeds kits in the early 70s – probably because they wore unusual number tags on their socks and beat Arsenal in the 1972 FA Cup final. My grandad, Frank Clayden, and my dad, also Frank, took me to my two first games.

One of our neighbours – a sales rep for Cadbury's and a nice guy who must have been pretty well off – was a season ticket holder in the West Stand. He was on holiday and we had his season tickets for consecutive home games, v Leicester City (22/9/73) and Burnley (6/10/73). I was 11 and blissfully unaware that West Ham were coming off the back of a very good season, in which we had finished sixth with Bryan 'Pop' Robson topping the first division score chart with 28 goals, and about to enter the 1973-74 season, which saw a relegation battle and Bobby Moore's departure.

Robert Wells: v Burnley (6/10/73). I was 12 and went with three friends from school, catching the bus from my home town of Orpington on a cold, wet day. It rained that hard, I feared the game would be postponed. I vividly recall the walk through the dark Woolwich tunnel and then catching the 69 bus to Canning Town, followed by the long walk up Barking Road until the floodlights came in to view. Paying the 15p entrance fee to the North Bank, then feeling the tingle of excitement as we came out of the dark onto the terraces, vivid green, claret-and-blue all around.

The outstanding memories of the game itself were seeing a curling shot by Bobby Moore saved by the keeper, Ted MacDougall being sent-off for headbutting Doug Collins and an 18-year-old Mervyn Day playing only his second game for Hammers. The result was a 1-0 loss, something I have had to get used to over the years, but so began a love affair with the club that has lasted more than 40 years and is now being carried on by my two sons.

Stanley Borgonha: v Derby County (27/10/73), 0-0. Aged 15, I was attending a rugby-playing school in Surrey at the time where there were only a few known West Ham fans, none of whom were able to visit Upton Park, so I went to the match by myself. Our two main strikers, Pop Robson and Ted MacDougall, were missing and Ron Greenwood pushed Trevor Brooking into attack. Although the game was not particularly entertaining, I remember my excitement at standing on the South Bank for the first time, near the away supporters.

Gerard Daly: I got interested in West Ham during the 1971-72 season at the age of seven – I think it was because I liked Geoff Hurst. My mum, Margaret, was from Forest Gate and my grandad was a West Ham fan but he died when I was three. I used to insist that I had supported West Ham before I knew Mum, then wonder what everyone was laughing at!

My first game was a goal-less draw v Derby County (27/10/73). Very few memories of it except being shocked at the length of the District Line journey, being bought a rosette and shaking with excitement at the sight of Bobby Moore casually leaning on a goalpost not far away from me.

Martin Scholar: My dad, Selwyn, was a fanatical West Ham fan since going in the 50s at the age of 12 or 13, right through to his passing away in his 70s, so I was always going to follow in his footsteps. And I was hooked by my first game, when I was six or seven, under the lights, sitting in the upper tier of the old West Stand, with maybe 500 people there for a reserve match v Arsenal in October 1973 or '74. I'm fairly sure we lost 6-0 but on a perfect autumn evening with smoke in the air, it was fantastic to hear the sounds of the players shouting and striking the ball. I couldn't wait to go back.

David May: All my family were avid West Ham supporters. Dad, John, took me to my first game, v Luton Town (19/8/74). Apart from falling asleep, he told me that all I did was stare at the North Bank! Also there that day was my uncle Micky May, the legendary amateur boxing coach

Bobby Gould, one of the game's great characters, about to celebrate with a fan.

at West Ham ABC. He spent 30 years at the club, bringing through many champions, including Kevin Mitchell, Matt Marsh and Dudley O'Shaunessy, to name but a few. He sadly passed away last year (2014).

Gary West: My dad, Jim, first took me when I was seven. The match was v Leicester City (21/9/74) and we won 6-2 (Bobby Gould and Billy Jennings both got two, plus one each for Billy Bonds and Keith Robson, on his debut). Dad told me not to expect that every week! He had first started going to West Ham when he was about eight, during the Second World War. His brother-in-law took him to see all the London clubs whenever he was on leave from the RAF and Dad chose Hammers as his team after they beat The Arsenal. It was only when he next went to Upton Park, and saw a terrible West Ham team get turned over, that he was told that all the players who played before were guests, and this was more like the norm. But he had made his decision and stuck with West Ham for the next 73 years, until he died in 2013.

His choice meant that my son, James, and I were also condemned to a lifetime of misery and frustration, interspersed with only the occasional highlight, but that is what being a Hammers supporter is all about. As a young boy, Dad used to cycle from Bethnal Green through the east London bombsites and pay an old girl a penny to leave his bike in her hallway while he watched the game, and then cycle back home afterwards.

When he first took me we stood in the Chicken Run, up the back against the wall to the upper tier, midway between the halfway line and the North Bank. He made me a little stool so I could see. As the 1974-75 season progressed, crowds got bigger due to our success in the FA Cup and Dad often had to pick me up when I had been knocked off my stool as the crowd swayed and sang *Bubbles*. I thought it was all marvellous.

I carried on going to home games with Dad until the 1991-92 season, when the board tried to bring in the bond scheme. Like many, he refused to pay for the right to buy a season ticket and gave it up in protest. After that, I continued to go to matches with my mates.

Nick Morgan: I grew up in west London in the 70s. Liverpool was the team, so everyone supported them, which seemed stupid to me. I loved footy, my dad didn't, so no guidance there. At school there was a book with all the clubs and their strips. I liked West Ham's claret-and-blue, so sold my heart and soul and devoted every fibre of my body to the club.

I can't recall my first visit to Upton Park but, after about three trips, Dad said: "Can we go and see my team now?" Astounded and thrilled he was now getting into football, I was very happy to go with him to Loftus Road and watch QPR. Honestly, it was only 20 years later that it finally dawned on me what he was doing. While Upton Park was a good hour's journey across town, QPR was just five minutes up the Westway. He didn't like football but, if he pretended to support his local team, then his wide-eyed son would be happy to go with him.

David Meagher: I grew up in Basildon, Essex, where my dad, Seamus, worked in Yardley's cosmetics factory. The social scene focused around snooker and football, which included regular trips up to the Boleyn Ground to watch an entertaining West Ham side that included Frank Lampard, Bobby Gould, Trevor Brooking and Billy Bonds. Supporting any other club than West Ham was unthinkable.

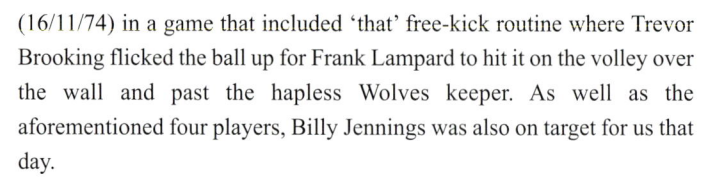

The first visit that I can recall was to see West Ham thrash Wolves 5-2 (16/11/74) in a game that included 'that' free-kick routine where Trevor Brooking flicked the ball up for Frank Lampard to hit it on the volley over the wall and past the hapless Wolves keeper. As well as the aforementioned four players, Billy Jennings was also on target for us that day.

I recall feeling pretty nervous in such a packed crowd but sitting up on the pitchside wall at the Chicken Run was a real thrill – even if I was wearing an embarrassing bright yellow anorak that Mum bought because of its high visibility!

Stephen George: My dad, Bob, was born in Plaistow and grew up on Harold Road, less than a stone's throw from the Upton Park gates. No doubt he would say he could see the West Ham floodlights from his bedroom window or at the very least hear the crowd roar on a match day. It wasn't like he needed to make a choice or anything; most of us know that with football you get what you're given. And to be fair, with Moore, Hurst and Peters on your doorstep every other week in their 60s heyday, why would anyone look elsewhere?

By the early 70s when I finally arrived, Mum (Sandra) and Dad had absconded to the footballing backwater of Chelmsford, Essex and two of the World Cup-winning triumvirate (Peters and Hurst) had also moved on to pastures new. It surprised quite a few people, therefore, that a largely experimental Hammers side would go all the way to Wembley to contest the 1975 FA Cup final, with the third of that famous three, Bobby Moore, playing for opponents Fulham (still doesn't sound right, no matter how many times I say it). I don't remember the game and, in truth, I probably never saw it – most two-year-olds aren't renowned for their patience. But I remember being told I was being taken to watch West Ham "bring the cup home", whatever that meant. And so on a bright Sunday afternoon in early May I joined the throng of men, women and children on the streets of Upton Park to watch the triumphant Hammers parade the world famous trophy. I remember being hoisted out of the window at my Uncle Harold and Aunt Maud's flat on the Barking Road, just along from Green Street, proudly holding up my cardboard replica of the FA Cup and being told by the elders to shout "Come on you Irons!" every five minutes.

And while my first visit to a Hammers match didn't come along for another six years – a 5-0 win v Preston in the old second division (31/1/81), it was on that May day in 1975 that the journey really began.

Ian Crocker: I was born and brought up in Dorset and followed my local non-league team Weymouth FC. In 1974, aged nine, I decided I should also support a big professional club. West Ham had the same kit colours as Weymouth. I clocked their results for a while and noticed that they beat Leicester 6-2, Burnley 5-3 and Wolves 5-2 in the space of a couple of months. That would do for me.

At the end of that season Hammers won the FA Cup thanks to Alan Taylor's double at Wembley and they repeated the feat in 1980, with

---

AUTHOR
IAIN DALE
Book: *When Football Was Football: West Ham*

I AM slightly embarrassed to say that I became a Hammer at the age of 10. It's not that I was embarrassed to become a Hammer, but it was the way it happened. Up to that point I had supported Manchester United. Well, it was natural, I lived in Essex! My best friend, Roger Sizer, supported West Ham and being easily led, I decided to follow suit. It seemed a good idea at the time. Luckily, in my adult years, I decided not to switch allegiances each time West Ham were relegated.

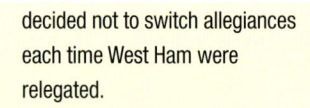

I vaguely remember going to see West Ham play Cambridge United in a testimonial game in 1972 and that was what finally did it. My first game at Upton Park came in 1975, when we lost 1-0 to Chelsea (29/3/75). Alan Curbishley made his debut. I stood in the lower tier of the West Stand, very near to where my current seat is. I remember walking along Green Street and seeing a series of fights. It's not like that now!

Trevor Brooking's magnificent world class header. Two FA Cups in five years was obviously a sign of more trophies to come. Not!

Mark Matthews: The main single reason that I support West Ham is Bobby Moore. I was born in 1963 at Bedford, where the nearest league club was Luton Town, who at the time were in the old fourth division and therefore not a particularly attractive option to a six-year-old. I had no idea where West Ham was, nor did I really know anything about the club, but this was at the time of the build-up to the 1970 World Cup tournament in Mexico with England, the holders, being led by West Ham's star player. Bobby Moore immediately became my hero and the image of him in the classic claret-and-blue strip was enough to get me hooked.

Unfortunately, my first visit to Upton Park was delayed for a further six years, as my dad wouldn't take me. At the time West Ham only accepted personal, not postal, ticket applications and, not being a fan himself, he wasn't prepared to trek to east London to purchase tickets. So my first West Ham games were away trips to Arsenal and Chelsea.

Anyway, I had a mate who was a Leeds fan and eventually his dad took us to the home midweek game against the Yorkshire side (23/2/76). All the seats had gone by the time we got to the ground, so we ended up packed into the West lower. It was a night game and, from what I remember, far from a classic, ending in a 1-1 draw (Alan Taylor).

Gary Osborne: Growing up in Romford, Essex, there was only one team to support. My first game was v QPR (23/8/76), which we won 1-0. I still remember the atmosphere and Graham Paddon's goal. I was hooked.

Kevin Pendegrass: I started going to Upton Park in 1976 and haven't missed a home game since September 1978, so I have many personal memories, good and bad, of Upton Park.

At the age of seven, I watched West Ham for the first time on *The Big Match* in November 1968, when they beat QPR 4-3 and, despite it being in black and white, I distinctly remember liking the colours we wore. From then on I always supported West Ham.

I lived in Norwich for much of my childhood and my first visit to Upton Park was for the visit of Norwich City (27/3/76). It was the year of our European Cup Winners' Cup run to Brussels but we only won one of our last 21 league games that season and plummeted down the table. I remember travelling down by train and getting the tube from Liverpool Street to Upton Park, then buying loads of badges outside the ground and queuing to get into the North Bank. We were dreadful that day and lost 1-0 to a Ted MacDougall goal. I travelled home wondering why I'd bothered – a feeling I've had many more times over the years.

John Ruane: An older lad by the name of Eddie Hayes led me to follow West Ham. I come from an estate located at the Elephant and Castle, deep into Millwall country. As a kid I was taken to watch them (Millwall) a couple of times by my older sister's boyfriend but the experience didn't do anything for me. One day I bumped into Eddie and told him of my visit to The Den and how bad it was. He then offered to take me over to watch West Ham.

So, one Saturday in 1976, we made our way to Upton Park. As soon as we were outside Upton Park station I knew it was going to be different. Eddie took me to the North Bank and bought me a hot dog. We were a bit early, so there weren't many inside at the time, but when 3.00pm came the players were out of the tunnel and the roar of the crowd went up. The goosebumps were all over me and the hairs on the back of my neck stood up. I knew at that moment I was home, this was my team and it has been ever since.

Gary Bush: Growing up in an East Midlands village was possibly about as far removed from east London as you could imagine. Like all kids of a young age back then, football was played at every opportunity, be it over the park or in the street, and during school holidays you'd be out playing until dusk with your mates. I wasn't surrounded by professional football clubs where I lived, so to start following a team such as West Ham was something different, certainly from my area. Bobby Moore played his part of course. I've followed the club from the late 60s and started going to matches in the 70s.

My first visit to Upton Park was as a 15-year-old and I couldn't have chosen a better one – the European Cup Winners' Cup semi-final v Eintracht Frankfurt (14/4/76).

Joe Morris: It was my grandad, Jack Rusman, who nurtured my West Ham along to Upton Park.

I was taken to a game when I was very young but don't really remember it. My first game for real was Leicester City (6/9/83) under lights, Gary Lineker scored first but we won 3-1 with goals from Steve Walford, David Swindlehurst and Tony Cottee. It was our fifth straight win at the start of the season and we were flying. I just remember the atmosphere, the noise, the thought that, at 15, I was doing something very adult. I went with my friend Neil Dobson and we were like celebrities at school the next day.

AUTHOR
ROBERT BANKS
Books: *An Irrational Hatred of Luton; West Ham 'Till I Die; The Legacy of Barry Green*

ONE of my earliest memories is of my dad, Bob, buying a colour TV and the first thing I saw was the 1975 FA Cup final. It's strange, because had I had a better understanding at the age of seven I would have wanted the underdog to win, but at that age I was more influenced by the colours and the noise. Dad also had a friend at work, Bob Hart, who supported West Ham and he was always encouraging me to go

Ham support. My grandparents used to live in Plashet Grove many moons ago and Grandad was the man who sighed despairingly when Hammers were beaten and would then just sit forlornly in his armchair until the rest of the classified football results were read out on World of Sport.

He was an industrious barber who took inordinate pleasure in cutting hair and styling it to the point of perfection. For years he worked tirelessly and diligently in a barber's shop called Kelly's in Green Street, Upton Park. I'll always treasure some of the funnier stories about him. Like her dad, my mum was fluent in Yiddish and would revel in the telling and re-telling of some magical moments.

There was the occasion when, after the final whistle had gone in the 1966 World Cup final, Grandad and his triumphant colleagues raced out of the shop and happily proclaimed that West Ham had won the World Cup. Their jubilant voices could be heard the length of the Barking Road.

Now here's another misty-eyed recollection from grandad's repertoire of stories. I've always craved a claim to fame. My grandad . . . wait for it . . . cut the hair of the fabled 1966 World Cup trio of Bobby Moore, Geoff Hurst and Martin Peters at Kelly's Barbers.

My first three games at Upton Park were all home victories, a 1-0 win v Stoke City (12/2/77), followed by Bristol City (2-0) and Manchester City (1-0), without conceding a goal.

Supporting the club has long required tolerance, faith, loyalty and an unwavering belief that one day we might just emerge with the Premier League title – or the old first division as we traditionalists might call it. At the end of the 70s I would take up residence on what would become known as the freezing South Bank terraces at Upton Park. Every fortnight I'd stand come rain or shine, shivering during the winter and then rejoicing at the merest hint of spring sunshine. I would make a special point of strolling into the ground at least three hours before the game. This may sound strange but I loved nothing better than the smell of hot dogs, hamburgers and the wonderful atmosphere in the ground. I would move about restlessly in anticipation of the 3.00pm kick-off, furiously stamping my feet on cold November afternoons and then breathing a sigh of relief when the players emerged from the tunnel. That tunnel was graced for 17 years by the elegant conductor and maestro who was Trevor Brooking, a player of exquisite playmaking gifts and a man singularly cool, calm and composed while others were losing their head.

Martin McCormick: v Norwich City (20/8/77), we lost 3-1 (Bryan Robson). I was seven and remember taking an old LP record case to stand on, so I could see over the advertising hoarding.

Dean Sutherland: As a 12th birthday present I got to choose any game in London to watch, so I went for West Ham v Man City (27/8/77) because, at that time, City were full of stars. Although they won 1-0 from a Joe Royle goal, by then I'd fallen in love with West Ham. It was the atmosphere that hooked me. A memory I still carry is the Westlers hamburgers being sold by vendors outside the ground – I loved them!

Adrian White: My big brother, Richard ('Chalky' to his mates), was born in September 1956, with me following six years later, in June 1962. We grew up in a relatively small Buckinghamshire village, some five miles north of the market town of Aylesbury, and 40 miles north of London. We have no family connections to the East End that I'm aware of, so why West Ham United? Well, it's quite simple really, the very young Richard quite simply liked the colours! And as the years followed Richard firmly nailed his colours to the Hammers mast, growing up on the triumphs of the 1964 FA Cup winners, followed by the European Cup Winners' Cup in 1965 and, of course, winning the World Cup the following year. I don't think I was ever going to have much choice as to who I would end up following as long as he had any influence in the matter.

The truth is I don't think I actually pledged my full allegiance until the 2-0 win over Fulham in the 1975 FA Cup final. Richard had tried, unsuccessfully, to get tickets for the final, so it was agreed between our mum, Vera, and dad, Cyril, that if Richard would pay half of the then very expensive colour TV licence fee, we could at least upgrade from the old black and white telly to watch the biggest match of the year at home in glorious colour.

Being six years younger than my brother and still at school, I had to wait a few more years before my first visit to Upton Park, to see QPR (10/9/77). I never considered it at the time but even a home game for us Home Counties-based supporters was quite a trek. The 11.40am train from Aylesbury into Marylebone, then walk down to Baker Street and head east, change at Whitechapel, and an Upminster or Barking train would take you on the District Line to Upton Park. I remember the train getting very packed as we stopped at Mile End, and my brother pulling me down at West Ham station as I very naively got up to get off! As we climbed the steps at Upton Park the excitement grew as I got my first view of Green Street, with the sellers of old programmes in the derelict houses on the left, the smell of the burger onions (God, those Westlers boiled hamburgers were bloody awful) and chips frying wafting down the street.

I don't remember that first game as being remarkable, other than it ended in a 2-2 draw, with Kevin Lock actually scoring for both teams and Pat Holland netting our other goal. Plus a spectacular tackle from Frank Lampard, almost putting QPR's Stan Bowles in the North Bank.

Andy Brooker: 'Who do you want to win, black or white?' It was May 3, 1975 and I was sitting in the front room of my gran and grandad's house in Borough Green, a relatively large village in Kent, on the A25 between Maidstone and Sevenoaks. A young Andy Brooker and football had not really been introduced yet and, as far as I can recall, I had shown no interest in either watching or playing the game that would become a massive part of my life.

In today's world, kids are saturated with football through every available media and, with live TV matches almost every night of the week, video games, internet and magazines, it is almost inconceivable that a youngster growing up now could avoid contact with the sport in any way until they were almost eight-years-old.

In 1975, however, things were very different. *Football Focus* on the BBC, presented by former Arsenal goalkeeper Bob Wilson, and *On the Ball* with Brian Moore on ITV provided the pre-match warm-up. On a Saturday evening it was Jimmy Hill introducing highlights of two games on *Match of the Day* and Sunday lunchtime wouldn't have been Sunday lunchtime without Brian Moore and *The Big Match*. That, however, was it. Apart from occasional highlights of a midweek game on the BBC's *Sportsnight*, presented by either David Coleman or Frank Bough, that was the extent of football coverage in the mid-70s.

"So come on," said Gran, as she continued pointing at the TV, "who is it to be? Who's going to win?" I paused momentarily before replying: "The blacks, I think."

I didn't know then that the black shirts on that rented Redifussion black and white TV were in fact claret-and-blue, the bearded warrior-looking figure leading the team out of the tunnel at Wembley was Billy Bonds, or that the team was West Ham United.

Like most eight-year-olds, my concentration levels for any amount of time were fairly non-existent and after 15 minutes or so, watching football had become boring and I needed a new stimulant. Gran and Grandad, ever willing to please, or just to get some peace, suggested we went for a walk in the woods, which adjoined their back garden. In the years that were to follow, it became almost unthinkable that at 3.20pm on FA Cup final day, the biggest day in the English football calendar, I would be walking among the bluebells through woods in Kent.

After running wild in among the trees and wildlife for an hour or so, we returned to find that the match was still on . . . and 'the blacks' were, indeed, winning as I had hoped, by two goals to nil. I somehow managed to sit still and watch the remainder of the game, and to this day I will never forget Billy holding aloft the FA Cup in front of thousands of adoring fans. I would find out in the many painful years that followed that West Ham do not win trophies very often and that players of the calibre of Bonds are a rare breed down at Upton Park. But one thing did happen that day that changed my life forever: I became a Hammer!

From that Saturday in May 1975, it actually took me another two-and-a-half years to attend my first game at Upton Park. My best mate at school at the time was Steve Williams and his dad, Derek, was a massive West Ham fan. In fact, one of his first dates with Steve's mum was to Wembley for the 1965 European Cup Winners' Cup final! One day, while I was playing at their house, his dad asked if I had ever been to Upton Park.

When I replied "no," he said: "We'll soon put that right then."

Soon after, I would be attending my first match, v Aston Villa (22/10/77). I remember the build-up to the game all week at school, getting more and more excited as the week went on. The excitement was almost unbearable by Friday but then eventually Saturday arrived. Derek and Steve picked me up at midday – he'd said that we had to be in the ground by 1.30pm in order to get on a barrier. We drove up the M2 that day in a red Mark 1 Ford Granada with a black vinyl roof, through the Blackwall Tunnel, where, coincidently, I'm sure I have spent as many hours queuing to get to a game as I have actually watching the match itself. We went through Stratford and then a little while after turned into Green Street.

The two things about walking to the ground I remember more than anything else are the little programme stalls set up in the porch of the houses on the left-hand side of the road and the smell of fried onions from the little burger carts. No massive vans back then, just an old bloke with a cart.

We were going to stand on the North Bank, so we went in through the main gates and walked up past the West Stand. Through the turnstile, up the stairs and there it was . . . the first time my eyes had clapped eyes on a place where so many dramas would be played out over the coming years. So many memories made, so many dreams shattered . . . Upton Park. We followed Derek to a barrier about 10 or so steps back to the right of the goal, which was obviously his regular spot, and I waited for what seemed like ages for kick-off to arrive.

At about 2.00pm, stadium announcer Bill Remfry climbed out of his little box on the front of the West Stand and disappeared. He returned about 20 minutes later, climbing back down the ladder into his box just before the LP that he'd left playing had finished. Where had he been? Long before mobile phones, pagers, seemingly even a basic radio, he had gone to collect the team-sheets. He then proceeded to read out the first West Ham line up that I saw live.

West Ham kicked towards us in the first-half and my first-ever goal at Upton Park came at 3.22pm, when a Tommy Taylor free-kick put us 1-0 up. I never actually saw the ball hit the net, as there were numerous heads and shoulders blocking my view, but the noise was deafening.

In many ways, my first game was just typical West Ham. They held the lead for five minutes before Ken McNaught equalised and then in the second-half went in front again through Derek Hales. Just as I was contemplating a win, Mervyn Day dropped a cross right in front of us and Andy Gray equalised. 2-2!

To avoid subjecting a couple of 10-year-old lads to a crush at the final whistle, Derek made us make a move about five minutes before the end of the game. We shuffled slowly back to the exit by the stairs, squeezing past people and desperately trying not to get lost. Looking up, I noticed the 'Remember Ibrox, Please Leave Slowly' sign that hung from the roof. It was a reference to the disaster at Ibrox Park that had claimed 66 lives and caused injuries to around 200 others on January 2, 1971, when hundreds of fans in a crowd of 80,000, who were leaving the ground early, suddenly rushed back up the exit staircase on hearing that Rangers had scored a late equaliser against Celtic. But I had no idea at the time what the sign on display at the Boleyn Ground meant.

So that was it, a portion of chips and back to the car. I managed to attend three more games that season – a 1-0 defeat to Leeds, 1-0 win against Newcastle and then the final home game, a 2-0 defeat to Liverpool that sent us down to the old second division. Typical!

We may have been relegated but the seed was sown and Upton Park would be a constant in every year of my life from that day to this.

Jason Stone: v Birmingham City (26/12/77), won 1-0. Alan Curbishley hit the ball through a ruck of players on the edge of the box to win it in the 88th minute. I was eight and went with Dad and my brother. I remember it was Boxing Day and I was sick on the way home in the car!

Heikki Silvennoinen: v Leicester City, (31/12/77), won 3-2. I was 21 and I watched the match from the North Bank, near the goal, so I had a very good view of the first two Hammers' goals by John McDowell and Derek Hales. Bobby Ferguson replaced Mervyn Day in goal after Day was dropped. We were comfortably leading 3-0 in the second-half when 'Fergie' conceded two soft goals, one of them being a 40-yard cross from Steve Kember which floated over his head. He later admitted that he had been very nervous but, fortunately, we managed to keep the lead.

Ian Smith: Up until the age of 12 I was an Arsenal supporter but had never been to a game. I liked their shirts and they were pretty successful even then (1970-78). I'd seen them win the FA Cup against Liverpool in 1971 on my grandad's colour television (we only had a black and white set). Charlie George was the hero and I will never forget how he laid flat out on the floor, arms outstretched, after scoring. The following year they lost to Leeds in the final and I remember not really being that bothered about it. My older brother, Steve, had also supported Arsenal but changed to West Ham after going with his mates for the first time (he had never been to a game before).

Anyway, suffice to say, he persuaded me to go to West Ham v Newcastle (21/1/78). It was a grey and cold afternoon and I was a couple of weeks away from my 13th birthday. We were on the South Bank, near the line of police that separated us Hammers from the Geordies (I still find it amazing that a thin line of Old Bill was all there was to keep two sets of fans with some reputation apart). I don't remember too much about the game other than it was a drab affair and we won 1-0 (Derek Hales).

We went crazy in the South Bank, the police line got breached and a few scuffles took place. This went on for most of the game and at one stage there was a huge surge and I found myself far too close for comfort next to a baying mob of Geordies.

The adrenalin rush from the fear was fantastic and more than I got from the pretty dull match itself, so I went home buzzing with my first experience of The Boleyn. I actually went down with the flu the following day and was off school for a week afterwards – the excitement must have lowered my immune system or something! From that moment on I was a Hammer and it's become a major part of my life for the 37 years since. As many fans say: "It's in the blood". But sometimes I wish it wasn't!

Steve Foster: My grandad, also Steve, was a Custom House boy, so really there wasn't much chance of supporting anyone else. My dad – again, also Steve! – started going in the 1957-58 season as a boy and had a season ticket for years, so it just carried on from there.

My first game was a birthday treat v Coventry City (1/5/78). I was seven and remember Geoff Pike getting taken off in the first half with a broken nose. Alvin Martin came on as a sub and Tommy Taylor, who had pushed into midfield, got the winner in a 2-1 victory. Patsy Holland got the other goal. Now working in football as a scout, I often see Pat at matches. He's a real genuine bloke and still has a great love for the game.

Liam Tyrell: Logically, it is right that I support West Ham. Born at Upney Hospital in 1967, I lived at Harold Wood, near Romford, before moving out to Canvey Island. My paternal grandparents were both born and bred on Evesham Road and Fairland Road in Stratford, close to West Ham Park, before moving to Dagenham and then Romford, where both my parents were from. My grandad, Herbert Tyrell, went to Park School in Stratford, where he was taught by Cornelius Beal, the games master who famously was directly responsible for *I'm Forever Blowing Bubbles* becoming our anthem. Grandad knew the boy the song was adapted for, William 'Bubbles' Murray, too, and always spoke fondly of 'Corney' Beal.

He also often talked of how his brother, Stan, went with his dad, Charles, to Wembley for the 1923 Cup final, having walked all the way there and back from E15. Great-Grandad Tyrell apparently losing most of the buttons on his suit from the crush in the estimated 200,000 crowd. He also remembered the score of the game being chalked up on a board outside a

Heikki Silvennoinen with wife Kaija and daughter Emma on a visit from Finland in October 2003.

shop nearby, their only means of knowing what was happening, as well as mentioning the illuminated West Ham Corporation Tram used to celebrate the cup final appearance.

At the age of six I moved north to Wakefield, West Yorkshire, where I was surrounded by Leeds fans. Luckily, there were one or two decent ones, like the brothers who lived next door and kindly went through their back catalogue of *Shoot/Goal* magazines, cutting out every West Ham poster and article for me. My maternal nan, meanwhile, always sent or saved the West Ham pages from *The Newham Recorder*, as well as nipping over to the club shop at times, too. I especially recall when she went to Upton Park just to get me the programme for the behind-closed-doors European game v Castilla in 1980.

I remember watching the first-half of the 1975 FA Cup final before 'playing' the second-half myself in a neighbour's garden, returning to see we had won 2-0, having missed both goals. In 1980, up bright and early and excited for the Wembley final, I spontaneously covered our front window entirely with posters, rosettes and scarves.

We travelled back to Romford often and it was on one such trip when I got my first taste of action at Upton Park. I knew the area reasonably well, as my other grandad, Alf, a grocer himself, had often taken us to Queens and Rathbone Street markets. He was from Kensington and a QPR man, so I have always had a big soft spot for them.

It was Dad's brother, David Tyrell, whom I have to thank for taking me and my brother, Sean, to our first West Ham game. He was a keen amateur footballer and by now living in Bow. He'd stopped going to games sometime in the late 60s, mainly due to escalating violence. He used to mention one game in particular, v Manchester United in 1967, when he spent more time looking out for, and dodging, incoming missiles than watching the game.

It was perhaps fortunate, then, that he took us to the opening game of the 1978-79 season, v Notts County (19/8/78). I remember we parked up around Plashet Grove and walked across the tin bridge over the railway, the high-rise flats prominent as we snaked our way through the back streets, before the first glimpse of the back of the stands as more and more crowds gathered the closer we got.

So many vivid recollections of the bright, sunny day have stayed with me. The squeeze through the turnstiles before we took our place on the North Bank, right down the front by the goalpost nearest the West Stand. The closeness of the pitch from the wall, the players in touching distance, the clarity of the noises, the intensity of the smells, the vibrancy of the colours all feel so fresh as I write these words. The experience stayed with me and in me. The white of the goalposts, netting, ball, shorts and socks. The pristine green of the lush turf. The warm glow of the sun, the perfect clear blue sky.

The smell of hot dogs, the peanut and programme sellers and the pre-match drone of chatter replaced by the roar from all four corners as the teams emerged. The black and white stripes of Notts County and the claret-and-blue.

Claret-and-blue, that distinctive combination everywhere. On the pitch, in the stands and on the people. The players I'd only known mostly from those magazines were all there right in front of me, just yards away. My hero, Trevor Brooking, effortlessly oozing class, linking so well with the waif-like whippet Alan Devonshire. The Trojan Billy Bonds and fellow warrior Frank Lampard looked invincible. Pop Robson and David Cross linking well as we raced into a 4-0 lead inside 20 minutes.

Half-time came and no thoughts about last season's relegation. Promotion would be a stroll. A fifth followed, 'Psycho' Cross completing his hat-trick before County threatened a comeback, the game ending 5-2. I was swiftly learning, there's always a twist with West Ham, nothing is ever that easy. I was hooked, though, that was it.

Lee Burch: v Stoke City (21/10/78), 1-1 (Trevor Brooking). I was four and the crowd was electric as I took my seat in the West Stand upper. I remember asking my uncle for a song-sheet, because I didn't know all the words to the songs!

Simon Hoppit: When I was around seven, I lived in Epping, Essex and

---

AUTHOR
KIRK BLOWS
Books: *Terminator: The Authorised Julian Dicks Story*; *The Essential History of West Ham United* (with Tony Hogg); *Fortune's Always Hiding*; *Bring Me the Head of Trevor Brooking*; *Hammers Heaven and Hell*; *Hammer Blows*; *Claret and Blue Blood* (with Ben Sharratt)

SAW four games in the 1978-79 season – our first back in the old second division following relegation – and, incredibly, they all resulted in draws, proving the point that watching West Ham dominate possession, create the lion's share of the chances and play the more attractive football doesn't necessarily guarantee victory!

My first match was a 1-1 v Crystal Palace (18/11/78) but far more memorable was the 3-3 with Sunderland three months later, in which goalkeeper Mervyn Day had an absolute nightmare and was not seen in a Hammers shirt ever again. The club splashed a world record £565,000 fee to sign a replacement in Phil Parkes just a few days later.

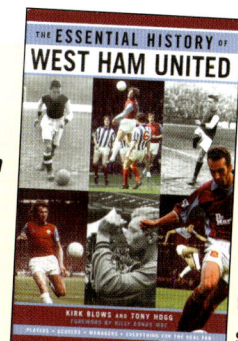

In the last of those four games, v Wrexham, visiting keeper Dai Davies was sent off for manhandling the referee after a goal had been awarded when the whole ground had clearly seen Pop Robson push the ball onto the head of scorer Billy Bonds with his hand. Typically, the Welshmen, despite being down to 10 men for more than an hour, levelled with just two minutes remaining!

UPTON PARK MEMORIES

AUTHOR
TIM CRANE
Book: They Played With Bobby Moore: The West Ham Years

MEMBERS of my family who supported Hammers can be traced back to the pre-First World War era of Danny Shea. My grandfather, Harry, was a regular at the old place from around 1912 and attended the 1923 FA Cup final. For much of his life he lived at No.38 Jedburgh Road, one of the many feeder roads to the ground.

His son, my uncle Sid, held a season ticket throughout the 60s, 70s and early 80s before declaring at a family gathering one day that: "When Brooking goes, I go."

The first game I went to was v Leicester City (26/3/79). I lied to my mother that I was playing Subbuteo at a friend's house – I was 11. In reality, we took the 277 bus from the Isle of Dogs and caught the No.5, 15 or 23 from Poplar to the ground. The match was under the lights and I remember being pushed around by the swaying crowd. I couldn't see hardly any of the pitch and windows of action just flashed in and out of my vision. Pop Robson scored a goal which gave us a 1-1 draw and it must have been at the North Bank end because I recall his celebration being close to where I was standing. I was super-scared and super-excited the entire game.

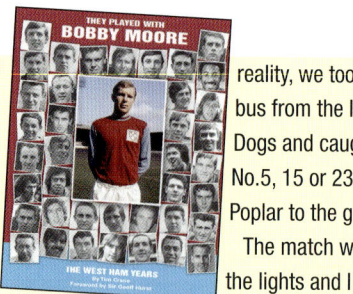

It was soon after that Uncle Sid ensured I used his friend's season ticket; he must have been mightily busy because I recall going to most games during my favourite season of 1980-81.

had a little den in the woods that I and a few friends would go to. One day some older kids were in there and said to me: "What team do you support?" Not knowing anything about football at the time, except that my brother had a Man United holdall, I said: "Er, Manchester United." They said: "We support West Ham!" So I turned around and said: "So do I!" From that moment on, I was a Hammer.

My first game was v Newcastle United (24/3/79). What a start to my addiction – we thrashed them 5-0 and I also won on the Grand National that day thanks to 20/1 second-placed Zongalero, after my dad put on a bet for me.

Jim Drury: West Ham 5 Newcastle United 0 (24/3/79). I was just under seven and remember the smell of cigarette smoke on the South Bank. Every time I smell smoke nowadays I am instantly reminded of that first match. The noise of supporters, especially when West Ham scored (John McDowell 2, Alan Devonshire, Frank Lampard, Pop Robson), and the sheer scale of the crowd. I stood on a wooden stool and my dad formed a barrier behind me and my brother whenever the crowd surged. I was also intrigued by the fact that grown men were singing rude songs constantly.

Mr R. Austen: Beat Newcastle United 5-0 (24/3/79). I remember thinking what a player Trevor Brooking was. Also the fans, the passion, that's why I loved West Ham after that.

Bjørn Arne Smestad: v Cardiff City (16/4/79), 1-1 (Pat Holland). Aged 17, this was my first visit to England after I had won match tickets in a competition in *Hammer*. I was also invited to the tea room after the game by programme editor/press officer Jack Helliar.

Neal Clark: v Wrexham (28/4/79). My outstanding memory of the game was when West Ham were awarded a penalty and the referee (K. Baker) sent off Welsh international goalkeeper Dai Davies for manhandling him. The penalty was converted by Billy Bonds but the game finished 1-1.

Colin Crowe: My uncle John moved to England from Ireland in 1958 and the first match he saw happened to be West Ham v Manchester United. Little did he know then but there was a young man also making his debut on that September evening, whose career would turn out to be slightly more remarkable.

Nine years later my dad, Gerry, moved to London from Cork. He was a Sunderland fan because of the Charlie Hurley connection but went to most other London grounds before trying out his brother's team. Once inside Upton Park's West Stand lower and watching the silky skills of Moore, Hurst and Peters, he was hooked.

I grew up always knowing and telling everyone that West Ham were my favourite team and my favourite player was Bobby Moore. I can remember before the 1975 FA Cup final my child-minder asking me who would I support now that Bobby Moore played for the other team. The name Billy Bonds had a great ring to it and he was now my favourite, even though I didn't have a clue what he looked like.

My dream finally became a reality when we faced Burnley in the League Cup (2/9/80). I loved every single minute of a 4-0 victory (Ray Stewart, Paul Goddard, Geoff Pike, O.G.).

Alex Dawson: v Watford (20/9/80), aged seven, Dad took me and my brother for the first time. I couldn't believe the atmosphere – claret-and-blue everywhere. West Ham won 3-2, Sir Trevor scored the winner from his trusty head. There was something about the players then – not superstars, just honest footballers, such as Lampard, Brooking and Bonds. Even though we were only a second division side that season, I was well and truly hooked.

Steve Smith: I was born into a mixed footballing family. My mum's side is Arsenal – in fact my late grandad took me to my first-ever game at Highbury against Fulham reserves when I was five or six. My dad lived on Barking Road and could see the South Bank floodlights from his bedroom window. His uncles and dad also followed the club since its inception. So when my interest in football kicked in during the 1978 World Cup in Argentina, Dad told me about West Ham, its history and its players. He would go to night matches at Upton Park and write the score on those unique, much-missed Helliar programmes and leave them on the kitchen

Ray Stewart wearing unusual blue shorts and socks for a home game but, for Tonka, a very familiar outcome – slamming home yet another penalty, this time against Politehnica Timisoara of Romania during the 1980 ECWC tie.

table so I could see how we got on when I woke up in the morning. I remember him, a mild-mannered man, going ballistic listening to the BBC Radio commentary of the FA Cup semi-final replay against Everton from Elland Road, when we reached Wembley in 1980.

The first game I went to was the European Cup Winners' Cup tie v Poli Timisoara (22/10/80), which we won 4-0 (Billy Bonds, Paul Goddard, Ray Stewart – pen, David Cross). I distinctly remember two things: a UEFA flag in the forecourt and the fact we wore sky blue shorts and socks at home. This was the time of our first Adidas kit and we normally wore white shirts and socks.

Richard Mumford: v Bolton Wanderers (25/10/80), won 2-1. Aged 13, I was taken on a long journey from home on the Isle of Wight by my dad. We had an early start: lunch in St James's Park, a quick look at Buckingham Palace and then took the tube heading out to Upton Park station. As the train neared our destination I was amazed at the large number of fans at each platform all donning the claret-and-blue – you don't see many Hammers' fans on the Isle of Wight!

I recall being overwhelmed by the long walk from the station and seeing the stalls selling West Ham merchandise, the aroma of onions from the burger vans and the police on horseback. I successfully squeezed my way to the counter of the portakabin club shop and exchanged my pocket money for an FA Cup winners' scarf.

We managed to get a couple of autographs on the way in when Ray Stewart and Geoff Pike scribbled on my programme, before taking our seats 45 minutes before kick-off in the West Stand.

John Lyall's men didn't disappoint. They were 1-0 up just before half-time, courtesy of a Mick Walsh own-goal, and a large number of supporters missed the second goal straight after half-time – 20 or so first or second-time passes from one end of the pitch to the other, ending with a 25-yard drive from Geoff Pike nestling snugly in the bottom corner. At

AUTHOR
NEIL HUMPHREYS
Books: *Match Fixer; Premier Leech*

It was a law in our house that we support our local side. My Forest Gate-born father, John, insisted on it (even though he had a brief dalliance with Tottenham as a kid until he bumped into Bobby Moore in Mooro's shop in Green Street and the legend pointed him towards the Hammers).

My first visit to Upton Park was with Dad to see West Ham beat Bolton 2-1 (25/10/80). I was six, we went in the North Bank and barely saw a thing, but it was like a dream. I had never heard such noise from so many people in one place before. I remember Dad sitting me on one of the crush barriers.

Years later, I came across the programme which delighted me (Dad rarely bought them) and of course I realised that I was essentially watching the 1980 FA Cup-winning side in a contest that involved the two sides from the first final at Wembley in 1923. As first Upton Park visits go, it wasn't a bad one.

106 UPTON PARK MEMORIES

South Africa-based supporter Greg Faasen in 1972, proudly wearing the kit that his mum had specially made by a tailor in their home city of Bulawayo. The other pictures were taken by Greg on his first visit to Upton Park in January 1982, while the shot of Paul Goddard in FA Cup action against Everton was a gift to him from West Ham secretary Eddie Chapman.

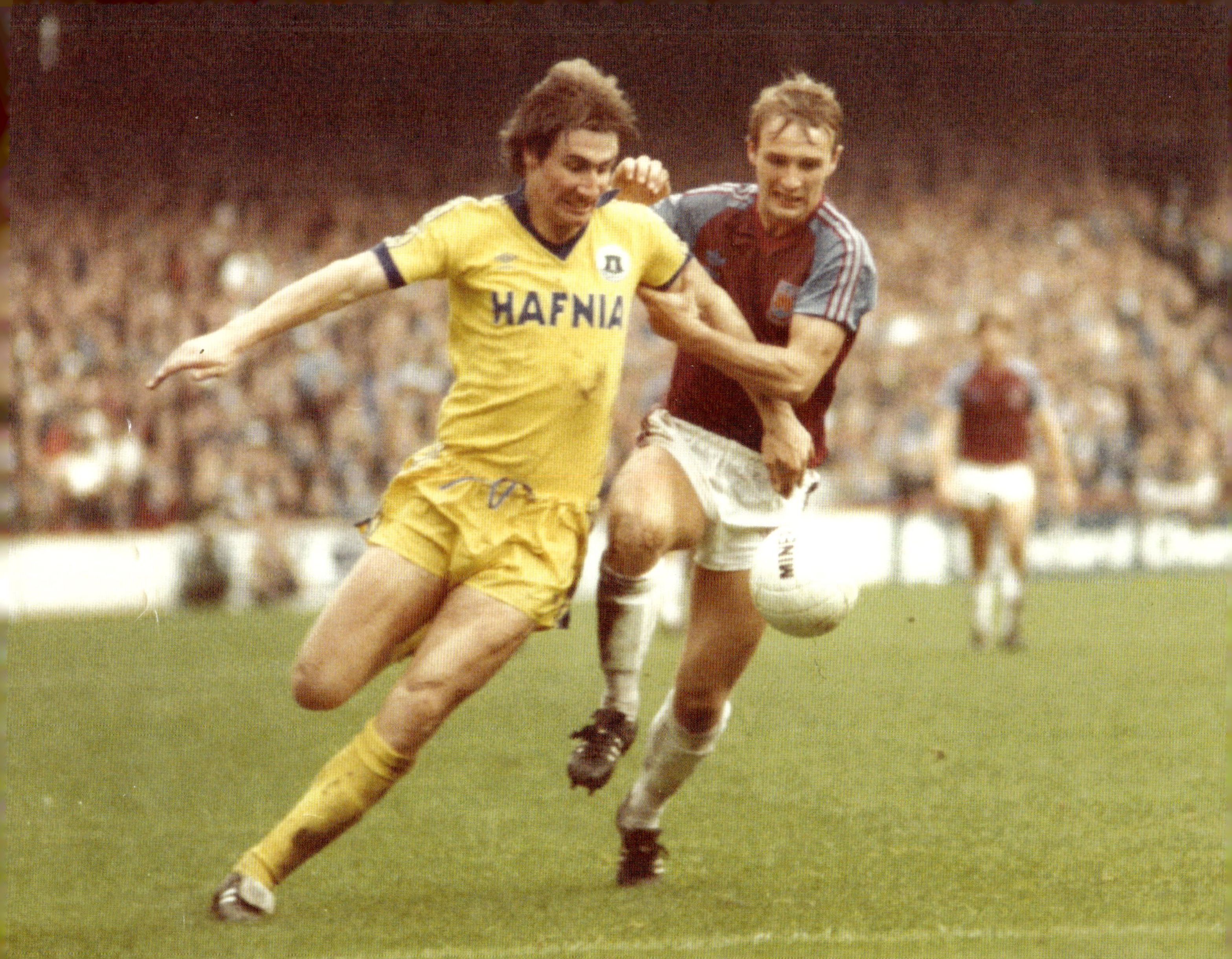
HAFNIA

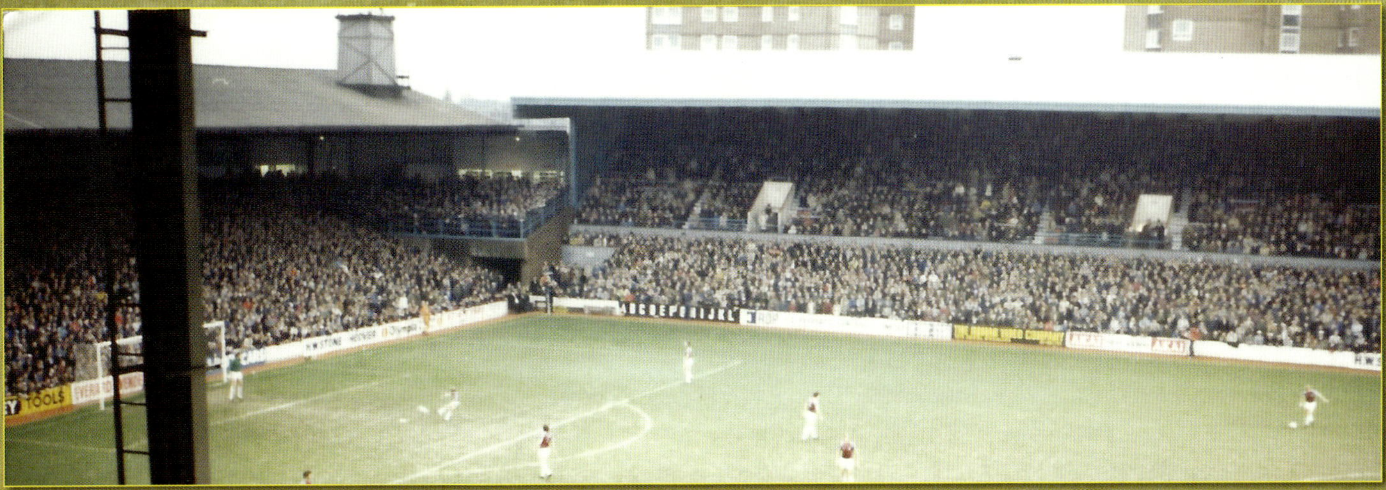

least the unlucky fans could console themselves that the TV cameras were present and the goal could be seen on ITV's *The Big Match* the following afternoon (I believe it became their Goal of the Season.) Brian Kidd managed a late consolation scissor-kick for Bolton but it stayed 2-1.

Mark Edwards: When I was at school in the late 70s and early 80s, everyone supported Liverpool. I was West Ham, I don't really recall why, I just was. Nothing sticks in my mind about what made me a Hammer but it made school hard. Liverpool were European champions – West Ham in Division Two. As my 10th birthday approached, my late father Michael told me that we were going to Upton Park as a treat, to see West Ham v Arsenal (5/12/81). We took our place behind one of the goals (I can't remember which) and I was captivated. The noises were thrilling, fans swaying side to side, front to back and I was clinging to Dad so as not to get lost.

Arsenal, unfortunately, took a two-goal lead and with about 10 minutes to go, Dad decided we were to leave to beat the rush at the tube station. This meant that I hadn't seen a West Ham goal but I did get a bunch of programmes that I studied on the train home, while Dad snored loudly. I arrived home and told my mum Cath the whole story of the day. I was given permission to watch the highlights on *Match of the Day* and somehow stayed awake to see that, in the 85th minute, Stuart Pearson had scored a consolation goal for Hammers. I was gutted, as I'd missed the chance to celebrate a goal at Upton Park. Little did I know that I would spend the rest of my life looking out of the same 10-year-old pair of eyes whenever I went to Upton Park. I'm 42 now but still get the same buzz as I did all those years ago.

Greg Faasen: Rhodesia was a colony of the British Empire – I remember *God Save The Queen* on TV at the end of scheduled shows and how many people just stuck up their middle fingers. Rhodesia was going to go alone, with or without the mighty Britain and Harold Wilson! This was Unilateral Declaration of Independence – November 1965 – and I was six-years-old. So, with this as the backdrop, how in heaven's name was I destined to support West Ham United?

Rhodesia in the 60s and 70s was full of ex-pats and a junior school friend of mine, Shaun Prescott, was a big Liverpool supporter. We lived in a small community on the outskirts of Bulawayo and kids regularly visited each other's homes to kick balls, play tennis and listen to music. Shaun said to me: "It's time for you to support an English football team."

I noticed that he was a regular reader of *Tiger* magazine and he said: "Why not look through some of the team groups and see if there is a team you might be interested in supporting?" Trawling through the pages, I said: "I like this maroon and blue kit." Shaun's dad, a big scouser, replied: "That's claret and sky you are referring to, lad. West Ham won the bloody World Cup, Moore, Hurst and Peters. Bloody cockneys, though, and the rest of the team are s***e – no good for you!"

However, that was going to be the team for me – the blond captain, shoulders upright, chin out . . . 'yeah, he looks like he means business'. I also loved the fact that the team picture was taken in a 'field' – at that time I did not know it was our Chadwell Heath training ground. These guys looked like they were a down to earth bunch and I could enjoy supporting them. Little did I realise what I was letting myself in for!

I finally made it to Upton Park – my first visit overseas – on Tuesday, December 29, 1981 to find The Human League at the top of the charts with *Don't You Want Me*. By now I was at university in South Africa and having played my first season as a professional for Wits University in the South African Professional Soccer League, I had managed to save enough money to make my pilgrimage to east London.

I had just spent a week with my ex-girlfriend's family in Gloucester, followed by Christmas with my pen-friend, George Anderson, and his family in Whittonstall, County Durham. Now I was in London and could not wait to get to my 'second home'.

I was staying with a fellow Wits University student and his family in Hendon and, on a murky December morning, I made my way to E13 to see if I could get a ticket for the FA Cup 3rd round encounter with Everton (2/1/82) the following week.

I remember the goose pimples I felt as I left Upton Park tube station and began the short walk down Green Street. The quaint houses on the right-hand side of the street, Bobby Moore's sports shop a little further down. Then, in all its glory, the Boleyn Ground, Upton Park. I stood in awe.

Viewed from Green Street, the stadium wasn't the prettiest building I had ever seen – it looked like it had been put together in bits and pieces over time – but, for me, it was just breathtaking. This is where I had listened to all those commentaries on BBC World Service, with Paddy Feeny, for all those years. This is where Ray Stewart had beaten Villa's Jimmy Rimmer in an FA Cup quarter-final in 1980 in front of the South Bank, where Keith Robson had scored that wonderful goal against Eintracht Frankfurt in 1976, and where Pop Robson had scored against Man United to keep us up in 1977. I had been listening – but not there. Now I was.

Determined to get a ticket, I joined the queue in the rain on that bleak morning. An hour later, a smiling lady came out of the club offices – I must have looked different, sun-burned or something – and she asked: "Where are you from?" I replied: 'South Africa," and she said: "Come with me." I followed her and, to my utter surprise, she walked me through to the office of secretary Eddie Chapman. A letter from my ex-girlfriend's uncle, the Archdeacon of Gloucester, to the club a few weeks earlier, may just have helped!

Eddie took me on a tour of the stadium, including John Lyall's office,

AUTHOR
DAN FRANCIS

Book: *Boys of '86: The Untold Story of West Ham United's Greatest-Ever Season (with Tony McDonald)*

SUPPORTING West Ham was simply a natural development, passed on by my dad, Roy, who grew up close to the ground and played in the same East Ham district schoolboys team as future Hammer Roger Cross. Dad lived in the high-rise flats behind the North Bank in Priory Court, and used to tell me stories about sneaking up on to the roof of the building to watch matches – although because his view was obscured by the North Bank roof, he could only see the pitch from the edge of the penalty area down to the South Bank, and often got a clip round the ear if the caretaker caught him up there!

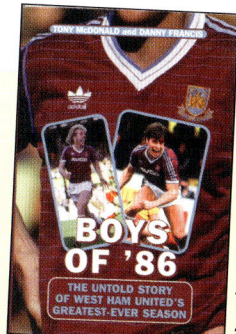

He followed the team home and away throughout the 60s and 70s and took me to my first game when I was six, a dull, uninspiring 1-0 defeat v Luton Town (24/8/85) at the start of what would turn out to be the greatest league campaign in the club's history. I remember being left slightly underwhelmed by the football itself, and the only thing that grabbed my attention was the shock of blond hair sported by West Ham's No.8.

The following day I was given a pack of stickers to start my new Panini 85-86 album . . . and the same blond West Ham player popped out. Hence Frank McAvennie became my boyhood hero, helped by the fact that he seemed to score every week that season!

---

the dressing rooms and on to the pitch – treated as royalty by someone who was royalty in my eyes. Getting back to his office after the tour, he handed me a Hammers tie and a photograph.

Then he handed me two tickets for the game. How could you not feel something extra special for the Hammers and all it stood for after this? I kept pinching myself – I was actually going to see my heroes in action.

When match day came, I took in every single aspect of the atmosphere. As I climbed the stairs into the West Stand, I looked back over the crowds lining up for the game and the players' car park below me with all the Ford Cortinas.

Then the players ran on to the pitch and began warming up. I remember the mascot having shots at Phil Parkes and every now and again, he would let one in, to the delight of the North Bank. Apart from 'Parkesy' in goal, we had Alvin and Billy as centre-backs and Tonka and Frank at full-back. In midfield there was Dev, Pikey and Trev. And up front, Sarge, Crossie and Jimmy Neighbour. Pancho was the sub. And Keith Hackett was the referee – Tony Gale, remember him?

The game was fantastic, with Trev setting up two headed goals for Bonzo and Psycho. Typical West Ham, though – we never do things easily. Eastoe pulled one back and then Tonka upended Sharp in the area in front of the South Bank – penalty! I was going to have my day spoilt after all. Parkesy, though, had other ideas – he was not going to let a young 22-year-old go back to Africa disappointed. The penalty was a poor one and Phil managed to block it with his legs.

Final whistle and the players trudged off the Upton Park mud – they had made my first visit to Upton Park all the more richer.

Matt Drury: My mum, Beryl, was originally from Walthamstow, east London before moving to Lincoln when she married my dad, Maurice. He wasn't a West Ham fan but would take my brother, Martin, and I to matches where possible. He felt Billy Bonds should be first name on the England team-sheet. Mum inherited her love of West Ham from her dad, Albert Keeble, who was originally from Stepney. He attended West Ham matches from the 1900s until the early 60s. Albert started going to Upton Park with a relative called Bert Davies. I cannot find Bert on any family tree, so am not sure if he was a blood relative. However, I understand Bert was on the board at West Ham. I have checked this with Tim Crane (West Ham historian) and he has confirmed Bert was, indeed, a director – and a controversial one at that.

My first match at Upton Park was a League Cup replay in 1982 v Lincoln City (29/11/82). The first match was rained off, although we only found out when arriving at the ground. We returned the following week to see West Ham win in extra-time with a Sandy Clark goal, after Ray Stewart had given us the lead.

Jason Fuller: My first visit was to see the 10-0 League Cup 2nd round, 2nd leg thrashing of Bury (25/10/83). I was nine and my parents had arranged a surprise for me – I didn't know that we were going to the match until 5.30 that evening. We sat in the West Stand lower, towards the South Bank end, and I remember standing on the seat twirling my scarf around my head with my dad continually telling me that it wasn't always like this.

Colin Walkinshaw: I was 13 and we beat Tottenham 4-1 on New Year's Eve, 1983. Standout memories were Ray Stewart's left-foot volley from the corner of the penalty box and seeing Trevor Brooking play.

David Steadman: My family have supported West Ham for generations and came from Plashet Grove, around the corner to the ground. My dad, Jim, captained East London Schoolboys in the mid-60s and had trials with the club at the same time as John McDowell. My grandad also supported the Hammers, so it's been in the family going back to the 30s, possibly even earlier.

My first-ever match was v West Brom (21/1/84). We sat in the old West Upper and I had my brand new scarf and cap. I still recall the buzz of seeing a big crowd for the first time, as well as the smells and excitement of the day. I don't recall much of the match, other than seeing the only goal scored by Tony Cottee, and that Bobby Barnes was pictured on the front cover of the programme.

Neil Roper: My dad, Terry, took my older brother, Ian, and I to our first game v Nottingham Forest (28/9/85), when I was four. West Ham won 4-2 (Frank McAvennie 2, Tony Cottee and Alan Dickens). We attended with my grandad, Horace Roper, who would've taken Dad to his first game some 30 years earlier, so it's fair to say there wasn't much choice with who I was going to support. I'm just beginning to realise how special a day it is to take your children to their first game – I'm aiming to get my two sons, Sam and Alex, to their first match before we leave The Boleyn, so they'll always be able to say they were there.

The one story Dad loves to remind me of is that he'd made it quite clear which way West Ham were shooting in the first-half so that my brother and I knew when to cheer if we scored. Unfortunately, he forgot to point out that the teams had changed around at half-time, so when Johnny Metgod scored for Forest early in the second-half, my brother and I jumped up to celebrate . . . only for Dad to quieten us down as quickly as he could before everyone around us thought we were Forest fans. Even in the old family section in the upper tier of the East Stand, he wasn't taking any chances!

Gjermund Holt: As a Norwegian guy born in 1966, all the boys in the street supported other teams, such as Leeds, Derby, Liverpool and Man United. At the age of about six, I pointed at the West Ham shirt in a magazine and, luckily enough, my mum bought it for me. I then started to find out about the Hammers and by the age of eight I was hooked.

I made my Upton Park debut the same day as Julian Dicks, a 0-0 draw v Everton (4/4/88). The atmosphere and whole experience was just fantastic. I remember it was an early kick-off on the Easter Monday. Me and a mate had a few too many beers the night before and switched the one-hour time difference from Norway the wrong way, so we were at Upton Park at 6.30 in the morning!

From that day on, I have travelled from Norway to see five or six games every season, home and away. My personal record was in 1999, when I saw 12 games live.

Chris Ludlow: v Brighton (17/11/90), who, ironically, are my local team. It was a cold winter's day and a friend of mine at the time, a West Ham fan, took me along. We arrived on the tube at Upton Park and from the minute I stepped off the train the feeling was something I had never experienced. We walked down Green Street and I got my first sight of the ground, an image I will have for the rest of my life.

We went down to the corner and had a couple of drinks in The Boleyn pub and the atmosphere was electric. We only spent about an hour or so in there but it was full of some real characters. At just about 2.40pm we made the short walk round to the South Bank.

From the minute I walked through the turnstiles I felt an instant sense of belonging. The buzz of the crowd was immense and I was instantly hooked. We stood on the terrace near the fence dividing the two sets of fans. The banter had already started and chants were being exchanged. Suddenly the sound of *Bubbles* started as the teams emerged from the tunnel and the hairs on my neck stood up.

Brighton took the lead through Hammer-to-be Mike Small midway through a half which West Ham had struggled to get into and trailed 1-0 at half-time. We made a change at the break when the hugely popular Stuart Slater came off the bench. It didn't take long until Slater received an Ian Bishop pass, wide on the left. Cutting into the penalty area, he dispatched an unstoppable shot beyond the reach of the despairing goalkeeper into the far top corner. The crowd erupted and the noise was incredible. From that moment you could sense there was only going to be one winner and, sure enough, a short while later Colin Foster headed us to a 2-1 victory.

Liam Corbett: My dad, Mick, moved over from Tipperary in the 60s, initially to Plaistow, then Ilford. As is the case with the traditional Irish sports, hurling and gaelic football, you basically have no choice but to support the team representing the place you're from. Dad, in his wisdom, decided to apply this to choosing a football team. So when my eldest brother, Ged, got to a certain age, he was given a choice of Leyton Orient or West Ham. In one of the few examples of a family supporting West Ham for glory-hunting reasons, the team in claret-and-blue was adopted by the Corbetts (by now living in Romford). That was passed down through the four younger brothers and the curse has since been passed on to our kids, so at the time of writing, and counting only the proper supporters, there's around 17 West Ham fans as a result of a bloke from Tipperary who thought football was a 'pansy's game' when he first moved over.

My first match was a 2-1 home defeat v Notts County (11/5/91) on the final day of 1990-91 season. I recall Mark Draper playing for County, and what seemed like a 50-man brawl but, in hindsight, was probably a 22-man brawl. Or maybe even 12 – them v Dicksy.

Mike Corbett: I don't actually remember our opponents for the first game I went to but I was taken by one of my elder brothers, Andrew 'Fingers' Corbett. I was pretty young and I have two memories from the game. The first was that, as there were no seats, and I was tiny back then, I couldn't see a great deal. Secondly, what little of the game I did view was pretty boring. And yet still that didn't put me off. Clearly, this backs up my theory that claret-and-blue is an incurable disease, rather than an addiction. People can beat addictions . . .

Matt Dynan: v Coventry City (11/12/93), It was an early Christmas present from my dad. We won 3-2 and I was standing in the corner between the old North Bank and the Chicken Run, pushing in front of everyone so I could get a better view. I remember thinking how big the ground was and that the players were actually real people and not just

Trevor Morley with Gjermund Holt, who edits and produces Scandinavian Bubbles magazine, in The Hammers pub at East Ham in May 2009.

stickers in an album.

I heard shouts of "Morley for England" from deep within the North Bank. He scored a penalty in that game, with Tim Breacker and Peter Butler getting the other two.

I came out of the ground as high as a kite, pumping with adrenaline. I'd supported Hammers since I was five or six but I was proper hooked now. I couldn't get to sleep for ages, thinking about how loud it was in the ground, and all the singing and chanting. I was now a Hammer for life.

Ivan Robeyns: My first visit to Upton Park was v Nottingham Forest (31/12/94), when we beat a strong Forest side 3-1 with goals from Tony Cottee, Ian Bishop and Michael Hughes. Having been a fan since 1981, it took me 13 years to get to Upton Park. I was 23-years-old that cold December day and very happy. Outstanding memories? So many to choose from. A packed stadium singing *Bubbles*, the noise when the players came out before kick-off, the roar that accompanied every goal, the chants aimed at Forest fans, the humour of the people sitting all around me, burning my tongue on a scorchingly hot pasty, the funny comments over the sound system before and after the game and at half-time, and walking back to the underground station, where we had to traipse all the way up and down the street next to the tracks to get to the entrance while nobody jumped the queue.

Jimmy Jacob: I didn't have much choice when it came to supporting the club, which I am not complaining about. I was pictured in the match day programme as a one hour-old baby, wrapped in a West Ham towel. The support runs in the family all the way back to my great great-grandad, so it really is in the blood. Main influence on me was my late great-grandad, Nick Hutchins, along with my father, Jason, and Auntie Zara, who I would attend the Boleyn Ground with on a regular basis. This now extends to my brothers, Denholm and Kaine, and cousin, Billy Ginn.

My first memory was a game v Nottingham Forest (31/12/94), when I was the match day mascot. Going into the dressing room, meeting my heroes – especially Julian Dicks – and then running out onto the pitch on

Jack McDonald, Connor Lewis and George McDonald.

a freezing cold day, to the roar of Hammers fans and the singing of *Bubbles* . . . what a feeling!

George McDonald: I have a small confession to make: at one stage in my life I used to follow Chelsea, despite my long family West Ham tradition. At the age of eight I was young, impressionable and also lucky enough to visit the Chelsea training ground and meet all the players. They had World Cup winners and world class internationals in their squad; the European glamour is what attracted me, I suppose, and West Ham didn't really have that at the time.

At first my dad, Tony, indulged my perversion. Begrudgingly, I imagine, he took me to Stamford Bridge a couple of times and to Wembley to see Chelsea lift the FA Cup in 1997. I believe Dad allowed this rebellion because he wanted me to enjoy football, see it played the right way. He wanted me to appreciate skill and flair. Chelsea fan or not, it's hard not to appreciate the abilities of players such as Vialli, Gullit and one of my footballing heroes, Gianfranco Zola. My slow switch from West Ham to Chelsea wasn't intentional but I had a taste of the Chelsea drug and became addicted.

Like an addict who can't help their addiction no matter how bad it is, who doesn't see what they are doing wrong to themselves or others, I needed an intervention. My support for the Blues was a disgrace to our claret-and-blue family and I felt like the ugly duckling. I guess Dad became sick of explaining to others how or why I was a Chelsea fan, was tired of apologising to our Hammers social circle for my crimes. So one day he sat me down and told me to "knock the Chelsea stuff on the head". I was born and bred to be a Hammer and it was time to come home. Being a kid, I couldn't afford to go and see Chelsea myself, nor buy tickets or replica shirts. Like all young lads, I needed my parents to provide for me and my provisions would cease unless they were West Ham. The threat of no football at all was enough to tempt me back to Upton Park. That, and fear of being locked in the attic!

Needless to say, I have been 100 per cent West Ham ever since and have been spending the rest of my life determined that, no matter how much silverware they accumulate, this Chelsea skeleton will stay locked indefinitely in my closet. Since I renewed my West Ham vows, they have been relegated from the Premier League twice and Chelsea have won every piece of silverware they have competed for. Thanks, Dad.

Deep down, though, I've always been a West Ham fan; I just veered a little off course along the way. My Grandad, Terry, played for West Ham's youth team and started professional career with Hammers, we were local and West Ham is in our blood.

I was a season ticket-holder at Upton Park for many years, experienced some highs and lows and have loved every second of it. West Ham is heart-achingly painful at times. Dad has said to me on more than one occasion, most memorably at the end of the 2006 FA Cup final: "West Ham will always let you down" but we still love them for it. Without those lows we wouldn't appreciate the highs. I wouldn't trade West Ham now for all the trophies Chelsea have bought in their trophy cabinet.

One of the many things I have learned from Dad is that a man's principles are worth more than anything else. Success without principles means nothing and this is how I regard Chelsea.

West Ham is a club of rich tradition, a community family club with values, history and principles. We have gone through some difficult times in recent years. And even though 'Big Sam' Allardyce was considered by some to be successful for getting us promoted back to the top flight and keeping us there for three seasons, it was achievement gained at the cost of our footballing principles. Is that really what the 'West Ham Way' is all about? I am proud of West Ham's history, traditions and values. Without them, we may as well all be supporting Chelsea.

Tom Fisk: v Coventry City, (31/1/96), won 3-2 after a goal-less first-half. The game had been postponed in December 1995, I was five, and so the first action I actually saw was the following January, with Dad, Grandad and Uncle Peter. Marc Rieper, Iain Dowie and Tony Cottee scored for us and Frank Lampard Jnr came on as a sub for his debut.

Arne Koellner: I was a 24-year-old shipping clerk from Germany, who had just started working at the local branch of a German shipping firm in Barking, of all places. It was my first time away from home and I was beginning to miss my hometown of Hamburg very much. I had trouble settling in, my colleagues spoke in an accent that sounded strange to my ears and I couldn't join in the banter. To fight my homesickness, I was looking for a home from home, a place that would give me stability and some joy, a new family so to speak. I needed a football team to support and since West Ham were just around the corner, just two stops on the tube, I chose them. In addition, a lot of my colleagues were West Ham supporters, so it felt like the natural thing to do.

My first game was a 4-2 win over Manchester City (23/3/96), who had Germans Uwe Roesler and Eike Immel playing for them. I was most impressed with the sheer noise, the passion of the fans, and *Bubbles* of course, even though I couldn't understand all the words at first. I also loved the claret-and-blue colours, while Julian Dicks was very impressive and I also instantly admired Tim Breacker as a player. Back then, I even thought that Iain Dowie (who scored two goals that day, with Dicks and Dani getting the others) was one of the best strikers in the world! The whole Upton Park experience made me want to come back for more. Today, Hammers are my number one football love forever – even ahead of my local club, St. Pauli.

Richard Nott: My parents, Christine and Frank, led me to support West Ham. My first visit, aged 12, was to see a 1-0 win v Leicester City (19/10/96). John Moncur got our winner.

Siobhan Hattersley: v Liverpool, (12/9/98), 2-1 (John Hartson and Eyal Berkovic). The tickets were a belated ninth birthday present from my dad, who had promised to take me to Upton Park but was unable to do so, because I had been through a serious illness in the months before. I remember being incredibly excited about seeing my hero Rio Ferdinand and was thrilled when Hammers beat Liverpool.

Jack McDonald: v Tottenham (8/8/99). We won 1-0 (Frank Lampard) but as I was only six, I can't remember much about the game.

I support West Ham because they are my local team and all my family supports the club. My grandad, Terry McDonald, played for the same West Ham youth team as Bobby Moore and John Lyall in the late 50s and then for the reserves, before being released following his national service in 1958 and joining our East End neighbours Leyton Orient.

No doubt a lot of older West Ham fans will read my answers throughout this book with pity. 'Poor sod' they'll be thinking, as I was born in 1993 and so haven't seen many of the great players in West Ham's history. My dad, Tony, always reminds me that on his first visit to Upton Park he saw Moore, Hurst, Peters, Brooking and Bonds, so sometimes I do feel like I missed out, especially when I think of the players I've seen – the likes of Julien Faubert, Gary Breen and Wayne Quinn (sorry for mentioning them all in the same sentence!).

James Clark: Living in Northfield, New Jersey, USA, I first attended a match at Upton Park with my brother-in-law, Charlie. Hammers v Watford (11/9/99), a 1-0 win thanks to a cleverly taken Paolo Di Canio free-kick. I was 29 and, to put it mildly, I was hooked. I sat in the old West Stand Upper and it was a brilliant, sunny Saturday. Even more than the goal, I remember Stuart Pearce crashing into a tackle, and you could seemingly hear the crack of his bone throughout the ground. Indeed, it turned out he broke his leg (for the first time that season; another break was to follow). The ground itself had not yet undergone the transformation we see today. As a virgin Hammers experience, it was first rate.

Charlie Beckwith: At the age of just 14, I have been a season ticket holder for 10 years. I sit in the East Stand at the back of the lower tier. My dad, Steve, made me support the Hammers – it wasn't optional. My first visit was v Burnley in 2003, a terribly boring game that ended 0-0.

Barry Hutton: West Ham v Nottingham Forest (26/12/04). I was 30 and came over from my home in Gauteng, South Africa. For some unknown reason I got the kick-off time for this game totally wrong – instead of starting at 3.00pm, it kicked-off at 1.00. Luckily, not knowing how bad the transport would be on a bank holiday weekend, I gave myself plenty of time to get to the ground for a three o'clock start. I got off the train at about 1.00, bought myself a programme and packet of chips and headed down the road to Upton Park. When I got closer to the stadium I was surprised to hear the crowd singing and cheering, so I quickly bought my ticket and ran up the stairs to find my seat. It was right at the top of the Dr Marten's (West) Stand, row HH, and as I was running up the stairs to my seat, something (must have been the football gods) told me to turn around and take a look at the field to experience my very first sight of live English football. May God be my witness, not even one second later West Ham scored the game's opening goal. A lucky goal, I might add (Forest's keeper tried to boot a backpass out of danger but it hit Teddy Sheringham and deflected into the net) but a fantastic moment for me nevertheless.

Bob Godbolt: My first visits would have been as a three-to-four-year-old before we moved from Custom House to Aberdeen when I was five. Even though I was a diehard Hammer, it wasn't until the 2002-03 season that I got back down, to see us lose 3-0 v Liverpool (2/2/03). David 'Calamity' James punching the ball away straight into the path of Gerrard saw us go 2-0 down and the fella next to me said: "You poor sod. You came all the way from Scotland to watch this shite? At least I only had to come from Barking."

I'm also a season ticket-holder for Aberdeen (not really a big fan, but it's a game to go to), and the people around me think it's hilarious that I'm there wearing a West Ham hat and scarf. A number of those around me now are at least West Ham 'aware'. Give me a couple more seasons and I'll have *Bubbles* echoing through Pittodrie.

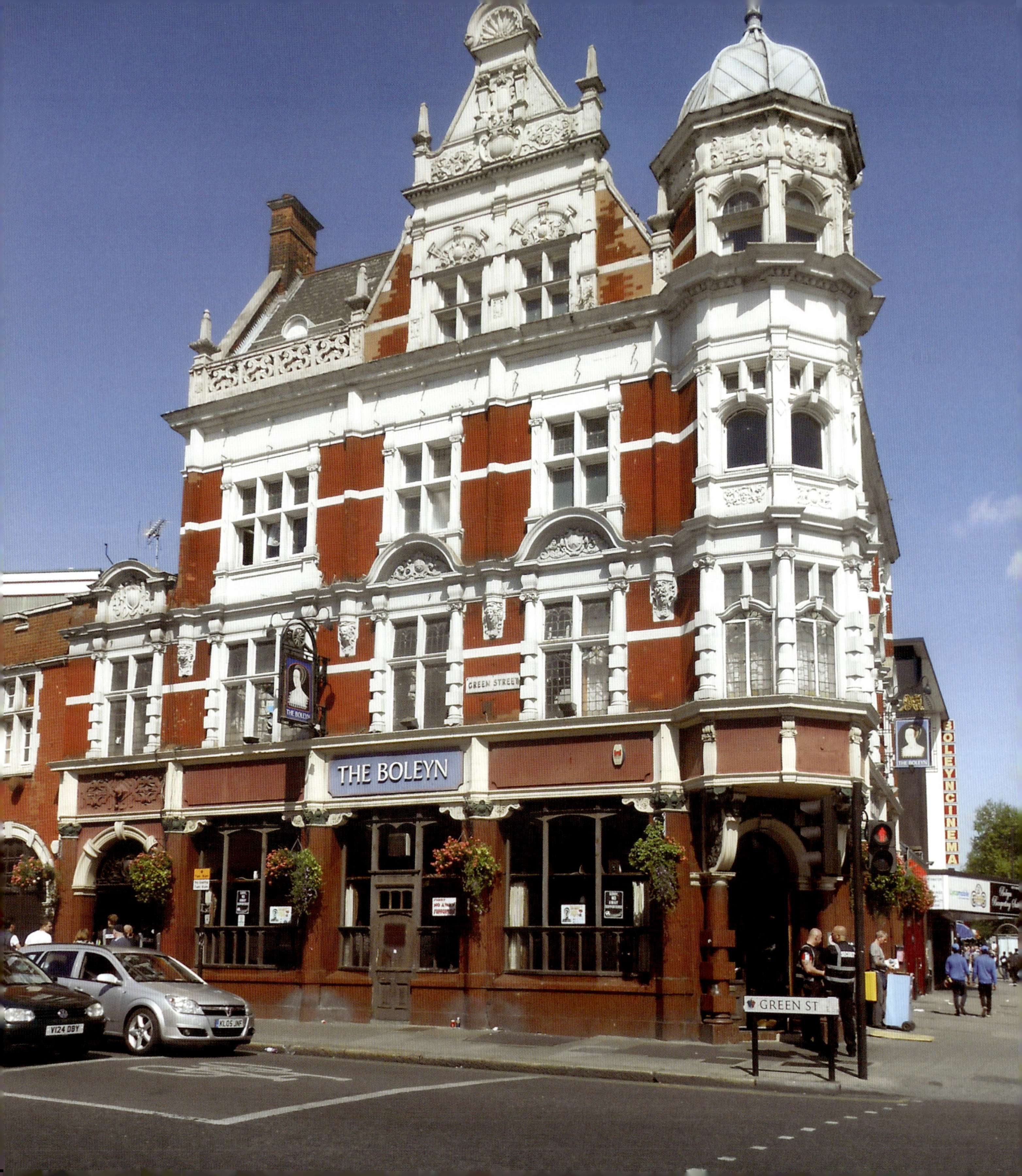
THE BOLEYN
GREEN STREET
GREEN ST
BOLEYN CINEMA

2 ROUTINES & RITUALS

FOR most of us, visiting Upton Park isn't purely about a 90-minute game of football. It goes much deeper than that. An opportunity to enjoy quality time and share a common love with family and friends, following traditions and customs that may have passed through several generations. Whether it be the pubs and cafes we visit before the match, the superstitions we follow once in the stadium, or even the journey to Green Street itself, these rituals are often the true foundations of our support – the comforts that have kept us coming back week after week when events on the pitch have truly tested our faith. And with the club preparing to move to a new home after 112 years, they are memories that will be treasured all the more . . .

Q: Describe any rituals that you followed, or a favourite haunt that you usually visited on your way to or from the Boleyn Ground?

Jim Wilder: I started going by myself as a schoolboy, with friends, during World War II. Our routine was to go to Barking or East Ham baths for a swim, then to Cooke's Eel and Pie shop in East Ham High Street for lunch before the match.

Reuben Gane: Sometimes after games my friends and I would call in at Ken Tucker's tobacconist's shop in Barking Road and hope to see Ken himself. We rarely did but we would buy some sweets, sherbet powder or liquorice sticks.

We also travelled by bike, which saved the bus fare, but we would then pay 6d (sixpence) to park our bikes in the front gardens of houses in the Barking Road or Priory Road. I favoured the Priory Road arrangement, as one householder used to let us park in the hallway of his house, which left room for motor bikes in the small front garden. Padlocks were always used.

Graham Wright: By the time I was 12 or 13, I was going fairly regularly with my friend, John. We used to buy *Treats* – little chocolate balls – before the game, which we didn't use to eat, but placed in the rims of hats being worn by men standing in front of us. When the *Treats* ran out, we used screwed up pieces of paper. It amused us to see the chocs and paper going round and round in the hats and suddenly fall off, to the surprise of the men. It whiled away the time until kick-off.

Rob Robinson: My mother always took me to home games when my dad, Bill, was looking after the junior teams. We would set off around 12 noon from our house in Welling, Kent, get the trolley bus to Woolwich, then either get on the free ferry or walk under the Thames via a tunnel. We would then board another trolley bus which would take us to East Ham Town Hall. From there we would walk. If we had had a good journey she would take me into the Green Street Cafe for a bacon roll. I always remember the owner having a parrot that he taught some naughty phrases about the opposing team we were playing.

Bobby George: After most games at Upton Park my brother-in-law, Dave, and I used to call in to see my Aunt Maud and Uncle Harold, who lived a few minutes from The Boleyn pub in Barking Road. Quite often, Aunt Lylie would be there, so between us we managed to put the world to rights along with the usual post-match analysis of the game we had just seen. The view from their living room window was of streams of traffic and football fans making their way towards the Greengate. Over the years from this window and their balcony we have watched the Hammers parade the cup on the way to East Ham Town Hall.

After leaving Barking Road, we more often than not made our way to The Black Lion pub in Plaistow for a swift half or two. Occasionally, some of the West Ham players had beaten us to it. I remember after one match there were several players in the bar celebrating a birthday, including Bobby Moore who looked very relaxed, and also John Cushley with his broken leg in plaster.

Mark Sandell: The Black Lion before the game; the banter, the hope and the round of predictions before we left. There was a bloke next to us in the East upper who ALWAYS left five minutes before the end, no matter how tense the game.

David Hughes: Walking through the North Street passages in Plaistow, passing the allotments and listening to the men predict how many West Ham would win by. Then I recall the walks back after the matches, either light of foot or the heavy trudge with my dad muttering "that's it, never again" (for the umpteenth time). I also recall him driving down Green

Street where, just past the old bus garage, there was a fishmonger who displayed on a large blackboard – not the cost of his cod or skate, but West Ham's score that day! Later years have seen many meets in The Boleyn, although these days it's The Black Lion, Plaistow.

Pete Gumbrell: I've tried them all, from NOT wearing claret-and-blue on a match day, to going through the same turnstile each game. I buy my programme from the same guy outside the same chip shop and park my car in the same street. I should really have learnt by now, though, that there is nothing I can physically do to change the score on the day other than sing *Bubbles* and shout the team on. It doesn't stop you following your rituals, though, does it!

Steven Mitchell: Bovril! Bovril represents as much about football to me as the rosettes, rattles, bobble-hats and scarves of my earliest days going to games. I often thought my father enjoyed his Bovril more than the match itself half the time. In those 'dim and distant days', I loathed the stuff and often shook in terror when he tried to order it at some dodgy away ground that only sold Oxo (Spurs) or, worse still, 'beef drink' (Chelsea), thereby disclosing our West Ham allegiance and putting us in mortal danger.

Still, I eventually came round and the thought of a visit to Upton Park without agonisingly burning my mouth with a plastic beaker of pre-match Bovril, suitable only for those boasting an asbestos throat, even on the hottest August or May day, is now complete anathema to me.

Michael Harris: I used to wear a claret-and-blue bobble hat and hooped jumper, knitted by my mum, which was festooned with badges showing photos of the players. I also took a rattle that I had painted myself, which in modern times would be considered an offensive weapon.

Martin Cearns: In recent years, tradition is to arrive an hour before kick-off and meet up with cousins, son Robin and friends at the bar at the north end of the West Stand upper. The beer is poor and expensive, surroundings uninviting, but company good and always a nice pre-match buzz. I will miss that and the sense of belonging which only comes from some 65 years of watching West Ham at Upton Park.

Pete May: I remember the roasted peanut seller in the North Bank in the 70s. You'd buy them in white paper bags and take the shells off and throw them on the terraces. From the 80s, when I started to write for *Fortune's Always Hiding* fanzine, I became a regular in Ken's Cafe. We sold our fanzine from a garden in Green Street and had post-match meetings in Ken's. Carol behind the counter is a great character and the egg, chips and beans is thoroughly recommended.

Eddie Parker: When I was a boy Dad would take me for pie and mash and a drink at the East Ham Working Men's Club in Boleyn Road, near Barking Road (well, he had a drink, I had something fizzy with an Arrowroot biscuit). Once I started going with mates, via bus and train, all

Programme seller Dennis Lamb has been a feature of the pre-match Green Street scene for many years, selling evocative old programmes as well as the latest edition.

PLAYER
ERNIE GREGORY
Born: 10/11/21, Stratford, east London
WHU career: 1946-60
Position: Goalkeeper
Apps: 406 **Goals:** 0

I WAS coached regularly by Dave Bailey, the understudy to Ted Hufton. He was also a terrific goalkeeper who specialised in handling low shots – he'd make a cup-shape with his hands.

He looked after me off the field, too. At lunchtimes, if we had a few bob, Dave, 'Woody' (the groundsman), team-mate Ron Cater and I would go over the road for a meat pudding, or up to Sandy's on Green Street for egg and chips or a Chelsea bun. Then we'd go back to the ground and practice on the field at the back of the West Stand. There was a cinder track and, out the back, a training field with trees and a sandpit area by the goal.

When I coached the keepers myself years later, I also used a sandpit, but the lads didn't want to know because the sand went all over them. But in my day, we always used the sandpit for goalkeeping practice – you could dive all over the place without hurting yourself.

our pocket money was reserved for a programme. A couple of times we would stretch to a plastic star badge with a black and white picture of one of the team, or a copy of *The Stratford Express* if it had freebie pictures of the players.

In recent times rituals have involved a couple of beers before the game. Over the years we have used The Central, The Black Lion, The Green Man, The Earl of Wakefield and The Denmark Arms. We have also sampled the delights of a bacon sandwich or two from Ken's Cafe and Lippies, to name but two. Visits to Dennis' old programme stall have always been well worthwhile.

Crispin Derby: When my two sons, Sam and Joel, reached drinking age we would meet in the Duke of Edinburgh opposite Upton Park station at 1.00pm for a pint before slipping round the corner to the Thai café in Plashet Road. We loved the old guy who ran it with his very young children assisting. Cooking was basic but good and cheap. As well as great Thai staples, he also provided standard British greasy spoon fare – every fried variation being accompanied by a huge pile of ready-buttered, sliced bread on a white plate.

Colin Kosky: My best mate, Tony, and I would get to the ground when the gates opened at around 1.00pm, both dressed in Beatles wigs and with umbrellas painted claret-and-blue, before rushing down to the front of the North Bank. The first song that came on the sound system was always Whistling Jack Smith's *I Was Kaiser Bill's Batman*, which I will always associate with an empty Upton Park.

Tony Hoskins: My mates and I would play for our school team on

Another well-known character synonymous with the match day experience on Green Street is Ellis Schwartz, who sells the official match day programme and also runs the programme stall, situated just before the main gates, with help from his father Sid and Fred Loveday (far left).

Tony Hogg: Me and my mates, Geoff Thompson, Barry Nunn and Jeff Cardy, used to go to Porky's Cafe in Green Street before the game. Then we would make our way to the ground, always buying a programme before paying our shillings to get in. We would often head for the old 'children's cage' to the right of the terrace and chuck peanut shells down on the heads of the older fans below. If we were near the corner flag we'd pelt the opposition's winger with orange peel as he took a corner. But that's as far as any misbehaviour went in those days.

Saturday morning and, as soon as we finished, it was a frantic bike ride to the train station, usually Westcliff-on-Sea. Bikes safely padlocked to the fence at the station, it was the eager wait for the train to Barking, then onto the underground, two stops up to Upton Park. In later years it would be a case of stopping off at The Barking Dog or The Spotted Dog (on opposite sides of the road next to Barking station) for a few beers before getting the tube.

We always went into the main entrance, round to the left to the North Bank turnstiles. We were normally there by 1.00pm. Another memory is the sound of the turnstiles being unlocked . . . in we go! It was a mad rush to get a prime position in the middle of the North Bank behind the goal. I can still hear the magical sound of Bill Remfry, playing what became his signature opening song of the day, *I Was Kaiser Bill's Batman* by Whistling Jack Smith.

Gavin Hadland: The whistling song really brings it all back. Sitting with my dad in the West Stand for two-to-three hours before the game, which was never boring for me, although Dad used to bring a book. For games against Man Utd we used to queue up from as early as 11-11.30am, and there was always a big crush outside the main entrance.

Richard Miller: We lived in Ilford and from 1954-55 until 1964, when I was old enough to drive, we cycled the four miles to the ground. In those days most of the houses opposite the ground allowed cyclists to leave their bicycles in their front rooms while they watched the game in exchange for three pence. I moved to Christchurch, Dorset in 1977 but have continued to travel the 290 miles there and back to Upton Park for most of the home games since.

Having parked in a side street as close as possible to Upton Park, we follow the same ritual: fish and chip lunch at Ercan Fish Bar on the corner of Barking Road and Priory Road, then we visit the sweet shop just a few doors along, at 21 Barking Road, to purchase the match day programme. The owner also saves the *Newham Recorder* for me – I have all the match reports dating back to when Trevor Smith first reported on West Ham games in 1954.

Kevin Radley: I went to most games with friends from Basildon, particularly Del Haigh and Jeff Holly, who were mates from Barstable Grammar School. We met up with other friends at the Bulls Eye pub in

118 UPTON PARK MEMORIES

The Black Lion, 59-61 Plaistow Road, Plaistow, E13 0AD.

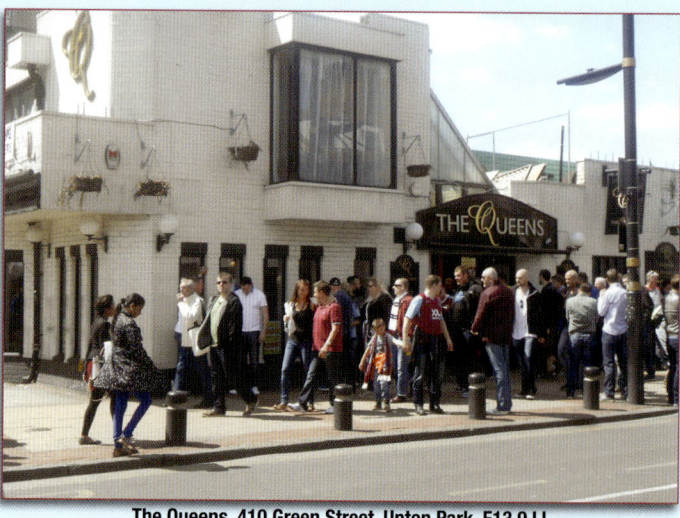

The Queens, 410 Green Street, Upton Park, E13 9JJ.

The Lord Stanley, 15 St Mary's Road, Plaistow, E13 9AE.

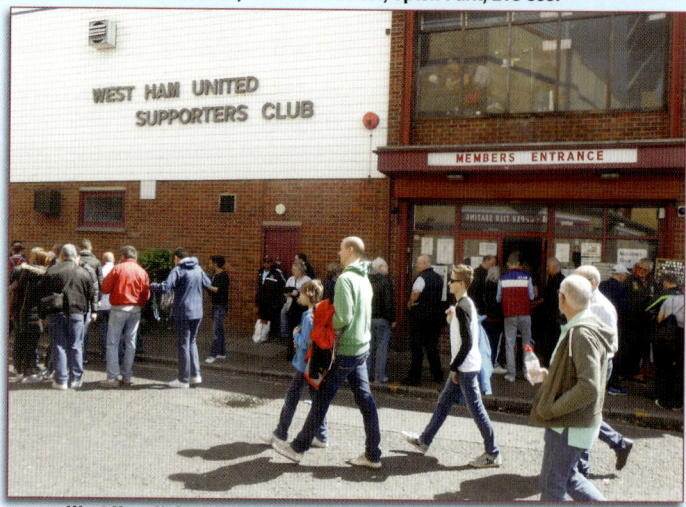

West Ham United Supporters' Club, Castle Street, Upton Park, E6 1PP.

The Duke of Edinburgh, 299 Green Street, Upton Park, E13 9AR.

East Ham Working Men's Club, 2 Boleyn Road, East Ham, E6 1QE.

UPTON PARK MEMORIES 119

The Boleyn Tavern, 1 Barking Road, Upton Park, E6 1PW.

The Central, 150 Barking Road, East Ham, E6 3DB.

The Denmark Arms, 381 Barking Road, East Ham, E6 1LA.

The Millers Well, 419-421 Barking Road, East Ham, E6 2JX.

The Victoria Tavern, 28 High Street, Plaistow, E13 0AJ.

Fans queuing before the game v Manchester United in January 1972.

PLAYER
KEITH ROBSON
Born: 15/11/53, Hetton-le-Hole, Northumberland
WHU career: 1974-76
Position: Forward
Apps: 87, **Goals:** 19

THE William The Conqueror at Manor Park was the pub us players in the 70s particularly liked to visit on a Saturday night, or the Burford Arms at Stratford.

After a few drinks there, we'd usually move on to The Room At The Top club in Ilford High Road, where I did some very daft things. I just couldn't handle it at all. I was young, single and having a good time. I had plenty of spare time on my hands.

When I moved into new digs in Coniston Gardens, Ilford, The Beehive became my local.

When I first joined West Ham from Newcastle I lived in digs in Lonsdale Avenue, Barking and I'd often pop into the bookies and The Boleyn for a pint after training in midweek. At first, I would walk home from the ground and no-one would recognise me. Then, when I started scoring goals and getting loads of publicity, there was always someone to drink with.

I've been back to Upton Park numerous times in the past 10 years or so. I'll always have a soft spot for the club, where I made a lot of friends.

Basildon, a stone's throw from the station. On the train we ran a sweep on the predicted score, the unwritten rule being that you could only predict a winning result for Hammers and you couldn't copy someone else's score. Any newcomers who didn't quite understand the rules and had the audacity to predict a West Ham defeat would be given a choice of 'seeing the light' or getting thrown off the train at Upminster. Given our somewhat patchy form over the years, there would often be a sizeable 'carry-over' fund!

On arriving at Upton Park, we headed straight for the Pie & Mash shop in Queens Market. Roy's pies (especially those that were slightly burnt) were the best around. The staff were great – very friendly and they always shared our optimism about the upcoming match. After double pie and mash with extra liquor, we headed to The Queens for more refreshment. Then it was off to the ground (North Bank or Chicken Run) where we arrived suitably fed and refreshed, in good voice and sometimes feeling ludicrously optimistic.

Ian McMaster: Head to Ken's Cafe for a cup of tea and fry-up before the game. I continue that tradition to this day on my occasional visits from Germany.

James Clark: When I'm visiting from the USA I buy a programme at Ken's Café after enjoying a plateful of fish and baked beans. Then I find an *Over Land and Sea* seller for another mandatory purchase before lingering outside the ground to watch for any celebrity arrivals, players or otherwise. A quick trip into the club shop, then inside the ground early to place a bet with Ladbrokes and watch the warm-ups – after a few beers, of course.

Afterwards, it's usually a long queue at Upton Park station. The horses used by the police always stick in the mind, as well as the overall look and feel (the buildings, the banter) of east London.

I once stayed at the Newham Hotel on Romford Road, so I got to know the whole of Green Street intimately. I love the bustle of the Indian/Pakistani shops and street stalls. I know that most of these residents don't fancy the football but I feel they are part of the experience, all the same.

This club will always occupy my heart, mess with my head and fire my soul. Come on you Irons!

John Burton: In the old days we had a ritual of putting money in the hat of the worst busker in the world, who used to play the penny whistle outside the North Bank. If West Ham lost we had to find the culprit who never put his money in.

Peter Lush: I always used to buy a programme at the station and then go to the bookshop on Green Street on the way to the ground. When it closed I then started visiting Newham Bookshop on Barking Road to get any new West Ham books. I still call in there now if I am in the area.

David Bernstein: It started in October 1982 when we played Liverpool at home. On a gloriously sunny day we were about to go into the Chicken Run when my friend, Phil, realised that he had forgotten to buy someone a birthday card. We walked back to Barking Road, bought the card and returned to our entrance. We always had our place saved by a lady and her son, so we positioned ourselves in our usual spot waiting for the team to come out. The sun was very strong and Phil removed his sweater, only to put it back on immediately as the clouds then appeared. But 10 seconds later the sweater was off again as the sun came back out.

We went on to beat Liverpool 3-1 and ever since, we always buy a birthday card from the same shop and remove/replace/remove our sweater before every game!

Marco Taviani: Usually a bite to eat in Al's Diner in Barking, then a few pints in The Barking Dog before the tube ride two stops to Upton Park. My friends and I have probably visited every pub from Barking to Plaistow at some point depending on what pub was 'in' at the time.

Ian Crocker: I loved the walk from Upton Park station to the Boleyn Ground. You could soak up the atmosphere perfectly and it was also obligatory to stop in the cafe for a sausage sandwich. When I got the job as match day stadium announcer (from 1986 to 1990), I used to get to the

> **Neil Humphreys:** This is embarrassing. There was a decent hairdressers opposite the ground, along from where the 1966 statue is today. When I got my first season ticket as a teenager, I had a huge crush on the girl on the counter. She leaned over the counter once to check the diary and suddenly the world was a brighter place. For almost an entire season, I seemed to get my hair washed and blow-dried more times than Liberace before games. She still never got the hint. But I don't regret it. This was the early 90s, during the Mike Small era. It was often the highlight of the afternoon.

ground a lot earlier and pop into John Lyall's office to get his team-sheet, so I could later pass the information on to fans. John was wonderfully welcoming and there were often famous football folk in his office. John used to introduce them to me and tell me to sit down for a sandwich and a cuppa. Priceless moments. He was a very special man and not a bad manager either.

Paul Clayden: In the late 70s I'd get to the ground an hour-and-a-half before kick off with my grandad and read every single word in the programme. To stand at the centre of the Chicken Run you had to get there early. By the early 90s I had discovered the wonderful Corner Cafe in Walton Road. Double egg on toast, double sausage, baked beans and mushrooms, a real treat. Then to The Lord Stanley for a pre-match beer. The ritual now is good old Ken's Cafe. I sometimes see my old school friend, Phill Jupitus, in there. Russell Brand was once a regular. I can't help but think that it should be transplanted to the Olympic Stadium.

Steve Wilks: At the age of seven, my friend Keith and I used to get there for around 11.30am so that we would be first in the queue to get in and take our favourite spot on the North Bank. After the game we would collect the special editions of the *Evening News* and *Evening Standard* which were left on the floor, containing lots of pictures of West Ham players which we collected for our scrapbooks.

David May: We used to meet at my great-grandfather, Mike Sullivan's, house in Sullivan Avenue (off Tollgate Road). Mike was known to all the family as 'Big Daddy'. He was also a Mayor of West Ham. We would set off from his place to the ground via the Beckton Dumps and Boundary Road. I remember having to have piggy back rides from my dad on the way home.

Gerard Daly: Pre-match rituals in adulthood would involve numerous pints in various pubs, mainly The Queens and The Boleyn, and sometimes a few at Waterloo station to break up the journey. I always had to get a sticker off the bloke collecting for Cancer Research. We'd sometimes lose when I did but we'd never win when I didn't. Or so I convinced myself.

Gary Bush: During my early years of following the club, after arriving at Upton Park station I would head to one of the programme sellers in Green Street and hand over my 10 pence for the latest edition of our

122 UPTON PARK MEMORIES

Queens Fish Bar, 406 Green Street, Upton Park, E13 9JJ.

Belly Busters, Green Street, Upton Park (opposite stadium).

Queens Market, Green Street, E13 9BA.

Green Street Cafe, 570 Green Street, Upton Park, E13 9DA.

Ken's Cafe, 467 Green Street, Upton Park, E13 9AX.

Nathan's Pies & Eels, 51 Barking Road, Upton Park, E6 1PY.

UPTON PARK MEMORIES 123

Ercan Fish Bar, 59 Barking Road, Upton Park, E6 1PY.

pocket-sized gem. Next it was a walk to the ground, while checking out the various goods on offer from the street sellers. The badge stalls always caught my attention. Badges all pinned onto boards shining brightly back at you, and it was always good to have a browse at the different designs on offer. I'd visited other grounds on my 'away days' but West Ham must have had more street sellers than any other club I could think of at the time.

Once through the main gates I would go to our small club shop, which was an Aladdin's cave of everything claret-and-blue but very small with just a couple of shop assistants serving behind the counter. It did make the most of every available space, though, there was stuff hanging from everywhere.

When entering the ground, I more often than not used the turnstile operated by George. How did I know his name? Well, the giveaway was his hand-knitted claret-and-blue jumper with 'George' emblazoned across the middle. He was always a cheerful bloke and made you feel welcome.

Far better than having some electronic device beeping back at you, that's for sure.

Stephen George: Upton Park was always a special place for me because my nan and grandad lived in a flat on the 14th floor of James Sinclair Point which, prior to its demolition, towered above Queens Market. And in that very same market was Roy's Pie & Mash shop – to my mind the best of the traditional pie shops that are, sadly, now an increasingly rare sight across London's East End (Roy's moved from Upton Park, where it opened in 1964, to Dagenham in 1994 and closed for good in 2014). In the 80s, when I started going to the games regularly, you could get a decent feed-up before the match AND a cup of tea for less than a pound.

Simon Hoppit: In the 90s, a group of us used to meet up behind the goal on the North Bank, where I would look out for Big Steve, who seemed to be about 8ft tall. In those days it was affordable and you could pay on the door, it was so much better. When I first started going to Upton Park, I used to try and bunk in as under-13 for quite a while, until one day

Cassettari's Cafe, just around the corner from the Boleyn Ground in Barking Road, was for many years the meeting place of West Ham players who gathered to discuss football theories and tactics over lunch. It was here, in the 50s, where the foundations for what became the famed 'West Ham Academy' were established, with Malcolm Allison, Noel Cantwell, John Bond and Dave Sexton, in particular, in the vanguard of that evolution. Those four are included in this picture taken at a reunion of ex-Hammers held in Cassettari's in the 70s, with Phil Cassettari senior standing between Big Mal and Bondy. The full line-up (left to right): Jimmy Andrews, Dave Sexton, Noel Cantwell, Malcolm Allison, Phil Cassettari, John Bond, Frank O'Farrell and Malcolm Musgrove.

a copper pulled me by the shoulder and said: "You are taking the piss, mate, join the proper queue."

Steve Smith: Dad had to have pie and mash before a game, either in Robin's or Duncan's, never Nathan's on the Barking Road. He hated their liquor and mash served from an ice cream scoop!

PLAYER
MALCOLM ALLISON
Born: 5/9/27, Dartford, Kent
WHU career: 1951-58
Position: Centre-half
Apps: 255, **Goals:** 10

WEST Ham decided to give us two shillings and sixpence so you could go and have lunch at Cassettari's.

We all had vouchers and that was abused because some guys did without lunch and copped the money instead to go to the dogs.

But the cafe used to be packed upstairs with a steady stream of players – who weren't always well behaved, I promise you.

We used to fill the room with our theories and disputes. But the result was that we were a nicely developing team. We had opened our minds and declared ourselves willing to try new things and be prepared to make some mistakes along the way. In 1956 and '57 we were emerging as certainties to eventually find our way to the first division.

Andy Brooker: The one thing that's been on my route for the majority of the time is The Best Turkish Kebab, just opposite Barclays Bank on Barking Road. In the late 80s I was hit with a really bad case of food poisoning, which I know was down to a dodgy frozen cannelloni. I lost weight and was really not well at all. My best mate, Stu, swore that it was from "that dodgy kebab house" but I knew it wasn't and I've been going in there pre-match now for nearly 30 years.

So when the curtain finally comes down on football at Upton Park, I've got to go and find a new kebab house in Stratford.

Mike Corbett: If I drive to the game, I will always stop at the sweet shop on the corner of Brampton Road and Masterman Road. The chap working there always asks how I think we'll do, and then wishes the team good luck. I generally like to get to the ground at least 30 minutes early, so I can buy and read a copy of the fanzine, *Over Land and Sea (OLAS)*, in my seat.

Liam Tyrell: I have never really had a set routine when it comes to match days. Early trips tended to involve being taken by other family friends as well as my uncle. When I first started to go independently I used to get the 252 bus from my nan's house on Mawney Road in Romford to Elm Park Station, then the District Line to Upton Park.

UPTON PARK MEMORIES

Tony McDonald: Fans who have only supported West Ham in the Premier League era wouldn't believe that for a little lad to have any chance of seeing much of the game in the 60s and 70s, they needed to be queuing at the turnstiles before 1.00pm, ready to rush down to the front of the terracing for a place on the wall surrounding the pitch. None of this strolling in at five-to-three to take your seat.

In my first season, aged eight, the ritual would be for Mum or Dad to drive me from home in Chadwell Heath to Aunt Maud and Uncle Harold's flat on Barking Road, where Maud would rustle up ham, chips and beans around midday. As I waited for their son, Dennis (who lived in a flat across the road), to call in to collect me and take me to the game, Harold would enlighten me on the qualities, or otherwise, of the World Cup-winning trio I was about to watch in awe. "Nah, Hurst . . . HURST! He's bleedin' useless, not fit to lace Victor Watson's boots. Peters? No mate, not as good as yer Jimmy Ruffell or Lenny Goulden. As for Bobby Moore . . . none of that lot are any bloody good."

It was like listening to Alf Garnett rehearsing his lines for *Till Death Us Do Part*. It's true what they say, though. Players were always so much better in 'our day' – and now I feel like I've turned into Uncle Harold when I tell my lads that Scott Parker wasn't in Geoff Pike's class, never mind that of Martin Peters!

Den would arrive and rescue me from his old man's pre-match sermon and then we'd walk round the corner into Green Street, where I'd call into Bobby Moore's shop to see what was on offer. That's where I bought my first pair of pukka football boots – Adidas Brazil.

The silly little things that go through your mind as a kid. My first priority as we entered Castle Street, and before reaching the South Bank turnstiles, was to see if there was a huge television truck with a gantry parked on the street at that end of the ground. If not, it meant West Ham wouldn't appear on TV all weekend. Imagine that now – your team is playing a Premier League game and you won't see a single moment's action from it unless you attend the game in person.

Unlike today, where Sky and BT Sport will bombard us with trailers of the matches they will be screening in the days ahead, BBC and ITV weren't allowed to mention who they would be featuring, in case it adversely affected attendances figures at those grounds. We didn't know any different back then.

If I did see a TV vehicle, my eyes would light up. My next thought would be, 'are we on BBC1 *Match of the Day* tonight, or will I have to wait until Sunday afternoon for *The Big Match* highlights?' Then, 'are we going to be the main game or just a token 10 minutes?' I tell you, us children of the 60s carried the weight of the world on our shoulders.

I think a lot of supporters today buy the match day programme simply out of habit. I doubt that they ever read a word of it, other than flick through glancing at the headlines and pictures before discarding it. In 1968-69 and for many years after, you had to buy a programme to know who was playing.

In the early 70s I was lucky that my girlfriend Joanne's dad, Brian Bond, was into speedway and also supported West Ham, my two passions in life at the time. He would take me, aged 10-11, and we'd stand on the new East Stand terrace that had replaced the original Chicken Run, which was unfortunately demolished in the summer before I started going to games.

The high East Terrace steps offered a perfect view but there was nothing better than standing by the perimeter wall, within touching distance of the players, where fans would drape their plain scarves over the wall.

I know avid anorak programme collectors will hate this, but as a young boy it made perfectly good sense to get home from the game and summarise events as I saw them. For a start, the result had to be inked in – if not on the front cover of the prog, then certainly next to the team line-ups on page three.

But I was more pedantic than that and would write a comment next to each player's name. I mentioned this absurd anally retentive behaviour to

Upton Park station in Green Street

Joe Durrell over a few pints the other year and he seemed pleased when I showed him the prog I'd kept for some 40 years. He saw with his own eyes that, for his debut game v Stoke City in 1971, he got a "Very good" from me, whereas Hurst was (probably harshly) marked down as "Bad" and Brooking merely "Fair."

As with everything in life, your habits change with age and circumstances.

In my early twenties, an older friend called Tony Lee – another West Ham football and Hackney speedway fan and a very successful insurance broker who was introduced to me by Brian Bond – drove us to games in his Alfa Romeo sports car. Tony could drink and it was he who introduced me to the warming half-time delights of Barley Wine sold from the West Stand bars at half-time in the early 00s. That stuff was rocket fuel – I swear Hammers had 22 players on the field in every second half.

After the game, to 'let the crowd die down', if it was a midweek game we'd invariably head off for a couple of pints at The Britannia in Stratford, which Frank Lampard part-owned. If not 'The Brit', we'd head further out to The Retreat in Chigwell, run by John Driver and his wife. We'd often see their son, Nick, a big Hammers fan, in the West Stand. Tony Lee drove us back to The Retreat straight from Wembley to celebrate victory in the 1980 FA Cup final.

Less than seven years later, I launched the club's official newspaper, *Hammers News* and, in the early 90s, edited the match day programme, which put me in the privileged position of having virtually unlimited access to the players, who were happy to receive phone calls on their land-line at home (in the days before mobiles).

The stark difference from now and that period in the late 80s/early 90s is that the most sociable West Ham players – the likes of Frank McAvennie, Julian Dicks, Ian Bishop, Trevor Morley, Kenny Brown, Allen McKnight, Ray Stewart and even the maestro himself, Liam Brady, who would occasionally venture out for a few quiet lagers after a midweek game – were generally relaxed about being seen out drinking with some of us who covered the club journalistically and they would also sup beers with fans in the trendy pubs and clubs of Essex, without fear of embarrassing pictures turning up on social media.

After home games there was a chance you'd bump into players socialising in popular late-night Romford haunts such as Hollywood's (next to the station in Atlanta Boulevard, now a block of flats) or Secrets (in the High Street), or get to meet them at the Phoenix Apollo steakhouse, owned by the Greek brothers, Panay and Gil, on Stratford Broadway, where 'Page 3 models' would literally hang out and love to be photographed with McAvennie, in particular.

There was a mutual trust and respect between players and the press back then but it rarely exists now. Those long-lost days of Mooro, Charlo, Cush and the boys having a carefree beer or three after a game in The Black Lion, or Frankie Mac, Bish and Dicksy knocking back bottles of Becks in their nearest nightclub or local pub in Essex, are just . . . well, distant memories.

The pirate t-shirt sellers in Green Street have attempted to cash in on the rivalry with Spurs.

Newham Bookshop, 747 Barking Road, Upton Park, E13 9ER.

Queens Fish Bar was often the first port of call and it's good to see the lads who served me all those years ago at away games now and again.

Much has depended on how I've travelled to the game, which station I've disembarked at or where I've parked the car. I miss Robins Pie & Mash at East Ham so try and make Nathan's if the queue hasn't quite made it up to The Boleyn.

It's sad how so many pubs have fallen by the wayside: The Green Man, The Prince of Wales, The Duke of Edinburgh, The Earl of Wakefield, The Castle, The Greengate, The Ruskin Arms – all places I liked to go.

Tony Hogg, author of three editions of the West Ham United Who's Who, *a top salesman and a real character. He works the local pubs on match days selling the retro EX magazine.*

The Lord Stanley, The Central, The Denmark Arms and, of course, The Boleyn are all OK but I like The Millers Well and The Black Lion. I love 'The Lion' for its impressive history, choice of ales, service and big beer garden.

I've always liked the fact you can use Plaistow, Upton Park or East Ham underground stations to get to the ground and have plenty of food and drink options on offer.

Mark Edwards: I'm not really a regular at Upton Park but I get to as many games as money allows with my father-in-law, Paul Milligan, and brother-in-law, Rob Milligan, or my best friend, Guy Johnson (who travels up from Cornwall). We always park up near Central Park, walk down to buy a programme and join the huge queue for pie and mash. I will then head towards the ground and get a copy of *OLAS*, as I like to read alternative views on the club.

Steve Burton: I always go into Ken's Cafe in Green Street for my pre-match fry-up and mug of tea. The place is a real West Ham United nerve centre.

David Steadman: I would always try to get in double pie and mash at Duncombes, or Duncan's (opposite Upton Park station) as it later became known (it closed in Jan. 2012). In later years a few of us would meet up for pre-match beers at The Castle pub along the Barking Road.

Gjermund Holt: Living in Norway, the journey to the game starts early. I have always liked to book hotels in the area, either in Barking, Ilford or

> **Steve Blowers:** In the mid-70s, my 35 pence per week pocket money got this four-foot nothing titch of a teenager to the Boleyn Ground and back – 3p on the high noon No.86 bus from Romford dog track to Forest Gate police station and then 2p on the No.58 all the way down Green Street.
>
> That meant I could be one of the first in the queue for the South Bank, where I'd pay 20p to click through the Juniors turnstile and sprint down to the front wall and read my 5p programme from cover-to-cover, while listening to the 'sounds' of announcer Bill Remfry, who was perilously-perched in his little box bolted high onto the West Stand. At 2.15, he would emerge through the roof and head off for the team-sheets before returning to meticulously announce the line-ups as the fans, hanging on his every syllable, penned the programme changes.
>
> With the band of the Royal British Legion subsequently taking over on the halfway line cabbage patch as kick-off neared, all we needed then was Remfry's pre-match cry of: "It's our *Bubbles* time!" Pure theatre.
>
> Win or lose, my last 5p would go on the two return buses home.
>
> All that for 35 pence per game – not a penny more, not a penny less.

UPTON PARK MEMORIES 129

at the stadium itself. I nearly always start out early at The Miller's Well pub in East Ham or The Black Lion in Plaistow. A few pre-match beers, a read of the programme and meeting other Hammers is very much a big part of the day, as well as a quick stop at the bookies. I always put a bet on the penalty-taker to score the first goal, so Dicksy won me a few bob.

Arne Koellner: No pre-match alcoholic drinks. I wanted to take the games in with all senses clear. So it was

just about putting on my Centenary shirt with Tim Breacker's name and number plus a scarf, two stops on the tube to Upton Park station and a slow walk along Green Street.

Jack McDonald: Before games, I used to help sell dad's *EX* retro magazine outside the supporters' club in Castle Street. We'd get there early, at around 11.30am, and had all kinds of people come up to us while we were selling.

Every Saturday home game felt like an episode of *Only Fools and Horses*, with my

Dan Francis: My happiest childhood memories are of going to Upton Park with my dad, Roy, on a Saturday afternoon in the late 80s and early 90s and, to be honest, it was the journey with him and our pre-match routine that I looked forward to as much as the game. We always took the same route by car from our house in Elm Park, through Dagenham and Upney, with Dad cursing the traffic as we crossed the A406 into Barking Road. If we had time, we'd pop into my nan and grandad's house, in St Dunstan's Road at the far end of Green Street, for a cup of tea, before parking somewhere near the ground and having pie and mash in Nathan's if the queue wasn't too long. A bag of chips from Ercan's if it was.

We'd then meet up with Dad's mates in the East Ham Working Men's Club. I'd be handed a lemonade and a packet of crisps and wander next door to the snooker room, where the same group of twenty-something lads would be playing every week. I'd have my head buried in the match day programme, pretending to read it but listening in to their conversations about football, music and girls as they hit balls around the table, thinking that they were the coolest blokes in the world!

At around 2.45pm, we'd leave the club and walk round to the West Stand entrance. That was my favourite part – the sights, sounds and smells that became so familiar and reassuring. Programme sellers, burger stalls, cigarette smoke . . . and manure from the police horses! I'd always beg Dad to let me have a quick look in the club shop – or portakabin as it was then – and then stand in amazement looking up at all the merchandise pinned to the walls, always hoping against hope that he would tell me to just pick whatever I wanted. He never did.

We'd then get through the turnstiles and walk up the steps to take our seats, right on the wall next to the directors' box in the middle of the West upper. After the game, we'd walk back to the car and then listen to the Capital Gold radio phone-in on the journey home. I never really appreciated it at the time but those Saturday afternoons spent with Dad were the foundation for the close relationship we've shared ever since – and so I have West Ham to thank for that.

As I got into my teenage years, I started to attend matches with friends and always stood on the North Bank. We'd get to the ground early and, when the turnstiles opened, race to try and secure our favourite spot – right at the front of the 'shelf' that used to hang over the corner next to the Chicken Run. I used to have enough money to cover my train fare, my match ticket (£5.00) and a programme, with £1 left over that I would use on a first goalscorer bet, asking a nearby adult to put it on for me at the booth. If it ever came in, I'd treat myself to a sausage and chips at Queens Fish Bar on the way back to the tube station.

Iain Dale: I leave my home in Tunbridge Wells, Kent around noon, make the 40-mile drive round the M25, up the A2 and then leave my car with the car wash crew in Barking Road, who've been looking after it for 15 years while I go to the game. I usually pay a visit to Viv in the Newham Bookshop on the corner of Barking Road and Green Street before heading along to Ken's Café. Carol, who takes the orders, is an avid listener to my LBC show, so we always have a good chat, before I order a good old fry-up. I meet my friend, Jo Phillips, there and we catch up on the gossip before heading down Green Street to buy a copy of *OLAS* from Gary Firmager.

brother, George (Rodney), carrying our purpose-built, wooden fold-up stand from our battered blue VW estate car, along Green Street. Once we reached our usual position and it was propped up against the wall outside the supporters' club in Castle Street, we'd fill up the shelves with back issues of *EX*. One day it was so windy the stand fell over, nearly decapitating a passing fan. Luckily, he accepted a free copy of the mag by way of apology!

Dad's worst mistake was buying some luminous yellow coats because he reckoned we would easily catch people's attention and it would increase sales. Unfortunately, the 'masterplan' backfired. People mistook us for stewards and were constantly asking us for directions or: "Do you know where the ticket office is, mate?" Those coats were not such a bright idea, after all, and we never wore them a second time.

George McDonald: Before spending a few hours before the game selling *EX* mag, we would sometimes visit Cassettari's for a pre-match fry-up. The place was steeped in West Ham history.

The 'Wine Bar' next door to Newham Bookshop was our regular post-match drinking haunt in the late 90s. It would get a bit rowdy in there after a win, beer guaranteed to go everywhere every time *Baggy Trousers* by Madness came on.

More sedate was the 'Plaistow Club' (Plaistow Park Community Centre in Queens Road West), a 10-minute walk from the ground through the allotments. The bar staff were always welcoming and as well as good-priced ale, you could catch the evening live Sky game on the telly.

William Lloyd: What I liked to do most was visit Cassettari's Cafe before the match to have something to eat and just sit and remember the old days when my Hammers heroes went to this same cafe after training to discuss football tactics along with their tea and bacon rolls.

Charlie Beckwith: We can't always do it but I do love a good Nathan's pie and mash before the game. If not, it's a Papa's Chicken all round.

Ian Smith: Before I could get served in pubs I always got the 147 bus from Ilford to Upton Park with my mate, Rich. We would sit smoking at the back on the upper deck in our green bomber jackets, jeans, Fred Perry polo shirt and 10 hole black Doc Martens, thinking we were hard. Fact is, we were just lads doing what most other lads did whether it be at West Ham, Arsenal or something completely different to football. We thought we looked cool – funny how you realise once you get older that you weren't really different at all.

Once we were relegated in 2003 I decided to buy a membership for the following season, as tickets would be easier to come by in the Championship. I managed to persuade two dads of my daughter's friends who, like me, were Hammers fans but hadn't attended for years. We initially drank at The Spotted Dog in Barking and would wax lyrical about our past but separate experiences as West Ham fans. Through these dads (Rich and Mark) we became friends with a bunch of Mark's old school mates and so we were 10-15 strong some games.

We began drinking in The Earl of Wakefield pre and post-match and soon got to know the landlord and bar staff there. Diane was the chief barmaid and wouldn't take any crap from anybody – she was good fun and actually a Gooner. We knew it was time to get to the ground when the urinals flooded and you were paddling in two inches of piss. You could set your watch to it – 2.30pm for a 3.00 KO.

We would regularly drink there post-match too – often to drown our sorrows and play pool while putting our favourite tracks on the jukebox. For some reason, and to this day I don't know why, the pub always sang Neil Diamond's *Sweet Caroline* before and after games. It would come on the jukebox and the whole pub would sing it with arms aloft: "Sweet Caroline, da da da…" The atmosphere was brilliant, with a few regulars

Tim Crane: For the past 10 years I ritually sat in with former club physio, Rob Jenkins, at his clinic opposite the main gates in Green Street. Rampaging buffalo would struggle to pull me away from that place which simply oozed West Ham. Can you imagine before every match, seeing the very cubicle used by Bobby Moore? Sometimes the nostalgia of Rob's colourful stories (and well stocked fridge) kept us in that clinic while the match was played out across the road – our season tickets used as beer mats instead.

Sadly, our good fortune came to an end in the spring of 2015, when the old place was converted into a flat.

Robert Banks: During my heyday of the 90s we would always go and have food and a few pints in The Miller's Well opposite East Ham Town Hall. These days it's more likely to be a pint in The Black Lion. I didn't have any superstitions as such, like lucky pants, but I did always try to park in the same place if I could, up behind Queens Market.

who sat in a corner by the bar (you know who you are) jumping on to tables and chairs to raucously sing it before, more often than not, falling off!

Sadly, the pub served last orders in November 2013 – a sign of the times and a nod to our imminent departure to Stratford. The last night there was fantastic – *Sweet Caroline* was sung constantly and the lights over the pool table were pulled out of the ceiling by an older drunken fan who inexplicably had his trousers round his ankles. His wife dragged him out, it was hilarious. Everybody wrote their thanks (and some abuse to Spurs) on the walls and eventually the place emptied out.

I would never say 'The Wake' was a good pub but it was our watering hole for footy and we had some tremendous times there. We drank with celebrities – Danny Dyer, Cass Pennant and Cerys Matthews – among others, as well as some away fans we might have invited to join us. We all miss the place, especially the carpet which your shoes or trainers would stick to, but times move on and now we're back at The Spotted Dog before no doubt finding a new watering hole at Stratford in due course.

Mark Matthews: Pre-match ritual nowadays always involves a few pints at The Lord Stanley in Plaistow, before the walk through the allotments to the ground, usually just in time to miss kick-off! Previously I used to frequent the now defunct Coach and Horses (also Plaistow) and, before that, The Earl of Wakefield.

Jason Stone: I always bought a cheese and bacon burger from Belly Busters mobile stall on Green Street and had a good drink in The Duke of Edinburgh or, in the early 90s, Charleen's wine bar.

Eamonn McManus: Coming from Manor Park, we would walk down to the ground stopping off at Tolani's café in Station Road for a good pre-game egg and chips, or we'd sometimes go upmarket to Peter's in High Street North for pie and mash. The Blakesley Arms, next to Manor Park station, and the Black Lion in Plaistow were pub stops on the way.

IT'S SNOW TIME

LET it snow, let it snow, let it snow!

Not that long-serving groundsman George Izatt was humming that little Christmas ditty in the bone-chilling winter of 1962-63, when Arctic conditions wiped out much of the British football programme in the coldest spell for more than 200 years.

During what became known as 'The Big Freeze', Britain stayed under a thick blanket of snow and ice for more than two months and the average temperature hovered around a mind-numbing minus-10 degrees Centigrade. No undersoil heating in those days to melt the snow and ice and keep the playing surface fully thawed. George and his hard-working groundstaff had to get to work with shovels to try and remove layers of the white stuff.

POSTPONED AND ABANDONED MATCHES

POSTPONED matches are always a source for discussion among programme collectors eager to confirm whether the club issued a programme for a game that was not played on its original scheduled date.

According to our Hammers historian Steve Marsh, West Ham programmes were printed for all of the first team postponements listed here. However, in the case of the game against Blackburn Rovers in February 1863, none were issued.

A programme was also produced for the original League Cup 2nd round tie against Aldershot Town, due to be played on August 9, 2011 but it's believed that only around 50 found their way into circulation after the game was postponed . . . due to the London riots, which severely disrupted traffic and transport in the capital and overwhelmed the Metropolitan Police. This rare edition is worth a few bob if you can get your hands on one.

Of course, the advent of undersoil heating and the latest advancements in pitch maintenance technology has resulted in far fewer postponed

SEASON	DATE	OPPOSITION	REASON
1936-37	12th December 1936	Aston Villa	Unconfirmed
1937-38	25th December 1937	Norwich City	Fog
1943-44	15th January 1944	Clapton Orient	Unconfirmed
1944-45	26th December 1944	Chelsea	Unconfirmed
1944-45	27th January 1945	Luton Town	Unconfirmed
1946-47	14th December 1946	Newport County	Fog
1948-49	27th November 1948	Grimsby Town	Fog – abandoned 50 mins (1-2)
1953-54	2nd January 1954	Stoke City	Fog – abandoned 83 mins (4-1)
1954-55	15th January 1955	Liverpool	Snow
1955-56	4th February 1956	Bury	Frost
1958-59	17th January 1959	Luton Town	Unconfirmed
1962-63	26th December 1962	Nottingham Forest	Frost
1962-63	14th January 1963	Fulham (FAC3)	Snow
1962-63	31st January 1963	Fulham (FAC3)	Snow
1962-63	9th February 1963	Blackburn Rovers	Snow
1965-66	28th December 1965	Aston Villa	Frost
1967-68	4th November 1967	West Bromwich Albion	Waterlogged
1967-68	13th January 1968	Sunderland	Unconfirmed
1968-69	28th December 1968	Arsenal	Frost
1968-69	18th January 1969	Wolverhampton Wanderers	Unconfirmed
1969-70	7th February 1970	Coventry City	Unconfirmed
1970-71	26th December 1970	Nottingham Forest	Snow
1976-77	29th December 1976	Coventry City	Unconfirmed
1978-79	13th January 1979	Burnley	Frost
1979-80	26th December 1979	Birmingham City	Unconfirmed
1981-82	19th December 1981	Wolverhampton Wanderers	Unconfirmed
1981-82	28th December 1981	Ipswich Town	Unconfirmed
1981-82	9th January 1982	Tottenham Hotspur	Unconfirmed
1982-83	12th February 1983	Arsenal	Unconfirmed
1984-85	12th January 1985	Chelsea	Snow
1985-86	28th December 1985	Southampton	Frost
1985-86	1st January 1986	Chelsea	Frost
1985-86	15th February 1986	Manchester United (FAC5)	Frost
1991-92	14th December 1991	Southampton	Frost
1995-96	26th December 1995	Coventry City	Frost
1995-96	31st December 1995	Newcastle United	Frost
1995-96	27th January 1996	Grimsby Town (FAC4)	Unconfirmed
1996-97	15th January 1997	Wrexham (FAC3R)	Fog
1996-97	19th February 1997	Newcastle United	Waterlogged
1997-98	3rd November 1997	Crystal Palace	Floodlight failure – abandoned 65 mins (2-2)
2000-01	30th December 2000	Chelsea	Frost
2009-10	10th January 2010	Wolverhampton Wanderers	Adverse local weather conditions
2011-12	9th August 2011	Aldershot Town	London Riots

UPTON PARK MEMORIES 133

matches at Premier League level over the past couple of decades. Now it is usually factors beyond the football club's control that result in a match being called off.

When the game against Wolverhampton Wanders was cancelled in January 2010, the pitch was perfectly playable . . . but icy pavements on many streets surrounding the Boleyn Ground would have made conditions treacherous for fans making their way to the stadium and it was this that caused West Ham to postpone the fixture on local authority advice.

Groundsman George Izatt measuring the depth of snow on the Upton Park pitch in the winter of 1962-63.

A blanket of snow covers the pitch in this view from the north-west corner.

134 UPTON PARK MEMORIES

Sign of the times . . . no snow, but a frozen pitch meant the Boxing Day, 1962 match against Nottingham Forest was cancelled.

Ronnie Boyce competing with Fulham's Bobby Robson during the FA Cup saga in that freezing winter of 1962-63. Amazingly, the third round tie at Upton Park went ahead on the evening of February 4 – exactly one month and six postponements after the date on which it should have originally been played. It was Hammers' first game in five weeks.

As this view from the north-east corner shows, the white stuff was back in 1985-86.

SOME PEOPLE ARE ON THE PITCH . . .

FOR many, making the pilgrimage to Upton Park in support of the Hammers has been more than just a way of life, it's almost a religious belief.

After all, it is the place where Trevor Brooking 'walked on water', Alan Devonshire rose from the dead to play brilliantly again despite a shattered knee, Paolo Di Canio performed the supernatural and Carlos Tevez worked a minor miracle to keep West Ham in the Premier League.

In June 1989, just days after a dispirited John Lyall had digested his last supper, evangelist Billy Graham hosted a three-day Christian mission on a stage erected on the hallowed turf.

Unfortunately, the organisers gave away too many free tickets, the event was over-subscribed, causing many to be locked out of the ground. After negotiations between the club and Graham's representatives, the crowd were provided with additional seats on the pitch.

Getting back to sport . . . the Boleyn Ground hosted a major heavyweight boxing match when David Haye and Dereck Chisora fought for the WBO International and WBA Intercontinental title in front of a reported 30,000 crowd on July 14, 2012.

The picture shows Chisora on the deck following Haye's left hook that proved the decisive KO blow in round five.

Finally, we go way back to the early 1900s for this shot of West Ham United defender Bob Fairman practicing his golf swing (out of the rough!) on the Upton Park pitch, in front of the Chicken Run.

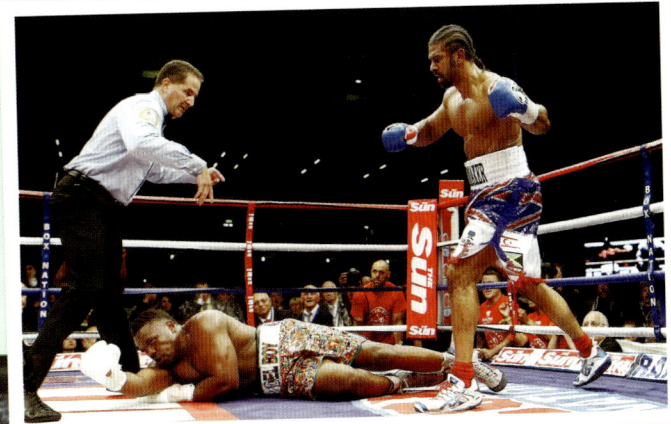

Poignant moment on March 6, 1993, the first game played at Upton Park following the death of Bobby Moore. Martin Peters and Geoff Hurst carry the symbolic No.6 wreath to the centre circle, accompanied by a solemn Ron Greenwood.

3 MEMORABLE MATCHES & MOMENTS

OVER the years there have been many classic and memorable matches at Upton Park, some involving triumphant victories for West Ham, others notable for crushing defeats.

From a demolition of the great Leeds United team of the late 60s and the unforgettable European Cup Winners' Cup semi-final victory over Eintracht Frankfurt in 1976, to a heart-breaking loss at the hands of Liverpool that confirmed relegation from the top flight just two years later.

Often, though, it's the little details or amusing personal anecdotes surrounding a match that stick in the memory more than the football itself.

A white duck holding up play for 15 minutes in the early 50s, an outfield goalkeeper's attacking heroics, a club legend supping a pre-match pint in The Boleyn pub, Bobby Moore showing supreme speed of thought to help out a stricken referee, or a dancing streaker during a freezing, snow-covered clash in the late 70s . . . our contributors have seen it all.

Q: What stands out as your most vivid memory from a game at Upton Park? This could be an unusual incident, or perhaps something bizarre, amusing or controversial.

George Hibbins: For atmosphere, the last match of the 1922-23 season, v Notts County (5/5/23) to gain promotion to the first division. We were about to appear at the first Wembley Cup final (I was there!) and needed to win our final second division game. The winners between ourselves and Notts County would be champions.

We did everything but score and, devastatingly, lost 1-0. County were league winners with 53 points and we finished on 51, so it was between us and Leicester City who would join them in the top flight.

The whole sell-out crowd of 26,000 stayed behind after the final whistle to wait for a telephone call to the directors' box, which came through confirming that our rivals Leicester had also lost . . . so West Ham went up on goal-difference.

Promotion and the Cup final – great days.

Jim Wilder: I recall a number of matches during the Second World War, particularly towards the end of it. The Germans had rockets which they aimed at London. The V1 (the doodlebug) was pilotless and had enough fuel to reach London. When they came overhead the match would stop and everyone would listen out for them. When the rocket stopped making its distinctive noise, that meant trouble – it was dropping. When we knew which area it had hit, if it was close to us, you could see spectators leaving as they rushed to see if their house had been bombed.

Upton Park itself was bombed a couple of times during the war. One wing of the main stand was missing and the East Stand caught fire.

William Lloyd: I was about 13 in 1946 and on the way to a game as I walked past The Boleyn. I saw one of my heroes, Dick Walker, coming out of the pub and I plucked up the courage to speak to him. I asked: "Dick, aren't you playing today?" – it was 2.30 pm and kick-off was in half an hour. "Course I am, son . . . I always play better after a pint."

And, of course, he went out and played his usual good game. A present-day manager would have a heart attack on hearing this anecdote today!

Eric Brown: Nearing the end of WWII, the fans used to donate money to the war effort or charity by throwing coins into a blanket held by a couple of men, going all around the pitch. A few small boys such as myself would pick up the coins that missed the blanket. I'm ashamed to admit this but one or two of the coins found their way into my pocket. Please forgive me.

Also, a man used to walk around the pitch after half-time carrying a board on his shoulders with the half-time scores written on in chalk. Modern technology! Fond memories.

Mr G. E. Hill: v Brentford Reserves in either the 1947-48 or 1948-49

WEST HAM UNITED 0
AC MILAN 6
Friendly
Tuesday, December 14, 1954

Reuben Gane: The friendly game against AC Milan, played six days after my 13th birthday, was one of the best I have ever seen at Upton Park. It was a really huge game for West Ham, probably the biggest since World War Two, and carried a similar feel to the great Moscow Dynamo games when they visited Britain in the late 40s.

I was living in Barking on the A13, not far from Bobby Moore's house in Waverley Gardens, and dashed home from my school, St Ethelburga's RC Secondary Modern in North Street, for a quick bite to eat and a cup of tea. After leaving home I ran up to town, intending to catch the No.23 at the East Street bus stop, but was alarmed when I saw the queue. People were four deep and going back some 75 yards around Blake's Corner into Ripple Road.

A quick change of plans were needed, so I dashed up to Barking Station to catch the District Line to Upton Park. I couldn't get onto the first train but managed to squeeze on board the next. Hardly anybody could get on at East Ham and it was even harder for any passengers that wanted to get off! The Upton Park stop seemed to discharge 95 per cent of its human cargo and I was carried along the platform and up the stairs without appearing to actually touch the ground.

The concourse was heaving with people and there was no sign of any of the normal programme sellers inside or outside the station. I always bought a programme but could not find any sellers in Green Street, nor outside the ground. I retraced my steps and found a vendor in Tudor Road, off Green Street. However, the programme turned out to be a pirate edition with very little in it.

It was around 6.15pm when I got to my normal South Bank turnstile entrance gates in Castle Street and Priory Road and saw masses of fans queuing to get in, boosted by those not able to get into the Chicken Run because the gates were closed around 6.30. On getting into the ground, you were met with a wall of people pushing upwards on the slopes that led to the terraces. I managed to get onto the terraces, about five rows from the back, but could not see a thing. Adults helped me push down to the front and, for safety reasons, many youngsters were placed over the pitch boundary and sat two deep around the pitch.

By this time you could see that Upton Park was completely full and the South Bank closed it gates around 6.45 for a 7.30 kick-off. Newspaper estimates put the crowd at 36,000 and others at 38,000. Many unofficially put the gate at well over 40,000.

When the teams came onto the field together, West Ham were in beige coloured tracksuits and AC Milan in their customary red and black striped shirts and white shorts. When Hammers took off their 'never seen before' tracksuits they were wearing off-white (or cream) shirts with white shorts and white socks. Maybe the shirts were originally white but had been washed with the tracksuits! In fairness, the shirts may well have been unbleached white cotton-drill.

Surprisingly, West Ham had George Taylor in goal instead of the regular keeper, Ernie Gregory, and our best player was right-winger Harry Hooper. His skill and speed troubled the Italians throughout the game and it was a big shock when he was sold to Wolves a few weeks later.

West Ham played well in the first-half and were a little unfortunate to go in at half-time 2-0 down. The second half was completely different, though, with Milan overwhelming West Ham with a level of football never seen before at Upton Park. Four more goals were scored by Milan without reply from Hammers, who were out on their feet at the end of the game. The Italian side's 6-0 victory was completely deserved.

Milan had several Italian international players in their side, plus goalkeeper Lorenzo Buffon, a distant relative of the current Juventus and Italian captain Gianluigi Buffon. Their centre-forward was Danish international Gunnar Nordahl, a huge, powerful and skilful striker who gave West Ham's defence a torrid time. The most outstanding player on the night, however, was South American inside-forward Juan Schiaffino. Milan had paid over $200,000 for the Uruguayan wizard and it showed when he gave a mesmerizing performance.

At the end of the game Milan were cheered off the field and West Ham were to gain huge experience in the style of play they, themselves, would try to emulate in years to come.

From left: Noel Cantwell, Malcolm Allison and Ken Brown under pressure from mighty Milan, with keeper George Taylor on the ground.

Terry Roper: It was Easter Saturday and West Ham were playing Arsenal (21/4/62). At half-time, the game was finely balanced at 1-1 but the second period produced one of the most remarkable comebacks in Hammers' history.

Early in the second-half, West Ham's Scottish international goalkeeper, Lawrie Leslie, broke a finger while repelling an Arsenal attack. To our absolute despair, he pulled off his green jersey after undergoing lengthy treatment and walked dejectedly to the players' tunnel, accompanied by physiotherapist Bill Jenkins. Clearly, Leslie was in a huge amount of pain.

There were no substitutes in those days and Hammers' left-back John Lyall donned the goalkeeper's jersey. Within a matter of minutes, Arsenal raced to a 3-1 lead and 10-man West Ham were in danger of being over-run. However, fate was about to play an unforgettable part in this match.

In the 70th minute, a great roar went up as Lawrie Leslie – resembling a latter day Braveheart – re-emerged from the tunnel wearing a numberless claret-and-blue shirt, black shorts with his damaged hand strapped-up and his arm hanging at his side. He was returning as an outfield player and took his place on Hammers' right-wing.

Suddenly, all was not lost and Leslie's unexpected reappearance had a galvanising effect on his team-mates. Almost instantly, the ball was played out to Leslie who showed deft control before setting off on a mazy run, leaving a trail of defenders in his wake before the ball was cleared for a corner. The damage had been done and, inspired by the heroics of Leslie plus the roar of the crowd, West Ham launched wave after wave of attacks on the Arsenal goal.

In the 75th minute, John Dick reduced the arrears with a header after good work by Martin Peters. It was now 3-2 and Upton Park seemed to be vibrating with noise and emotion as West Ham sought an equaliser. As the minutes ticked agonisingly by, it appeared their efforts would come to no avail but Leslie would not be denied.

With minutes to go, his dogged perseverance won yet another corner and as the ball floated over, Bobby Moore was the first to rise and send in a powerful header which was blocked by a defender. The ball ran loose and Hammers' centre-half Bill Lansdowne toe-poked it towards goal, falling backwards as he did so. For a split-second, it seemed that an Arsenal defender, standing on the goal-line, would clear it but the pace of Lansdowne's shot – or lack of it – deceived him and, astonishingly, the ball squirmed under his foot and over the line. It was 3-3 and the deafening roar that greeted the goal must have been heard for miles around.

Suddenly, it was all over and as the players walked from the field, the fans rose as one to applaud their heroes and, in particular, to salute the bravery of Lawrie Leslie who, not surprisingly, was voted Hammer of the Year at the end of the season. It was an amazing match and one that will live in my mind forever.

season. During a snow-storm, Brentford's goalkeeper was lying on the ground with the ball in his midriff. Almer Hall, West Ham's inside-right, then knelt down and pushed the keeper over the line with his head against the ball – and a goal was given.

Rob Robinson: It's not very often that the game is held up by a large white duck but that is what happened when Blackpool were the visitors for an FA Cup 3rd round tie (12/1/52). Blackpool had brought the duck as a mascot and I can still picture it being chased all over the pitch by stewards, who took 15 minutes to recapture the animal. In those days all the youngsters were passed over adult's heads and allowed to sit in front of the fencing around the pitch. Some of them also ended up chasing this duck.

Blackpool included a certain Stanley Matthews but even he couldn't stop us winning 2-1 (Jimmy Andrews, Frank O'Farrell).

Keith Martin: I recall witnessing the innovation of floodlights at Upton Park, with a friendly v Spurs (16/4/53). At half-time the lights went out and my companion shouted: "Put another shilling in the meter!" A reply came back: "No, mate, we're saving up for a new centre-forward."

Richard Miller: Ernie Gregory rolling the ball out to Malcolm Allison at the South Bank end in a game v Leyton Orient in 1956. Malcolm then proceeded to sit on the ball and started waving to the Orient players before quickly getting up and clearing it upfield as a couple of their forwards rushed towards him.

Reuben Gane: FA Cup 3rd round v Preston North End (7/1/56), 5-2. Hammers were in the second division and Preston were a powerful first division outfit and much fancied to go a long way in the cup. Tom Finney was in the Preston line-up and, I think, Eddie Lewis, the ex-Busby Babe who later joined West Ham.

Took my normal place on the South Bank with my claret-and-blue rosette and hat that Nan had knitted for me. She also gave me cheese sandwiches, an apple and a flask of tea, as I had a long wait to get in the ground.

Preston were the better side in the first-half but I was annoyed when they were given a penalty late in the half that was to put them 2-1 up. It wasn't the penalty that upset me but the manner in which Tom Finney netted. He ran up and checked, half stopping, which sent our goalkeeper, Ernie

John Powles: Having been a regular at Upton Park for 72 years, it is extremely difficult to select any specific event that has been controversial, bizarre or amusing, as there are many.

West Ham were obliged to play a midweek afternoon fixture against Doncaster Rovers (24/2/55). I was on leave from HM Forces, so I took the opportunity to be there despite snow having fallen heavily.

Despite a pitch covered by about six inches of white stuff, the game went ahead. We lost by a single goal and from memory, it was a farce. It was watched by the lowest-ever Football League gate at the ground, 4,373.

Gregory, diving to his right. Finney calmly slotted the ball inside the left post. I had never seen this form of professionalism-cum-gamesmanship before. It shocked and annoyed the 29,000 crowd.

The second-half saw a different Hammers, who completely dominated in a manner they would show a couple of years later when 'Fenton's Furies' would gain promotion at the end of the 1957-58 season.

Inside-right Albert Foan gave the performance of his career, scoring a super hat-trick to give Hammers a richly deserved 5-2 victory. Billy Dare got the other two goals but the memories that have stayed with me are Foan's goals and him being lifted shoulder-high off the pitch. Unfortunately, so does that of such a great player like Tom Finney scoring the way he did.

Crispin Derby: A real cracker v Swansea (18/1/58) who were full of famous Welsh international players such as Cliff Jones, Ivor Allchurch and Mel Charles. It never stopped, with play swinging from end to end as all 22 players seemed intent on attacking. Our goals in a stunning 6-2 win came from Vic Keeble (2), Bill Lansdowne, John Dick, John Bond and Noel Cantwell.

The stand-out memory was Noel's fantastic goal – that classic double act of a Bond free-kick on the right touchline close to the halfway line, with Noel running in from the left side and arriving at top speed just inside the penalty area to power a header past a helpless goalkeeper. Magnificent.

John Pocklington: Watching our full-backs, John Bond and Noel Cantwell, pass the ball back and forth in front of goal, with goalkeeper Ernie Gregory going mad at them.

Ed Gillis: First home game following promotion to Division One. The opposition were reigning champions Wolverhampton Wanderers (25/8/58) but Hammers earned a magnificent 2-0 win (John Smith, John Dick). The Chicken Run was really rocking and we swayed devotedly to *Bubbles*.

John Pocklington: v Wolverhampton Wanderers (25/8/58). I lost my autograph book at the ground. I went back first thing the next day and the groundsman let me in to look for it. I couldn't find it but as the ground had not been swept up, I found more than enough money to replace it!

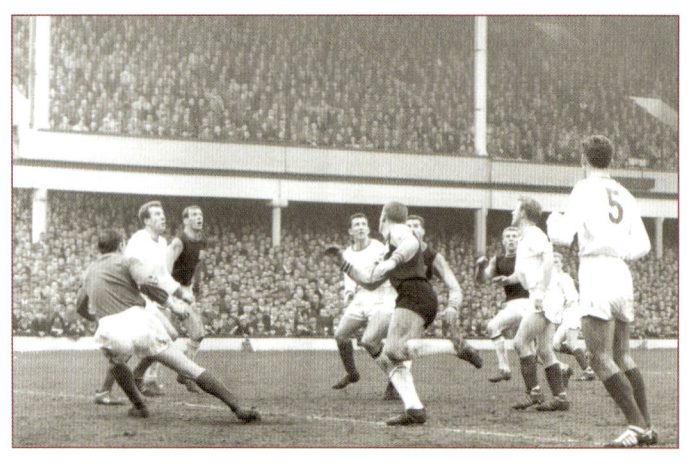

Pictures from Lawrie Leslie's extraordinary heroics against Arsenal in 1962. West Ham's equaliser: The ball is crossed into Gunners' goalmouth, where Lawrie (in black shorts) is causing panic. Other players (left to right) are: Jack Kelsey, Laurie Brown, John Dick, Johnny Macleod, Bill Lansdowne (almost hidden by Leslie), Bobby Moore, John Petts and Terry Neill (5).
Bill Lansdowne (on ground) toe-pokes the ball goalwards, eluding both Arsenal keeper Jack Kelsey and Ted Magill (2), as Lawrie Leslie watches.

Brian Belton: Visit of Ron Greenwood's hometown club, Burnley, to Upton Park in the FA Cup 5th round (29/2/64). It was a truly great match in that it was a game with goals that had the quality of flowing from end to end in the best traditions of English Cup football; it was a crucial encounter on the road to the Hammers' first major trophy; and, as such, was a seminal moment in the club's history.

Burnley were greeted by an all-ticket crowd of 36,651 (including England manager Alf Ramsey), a club record at the time. John Connelly gave them a half-time lead, John Sissons pulled one back from a very tight angle at the South Bank end and two goals in eight minutes put Hammers 3-1 up, before Ray Pointer induced a nervy finale by reducing the arrears in the 80th minute. But Hammers held out and joined Manchester United, Preston and Swansea in the semi-finals.

For Hammers' third, Byrne looked a tad offside and appeared to push Brian Miller over before he scored. As soon as Worcestershire referee, E. Jennings, awarded the goal, Burnley players went into a frenzy that included Gordon Harris striking John Bond. For all this, Budgie's effort – shrugging off Brian Miller and dribbling around keeper Adam Blacklaw – had been impressive.

The league win at Ewood Park in the last game of 1963 had been the season's turning point for West Ham but the match against Burnley marked the moment when Hammers came of age. The side demonstrated a ruthless determination that had often been lacking in their make-up.

Byrne played wonderfully and his performance dominated the headlines of the morning papers. He was, probably quite correctly, given the credit for taking West Ham into the last four. His alacrity and control on a muddy surface had, indeed, been the difference between the two sides.

Fans queue on the main forecourt for tickets to the 1964 FA Cup final.

Dave Satchell: Still makes me feel emotional when I think about it – most memorable game – it was the season after Spurs won the double (28/8/61) and they had Mackay, Blanchflower and all the other great players but we beat them 2-1 and the crowd never stopped singing throughout the game. Tremendous.

Funniest thing I can remember at the ground was during a match attended by nearly 40,000 in the early 60s. I was on the South Bank, in the middle, and this bloke wanted to go to the toilet but nobody would (or could) move to let him through. Despite asking the man in front of him to move, the man would not co-operate at all. Being really annoyed, the man who was bursting deliberately peed in the other man's overcoat pocket.

Michael Harris: When fans swarmed across the pitch to mob Lawrie Leslie (my favourite goalkeeper) after he had inspired Hammers to come from 3-1 down and grab a 3-3 draw with Arsenal . . . from the right-wing!

Roy Thomas: We played Southend United in the Essex Cup and when the teams went off at half-time there was a terrific snow-storm. The teams dutifully reappeared after the break and kicked off. All of a sudden the referee stopped the game, realising nobody could see the ball which was white and, hence, exchanged for an orange one.

Peter Jones: We all know how peerless Bobby Moore was in the 60s for West Ham. However, one incident that never seems to be recalled, highlighted for me that he was human after all. In the 1963-64 season, West Ham were seeing out their league games before the FA Cup final against Preston.

Hammers entertained Bolton Wanderers (4/4/64) and a long ball forward found Moore sweeping up very deep. It was then that he tried a bit of showboating. He put his foot on the ball awaiting the onrushing Bolton forward, then tried to flick it round him. But the Bolton player got the ball, ran on and scored past Jim Standen. Embarrassment all round, a 3-2 defeat (Alan Sealey, Johnny Byrne) and a wake-up call for the team one month before the final.

Howard Dawson: A match during the 60s when Bobby Moore was outpaced (no surprise) along the touchline by an opposing forward and managed to slow him up by placing his finger in the other player's shorts and pulling the elasticated waistband so that he could hardly run. The referee and linesman were oblivious to his antics.

Mr G. Pope: For a few seasons I used to stand in the lower West, quite near the tunnel on the South Bank side. There were a group of blokes there who, nearly every match at some point in the second-half, broke into a medley of Beatles songs, particularly *Twist and Shout*.

Don Hanley: Queuing all night for FA Cup quarter-final tickets in March 1964. We were playing football at 3.00am outside the old West Stand and a policeman told us to stop, as we were making too much noise. The people queuing all booed him and he went away with a smile on his face. Real East End humour.

David Axtell: My first visit, aged seven, was with my younger brother, dad and uncle. No game to see but we spent four hours queuing around the ground to get tickets for the 1964 FA Cup final. As soon as my hand reached up to the ticket office to get the maximum two per person, the tickets disappeared from my hands into my dad's. I assume him and his mates had a good day out that May. I was taken on a regular basis from the next season, usually sitting on various people's shoulders in the Chicken Run.

Graham Arnold: In 1964 I had already been going regularly to the Boleyn Ground for the last four years with my mum. In the May I had even seen my glorious Hammers win the FA Cup at Wembley and I was eight-years old. It was probably only then that I realised how privileged I was because my dad (Dick Arnold) worked part-time for West Ham and that was to have a magical impact on me.

He was an 'expenses only' backroom boy, a 'bucket and sponge' man, who, along with a few others, scouted and kept the Metropolitan League and the two South-East Counties League teams running. He would pay the bus fares to the budding stars of the future after training on a Tuesday and Thursday night but, more important to me, was the fact that he had entry to the inner sanctum of the ground.

On Saturday mornings, when the youth team were playing away, they would meet at the ground to pick up the coach. Walking to the kit room under the ground, I would take in the smells, especially on match days, cut grass and white paint. I would poke my head around the door into the home team's dressing room and gaze at the claret-and-blue hanging up, my eyes scanning for the No.6 shirt worn by my hero, dreaming of the day I would pull that kit on.

More smells wafting through my nostrils, the baths and floors clean and sparkling, and on the treatment table, arnica, white horse oils and liniment. At this point I would always slip away from Dad, go down the tunnel onto the pitch and sometimes old Jock, the groundsman, would let me walk to the centre spot where my imagination would run riot.

But the really special event were the evening youth games. Dad would sometimes be the trainer and I would sit in the corner of the dug-out. I was even allowed to sit in the corner of the dressing room and listen to either Billy Lansdowne or John Lyall, when they were the youth team managers, give their pre-match and half-time instructions.

This wonderland stopped for me at 14. I was getting close to the ages of the apprentices and realised, as did my dad, that I was never going to become a professional.

Dad worked for the club right up until his death in 1981. In the *West Ham United Football Book No.3*, Wally St Pier, West Ham's greatest scout, said: "There is nobody at Upton Park more West Ham-minded than Dick." I'm proud of that, and the Boleyn Ground is where his spirit lies.

UPTON PARK MEMORIES 143

FOR WEST BROM IT WAS...

Oh, Dear!
Oh, Dear!
Oh, Dear!
Oh, Dear!
Oh, Dear!

By MICHAEL BROWN

MORE than 27,000 football fans stood up yesterday and cheered the man they liked to tease—inside forward Brian Dear.

For the 21-year-old player made the barrackers at Upton Park—who have sometimes ragged him by chanting "Oh, Dear, what can the matter be?"—change their tune.

He scored five of West Ham's six goals against West Bromwich—so this time it was a case of "Oh, Dear" five times for the visitors.

Big kiss

Afterwards, the team presented him with the ball, autograph-hunters hung around the dressing-room door, and there...

Brian Dear gives West Brom goalie Potter no chance as he bags the second of his record five-goal haul on Good Friday, 1965. Brian and wife Janice pictured with the historic match ball.

Dear leaves Potter without a hope of saving West Ham's third goal and the second of his personal haul of five at Upton Park

On match days he is there with me and my mum, who in spite of her 88 years, still sits next to me, as she has done for the last 44 years.

Stephen Cain: Even after 50-plus years, a match that sticks in my head was v Man Utd, (24/8/64) 3-1. I was only eight but I still remember West Ham gave the likes of Charlton and Law a real football lesson. I recall the late, great Johnny Byrne scored for us (along with Geoff Hurst and John Sissons). We were world class that night in the season that brought West Ham European glory.

Danny Cooper: Before progressing to the North Bank with the big boys, we started out in the Chicken Run to keep out of trouble. There were always 'conversations' going on between the crowd and whoever was playing on the wing. I remember, even then, Harry Redknapp used to take his fair share of stick. I also remember a certain respect for John Bond who always seemed to be able to walk the ball well into the opponent's half before anyone plucked up enough courage to try to tackle him. Well, that's how it seemed.

In terms of memorable games, I would lump together the floodlight European ties of the mid-60s. There was always something special about those nights against teams with funny names. The games always seemed faster, the colours brighter and the players bigger. The sight of Bobby leading out the team, immaculate and legs glistening with oils, always comes back to me when I see a floodlight game.

Paul Walker: I am a child of the 60s and my greatest memories are of that 1964-65 side that won the FA Cup and the European Cup Winners' Cup . . . times that are hard to explain to fans today, who have never experienced such success. For me, the two most vivid memories come from that era.

Brian Dear's amazing five goals in 20 minutes v West Brom on Good Friday (16/4/65), including a six-minute hat-trick, had to be seen to be believed. I was late getting there and ended up in the West Stand lower terracing, not my favourite place because it was below ground level at the front and difficult to see. I was stuck at the front, in line with the penalty spot in front of the North Bank, just where Dear scored all his goals. A perfect view, in fact.

Ian Nunney: I was lucky enough to go to the 1965 ECWC final at Wembley. We started in The Boleyn for a drink or two. I was only 11, so no beer for me, but the landlord did give me an empty beer box to stand on at the game.

Alan Chapman: One incident that stands out was before a match v Blackpool (27/12/66). It was a bank holiday and my friend, Keith, and I assumed it was a 3.00pm kick-off, arriving at a deserted ground to discover it was actually a 7.30pm start! So we had about five hours to kill before the match.

During the afternoon we found ourselves in Priory Road, round the back of the old Chicken Run. There were some boys there playing football and we joined in for a while. One of them had a glossy team photo, fairly battered, from the previous season which he offered to sell to me for half-a-crown. As this was more than it cost to get in and I could easily buy an up-to-date photo for less, I declined. He then said that if I didn't buy it, he would tear it up. I said that if he was going to do that he might as well just give it to me. But he refused and tore it up there and then, throwing the pieces into the gutter!

Paul Morgan: v Stoke City, (7/10/67), THAT unbelievable 4-3 defeat! Geoff Hurst (2) and Martin Peters put Hammers 3-0 up in 40 minutes but Stoke scored four in the last 25 minutes.

Tony Hogg: I remember Johnny Byrne hitting a ball so hard it knocked a little lad unconscious during one match. Like a true hero, Johnny was very concerned and lifted him out of the crowd into the care of the St. John's Ambulance people. I think there was a picture of the incident in the local paper.

Andrew Smith: One of the matches I particularly remember was v Manchester United (6/5/67). Their team included Denis Law, Bobby Charlton and a young George Best. Although we had the World Cup winning trio, the score was a 6-1 home defeat, with Man United also winning the first division title. It was a sombre journey back on the District Line that day.

WEST HAM UNITED 7
LEEDS UNITED 0
League Cup 4th round
Monday, November 7, 1966

Terry Connelly: Of all the games that I have witnessed over the years at Upton Park, the most vivid in my memory is the 7-0 annihilation of Don Revie's much-lauded Leeds United. I believe it was the most complete performance I have ever seen from 11 players in the claret-and-blue. It was a magnificent display with the strings being pulled by the outstanding 'Budgie' Byrne, who was simply unplayable on the night.

Many years later I attended Malcolm Musgrove's testimonial dinner and spoke with the guest speaker – a certain Jack Charlton – about that night. He recalled that he had never experienced anything like it. "We never knew what hit us," he said. "We were three down inside half-an-hour, all identical goals from the young blond kid Sissons. We were four down at half-time and were given a complete run around. The gaffer was not happy."

Bobby George: Once in a while a game comes along that stays in your memory for the rest of your days. Such a time was on a November evening in 1966, when West Ham beat the great Leeds United 7-0. Not only was this the happiest I have felt after

'Budgie's' class wrecks cocks of the north

By Tony Smith

League Cup – 3rd Rnd.
W. HAM 7
LEEDS 0

Johnny Byrne earned most of the post-match plaudits.

a result, but the football was outstanding. Johnny Byrne played the game of his life – I have never seen him play better. Leeds had all of their top players in, Bremner, Hunter, Clarke, Giles and Charlton, and they could not get the better of him.

Budgie did not score in the game but I think he made most of them.

Derek Price: Individually and collectively, the whole performance was sheer perfection. West Ham played classically, like an orchestra, and 'Budgie' Byrne was the supreme conductor.

Howard Dawson: Memorable in every way and probably Johnny Byrne's finest hour without scoring. Three months later he had left Upton Park and gone back to Crystal Palace.

Paul Walker: I can still recall Billy Bremner screaming at his players in front of the Chicken Run for more effort – and they were already seven down.

PLAYER
GEOFF HURST

Born: 8/12/41, Aston-under-Lyne, Lancashire
WHU career: 1960-72
Position: Forward
Apps: 503, **Goals:** 249

BUDGIE was fantastic that night. Unplayable. To win 7-0 against the mighty Leeds was an unbelievable achievement.

The first and foremost thing is that we won. Then we can consider the personal achievements involved and it was great for 'Sisso' and I to both score hat-tricks and Martin to get the other.

I think the week before they had drawn against Arsenal and were top of the league. It was a really heavy pitch that night, which should have suited Leeds more than us, but the team was magnificent.

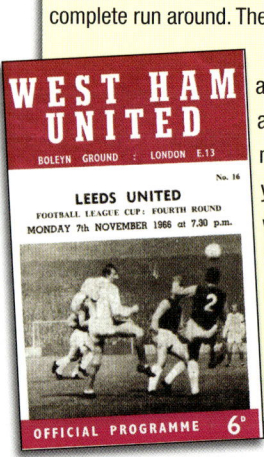

Alan Deadman: Beating Sunderland 8-0 (19/10/68) and Sir Geoff bagged a double hat-trick. I had been given complimentary tickets for the game by Mrs Charles, whose two sons John and Clive were playing for Hammers at the time. Mrs Charles used to live near my aunt Elsie and I'd run errands for her. I can remember running to the butcher's to get Clyde Best a steak for his tea while he was lodging with the Charles family.

Terry Foster: Most unusual memory was v Stoke City (8/4/69). A terrible, goal-less game enlivened only by a woman spectator running onto the pitch at the end and decking the ref (T.H.C. Reynolds of Swansea).

Tony Clement: I think it was v Burnley in the late 60s, when at half-time they put out an appeal to the crowd for a 'linesman in the house', because the ref was injured. They found one and the game resumed.

The guy who I found amusing was the man who put up the half-times on the 'ABC' board on the low brick wall of the North Bank. He'd come out with his piece of paper and his numbers and start putting up the half-time scores. There would be murmurs around the ground. Could the mighty Wolves be losing at home? How could The Arsenal be losing their game and so on. All was resolved as the second half was in progress, because this man would re-appear with another piece of paper and correct most of the scores! You can imagine the comments from the wags in the Chicken Run.

Ian McMaster: Among my most vivid memories is the 1-0 defeat of Liverpool (28/3/70), when Pat Holland scored the winner past Tommy Lawrence. It seemed almost unbelievable for me that we had beaten Liverpool.

John Reynolds: I went with my dad to an entertaining 3-3 draw v Wolves (14/11/70). I was nine at the time and while sitting on the wall behind the North Bank goal, a corner came over right in front of me. Bobby Moore then headed a clearance that slammed Welsh referee Gerrard Lewis full in the face at point-blank range and knocked the poor man clean out.

As West Ham broke upfield on the attack, our cool captain picked up the whistle and, with a couple of blasts, halted play. The ref recovered after treatment and, with seven minutes to go, we lost a 3-1 lead (Clyde Best 2, Bobby Moore), with Hammer-to-be Bobby Gould equalising two minutes from time.

I remember hurrying away from the ground in the pouring rain with Dad cursing about the lost lead – a tradition I would carry on in later years with my children. It was a great game, though, superb entertainment.

John Burton: A 3-3 draw against Celtic in Bobby Moore's testimonial (16/11/70). The result makes this seem like a typical testimonial match but both teams were playing their hearts out as if it was a European Cup tie. My lasting memory was little Johnny Ayris being marked by the giant Tommy Gemmell.

Kevin Courtney: Seeing my boyhood hero Bobby Moore scoring past Gordon Banks via a deflection in the 2-1 victory v Stoke City (25/9/71). His celebration was typically muted but after that I proceeded to copy him whenever I scored a goal at school!

John Burton: It happened in the North Bank in a League Cup tie v Liverpool (27/10/71). I was wearing a pair of Hush Puppies that had elastic sides and no laces. When West Ham scored (we won 2-1 – Geoff Hurst, Bryan Robson), we all went daft as usual, and after we had all calmed down I discovered that one of my shoes had come off. My mates started chanting: "He's lost his shoe, he's lost his shoe, Ee Aye Addio, he's lost his shoe!". About 15 yards in front of us came the reply: "He's found your shoe, etc . . ." My shoe was then handed back to me over everyone's head.

Dave Spurgeon: If I am tied down to one choice only, then not for the happiest of reasons it has to be me being among that throng of fans on the North Bank when Gordon Banks saved Geoff Hurst's penalty in the dying minutes of extra-time to deny us a place in the League Cup final at Wembley. Inside 60 seconds every Hammers fan there that night rode the emotional rollercoaster of euphoric anticipation through to dismayed disappointment and disbelief, pretty typical over the decades, one could say.

There was celebration and noise when the penalty was awarded (Banks dropped a cross and then brought down Harry Redknapp while trying to retrieve the ball) akin to an actual goal being scored. As Hurst placed the ball on the spot the crowd and mood seemed to change in a matter of seconds. Even the more exuberant and vocal elements on the North Bank steadied themselves in anxious anticipation. Hurst had scored from the spot against Banks in the first leg. Could he do it again with the Twin Towers in sight?

My vivid memory is of looking down the length of the pitch to see Tommy Taylor and John McDowell crouched down, covering their eyes with their hands facing the South Bank and not daring to watch. Some prophet of doom from about three feet behind me on the terrace then shouted: "Give it to Robson, for f*** sake, Hurstie, we all know where you gonna f****** put, it let alone Banks!"

Well, Gordon Banks certainly knew and as the ball flew off Hurst's boot at such power and speed, I could not actually say I could follow it with the naked eye. My eyes, however, did not see the desired result of the ball smashing the net, only it's return from orbit via Gordon Banks fists and the look of disbelief on Geoff's face.

My ears were filled with groans and foul mouthed curses from 10,000 fans around me. I was probably too numb to shout anything but if that prophet of doom from behind me had been identified, I may well have had a word in his ear.

A vivid memory, indeed, but not one to cherish.

Steve Wilks: v Leeds (14/4/73). Bobby Ferguson was in goal and came out for a long ball down the middle. He seemed to go over the top of a Leeds player and his team-mate John McDowell before hitting the ground,

146 UPTON PARK MEMORIES

Tony McDonald: Too many personal memories from different stages of my time supporting and writing about the club to mention even a fraction of them all but here are some random thoughts . . .

The song that Bill Remfry always played before kick-off, which sticks in my head from my earliest games in 1968-69, was the No.1 hit, *Those Were The Days* by Mary Hopkin. The melancholy lyrics and homely sound of the little blonde Welsh lass encapsulates what this book is all about and whenever I hear it now I'm instantly taken back to happy days leaning on the wall of the South Bank and that moment of sheer anticipation when Mooro and co. emerged from the tunnel. 'Yes, those were the days, my friends, we thought they'd never end . . .'

Not many results seemed all that gut-wrenching to this 11-year-old but to be stood very adjacent to the North Bank goal, leaning right on the front wall, when Stoke keeper Gordon Banks somehow diverted Geoff Hurst's thunderbolt penalty over the crossbar in the League Cup semi-final, 2nd leg (15/12/71) was one such occasion. Having won the first leg 2-1 at the Victoria Ground, we were foolish to count our chickens and start dreaming of meeting Chelsea in the final at Wembley – in the days when the League Cup had credibility and was well worth winning. To add insult to injury, our defence gifted John Ritchie a soft winner on the night. It took two replays, at Hillsborough and Old Trafford, before the dagger was fully imbedded in Hammers' hearts but this was an early taster for me of how cruel supporting West Ham can be, or appear to be in those moments when we lost touch with reality and mistakenly believe that football really is the be all and end all of life.

For the 1971-72 season, I went up in the world – well, to the front row of A Block in the West upper, where Dad managed to secure a couple of season tickets from Jack Turner, who was Bobby Moore's agent and also acted on behalf of several other players around that time. Turner had been quite influential behind the scenes at Upton Park, although I think he was pushed into the background more when Ron Greenwood arrived as manager in 1961.

Those first few rows of seats were taken by the players' wives and girlfriends and one or two others associated with the club but my uncle, Eddie Hollingsworth, and me were there among them, too, for a few seasons.

Except on the day those non-league upstarts Hereford United came to town for the FA Cup 4th round replay (14/2/72) and our usual seats were not available. Britain was in the midst of an industrial crisis, with workers out on strike, factories operating a three-day week and power supplies limited. For a while football clubs were forbidden to use their floodlights, so this game against Southern League Hereford – who played in the fifth tier of the English pyramid system – had to be played at 1.30 on a Monday afternoon.

Unlike today, FA Cup ties were virtually unmissable back then; you wanted to follow your team all the way to Wembley for the biggest game in the domestic football calendar. And if your team didn't make it there, you were still glued to the telly on Cup final day, taking in all the pre-match build-up and the game. It's importance magnified by the fact that, for many years, it was the ONLY domestic game of the season shown live on television.

So we were all eager to see us play Hereford, who had caused a national sensation by knocking out first division Newcastle in the previous round, just nine days earlier.

My problem was, my mum didn't share my enthusiasm. When I asked her if I could have that Monday afternoon off school, she flatly refused and there was no room for negotiation. I thought, 'Christ, what can I possibly learn in Mr Skinner's woodwork lesson (Mayfield Boys secondary school in Goodmayes) that was so bloody important!' It was obvious from the classroom banter on the morning of the game that more than half the class were intending to bunk off after the lunch break and board the 238 bus in Goodmayes Lane that went all the way to Green Street.

After a lot of soul-searching I decided to defy Mum's wishes and join class-mate, Steve Kidd, on the 238 to Upton Park. Mr Skinner would have to do without lecturing me on how to bang a nail into a piece of wood for another week. I don't know whether we needed Uncle Ed to lend us a few quid to get in or what, but I remember phoning him from a call box outside the school to arrange to meet him outside the ground. Good, old Ed, he was like a father figure to me and I knew he wouldn't mind being complicit in my truancy and deceit of Mum (his niece). Sure enough, this kindly old man in his sixties came the one stop on the tube from his home in Plaistow to meet me and Steve.

It seemed chaotic outside the ground, with 42,271 evidently bunking off either work or school to see if mighty Hereford could repeat history. We joined a lengthy queue for the North Bank and somehow managed to find a small gap on the wall down by the north-west corner, where the view was so poor that I couldn't see Geoff Hurt net the first goal of his hat-trick in a comfortable 3-1 win.

I was taught that honesty is always the best policy, so I decided I would tell Mum that I had been to West Ham. Mistake! She took away my season ticket and imposed a one-game 'ban', which saw me miss the next home game v Crystal Palace five days later.

She also vehemently refused my request to write me a sick note that I could hand in to my form teacher, Mr Ashwell, the next day. I promised to run all sorts of errands for her, clear up the dog poo in the garden, go fetch her usual packet of 20 Silk Cut from Arthur's off-licence (even offered to pay for them with my pocket money) . . . anything, but she could be stubborn at times and wouldn't budge an inch.

So Tuesday morning registration descended into farce, as each 11/12-year-old kid in turn produced a pathetic hand-written sick note from his mother verifying that he had been ill, gone to the dentist, was knocked over by a bus, had suffered an unexpected bout of bubonic plague . . . every excuse in the book. Until Mr Ashwell got to me. "McDonald! So why were YOU absent yesterday afternoon?"

Without a sick note, I didn't have a leg to stand on, so I just came out with it: "Went to West Ham, sir."

The room went deathly silent apart from a few sniggers at the back of the classroom. "See me outside afterwards, lad."

I was fully expecting to be punished with the rubber slipper across my backside or, worse, the cane on the

Malcolm Allison (right) explaining the 'West Ham Way' to Philip Evans (left), publisher of the second edition of the *West Ham United Who's Who*, and co-author Tony McDonald at the book launch held at Upton Park in December 1994. Stephanie Moore is behind 'Big Mal'.

hand. But, to be fair to Ashwell, he knew the score; that all those with notes were lying and that they, too, had gone to the game – there were only about half-a-dozen nerdy kids who preferred woodwork to a Hurstie hat-trick, but each to their own – so he let me off and appreciated my honesty . . . which is more than can be said for my highly principled Mum!

This is not exactly original but being one of the 11,721 who froze v Cambridge (21/12/79) was definitely unforgettable. The sight of men jumping up and down on the half-empty terraces, desperately trying to get warm to the instrumental sound of Mike Oldfield, was surreal. If only the TV cameras had been there on that icy Friday night – how good it would be to replay it again and also enable those who were not part of this bizarre experience to enjoy now on YouTube.

John Lyall was, in my view, the best all-round manager in the Boleyn years, so it was heart-warming to see the pride on the faces of John's widow, Yvonne, son, Murray, and other members of his closest family when a large and distinguished group of ex-Hammers (and Yes keyboard player Rick Wakeman) gathered outside the main entrance (20/1/08) for the unveiling of the Blue Plaque in his honour.

Not exactly an 'I was there' occasion but I did happen to be at the Boleyn Ground on the night of the 'Great Storm' (15/10/87). Because there was no football being played, none of us in the warmth of the corporate lounge inside the stadium were aware of the significant damage in the process of being wreaked until leaving there late on that Monday night. Hurricane-force wind speeds of up to 100-plus mph had been observed across the worst-hit area of south-east England.

It really was a strange, old night in more ways than one. West Ham's commercial manager, Brian Blower, had invited about 50 local Asian newsagents to a meeting for the launch of his new Cockney Cashline draw tickets, which he hoped to persuade them to sell in their shops. He asked me to join him and them at the stadium and do a write-up for *Hammers News* (how interesting).

Brian was a smooth and canny operator who transformed the club's commercial income from next to nothing and established it as one of the most successful in the English game. He could sell ice cream parlours to the Eskimos on a cold day but there were a lot of Mr Patels and Mr Singhs there on that stormy night who didn't look too blown away by his latest money-making enterprise.

I felt very proud and privileged one night in December 1994, when so many ex-players turned out in one of the main West Stand lounges for the launch of the *Who's Who of West Ham United* book co-written by my old mate, Tony Hogg, and me, and published by our boss and my good friend, Philip Evans.

Among our many special guests of some 30 or 40 ex-Hammers were Malcolm Allison and Noel Cantwell, who were accompanied by Stephanie Moore. My dad has always emphasised to me what a pivotal role the pioneering 'Big Mal' played in the transformation of the club in the late 50s. Although I abhor modern celebrity culture and there are very few people I wish to be photographed with, it did mean a lot to have a picture taken with Malcolm and Dad.

It was a thrill to actually play in an 11-a-side supporters' match on the full-size Upton Park pitch, with several thousand in the stadium watching (and sniggering). The players had to donate £250 each to charity and we were all given a replica fully-numbered West Ham kit to wear and keep as a memento.

The 60-minute game took place immediately before Hammers' centenary friendly v Sporting Lisbon (7/5/96). Although the pitch was a bit wet and spongy and nothing like the immaculate surface they play on today regardless of weather conditions, it was an experience of a lifetime.

Geoff Hurst scoring the second of his three against Hereford in 1972.

and looked to be really seriously injured. I have never known a crowd go so quiet.

After what seemed like an age, he was put on to a stretcher and taken off with concussion. Clyde Best took over Fergie's green jersey and although Allan Clarke headed Leeds in front with seven minutes left, Pat Holland got our equaliser in the dying moments.

Mick Melbourne: Possibly when Bobby Moore pole-axed the referee with a clearance and picked up his whistle to stop the game. There was Billy Bonds' dance with the 'werewolf', Peter Withe, and Eric Morecambe throwing us cigars when Luton came to town. And Hurstie's six goals against Sunderland.

Mark Harknett: There are so many but the most amusing really stuck in my mind. It was sometime in the mid-70s. By this time we had moved to the Chicken Run and were stood near the halfway line. The ball ran loose near to where we were standing and Frank Lampard moved forward to the ball from defence just as Keith Robson moved back from attack. Lampard waved him away and shouted: "F*** off, f*** off", at which point a wag in the crowd shouted out: "Don't listen to him, Robson. We've been telling him to f*** off for years!"

Stuart Allen: I remember being ill one weekend and, unusually for me, going into the South Bank. Billy Bonds was named as Player of the Month by various newspapers before the game v Chelsea (2/3/74). He then proceeded to score a hat-trick, if memory serves me correctly, all at the South Bank end.

David Meagher: I remember going with my dad to a midweek match v Liverpool (19/2/75) that ended 0-0. As I was positioned right on the wall at pitchside, I got to pat Frank Lampard on the back as he took a throw-in. As a consequence, it was caught on camera and featured on *Match of the Day* – something my school mates spotted, which brought celebrity status for a few weeks and contributed to my getting selected for the school's first XI football team!

Richard Miller: An ill-tempered match v Ipswich (27/12/75), when Keith Robson was sent off just in front of where I now sit in the East Stand. Having already been subjected to several crude tackles from Ipswich full-back George Burley, Keith was again halted in his tracks by yet another foul from behind, to which he responded with a punch that completely flattened the Ipswich defender.

Roger Hillier: The most exciting match I attended was the ECWC quarter-final, 2nd leg v Den Haag (17/3/76). After losing the first leg 4-2, West Ham had to win by two clear goals. Fortunately, we only had to wait until the 33rd minute for Alan Taylor and Frank Lampard to score the first two of West Ham's three goals on the night. A 3-1 win that evening was an amazing achievement, especially when you consider Hammers were 4-0 down at half-time in the away leg.

Gary White: I took a girl called Jane into a packed North Bank to see the European match v Den Haag (17/3/76). We were right in the middle with all the lads with scarves tied to their wrists and painted Doc Marten's boots. Due to crowd surges, we got separated for a while early on but I was pretty keen on her and we found each other again. She was great looking and loved football. At the end of the game I asked her how she was, expecting her to have the right hump, but she said she loved it and "could she come to the next round?" Needless to say, that girl is still my wife to this day!

I guess Jane and I were always destined to be together after she enquired, on New Year's Eve, 1979-80, as to when we may get engaged. I replied: "When West Ham win the FA Cup!" And what happened . . . five months later we beat Arsenal at Wembley and no club from outside the top flight has won the FA Cup since! It was fate and Jane was there with me and the massed hordes of Hammers behind the goal to witness that famous 1-0 victory.

Jane is also our good-luck charm away from home, Hammers having won nine out of the 10 away games she has accompanied me to over all those years. We were desperate for a win at Stoke the other year, so I took her up there and, hey presto, we won 1-0!

I actually appeared on TV in 1996 when they were making a TV programme about the 1966 World Cup final. I noticed in the West Ham v Newcastle programme they were asking for people to come forward who had special memories of the day. As it was my seventh birthday on that momentous day of July 30, 1966, I rang the TV company and told them of my connection to that date. They invited me to the Boleyn Ground for a filmed interview. I was joined in the lounge in the Bobby Moore Stand by my two daughters, Katie and Lucy, who were four and two at the time. They sat there watching their dad being filmed on TV, talking about his birthday party which was postponed until after Bobby had lifted the Jules Rimet trophy!

Gerard Daly: I remember when I was about nine, my dad, John, was reading his programme and the ball came over and hit him straight on the head, making his eyes water. I wanted the North Bank terrace to swallow me up.

Danny Waller: Before smoking was banned from football grounds and other public places, my dad accidentally set fire to his trousers at Upton Park. We used to arrive about 1.30pm to get into the Chicken Run terrace when the gates opened and take our usual place at the back on the halfway line. For the first hour or so, until the stand began to fill up, you could sit down. I'd be chatting with my mates while Dad would sit on the steps reading his newspaper having a smoke.

At one match he didn't put his fag out properly when he trod on it – it was a baking hot afternoon and we were all enjoying sitting in the sunshine – and then he asked: "Can you smell burning?" We noticed the hem of his jeans leg was smouldering!

UPTON PARK MEMORIES   149

Alex Dawson: My first ever game and Dad didn't have tickets. He tried to give the lady in the ticket office a sob story about the car breaking down and not wanting to break his little boy's heart. It was all going to plan when I started tugging on Dad's coat. "But we didn't break down, Daddy, we came straight here!" I got a big kick but, luckily, we got our tickets in the end.

John Goff: I was standing at the top of the stairwell and an old lady, who couldn't have been less than 90-years-old, was taking ages to climb a few steps when I caught sight of her. "Do you want a hand, darling?" I asked her. "It's all right, dear, I have to take it easy as I've got a dicky heart."

An old lady with a heart condition watching West Ham – they've always given my young, healthy heart a very testing time!

Ian Heywood: I used to cycle from Edmonton to the Boleyn Ground – about a 12-mile journey. On one occasion, after a couple of miles it started snowing and I eventually arrived at the ground covered from head to foot in snow, freezing cold. The banter and the humour directed at me, all taken in good fun.

Richard Golby: A particular memory of an incident on the way to Upton Park concerns the giant inflatable pig anchored to Battersea Power Station as I went past on the train. This was the day they were supposed to be photographing the cover shot for Pink Floyd's *Animals* album (I think it was 4/12/76, West Ham 0 Middlesbrough 1), which was released in January 1977. There was no sign of the pig by the time I made the return journey. It was only later that I learned that it had in fact broken free from its moorings and floated off towards the Kent coast!

Alan Byrne: The 4-2 rout of Manchester United in our last match of the season (16/5/77), after Reds had taken a first minute lead through Gordon Hill and 'Pikey' missed a penalty just before half-time.

'We're staying up' read the back-page headlines the next day, and of course we had, with Pop Robson grabbing a brace and goals from Geoff Pike and Frank Lampard.

Bill Drury: Beating Man Utd 4-2 to avoid relegation. Just about stood in West Side lower. Geoff Pike scored playing as a makeshift centre-forward.

Gary Bush: I used to see this one particular fan in the late-70s standing on the North Bank in a pair of slippers. The first time I spotted him I was amused by the fact that he would probably be back home eating his tea before I had even got to the underground station. I resisted the temptation

It was a measure of the respect so many people had for John Lyall that the list of ex-Hammers who attended the Blue Plaque unveiling in 2008 read like a West Ham's who who. Back row, left to right: Alvin Martin, Billy Bonds, Ray Stewart, Alan Devonshire, Bobby Barnes, Phil Parkes, Stuart Slater, Chris Kiwomya (Ipswich Town), Tony Gale, Frank McAvennie, Mick McGiven, David Cross. Front: Pat Holland, Sir Trevor Brooking, Rick Wakeman (only an old rocker would wear white trainers!), Martin Peters, Sir Geoff Hurst, Rob Jenkins, Tony Cottee, Frank Lampard, Terry Venables (England).

John Lyall
1940-2006
Manager of
West Ham United
1974-1989
SPORTS HERITAGE

Neil Humphreys: I've got an absolute cracker. In my mid-teens, when I was West Ham crazy but usually skint, I often went along to the reserve games, which was all I could afford at the time. It was a couple of hundred fans in the old West Stand, I seem to recall, many of them were pensioners wrapped in blankets, drinking from flasks of tea and moaning that it had all gone to pot since Bobby Moore.

The atmosphere was entirely benign. If I were lucky, the old man beside me would offer a Werther's Original. It's important to stress that there was more chance of being mugged in Mothercare than something untoward happening at a reserve match at Upton Park.

And yet, at a West Ham-Millwall game, played out before a hundred fans, the unthinkable happened.

A drunken West Ham fan lurched towards me at the top of the staircase near the tea stall, shouted "oi, you're f****** Millwall," and punched me in the face.

I was 16. He was at least 60. He was also on crutches.

Before I had a chance to explain that I was in fact a fellow Hammer and had the fan club membership to prove it, two burly stewards grabbed me in an arm lock and said: "What are you playing at, son? He's old enough to be your grandad."

And they threw me out of the ground. It remains one of the surreal highlights of my life, chinned by an OAP on crutches and thrown out of Upton Park.

Tim Crane: As a young lad of 12, seeing Ray Stewart convert a last-minute penalty against Aston Villa (8/3/80) to take us to the FA Cup semi-final was simply too much excitement for my small frame to handle. I suppose I have been trying to replicate that high ever since. I have a DVD of the game and I love the interview with Ray afterwards – the very first time he reflects on the achievement.

I have mixed emotions about our FA Cup success that year. I queued up all night to get a ticket but my dad convinced me to sell it to an elderly gentleman who operated the foot tunnel in Greenwich. At that age a father is like a God, so I believed his words to be true. "This man is getting on in age and won't have any other chances to watch West Ham at Wembley. There will be plenty of other chances for you . . ."

One saving grace is that little did I know I would interview most of our cup heroes from 1964, '75 and '80 for *EX* magazine.

of treading on his toes as we left the terrace – it wasn't his fault I had another 120 miles to go home to Leicestershire!

Kevin Pendegrass: I have a few memories but the main one is of Phil Parkes looking away as Ray Stewart prepared to take the last-minute penalty v Aston Villa (8/3/80). He was crouched down right in front of me at the North Bank end, not bearing to look. The roar of the crowd told him it was in and he jumped up punching the air.

Other memories that stand out: v Oxford United (5/3/88). Absolutely awful game, then a fan runs out of the Chicken Run and smacks the ball from 25 yards into the top corner at the South Bank end, getting the biggest cheer of the day.

Bill Remfry struggling to pronounce the names and taking ages to read out the Dinamo Tbilisi team (4/3/81).

And the absolute hatred permeating from practically the whole stadium

Heartbreaker: Gordon Banks fists Geoff Hurst's penalty into the night sky to deny Hammers a Wembley date with Chelsea.

directed at Paul Ince on his first game back for Manchester United (26/2/94). Ince had the last laugh, though, equalising late to make it 2-2.

Gary Bush: It was the last Saturday home game of the season, v Shrewsbury Town (26/4/80), before glory beckoned at Wembley a few weeks later. I was a regular on the North Bank that season and travelled to the game from where I lived in the East Midlands. Tickets for the FA Cup final were to go on sale on the Sunday but, due to the distance, it would have proved difficult for me to get back again the next day to join the masses queuing up at the ticket office. I'm sure the tickets would have been all snapped up for that first allocation long before I'd have got there. I had a voucher, given out at a previous game, which had to be presented at the time of purchasing your ticket. I knew the Boleyn vaults wouldn't be opened up on the Saturday of this game just to give this East Midlands Iron his ticket but, somehow, I had to make inroads to get one of the prized possessions. So I thought, 'let's go to the top . . . John Lyall!'.

My plan was to hang around after the game in the hope of seeing John but this plan of action was put into operation sooner than I thought due to us losing the Shrewsbury game 3-1 (Trevor Brooking).

Towards the final minutes of the match I made my way from the North Bank down to the refreshment area and carried on through a door, where nobody was about to stop me. I hadn't a clue where I was going but just carried on regardless. The next thing I know, I've ended up in the players' tunnel looking out at the game still in progress.

The referee's whistle blew for full-time and, suddenly, Trevor Brooking and the boys are all walking past me back to the dressing room. I saw John go by but thought it best not to introduce myself at that particular moment. Given the result, he didn't look too pleased.

I spotted someone official-looking in his club blazer and went over to him to confess my reason for being stood in the tunnel. I thought he may have just thrown me out but, with this being the best family club in football, he said to wait where I was and he'd get someone to help me. A little while later, as I stood gazing around the

Kirk Blows: I used to stand against the front wall at the bottom of the West Stand and a friend of mine used to take great delight in verbally abusing opposing players whenever the opportunity arose. On one occasion (11/3/80), my pal had spent a great deal of time trying to remind Notts County midfielder Don Masson of his terrible experience at the 1978 World Cup finals with Scotland.

This was all very entertaining until such time when play was stopped because of a player injury and Masson, ball in hand, decided to wander over to us to introduce himself. "Hi, I'm Don, are you enjoying the game?" he enquired of my mate as he parked his backside on the wall in front of us.

Needless to say, my friend suddenly went very quiet and his face turned a very deep shade of claret...

Goalkeeper Bobby Ferguson receives attention after suffering concussion v Leeds in 1973. Manager Ron Greenwood and his assistant John Lyall show concern, along with physio Rob Jenkins, his Leeds counterpart Les Coker (in the white tracksuit top), plus players Kevin Lock, Clyde Best, John McDowell, Trevor Brooking and Leeds skipper Billy Bremner. Clyde Best donned the green jersey after Fergie went off.

empty stands, a bloke came up behind me and introduced himself as Denis Smith from the ticket office. He told me that John was still in the dressing room, apparently giving the players a rollicking over the result. Good job I didn't approach him, then.

Denis said he'd let John know about my search for a ticket and that I should post my voucher and ticket money (all £3.50 of it) to John as soon as I could. West Ham United's manager would make sure I got my ticket.

This I did and, sure enough, the following Thursday my ticket duly arrived with a compliment slip signed by John himself. What a top bloke he was.

Richard Mumford: My 16th birthday holds my fondest memory of the Boleyn Ground. Mum had written to Trevor Brooking who had agreed to meet us there for a couple of photographs. Despite being the legend that he is and a very busy man, Trevor gave up an hour-and-a-half to show us around the ground, the players' lounge, directors' box, the changing rooms, you name it, he took us there. Trevor displayed such a pride in showing us around his club, his affection for West Ham and The Boleyn Ground was unashamedly there for all to see. The best 90 minutes at the world's greatest stadium and not a ball was kicked!

Neal Clark: League Cup semi-final, 2nd leg v Coventry City under floodlights (10/2/81). We were trailing 3-2 from the 1st leg at Highfield Road, having been 2-0 up. Typical West Ham. With time running out and leading 1-0 courtesy of Paul Goddard, extra-time was looming. Then in the dying minutes, Jimmy Neighbour scored to make it 2-0 on the night and 4-3 on aggregate. I can still remember seeing a very young Les Sealey, the Coventry keeper, sitting in his goal crying after the final whistle was blown.

John Lawrence: A second division game v Chelsea (14/2/81). Both teams were in the top four (we were top and nearly promoted). The North Bank was absolutely packed when we went in, and more people kept arriving. It got very uncomfortable, kids were crying and it got worse and worse. My mate, Phil, started shouting "help me, help me." I was only a few feet away but I couldn't even get my arms up, it was that bad.

I remember thinking, 'what do I say to his mum? Why couldn't I have helped him?' Then a guy to my right managed to free one arm and pointed at the nearest policeman, who seemed oblivious to everything. "Oi you!" he shouted. "I want your f****** number, 'cos I'm going to report you when I get out!"

The look on the officer's face was an absolute picture. Probably in fear of his job, and an impending right-hander, he summoned reinforcements, and hundreds of people were pulled out and sent to sit in front of the wall by the East Stand, where I found a very pale version of my mate.

With only seconds remaining of the FA Cup quarter-final against Aston Villa, ice cool Ray Stewart steps up to score the penalty that sealed Hammers' place in the semis and Tonka's place in claret-and-blue hearts.

We won 4-0 (Trevor Brooking 2, David Cross, Alan Devonshire), the game rounded off by a second from Trevor, who was applauded by the Chelsea keeper Petar Borota as the ball curled around him and into the net. All the lads had tickets for a 'do' that night in Chadwell Heath but Phil was still feeling too unwell to come.

Steven Mitchell: Not wishing to sound disloyal, but the greatest game I have ever seen at Upton Park was the 4-1 ECWC defeat at the hands of Dynamo Tbilisi (4/3/81). It is all too easy to select a brilliant West Ham win from the past but that particular night was strangely special. I normally leave Upton Park after a defeat in a fog of frustration, disappointment, angst, aggression, misery, you name it. However, that night was different. It was almost an education, with several of the Georgian players producing football performed at a level beyond the capacity of even our (then) quality side. The captain, Chivadze, was awesome, a sweeper/central defender in the class of the likes of Moore, Beckenbauer and Krol. The standing ovation our appreciative crowd gave him and his team-mates at the end of the match was a credit to our club.

Ian Smith: Tbilisi won 4-1 and were applauded off the pitch. I had never seen this before, nor since. They thoroughly deserved it, too, and it was then I realised that West Ham fans are a pretty educated lot when it comes to appreciating good football.

Alan Byrne: Matches under the floodlights always had that special edge. Even during the pre-match warm-up you could see it was going to be a difficult match for us, just by the way Dynamo Tibilisi were thumping the balls into the back of the net.

I was one of the many faithful who were happy to clap them off at the end of the game after a masterful display. It was no surprise that they eventually won the competition that year.

Dave Satchell: The best performance from any visiting team was by Dynamo Tbilisi. They were fantastic on the night and I was proud of our supporters when they gave the Georgian side a standing ovation as they left the pitch. Typical Hammers fans giving credit where due, even after a 4-1 thrashing. Tbilisi played us off the park that night.

John Reynolds: I went to a few games in the early 80s with my sister, Lynn. The last game of our second division championship season in 1981 we played Wrexham (2/5/81). On our way to the game, my sister tripped over but assured me she was OK. We were standing at the back of the old South Bank when Lynn fainted. I alerted a policewoman and the St John's Ambulance staff, who took her on a stretcher around the pitch and down the tunnel to a first aid room.

The time was by now approaching 2.45pm, when manager John Lyall, goalkeeping coach Ernie Gregory and chief scout Eddie Baily walked past me to collect an award for winning the league. I watched the presentation at the players' tunnel entrance, with the injured Paul Allen and Bobby

Frank Lampard, Stuart Pearson and Trevor Brooking (mainly hidden) are the first to congratulate the nerveless match-winner.

WEST HAM UNITED 3 EINTRACHT FRANKFURT 1
European Cup Winners' Cup semi-final, 2nd leg
(West Ham win 4-3 on agg.)
Wednesday, April 14, 1976

Gary Bush: At the age of 15, this was the first match I attended at Upton Park. Fans often talk about this as being one of the best games ever played under those famous old lights of ours. And having been there, I wouldn't disagree. I arrived mid-afternoon and there were already plenty of fans gathering for what was to be a 7.30pm kick-off. I headed down to the ground from Upton Park tube station and it's one of those places that just looms out at you once you get closer to it. At last, I'd made it to the home of my heroes.

I left briefly in search of some East End grub – Ken's Cafe did the trick – and headed back to the ground. It's then that I realised I should have eaten a bit quicker, because there were now queues of fans lined up where I'd been standing earlier. It wasn't an all-ticket game, so I thought it best to join the line and stay put.

Once through the turnstile it was up the steps and onto the North Bank. When that first sight of the pitch becomes visible, that's when it hits you. Finally, after all those years of having your heroes plastered around your bedroom walls, they are now going to be performing in front of you.

The ground filled up quickly and soon there wasn't any space to be seen. Fans were tightly packed together on the terraces and I recall watching the Chicken Run swaying as one to the singing of *Bubbles*. What a sight. The atmosphere was electric.

On a pitch that was a complete mudbath, Trevor Brooking was brilliant and Keith Robson scored a blinder. A 3-1 win sent us through and in good old Irons tradition, we did have to hang on a bit at the end. At one stage Tommy Taylor pretended to be swimming in the mud as he lay on the floor and the whole crowd laughed. The pitch was really that bad.

When the game had finished everyone was celebrating a great night. For a moment my feet left the ground as the tidal wave of fans left for the exit. It was that tightly packed, you had no choice but to just go with the flow. The streets outside were buzzing as I made my way back to the tube station. You could hear *Bubbles* being sang everywhere.

What a night. What a first visit. Incredible. The next day I must have read the newspaper report of the game 10 times over. I couldn't wait to go again and that walk up to the ground, when paradise finally comes into view, is one I never tire of. Just like my first time, Upton Park, for me and thousands of others, will always be special.

Richard Golby: Fantastic atmosphere, edge-of-the seat (or whatever the standing equivalent is) excitement and tension as West Ham, 2-1 down from the first leg but with the benefit of an way goal, scored three in the second half (including one of Sir Trevor's rare but significant headers and a cracker from Keith Robson) to make it 4-2 on aggregate, before the Germans scrambled a goal in the 87th minute to set up a nervy, last few minutes.

Mr G. Pope: Torrential rain, fantastic atmosphere and the performance of his life by Trevor Brooking. Unforgettable.

MANAGER
JOHN LYALL
Born: 24/2/40, Ilford, Essex
WHU managerial career: 1974-89

IF one game stands out in my mind, I would have thought that was it. It was a perfect night for West Ham . . . a fast, wet pitch, the floodlights and we knew that the crowd would frighten the Germans in a positive way for us. On any given night, we would present any team with problems.

Our lads deserved great credit for that performance, because Eintracht were a very good team.

Gary Casson: Trevor Brooking was simply sublime that night. It was pure magic . . . the atmosphere, the performance, the goals. Unsurpassable for those privileged to be there.

Robert Wells: This is the easiest question to answer and I am sure will get the vote of most who were there. From the moment we caught the bus straight from school, arriving at the ground around 5.00pm where the streets were packed outside the still closed gates. No tickets in those days – just queue at the gates and hope for the best. Something like 40,000 people (officially 39,202) packed into the ground on a filthy night, the floodlights reflecting off the shiny mud pitch (there was never any grass left at that time of the year).

You could almost smell the fear of the German players as they walked out to an atmosphere of

The German keeper grabs hold of the ball as Keith Robson gets ready to pounce, with Billy Jennings looking on.

Trevor Brooking's header finds the top corner of the Eintracht Frankfurt net.

hostility – not towards them as people, but as the opposition. The crowd was close enough to reach out and touch them, something completely alien to those who were used to having vast running tracks surrounding their pitches.

Two from Tricky Trev and a screamer from Keith Robson sent us home deliriously happy, soaked to the skin but not caring – on to Brussels a few weeks later.

Roger Jacobson: I've never seen a West Ham team play better and the atmosphere was amazing. I could barely talk for days afterwards.

Tony Hoskins: I was standing in the Chicken Run, towards the South Bank. When Sir Trevor Brooking headed in our first goal the place erupted with a noise that must have been heard back in Frankfurt itself!

I am a very privileged man to be able to call Keith Robson a personal friend, and to this day I still tell him that he miscontrolled the ball before firing home that unstoppable 30-yard shot into the top corner! If you look at it, he did so well to control the ball on such a muddy surface.

The main moment came when Sir Trevor got into the box, turned the defender and calmly passed the ball into the far corner…that memory will stay with me forever.

Jack Fawbert: I stood in the Chicken Run for the one and only time that night. Keith Robson ran his socks off. He was the real star on the wing, showing the sort of determination and commitment that all West Ham players ought to show (though often don't).

Gerard Daly: Torrential rain, enormous queues and fear that we wouldn't get in. We gave up on the North Bank and ended up in the Chicken Run. I remember the huge German flag and the relief when the magnificent Brooking finally broke the deadlock with his less famous big-match header, the delirium when Robson's 25-yarder flew in seconds after he'd failed to control the ball, to a loud groan, before Brooking feinted and weaved through the German defence and the puddles to make the game safe.

Safe? Ha! This is West Ham. Inevitably, the Germans pull one back. One more and they go through. The ball pings about our box. My legs shake violently and my throat tightens, I fear I'm going to be sick. I look up at my dad for reassurance. His face is covered by both visibly trembling hands. He peers through his fingers as if watching his whole family face a firing squad. This is the first time I experience how ill watching 11 blokes kick a ball about can make you feel. Eventually, at about midnight, the whistle blows and we're through.

We stop off at The Hole in the Wall at Waterloo on the way home, Dad clearly desperate for a drink as, in adulthood, I so often would be upon leaving a game. I stand in the doorway with my Coke and crisps and people see our claret-and-blue scarves and congratulate us as if we had been playing. People ask if we're going to Brussels and I feel important. But there's more chance of my mum letting me smoke.

Kevin Courtney: What a night. Fantastic to feel the hairs stand up on the back of your neck when almost 40,000 are singing *Bubbles*.

Steve Mortlock: Although we had only lost 2-1 in Germany, many experts felt the 2nd leg would be beyond us. However, we played superbly and in my opinion Trevor Brooking had his greatest game in a West Ham shirt that night.

Tony Clement: It was a night Upton Park was built for. Pouring down with rain, windy, very heavy pitch, very vocal full house and played under floodlights. Goal-less at half-time, Brooking turns it on in the second-half and The 'Ammers go into a 3-0 lead (4-2 on aggregate) but with a few minutes to go, in true West Ham fashion, the Germans score. We'd done enough though. Wild celebrations at the final whistle.

That's why we go – never the same two games running, so unpredictable. Sometimes we leave in frustration, other times in goose bumps.

Gary Price: The memory is still spine-tingling. View what bits there are on video and be transported to a magical place.

The German keeper grabs hold of the ball as Keith Robson gets ready to pounce, with Billy Jennings looking on.

WEST HAM UNITED 3
CAMBRIDGE UNITED 1
Football League Division Two
Friday, December 21, 1979

Ian Puxley: The fantastic atmosphere for the Cambridge Utd game. Played on the last Friday night before Christmas, I stood with my friends in the West Side. One of us (not me) had smoked dope and drank a few too many. He leant over a crash-barrier and spewed for England, creating a BIG space around us!

Then the compulsory, but completely spontaneous, dancing to In *Dulci Jubilo* played by Bill Remfry (RIP), Hammers' DJ at half time. As the blizzard fell it was a fantastic moment.

And Hammers recovered to win 3-1 (Stewart, Pearson, Neighbour) from being 0-1 down at half-time.

Not many fans got this clearer view of Stuart Pearson scoring in the blizzard.

Billy Bonds returns to the pitch at the start of the second-half to find a trouser-less fan entertaining the sparse crowd.

Trevor Brooking just manages to keep his feet on the slippery surface, leaving one Cambridge defender to sit it out.

Kevin Courtney: I stood in the West Enclosure at the North Bank end, having decided it was too cold to stand in my usual spot in the Chicken Run. It was almost impossible to see the other end of the pitch.

At half-time a male streaker (wearing only his boots and a hat) ran onto the pitch and did a jig to a track from Mike Oldfield's Tubular Bells album being played over the PA.

Imagine that happening now. For a start, the game would be called off. The streaker would have half-a-dozen stewards drag him off the pitch and he'd be banned for life.

Mark Sandell: Small crowd, it snowed and we couldn't see any of our three goals as it was too misty to see from the North Bank.

At half-time, whole lines of fans linked arms and danced up and down the terraces to Mike Oldfield's Xmas hit In *Dulci Jubilo* ('In Sweet Rejoicing').

Afterwards, we were walking down Green Street and a police van came past, the back doors opened and they started throwing snowballs at us. All good natured but bizarre.

Richard Goldby: The lowest attendance for 25 years (11,721) were warmed up by the announcer playing Mike Oldfield's In *Dulci Jubilo* – twice! The players came out for the second-half to see everyone on the terraces jumping up and down in time to the music and on the pitch a (male) streaker, clad only in a thick sweater and Doc Martens. Within a couple of minutes of the restart, Ray Stewart had tonked in the equaliser and West Ham went on to win 3-1 after going ahead when an attempted clearance went in off Stuart Pearson's backside.

Martin Cearns: I was concerned that I was going to miss kick-off. Travelling from work, the underground was busy with passengers who had thoughts of office parties rather than football. An abandonment looked certain but referee Clive Thomas kept it going. It is not the goals that I remember, but looking down from the West Stand upper and realising that winger Jimmy Neighbour was dribbling at least a yard in touch. The official's view at ground level must have been obscured by the snow.

Ferguson, who was leaving the club that summer. I couldn't believe my luck. One moment I was at the back of the stand, the next I was in the thick of our title celebrations.

While my sister's cuts and bruises were being tended to, Billy Bonds appeared, looking like a giant with the tiny mascot in front of him. I congratulated the team – probably our best ever – as they ran out, and followed Trevor Brooking, who always went out last, up the tunnel. A dream come true.

Heikki Silvennoinen: v Coventry City, (10/9/83), 5-2. This was West Ham's fifth win in a row from the start of the season. Hammers missed a penalty early on and after Coventry scored two quick goals inside 15 minutes, West Ham responded with three in three minutes. Dave Swindlehurst scored a hat-trick and Steve Whitton two (one a 25-yard rocket).

At the end of the match the fans gave BOTH teams a standing ovation (you hardly see that nowadays). Coventry manager and former Hammer Bobby Gould said: "Anyone who says Brooking's and Billy Bonds' legs have gone had better think again!"

My all-time favourite player, Alan Devonshire, was superb, controlling the game from midfield.

Mark Matthews: During the early 80s I used to work with a Football League linesmen who invited me as his guest to the home game v Arsenal (10/12/83). I went with my cousin and had a very pleasant day, going on the pitch before the game, having met the match referee, Eric Read, and his wife before the game in one of the lounges. We had great seats in the West Stand next to Mrs Read and saw Hammers win 3-1 (Trevor Brooking, Chris Whyte own goal, Geoff Pike).

However, the game was not short on controversy and after only about 15 minutes there was a flare-up in front of the Chicken Run between David Swindlehurst and Arsenal defender John Kay. As a result, Mr Read showed both players a red card, much to the disgust of West Ham fans around us, who proceeded to direct a volley of abuse at the hapless referee for the rest of the match. It was a little embarrassing for me sitting next to his charming wife!

Ian McMaster: The best performance I ever saw was the first half of the game v QPR (31/3/84), We went 2-0 up (Geoff Pike, Tony Cottee) and Trevor Brooking, in his last season, was absolutely unbelievable. As you know, the game ended 2-2 (Hammer-to-be Clive Allen got both of theirs) which, was a real disappointment after the way we played. But those first 45 minutes would be hard to beat.

Greg Faasen: I've been to Upton Park three times – a 2-1 win v Everton in the FA Cup 3rd round in 1982, a 3-1 defeat by QPR (1/1/85) and then when I brought my whole family across from South Africa to watch Hammers beat Middlesbrough 2-1 at the end of 2008-09 season.

The game v QPR was the first time my then girlfriend (now wife) watched Hammers with me. We stood in the North Bank and at the time John Lyall was taking some barracking from the fans. With the likes of Steve Whitton in the side, alongside players such as Swindlehurst, Hilton and McAlister, it was not the best of times to be a fan.

After starting brightly with a rare Paul Brush goal, West Ham quickly conceded three and not even the likes of Paul Allen could help us. On the tube back to London, we inadvertently stepped into a carriage full of QPR fans and it is the only time I have ever told my wife to hide her claret-and-blue scarf.

Spencer Dodd: It has to be my appearance as a match day mascot before a home win v Aston Villa (23/4/83). My overriding memory was in fact the smell of the changing rooms. I met the players, manager John Lyall and got them all to sign the album of photographs I was given on the day. I still have all the photos, the programme, the album, their signatures and the 10p piece that was tossed to decide who would be kicking off the game.

I remember kicking the ball to Phil Parkes in the warm-up and the cheer from the supporters behind the goal when I scored, with my family and friends cheering on in the crowd.

Sadly, it's the closest I ever got to becoming a professional footballer but as the game – a 2-0 win (Billy Bonds, Dave Swindlehurst) – was featured on *Match of the Day* that night, I was able to watch myself over and over again as the years went by. Alas, the VHS tape has gone along with the VHS recorder.

David Bernstein: We were playing Aston Villa (23/4/83) and the controversial Clive Thomas was referee. Peter Withe and Billy Bonds clashed on the halfway line and squared up to each other, only to look and see Mr Thomas watching every move. 'Bonzo' then took Withe's arm and they both danced away along the halfway line, much to the amusement of the crowd. This scene featured in the opening shots of *Match of the Day* for years.

Stephen Cain: v Arsenal (10/5/83), who played for one season only in a green-and-blue away strip. Gunners won easily 3-1 but because of their shirt colours, both keepers, Phil Parkes and Pat Jennings, wore white shirts. I think Phil was in all-white kit. Have not seen both keepers, before or since, wearing WHITE shirts and certainly none in all-white.

Marco Taviani: I attended the 10-0 battering of Bury in the League Cup (25/10/83) and 8-1 victory v Newcastle United (21/4/86), when Alvin Martin scored a hat-trick against three different goalkeepers. Both quite bizarre results.

John Ruane: Trevor Brooking's final match, v Everton (14/5/84). When the final whistle sounded the players went down the tunnel but not one person left the ground. After they cleared the fans who ran on the pitch, they announced Trevor would be coming back out to do a lap of honour.

When he did I was one of the first over the wall and onto the pitch and helped another lad to lift Trevor up onto his shoulders and do the lap of honour with him.

Jimmy Neighbour nips in to put Hammers through to the League Cup final with this goal against Coventry City in 1981.

Ian McMaster: Most emotional game was Trevor Brooking's last. I was in the South Bank for that one with an Everton supporter. Trevor's run around the ground in his socks was sublime.

Dean Sutherland: We were one down to Everton (2/11/85) with about 15 mins to go but came back in style to win 2-1, with Frank McAvennie scoring two past Neville Southall. Pure theatre.

John Goff: The 8-1 demolition of Newcastle United (21/4/86), including a hat-trick from centre-half Alvin Martin. Constant pressure from the first minute and amazing, flowing, entertaining football.

Billy Green: The greatest match I've seen at Upton Park for atmosphere was the 2-1 win over Ipswich (30/4/86). We were 0-1 down with 20 minutes left, and after such a great season the title seemed to be slipping away. A great Alan Dickens goal levelled the scores, then with four minutes left 'Tonka' (Ray Stewart) was as calm as you like to give us the victory from the penalty spot. The ground was bedlam at the final whistle as everyone poured on to the pitch singing "We're gonna win the league". OK, so a week later Chelsea failed to beat Liverpool and our dreams just faded and died but for that one night, and the only time ever, I truly believed we WERE gonna win the league.

Jim Drury: When we beat Ipswich 2-1 with a dodgy penalty in the closing minutes was the best, because I genuinely thought we were going to win the league the next week.

Bjørn Arne Smestad: v Ipswich Town, last home game of a memorable 1985-86 season, and all the players appeared in the directors' box to acknowledge the support of thousands of fans on the pitch. Not very unusual but a great moment.

Jason Stone: v Chelsea, (11/10/86), 5-3. Goals, penalties (three), drama – everything.

Martin McCormick: v Chelsea, (11/10/86), 5-3. The game had everything – passion, loads of goals and a great last goal from Tony Cottee. The atmosphere was electric.

Steve Smith: My most vivid memory was the end of 1986-87, v Man City (9/5/87). We won 2-0 (Tony Cottee, Liam Brady) and they were relegated. As was the tradition then, we went on the pitch after the last game of the season. Expected trouble with the City fans then turned into a moment of mutual respect, with scarves and hats being swapped – even though they had just been condemned to the second tier. I held them in high regard from that day since and don't begrudge their fans the success they're having now. Chelsea, on the other hand . . .

David Steadman: Loads of great memories. I suppose from a game it would be Di Canio's wonder goal v Wimbledon, Kanoute's amazing debut in the same game and my most memorable match, the 2-1 win over Ipswich in 1986 to keep us in with a chance of winning the title.

My best memory, though, is being picked as a Junior Hammer to walk the 'Join the Junior Hammers' banner around the pitch before a Simod Cup match v Chelsea in the late 80s. We all got to see the match for free and were given a West Ham tracksuit. The biggest thrill was waiting in the tunnel as the players walked in and seeing my hero, Alan Devonshire.

Hammers wait to kick-off after Dynamo Tbilisi had scored again in their brilliant 4-1 victory that earned the respect of the Upton Park crowd.

Without thinking, I remember saying: "All right, Devo" and he replied: "Hello, son." As you can imagine, being aged 11 or 12, it was amazing to say I'd spoken to my hero.

Colin Walkinshaw: A dismal 1-1 draw v Oxford Utd (5/3/88) conjures up the funniest memory. The ball had gone out for a goal-kick and rolled back on to the pitch. A fan jumped out of the Chicken Run, ran for the ball and dribbled it to the penalty spot. The crowd egged him on to shoot. He shot, scored and the crowd erupted while he ran off in celebration. His mate then jumped on to the pitch to give him a congratulatory hug. The whole crowd was jumping up and down. They both ran back into the crowd, who hid them from the police in pursuit.

Most unusual memory? I was 17 and walking towards the West Stand upper to buy a ticket when an elderly man approached me at the turnstile and offered me his friend's season ticket. I offered to give him some money but he flatly refused to take it. "All I'll ask is that you take me to the bar and buy me a drink," he said. So to the bar we went. I bought him a scotch and listened to his stories of Bobby Moore and Geoff Hurst. We went to the seats – they were fantastic, front row, right next to the directors' box on the halfway line. We beat Charlton 2-0, Tony Cottee scoring both goals. I was touched by the man's kindness and generosity.

Gary Price: v Oxford Utd (5/3/88). During a break in play a fan ran on from the Chicken Run to plant a 20-yard wonder shot past our startled keeper Tom McAlister. The goal-starved fans had seen a paltry 28 goals in the previous 29 games.

Lee Burch: v Aston Villa (17/9/88), 2-2 (Derek Mountfield own goal, David Kelly). We were two-nil down with about 25 minutes left when substitute Alan Devonshire sparked a comeback He lobbed Nigel Spink from near the halfway line and the ball hit the post before rebounding in off Mountfield.

Kristian Hall: My memories of West Ham fans doing the hokey-cokey in the South Bank in the late 80s/early 90s probably wouldn't get printed,

Paul Goddard challenges David Kipiani, one of the most impressive of Tbilisi's star-studded side.

as there was a copper in the middle! The crowd in those days were a large chunk of the whole experience. I'm glad I never saw anyone get hurt but I saw a lot of funny things. Without meaning to sound like an old git, will it ever be that much fun again?

Ian Crocker: Having stood in the pouring rain watching us get pumped 6-0 at Oldham in the great Valentine's Day massacre of 1990, I always remember how close we came to a remarkable recovery in the second leg (7/3/90) – Billy Bonds' first match as manager after Lou Macari had resigned. It was 3-0 (Alvin Martin, Julian Dicks, David Kelly) but I'm pretty sure we hit the post and bar and gave it everything.

I also remember a League Cup defeat to Barnsley (6/10/88), when we were 2-0 up and strolling, got pegged back to 2-2 and then somehow contrived to get walloped 5-2 (Kevin Keen, Stewart Robson) in extra-time. How very West Ham!

I was working as the stadium tannoy announcer and said something like: "Today's attendance is 12,403 and we'll be lucky to get the 403 on Saturday." It raised a laugh among the fans but someone from the Football League heard it and issued instructions to clubs for their PA announcers to be professional at all times. West Ham's commercial manager, Brian Blower, rang the League for some gossip as to which announcer had been naughty, only to be told it was his own!

Lee Burch: Paul Hilton's testimonial v Crystal Palace (13/5/91), when

Dan Francis: There have been so many over the years. Ray Stewart's penalty winner against Ipswich in April '86 when it felt like Upton Park was going to explode; a 4-1 League Cup win over mighty Liverpool in '88, Frankie Mac's farewell hat-trick v Forest in '92 and Paolo's meltdown against Bradford in 2000. The one that really stands out for me personally, though, is the final home game of the 1992-93 season, v Cambridge United (8/5/93), when we needed to win to ensure automatic promotion to the new Premier League.

I was 14 at the time and took my younger brother, Scott, to the game. We were a bit late getting to the stadium and by the time we got on to the North Bank, it was absolutely heaving. We couldn't see a thing, so I hatched a plan to get us a better view. Telling Scott to do his best 'ill' impression, I squeezed us down to the front at the corner of the Chicken Run, where the St John's Ambulance cadets were situated, and told them that my little brother wasn't feeling very well and needed some space. It worked. They allowed us to sit on their little bench for 10-15 minutes until he was feeling okay, then ushered us into the relative space and comfort of the Chicken Run.

When Clive Allen scored the winning goal in stoppage time, the crowd went mad and it seemed like everyone was storming on to the pitch to celebrate. I wasn't going to miss out, so grabbed my brother and told him to jump over the wall. Trouble was, Scott was only tiny, and a bit tubby at the time, so he was really struggling to clamber over. It was like trying to lift a baby elephant above your head.

By the time I eventually rolled him over the wall, the moment had passed and people were making their way back to the terraces. We did a little jig by the side of the pitch anyway, then turned to head back to our spot.

I'll always remember glancing over and seeing the St John's Ambulance staff shaking their heads at us in disgust!

Martin Allen entertained us in the Chicken Run and took the 'mickey' out of Kevin Keen.

Mark Edwards: My most vivid memory is more personal than unusual. West Ham v Tottenham (26/10/91). My great friend, Neil Reed, invited me to join him and his father, Alan, in the Chicken Run as his brother, Stuart, was unable to attend. They were all long-term season ticket holders and I was delighted to join them.

Neil was West Ham mad. I played football on Sundays with him and he was a truly great man and great character. We spent the day laughing and it was one of those days on the pitch . . . a 2-1 home win, with Gary Lineker scoring for Spurs and the less prolific Mike Small and Mitchell Thomas scoring for Hammers.

Neil was one of those people whose company often made a bad performance bearable. He saw all that was good in the world and I miss him greatly. Neil Reed 1971-2009.

Jim Drury: When George Parris collapsed near the centre of the pitch v Arsenal (14/3/92), 30 seconds after coming on as a substitute, and everyone thinking he was dead. Turned out he had a heart condition but, thankfully, recovered and the problem never arose again during his playing days.

Stephen George: I was lucky enough to have a ticket to the match v Wolves (6/3/93), billed as a tribute to the legendary Bobby Moore, who had sadly passed away two weeks earlier. The gates to Upton Park were a shrine to the great man with a sea of scarves and memorabilia, each a small token of what his memory meant personally to supporters both young and old, and collectively a reminder of the impact his legacy had on the game as a whole.

Before the game I recall a West Ham fan ran on to the pitch which, given the sensitive nature of the occasion, even managed to offend the most lively of West Ham fans. As this fan made a beeline towards the massed ranks of Wolves fans packed into the corner of the South Bank, we waited for the stewards and police to invoke the customary heavy-handed and undignified exit from the ground, only to watch in amazement as he stood applauding the Wolves fans for their own show of respect to Bobby's memory.

As I recall, the whole ground stood applauding for several minutes, which made the hairs stand up on the back of my neck, such was the outpouring of emotion that day.

Steve Foster: Most vivid memory has to be v Wolves (6/3/93), the first home game after Bobby Moore's death. It was such an emotional

John Northcutt: One memory that will never leave me was the day we all said goodbye to Bobby Moore. Our hero had sadly died of bowel cancer some 11 days before and the biggest crowd of the season had turned up to pay their respects before the game v Wolves (6/3/93).

A giant floral No.6 shirt was carried on to the pitch by Geoff Hurst, Martin Peters and Ron Greenwood. A chant of 'There's only one Bobby Moore' arose from around the ground. Some Hammers fans came on to lay their own flowers and in a nice gesture, two Wolves supporters laid their own black and gold wreath.

A hush fell over the ground as the PA system broadcast a commentary of the moment when Bobby lifted the European Cup Winners' Cup, West Ham's finest achievement. A minute's silence followed with players of both teams gathered around the centre circle. I said a quiet farewell to the finest footballer that wore our claret-and-blue.

Earlier thousands had passed through the gates, filing past the long wall of tributes left by fans. On an afternoon filled with sadness, it was fitting that West Ham ended with a 3-1 (Trevor Morley, Julian Dicks – pen, Matt Holmes) victory.

Our bubbles have often faded and died at Upton Park but the spirit of Bobby Moore lives on.

Tony Cottee heads his fourth goal in the 10-0 League Cup battering of Bury in 1983.

atmosphere and seeing Ron Greenwood, Geoff Hurst and Martin Peters carry the wreath to the centre-spot will stay with me forever. The Wolves fans were first class that day as well.

Matt Dynan: We were 2-0 down v Norwich City (11/3/95) with about eight minutes left. Ref Alan Wilkie had already gone off injured and his replacement (M. Sims) sent off the wrong Norwich player – Johnson when it should have been Prior – for a second yellow. Apparently, he got confused as they both had skinheads.

I was sitting in the West Stand upper and on the other side of the aisle from where I was sitting were two father and son Norwich supporters – not trying to hide the fact and proudly wearing the yellow and green hats. The look on their faces when Tony Cottee popped up to grab two late goals is one I will never forget. To them, they might as well have lost the game.

Neil Roper: It was the day we denied Manchester United the league title at Upton Park for the second time. I didn't attend the first time it happened, in 1992, when Kenny Brown scored the only goal of the game, nor the infamously hostile encounter in February 1994, when Paul Ince popped up with a late equaliser, so this was the first time I'd seen Manchester United live (14/5/95). It was the last game of the 1994-95 season. The Red Devils had won the double the previous season and were on course to repeat the feat when they came to Upton Park, needing a win (and Blackburn Rovers to lose at Liverpool) to take the league title, with an FA Cup final against Everton to come the following week.

I was a Junior Hammer at the time but we weren't season ticket holders, so I'd got used to popping over to the stadium to buy match tickets. The day they went on sale for this fixture my dad, Terry, and I queued for almost an hour inside the main entrance on Green Street to get them.

The game stands out most for its sheer magnitude. Everyone around us had headphones in or radios glued to their ears. Huge cheers went up when Blackburn scored at Anfield, and I also remember quite a few occasions when word had obviously incorrectly gone round that they'd scored again and small pockets of fans would start jumping up, leaving others looking quizzically at their radios.

West Ham were fantastic in the first half, with every player putting in

TREVOR BROOKING

MY final game was at home v Everton (14/5/84). It was a Monday night and Everton were due to play Watford in the FA Cup final the following Saturday, so it was disappointing to lose that game 1-0.

John Lyall kept us all in the dressing room and was telling the younger players like Alan Dickens and Tony Cottee what they needed to learn from the experience. Mick McGiven was holding the dressing room door closed but our chairman 'Mr Len' (Cearns) was trying to get in to ask John if I could re-take the field to say a final farewell.

When I eventually went out there, I couldn't believe that everyone had stayed behind to acknowledge my final game and I ended up doing a lap of honour.

It was a perfect way to sign off with the fans.

Trevor Brooking salutes the crowd on the occasion of his final game in 1984.

fantastic performances and when Michael Hughes met Matty Holmes' cross with a first time volley past Peter Schmeichel into the bottom corner, I'd never heard a roar like it. The atmosphere of the whole game will always stay with me but the second half was a completely different story.

Manchester United brought Mark Hughes off the bench at half-time and they dominated the second half, eventually equalising with a header from Brian McClair. This was followed by one of the greatest performances I've ever seen from a West Ham player: step forward Ludek Miklosko. A couple of the saves he made from Andy Cole to deny them the win, and the title by a single point, were incredible.

Although the game meant little to us in terms of league position (we finished 14th), the atmosphere was on a knife-edge and Ludo's performance kept us in the game. A truly memorable performance from the whole team and an atmosphere that will stay with me forever – and all for a 1-1 home draw!

George McDonald: The day Rio Ferdinand signed professionally for West Ham. I believe it was during half-time at a night game that a fresh-faced and suited Rio stepped out onto the Upton Park pitch, where they had set up a table, and he signed his first contract for the club overseen by assistant manager Frank Lampard. I think Rio's younger brother, Anton, also may have been present and eventually became part of the deal.

Rio obviously later became the most expensive defender in history, so the day he signed always stuck in my mind as unusual and memorable. Not many schoolboys sign for clubs during half-time in a first team match, so you knew he was going to be something special.

Arne Koellner: It wasn't actually during the game itself – a 2-2 home draw v Man United (8/12/96) with Florin Raducioiu scoring one of his very few goals for us – but only after I went to my local pub in Barking the following day. The other people in there started cheering and I couldn't figure out why. I then learned that I had been on screen, close up, for several seconds on Sky Sports, who had obviously shown the game live, and those who knew me in the pub had recognised me.

I've never seen the TV footage, so I don't know if I was picking my nose or shouting some obscenity at the referee at that point. All I know is I wore the legendary 'ecru' third shirt of that season. I don't know what came over me – I really should have worn claret-and-blue that day – and I never really liked that beige shirt anyway.

Stanley Borgonha: Many of my funny memories from The Boleyn wouldn't make for family reading. One worth mentioning occurred during a Premier League game v Manchester United (8/12/96). Phil Neville, who could not be described as handsome, was warming up near the Bobby Moore lower tier when someone shouted: "Oi, Neville, get that mask off!"

Neville pretended not to hear the comment and jogged up to the touchline. When he approached the BM Stand again, the same person shouted: "Oi, Neville, I thought I told you to get that mask off!"

Neville's face turned bright red, much to the amusement of the West Ham fans within earshot.

Liam Corbett: John Hartson's 83rd minute equaliser against Arsenal in an FA Cup quarter-final replay (17/3/98) was the most I'd ever celebrated a goal – the whole stadium just went insane. I was close to tears by the end of the penalty shoot-out, though. Arsenal beat us 4-3 on pens and went on to face Wolves in the semi-final.

I actually also saw Marco Boogers score a goal at Upton Park – in Alvin Martin's second testimonial, when Steve McManaman, Jamie Redknapp and Chris Waddle all wore claret-and-blue.

Gjermund Holt: v Crystal Palace (3/11/97), when the floodlights went out, I had a front row seat in the West Stand. Attilio Lombardo lost the ball over the touchline just in front of me, so I jumped towards the wall to laugh at him, only to hit the small gate and fall over. This was quite close to the corner flag and the Palace supporters, who laughed their heads off, started singing "She Fell Over!"

I have presented the Scandinavian Hammer of the Year award pitchside a few times before kick-off, which was great. It was also a proud moment when I was interviewed on the screen before a game with my two kids.

Tom Fisk: v Crystal Palace (3/11/97), when the lights went out in the 65th minute, just after we made it 2-2. The banter was even funny for a seven-year-old. An interesting experience.

John Reynolds: My greatest match at Upton Park was when my son Stuart was mascot v Tottenham (28/11/98). We met the whole squad – players like Rio, young Frank Lampard, Steve Potts, John Hartson, Ian Wright, etc – and then went into manager Harry Redknapp's office, where his assistant Frank Lampard Snr and Sir Geoff Hurst were sitting with him. The day just got better and better. My son led the team out and we beat Spurs 2-1 (Trevor Sinclair scored both goals), to go second in the Premier League behind Aston Villa. Those were the days.

Jason Stone: A 24,000 crowd (v Aston Villa, League Cup quarter-final, 15/12/99) not realising Manny Omoyinmi was cup-tied.

R. Austen: Watching substitutes John Moncur and Ian Wright warming up and copying everything the linesman did. The crowd loved it – they were real characters.

Billy Green: John Moncur warming up as a substitute. He always used to run behind the linesman and mimic everything he did. But whenever the linesman turned around, John would act all innocent. On one occasion there was a female on duty with the flag. 'Moncs' was pretending to try and kiss her while she tried to run the line, totally oblivious to what was going on behind her.

Bill Drury: UEFA Cup, 1st round, 1st leg v Osijek (16/9/99) – our first time in the competition and hadn't been in Europe since 1981. Quite emotional when teams came out to Prokofiev's *Dance of the Knights* and then celebrating Paolo's goal to the sound of Pavarotti's *La Donna E Mobile* ("Paolo Di Canio, Paolo Di Canio, Paolo Di Canio, Paolo Di Canio"). Paulo Wanchope and Frank Lampard scored the others in a 3-0 win over the Croatian side.

Matt Drury: Most vivid memory would be Paolo Di Canio scoring twice in a 2-1 win v Arsenal (3/10/99). This was also the match that Patrick Vieira was sent off and spat at Neil 'Razor' Ruddock. It is also the day I met my wife, Wendy!

It's not an interesting story, I'm afraid. I went to the match, drove home to Lincoln, went out for a few celebratory pints, got drunk – and met my future wife.

I recently got the match programme from that game signed by Tony Adams at a sportsman's evening. He spoke very highly of Steve Potts (having known him since the age of six when they played together for Dagenham United). He also confirmed Vieira wasn't a huge fan of Ruddock.

Jimmy Jacob: My most vivid memory was a few seasons back, singing *Bubbles* when the players came out and I got all emotional (with tears) which had never happened before. Weirdly I felt as though my great-grandad was there enjoying the atmosphere with me.

David Meagher: Having moved to live in Ireland and reduced to twice-yearly trips to Upton Park, I was lucky enough to choose the home game v Bradford City (12/2/2000) that ended in a 5-4 thriller. I attended the match with my best man, John Browne, but we had gone on a bit of a bender the night before, which ended in a bout of fisticuffs over some minor point of disagreement about who was the more naturally gifted player (both of us are pretty awful, as it turns out).

Happily, we made up on the morning of the game and headed off to the match well hung-over. Little did we know the treat that was in store as an injury to Shaka Hislop triggered a defensive implosion for West Ham and we were left having to try and outscore a rampant Bradford after being 4-2 down.

Although everybody remembers the argument between Frank Lampard junior and Paolo Di Canio about who would take the penalty, some folk

View from the East Stand as jubilant fans invade the pitch to celebrate Hammers clinching promotion in 1993.

seem to have forgotten that prior to that, Di Canio had asked to be substituted as he was unhappy about a succession of unsuccessful penalty claims turned down by the official, Neale Barry. In protest, he decided to sit down in the centre circle and kept his head down, sulking, as the crowd broke into the Di Canio chant.

What I loved most was that the ball actually cannoned off him while he was sitting down and the referee and other 21 players all carried on playing!

Mark Sandell: I loved the 5-4 v Bradford City (12/2/2000) for a brilliant 90-minute summary of the magic of Paolo Di Canio: petulant, dramatic, funny . . . and, ultimately, wonderful.

Trevor Treharne: I think it was a cup match and a fat male streaker ran onto the pitch to loud cheers. However, no-one stopped him and he ran out of ideas. The crowd went quiet and everyone just looked at him. I think he rolled on the pitch for something to do. Di Canio went over to him and gave him a hug before he finally left the pitch.

Sally Roberts: Funniest Memory? Ah! Good old Cockney humour. All honours here have to go to fellow fans for their many ribald, bawdy and slanderous comments. To chose one is difficult, but I will plump safely for witnessing the collective destruction of a single ego. The game was v Middlesbrough (2/12/2000), who were having a tough time under Brian Robson. Boro fans were loudly and visibly up for it, being ensconced close to the West Stand Lower supporters, and if they thought they'd get a break from the barracking of the Chicken Run, they were in for a surprise.

One chap, in particular, was leading the offensive. Shaven-headed, glasses, lots of aggressive finger-pointing and much bawling of threatening promises, he obviously wanted it. At first, he appeared to be ignored, but not being deterred from his task, he kept making a nuisance of himself.

Then the singing started.

It's got to be embarrassing when a few hundred people begin singing to

Scorer Michael Hughes is congratulated by Trevor Morley, much to the dismay of Paul Ince, on another day when Hammers stopped Manchester United from winning the league title.

Iain Dale: The most bizarre game I can recall is our 5-4 home victory v Bradford City (12/2/2000). Stephen Bywater had to make his debut in goal after Shaka Hislop went off after two minutes and he had a nightmare, at fault for most of their goals.

But it was Paolo Di Canio's extraordinary behaviour that makes the match memorable. He had three cast iron penalty calls rejected by the referee and in the end sat down on the pitch in protest and signalled to manager Harry Redknapp to sub him. Redknapp refused.

Moments later, West Ham were awarded a penalty and we were treated to the sight of Frank Lampard and Paolo scuffling for the ball. Guess who won. And he scored.

The match was also memorable for Joe Cole scoring his first goal for West Ham at Upton Park. What a game!

you. Right? Singing about you. Very personally about you. In complete harmony and unison.

Watching his body language change from foaming anger, to a startled 'huh?', to blushing, to feet-shuffling, to the final slumping of the shoulders, was a picture. By the time he had his own circle of space around him he was grinning and applauding the banter. Especially when the Hammers joined in with the calls for Robson's head. Football camaraderie at its best.

Siobhan Hattersley: v Tottenham Hotspur, FA Cup quarter-final (11/3/01), lost 3-2. It was the first time I saw West Ham lose and I was heartbroken that even my lucky bear wasn't enough to see Hammers through to the next round. I was so gutted we lost that I decided to write a story about it, which was later printed in the match day programme (3/5/03).

Paul Kavanagh: Taking my seat for the first home game of the 2003-04 season, a goal-less draw v Sheffield United (16/8/03). It felt very unusual sitting there and not seeing the likes of Di Canio, Cole, Kanoute or Sinclair. These were players who'd graced Upton Park with their skill and flair in the late 90s and in to the new millennium. It was the price of relegation.

Ivan Robeyns: Even though I was witness to some enthralling games, resulting in victories against Arsenal, Manchester United, Liverpool and Chelsea, the greatest match I have ever seen at Upton Park was the game v West Bromwich Albion (8/11/03). Leading 3-0 after only 20 minutes, West Ham managed to throw it all away and end up losing 4-3.

Going through all possible human emotions in 90 minutes is, to me, a part of what being a Hammers fan is all about. There isn't a play, a film, a book, or a work of art that can cause an emotional rollercoaster like it. Never a dull moment.

Also, it was the first time my girlfriend accompanied me to a game at Upton Park. Coming out of the ground, I was completely gobsmacked at what I had just witnessed, unable to comprehend what had happened after those first 20 minutes. Joining the 'effing and blinding' supporters on the Barking Road who had lost all will to live, my girlfriend hooked her arm into mine, giggled and naively said, without a hint of sarcasm: "Wow! When can I come again?" Bless her, the poor girl.

Nick Morgan: The first game I took my eldest son, Alex, to. We were in the Championship and all our star players had gone, except for Michael Carrick. We played Walsall (6/3/04), which I thought would be a goal-fest to help secure his devotion and faith. Instead, it was rubbish and goalless.

Behind us were some young lads, no older than 13. They talked throughout the game, barely watching, until one of the Walsall players got injured. Then they all got up and chanted: "Let him die, let him die, let him die!" I turned to Alex and said: "That's not very nice, is it?" He replied: "No, but it is funny, Dad!"

And then I realised he'd got it – what it's like supporting West Ham. Disappointing and frustrating, but plenty of banter and humour. Plus we stick together.

Liam Tyrell: Many of the events that happened around the time of the ill-advised bond scheme were quite unique. It feels good to think that, by being part of some of those protests, I did my bit to highlight the unfairness of the sorry affair. I struggle to see a time when our fans would be as organised and generally bothered to fight any such injustice again. Seems to be too much apathy these days and acceptance that the powers that be will get their way.

One thing that stands out for me as unique involves a song for a player. As is often the norm when there's a new signing, there are calls to make up a song for the new arrival. During the January transfer window in 2004 we signed Bobby Zamora. I was looking at various attempts to find a song for him on www.kumb.com and thought I'd have a go myself.

The 'Vieira song' (sung by Arsenal fans in honour of Patrick Vieira), to the tune of the Dean Martin classic Amore, was in vogue at the time, so I set about thinking of something to fit that tune. 'He comes from Senegal, he plays for Arsenal' How hard could that be?

Let's see, Zamora. He came from White Hart Lane (as part of the deal that saw Tottenham sign Jermain Defoe from West Ham). He's better than Jermain. Voila! OK, while he may not have been better than Defoe, it at least made him and us think that was the case.

So, the first game for 'Barking Bob' was away at Bradford City a few days later. Zamora came on as sub and I instinctively started the chant, assisted by my brother. We had a few friends sat around us too and as Bobby started to assert himself impressively the song began to get louder as more and more joined in. He scored and before you knew it virtually the whole two tiers of travelling Hammers were singing it!

The next game was at Norwich, where we got it going again before the next test at home to Cardiff. Another Zamora goal helped and the chant became his song. Hearing it sung by more than half of the 70,000 crowd at the Millennium Stadium in Cardiff, where Bobby Zamora scored the winning goal in the 2005 play-off final v Preston, was a special moment indeed. Special enough for what the goal meant but extra special that I had made the song up. I know it's not exactly the same but it felt like how I would imagine a rock star feels hearing songs they've written being sung back at them in a big stadium or arena.

Jack McDonald: One that was not memorable for football reasons. It was the notorious League Cup clash v Millwall (25/8/09). My cousin, Connor Lewis, and I got the train from Barking to Upton Park and we must have arrived just in time, because I remember that the Millwall fans turned up literally five minutes later. I bumped into a few of my mates, Brandon, Alex and Gillard, who were stood in Green Street outside The Queens pub. It was a weird atmosphere at first, as if all the West Ham fans were waiting for Millwall to arrive, the calm before the storm.

It didn't take too long for the fans to get into full voice. I remember the 'Sit down if you hate Millwall' chant, where most West Ham fans sat down in the middle of Green Street, despite cars and buses trying to get past. I was on my way to buy a programme at the time when everyone sat down around me. My cousin pulled me down and said: 'We'd better sit down otherwise they'll think we're Millwall'. So, after checking to see

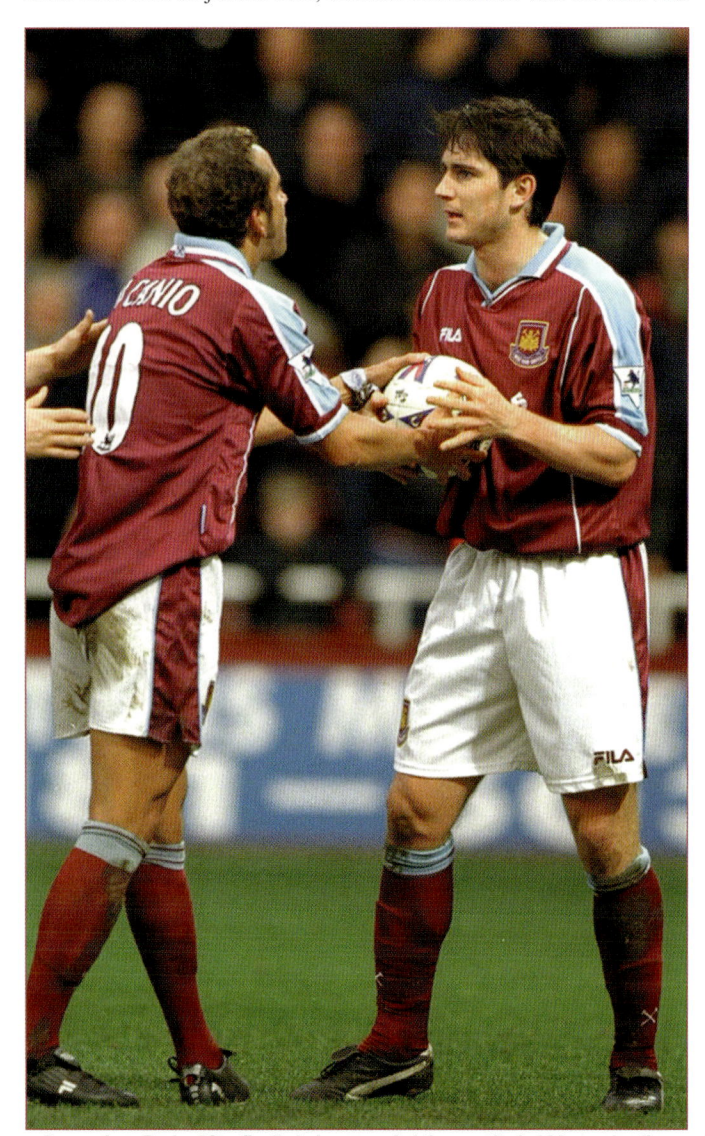

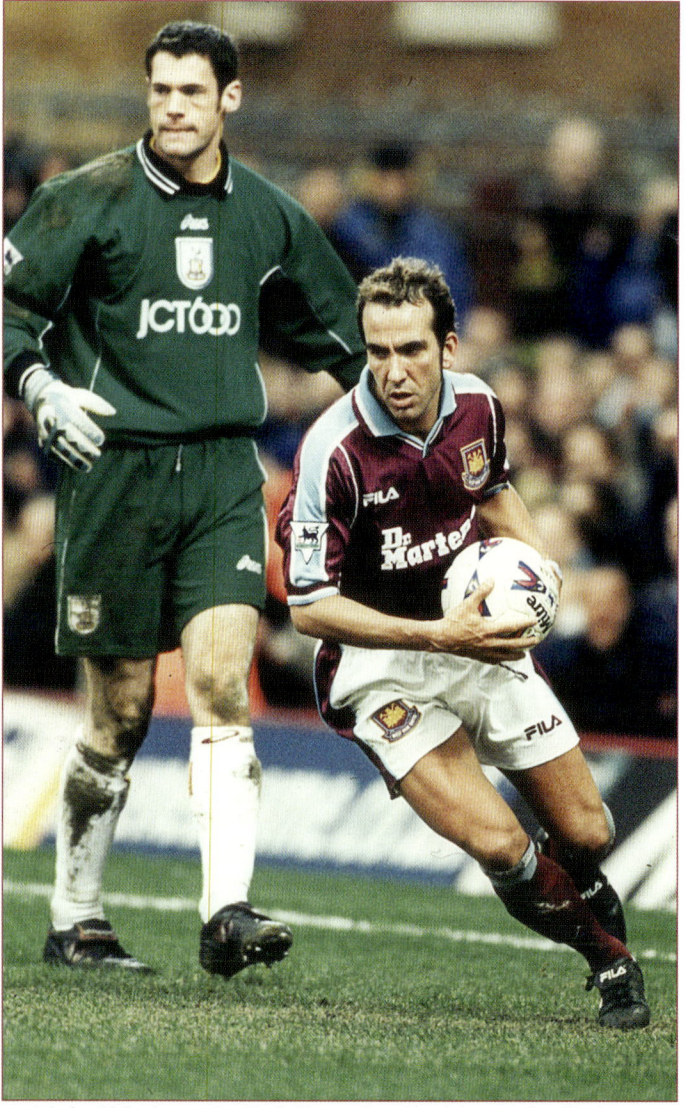

Pumped-up Paolo: After finally being awarded the penalty he'd been pleading so desperately for, Di Canio wrestles the ball away from Frank Lampard and insists on taking it himself. Goal! The Italian wheels away from Bradford keeper Aidan Davison and leads West Ham's incredible fightback like a man possessed.

there was no horse shit around, we crouched down until the fans sang the 'Stand up' version.

The game itself generated probably the most exciting atmosphere that I've experienced at Upton Park. Even with only 20,000 fans in the stadium, the noise was incredible. The pitch invasions were surreal. I'd never seen one at West Ham before, so to witness three in one game was something I won't forget.

I managed to avoid all the trouble, quietly making my way to Upton Park station as the Millwall fans were kept behind inside the ground. As I got to the station, me and Connor checked our phones to see all the texts and missed calls. We were told that our journey back to my home in Romford via Barking wasn't safe, so my auntie Lisa (Connor's mum) met us outside The Boleyn pub and drove us back to their house in Chadwell Heath.

A classic story was when my great uncle Dennis Farrow (grandad's cousin) went down to the kiosk to buy two hot dogs during half-time of the infamous League Cup quarter-final replay v Aston Villa (11/1/2000). He came back to his seat in the West upper and when the whistle blew to signal the end of 90 minutes, he stood up to leave . . . only to realise both sets of players were sitting down on the pitch and about to have a team-talk. "What are they doing?" he asked, all perplexed. It was then explained to Dennis that he had missed Frank Lampard's 47th minute goal while in the queue for hot dogs and so the game was now going into extra-time . . . he hadn't realised that Ian Taylor's 80th minute strike was in fact Villa's equaliser, not their winner!

Charlie Beckwith: Some favourite games of mine range from beating Millwall 2-1 in the Championship in 2012, to beating Tottenham 2-0 at The Boleyn in 2014. Another favourite has to be the 1-0 win over Man United in Alan Curbishley's first game in charge.

Floodlight failure caused the 1997 match against Crystal Palace to be abandoned with the score at 2-2 in the 65th minute, moments after West Ham midfielder Frank Lampard had sealed his side's fightback from two goals down. Referee David Elleray took the teams off and despite electricians getting the lights to flicker briefly back into life, they went out again, and the game was abandoned after a half-hour delay. West Ham MD Peter Storrie said at the time: "The floodlights at the south end contracted a fault which was impossible to find in the timescale. This end controls the floodlights for both ends of the ground, that is why the whole system went down." But the power loss was no accident, it was sabotage. Subsequent police investigations revealed that the plug had been pulled by criminals working on behalf of an illegal Far Eastern gambling syndicate.

**WEST HAM UNITED 2
IPSWICH TOWN 0
Division One Championship Play-off semi-final, 2nd leg
(West Ham win 2-1 on agg.)
Tuesday, May 18, 2004**

Paul Kavanagh: Fans showed tremendous pride, passion, courage and belief to lift the players from a 1-0 deficit in the first leg to a 2-0 (Matthew Etherington, Christian Dailly) victory in the return under the lights. I don't believe the players would have achieved this victory without the fantastic support the fans showed that evening. A game which will live long in the memory of the Hammers faithful who watched their team perform heroically.

Ian Smith: The crowd was rocking before KO and it only got louder as the game progressed. Etherington put us level on aggregate and I remember a complete stranger lifting me up and kissing me when Dailly made it 2-0. Ipswich hit the post right at the end but we won through and the noise in the ground that night was second-to-none. I've witnessed some great crowds at The Boleyn in the past but since we've had all-seater stadia the atmosphere has been poor. That night ranks as one of the best-ever at Upton Park.

Matt Dynan: It's a long time since the crowd has been so behind the team to the point they helped earn the result.

Pete Gumbrell: For atmosphere alone, it's got to be the play-off semi-final v Ipswich. There was so much to play for, the fans and team were up for it on the night and the result was just fantastic.

Tim Evans: The atmosphere was something else, everything was bouncing, it was the best night I can ever remember and I didn't get home until about 3.00am.

Matty Etherington is congratulated by Hayden Mullins, Bobby Zamora and Marlon Harewood after scoring in the play-off semi-final against Ipswich on a raucous night under the lights.

Special Guests

The Queen receives flowers as West Ham chairman Terence Brown looks on.

THURSDAY, May 9, 2002 . . . no game was played on that day but West Ham United described this special occasion as the "most important non-footballing event in the history of the club".

Her Majesty The Queen, who was 76-years-old at the time and accompanied by the Duke of Edinburgh, arrived at Upton Park to officially open the new Dr Marten's Stand as part of her visit to east London.

She also met West Ham's young stars Joe Cole, Jermain Defoe and Glen Johnson.

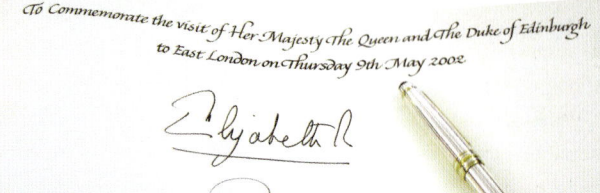

After the formal ceremony, Hammers' chairman Terence Brown hosted a Golden Jubilee Luncheon on behalf of the London Borough of Newham, Barking & Dagenham, Havering, Redbridge, Tower Hamlets, Waltham Forest, Greenwich and Bexley.

To Commemorate the visit of Her Majesty The Queen and The Duke of Edinburgh to East London on Thursday 9th May 2002

Elizabeth R
Philip

UPTON PARK MEMORIES 169

Her Majesty meets Jermain Defore while Glen Johnson looks on.

Joe Cole shakes hands with the Duke of Edinburgh.

The official opening of the new main stand completes the final redevelopment of the Boleyn Ground.

Harry Hammers one in!

THE Club received its second royal family guest just a couple of months after HM The Queen's visit, when Prince Harry called in to Upton Park on Thursday, September 12, 2002, three days before he turned 18.

It was part of his first solo royal public engagement to honour the memory of his late mother, Diana, Princess of Wales, who had died five years earlier.

Prince Harry was out and about in London visiting a centre for vulnerable young people, then a primary school, before stopping off for a more light-hearted interlude at the Boleyn Ground and completing his day at Great Ormond Street Hospital.

At West Ham the Prince had a kickabout with young people involved in a community project. Despite his suit, tie and shiny shoes, Prince Harry took a penalty against Anton Ferdinand, the younger brother of former Hammer Rio, who made his first team debut as a defender a year later.

"He was going on as if he couldn't hit a ball but he smashed it into the top corner. I couldn't get near it," said defender Ferdinand, who made his first team debut a year later.

Prince Harry was presented with a West Ham shirt with 'Harry' and '18' on the back, even though he is an Arsenal fan.

170 UPTON PARK MEMORIES

DANCING
IN THE STREETS

THE Cockneys love a good, ol' knees-up and there's nothing like victory in the FA Cup Final to set the streets throughout east London ablaze with jubilant Hammers, blowing bubbles and determined to enjoy the celebrations to the full. So let's grab this opportunity to remind ourselves of those heady far off days, in 1964, 1965, 1975 and 1980, when, briefly, we were the happiest people alive. Look very closely at the street parade pictures and you might just spot yourself or someone you know!

1964

UPTON PARK MEMORIES 171

172 UPTON PARK MEMORIES

UPTON PARK MEMORIES 173

1965

174 UPTON PARK MEMORIES

1975

UPTON PARK MEMORIES 175

176　UPTON PARK MEMORIES

1980

UPTON PARK MEMORIES 177

Despite ill health, Jeff O'Brien, West Ham's most memorable programme seller, still attends under-21 home games at Rush Green, where this picture was taken in October 2015. He was at both the 1975 and 1980 FA Cup Final and also travelled to Holland, Germany and Belgium to see the team play Den Haag, Eintracht Frankfurt and Anderlecht respectively in the 1975-76 ECWC.

CHARACTER
JEFF O'BRIEN

I FIRST started going to West Ham as a fan in 1964 – we drew 1-1 with Blackburn Rovers – and sold programmes there from 1971, when Tom Jenkinson of the Supporters' Club got me a job working outside the ground.

Then Nobby Greenhill, who was employed by the club on the commercial side, asked me to sell programmes from inside the stadium.

I used to sell walking round the edge of the pitch with a lady called Gill – but she found a new boyfriend and we've lost touch.

Fans used to throw things at me – peanuts and bananas, that sort of thing.

I sold programme for West Ham until I was sacked by a bloke called Tim in 1997. I didn't return to work for the club until Boxing Day last year (2014). It's a voluntary, unpaid job but at least it means I get in for nothing.

A lot of people who knew me thought I had passed away because they hadn't seen me for so many years. I just couldn't afford to go to games during all those years when I wasn't selling programmes.

In the 80s I worked as a porter for Selfridges, at the same time as ex-Hammer Johnny Ayris, but they sacked me after a week! I then worked as a roadsweeper in Newham . . . for a couple of weeks!

I was born in Dagenham in 1951 and still live there.

I suffer from type 2 diabetes and two years ago I was diagnosed with non-Hodgkin's lymphoma. I watch the under-21 games at Rush Green, which is not far from where I live, and hope I'll be well enough to go to the Olympic Stadium.

4 CHARACTERS

WHILE the players may be the main attraction, it could be argued that just as much entertainment has been found off the pitch on a match day at Upton Park over the years. From the cutting wit and humour heard on the old terraces and in the stands, to the unique individuals who may have worked in and around the ground over a long period of time. Here our contributors recall those characters, without whom the Boleyn Ground would have been a far duller place . . .

Q: Describe any 'characters' in the crowd and why they stood out.

Kevin Mansell: The Leyton Silver Band played on the pitch near us for 40 minutes before the start. The bandmaster was a small man wearing a peaked cap standing on a podium. Next to one of the band men was an inverted post-horn. At about 2.50pm the band played *I'm Forever Blowing Bubbles* but I don't remember anyone singing along. That only happened when the Chicken Run swayed back and forth when we were winning cup games.

After *Bubbles*, groundsman Paddy O'Leary would wave frantically to the conductor and they would play *The Post Horn Gallop* as the teams ran out.

Reuben Gane: 'Monty' was famous at Upton Park in the late 50s and early 60s. An elderly chap in British army uniform, sometimes with an overcoat, who was the spitting image of our World War Two hero, Field Marshall Montgomery. Monty would march around the perimeter of the pitch giving over-the-top salutes to the crowd and blowing an ancient bugle. Sometimes he would be accompanied by a little scruffy dog.

When an over-zealous policeman would try to escort Monty out of the ground, supporters would shout and boo and the copper would relent and let Monty go over the wall and disappear into the crowd.

Terry Connelly: 'Monty' used to come onto the pitch wearing army beret, battledress, socks and boots, along with a grass skirt. He used to place an imaginary ball on the penalty spot, take a run up and then throw his arms in the air as the 'ball' hit the net. This was followed by a blast from his bugle which he would blow throughout matches.

Dave Spurgeon: 'Monty' would stand on the South Bank dressed always

The most memorable character of the 50s, 60s and 70s, 'Monty' gets his collar felt and is thrown out of the South Bank.

in a maroon track suit and wearing an identical military large black beret complete with military badges.

Over his right shoulder he carried a military brass bugle and if West Ham conceded a goal, or if the crowd were unusually subdued, he would give a perfect rendition of The Last Post.

After the game he could be seen marching, military style, down Green Street, occasionally halting, playing the bugle and then marching off again. The epitome of a harmless and entertaining eccentric.

Steve Derby: At the end of the match, 'Monty' would stand on the dividing wall between the South Bank and Chicken Run and salute us all as we left. Of course, we saluted back.

Richard Miller: 'Monty' became a favourite among the crowd, with many supporters readily throwing cash, which he gleefully collected.

David Barnard: Before each match 'Monty' was allowed to march up and down the centre of the pitch, from goal to goal, with his small dog (possibly a Jack Russell) and two balloons (guess what colour they were).

And then, in the 60s, his pre-match appearances were curtailed. But I was standing behind the goal in the South Bank – it was a sell-out and could have been against Manchester United – and a few barriers in front of me was an elderly guy who, during the match, started to blow his bugle as if his life depended on it. Yes, it was Monty.

The police decided that he was a threat to the peace – maybe they thought the referee would mistake his bugle for the sound of the whistle? – and he was yanked unceremoniously out of the crowd by the law, to widespread booing from the South Bank faithful.

Bobby Moore, to his credit, saw what was going on and interceded on his behalf. No success, though, so in his 80s, Monty must have been the oldest spectator ever to have been ejected from the ground.

Monty made a brief reappearance a few years later in the *Ilford Recorder*, which published a photo of Monty and his beloved from the same old folks' home tying the knot.

Monty's impact on the local community is also evident from these online messages posted on the popular Newham Story Forums (www.newhamstory.com), which provide more insight into this famous, old character. They also confirm his real name as Percy Sparks.

Ed Styles (August 2008): 'Monty' certainly was a local character around the docks and at West Ham United football ground in the 60s. He could also be seen marching up and down the High Street in East Ham.

Around the docks he would entertain us dock workers in the pubs and cafes with his excellent marching skills. One time I remember we copped a dreaded 'bridger' at the swing bridge by the Albert Dock Basin, just outside the Manor Way Canteen (also known as 'Dirty Ben's Cafe'), so along comes Monty who gladly entertained us with his dancing skills to the music on the jukebox.

When the ship had passed through the cutting and the roadway became Woolwich Manor Way again, the captive audience, including some passengers on the 101 bus, carried on their way. And Monty saluted us all, blew his bugle and marched off towards the ferry.

I believe Monty's real name was Ron and that he was an ex-soldier who became badly disturbed after the war.

DougT (March 2011): I certainly remember 'Monty' as a familiar sight around East Ham and Upton Park during the 50s and 60s. Although I cannot now verify this, my mother, who worked in Caters in High Street North, told me of an occasion when Monty, probably refreshed by a certain amount of alcohol from The Cock Hotel, decided that his 'enemy' that afternoon was to be a bus travelling along the High Street. He stepped on to the pedestrian crossing at the corner of Myrtle Road and held the bus, and other traffic, up with his imaginary rifle for almost 10 minutes before a member of the local constabulary encouraged him that it was time for a ceasefire.

leydaf (March 2011): Does anyone remember his little dog that he had for a time? One day, Monty was proceeding along the High Street at quick march pace, bugle in one hand, little dog on the lead in the other. Just as he was passing Johnny Bolton's and the British Home Stores, the little dog, not to put too fine a point on it, needed the loo and proceeded to squat. Monty, oblivious to this, proceeded undaunted and the poor little chap was unceremoniously bounced along on his behind as he tried to do his business!

westham John (July 2011): I also remember 'Monty' (real name Percy Sparks). We were playing about one day in Queens Market and a friend of mine got a bit saucy and upset Monty, so he clouted him. A court case ensued but he got off with a warning. What a lovely old chap, miss him a lot.

Leigh (Jan 5, 2015): Hi, I would just like to ask if anyone has any photos of Monty (Percy Sparks), as he was my grandad and I never met him. He left his family and moved London way. I would love to see a photo of him, seems he was quite a character. I know he was a massive fan of West Ham and did the London-to-Southend walks with the police.

I really want to find out more about him and would like to know where he's buried, so that my sister and myself could go and pay our respects to him. Do you think anyone would know when he passed away?

Bob L: Hi, Leigh. The death of a Ronald James E. Sparks was registered in Newham in 2001, with 1926 given as the estimated year of birth.

Crispin Derby: I was privileged to see 'Monty' in his red-faced prime but a bigger memory is from some games in the 2003-04 season, where my sons and I found ourselves in the East Stand near the away supporters. There we felt very much at home sitting with a large family who I think were all season ticket holders. Supreme among them was the guy my boys christened 'Coach'.

Clad in his grey mac and seated in line with the edge of the penalty area, he would spend the entire game monotonously advising the West Ham team what to do next, what their strategy should be and particularly how to play the opposition offside. All this with meticulous and frequent gesticulations.

Another member of the family would be more vociferous in an explosive way and held particular grudges against various partially-sighted linesmen. On one memorable occasion he broke off a conversation with a female family member to violently upbraid yet another official. 'You f****** stupid, f****** lino, can't you see he was played on you f****** ****' he bellowed, before turning back to the girl to resume conversation absolutely calmly '...and how is Elaine now?'

David Hughes: All the Chicken Run as they the swayed to *Bubbles*, arms by their sides – a sight to behold and unique to our club, to our ground, alas sadly gone.

I also used to be fascinated by the greatly overweight drummer of the Leyton Silver Band and the little fellow who somehow managed to faultlessly play *The Post Horn Gallop* as Hammers took to the field.

Graham Wright: When I used to go to reserve matches as a teenager, I would always buy a programme – a single piece of paper with just the team-

> **John Powles:** In the days of the old Chicken Run, humour was rife and a number of underperforming home players really took some stick. I was a bit too young at the time but I wish I had made a note of some. Sitting now in the East Stand upper there aren't too many individual comments these days but one that came out recently involved the bloke next to me who was angry at the team's lack of effort. He yelled out a couple of times: 'Who wants it then? Who wants it?' A woman just in front yelled back: 'It depends on what you're offering.'

PLAYER
BRYAN 'POP' ROBSON
Born: 11/11/45, Sunderland, County Durham
WHU career: 1971-74 & 1976-79
Position: Forward
Apps: 254, **Goals:** 104

ON my debut v Nottingham Forest (24/2/71), I was buzzing about all over the place, chasing balls from one part of the pitch to another and generally trying my hardest to impress.

After about 20 minutes, I made a good tackle and knocked the ball over the touchline in front of the Chicken Run. It was dead quiet in the crowd until this bloke piped up: "C'mon, Robson, f****** liven up a bit."

That was absolutely brilliant!

---

sheets on – costing 1d or 2d. The bloke who sold them was about 109 and always had gallons of snot hanging down from his nose! He used to lick his fingers before grabbing hold of one of these programmes, scrunching them up before handing them to you. When you un-creased them and made sure there wasn't anything unsavoury on them, you were lucky if they were still readable!

Doug Barrett: Characters in the crowd? The whole bloody lot. I can't remember anyone in particular but there was the usual crowd of lunatics who frequented the North Bank in the late 60s. The ones who bring to mind my fondest memories were the comedians in the Chicken Run around the time Harry Redknapp started his career on the right wing. Our 'Arry really got some stick but generally gave as good as he got and would often stand chatting with members of the crowd when there was a lull in play – and sometimes even when play was ongoing!

Reuben Gane: I used to buy my peanuts inside the ground from a youth, much the same age as me, who used to toss his bags of Larkins Roasted Peanuts into the crowd. Fans, in turn, would throw their money down to this chap who I learned was called Terry Creasey.

I saw him over many years, long after his peanut ventures ended, and was able to give him some work in the family haulage business. Terry became a good mate and even turned out for my Sunday morning football team, Tow FC.

PLAYER
HARRY REDKNAPP
Born: 2/3/47, Poplar, east London
WHU career: 1965-72
Position: Right-winger
Apps: 175, **Goals:** 8

As my form dipped, so did my popularity at Upton Park. My confidence was draining and for a long spell the punters hated me.

And Upton Park was a difficult place to play if you were a winger. A section of the ground called the Chicken Run was right on top of you, the crowd could almost touch you, and every time you got the ball they expected you to turn the full-back inside out and get a cross in.

I had some banter with the fans, though. There would be a stoppage in the game and I'd turn round and ask the Chicken Run who had won the 3.30 race somewhere!

He always insisted on playing left-half in the No.6 shirt, the same number worn by his great pal, Bobby Moore. Terry also brought along ex-Hammers John Charles and Georgie Fenn to play for me. Frank Lampard would come and watch our games at Central Park, Dagenham and when we switched to Barking Park as our home base, Ernie Gregory would come over to watch us.

Terry's brother, Pat, also turned out for me before he lost his life in a car accident. Patsy also played for West Ham's youth team. He was a really smashing lad. It was a very sad loss.

Paul Walker: Everyone in the Chicken Run was a character back then. Visiting players looked terrified because we were so close to the touchline and I recall Harry Redknapp also looking a little white when he was out on the line, such was the stick he was getting.

Characters who stick in your mind are the peanut seller who walked around the touchline catching money thrown down to him, and hurling bags of nuts back. And the little lads who walked around with the half-time raffle results.

Peter Jones: The main characters that I remember are the guys who used to come round the terraces pushing through the crowds, shouting "roasted peanuts" as they tried to sell their wares.

My future wife was also a character when, in a fiery match, Geoff Hurst was booted up in the air and came down to land heavily on the opposition

Winger Harry Redknapp had banter with the Chicken Run.

182 UPTON PARK MEMORIES

player who had challenged him. I said something to the effect of: 'Wow, fancy having Geoff Hurst on top of you like that!' To which she replied to the amusement of all around us: 'Yes, please!'

PLAYER
KEN BROWN
Born: 16/2/34, Forest Gate, east London
WHU career: 1952-67
Position: Centre-half
Apps: 455, **Goals:** 4

I COULD never do any wrong according to some of our fans. Even if I'd scored three own-goals, it wouldn't have been my fault in their eyes. The supporters were terrific to me.

I was always in the habit of coming out of the tunnel and running straight across the middle of the pitch towards the Chicken Run. I'd kick-about over that side and would hear the loud voice of a certain fella, who would wait until it all went quiet and shout: "Brownie, Brownie."

I'd see the people around him laughing and then I'd look up and see this black man with big, wide eyes smiling at me. He'd say: "All right today, Brownie?" I'd acknowledge him with a little wave ... this used to happen quite regularly.

One day I could hear the fella's voice rise up above the crowd again as he shouted the usual: "Brownie, Brownie". But then he suddenly added: "I'm not on your side today."

So I gave him a puzzled look, shrugged my shoulders and thought, 'what the hell is all that about?'

And then it dawned on me ... we were playing BLACKburn Rovers. I cracked up!

Tony Hoskins: As a youngster there were so many characters around where we stood on the North Bank, and later in the West Stand lower. There are two that I remember so well. The man who sold the peanuts. He was amazing. He would throw them up to whoever asked for them and he just didn't miss, the bag of nuts would land in the hand of the person buying them, wherever they stood.

The other was 'Quasimodo', the programme seller. I will never forget the night he walked between the goal and the wall of the North Bank and tripped over one of the goal supports. He went flying and so did most of his programmes. Legend!

Colin Crowe: I have been to hundreds of games since 1980 but the one I recall is when the programme seller, Jeff, who used to get a bit of stick, was giving some digits to the North Bank when he was going past. Feeling pleased with himself, he managed to trip over a peg behind the goal and fall flat on his face, much to the amusement of the crowd.

Gjermund Holt: There have been so many funny characters in the stands. For a guy from the Norwegian countryside, it was unbelievable to see the first guy who sold me a programme, with 17 earrings, long hair and nearly no teeth. He was smiling, though, and made me feel very welcome!

Chris Ball: A character I remember, but not in the crowd, was the programme seller who went around the outside of the pitch. In the Chicken Run he was affectionately known as 'Ugly'. People would ask for a programme and throw the money at him so that it went over his head and

---

Dan Francis: Having been an employee of the club in the past, I've been lucky to get to know many of the characters behind the scenes at Upton Park – people who may not be widely known to supporters but have played their part over the years in helping to create that 'family' reputation the club were once renowned for.

The likes of Jimmy Frith, quite possibly the nicest man I've ever met, who has been coaching youngsters and supporting the first team staff since Ron Greenwood was manager. Or Pete Williams, a long-serving kit man whose smile would always light up a room, and Jimmy and Betty Webb, a lovely couple who helped run the supporters' club in the 60s and later worked for the club in a number of roles.

Then there were those who helped make the match day experience a memorable one for me as a young fan. When I attended matches with my dad, we would meet up with his mates and I always looked forward to seeing one in particular, a guy named Ken Goodman. It was Ken who educated me on the history of West Ham United - what he doesn't know about the club isn't worth knowing. He also happens to be the funniest bloke in the world, and some of his comments and one-liners about players, referees or opposing fans used to have me in stitches. I still love meeting up with him now whenever I can to discuss West Ham – he's got more hilarious as he's got older!

When I later stood on the North Bank, there were several instantly recognisable supporters who you would often hear before you saw. One guy used to stand near me shouting the same thing every week once the season got to January: 'West Ham, you're like the bloody Christmas decorations!' For some reason, he also had a mild dislike of Steve Potts, and would constantly shout 'Potts and pans!' whenever he was on the ball. Strange the things that stick in your mind.

And who could ever forget the programme seller who would pace around the edge of the pitch before every game? Clad in leather biker gear, he possessed a set of teeth that could eat an apple through a tennis racket.

I recall his name was Jeff, but he was known by various other monikers such as Igor, Nobby, Quasimodo, Catweazle and Ugly. One Saturday afternoon, I was standing at the front of the North Bank, minding my own business, when Igor suddenly pointed at me and flashed that toothy grin, before saying: 'I know who you are ... you're Paul Hilton's son!'

Thinking on my feet, I asked if that would entitle me to a free programme. He said 'no' and just carried on walking, then said the exact same thing to me at the next home game! Despite my denials, he wouldn't have it and insisted he was right. I often wonder what old Igor would be up to these days ...

onto the pitch. He had a colleague who was known to the crowd as 'Lurch'.

I also remember the peanut seller before the game. Whenever I have roasted peanuts now, I can hear him in my head saying 'Peeeeea-nuts.'

Stephen George: Who can ever forget the shouts of 'Peanuts' before (and during) games in the 80s, as a scruffy little fellow with long hair, drainpipe jeans and winkle picker boots weaved his way seamlessly in an out of the packed terraces with his match day fare.

And who could miss Stevie Bacon, an almost omnipresent on the touchline with his Nikon camera flashing away throughout.

David Bernstein: There were a pair of female twins who used to stand in the South Bank near the Chicken Run and wore long scarves full of badges. If a player from the opposing team fouled one of our players particularly badly, Billy Bonds would run over to them for information on the culprit in order to go and dish out his own retribution.

John Reynolds: I cannot recall many characters inside the ground but I do remember vividly an old WWII veteran who used to play a mini accordion in the alley by the flats behind the North Bank. We used to park behind the old Upton Park bus station and walk through to the turnstiles, and at every home game we saw this old boy with one leg missing, on crutches,

Former PE teacher Jimmy Frith, one of the unsung heroes behind the scenes, has coached countless young players in his many years at West Ham.

> **Steve Blowers:** The Percy Dalton peanut man, who walked around the cinder track yelling: "Peanuts, roasted peanuts." Upon hearing a cry from a willing punter, he would skilfully launch his laser-guided, paper bag of monkey nuts high onto the terraces, faultlessly catch the coins coming the other way and then chuck the change back up into the crowd.
>
> One of the great stalwarts of Upton Park . . . or so I thought until I went to White Hart Lane for an away game and saw him doing exactly the same thing at Spurs!

churning out old classic musical tunes. My brother and I always dropped a tanner each into his hat on the ground in front of him, much to his delight.

Steve Perry: Now that I am a season ticket holder, I get to hear a lot of great banter but one that did make me chuckle was from a fan who had just seen one of our players miss a sitter and shouted: "My mum could have scored that." There was silence before he finished with: "And she has been dead for five years."

Mark Harknett: A bloke on the Chicken Run called Paul. Loud, abusive and hilarious. At a game against Burnley in 1974-75 they handed out vouchers to get cup tickets. One appeared on the touchline and the Burnley winger, Leighton James, picked it up. Paul had been abusing James all game and shouted: "Oi, James, give me that fucking voucher." Not surprisingly, James smiled and ripped it up!

Peter Tydeman: We went on a stadium tour which was conducted by a guy called Wally Morris. He had a bubbly Kevin Keegan haircut and you could see he loved the club. He had worked there for a long time and had done some scouting. If you'd cut him he would have bled claret-and-blue.

Gary West: One guy, who stood near us in the Chicken Run, always had the hump with Alan Devonshire. He used to scream abuse at him and 'Devo' would look incredulously into the crowd because he, along with Trevor

> **Tim Crane:** There were many people who loved to stand in the same place on match days. I remember two old girls with scarves full of badges who always stood on the wall behind the goal at the South Bank.
>
> I loved the singing and my all-time favourite is:
>
> *She wore, she wore, she wore a claret ribbon*
> *She wore a claret ribbon in the merry month of May*
> *And when I asked her why she wore that ribbon*
> *She said it's for my West Ham and we're going to Wembley*
> *Wembley! Wembley!*
> *We're the greatest West Ham and we're going to Wembley!*
>
> I would love to dream up a song which was adopted by West Ham fans. I think the following, sang to the same tune as 'He scores when he wants', could have a chance:
>
> *We love the Boleyn. We love the Boleyn*
> *Bobby Moore played there. We love the Boleyn*

> **Pete May:** When I used to stand in the Chicken Run there was a man in a suit whom we nicknamed 'Lino', because he was always shouting "Oi, Lino!" He used to give poor Kevin Keen some terrible stick. And I came across a bald bloke in a leather jacket called Steve Rapport, aka North Bank Norman, shouting: "Remember goals, West Ham? They were big in the 70s!"

Brooking, was on a different planet, skill-wise, to all the other players on the pitch and couldn't understand why this bloke had it in for him. None of us could either but the man was big and drunk, so we always let him get on with it and it was just funny seeing the look on Devo's face.

Gary Bush: Night games under those Upton Park lights were special and it was during my visits to a few of these that I noticed a particular character who, like myself, stood on the North Bank. He was an elderly gent and would appear wearing what can only be best described as a well-loved cardigan. Nothing particularly strange in that but what was a little different from what your average fan on the terrace had was his footwear. He'd got his slippers on! Now that's what I call a local – it was like he'd just left his armchair to nip over to the game.

Kevin Pendegrass: A bloke used to stand near us in the Chicken Run in the 80s and 90s who everyone called 'Lino'. He would give the linesman on our side dog's abuse every time he made a mistake but, to be fair to him, he would always compliment him if he made the right decision or gave it our way.

Mike Corbett: There's a chap that sits in front of our seats, probably in his 60s. He gets so worked up about every decision, and he will often stick his finger up at the ref, although, bizarrely, it's not usually his middle one! It doesn't sound like much but it's very entertaining – he's worth the price of admission alone.

Liam Tyrell: The peanut seller was always a mainstay from my early games in the late 70s and through the 80s. I was fascinated hearing the 'PEANUTS!' cry from afar and watching how he worked his way through the crowd. Funny how I don't seem to remember that many people purchasing peanuts but often walking through a sea of discarded shells.

'Quazi', the programme seller, or 'Igor' as some referred to him, was a familiar sight. I remember one weekday spotting him in Barking and thinking it was odd seeing him without a bundle of programmes under his arm.

> **Neil Humphreys:** I loved a father and son duo who sat beneath me every game. The son, always eager to impress the father, parroted everything he shouted. My favourite one was when the Dad stood up and screamed: "Get off, Kevin Keen, you're f****** useless."
> So the boy stood up and added: "Yeah, Keen, you're f****** useless."
> His Dad clipped him round the ear for swearing and everyone cheered.

Stephanie Moore and Terry Creasey in 2012.

Tony McDonald: I didn't know Terry Creasey as a peanut seller, but rather as the go-to man for tickets for football matches, pop concerts, theatre shows, you name it, he would usually come up trumps. Terry went to the same school, Harold Road in Upton Park, as my dad and 'Uncle' Dennis. He's a true cockney character, claret-and-blue through and through.

He can usually be seen socialising at functions in the company of ex-Hammers who have been his long-time friends, particularly Frank Lampard senior. When Harry Redknapp and Frank worked in tandem as manager and assistant, Terry was a frequent visitor to the Chadwell Heath training ground, where he would sit and have tea and a bit of grub with his old mates, although he was not impressed when Glenn Roeder made him unwelcome there as soon as he succeeded Harry as manager in 2001.

I was on the same table as Terry at the dinner in honour of John Lyall and Ron Greenwood, held at Upton Park in 2008, and recall an amusing scene on what was otherwise a serious occasion. To avoid queuing later for Sir Geoff Hurst's autograph, before starters had even been served, Terry leant across to Geoff, who was seated with fellow West Ham legends at the next table, passed him the menu and nonchalantly asked: "Can you sign that for me, please, Geoff?"

Now Terry had known Geoff since he was a youth team player and didn't expect any problems, so he was visibly taken aback when the World Cup hat-trick hero politely declined, explaining that he would be happy to sign it later.

"Oh, c'mon, Geoff, don't mess abaht, mate . . . " Terry replied, thinking Geoff was joking.

But he was serious. Geoff was enjoying a chat with his former team-mates, including Lampard, Martin Peters, Sir Trevor Brooking and Billy Bonds, and didn't want to be interrupted. He probably also suspected that if he made an exception for Terry, before you knew it many others would descend on him, which could have annoyed the others on his table.

When Terry's persistent polite requests drew a blank, he threw his arms in the air, sat back down at our table and his parting comment was priceless: "OK, Geoff, I'll remember that the next time you want tickets to see Take That . . ."

We all laughed, including Geoff.

Larger-than-life West Ham characters don't come any bigger than Steve Bacon, who had to give up his long-time role as the club's official photographer due to diabetes. In 2015 he had his left leg amputated, although it's a measure of Steve's popularity that some of the biggest names in Hammers' playing history immediately offered to appear at a fund-raising dinner in his honour.

No-one can have photographed more West Ham games than Stevie, who has become quite a celebrity in his own right. He now seems to spend as much time being photographed than he does taking pictures and he will be remembered long after many who have played in the shirt have been forgotten.

There can't be another football photographer in the land who's had his name chanted by thousands of fans ('There only one Stevie Bacon . . .') or been the subject of a fanzine cartoon strip.

His successor as official Hammers 'snapper', 'Arfa' Griffiths, will probably never emulate Steve's legendary status but he, too, is a character with a good sense of humour (which is always handy when covering West Ham). Arthur is such an obliging bloke – to the extent that he allowed me to persuade him to go to the rooftop of flats behind the East Stand one dark, blustery night a few years ago to take the picture that dominates the front cover of this book.

Finally, I must mention my good friend and one of our contributors, Terry Connelly. For more than 60 years Tel has supported Hammers, during which time he accumulated the most extensive and impressive autograph collection you will ever see. I think he stopped, or at least tempered, his pursuit of signatures when players of the modern era could only muster an indecipherable squiggle with their shirt number added for identification purposes.

Through his autograph-collecting, Terry got to know many ex-players who became personal friends of his and would entertain him in their homes. John Lyall and Harry Redknapp, in particular, have both had a lot of time for Terry over the years.

I've seen the many handwritten letters he received from them, thanking him for his interest in their well-being and for remembering their time at the club. He still makes a point of keeping in touch with numerous former Hammers, which means a lot to them. He enjoys a mutual respect with many of our 'old boys'.

Although Terry is now retired, it was not so long ago that the London catering company he worked for, Russell Hume, supplied West Ham with meat. As the club's point of contact, he would regularly meet the head chef and catering management to discuss their requirements.

Despite remaining a die-hard supporter, Terry doesn't wear claret-and-blue

Happy snappers Steve Bacon and 'Arfa' Griffiths in 2010. Looks like Steve is signing another autograph!

blinkers and, at times, has been vitriolic in his condemnation of certain managers whom he felt weren't paying enough attention to the ethos laid down by Greenwood and Lyall. I'll never forget those dire days, during Alan Pardew's lowest moments as manager, struggling to make it out of the Championship, when the ground would fall silent during a break in play. Terry would rise from his padded seat in the executive section of the West Stand, within earshot of the dug-out, to deliver those familiar words in a loud, booming voice: "Pardew, Pardew . . . out, out, out!"

West Ham United needs characters like Terry Connelly . . . and Tony Hogg.

It was through our mutual friend, 'Hoggy', that I got to know Terry Connelly. Hoggy wrote occasional pieces for *Hammers News* and in the early 90s we became work colleagues as well as good mates, when he was appointed as our advertising sales manager. He excelled in the role.

He was so good at his job that when he offered to sell copies of our retro EX magazine at home games, we'd have been silly to have turned him down. If you've frequented any of the pubs in the vicinity of Upton Park in the past 13 years you couldn't have failed to have come across Hoggy meandering through the bars, or in the streets around the ground.

Tony Hogg, former Hammer Eddie Bovington and Terry Connelly.

ALF GARNETT: "Yer actual West Ham"

TELEVISION characters and so-called West Ham fans didn't come any louder or larger-than-life than Alf Garnett, star of the long-running BBC sitcom, *Till Death Us Do Part*.

Played by actor Warren Mitchell, Alf was probably the most famous - or should that be infamous? - Hammers fan on TV in those far off days before political correctness.

Created by Johnny Speight, *Till Death Us Do Part* ran on BBC1 from 1965 until 1975. It centred on the East End Garnett family, led by Alf, a reactionary working-class man who held racist and anti-socialist views. His long-suffering wife, "silly moo" Else, was played by Dandy Nichols and his daughter, Rita, by Una Stubbs. Rita's husband, Mike Rawlins (Anthony Booth), was a socialist layabout and a Liverpool fan – a "long-haired scouse git", according to his father-in-law.

Alf's passion for West Ham was highlighted in numerous episodes that featured him wearing a claret-and-blue scarf to the pub and West Ham matches. Lines in his script referred by name to "yer actual Bobby Moore", Geoff Hurst, Martin Peters and Ron Greenwood.

The episode titled 'A Wapping Mythology' (series 2, episode 7), broadcast on February 6, 1967 but since wiped by BBC archivists, featured Hammers Peter Brabrook, Johnny Byrne, Ken Brown, along with Moore, Hurst and Peters. The plot saw Alf - the "four-eyed old git" - win two free tickets to see them play against Liverpool at Anfield. He blamed Hammers' defeat on Labour leader Harold Wilson for "having referees in his pocket".

Some scenes from the TV series, plus a film adaptation of the same name released in 1969, were recorded in and around the Boleyn Ground. Bobby Moore, George Best and Mooro's black actor friend, Kenny Lynch, appeared in a scene shot at the Black Lion pub, Plaistow.

In another scene from the early 70s, Alf was filmed in the directors' box at Upton Park, apparently watching the home game against Manchester United in which Clyde Best – one of the first black Hammers – featured prominently.

Action sequences from the home game v Stoke City in 1971 were used in the episode in which Alf takes his baby grandson to the match. As Alf blurted out the awful words: "Oi, you c****, pass it!" viewers saw a clip of Clyde Best slamming a shot against the post.

Garnett's strong allegiance to West Ham continued when the BBC produced a sequel, *In Sickness and in Health*, from 1985 to 1992. In one episode, Alf feigns disability to gain access to the disabled enclosure at Old Trafford for a better view of the 1985 FA Cup tie which Man United won 4-2.

Alf was known to make derogatory remarks about "the Jews up at Spurs". This was a 'playful touch' by Speight, knowing that in real life Mitchell was both Jewish and a Spurs supporter.

In interviews, Speight explained he had originally based Alf on his father, an East End docker who was staunchly reactionary and held "unenlightened" attitudes toward black people. Speight made clear that he regretted his father held such attitudes – beliefs Speight regarded as reprehensible. Speight saw the show as a way of ridiculing such views and dealing with his complex feelings about his father.

The house seen in the opening and closing titles to the 60s episodes was located on Garnet Street in Wapping (from where Speight took the Garnett family name) but this terrace was demolished in the 80s.

To quote the Wikipedia website: *"Till Death Us Do Part* became an instant hit because, although a comedy, in the context of its time it did deal with aspects of working class life comparatively realistically. It addressed racial and political issues at a difficult time in British society. The attitude of those who made the programme was that Alf's views were so clearly unacceptable that they were risible but some considered the series uncomfortable and disturbing.

"Some were oblivious to the fact that Johnny Speight was satirising racist attitudes. Ironically, many who held similar opinions to the character enjoyed the show, perhaps missing the point that Alf's opinions were considered offensive and that they were being ridiculed.

Alf Garnett stirring up the crowd in the West Stand during the 60s.

"Mitchell imbued the character of Alf Garnett with an earthy charm that served to humanise Alf and make him likeable. According to interviews he gave, the fact that some viewers overlooked Alf's views and regarded him as a rough diamond disappointed Speight.

"The show captured a key feature of Britain in the 60s – the widening generation gap. Alf represented the old guard, the traditional and conservative attitudes of the older generation. Alf's battles with his left-wing son-in-law were not just ideological but generational and cultural. His son-in-law and daughter represented the younger generation. They supported the aspects of the new era such as relaxed sexual morals, fashions, music, etc. The same things were anathema to Alf – and indicative of everything that was wrong with the younger generation and the liberal attitudes they embraced.

"Alf was an admirer of Enoch Powell, a right-wing Conservative politician known particularly for strong opposition to the immigration of non-white races into the UK."

Mitchell played the Garnett character on stage and television up until 1998, when writer Johnny Speight died.

And on November 14, 2015, Warren Mitchell himself died at the age of 89. Episodes of *Till Death Us Do Part* and *In Sickness and in Health* can still be viewed online at www.youtube.com

Warren Mitchell (centre) and fellow actors filming a scene for *In Sickness and in Health* from the Boleyn Ground in the 80s.

Robert Banks: There was a guy who used to sit behind me in the Bobby Moore lower when I had a season ticket there. He had a very dry sense of humour and would make up fantastic nicknames for the players that no-one else used. He called Craig Forrest 'Superglue'.

The humour in the crowd is one of the main reasons I love the place. I remember in the early 80s there was a hold-up in the game for an injury and someone shouted: "Don't just stand there West Ham – practice!"

Another character was a guy whom I first noticed at Highbury one day. When everyone was taunting the Gooners with 'One Trevor Brooking...' he stood up and headed an imaginary ball. I later got to know Mick, a true Hammer.

Jack McDonald: When the PA announcer used to say: "Mr Moon is now in the stadium" (code to stadium staff for a possible security alert somewhere inside the ground), there was a bloke who would always respond by shouting: "Alfie's here!" in a reference to the *Eastenders* character Alfie Moon. When the announcement was followed minutes later by "Mr Moon has now left the stadium", the same bloke would reply: "I don't blame him!"

I should also mention my grandad, Terry. When he had a season ticket with us, he used to get frustrated with the people in front of him, who kept standing up every time West Ham had the ball anywhere near the opposition penalty area. He used to shout: "Anyone wanna buy a seat?"

He always carried his transistor radio with him and would listen to BBC Radio 5 Live score updates through an earpiece to keep tabs on how the teams he had put bets on were doing. He would occasionally blurt out unwelcome things such as "Chelsea . . . 1-0 . . . Lampard", much to the annoyance of fans around us, who certainly didn't want any reminders of how Chelsea had raided our club and taken Lampard, Joe Cole and Glen Johnson from us. "Millwall are winning" was another announcement that, strangely, never went down too well either!

Although West Ham and Leyton Orient, the two main clubs he played for longest, are his teams, I don't think he realised quite how loud his regular verbal score updates were with his earplugs in, or to what extent the news he was imparting might offend Hammers fans. But on some occasions, usually when West Ham were losing or playing badly, people would turn round to him and shout: "We don't give a f***, mate!"

Peter Thorne: Almost too many to recount but mainly deriding from fan chants or spontaneous terrace humour. Most would come under the heading of 'You Should Have Been There'. "Oi, Gould! – you couldn't trap a bag of cement."

Even so, Rodney Marsh bearing his arse when the North Bank fans chanted 'We all hate Marsh and Marsh and Marsh', to the tune of the Dambusters march, was very funny. When it got to the rousing last line 'We all f****** hate Marsh', Rodney himself applauded and laughed - then scored the winner!

DARKEST DAYS

WHEN reflecting on the Boleyn Ground years, let's not pretend that Hammers' home ground as always been a family-friendly environment where men, women and children could watch a game in safety without the threat of being engulfed by violence on the terraces.

Like every other club, West Ham United has suffered its share of crowd disturbances of varying seriousness over the past 50-plus years. Terry Roper recalls when the scourge of hooliganism first reared its ugly head at Upton Park . . .

LARGE scale football hooliganism in Britain has thankfully been eradicated. Apart from a few isolated incidents, stadiums have largely been a thug-free, family-friendly environment since the Taylor Report into the 1989 disaster at Sheffield Wednesday's Hillsborough ground which paved the way for all-seater stadia, CCTV surveillance, improved stewarding and police vilgilance to further deter the mindless minority. It has to be said, too, that wallet-busting admission prices have also kept away an unruly element.

When we reflect on the past, there is a shocking realisation that hooliganism affected football in this country more than 50 years ago. In the very darkest days, it dragged the game into the gutter and football was at its lowest ebb – a stinking pariah of our society. At times, the degree of violence among opposition fans on the packed and urine-soaked terraces was simply horrifying, as we impotently watched the terrible events unfolding before our very eyes.

In a sense, football hooliganism, as we know it, was first 'conceived' in the early 60s and although it had relatively meagre beginnings, it quickly gathered momentum and spread like wildfire throughout the ensuing decades. It left behind mayhem, carnage and, occasionally, death in its frightening wake.

For the more elderly among us, it is easy to pinpoint when hooliganism first reared its ugly head at Upton Park. The date was Saturday, September 16, 1961 and the occasion was a first division match between West Ham United and Chelsea.

Under their new manager, Ron Greenwood, West Ham displayed all their very best attributes from the very first minute of this London derby in the Upton Park sunshine. Hammers were quickly into their stride, overwhelming the opposition, setting a high tempo and racing to a two-goal lead inside 25 minutes, thanks to strikes from John Dick and Malcolm Musgrove.

Throughout the first-half, Hammers' captain and Welsh international midfield maestro, Phil Woosnam, was simply magnificent. His passes zipped across the turf. He pointed; he urged; he demanded the ball; he ran the game from the middle of the pitch. To watch him in that form was to see a demonstration of what the experts of that period had drooled about his abilities for so long. The vision, the precision, the way he knew what he was going to do with the ball long before he received it; he delivered a master-class for any aspirant midfielder.

Clearly, Chelsea also thought that Woosnam was the major factor in their ongoing demise that afternoon. During the half-time break and still 2-0 down, Chelsea set out their stall accordingly for the second period. Within their ranks, Blues (or The Pensioners as they were nicknamed back then) had a Scottish international midfield dynamo called Tommy Docherty who, admittedly, was in the twilight of his career, but still possessed a ferocious tackle and was not afraid to use it when the occasion arose.

Early in the second-half, the combative Docherty finally caught him with a tackle that was so late, it would not have gone amiss in the following week's fixture list. As a result, Woosnam crashed to the turf, clutching his knee and, clearly, in considerable pain.

Unprecedented scenes from September 1961, which show Hammers' Malcolm Musgrove and Ken Brown trying to talk sense to a couple of irate fans who had invaded the pitch during the Chelsea game. Geoff Hurst, Tony Scott and Joe Kirkup are the others in view, while in the background members of the St. John's Ambulance Brigade have loaded injured keeper Lawrie Leslie onto the stretcher.

After several minutes of on-the-pitch treatment from Hammers' physiotherapist Bill Jenkins, the distressed Woosnam was carried from the pitch to the dressing-room. It should be remembered that the use of substitutes in Football League matches was still four years away and, hence, West Ham were reduced to 10 men.

These were also the days when players had to seemingly commit first degree murder before they were disciplined on the field of play and Docherty's only punishment for his appalling challenge was to receive a 'finger-wagging' type telling-off from referee Les Hames.

The game restarted amidst a chorus of booing and whenever the errant Docherty was in possession, the cries of derision grew to a crescendo. At the same time, the game itself was beginning to turn ill-tempered which seemed to reflect the antagonism that was starting to surface from within certain sections of the crowd. Things were, indeed, turning nasty and a mightily unpleasant atmosphere was suddenly prevailing that had not previously been experienced by Upton Park and its patrons.

Nevertheless, although West Ham had been reduced to 10 men, it says much for their superiority that Chelsea could not force their way back into the game.

However, with 30 minutes remaining, an explosive incident occurred which triggered a chain of events that would catapult this particular football match onto the front pages of every national newspaper.

A sporadic Chelsea attack saw a low cross fired into West Ham's penalty-area, which their Scottish international goalkeeper Lawrie Leslie claimed with ease. At that precise moment, Chelsea's young striker Bobby Tambling came racing in with his left boot raised and studs showing in a vain and desperately late attempt to make contact with the ball.

The momentum of Tambling's futile run and subsequent lunge propelled him through the air and his boot crashed into Leslie's unprotected face.

Hammers' keeper fell backwards, pole-axed, and as the ball ran loose, Chelsea's Barry Bridges rifled it home into the unguarded net from 10 yards. Incredibly, the referee immediately pointed to the centre-circle, thus indicating that the goal had been allowed to stand.

Hames' decision triggered a furious eruption of anger among Hammers' outraged fans, particularly those at the South Bank end.

It was there that the stricken Leslie lay unconscious on the Upton Park pitch with his arms spread-eagled in the crucifix position and blood beginning to seep from a horrific gash on his forehead. Geoff Hurst was the first to reach him, bending over his prostrate team-mate before frantically signalling to the touch-line for urgent medical attention.

The whole of Upton Park began to vibrate as the deafening sound of booing and cries of derision reverberated from all areas of the packed ground. Suddenly, an even greater roar – this time, one of incredulity – rose up as a shirt-sleeved fan clambered over the low perimeter wall from the South Bank and started running menacingly towards the referee. A second fan quickly followed him onto the pitch and, suddenly, a dozen or so more appeared – each with the apparent intention of attacking the referee or, at least, seeking retribution against the other perceived 'villains' of the afternoon, namely Tommy Docherty and Bobby Tambling.

Several policemen quickly entered the playing area in hot pursuit of the transgressors but the latter were already being met with the restraining hands of a number of West Ham players, most notably Ken Brown, Malcolm Musgrove and Alan Sealey. Punches were thrown by several of the pitch invaders as they tried, in vain, to target the referee and certain

Chelsea players but, by now, the police were also in the thick of the action.

The most aggressive of the hooligans were grappled to the ground and held there until sanity prevailed, when they were all frogmarched away down the players' tunnel with their arms held excruciatingly behind their backs in vice-like grips by the law. The rest were treated in a similar fashion, although they appeared to accept their fate more readily and their acts of defiance towards the police were not as great as some of their raging counterparts.

The modern perception of football hooligans is one of shaven heads, tattooed arms and bulging beer guts (and that's just the women in some parts of the country) but the reality was considerably different on that day at Upton Park in 1961. Naturally, the main protagonists were young, loutish hot-heads but one 'hooligan' was actually a middle-aged man incongruously wearing a suit with collar and tie, while another was a man of similar age in a jacket and flat-cap.

How times and fashions have changed at football matches in the course of half-a-century.

Nevertheless, irrespective of the dress-code, this was a serious and potentially dangerous situation. In preceding years, English fans had scoffed at occasional newspaper pictures and reports denoting riots and pitch invasions at football grounds in far off places, such as South America. In truth, it was a pious attitude because the general consensus of opinion was that such an occurrence could not possibly happen here.

Admittedly, the events at Upton Park did not constitute a full-blown riot but the fact remains that a considerable number of fans – all of them with seriously aggressive intent towards the referee and opposition players – had invaded the playing area during a game in the top sphere of English football. It was an unprecedented event and it sent shockwaves throughout the game.

For the record, the pitch invasion lasted just five minutes from start to finish before the last of the hooligans disappeared from view down the tunnel 'escorted' by the police.

The abiding memory thereafter was the incongruous sight of Alan Sealey picking up several police officers' helmets from the Upton Park pitch, since they had become dislodged and fallen to the ground in the fracas.

Meanwhile, Leslie had already been carried from the field on a stretcher and 20-year-old Bobby Moore was pulling on the green jersey and preparing himself to take over as Hammers' emergency goalkeeper.

An ambulance rushed Leslie to the London Hospital in Whitechapel, where he later recovered consciousness and had 18 stitches inserted in the head wound.

Not surprisingly, the shocking events made headline news the following day. with several of the newspapers jointly labelling it 'The Battle of Upton Park' in their banner headlines. It even prompted one of the papers to demand the introduction of fences or moats around pitches to avoid repetitions at other grounds in the future. It did not make good reading for those of us with claret-and-blue blood coursing through our veins.

Fortunately, the only punishment meted out was when West Ham later received a written warning from the FA about the future conduct of their fans. No further action was taken. Nevertheless, it was a close call and the club was fortunate to escape so lightly.

There is no doubt that if such an incident had occurred at Upton Park in later years, when hooliganism had taken its vice-like grip on the game, the repercussions would have been considerably greater.

ALTHOUGH the Chelsea game in September 1961 marked the start of crowd trouble at Upton Park, numerous other outbreaks of violence caused the club to be embroiled in unwanted bad publicity it was often powerless to quell. Here we look back at some of the worst 'trouble spots' . . .

September 9, 1966
West Ham United 1 Liverpool 1

Play was held up for several minutes in the second-half so that broken glass thrown by Liverpool fans could be swept from the goalmouth. In his match report for the *Newham Recorder*, Terry Hopley wrote: "The disgraceful behaviour of a bunch of Liverpool louts (standing in the North Bank) played a major part in preventing West Ham picking up their first win of the season. For after the game had been held up while fragments of a smashed brandy glass were removed from the goal area Hammers suddenly lost their iron grip they had held for three quarters of the game. And it was during the time added on for the hold up that Liverpool broke away to snatch a last-gasp equaliser.

"These so-called soccer supporters had already riled the 35,000 Cockney crowd by chanting: 'If you want a fight so do we' – and throwing missiles including an empty whisky bottle and a coca-cola tin at Jim Standen.

"Referee David Corbett had to ask for police support behind the West Ham players' goal after players had assisted in clearing fragments of glass from the penalty spot."

The worst excesses of hooliganism at Upton Park in the 60s and 70s inevitably involved Manchester United fans, bolstered by a large contingent of London-based followers known as the 'Cockney Reds'. The swashbuckling United team of the 60s, starring George Best, Bobby Charlton and Denis Law, regularly attracted the biggest away support and capacity crowds wherever they played.

May 6, 1967
West Ham United 1 Manchester United 6

With this emphatic victory Matt Busby's team clinched the league championship in style but their fans among a crowd of 38,424 – a post-war record – marred what should have been a joyous occasion. The *Newham Recorder's* Lawrie Hacker wrote: "Could the louts on the North Bank who were busy throwing broken bottles really have appreciated the magic and mastery of this Manchester side? They came to Upton Park needing just one point to clinch their fifth first division championship since the war."

West Ham's programme editor, Jack Helliar, was an old school fellow never prone to hyperbole, so if a reference to crowd trouble appeared in his editorial comment, you can assume the club were sufficiently disturbed by what had gone on. For the programme immediately following the United game (v Man City, 13/5/67), Jack referred to a post-match pitch invasion by jubilant visiting fans who called for the re-appearance of Busby and his players in the main stand. Jack wrote: "The greater majority of those who demonstrated their fanaticism were 'all good lads' but it is difficult to put on paper opinions of the minority who made this an excuse for other outbursts that are certainly not representative of true soccer 'fans'.

"We are very well aware that Upton Park has 'followed the trend' by attracting an unruly element in the past couple of years, and it is sad to think that this appears to be one of 'the penalties of success'; but unfortunately it went much further than normal on this occasion, and the names on the hospital casualty-list gave sufficient evidence that there were no distinctions between friend or foe as far as home addresses or sex were concerned; certainly some innocent bystanders were unwilling victims, and this might have applied to some of the players had some of the missiles found their target."

There were echoes here of the glass-throwing incident in the Liverpool game some two years earlier. Clearly, crowd trouble was on the increase as the 60s evolved, mirroring the growing mood of contemporary youthful rebellion. With its tribalism, football was a natural outlet for pent up aggression among youngsters on the terraces.

Jack went on: "In the latter respect we can be pretty sure that it was not a Hammers' fan who threw a bottle into the goalmouth we were defending in the first-half and the youngsters who left our goalposts out of shape were certainly not wearing claret-and-blue!"

Jack made the point that anarchy and vandalism were not confined to football grounds when he added:

"Similarly, the police could vouch for the destinations of those who caused additional disturbances en route to home. Nevertheless, there were many Londoners among those who have already appeared in court as a result of the melee, and obviously some of these have regularly attended the Boleyn Ground this season."

September 2, 1967
West Ham United 1 Manchester United 3

The expressive 'summer of love' and flower-power hippy movement in

America had done nothing to bring peace and harmony to English football grounds. Four months on from Manchester United's previous visit to Upton Park, this early season encounter brought another series of crowd disturbances and arrests.

Whether West Ham's hierarchy were attempting to play down the latest trouble at the Boleyn Ground is not known but there was scant mention of it in the programme that followed United's visit, other than a few lines tucked away at the back to record punishment meted out to troublemakers.

It read: "As a result of police action against offenders at our match v Manchester United on September 2, the following fines were imposed by local magistrates: One of £28 for threatening behaviour and assaulting a policeman. Four of £10 each for insulting behaviour.

"The police took a firm line at our last home game, and in addition to those charged a considerable number were also ejected from the ground."

By the mid-70s, trouble inside and outside football grounds the length and breadth of the country has escalated out of control. The terraces became a breeding ground for gangs of thugs who went to matches intent on causing mayhem and fighting with opposition fans.

It has to be said that West Ham had its own groups of hooligans, most infamously the feared Inter-City Firm (ICF), who became more sophisticated in their approach. Showdowns with rivals fans were pre-planned, often some distance from the football ground, before battles were won and lost and 'calling cards' were left.

Members of the notorious ICF group, including its most well-known former leader, Cass Pennant, went on to become successful and respectable businessmen – celebrities in some cases – who have in more recent times attracted a cult following through their association with films such as *Green Street* and books of the hooligan genre. Some former ICF members are now grandfathers and their once violent activities, that brought fear to the streets, shopping centres and football grounds at the height of hooliganism in the 70s and 80s, have passed into football folklore.

By the end of the 60s, the club decided to try and confine ticketless away fans to the South Bank, although with little or no segregation in place and very few advance tickets sales, fans without season tickets for the seated areas would rock up at the turnstiles, pay their admission money, go in and more or less stand wherever they liked.

While West Ham's most vocal supporters tended to stand on the North Bank, where most chants and songs emanated from in the early post-Chicken Run days, a group of home fans more intent on seeing off their unwelcome visitors would join forces at the back of the South Bank, where isolated scuffles and crowd surges were usually dealt with fairly quickly by police.

But when Manchester United were in town, the sense of menace in the air always went up a few notches and violence was very much on the agenda . . .

> **West Ham United Football Co., Ltd.**
> BOLEYN GROUND, GREEN STREET, LONDON, E.13
>
> AN APPEAL BY THE MANAGEMENT TO A VERY, VERY SMALL SECTION OF OUR CROWD
>
> ## WHAT DO YOU THINK YOU ARE DOING?
>
> Following our F.A. Cup win in 1964, we received a letter from British Rail commending us for having the best-behaved supporters of any club in the country. During the next two seasons we travelled extensively in Europe with a large following of supporters. Once again, wherever we went we were told how much everyone was admired for their excellent conduct. In fact, at home and abroad, "West Ham United" had built up a solid reputation for sportsmanship and good behaviour—one they thoroughly deserved.
>
> **But what is happening now?**
>
> This season a particularly nasty lot of young hooligans have suddenly appeared who are doing their best, and with some success, to completely ruin our good name. What have they been up to? These are just a few incidents. On the way home from Manchester they "called in" at Luton and ran amok, causing considerable damage and bringing a pile of letters to the club from people who had suffered from their actions. At Norwich they invaded the pitch, causing a lot of trouble to the home club. On the way home from Aston Villa they kicked in a plate-glass door of a shop at the Newport Pagnell service station, with the intention of helping themselves because it was closed. After the match at Tottenham on the 7th February they rampaged through the streets, smashing windows, and in one street damaged a car, clearly marked "DOCTOR" and parked at his surgery, rendering it unfit to drive! The Doctor's patients in his Clinic and old people living nearby were scared out of their lives.
>
> **It is bad enough to behave like that at all, but to do it wearing the colours of this Club makes it even worse as far as we are concerned.**
>
> The definition in the dictionary of the word "Support" is "to uphold" and "to represent in acting." Neither of these you do, therefore you are not supporters. In fact you are a disgrace to the Club, a disgrace to the team, and a disgrace to yourselves, and we can do without you.
>
> So unless you change your ways and cut out the rough stuff, our message is loud and clear . . .
>
> **"GET OUT AND STAY OUT"**

After a spate of incidents during the 1975-76 season, the club published this appeal notice in its programme.

A female fan is escorted out of the Boleyn Ground during trouble at the Manchester United game in September 1967.

October 25, 1975
West Ham United 2 Manchester United 1

It should have been a mouth-watering occasion. John Lyall's third-placed Hammers against Tommy Docherty's table-toppers, in front of 38,528 – the biggest of the season at Upton Park. Alas, inevitably, most of the press coverage focused upon the unsavoury scenes . . . crowd surges, fans pilling onto the playing area which caused a near 20-minute stoppage early in the second-half.

It got a bit spicy on the field, too, where Hammers' match-winner Bobby Gould scrapped with Reds' skipper Martin Buchan after Gould robustly challenged United keeper Alex Stepney for a loose ball.

In fairness, most of those who clambered over the low perimeter wall at the South Bank end and onto the pitch did so simply to avoid being hurt in the crush on the terraces. Even so, some of the injured had to be carried away on stretchers.

It didn't look good and it was not difficult to see why the tabloids took the more sensationalist angle. From reports originally filed by a UK press agency, one Australian newspaper even quoted someone claiming to be the chairman of the Man Utd Supporters' Club, who branded West Ham fans as "evil".

On this occasion, West Ham launched a counter-offensive, using the next home programme to submit a lengthy defence of precautions taken to avoid trouble at the United game. With clubs footing the bill for policing, they pointed out that 500 police were on duty at the game and were "also to keep down the aggro to a moderate level outside the ground".

They pointed out that they restricted capacity, stating: "Although the capacity of our South Bank is 9,500, only 7,874 were admitted there that afternoon. All 13 turnstiles were closed by 2.30pm (prior to the 3.00pm kick-off)."

West Ham defended their decision not to make the match all-ticket, on the basis that they still wouldn't have been able to guarantee segregation of supporters because many visiting fans were based in the south and could have bought tickets posing as home fans.

They added: "The sale of intoxicating liquor on the ground was suspended for the day and local publicans did not open their premises until 7.00pm.

"Much was made of the opening of an exit gate but this was quickly checked by police and only a few dozen gained illegal entry (not hundreds or thousands, as erroneously reported).

"There had been a few clashes of rival mobs earlier on but the main cause of the fracas was the pushing-forward of those at the back of the South Bank.

"Sensibly enough those in the front who were in danger moved on to the pitch."

Without photographic evidence or access to old footage on the Internet, supporters who only began attending games in the Premier League era would probably not believe that fans used to be herded like cattle onto crowded – sometimes over-crowded – terraces surrounded by metal railings that kept them caged in like animals.

Unlike many other grounds in the late 70s and early 80s, including Manchester United's Old Trafford, Liverpool's Anfield and the London grounds of Tottenham, Chelsea, Millwall (of course) and Leyton Orient, West Ham never did erect fencing to prevent fans from entering the playing area. (Chelsea chairman Ken Bates even went so far as to suggest the introduction of electric fences at Stamford Bridge – and he was probably deadly serious!)

For years, the *Hammer* programme carried notices urging fans to behave and 'keep fences away from Upton Park', an appeal often verbally reinforced by announcer Bill Remfry, too.

Some 14 years before the Sheffield tragedy that changed the face of crowd safety conditions forever, Hammers continued their response to media criticism of their handling of the 1975 Manchester United game by pointing out: "Had there been a larger space available between the wall and the goal-line this would have created fewer problems but one can well envisage what might have occurred had there been an un-climbable fence in that area."

In the aftermath of Hillsborough, fences at football grounds throughout Britain were taken down.

Winter of discontent

How fans hammered the bond

NOWHERE was the effect of the far reaching Taylor Report that followed Hillsborough felt more acutely than at West Ham.

The decision, agreed by the board of directors in 1991, to expect Hammers' loyal supporters to fund most of the cost of their projected £15.5m stadium improvements provoked unprecedented anger on the Upton Park terraces and drove an irreversible wedge between the club and many of its loyal supporters who felt they were being taken for mugs.

West Ham's plan was to sell 19,301 debenture bonds costing between £500 and £975, which would account for three-quarters of the capacity of a new-look, all-seater stadium – the Football Licensing Authority's requirement of all first and second division clubs by the start of the 1994-95 season.

The bonds would mainly entitle the holder the *right* to buy a season ticket – although, crucially, not actually to buy one – for a minimum of 50 years and have priority call on tickets for away matches and cup ties.

Timing is often key in such matters. As it happens, on the day the Hammers Bond Company scheme was launched, at the home game v Liverpool on November 17, West Ham fans could hardly have felt much happier. Their team had just beaten Arsenal 1-0 at Highbury and arch rivals Spurs 2-1 in their previous home match.

Billy Bonds' summer signing from Brighton, striker Mike Small, was in the form of his life, scoring 13 times in the first 18 league and cup matches of the season.

After achieving promotion the previous May, there was genuine hope that after a slow start (only one win in their first eight first division games), Hammers could re-establish themselves in the top flight.

But then the Bond dropped. And the fall-out damage was devastating, on and off the field.

Hammers failed to win another game in the two months following the expensive bond launch. Small's golden touch deserted him, never to return, and the side were soon fighting a relegation battle they were ultimately destined to lose.

So, faced with a team rapidly drained of confidence and in freefall, with no money to fund new signings (on the contrary, 'Bonzo' was told he would have to sell his best assets before he could buy), the mood on the terraces turned ugly.

Angry fans directed most of their venom at the six-man board made up of chairman Martin Cearns, his father, Len (whom he had succeeded in February 1990), his uncle Will Cearns, Charles Warner, Peter Storrie (MD and widely viewed as the official club mouthpiece) and recent newcomer Terence Brown. Apart from being appalled by what they perceived as the board's disdain, fans argued that if they were expected to finance the ground improvements, then they should at least be able to purchase shares in the football club, not pay out of their own pocket to boost the share value of the existing stakeholders' on the board.

West Ham attempted to offer its customers a variation on a similar bond debenture previously unveiled at Arsenal and Glasgow Rangers. Long-time supporter Terry Connelly spoke for the majority of irate fans when he pointed out in an interview with the *Evening Standard's* Ken Dyer: "The scheme is ill-conceived from start to finish. Where else are you asked for a non-returnable loan? It seems to me, we are being asked by the board to invest in their future."

Although there was no denying the team – which would finished rock bottom 22nd, winning just six home games out of 21 – wasn't good enough, the toxic atmosphere pervading Upton Park throughout that bleak winter of 1991-92 only further affected performances and results.

Bonds, appointed 18 months before the bond fiasco, publically distanced himself from the club's audacious proposals, while club captain Julian Dicks openly opposed it, which only served to galvanise supporters in their sustained campaign against what they considered to be an outrageous, ill-conceived, con.

It may be difficult for those who became fans later in the Premier League era to imagine the level of vitriol and hostility unleashed from the terraces in those dark days when a determined group of supporters still had a voice that was heard.

Several matches were disrupted by protestors who

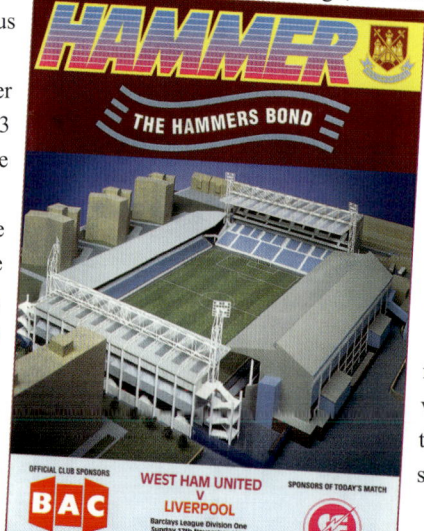

took to the pitch to vent their feelings. Surprisingly, the club escaped punishment by way of a points deduction (although they were relegated anyway in May 1992, deferring a loss of points the following campaign could have seriously damaged promotion hopes).

Some of the worst demonstrators crossed the line – the verbal abuse endured by former chairman Len Cearns was unacceptable – but thousands more presented a united front in their campaign to crush the bond.

A protest group called the Hammers' Independent Supporters' Association (HISA) was set up to co-ordinate a more structured battle plan. In conjunction with *Fortune's Always Hiding* fanzine, they produced thousands of A4-size red cards with the word 'RESIGN' printed in bold, black letters that were held up in the faces of the beleaguered board members at the home game v Sheffield United (21/12/91).

The board attempted to placate fans by offering a season ticket at a discount of £100 per season for anyone who bought a bond but it made little or no difference. HISA released thousands of red balloons in a peaceful protest at the home game against Everton on February 29 but the afternoon turned sour again.

The fact that fanzines were then at the height of their hard-hitting powers (see p263) also helped to get across the unequivocal message that West Ham fans were having none of it.

Looking through our newspaper archives, we present extracts of how the press covered that horrible winter of discontent in E13 . . .

January 1, 1992
West Ham United 1 Leeds United 3

Harry Harris (Daily Mirror): Life is tougher at the other end of the table as the Hammers embark on a New Year deep in crisis. 'What a load of rubbish' and 'Sack the board' echoed round the ground near the end.

January 4, 1992
West Ham United 1 Farnborough Town 1 (FAC 3)

Trevor Smith (Newham Recorder): The growing bitterness was highlighted after Saturday's FA Cup draw with non-league Farnborough, when hundreds of supporters stage a mass sit-in on the Upton Park centre circle. Hammers' managing director Peter Storrie invited a six-strong deputation from the demonstrators to talk with him.

January 11, 1992
West Ham United 1 Wimbledon 1

Lee Clayton (The Sun): There were more West Ham fans on the pitch on Saturday than Wimbledon get on the terraces. West Ham's average home league attendance this season is 22,183. More than 250,000 fans have watched them at Upton Park, raking in gate receipts of around £3million. Yet they are in turmoil – with no money to spend and every player for sale. Why?

Roy Collins (Sunday Telegraph): West Ham fans seemed to have only the after-match demo to look forward to, which went ahead despite the late equaliser, despite a meeting between fans and directors before the match and despite a three-page defence of the bonds scheme in the programme.

Unattributed: Angry supporters got as far as the directors' box, where manager Billy Bonds was called on to make an abortive plea for calm and commonsense.

January 14, 1992
West Ham United 1 Farnborough Town 0 (FAC 3R)

Before the replay, West Ham United issue A4 leaflets at the ground, which stated:

As West Ham supporters who want the best for the club, let us please be constructive.

Regrettably, last weekend's demonstration was not as 'peaceful' as many of the reports indicated. Seats were damaged, parts of the pitch are a mess (as you will see tonight) and some of the club stewards were injured. The safety of many supporters was jeopardised.

No-one doubts that those of you who have demonstrated have the club's interest at heart, but you must realise that further protests would be counter-productive.

In the last few weeks we have had a number of meetings with supporters, all of which were constructive and at which progress was made. The most recent was with those who emerged

196 UPTON PARK MEMORIES

after the first Farnborough Town match.

A number of ideas relating to the Hammers Bond Scheme have been put forward but the club now needs some time to consider these with their advisors. We will then communicate further with you.

We now have your views and opinions – give discussions a chance.

Home FA Cup ties v Wrexham and Sunderland, as well as the league match v Oldham Athletic passed off without crowd trouble but the worst was still to come. The visit of Everton, including ex-Hammers Tony Cottee and Mark Ward, was arguably the blackest day in West Ham United's history.

February 29, 1992
West Ham United 0 Everton 2

Trevor Smith (Newham Recorder): The day began with the nation-wide

Fans made paper planes out of the club's leaflet and threw them onto the pitch in the Farnborough replay.

PLAYER
JULIAN DICKS
Born: 8/8/68, Bristol
WHU career: 1988-93 & 1994-99
Position: Left-back
Apps: 326, Goals: 65

(Speaking immediately after the Everton game on 29/2/92):

I AGREE with what they are doing, even if I don't agree with the way they are doing it. Their actions could cost us points. But it's their way of showing the club they are unhappy.

I think they are totally justified in doing that. They pay our wages and pay to keep this club alive.

The bond scheme is wrong. You can't ask an ordinary bloke to pay £975 just to watch his football team.

It's up to the board to put it right, because the fans have made it very clear they won't accept it any longer.

anti-Taylor Report protest which flooded the area with red balloons. A terrace sit-down was then followed by a spontaneous second-half pitch invasion.

Martin Keown was down for several minutes and the hold-up resulted in the pitch invasion, sparked off by one individual who uprooted a corner flag and, unchallenged, planted it on the centre spot, where he sat in mute, cross-legged defiance.

Home skipper Julian Dicks retrieved the flag stick, while team-mate Martin Allen squatted in animated conversation with the demonstrator, whose refusal to move prompted several hundred like-minded fans to swarm afield and gather in front of the directors' box, baying for blood.

Happily, it was all over in no time and, not least because of a deliberate low police profile, with least damage.

Lee Clayton (The Sun): The club is deep in the biggest crisis in its history. And the actions of the fans overshadowed another totally inept West Ham performance. They are lacking character and commitment and their furious followers are sick of it.

A section of them invaded the pitch midway through the second-

A fan makes his point to Julian Dicks.

JUST PLAIN DAFT

Steve Bacon photographed protestors for the Newham Recorder.

Bonded by their sense of outrage

half, stopping the game for more than seven minutes.

Neil Harman (Daily Mail): Between them in six months, these two clubs have managed to disaffect more supporters with the schemes for their ground redevelopment than the average attendance of most clubs in the Football League.

When the Arsenal fans unfurled their 'Stuff The Bond' banner, it was greeted with acclaim from all sides. Not to be outdone, the Cockneys responded with 'Wanted – For The Murder Of West Ham', listing in small print beneath the identities of the six directors.

Rob Shepherd (Daily Mail): Where there was always banter even in adversity, now there is bitterness . . . the consequence of the bond issue.

In stark contrast, there was a triumphant end to the following 1992-93 season, when the club regained its top flight status. But the promotion campaign began badly, when only 11,921 turned out to see the home win v Watford, followed by 11,493 for the live televised match v Derby County and a mere 10,326 – the worst home league gate in 35 years – for the 6-0 demolition of Sunderland on October 11.

Clearly, increasing ticket prices following relegation and the most disastrous season in the club's 92-year history, compounded by the worst

MANAGER
BILLY BONDS

I STILL say the bond scheme had a big and damaging effect on us that season – we were halfway up the table when the club brought it in. We'd just beaten Arsenal at Highbury and drew at home to Liverpool on the day the scheme was announced. We were doing OK but when the bond scheme came in all hell broke loose. It was never easy after that.

I recall the former chairman, poor, old Len Cearns, being abused by fans who came up to the edge of the directors' box to have a go at the end of one home match. He was trying to pacify them while the other directors had already shuffled inside to the comfort of the boardroom. I was asked by the police to try and calm a nasty situation and I'm not so sure that all of them who were hurling abuse at Len – God rest his soul – were actually West Ham fans. It seemed to me more like a case of rent-a-mob.

I remember walking down the tunnel after we'd lost at home to Crystal Palace and the fans were spitting blood at me. It was a bit hard to take but that's football management for you. As a player, I'd had a situation with our fans after the crowd trouble in Madrid where we were playing a European Cup Winners' Cup tie against Castilla, After the trouble out in Spain, the papers said I'd have called our fans 'scum'. The Chicken Run had a pop at me about it but I'd been misquoted in the paper, so I'd had stick from some of them before.

But that was not as bad as the stuff that was going on at around the time of the bond scheme. It became very abusive but then it wasn't the majority of the fans who were behaving like that. It was a minority.

> **Neal Clark**: I can't remember who we were playing but we were losing and the crowd were restless. As the ball went over towards the corner of where the Chicken Run met the South Bank, a guy jumped onto the pitch, ran about 15 yards with the ball and leathered it into the top corner past the keeper. It got the biggest cheer of the afternoon. He then ran back to the Chicken Run, where he was pursued by a steward and a copper. As he was running away he started to take off his brightly coloured coat, to try and blend in with the rest of the crowd. He was eventually nicked, amid much loud booing from the crowd.

recession in modern times, was another big mistake. With fans still raw from the bond debacle and the average attendance down by around 8,000 on the previous disastrous campaign, the club had no option but to apologise for their over-pricing folly while announcing that they were reducing season ticket seated prices by up to 25 per cent and slashing match day seat prices by as much as 18 per cent.

The facts indicate that the bond scheme was a huge flop, a massive PR own-goal. Only 808 of the original 19,301 target figure were actually sold, raising just £600,000. At the end of the season Martin Cearns, who, like his father, was also the subject of abuse from fans, stood down as chairman (though remained on the board) and was succeeded by Terry Brown.

Although the fans effectively won their battle, if not quite destroying the Hammers Bond, then discrediting it and forcing the club to revise its original plans, there was probably more hand-wringing among the hierarchy at the Royal Bank of Scotland – who were persuaded by West Ham to underwrite 75 per cent of the bond offer, a reported £11.6m – than within the stained corridors of power at Upton Park.

But then again, football used to be about much more than money. What West Ham's bond scheme did was alienate thousands of long-term supporters forever, many of them never to return.

Police attempt to remove a couple of sit-in protestors during the Arsenal game.

GETTING THE MESSAGE ACROSS

THE banners displayed by bond scheme protestors in 1992 were by no means the first to be unfurled by unhappy fans at Upton Park.

In January 1971, supporters on the East Terrace unveiled a banner which read: 'MOORE SUB THE FINAL SICK JOKE', after Ron Greenwood dropped his captain in the aftermath of the Blackpool incident earlier that month, when Bobby Moore and several team-mates were seen out drinking in a Blackpool club on the eve of Hammers' 4-0 FA Cup 3rd round defeat by the Tangerines.

Other banners, including 'GREENWOOD OUT' and 'HAMMERS HOLIDAY CAMP' were also brandished by fans trying to get their message across to those in authority.

Although members of the Cearns family were vilified during the worst of the Hammers Bond protests, no West Ham United chairman endured more scathing or sustained vocal attacks than Terence Brown when the club flirted with relegation again in 1997. A blue-and-white 'BROWN OUT' banner was prominent in the East Stand before it appeared in a photograph on the cover of a biography about the embattled former major shareholder.

Another 18 years elapsed before anti-protest banners were next draped from the stands, this time calling on owners David Sullivan and David Gold to sack manager Sam Allardyce. Early in his four-year tenure (2011-15), 'Big Sam' once publicly referred to Hammers supporters as "deluded".

'Come on, you Irons!'
Songs and chants through the years

Bubbles
I'm forever blowing bubbles
Pretty bubbles in the air
They fly so high, nearly reach the sky
Then like my dreams they fade and die
Fortune's always hiding
I've looked everywhere
I'm forever blowing bubbles
Pretty bubbles in the air

I'm dreaming dreams, I'm scheming schemes
I'm building castles high
They're born anew, their days are few
Just like a sweet butterfly
And as the daylight is dawning
They come again in the morning

(Repeat first verse and chorus)

When shadows creep, when I'm asleep
To lands of hope I stray
Then at daybreak, when I awake
My bluebird flutters away
Happiness, you seem so near me
Happiness, come forth and cheer me

(Repeat first verse and chorus)

She wore, she wore, she wore a claret ribbon
She wore a claret ribbon in the merry month of May

And when I asked her why she wore that ribbon?
She said it's for my West Ham and we're going to Wembley

Wem-ber-lee! Wem-ber-lee!

We're the greatest West Ham
And we're going to Wem-ber-lee!

To the tune of *Bye Bye Blackbird* and sung in more respectful times at the 1956 FA Cup 6th round tie, watched by nearly 70,000, at White Hart Lane

Take no notice of old Harmer's story
Cantwell is the boy to scotch his glory
Dick's on form, so is Foan
Billy Dare's the boy to roam
Tottenham, goodbye!

We are the West Ham boys
We march down the street
Stamping our feet
Coz we are the West Ham boys

When we're walking down the Barking Road
Doors and windows open wide
We knows our manners
We spend our tanners
We are the West Ham boys

ITo the tune of *Land Of Hope And Glory*

West Ham pride of London
Greatest of them all
There's no finer team
Who can play football

Byrne at centre-forward
Batman on the wing
Standen is the goalie
Saving everything

Peters is a link man
Boyce's with him too
Brownie's in the centre
Letting nothing through

The bells are ringing
For the claret and blue
The North Bank's singing
For the claret and blue
When the 'Ammers are scoring
And the North Bank is roarin'
And the money is pouring
For the claret and blue (claret and blue)

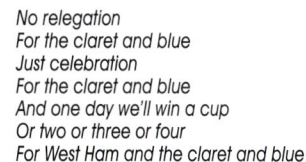

No relegation
For the claret and blue
Just celebration
For the claret and blue
And one day we'll win a cup
Or two or three or four
For West Ham and the claret and blue

You are my West Ham, my only West Ham
You make me happy when skies are grey
You'll never known just how much I love you
Until you've taken my West Ham away
La la la la la la la la

You never felt more like singing the blues
When West Ham win and Tottenham lose
Oh West Ham, you've got me singing the blues

Stamford Bridge is falling down
Falling down, falling down
Stamford Bridge is falling down
Poor old Chelsea
Build it up with claret and blue
Claret and blue, claret and blue
Build it up with claret and blue
Poor old Chelsea

Up your arse and up your arse
Stick the blue flag up your arse
From Stamford Bridge to Upton Park

Stick your blue flag up your arse

To the tune of *Ten Men Went To Mow*

One man couldn't carry
Couldn't carry Lampard
One man and his fork lift truck
Couldn't carry Lampard

Two men couldn't carry . . .
(All the way to ten)

Big fat, big fat Frank
Big fat, big fat Frank
Big fat, big fat Frank
Big fat Frankie Lampard

Come on, you Irons . . .

South Bank, South Bank do you job
South Bank, do you job

(Response from the opposite end):

North Bank, North Bank do you job
North Bank, do you job

We're not the North Bank
We're not the South Bank
We're the West Side Upton Park

The Chicken Run (The Chicken Run)

You'll never make the station

We never run from Tottenham

You're going home in a Cockney ambulance

Tip-toe, thru the North Bank
Get yer boots on, get yer head kicked in
So tip-toe thru the North Bank with me

Chim chim-in-ey
chim chim-in-ey
Chim chim cher-oo
We are those bastards in claret and blue

To the tune of *Chirpy Chirpy Cheep Cheep*
Where's the money gone?
Where's the money gone?
Where's the money gone?
Where's the money gone?
Far, far away . . .

To the tune of *This Old Man*

U-N-I . . T-E-D, West Ham are the team for me
With a nick-knack paddywhack, give the dog bone
Why don't Tottenham f*** off home

We are the West Ham
The pride of the south
We hate the Arsenal
Coz they are all mouth
We took their North Bank
But that was f***-all
The Hammers will rise
And the Gunners will fall
La la la la la la la la

To the tune of *Deck The Hall With Boughs Of Holly*

West Ham are the pride of London
La la la la la la la la

To the tune of *When the Saints Go Marching In*

Oh east London
Is wonderful
Oh east London is wonderful
Full of t**s, f***y and West Ham
Oh east London is wonderful

PLAYERS

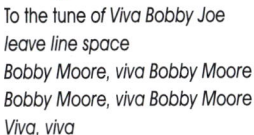

Bobby Moore
To the tune of *Viva Bobby Joe*
leave line space
Bobby Moore, viva Bobby Moore
Bobby Moore, viva Bobby Moore
Viva, viva

Bobby Moore's football machine (yeah, yeah, yeah)
Everybody knew they'd seen a sensation (a sensation),
Hear what I say now

Bobby Moore, viva Bobby Moore
Bobby Moore, viva Bobby Moore
Viva, viva

Billy Bonds
Six foot two, eyes of blue
Billy Bonds is after you
La la la la la la la la!

He's here, he's there
He's every f****** where
Billy Bonds, Billy Bonds

Billy Bonds' claret and blue army
Billy Bonds' claret and blue army
Billy Bonds' claret and blue army

(Also sung in the name of Johnny Lyall)

Harry Redknapp
We've got 'Arry, 'Arry, 'Arry Redknapp on the wing,
on the wing
We've got 'Arry, 'Arry, 'Arry, 'Arry Redknapp on the wing,
on the wing
'Arry, 'Arry Redknapp
'Arry Redknapp on the wing
'Arry, Harry Redknapp
'Arry Redknapp on the wing

Bryan 'Pop' Robson
Pop, Pop, Pop Robson
Score a little goal for me

Trevor Brooking
Trevor Brooking walks on water
La la la la la, la la la la...

We all agree . . .
Trevor Brooking is magic

Frank Lampard (Snr)
I'm dreaming of a Frank Lampard
Just like the one at Elland Road
When the ball came over
And Frank fell over
And scored the f****** winning goal

Frank McAvennie
One Macca-vennie
There's only one Macca-vennie
One Macca-vennie
There's only one Macca-veneeeeee

Also sung in the name of Tony Cottee and club photographer Steve Bacon

Alvin Martin
Alvin Martin, Alvin Martin
Alvin, Alvin Martin
He's got no hair
But we don't care
Alvin, Alvin Martin

George Parris
Oh Georgie takes no, no s***
Oh Georgie takes no, no s***
Oh Georgie takes no, no s***
Oh Georgie takes no s***

Leroy Rosenior
You don't know what I've been told
Leroy's boots are made of gold

Ludek Miklosko
Oi, big boy, what's your name?
My name is . . . Ludo Miklosko
I come from near Moscow
And I play in goal for West Ham (West Ham)

When I walk down the street
Everybody I meet
They go, 'oi, big boy . . .
. . . what's your name?'
My name is Ludo Miklosko . . .

Trevor Morley
Ooo, Morley, Morley
Ooo, Morley, Morley

Don Hutchison
Ooo, aah, Budweiser!
Ooo, aah, Budweiser!

Paolo Di Canio
To the tune of *La donna è mobile* by Luciano Pavarotti

Paolo Di Canio, Paolo Di Canio
Paolo Di Canio, Paolo Di Canio
Paolo Di Canio, Paolo Di Canio
Paolo Di Canio, Paolo Di Canio

Joe Cole
To the tune of *Gold*

Joey Cole – COLE!
Always believe in your soul
You've got the power to know
You're indestructible
Always believe in
Joey Cole – COLE!

Christian Dailly
To the tune of *Can't Take My Eyes Off You*

Oh Christian Dailly, you are the love of my life
Oh Christian Dailly, I'd let you sh@g my wife
Oh Christian Dailly, I want curly hair too.

Bobby Zamora
To the tune of *Volare*

Zamora, oh oh
Zamora, oh oh oh oh
He came from White Hart Lane
He's better than Jermain
Zamora, oh oh
Zamora, oh oh oh oh

Mark Noble
Mark Noble, oh oh
Mark Noble, oh oh oh oh
He comes from Canning Town
He stopped us going down
Mark Noble, oh oh
Mark Noble, oh oh oh oh

Thanks to the following for their lyrical contributions via the *EX* Hammers Facebook page: Micky Hastilow, Keith Charles, Liam Tyrell, Gareth Stewart, Jeff MacMahon, John Walsh, Paul Gough, Marco Taviani, Ian Gowans, Dave Clements, Jeff Garner, Tony Hoskins, Tony Cullen, Trevor Higgins, Steve Gunter, David Gregory, Michael Pocock, Michael Fendick, Doug Barrett, Michelle Gabriel, Gary Miller, Graham Harris, Kerry Evett, Steve Burton, Ray Swift, Jeff Woolnough, Simon Lord, Russell Hughes, Wayne Hever, Nicky Thorne, Mark Evans, Andy Brooker, Phil Kirk, Jason Stone, Kevin Kersse, David Grant, Ian Arkesden, John Robinson, Jon Boreham.

Popular Frank McAvennie celebrating the last of the many goals that made him such a big crowd favourite.

5 GREAT GOALS

MUCH as we admire well organised defence, goalkeeping heroics, tough tackling, creative midfield enterprise and nippy wingers who can deliver searching crosses with pinpoint accuracy, nothing gets us excited quite like a goal.

Volleys by Martin Peters, Keith Robson's wonder strike in the 1976 European Cup Winners' Cup semi-final, several Trevor Brooking specials, ice cool Ray Stewart penalties and Paolo Di Canio's beautifully executed volley against Wimbledon in 2000 featured prominently among our contributors' nominations. But there have been a number of other great Hammers goals to savour.

Q: Greatest goals you've seen scored at Upton Park by West Ham players?

Jim Wilder: In the 40s there was a right-winger called **TERRY WOODGATE**. In one match he took three corners in a short period of time. The first two went straight into the back of the net. The third hit the crossbar and came out. I have never seen three better corner-kicks.

John Powles: A special goal was in the 1957-58 promotion season in a match v Derby County (7/9/57). **NOEL CANTWELL** collected the ball from his own left-back position and ran with the ball diagonally across the pitch to an outside-right spot, winding his way past three opposition players before cutting inside and lcashing a shot into the top right-hand corner of the goal at the South Bank end.

Ed Gillis: West Ham v Liverpool (19/4/58), an important game, with promotion to Division One a distinct possibility. I was standing directly behind the goal on the North Bank, my head appearing just over the wall. We were 1-0 down but awarded a free-kick just outside the Liverpool penalty area. 'Muffin' **JOHN BOND** laced a free-kick towards the goal, which looked set to knock my head off, until the net intervened. Glorious!

Kevin Mansell: It's hard to specify one that stands out – there are so many – but some **JOHN BOND** goals live on. A bullet free-kick from 25-yards in a floodlight friendly against the Brazilian club Fluminense (24/4/60), which was greeted with a collective gasp of astonishment from the Chicken Run. And a goal at the South Bank end v Everton (4/4/59) that he scored with his left foot on the turn from 35 yards, during a season when he had a spell as our centre-forward.

Paul Walker: I was unfortunate to be working in Cardiff and watching on TV when Paolo Di Canio scored his amazing goal against Wimbledon in March 2000, so I have to look back to the 60s for a very special goal scored by **JOHNNY BYRNE** as the greatest I have seen – for the emotion it generated as much as anything else.

It was in the 1964 FA Cup quarter-final (29/2/64) against what was then

John Bond scored spectacular and important goals from his usual right-back role and also when pushed forward into an attacking position.

204 UPTON PARK MEMORIES

a very good Burnley side. We had been behind at the break before John Sissons raced down the left and squeezed along the byline to score the equaliser from an acute angle.

Then came Byrne, a brilliant player who would have graced any generation. He scored two in eight minutes to secure what was eventually a 3-2 win. That second goal was a perfect volley from just outside the box – he was off the ground and struck it so sweetly.

Another great goal came from the thunderous boot of right-back **JOHN BOND**, known as 'Muffin' to us all because of the power he generated. His special goal came in the ECWC 2nd round, 1st leg v Sparta Prague (25/11/64) the following season. We were getting nowhere against a tough, physical Czech side until Bond struck a 25-yarder in the 58th minute. John was right in front of me in the Chicken Run when he hit the ball. To a small boy, it seemed miles out but crashed into the far corner.

Terry Connelly: Scored by **JOHNNY BYRNE** v Burnley, FA Cup 6th round (29/2/64). Burnley had been putting us under a lot of pressure. We broke quickly upfield and Byrne absolutely belted a volley past Adam Blacklaw in the Burnley goal to put us 2-1 up, having been a goal behind early in the game.

John Byrne and John Sissons (on the far side of the goal) raise their arms to signal a goal in the 1964 FA Cup sixth round against Burnley, while the South Bank goes wild.

PLAYER
MARTIN PETERS
Born: 8/11/43, Plaistow, east London
WHU career: 1962-70
Position: Right-half/Midfield
Apps: 364, **Goals:** 100

BY pure coincidence, when Martin Peters was writing his first autobiography, *Goals From Nowhere*, his editor/publisher asked him to cover one West Ham home match in diary form. The game Martin chose to write about was v Leicester City (16/11/68), played just a few months before the book went on sale.

The most versatile player in Hammers' history scored 100 goals for his local club, including some absolute belters, but none are more fondly remembered than the one he netted in such spectacular style on this day. In his words, this is how he remembered it:

SECOND-half we start giving them a right chasing, but we should be getting a couple more. Shilton's still playing well. But we are not taking our chances. I could have had one or two but I hit my best chance wide of the far post. Tried to volley the ball as it came over but I didn't turn my foot enough. Called myself all things under the sun.

Andy Lochhead went off about half-hour from the end. Second time this season we've sickened him.

Then they get a free-kick on the edge of our box. I go back with Geoff Hurst to help form a 'wall' in front of our goal. The ref tries to get us to move back. 'He's joking, we must be 20 yards away already.' But they make a mess of the kick and Manley hits a tame shot. I'm appealing for offside when John Charles gets the ball. He hits it long out to 'Siss' and I'm running like hell with Geoff just in front of me. There's no-one up there.

I saw the full-back waiting for Siss. He won't take him on, I think, he'll pull it back and cross with his right. I see his boot swing but I lose sight of the ball behind a player.

Then I see it high in the air. There's a defender on my left but I think it's going to beat him and it's coming on my right foot. I'm on the edge of the box. Shall I push it forward? No, I'll hit the bloody thing first time. On the volley, wham, just right. He's not even seen it. It's in the back of the net and I run on and belt it as it rolls back out again.

'Go on, my son,' I'm shouting as the boys come running up, all shouting and jumping on me. The crowd's gone potty. Must have looked great.

That's Leicester gone. Not much doubt left in the game now. I'm walking about two foot above the ground. I can promise you there's no feeling like it. Then Brian Dear, who's had a blinder, bangs in the fourth goal just before time.

Whistle goes. Shake a hand here and there. Leicester are sick. Still, if it hadn't been for that goalkeeper of theirs we might have had six or more.

Clatter of boots up the passage. Ron comes into the dressing room after us. "Well played, lads. Great goals."

I forgot to mention that I was wearing No.7 this game because right-winger Harry Redknapp was injured. Harry comes in beaming. "It's the shirt, Mart, can't go wrong in it."

Then we all lie in the bath and when you've had a good win that's probably the best part of the day. Lying back, soaking out the bumps and bruises and chatting away nineteen to the dozen.

Then as we dry ourselves the results come over the tannoy, punctuated by our 'oohs' and 'ahs'. Chelsea got beat – 'great'. Arsenal won away – 'sods'.

After changing, it's into the players' bar – a nice place where we can go with our guests and have a drink on the club. I have a light and lime because they had run out of lager. Jimmy Tarbuck is there – he always seems to be around when I score.

"What a great goal, Mart," he says.

Then it's out into the cold evening. Still a few people around to slap your back and get an autograph. Tonight I've got to pick up the mother-in-law to take her up to the house where she babysits for Cath and I to go out.

A meal first and then on to a friend's house for a party. Siss and Ron Boyce are there, so we play the game three or four times over. The party goes on till three in the morning but I last well with the dancing. Cath, the life and soul of the party early on, fades badly.

Sunday morning and eyes down for a long study of the papers. Like to read the reports of other games – and ours, of course, but I'm not really bothered what they say about me.

I had a good press this time. Dick Milford in *The People* wrote: 'Perfection! West Ham, the most imaginative side in the First Division, strive for it all the time. Just after the hour at Upton Park they achieved it with the finest of Martin Peters' 13 goals this season. Maybe the finest of his life. Maybe West Ham's finest.'

R.D.F. Green in the *Sunday Telegraph* said: 'A gem of a goal, fashioned in equal parts of beauty and power, set the crown on this attractive game...

'Full-back Charles put through a long, fast ground pass to Sissons. He, in turn, evaded two converging defenders and sent a pass of hand-tooled precision over the head of the marked Hurst and on to Peters. With some of the inevitability of a law of physics, the ball dropped just so far in front of the fast-moving Peters for him to volley it into the net like a rocket.'

I won't pretend I wasn't flattered by all the praise. But the game was on the television on Sunday afternoon and I wanted to see if it looked as good as they said it did.

Just as the game was going to start, some photographers arrived. They wanted some pictures and as much as I wanted to help them, I urged them to be as quick as they could.

I missed a lot of the game but arrived back in front of my set in time to see the goal. Even if I do say it myself, it wasn't a bad one. They showed it four times altogether – Brian Dear was in the studio going over the game with them. He had to admit that it was a Leicester player who put the first goal in, so he didn't get the hat-trick the players credited him with. He deserved three, anyway.

I was lucky, really – picking a good Saturday to talk about in this book.

Peter Jones: I am a little biased in naming my best goal. In 1965 my neighbours in Elm Park were related to **EDDIE PRESLAND**, the West Ham defender who played six league games in the 60s. He used to bring me programmes back from away games and made his debut v Liverpool (27/2/65). I can recall standing behind the North Bank net at the front, cheering him on. He hit a speculative ball forward from just outside the box, which took one bounce over the head of Gerry Byrne, a Liverpool full back, for a debut goal in a 2-1 victory.

Dave Spurgeon: MARTIN PETERS' volley in the 4-0 win v Leicester City (16/11/68) was simply breathtaking in its technique and execution, typical of that player. Bobby Ferguson started the move by throwing the ball to left-back John Charles, who played it down the left-wing to John Sissons. After a burst down the touchline, he sent over a lofted cross into the Leicester penalty area. Peters timed his run to typical perfection and volleyed the ball, sidefoot, but got such power on the contact that the ball seemed to be rocket-propelled as it flew past Peter Shilton.

Bobby George: From my view, standing on the South Bank, I saw **MARTIN PETERS** score one of the best goals I have ever seen at Upton Park, v Leicester City. Peters hit the ball right-footed on the volley without breaking stride. It was a quite magnificent goal.

Norman Roberts: One goal which always comes to mind was when John Sissons put in a cross and **MARTIN PETERS** caught it on the volley and nearly broke the net v Leicester City. Footballs were a lot heavier then and nothing like the balloons they play with today.

Tony Cullen: I believe **MARTIN PETERS**' strike v Leicester City was voted ITV's *The Big Match Goal* of the Season. I recall he ran the full length of the field before his perfect volley.

Eddie Parker: **MARTIN PETERS** scored an acrobatic screamer v Stoke City (7/10/67). It was a right-foot volley from outside the box from Harry Redknapp's cross.

In the early 80s, **GEOFF PIKE** once took a free-kick, lobbed the wall with back spin on the ball, and then ran on to collect it and score. Someone else must have touched it on the way but it was a brilliant goal.

Rob Robinson: The best goals that I have seen at Upton Park came from the combination of **MARTIN PETERS** and **GEOFF HURST**. Their usual ploy was to play out from the back up to Peters. He would ghost up the wing on either flank and whip in crosses for Geoff to get in front of defenders at the near post and score with powerful headers. One of his six goals v Sunderland (19/10/68) was scored in this manner.

Crispin Derby: **GEOFF HURST** in a 3-2 win v Chelsea (12/4/65). I was behind the goal he scored in, so watched it all the way from his left foot, 25 yards out, past a helpless Peter Bonetti. He did it all the time but this was the best I saw.

Tony Hoskins: Apart from the Di Canio goal v Wimbledon, my favourite came in the League Cup 4th round tie v Liverpool. It was 1-1 and very late in the game when Harry Redknapp ran down the right wing. As he got to the byline at the South Bank end, it looked like the ball had gone out of play but he got his cross in and **BRYAN 'POP' ROBSON** was there at the near post to secure a 2-1 victory. There were nearly 41,000 people packed in that night and the noise they made when we scored was incredible.

Michael Harris: **TREVOR BROOKING** v Spurs (1/4/72). Bobby Moore intercepted the ball and played a superb pass down the left with the outside of his right foot to Trevor Brooking. He jinked his way into the penalty area, turning Peter Collins inside out, before curling a right-footed shot past Pat Jennings and inside the far corner of the net at the South Bank end.

Dave Spurgeon: Long before *Bend It Like Beckham*, there was bend it like Brooking. His goal in the 2-0 win v Spurs (1/4/72) was memorable just as much for the way Bobby Moore majestically dispossessed Alan Gilzean in the West Ham half, by flicking the ball over the Scot with his right foot, knocking it forward a touch and then playing an inch-perfect pass with the outside of the boot, Beckenbauer-style, to **TREVOR BROOKING**.

Clever Trevor then teased Peter Collins, trying to tempt a tackle that never came, before looking up and curling the ball past the world class goalkeeper that was Pat Jennings. Guinness should use the skills displayed by Bobby and Trevor in this goal – it was 'pure genius' in double measure!

Vic Lindsell: **CLYDE BEST** v Leeds United in a 3-1 victory (30/3/74). I fainted that day, due to rushing down my pie and chips and then being exposed to glaring sun in the lower West side. After recovering in the medical room, I walked back out of the tunnel at the time of the final whistle and had the opportunity to pat my heroes on the back as they left the pitch.

Alan Byrne: Leeds had taken a half-time lead through Allan Clarke and looked comfortable but we came out a different team in the second-half. **CLYDE BEST** collected a pass from midway in the opposition half and waltzed towards the Leeds goal before planting a lovely shot past the impressive David Harvey. That was the catalyst for a famous Hammers fight-back.

Kevin Radley: Three goals from the same game stick in my memory. It was the ECWC semi-final, 2nd leg v Eintracht Frankfurt – probably the best game I ever saw at Upton Park. Trevor Brooking's performance and two great goals were fantastic but sandwiched between them was a corker from **KEITH ROBSON**.

The way I remember it was that a pass landed in front of 'Robbo' about five yards outside the penalty box down the right side. The ground was wet and skiddy and he appeared to let the ball get away from him before turning and smashing the ball with his stronger left foot into the top left corner of the goal at the South Bank end. The goalie's feet were firmly planted in the muddy ground as the rocket flew by him.

After his dramatic ECWC semi-final goal in 1976 Keith Robson didn't have any trouble finding new friends around Upton Park!

It put us 2-0 up (3-2 on aggregate) and there were wild celebrations on the terraces – we were on our way to Brussels for the final. That's how I remember the goal – I daren't check it out on YouTube in case it was any different!

Jeff Garner: Without doubt, **KEITH ROBSON**'s goal v Eintracht Frankfurt. Because of its importance, the atmosphere and the conditions. A truly stunning strike into the top corner of the net.

Phil Garner: Has to be **KEITH ROBSON** v Eintracht Frankfurt.

Gerard Daly: My favourite would probably be a mostly-forgotten 25-yarder by **GEOFF PIKE** in an otherwise dull 1-0 win over Norwich City (11/4/77). It also sticks in my mind because, sadly, it would prove to be the last time I ever went to Upton Park with my dad, John.

John Reynolds: If not the best goal ever, it is certainly my favourite. It came in a 5-0 win v Newcastle United (24/3/79). Paul Brush won a sliding tackle on the halfway line. Trevor Brooking and **BRYAN 'POP' ROBSON** combined with a deft one-two before Brooking conjured a wonderful inswinging pass behind the defence. Robson ran on to the return pass and slapped the ball with his left foot high into the roof of the net.

Peter Lush: The last-minute penalty by **RAY STEWART**, v Aston Villa, FA Cup 6th round (8/3/80). He was so cool. It was at the South Bank end where I was standing.

Another favourite of mine is **JIMMY NEIGHBOUR**'s winner v Coventry City, League Cup semi-final, 2nd leg (10/2/81). I didn't get a ticket for the 1980 FA Cup final, so when we beat Coventry I knew I would get to see West Ham at Wembley in a cup final.

Finally, **LIAM BRADY**'s winner v Wolves (5/5/90) in the last minute of his final game. It rounded off a good 4-0 win and was a wonderful way for one of the game's greats to finish his career.

Spencer Dodd: Every one of **RAY STEWART**'s penalties. As a right-back myself growing up, I'd always watched out for the right-back and how he played the game. For me there were few better than Ray. Hard but fair, never shirked a tackle and with a hammer of a right foot. Whenever he stepped up to take a penalty there was no question of him placing it, he just thumped it as hard as he could and the ball was generally past the keeper before he'd had a chance to react. He hardly ever missed and at that time we were winning a few.

Bonds would invariably break up the play and win the ball, passing it on to Brooking who would then ship it out to Devonshire on the wing. Devonshire would dance into the box before dropping a shoulder and going past the defender. However, more often than not he'd be taken down before he could get his cross in or get a shot away. Defenders knew what was coming but seemed helpless to do anything about it.

Given the regularity with which it would happen, my dad was always up on his feet telling him to "get in the box" and bemoaning the fact that he didn't do it more often!

Kevin Pendegrass: RAY STEWART's volley from the right touchline v Spurs on New Year's Eve (31/12/83) went in like a tracer bullet and I don't think Ray Clemence even saw it. Shame it wasn't on TV.

TONY COTTEE's superb overhead scissor-kick v Nottingham Forest (21/11/87) – a goal any Brazilian would have been proud of.

Michael Oliver: I'm going to pick three goals, all long-range efforts, which weren't captured on camera, so they're probably not quite as good as I remember! The first two were v Brighton (5/3/83). We went behind in the 82nd minute (to what I seem to remember was a pretty good goal itself by Ryan) but **ALAN DICKENS** equalised from about 30 yards a minute later and almost immediately **TONY COTTEE** scored from similar range.

Steve Blowers: My choice is **KEITH ROBSON** v Eintracht Frankfurt, ECWC semi-final, 2nd leg (14/4/76).

The mud-splattered Trevor Brooking sends 'Robbo' clear with an inch-perfect, defence-splitting pass from the halfway line. The flag stays down as the Geordie striker contends with the skidding ball deep behind German lines. "Oh no, he's let it run a yard too far," groans disconsolate ITV commentator, the late, great Brian Moore.

But 25 yards out, Robson quickly composes himself and lets fly with a simply sensational strike that dips under the far angle.

"Oh, what a goal!" announces the back-tracking Moore, quickly eating his words.

Pete May: A **TREVOR BROOKING** curler into the corner of the Derby County net stands out. It was a 3-3 draw (22/1/72) and Trev scored at the North Bank. He also scored another cracker against Eintracht in the 1976 ECWC semi-final.

I'll never forget a diving header by **BOBBY GOULD**, from a Frank Lampard cross, in a 6-2 win v Leicester City (21/9/74) and how he celebrated right in front of me.

A **BRYAN ROBSON** glancing header from the edge of the box against the then-mighty Leeds was another great goal, while **PAOLO DI CANIO**'s volley v Wimbledon was the best for sheer technique, just beating Steve Potts' effort against Hull (6/10/90)!

PLAYER
KEITH ROBSON

IT was a wonderful experience to play in those European games – it was magic under the lights at Upton Park.

We went 2-1 up and Trevor (Brooking) put a fabulous ball through the middle. I was just about to shoot when the ball hit a divot and bobbled up.

I kept running and I remember Brian Moore saying on the commentary that I'd misjudged it.

But I doubled back on myself, turned round, looked up and hit this ball from about 35 yards and it flew in the top corner.

Unbelievable! I just went mad! It was a one-off, a wonder goal.

We had some party that night!

The following season, v Tottenham on New Year's Eve, **RAY STEWART** hit an absolute screamer from even further out, somewhere near the right touchline, and it flew in via the underside of the bar, which always makes goals look more spectacular somehow.

John Ruane: One that sticks in my mind was scored by **MARK WARD** v Manchester United (2/2/86). We were 1-0 down at the time. He won the ball near the halfway line and sprinted down the wing, then let fly with a rocket that nearly broke the net. We went on to win the match 2-1 with yet another Tony Cottee goal.

Ian McMaster: Our fourth, by **TONY COTTEE**, in a 5-3 home win v Chelsea (11/10/86). Alan Dickens' flick of the ball over the opponent's head was just sublime.

Gary West: It might not have been the best, technically, but **GEORGE PARRIS'** goal v Watford (28/3/87). We were desperately in need of a win to avoid relegation and on a mudheap of a pitch George bashed one in from 20 yards at the South Bank end to win the game.

Ian Crocker: I can still see in my mind **PAUL INCE's** magnificent

PLAYER
RAY STEWART
Born: 7/9/59, Stanley, Perthshire, Scotland
WHU career: 1979-90
Position: Right-back
Apps: 431, Goals: 84

THE goal I scored in our 4-1 home win v Spurs (31/12/83) was the greatest of my career.

The ball was about 25 yards out from the Tottenham goal, on the right-hand corner of the penalty area. Steve Whitton was lining up a shot and shouted to me to 'leave it' – but I ignored him and cracked it myself.

The ball flew past Ray Clemence – one of England's all-time greatest keepers – and into the top corner of the South Bank net. I've never scored another goal like it and if they had opened the gates at Upton Park there and then, I would have ran the length of Green Street, I was so pleased!

Of all the penalties I scored, the one that beat Aston Villa in the FA Cup quarter-final (8/3/80) was my best.

Just seven days earlier I had missed from the spot against Luton (even though I tucked away the rebound) and although I knew that if I missed this one in the last minute or so of the sixth round tie I probably wouldn't be asked to take another penalty, I had no hesitation in grabbing the ball and placing it on the muddy spot at the South Bank end.

The buzz of anticipation among the 36,393 crowd was incredible but I had to block out that and all the fuss that was going on around me as Villa players protested to referee about his controversial decision to give handball against Ken McNaught.

Villa keeper Jimmy Rimmer was one of the best in the business, an experienced keeper, but the thought of missing never entered my head.

I rate that as my greatest-ever penalty, because of the importance of the occasion and the fact that it put us into the semi-final against Everton.

It was at that moment when the ball hit the back of the Villa net, and the fans went wild, that I truly felt accepted by the West Ham supporters. It was as if a young Scot, who had signed for the club the previous September, had become a 'Jock-ney' or an East Ender for life that day! It was such an incredible thrill.

Ironically, only seconds after the re-start, I gave away a free-kick just outside our penalty area. The shot got through our defensive wall but Phil Parkes saved the ball and my neck!

After the match I was treated like a hero. One newspaper got me to walk back out to the penalty spot and pose for photos sitting on the match-ball. My name was suddenly up in lights and I've got to admit, I loved it.

We celebrated afterwards with a few drinks at Frank Lampard's pub, The Britannia, in Stratford. I think everyone in the place wanted to buy me a drink.

PLAYER
TONY COTTEE
Born: 5/7/65, West Ham, east London
WHU career: 1983-88 & 1994-96
Position: Forward
Apps: 336, **Goals:** 146

BILLY Bonds made his first home appearance of the season against Nottingham Forest (21/11/87) at the age of 41 and stole the headlines with a typical swashbuckling display made all the more heroic by his head bandage. But the game turned into a personal triumph for me, too, as I scored twice in an exhilarating 3-2 victory.

My winner from about 12 yards out, an acrobatic overhead kick from Mark Ward's driven chest-high cross that flew into the top corner, is the best goal I've ever scored.

The fact that England manager Bobby Robson was watching from the stand made it even sweeter.

Neil Humphreys: My greatest goal needs to be accompanied by a string quartet because it's impossible not to get the violins out. After my parents divorced, money was tight so regular trips to Upton Park were out of the question. But once a season, my uncle took me to West Ham as a birthday present. The closest fixture in 1987 fell on November 21, at home to Nottingham Forest.

The game was a classic for many reasons. Firstly, Hammers won, which they usually conspired not to do on my annual birthday treat. The score was 3-2, so we got five goals and the game was end-to-end, first-touch stuff; sumptuous football that West Ham has rarely witnessed in recent years.

And then, there was THAT goal.

From the right flank, Mark Ward sent a cross towards the far post but it was too deep, too far from goal, and drifting away from **TONY COTTEE**. The petite poacher had a decent leap but he was not David Cross. Even from my vantage point, I expected the cross to drift out for a throw-in.

But Cottee turned contortionist, twisting in mid-air like a corkscrew, his back to goal, taking flight. With those trunk-like legs of a stallion, he turned into Pegasus. Part ballerina, part butcher, he executed the perfect scissor-kick. The ball left his boot like a bullet, still accelerating as it hit the roof of the net.

The memory always deceives. In my mind's eye, Cottee took off somewhere near the corner flag and the ball followed an impossible trajectory. Of course, he was a little nearer to goal but the finish was no less magnificent. Watch it on YouTube. That kind of take-off usually requires four engines and an airport runway.

Many years later, circumstances brought Cottee and I together at a restaurant table in Singapore. I told him about the annual birthday treat, the soaring scissor-kick and what that goal meant to me as a poor kid from a council estate. He understood. He was a West Ham fan whose day job happened to be scoring goals for our beloved club. I bought him dinner that night.

He gave me my favourite Upton Park goal of all-time.

I think I owe him a few more dinners.

---

volley flying into Liverpool's net when we trounced them 4-1 in the League Cup 4th round (30/10/88). Ince was outstanding that night but **TONY GALE's** free-kick wasn't bad either. It was good not just to beat Liverpool for a change but to wallop them. Of course, we got knocked out by Luton in the semi-finals and were relegated at Anfield that season. Well, there's always a payback, isn't there!

Mark Edwards: STUART SLATER, v Sunderland (18/10/89). 20,901 fans saw a 5-0 victory which included a wonder strike from Slater. A long goal-kick from Phil Parkes was headed on by Eamonn Dolan to the chest of Slater, who then volleyed over the Sunderland keeper. It was a fantastic goal by an exciting young player.

Roger Hillier: One not often mentioned, a **JIMMY QUINN** effort in a hat-trick v Sheffield United (21/3/90). The goal was memorable, not so much for Quinn tapping it in from the six-yard box, but for the scintillating run by Stuart Slater. Slater picked the ball up on the left-hand side close to the halfway line and ran with it, beating several opponents to race into the penalty area and square it to Quinn for the simple tap-in. It all happened so quickly.

Marco Taviani: The obvious choice would be Paolo Di Canio's goal of the season volley v Wimbledon. However, I also enjoyed **LIAM BRADY's** farewell goal v Wolves (5/5/90). I was standing on the North Bank with my nephew and it was nearing the end of the game when Brady picked the ball up in midfield and ventured forward. As I recall, he seemed to go forward unchallenged, gracefully, as all left-footed players seem to do, and then let fly. The ball went swerving sweetly in to the top left-hand corner of the net as we were looking at it.

This signalled a pitch invasion from all four sides of the ground. Brady, who was running towards the Chicken Run to celebrate, later said that he stopped because he saw the Chicken Run running towards *him!*

Liam Tyrell: Several goals are hard to forget. One favourite was the **LIAM BRADY** goal in the final moment of his final career game. Home to Wolves, final game of the season, scorching hot day, 3-0 up and cruising. 'Chippy' had always been my favourite non-West Ham player so it was pretty special when we signed him. Yes, he was past his best and he suffered a couple of bad injuries but still showed his class and scored some screamers, too. This one was pretty special, a typically brilliant left foot shot bending into the top corner, prompting a pitch invasion and the ref ending the game a couple of minutes early. What a way to go!

Undoubtedly the **PAOLO DI CANIO** wonder goal was not only my best Upton Park goal but the best I have ever seen in the flesh. It was one of those 'Did I really just see that?' moments. It all happened at the other end of the ground from my season ticket seat in the Bobby Lower, so it was not until I saw the TV replays that I was able to see quite how special the goal was. The precise Sinclair delivery, the leap, the eye on the ball concentration, the scissor-style connection and the exemplary execution.

In real time the audible gasps of breath confirmed you'd seen something special and it sure was.

Chris Ludlow: Ones that stand out for me, in no particular order, are: **STUART SLATER,** v Brighton (17/11/90). Cutting in from the left and smashing it right-footed into the far top corner, it was the first West Ham goal I witnessed at The Boleyn.

TREVOR SINCLAIR's 30-yard volley v Charlton Athletic (26/12/2000), the pick of some great goals in a 5-0 Boxing Day thrashing.

A year later, we were treated to another Boxing Day cracker from **TREVOR SINCLAIR.** This time a fantastic 25-yard scissor-kick from a Joe Cole cross, v Derby County (26/12/01).

MATTY ETHERINGTON, v Ipswich Town, play-off semi-final, 2nd leg (18/5/04). Cutting in from the right, he smashed it left-footed into the top corner at the Bobby Moore Stand end.

PAOLO DI CANIO came on as a late sub to grab a 1-0 win in his last game at Upton Park v Chelsea (3/5/03).

One of the two **JULIAN DICKS** scored v Oxford United (21/11/92). Left-foot belter from 25 yards from the left-hand side into the top right-hand corner at the North Bank end.

JULIAN DICKS, v Manchester United (8/12/96). Trailing 2-0 with a little over 10 minutes to go and seemingly dead and buried, we got a lifeline with a Florin Raducioiu goal. Two minutes later we were awarded a penalty and the chance to level the game. Up stepped Julian to smash home the spot-kick into the roof of the net (BM Stand end) with what can only be described as the most fiercely-struck penalty I have ever seen, to send the crowd delirious.

Liam Corbett: **JULIAN DICKS** v Manchester City (23/3/96) – a pile driver from 25 yards into the top corner from the left-hand side of the area in our 4-2 victory.

Mike Corbett: Any **JULIAN DICKS** penalties. I always felt a little sorry for the opposing keeper – and you had the feeling that he was aiming for them!

Ian Nunney: All goals at Upton Park are special to me but three that come to mind were all scored by **FRANK McAVENNIE,** in what turned out to be his last game for the club. He was named as a substitute for the final match of the 1991-92 season, v Nottingham Forest (2/5/92). I loved 'Macca' as a player and was a bit miffed to see he was on the bench for what was my only visit that season. He was brought on for Mitchell Thomas at half-time and suddenly the game came to life. He scored a memorable hat-trick and we had another great win under our belts. It was a fitting way for him to finish a great career at West Ham.

Matt Drury: A crashing **JOHN HARTSON** header from a corner v Spurs (24/2/97). The match was played on a Monday night in torrential rain. We won 4-3.

Terry Roper: The greatest goal that I have ever seen at Upton Park was

Classy Liam Brady bowed out in style in his final game against Wolverhampton Wanderers in May 1990. In the first shot we see the Irishman letting fly with an unstoppable shot that sparked these jubilant scenes. In the second picture Leroy Rosenior (9) is heading towards the Chicken Run to join in the celebrations ... but the fans were already heading the other way!

PAOLO DI CANIO's airborne volley v Wimbledon (26/3/2000). The build-up was simplicity itself – a cross from the right by Trevor Sinclair and there was Di Canio at the far post to score his 'wonder goal'.

In a sense, that unforgettable strike typified everything about him. He was an original talent, audacious and gloriously inventive. He was both brilliantly preposterous and preposterously brilliant.

He was disruptive, narcissistic and the proverbial pain in the arse, but he was also subtle and cunning. He scored brilliant and unorthodox goals and created opportunities for his team-mates with a dexterity that was simply breathtaking.

Di Canio's time at Upton Park was vivid, unforgettable and, at times, every bit as glorious as it was ludicrous, but he will always be revered as one of West Ham's greatest players.

Alan Porter: It has to be **PAOLO DI CANIO's** wonder goal v Wimbledon. My father and I were season ticket holders in the East Stand, just underneath the old camera scaffolding, and we were right in line with Trevor Sinclair's cross. It seemed as though the ball hung in the air for an age after it left Trev's boot and then sped up dramatically after Paolo's scissor-kick shot. Truly magnificent.

Chris Ball: The best I've ever seen. It doesn't need describing.

Steve Perry: Pure genius.

Andy Brooker: There have been some fantastic goals that I have witnessed during my 37 years of attending games at Upton Park. The obvious one being **PAOLO DI CANIO** v Wimbledon. Viewing it from the Bobby Moore lower, I don't think I realised the full beauty of the goal until I saw it again on TV.

David Steadman: Has to be **PAOLO Di CANIO's** v Wimbledon, which I was right behind. He seemed to almost hit it in slow motion and the whole stadium knew they'd seen something pretty special the second it hit the back of the net.

Di Canio's double in a 2-1 win v Arsenal (3/10/99) – our first at home against them for 12 years – were also memorable, particularly the one where he skinned Tony Adams and Martin Keown before slotting home in front of the Bobby Moore Stand.

Ivan Robeyns: PAOLO DI CANIO's final game at Upton Park, when his goal ensured a 1-0 victory v Chelsea (3/5/03). After he scored he ran towards where we were in the West Stand lower. He seemed more emotional than ever. And even though I was so happy, I felt this sadness somewhere inside of me. I could sense it would be the final time I would see him weave his magic in claret-and-blue.

Adrian White: One of the best goals would have to be the 20-yard strike by **BOBBY ZAMORA** v Everton (21/4/07) in the 'Great Escape' season of 2006-07. Yossi Benayoun flicked the ball back to Zamora, who curled a venomous left-foot shot into the top corner at the Trevor Brooking Stand end, past a static Tim Howard, to seal the all-important 1-0 victory.

Iain Dale: I'd like to say the Paolo Di Canio volley v Wimbledon but, due to severe congestion, I was stuck in the Blackwall Tunnel at the time.

I was a big fan of **MATTHEW RUSH** and remember a cracking goal he scored v Ipswich Town (2/4/94). The ball was whipped in to the box from the left, an Ipswich defender headed it clear, then in came Matthew Rush, 30 yards out on the right. He hit it on the volley straight into the top left-hand corner of the Bobby Moore Stand net. Surely one of the finest goals ever scored at West Ham.

Rush was a silky winger and I ached for him to be given more of a chance by Billy Bonds and then Harry Redknapp. I felt he had the potential to become a top class player but, sadly, he never made it.

A few adoring fans came on to the field to congratulate Julian Dicks after he nearly knocked Peter Schmeichel's head off with a typically rasping penalty kick in the 2-2 draw with Manchester United in 1996.

Dan Francis: I was sat in the West Stand press box directly behind Paolo Di Canio when he produced his Goal of the Season volley against Wimbledon in March 2000 and it took my breath away. For technical brilliance and sheer quality, it would be hard to beat that.

However, my personal favourite was **FRANK McAVENNIE's** hat-trick strike v Nottingham Forest on the final day of the 1991-92 season (2/5/92).

The goal itself wasn't particularly memorable – Frank chested down a long pass forward from Julian Dicks and rolled the ball left-footed past Mark Crossley – but the circumstances around it were unforgettable.

I was due to be attending the game with my dad, as usual, but at the last minute he got called to work and so I went to the match with a friend instead. It was the first time I'd been allowed to stand on the North Bank – an experience that was both terrifying and exhilarating in equal measure – and I recall even before the game having a feeling that something special was going to happen that day.

For seven years I had waited for my hero to score a hat-trick – he had grabbed a brace on numerous occasions – and to see him finally achieve it on his last appearance for the club, after coming on as a half-time substitute, was real Roy of the Rovers stuff.

I'll admit I had tears in my eyes as Frank raised both arms aloft and walked towards us behind the goal to say his farewell in the most fitting way possible. What a way to go.

"Who writes your scripts?" manager Billy Bonds asked Frank McAvennie after the popular Scot 'signed off' on his turbulent Upton Park career with an astonishing second-half hat-trick on the final day of the 1991-92 season against Nottingham Forest. The fact that Hammers had already been relegated from the top flight at the end of an acrimonious campaign blighted by the bond scheme protests made his last day heroics all the more remarkable. Frank later revealed that team-mate Mitchell Thomas feigned a hamstring injury at half-time so that he would be brought on as a substitute.

Tim Crane: I was in the Bobby Moore Stand for Paolo Di Canio's goal, which wasn't the best vantage point.

ALAN DICKENS' goal v Ipswich Town (30/4/86) unlocked a lot of happiness, as did **STUART SLATER'S** v Everton in the FA Cup 6th round (11/3/91). Every goal is a joy really but my love of records, history and statistics laments the fact that I missed out on the Geoff Hurst era. Come to think of it, plonk me in the ground for Victor Watson's debut and subsequent career and I'll die happy.

One goal I would love to have seen at The Boleyn would be **KEITH ROBSON'S** v Eintracht Frankfurt. When I managed to get a DVD of the footage I watched it every morning at breakfast for about a year! All things considered, it must be one of the greatest ever scored at the old place.

George McDonald: Exciting and controversial, South American superstar **CARLOS TEVEZ** places the ball on the turf just outside the box at the Centenary End (Trevor Brooking Stand). Hammers are leading Tottenham 1-0 thanks to an early strike from a young Mark Noble. Tevez, yet to score for West Ham, loops his right-footed free-kick up over the wall, dips it just under the crossbar and over the hand of snail-like goalkeeper Paul Robinson. The crowd went absolutely wild.

Although not the best goal I've ever seen at Upton Park – a marginally more adequate keeper probably would have saved it, but we had gone 2-0 up against our nemesis and, more importantly, Tevez had scored his first goal for the club.

Tevez was an anomaly at West Ham. Everyone knew that the magical deadline day signing of the Argentine duo of Tevez and Javier Macherano probably wasn't kosher but we didn't care, we had a world class striker for the first time in a very long while. Amazingly, up until that point, he wasn't picked regularly by manager Alan Curbishley and would often start as a sub while forwards Bobby Zamora and Marlon Harewood got on the team-sheet ahead of him. West Ham were probably scared to use him because of the legal implications, which came to light in a big way at the end of that season, when West Ham just managed to avoid relegation thanks to Tevez's winner at Old Trafford on the final day.

That goal against Spurs sent elation and relief around the stadium. We ended up losing the game 4-3 but 'Carlitos' had become a cult hero already, and he could no longer be ignored. The fans demanded he was played and, almost single-handedly, he performed one of the greatest escapes in Premier League history.

Jack McDonald: **CARLOS TEVEZ's** free-kick v Spurs (4/3/2007). I remember him jumping over the advertising hoardings and reaching out to the crowd not too far from where we were sitting in the West lower. The whole of The Boleyn was jumping up and down.

He scored a similar free-kick from the same place v Bolton a few weeks later but my favourite goal was the one he got v Chelsea. After receiving the ball from a throw-in out by the East Stand, he played a neat one-two before cutting inside and unleashing a swerving right-foot shot that Petr Cech could only fingertip into the far corner of the net from about 22 yards. Despite losing the game, it was a lovely bit of magic from the little Argentine.

Another great goal was **ANTON FERDINAND's** volley v Fulham (I remember it well because it was Tomas Repka's last match for the club) – a great strike from a defender on the turn.

Gjermund Holt: I have seen around a hundred games at Upton Park, and there have been so many great goals. If I have to pick one, it would have to be **CARLOS TEVEZ's** free-kick v Spurs in (4/3/07), because it meant so much at the time.

Carlos Tevez leaps towards fans in the lower West after scoring from a free-kick against Spurs in 2007.

PLAYER
PAOLO DI CANIO
Born: 9/7/68, Rome, Italy
WHU career: 1999-2003
Position: Forward
Apps: 140, **Goals:** 50

MY goal against Wimbledon (26/3/2000), it was a great pass from Trevor Sinclair. Without a great pass, I would not have scored a great goal.

If am honest, yes, it was technically the best goal I have ever scored.

I speak about Di Canio in a good way or a bad way, but always honestly, whether I have played bad or good. I criticise myself for bad things, so it is fair that I say: 'Well done, Paolo' for good things and this was not just one of the best goals I have scored, but one of the best I have seen.

It looks technically impossible. It is in a strange position and the bicycle kick with the right foot, because normally you would control it or volley with the left foot.

If you hit the ball just one or two centimetres either side, it could end up out of the ground, or back near Trevor Sinclair!

I knew it was going to go over the defender's head and in that split second I decided to volley it. Maybe next time I would control it, but I knew then I could volley it. I like that technique and I try it all the time in training.

Belissimo! Paolo Di Canio watches the ball leave his right boot on its way over Wimbledon keeper Neil Sullivan and into the net for one of the greatest goals ever seen at Upton Park, or any other ground.

Hammers' ultimate high . . . Bobby Moore lifts the European Cup Winners' Cup after the 2-0 victory against TSV Munich 1860 at Wembley in 1965. Two-goal hero Alan Sealey is on the left, with Martin Peters, Brian Dear, Ron Boyce, Geoff Hurst, Jack Burkett and John Sissons also in shot.

6 HIGHS & LOWS

WHEN it comes to 'ups and downs', not many do it better than West Ham United. Five promotions and five relegations since 1978, seven Wembley appearances in the space of 17 years and then not a single one for the next 31, plus unforgettable victories and heart-breaking defeats in equal measure . . . the phrase 'roller-coaster of emotions' could have been invented at Upton Park. And if you've followed the claret-and-blue for any length of time, you'll know just what a crazy ride it can be.

Q: The happiest and lowest you felt after watching a match at Upton Park – and explain why?

Ed Gillis: Happiest – West Ham United 2 Wolves 0 (25/8/58), newly-promoted, beating the champions, Billy Wright *et al*, in our first home game of the season and realising that we had just beaten the best.

Lowest – West Ham United 3 Newcastle United 5 (20/2/60). A crazy score and a crazy match! As a callow youth, I had observed that Magpies' George Eastham had played well and that our goalkeeper, Noel Dwyer, had been less than efficient. Subsequent insinuations that the result had been 'manufactured' for betting purposes and that West Ham player(s) were implicated meant a loss of innocence and a welcome to the world of the cynics.

Colin Kosky: Happiest had to be after beating Eintracht Frankfurt in (14/4/76). That night was electric.

Lowest was losing 6-1 at home to champions-elect Man United (6/5/67) with George Best, Bobby Charlton, Denis Law, etc, when their

West Ham keeper Noel Dwyer and his team-mates came under suspicion after a heavy defeat by Newcastle United in this eventful match from 1960. Noel Cantwell and Andy Malcolm are the other Hammers in view, along with Magpies' George Eastham.

John Powles: The happiest was after West Ham's 7-0 drubbing of the great Leeds United side in a League Cup tie (7/11/66). Clubs then played their full first team players in the competition, so the result was no fluke, and was executed with football of a top class ability. I could honestly say this was the most satisfying night.

The 2-0 defeat v Everton (29/2/92) was the lowest I've felt. It came in the middle of all the furore over the ill-fated bond scheme. A large number of fans were incensed that, in order to obtain a season ticket for the following campaign, a bond had to be purchased, the cheapest at £500. Not only was the Everton game appalling, no less than seven balls went into the crowd and were not returned. And there was a pitch invasion which halted the game for a period of time, during which a fan grabbed a corner flag and stuck it in the centre circle. Fortunately the West Ham board relented regarding the season tickets but my support was at its lowest ebb at that time.

fans 'took' the North Bank after a running battle. We were at the front and went berserk when John Charles scored our goal.

Richard Miller: Happiest was beating Burnley 3-2 in the FA Cup 6th round (29/2/64), which meant Hammers had reached the semi-final for the first time since I had started supporting them. From being a goal down, a magnificent goal from a very narrow angle by Johnny Sissons and two superb goals from Johnny Byrne secured a well-deserved meeting with Manchester United at Hillsborough, which will always be remembered as a truly unforgettable day for every Hammers supporter privileged to be there.

My lowest memory is losing to Chelsea in the FA Cup 4th round

John Sissons looks about to fall on the photographer who captured the moment his effort from a tight angle ended up in the net after a failed attempted goal-line clearance by Burnley defender Alex Elder during the epic FA Cup quarter-final of 1964. Johnny Byrne scored Hammers' other two goals in the 3-2 victory.

(30/1/65) on the same day as Winston Churchill's funeral. A Bobby Tambling goal after just 10 minutes, following a dubious free-kick awarded against Joe Kirkup, meant we were no longer FA Cup holders.

Doug Barrett: Happiest was probably watching Geoff Hurst score six goals in our 8-0 thrashing of Sunderland (19/10/68).

Strangely enough, the lowest point involved the same player, in the League Cup semi-final, 2nd leg (15/12/71). This match demonstrated how high can turn to low in a split second. We had won the first leg, 2-1, at Stoke, so needed only to draw at Upton Park in order to reach the Wembley final. Last minute of normal time and West Ham are awarded a penalty after Harry Redknapp is brought down by Gordon Banks. Geoff Hurst to score and put us into the final. Hurst belts a thunderbolt towards the top corner of the net, only to see it pushed over the bar by his England colleague and fellow World Cup winner, Banks. It took two more matches to divide the two teams and unfortunately it was not Hammers who eventually came out on top.

Mark Harknett: After beating Eintracht Frankfurt (14/4/76). Elation and relief. Elation, because we'd reached a European final. Relief, because it was a tense, nail-biting finish. We were 3-0 up at half-time but a second-half goal for Frankfurt meant that if they scored again we'd be out on away goals.

Lowest was losing 2-0 to Liverpool in the last game of the 1977-78 season (29/4/78). We went into the game thinking we needed to win to stay up, although as it turned out, a draw would have been enough. For me and many others, our first relegation and terribly depressing.

Dave Spurgeon: As single match examples, the happiest has to be v Eintracht Frankfurt (14/4/76), when we won our way to the European Cup Winners' Cup final. The atmosphere and noise under that special magic spell that cup games under the Upton Park floodlights seemed to have generated over the years was never as great as that night. I had spent a week's salary on two occasions earlier in the 1975-76 season following the team to Den Haag and Frankfurt for first leg ECWC games, so the realisation I was now going to Brussels for the final, along with my brother and friends who stood alongside me that memorable night, made it my happiest post-match feeling.

The League Cup semi-final, 2nd leg v Coventry (10/2/81) came closest to matching it.

My lowest feeling was towards the very end of the 1966-67 season when we were completely humiliated by the Manchester United team (6/5/67), who clinched the league title with a 6-1 thrashing of a completely inept and seemingly disinterested West Ham team. This turned out be our sixth consecutive defeat at the end of a season which had promised so much in the immediate aftermath of the 1966 World Cup triumph.

The day did not bode well for me or my friends who attended the game, three of whom were United fans. Despite arriving at the ground two hours before kick-off, our preferred vantage point of the West Enclosure was not available to us. Police and stewards diverted queuing fans to other parts of the ground, indicating the West Enclosure and Chicken Run would soon be filled to capacity and turnstiles shut. We ended up in the South Bank at the corner adjacent to the Chicken Run with no sight at all of a third of the pitch.

West Ham keeper Colin Mackleworth stops Denis Law from adding to Manchester United's six goals in the 1967 game that was marred by crowd trouble and saw the visitors clinch the league title.

> **Tony Hogg:** The happiest I've ever been after watching a game at Upton Park would have to be following the 2-1 victory over Real Zaragoza in the semi-final, 1st leg of the European Cup Winners' Cup (7/4/65). The Spanish forward line was known as the 'Magnificent Five' but Hammers paid scant regard to their reputation by putting them to the sword 2-1, with a diving header form Brian 'Stag' Dear and another goal from 'Budgie' Byrne.
>
> The following season, at the same stage of the same competition, Hammers battled against the formidable Germans Borussia Dortmund as they attempted to retain the Cup. In one of the greatest displays I've ever witnessed from a West Ham team, Martin Peters put us in front with a low shot from outside the area which evaded Hans Tilkowski and went just inside his left-hand post at the erupting North Bank end. But winger Lothar Emmerich broke our hearts with two late goals in the 86th and 87th minutes to put the Germans in a commanding lead for the return in Dortmund.
>
> I'll never forget the almost deafening silence as the West Ham fans trooped back down Green Street towards Upton Park station in the realisation that the European dream was finally over.
>
> It was little consolation that Borussia defeated Liverpool in the Hampden Park final and that Tilkowski and Emmerich were on the losing side when England defeated West Germany in the World Cup Final at Wembley two months later.

Terry Roper: For a very personal reason, the happiest that I have ever felt at a game at Upton Park was when West Ham beat Nottingham Forest 4-2 with goals from Frank McAvennie (2), Tony Cottee and Alan Dickens (28/9/86). It was the season when the 'Boys of 86' came so close to winning the League championship for the only time in the club's history.

What made the game so special was the fact that it was the first time I had taken my two sons, Ian and Neil, to Upton Park to watch my beloved West Ham. They were both very young at the time (seven and four respectively) and it was a memorable occasion as we took our seats in the West Stand. It was the day that my sons became the fourth generation of West Ham fans in my family.

My lowest ebb at Upton Park came, not after just one match, but throughout much of the 1991-92 season, entirely due to the disgraceful implementation of the bond scheme by the board of directors. Manager Billy Bonds had no money to strengthen his squad, since all available funds were earmarked for ground improvements following the Hillsborough disaster and the resultant Taylor Report.

Redevelopment at Upton Park was expected to cost £15m and to finance the project, the directors launched the Hammers' Bond Scheme which, in effect, was a scurrilous plan to get the fans to pay the requisite modernisation out of our own pockets. We were expected to pay between £500 and £975 for a bond which merely gave us the right to purchase a season ticket for the next 50 years. It did not pay for the ticket itself, which came at an additional cost each season. It was an appalling decision and a shocking insult to our undying loyalty.

Quite rightly, we were outraged. Protests and pitch invasions duly followed. Our outrage was confirmed by the fact that only 808 bonds were sold out of an initial target figure of 19,301, which equates to a take-up of approximately 4 per cent.

Unfortunately, the venom aimed at the directors appeared to have a demoralising effect on the team who, in any event, were clearly not good enough for the top sphere of English football. West Ham won just nine games all season and finished bottom of the table.

There have been some shameful episodes in West Ham's recent history, such as the hugely embarrassing Tevez affair; the appalling and crass use of Bobby Moore's name for advertising purposes, particularly bearing in mind the club blatantly turned its back on him after his playing days were over; plus the shocking profligacy of manager Alan Curbishley and his chairman Eggert Magnusson who both totally ignored the laws of economic gravity by almost bankrupting the club with a string of ludicrously overpriced and, in some cases, injury-prone signings, all on huge contracts.

However, the bond scheme remains, arguably, the most shameful episode of all. It was a disgrace and an affront to those of us who have supported the club through thick and thin.

I have selected this as the lowest moment, even over the relegation-related experiences over the years, because it epitomised the worst end of the West Ham enigma in a season when we took the term underachievement to a new level.

Paul Ford: Happiest was the night match v Man United (16/5/77), where a win in our last match of the season would ensure safety from relegation. A rollercoaster of a game which my girlfriend wanted to come to. I took her along and found her football knowledge sadly lacking when I had to explain the kick-in/warm-up was a form of practise prior to the start. When Man Utd kicked off they contrived to score through Gordon Hill within 20 seconds. You could hear the proverbial pin dropping as we could see impending relegation looming. The hush was broken when a voice beside me asked: "Does that one count or are they still practicing?"

Robert Banks: I remember coming from a goal down to beat Norwich 2-1 in the FA Cup 4th round (4/2/84). We danced and sang all the way down Green Street after the game like we had won the cup itself. The Everton quarter-final (11/3/91) was a special night too. It's cup nights that I remember being the happiest.

The lowest would probably be the whole bond scheme episode and turning up to games expecting to get beaten. In other relegation seasons I have gone to each game with a crumb of hope – but not in the latter half of 1991-92.

Gladly, the team rallied and we ran out 4-2 winners thanks to Frank Lampard equalising, a brace from Pop Robson, plus one from Geoff Pike (who also managed to miss a penalty). Stuart 'Pancho' Pearson also scored for Man Utd to keep our nerves jangling. I remember referee Clive Thomas playing what seemed like 10 minutes stoppage time before our safety was finally confirmed.

For my saddest moment, fast-forward 12 months to the last match of 1977-78 when a 2-0 loss at home to Liverpool (29/4/78) saw us relegated for the first time in my lifetime. It felt like the world had ended. If I had known that this would be the start of our revival, which would include two Wembley finals as a Division Two team, I may not have been quite so devastated.

Ian McMaster: Happiest was probably after the FA Cup quarter-final victory v Aston Villa (8/3/80), thanks to Ray Stewart's last-minute penalty. I was standing at the other end, in the North Bank. The guy next to me, who I didn't know, practically kissed me when that penalty went in.

Lowest was after the 2-1 defeat by Chelsea (15/4/86). We were on such a great run but just didn't hit it off that evening. I had the awful feeling that we had just blown the league championship and, although we strung together more victories at home that season, those missing points really killed us. Such a miserable journey home to Dulwich.

Martin Scholar: Happiest when we beat Aston Villa in the FA Cup quarter-final (8/3/80). For a second division team to be in the semi-finals was fantastic.

Lowest was a very West Ham moment . . . getting promoted in 1991 but being pipped by Oldham to the (second division) championship in the final moments of the season, thanks to a 2-1 home defeat by Notts County (11/5/91). Hammers needed to match Oldham's result at home to Sheffield Wednesday to clinch the title and the celebrations were almost beginning at Upton Park when we heard Oldham were 2-0 down after an hour . . . only for them to fight back and grab a last-minute winner.

Adrian White: I have to say one of the happiest times was the second leg of the 1981 League Cup semi-final v Coventry City (10/2/81). We had lost 3-2 in the first leg at Highfield Road but a 20-yard belter from Paul Goddard and an 89th minute winner from Jimmy Neighbour sent the 38,551 present that February night mental as we celebrated what would be our third trip to Wembley in 10 months.

The lowest moment has be after Trevor Brooking's final game, v Everton (14/5/84). The team that I had followed home and away for the previous seven seasons was breaking up, and I recall Brooking's retirement being a major blow to me.

Michael Harris: The happiest I have felt after watching a game at Upton Park was v Newcastle United (2/2/85), a 1-1 draw. The game wasn't very good but I had taken my six-year-old son, Paul, to his first game and that meant he was now condemned to a lifetime of suffering along with all of us Hammers fans.

The lowest I have felt was when Geoff Hurst's penalty was saved by Stoke's Gordon Banks in December 1971. It is the best save I've ever witnessed and, had Hurst scored, we would have been back at Wembley in the League Cup Final.

Steve Smith: Happiest was after we beat Ipswich Town (30/4/86). We had been through the mill that night and when Ray Stewart scored a last-minute winner from the penalty spot, I genuinely thought we were going to win the league.

The saddest day will be when we play our last match at The Boleyn Ground. I'll be in bits.

David Steadman: Happiest feeling was after the 2-1 win against Ipswich (30/4/86), a late Ray Stewart penalty winning the match and keeping our dreams of winning our first ever title in place. My dad was a steward at the time and told me that Ipswich skipper and legend Terry Butcher had punched a hole in the dressing room door after the match, as it more or less condemned Ipswich to relegation.

Mark Matthews: The happiest watching a game at Upton Park would have to be the final home match of the 1985-86 season, v Ipswich (30/4/86). After coming from behind to dramatically win 2-1, West Ham moved up to second in the league, four points behind leaders Liverpool with a game in hand. At the end I, along with thousands of other fans,

Ray Stewart leads the celebrations, followed by Frank McAvennie and a leaping Paul Goddard after scoring the penalty that beat Ipswich Town in April 1986 and kept alive dreams of the league championship.

flooded onto the pitch to applaud the team in the directors' box and there was a feeling of euphoria and a real belief that the team were on the brink of winning the first ever league title in the club's history.

I don't really want to dwell on the lows at Upton Park – with five relegations during my time there has unfortunately been a few! The most recent one that comes to mind, though, was the 3-0 defeat by Sunderland (22/5/2011) on the last day of the season after Avram Grant had been sacked and we had already been relegated. At that point there appeared little hope for the future.

Gjermund Holt: I think I have never felt happier than I did on my first visit, v Everton (4/4/88). I was so over the moon. I was 21, and had saved my money to travel from Norway. I remember I cried when the game kicked off, it meant so much to me.

The lowest was maybe when the ref blew the whistle and we'd lost 4-3 to Spurs (4/3/2007). Everyone in the Bobby Moore lower was so down. We were almost relegated, then Mark Noble came towards us with tears in his eyes. It was like something happened at that very moment. The crowd began singing, 'Nobes' started to cheer up with his hands in the air. I still believe that was the moment when the 'Great Escape' really started.

Peter Lush: The 4–1 victory in the League Cup v Liverpool (30/11/88). We were having a terrible season that ended with us getting relegated but that night we destroyed Liverpool, with a young kid called Paul Ince scoring two goals and running the game from midfield.

Stuart Slater is congratulated by Tony Gale after his FA Cup match-winner against Everton in 1991. Jimmy Quinn, Colin Foster, Tim Breacker and Ian Bishop are also part of this happy scene.

Lowest: Whenever we've fallen apart to lower grade opposition in cup ties.

The saddest was the game after Bobby Moore died, v Wolves (6/3/93), with all the tributes outside the ground and before the match. I made a collage of the photos I took that day and still have it on my bedroom wall.

Michael Oliver: The happiest (apart from every time we beat Tottenham) was probably when we beat Manchester United 1-0 with Kenny Brown's goal (22/4/92). Even though we were all but relegated, the atmosphere was amazing and I desperately wanted to win. It was a great performance too, the team seemed determined not to lose. And it effectively stopped Man United from winning the title.

I should also mention the play-off semi-final, 2nd leg, against Ipswich Town (18/5/2004). Brilliant performance, great atmosphere, and I was convinced we were going up.

The lowest was probably after losing 2-1 to Sunderland on a Friday night (29/4/2005), the penultimate game of the season. We'd been 1-0 up at half-time through Marlon Harewood and heading for the play-offs but defeat appeared to have put them out of reach. The prospect of another season out of the Premier League, with our better players having to be sold, was truly depressing. I went away for the weekend wanting nothing to do with football and avoided seeing all the other results until Sunday night. Of course, they all went our way and the season had a happy ending.

Alan Porter: Happiest? It doesn't seem right to hold bad feelings about another team. It's only a game. However, we were virtually alrerday relegated and Manchester United had to beat us (22/4/92) to win the league. Memory tells me that we had stacks of injuries. Our team was full of reserves and people playing out of position. It wasn't so much the fact that we won, it was Sir Alex Ferguson's post-match claim that West Ham's efforts had been 'obscene'. Indeed, they were!

Saddest? My dad introduced me to West Ham. He was still a season ticket holder at 93. Every game I go to I still look at 'his' seat: K123, East Stand upper. Wonderful memories, I wish he was still there.

Ian Crocker: I felt at my lowest at the first game after Bobby Moore's death, v Wolves (6/3/93), mainly because of the emotion involved. The club and fans were brilliant in the aftermath but it was a tough time having worked with Bobby at Capital Radio. He was such a great bloke. You would never have guessed he was the man who lifted the World Cup for England. He was unassuming and more interested in others than himself.

I remember covering West Brom v West Ham at The Hawthorns and Bobby dropped me off at the media room before going off to park the car. I asked for passes in the name of Capital Radio and the guy on the door said, in all seriousness, not realising his error: 'Which one are you? Bobby Moore?' I wish!

Graham Wright: The happiest I ever felt was after the final game of the 1992-93 season v Cambridge United (8/5/93), when we clinched promotion back to the top flight. The last few weeks had been very tense, with Portsmouth going through a purple patch to seriously endanger our chances of going up. It all depended on the Cambridge match and Portsmouth's final game the same day. West Ham went ahead but it could all have gone wrong at any time, until a couple of minutes from the end, when Julian Dicks went marauding down the left-wing, cut inside and laid the ball on a plate for Clive Allen to clinch the 2-0 win. Many of the crowd prematurely invaded the pitch, and I thought the referee might abandon the game. Fortunately, the pitch was cleared, the last minute or two was played out and the final whistle blew. We then went mad!

I have never been present when West Ham have been relegated but I have felt very low after some of our painful defeats. The worst was a match v Stoke City (7/10/67). I was behind the South Bank goal where

---

Steve Blowers: Happiest: That fantastic, floodlit, FA Cup 6th round victory over first division Everton (11/3/91), when Stuart Slater announced his arrival on the big stage with a stunning, scoring performance that saw the Toffees come unstuck as second-tier West Ham United booked a Villa Park semi-final against Nottingham Forest. We may have been in Division Two but, boy, we were still good.

Lowest: Having already won at Manchester United and Sunderland, it was simply heartbreaking to slump to an FA Cup 6th round defeat in the late kick-off at home to Tottenham Hotspur (11/3/2001). The stage was all set for the hyped-up Hammers to progress to an Old Trafford semi-final but with PA announcer Jeremy Nicholas prematurely announcing during the warm-up that West Ham United – and only West Ham United – would be facing Arsenal in the last four, the bubbles burst for Harry Redknapp's favourites as a now fully-fired Spurs unexpectedly ran out 3-2 winners.

PLAYER
KENNY BROWN
Born: 11/7/67, Barking, Essex
WHU career: 1991-96
Position: Right-back
Apps: 79, **Goals:** 6

WE went into the Manchester United game (22/4/92) bottom of the table, knowing we had to win our last three matches – and hope that our relegation rivals Coventry, Luton and Notts County lost their games – to survive.

On the other hand, Man United were one point behind the leaders, Leeds, with a game in hand, so they were close to winning the title.

Ludo Miklosko had one of those great games that he always seemed to have against United. He stopped everything and the longer the game went on, the more we sensed we could win. In the second-half, Ludo made a fantastic save from a Mark Hughes scissor-kick following a corner, where it was my job to defend the near post. As Ludo rolled the ball out to Stuart Slater to start our attack down the left, I started my run upfield.

Stuart burst away down the left but his final ball into United's penalty area wasn't good. Neither was Gary Pallister's clearance, though, because he seemed to slash at the ball and it came flying at me just as I arrived in their box. All I could do was 'open up'

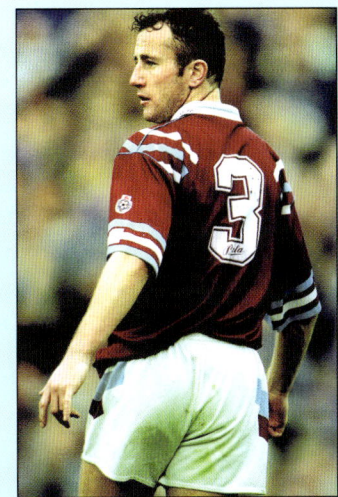

Kenny Brown wrecked Manchester United's title plans in 1992.

the inside of my foot and steer it straight back into their net past Peter Schmeichel. It was more instinct than anything, but I knew what I was doing.

After the game, Bill (Bonds) came up to me and said: "The press want to know if you meant it." And, of course, I said I did.

But the next morning there was all sorts of stuff written. I had to laugh because one paper said it was a ricochet off my shin and that the ball had bounced into an empty net.

It didn't really bother me. I was just happy to have scored the winner. Unfortunately, the euphoria didn't last long, though, because we lost at Coventry the following Saturday and that sent us down.

West Ham scored three times before half-time. Another great win wrapped up – or so we thought. Stoke scored four times in the same goal in the second half to win 4-3! We went home in a daze.

Matt Drury: Happiest moment was invading the pitch when we beat Cambridge to be promoted to the Premier League (8/5/93).

Lowest was probably a 5-1 defeat to Leeds (1/5/99), when we had three players, Ian Wright, Shaka Hislop and Steve Lomas, sent off.

Tony Hoskins: The Cambridge United game when we clinched

Dan Francis: I was too young to really appreciate what was happening towards the end of the 1985-86 season. I recall there being an electric buzz around the ground but at the time I didn't know any different and so wrongly assumed it was just the way things were at Upton Park every year!

By the early 90s, I was more aware of the true meaning of being a West Ham fan, of the highs and lows, of fortunes always hiding, of dreams fading. In 1990-91, I was at an age when my obsession with West Ham and football in general was at a peak. I literally lived and breathed the game, and I don't think I've ever been happier than I was the night we beat Everton 2-1 in the FA Cup quarter-final (11/3/91), when I genuinely believed I was finally going to witness my heroes play in a cup final at Wembley. Stuart Slater scored a stunning solo goal to win the game and, as the strains of 'We're on the march with Billy's Army, we're all goin' a Wember-lee!' reverberated around the stands, I was bursting with absolute pride and joy, completely in love with the game.

From a footballing point of view there are many dismal defeats and performances to reflect on, but I recall being particularly crushed on the final day of that promotion-winning campaign, when a 2-1 defeat v Notts County (11/5/91) denied us the old second division title. After Keith Hackett had ripped apart our FA Cup dreams just a few weeks previously at Villa Park, the opportunity to win our first piece of silverware since the same achievement exactly 10 years earlier would have helped to soften the blow and, from my seat right next to the directors' box, I was looking forward to being in the thick of the celebrations. Sadly, our defeat and Oldham's 3-2 win over Sheffield Wednesday earned the Latics the title, a scenario that left me in tears.

Personally, though, the lowest moment I've ever experienced at Upton Park came with the tragic loss of a friend and colleague, on January 2, 2006, the very first day that I began working for the club's media department. That afternoon, we were playing Chelsea at Upton Park and lost 3-1 but the result paled into insignificance when I was told just a few moments after the final whistle that Ian Jackson, a member of the club's groundstaff, had died suddenly a few hours earlier.

Ian was only in his late 30s but had worked at Upton Park and Chadwell Heath since leaving school in the 80s. I got to know him well during my frequent visits to the training ground and also played football with him on a Sunday morning for the Havering Nalgo amateur side that Trevor Brooking and Billy Bonds graced in the late 80s. Ian was an infectious character, always laughing and joking, and like many others at the club in those days, would do anything he could to help you. He left a wife and three young children whom he was completely devoted to, and his loss had a profound effect on everyone who knew him. I still miss Ian now, and when the lights go out at Upton Park next summer, I'll be remembering him as much as the football.

promotion (8/5/93) was all the more special as I was with my dad and we celebrated on the pitch.

Lowest I ever felt came when one of my schoolboy heroes, Stoke City's Gordon Banks, saved Geoff Hurst's penalty (15/12/71) to deny us a place at Wembley in the League Cup final. I was stood against the wall just to the right of the goal and when Geoff hit the ball we were already starting to jump and punch the air but, somehow, Banks made one of his trademark saves and our dream ended.

Mike Corbett: Beating Man City 3-0 (17/12/94). Tony Cottee scored a hat-trick, and we just played really well. There was such a great atmosphere in the stadium that day.

The worst is a long list, but I've chosen a recent game that we won, which may seem odd. We played Southampton (22/2/2014) and beat them 3-1. But our football was so terrible, I honestly came away with the feeling that we'd lost. At that point I seriously considered not renewing my season ticket, or even going to another game. No pleasing some people, I suppose, although, in my defence, I think the stats of that game showed that we only had 30 per cent possession.

David Meagher: Happiest was when we beat Blackburn Rovers in their end-of-season run towards the Premier League title in 1995 – a game we needed points from to boost our survival efforts. Against all odds, we put in a stunning performance – keeping the SAS (Shearer and Sutton) pairing quiet to win 2-0 with goals from Marc Rieper and Don Hutchison. Leaving the ground, we knew we would survive but little did we know how dramatically the season would end with Man United 'frustrated' on the final day by our heroes!

The lowest was after a sickening home 1-0 defeat to Southampton (2/12/2002) when, after pummelling a poor Southampton side for 80 minutes without scoring, we were suckered by a last-minute James Beattie goal. It dawned on all concerned that the stunningly talented squad Glenn Roeder had assembled was truly jinxed.

Chris Ludlow: The lowest I have been was after the 2002-03 season, when we were relegated with one of the best squads I have seen. Another low point was the last day of the North Bank, knowing that the game v Southampton (7/5/94) would be the last time I would stand on the terraces that were such a big part of the early days following Hammers.

Neil Roper: Happiest I felt was the night we beat Spurs 4-3 (24/2/97). This was the first season my dad and I had season tickets and was actually the first time I'd seen West Ham play Spurs. Most notably it was also the night John Hartson and Paul Kitson made their home debuts, both having been signed a few weeks earlier to try and save us from relegation. For me, this was the greatest game I've ever seen at Upton Park and I remember walking home that night feeling 10 feet tall because, not only had we just beaten Spurs, but I also felt like one of the chosen few who was there to witness just what an incredible game football can be.

If anything can demonstrate just what an incredible game football can be, then my lowest point I can remember came just a couple of months earlier. On New Year's Day, 1997, we played host to Nottingham Forest, who were bottom of the table, just below us. Not only did West Ham put in a truly abysmal performance, barely recording a worthwhile effort on goal, but Marc Rieper's error towards the end of the first-half allowed Kevin Campbell to score the only goal of the game. Dad and I still maintain it was the coldest day either of us have ever experienced at Upton Park – the pitch was icy and half-time was even shortened to 10 minutes because of the freezing temperature. The terrible performance certainly didn't help and we both headed for the car after the game wondering whether we were going to witness relegation in our first as season ticket holders.

Gerard Daly: Happiest would be the 3-2 win v Chelsea (12/3/97). We conceded a late equaliser to Mark Hughes but Paul Kitson got a last-gasp winner. I grew up in Kingston, Chelsea territory, so always considered them the main enemy.

Neil Humphreys: The happiest Upton Park memory was a bit of a cheeky one. I bunked off work and nipped into the stadium for free. On May 8, 1993, I told the manager at the Iceland supermarket in East Ham's high street, where I had a part-time job, that I needed to take an extended lunch break. I joined a mate for a couple of pints and by the time we reached Upton Park, it was a lock-out. So we followed the game in The Boleyn pub, waited until the final 10 minutes when they opened the gates, joined the crush trying to get in and ended up sitting on the touchline near the corner flag, just in time to see Clive Allen tap in to seal a 2-0 victory against Cambridge United. The result confirmed West Ham's promotion under Billy Bonds, our lifelong hero.

As for the lowest memory, I was one of those on the pitch protesting against the idiotic bond scheme and that entire season was dreadful.

But a turgid game a few seasons ago was a personal low point. Going into the stadium, I was buzzing. On January 30, 2010, I had just launched my first novel at the glorious Newham Bookshop and posed with the book for a photo shoot in front of the World Cup 1966 statue. So I was really up for the game against Blackburn Rovers. It ended 0-0 and was utterly dreadful.

The fact that I can recall nothing about the game tells only part of the story. I didn't recognise the stadium or the exorbitant, corporate cocoon it had become. Everything was expensive, the football was dire and the increasingly white-collar crowd generated about as much atmosphere as a dentist's waiting room. I'm no inverted snob. But the ticket cost almost 50 quid and felt overpriced, 10 times over.

I didn't recognise the stuttering football on the pitch or the stadium itself. It was awful.

Marc Rieper scored in the 2-0 win against champions-elect Blackburn Rovers in 1995.

Paul Kitson scored vital goals that helped keep Hammers up after signing in 1997.

The lowest I felt, and there's plenty to choose from, would possibly be after a 2-1 home defeat to Hull City (20/1/90). There seemed a real feeling that serious decline was setting in but a few weeks later Billy Bonds took over from Lou Macari and things seemed a lot more hopeful.

John Reynolds: Perhaps my happiest moment at Upton Park was also my worst. A League Cup quarter-final v Aston Villa (15/12/99). I mean, West Ham never win on penalties when it matters. And when we eventually did, it got taken away from us two days later after a Football League inquiry into what became known as the 'Mannygate' affair.

I was the last person to leave the stadium after Shaka Hislop saved a sudden-death penalty from Gareth Southgate. I was dancing joyously on my seat in the Bobby Moore lower and so high on euphoria that I had to be removed by stewards.

Two days later, we learned that the game would have to be replayed because Manny Omoynimi (a youth/reserve team forward who played for only 10 minutes) was deemed ineligible, having played for Gillingham in an earlier round of the competition while on loan. I so nearly didn't go to the replay. I, and every other West Ham supporter, knew what was coming. Graham Mackrell, the club secretary, was sacked for a 'slight' oversight. Slight? It was typical West Ham.

Spencer Dodd: Beating Spurs and Chelsea was always a highlight but for me it has to be the play-off semi-final, 2nd leg v Ipswich Town (18/5/2004). My dad, Jeffrey, was by this stage pretty ill and had been in a wheelchair for some time. Driving to the game, parking, getting him in and out of the wheelchair, to the stadium and then to and from our seats, etc, made it quite an ordeal. As a result, we'd been going less and less frequently. To be fair, everyone was always very helpful, very respectful and hugely supportive, which only ever strengthened my respect for the fans and deep love I have for what to me has always been a family and community-lead club.

Anyway, I sensed it was going to be a cracker in advance and Dad and I wouldn't have too many more opportunities like this, so I splashed out on hospitality tickets for us. We could get there early, have dinner at the stadium, and take our seats, which I'm pleased to say were still in amongst

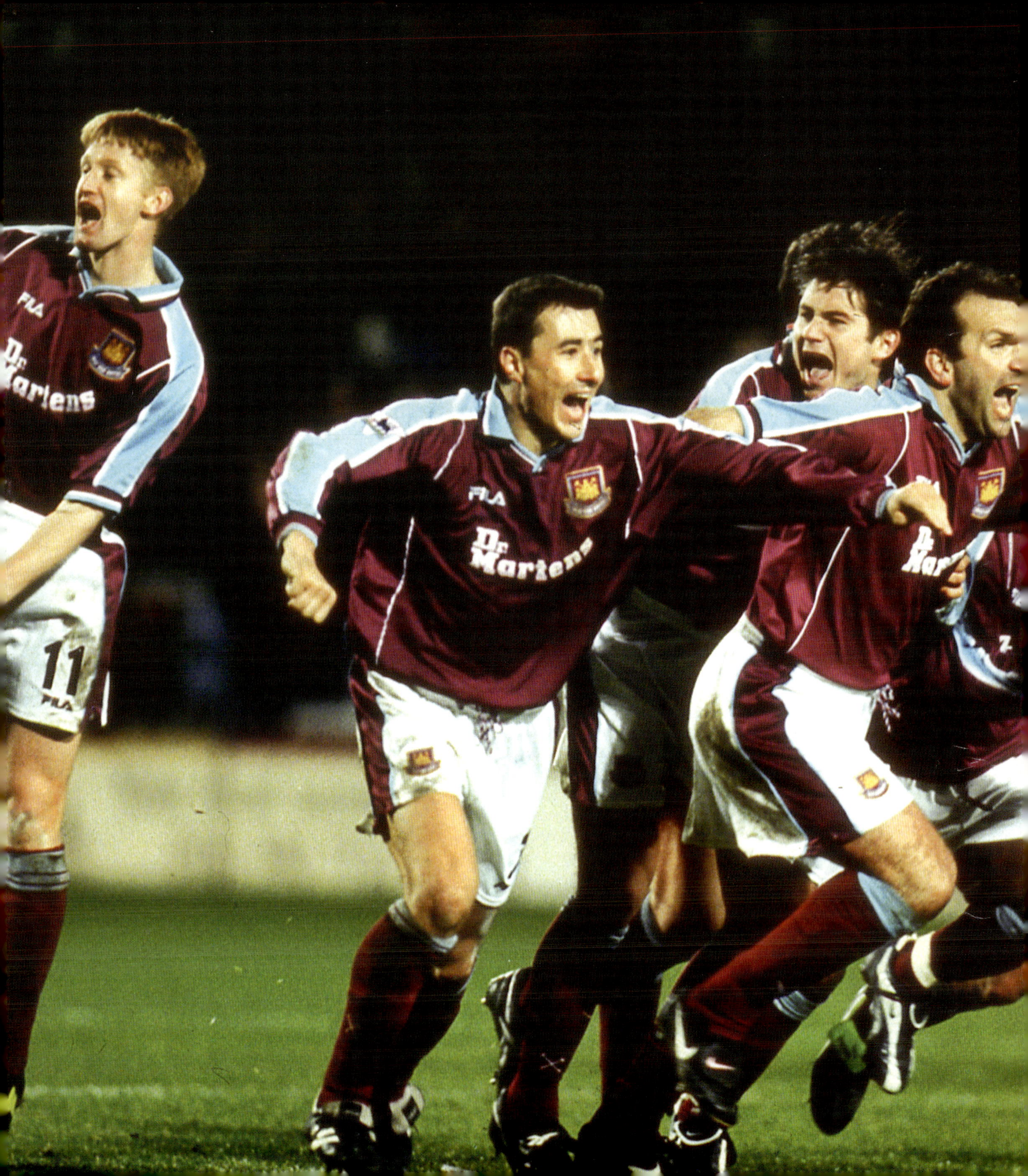
FILA
Dr Martens
11

Shaka Hislop's penalty save sparked triumphant scenes at the end of the shootout in the infamous League Cup quarter-final against Aston Villa in 1999. Exploding with delight and rushing to congratulate the keeper are (left to right) Steve Lomas, Marc Keller, Frank Lampard, Neil Ruddock, Trevor Sinclair (partly hidden), Javier Margas and Manny Omoyinmi. The latter was subsequently found to be cup-tied and the game had to be re-played at a bitter cost.

the fans, so we didn't feel too detached from it all.

Manager Alan Pardew pulled out every trick in the book and drew upon everything at his disposal to get the crowd going . . . the smoke, the horns, the singing, bubbles . . . and he succeeded in whipping the crowd up into a real frenzy. The way we attacked the game helped but it was non-stop noise from start to finish.

Dad and I both left with a smile on our faces and a memory to cherish.

Eamonn McManus: Happiest, for many reasons, would have to be the Ipswich play-off semi-final (18/5/2004). That night my son was ill and I asked a 'Spud' friend, Dave O'Grady, if he would like to come and he could not believe the atmosphere and how we kept going all night. I think

Tim Crane: There have been surprisingly few occasions when I have been pulse-poundingly happy after a game but there are a few which stand out.

The Aston Villa FA Cup 6th round (8/3/80), and Coventry in the League Cup semi-final (10/2/81), when Paul Goddard and Jimmy Neighbour took us to Wembley.

I was permanently happy during that 1980-81 period. I remember we beat league leaders Blackburn 2-0 (11/10/80) and Nobby Stiles' Preston 5-0 (31/1/81). We were unplayable and took that form into the top flight for a while.

I was tickled pink when we beat Aston Villa in the quarter-final of the League Cup (15/12/99). I was off to New York the following day and the thought of a semi-final against Leicester City for a place at Wembley was exhilarating. By the time I came home 'Mannygate' had unfolded and we lost a re-match.

I was fairly low when we lost our final home game to Notts County, 2-1 (11/5/91). It allowed Oldham to pip us to the number one spot for promotion. Sure, we still went up but I had a decent amount on us at 5/1 to be champions and had already booked a trip to the States on the strength of it!

Anytime we beat Spurs, Arsenal, Liverpool and Man Utd is an obvious thrill. The 4-1 pounding of Liverpool in the League Cup (30/11/88) during the Paul Ince years was mesmerising, as was the 4-0 in the League Cup against United in more recent times (30/11/2010), with Jonathan Spencer nabbing a brace.

There was a time during the mid-80s when we beat Arsenal at home more often than not and ruining Spurs' Champions League aspirations in 2006 is another fond memory.

Most recently, I found myself punching the air with happiness after the thrilling FA Cup replay against Everton (13/1/2014). Winning 9-8 on penalties with a goalkeeper, Adrian, scoring the winning goal was a first and I do enjoy watching history.

It must be said that I would trade all these experiences in to be taking my place in the stands for my first ever game at The Boleyn, v Manchester United (8/9/58), when a certain young Bobby Moore took his place in the line-up for his debut.

Unquestionably, those West Ham fans during the Bobby Moore era had the best of it.

'Oh, Christian Dailly...' The goalscoring defender celebrates victory in the electrifying 2004 play-off semi-final v Ipswich Town.

he might even have a soft spot for us now.

Eintracht Frankfurt (14/4/76) was also a good night game. I remember blagging duty-free cigarettes from German women sitting in the East Stand above us in the Chicken Run. A good night and good banter.

Liam Tyrell: Play-off semi-final, v Ipswich (18/5/2004) was a particularly satisfying occasion under the lights at the Boleyn Ground. I cannot recall a time when the ground was rocking like that, it was an electric atmosphere. Nights under the lights can be special and that really was. Turning around a first leg deficit with the added bonus of celebrating reaching a final added to the event.

The relegations have been obvious low times. For some of those dark times there was a sense of inevitability where we'd been doomed for many weeks. On other occasions, like the drop being confirmed at Anfield in '89, there was a true sense of pride at almost achieving the impossible after a fine late run of form.

One of the saddest occasions was the first home match following the death of Bobby Moore, v Wolves (6/3/93). I drove down from Yorkshire the previous night and, without thinking, found myself in the early hours heading straight to the main gates instead of my Romford destination. It felt like I had to pay my respects to the growing mass of memorabilia and flowers. That respectful stillness stayed for days. The sight of Hurst, Peters and Ron Greenwood laying the wreath on the pitch hit home the loss of West Ham's most famous son.

Ian Smith: That Ipswich play-off semi-final (18/5/2004). Christian Dailly got the ball in his nether regions but still managed to put it into the net for our winner before collapsing to the ground in agony! I also remember Ipswich hitting the bar in the final seconds and the relief all around the ground when Stephen Bywater got hold of the ball and the final whistle blew. What with the atmosphere and coming back from a first leg deficit, we were going to the Millennium Stadium for the first time. The excitement was tangible and the crowd were so happy, they sung on the trains all the way home. We all thought that West Ham would soon be back in the Premier League, where they belong. We couldn't have been more wrong.

There have been plenty of low moments at Upton Park, especially during relegation seasons, but the most recent one was losing to Spurs (25/2/2013), when Bale scored in the last minute with a 25-yard screamer. We had managed to turn around a 1-0 deficit to go 2-1 up before Spurs equalised with about 15 minutes to go. There were chances at either end but I vividly remember Bale getting knocked down and looking for the free-kick. When play continued with no free-kick, he got up, received the ball and smashed it into the corner. I was truly gutted. I hate losing to Tottenham but to do it in the last minute was unbearable.

George Reynolds: Happiest is without a shadow of a doubt the 4-0 thrashing of Manchester United in the League Cup quarter-final (30/11/2010). My favourite player, Carlton Cole, turning and destroying Jonny Evans on a regular basis during the game, Jonny Spector playing out of his skin in a game where everything seemed to go right. Of course, the next day at school, I walked in with a VERY large grin across my face to greet everyone! When we called my grandparents after the game, they said they had initially thought Sky had got the score the wrong way round and couldn't believe it.

Lowest was after watching us fall apart v Wolves (23/3/2010) under Gianfranco Zola. I think James Tomkins mis-hit a backpass, which allowed Wolves to score, and we were woeful. After the 3-1 defeat I came out of the ground in tears, absolutely convinced we were down with no chance of us being saved. Having been too young to remember the previous relegation in 2003, and confusingly optimistic when we only just stayed up in 2007, this was the first time I thought I would watch us get relegated. Although crying as I came away from the stadium, I remember a man walking past us down Priory Road, who came over and consoled me and said: "Don't worry, we'll do it and stay up." Fortunately, that year he was right!

Paul Walker: The 3-1 home win v Chelsea (1/12/2012), a great result against a club obscenely rich, with us just back in the top flight, was very pleasing. As has been any win over Spurs. But for me the happiest days were under Ron Greenwood and John Lyall in the 60s and 70s. And you have to go some to match the feeling when Ray Stewart's 89th minute penalty crashed home in the FA Cup quarter-final v Aston Villa (8/3/80). It secured a 1-0 win and from way up at the back of the North Bank that day, watching the whole stadium go crackers was wonderful.

Iain Dale: The lows seem to merge into one big morass. However, the one that sticks in my mind is the 3-0 defeat to Sunderland (22/5/2011) at the end of the 2010-11 season when we were relegated. We were already down but we just wanted the team to show us some pride. It was clear that Avram Grant had lost the dressing room and should have been shown the door in January. Hindsight is a wonderful thing, It was an abject performance from a team whose self-belief had disappeared. Another low was when we contrived to throw away a 3-0 lead v Wimbledon (9/9/98) and went on to lose 4-3. Only at Upton Park, eh?

But let's not forget the highs too. Beating Man U 4-0 in the League Cup (30/11/2010) was a bit special, and the 3-1 win against Chelsea (1/12/2012) was memorable. Perhaps I was happiest when we beat Aston Villa in the League Cup quarter-final (15/12/99), having gone 2-1 down in the 90th minute. Paolo Di Canio then scored a penalty and we then 'won' the game on penalties.

When I say won, it was a pyrrhic victory, since it was later discovered that Manny Omoyinmi was cup-tied. The game had to be replayed (11/1/2000) and, of course, being West Ham, we lost 3-1 after extra-time. Just like my dreams . . .

The lowest I and my late brother, David, ever felt leaving the ground was after the League Cup semi-final, 2nd leg, v Stoke City (15/12/71). Geoff Hurst could have sent us to Wembley had he scored a last-minute penalty in front of the North Bank. He always smashed them but somehow Gordon Banks managed to stick up a hand to divert the Hurst thunderbolt over the bar. Two more replays with Stoke ended with us being knocked out after losing 3-2 at Old Trafford. That night at The Boleyn was a horror. We drove home to west London without saying a word to each other all the way. We had been so, so close.

Alan Deadman: My lowest point has to be the last game of 2010-11 when we lost 3-0 at home to Sunderland (22/5/2011). We had gone 10 games without a win and were relegated, rock bottom, with only 33 points. An awful season and a lack-lustre end to Avram Grant's management.

Charlie Beckwith: The happiest feeling I've had at Upton Park is when we beat Tottenham 2-0 (3/5/2014), singing 'It's happened again!' to the Spurs fans who were almost in tears.

Lowest moment was when Gareth Bale scored a screamer to put Spurs 3-2 up (25/2/2013).

Spec-tacular! Another memorable night under the lights. Jonathan Spector enjoying a rare moment of glory as he celebrates scoring in the 4-0 League Cup quarter-final win v Manchester United in November 2010.

PROGRAMMES
Helliar family history

FOOTBALL programmes have come a long way since the one penny sheet was standard issue at grounds up and down the country.

Nowadays, West Ham fans get a 100-page, glossy, full colour, perfect-bound, lavishly produced magazine for £3.50 and no-one can dispute that it is among the best in world football.

Apart from all the many features you would expect to find on current Hammers teams and players and what's going on in and around the club, there is also plenty of nostalgia for older generations to enjoy and younger fans to learn about.

The club's idea to replicate a different old-style cover design from years gone by for every home programme of the final 2015-16 season at Upton Park was a timely nod to history and a neat touch.

Supporters, not just avid collectors, will be familiar with most of the various front cover designs illustrated over the following pages and associate them with their own period of attending home matches.

In praising the club for its modern, professional approach to high quality programme design and production, we cannot fail to recognise the enormous part the Helliar family played in the pre-colour era to establish Hammers' programme as one of the most respected in the land.

Samuel Wallace Helliar was a brass founder at Thames Iron Works and a member of the football committee which, in 1895, laid the foundations that led to the formation of West Ham United FC in 1900.

The family printing business, founded in 1902, had for many years printed general items of stationery, tickets, etc, for the football club and in 1919 began printing the match day programme.

Three years earlier, in September 1916, Jack Helliar, was born in Humberstone Road, Plaistow, within sight of the Boleyn Ground, and so began an association that that was to influence his life for the next 75 years.

A pupil at Denmark Street Elementary and then West Ham Secondary, on leaving school in 1933 Jack joined his father, Frederick Samuel, and uncle, Henry William, in the business while continuing his studies at the London School of Printing.

During the period of the 'phoney war' in 1939-40, he and many of the West Ham playing staff joined the Essex Regiment Territorials. On Boxing Day, 1942, he married his wife, Ellen, and their only child, John, was born in July 1945.

Jack Helliar, a larger than life character whose family printed the programme for 65 years.

At the end of the war Jack returned to the family business and in 1946 commenced writing the West Ham programme as well as printing it.

He would take the short drive from Helliar & Sons Ltd at 235-237 Barking Road, Canning Town (the last of its three different locations in close proximity), to the Boleyn Ground, where he met club secretary Frank Cearns to collect copy for the next programme. There came a point where Cearns realised that, in Jack, they had a well-educated man whose vast knowledge of the club made him the ideal candidate to take over as editor, for which he was paid 10 shillings and sixpence (half a guinea).

By the mid-60s Jack regularly accompanied West Ham squads, first XI and youth sides, on tours all over Europe, including cup ties behind the

Iron Curtain, and was present at the Houston Astrodome in Texas, USA in April 1967 to see Hammers face Real Madrid in the first football match played on a full-size pitch under cover.

It was promotion achieved in May 1958 that proved the catalyst for the club's switch from the traditional four-page white programme to the distinctive, pocket-sized (approx 180mm x 125mm) design which incorporated the club colours. The popular new-look, designed by Jack, appeared from the start of the 1958-59 first division season and was retained for the next 25 years.

In the late 60s, West Ham became one of the first clubs to include full-colour photos in their programme using a four-colour print process. Initially, they appeared as four-page centre inserts, before colour was used on the front and back covers for games against London rivals in season 1969-70.

Ironically, when Helliar & Sons were unable to meet the club's demands for a larger, full colour production throughout, which became standard at the big clubs by the early 80s, they lost the contract to produce the programme. At the start of the 1983-84 season, West Ham broke with a tradition that dated back 64 years when it went outside Helliar for its printing and appointed Maybank Press to produce and print its programme. A new editor, Colin Benson, a freelancer with no affinity to West Ham, was also brought in to mark the start of a new era.

Jack's son, John Helliar, had joined the family printing company in 1965. By the time they lost the contract, John's mother, Ellen, and his wife, Betty, were also helping out at the factory, where the whole process of printing, folding, collating and saddle-stitching took place.

John explained: "We could see that the club was possibly looking to make changes for two or three years before it eventually did but managed to keep the contract. We had Heidelberg presses but really needed to invest in more modern machinery to keep pace with changing times.

"When Jack Petchey joined the board of directors, he had new ideas about how the club should go forward, including a more colourful and larger programme, and in the end we lost out when the club decided to change printer.

"Although we continued to print other items for West Ham, including season ticket books and match day tickets, plus reserve and youth cup programmes and stationery, the programme was our biggest job and the club one of our largest clients.

"Dad retired from his active role in the company at that time, I took over the day-to-day running and we had to make quite a few others redundant."

The personal touch had gone. Maybank Press, based at Hainault, Essex, also printed programmes for numerous other football clubs, as did the various other printers who followed them over the years. Modern four colour web offset presses meant faster production, more flexible deadlines and a full colour programme.

Not that many didn't lament the loss of those small but popular editions of *Hammer* that fitted neatly inside fans' jacket pockets without being folded or creased. It had a uniqueness that all the other programmes West Ham put out since have never had.

However, the Helliar's connection with West Ham didn't end with the loss of the programme contract. Jack continued to write a regular historical column for the programme and, as the club's recognised historian, dealt with countless correspondence from supporters and media questions relating to West Ham past. He also remained as popular host of the press room at Upton Park, a role he took on from the early 60s.

Following the death of his father in January 1992, aged 75, John Helliar took over managing the press room and still contributes history-themed editorials for the match day programme.

And in the final season at Upton Park, John acted as a tour guide, showing supporters and other curious visitors around the stadium.

John Helliar was still writing for the programme and taking stadium tours in the final season.

232　UPTON PARK MEMORIES

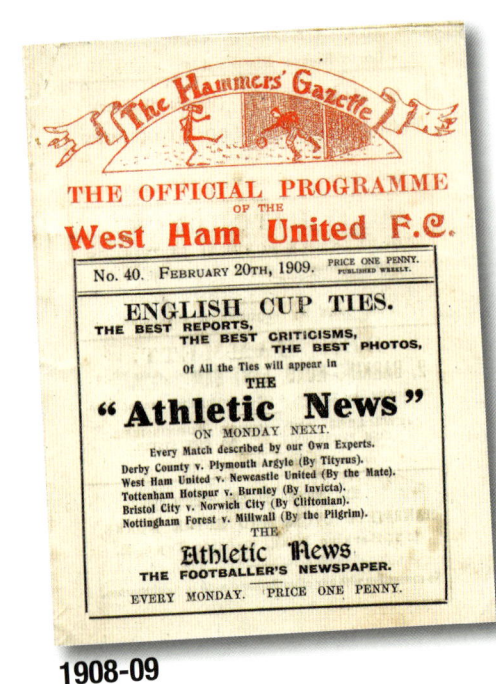

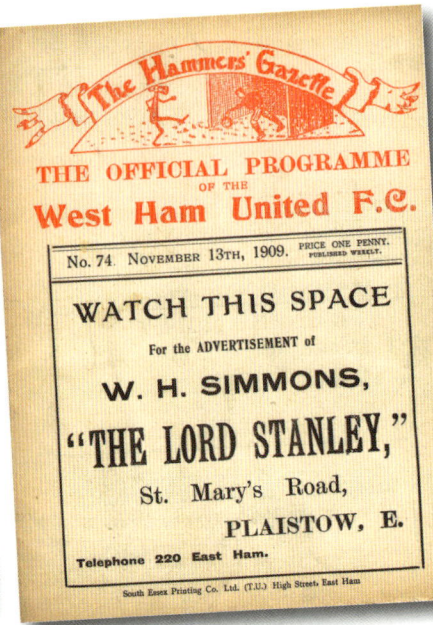

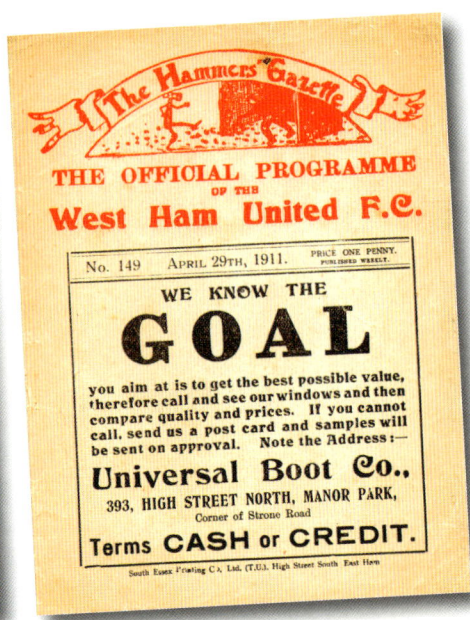

1908-09

1909-10

1910-11

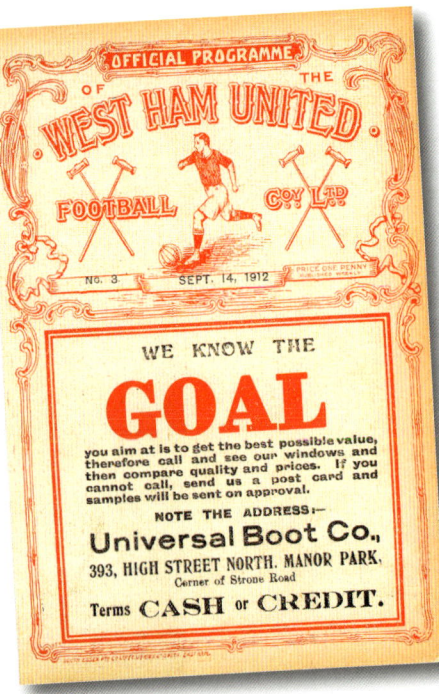

1911-12

1912-13

1913-14

UPTON PARK MEMORIES 233

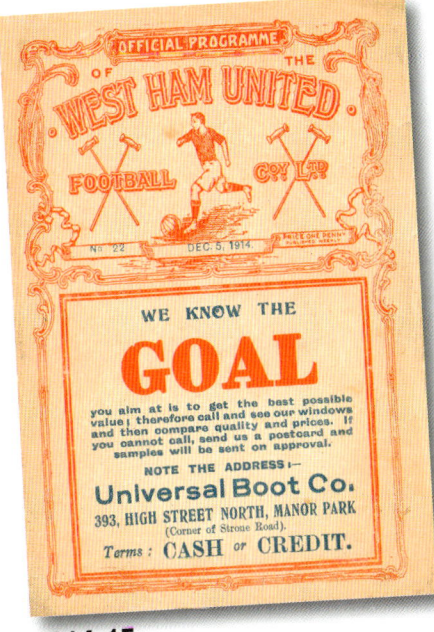

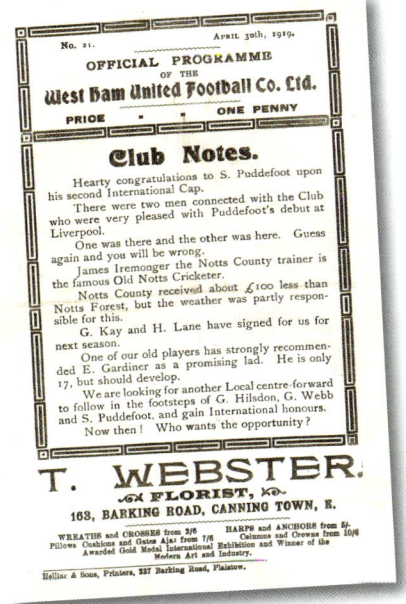

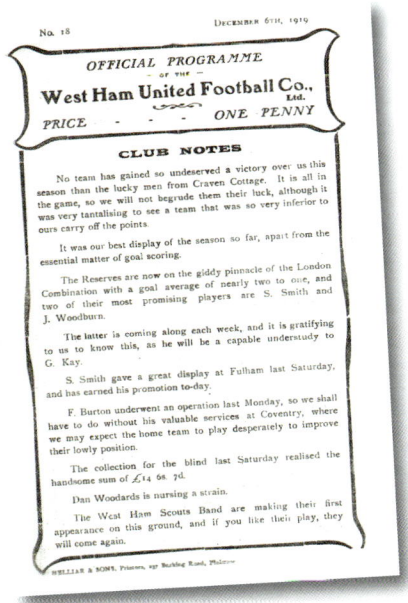

1914-15

1918-19

1919-20

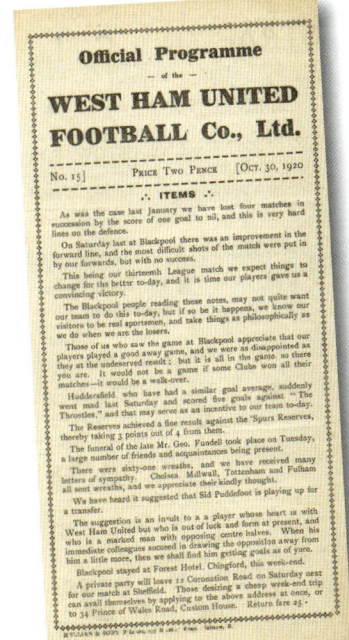

1920-21

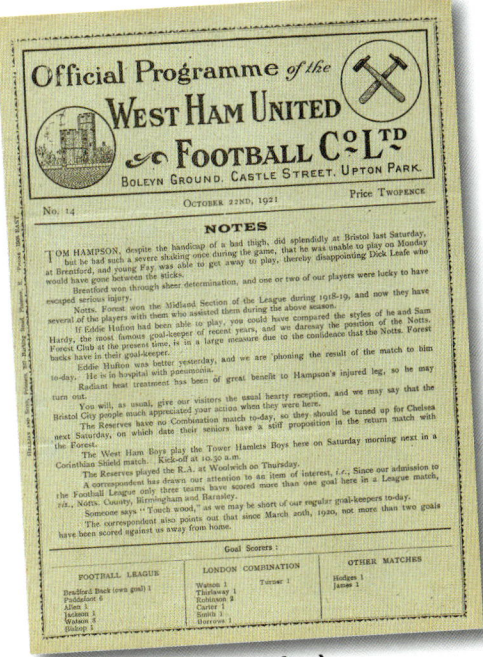

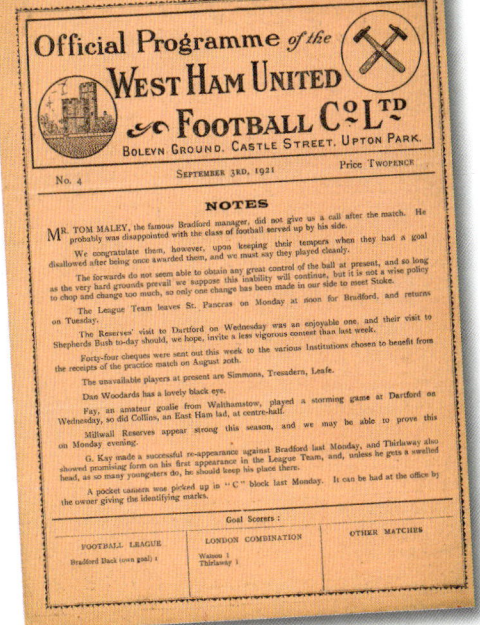

1921-22 (Green version)

1921-22 (Orange version)

1922-23

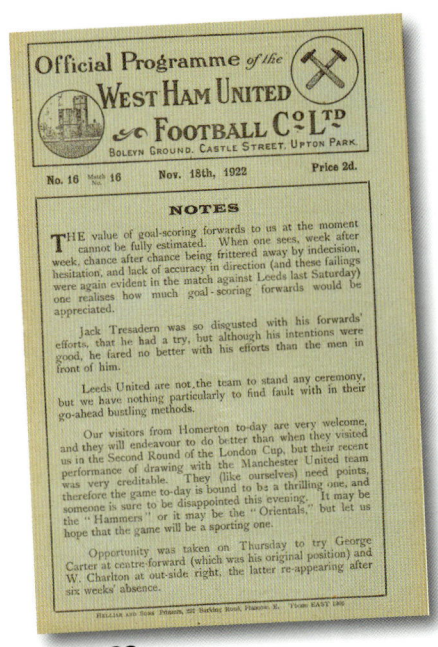

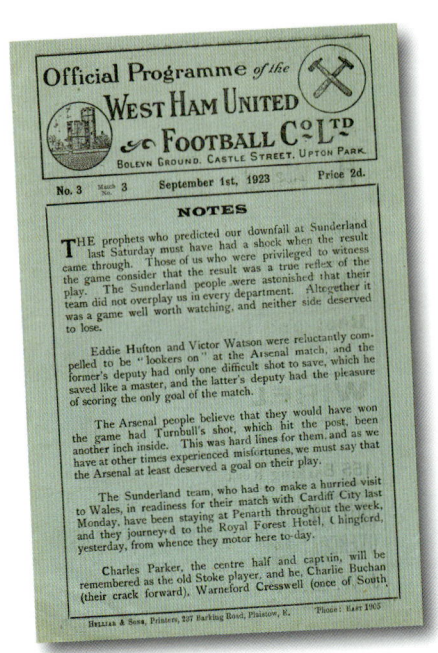

1923-24

1924-25

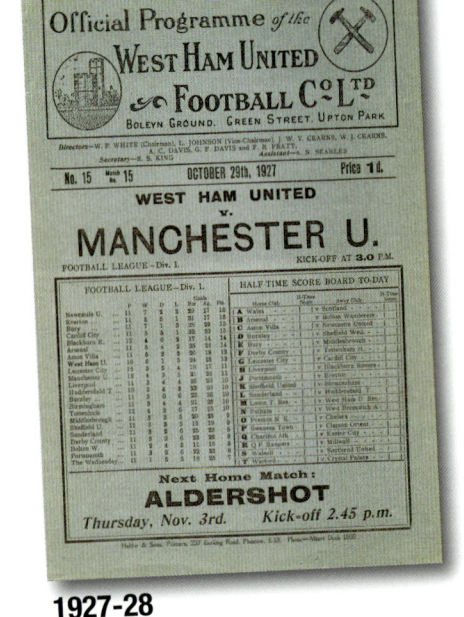

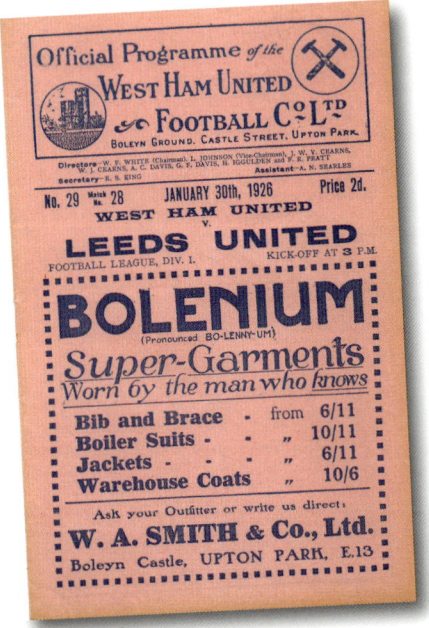

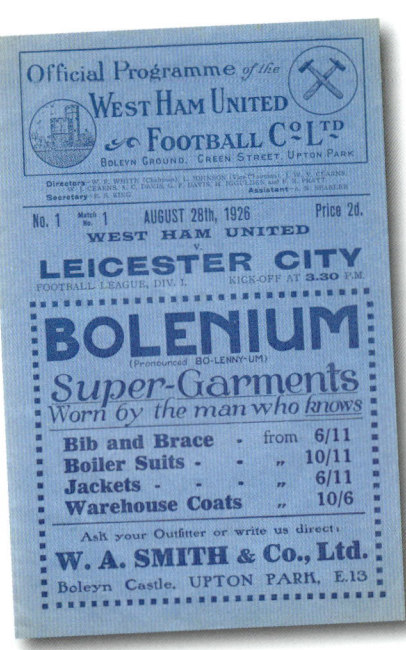

1925-26

1926-27

1927-28

UPTON PARK MEMORIES 235

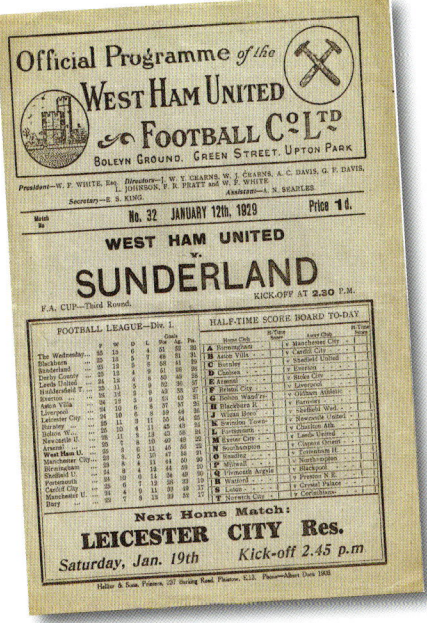

1928-29

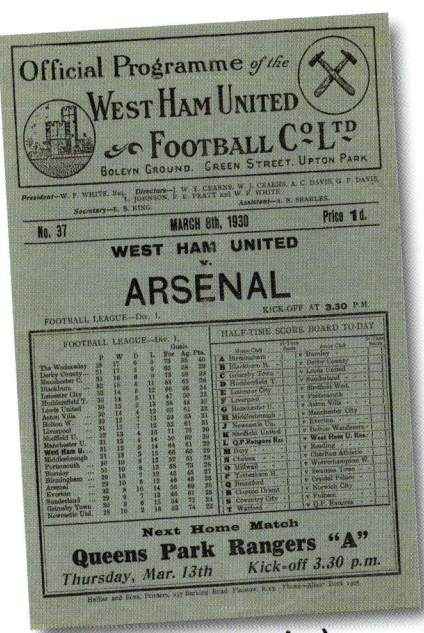

1929-30 (Green version)

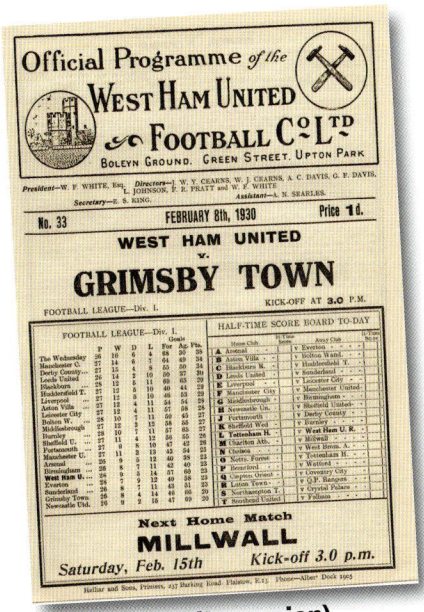

1929-30 (White version)

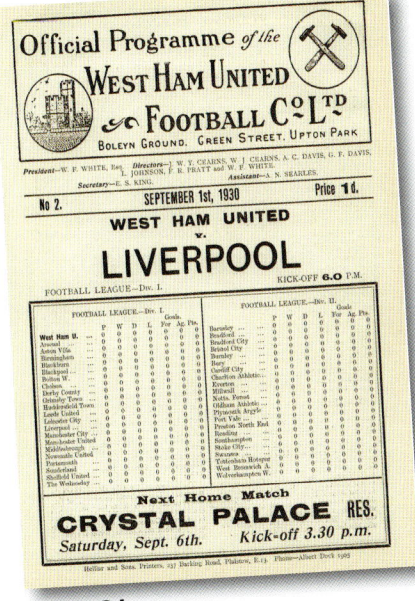

1930-31

1931-32

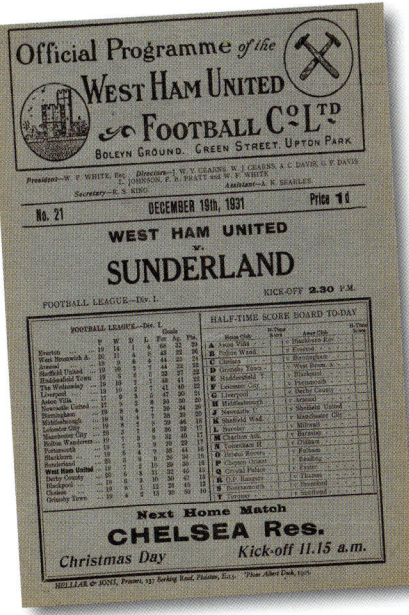

1932-33

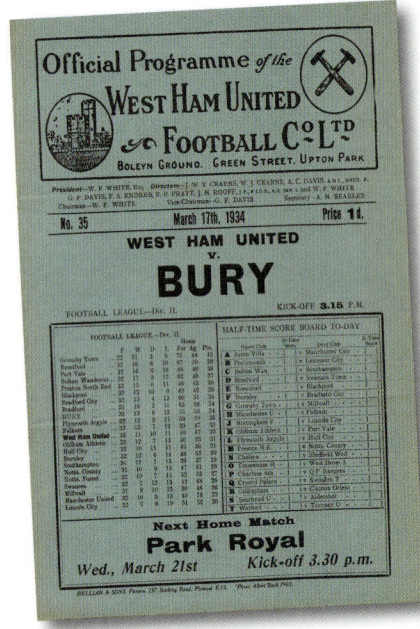

236 UPTON PARK MEMORIES

1933-34

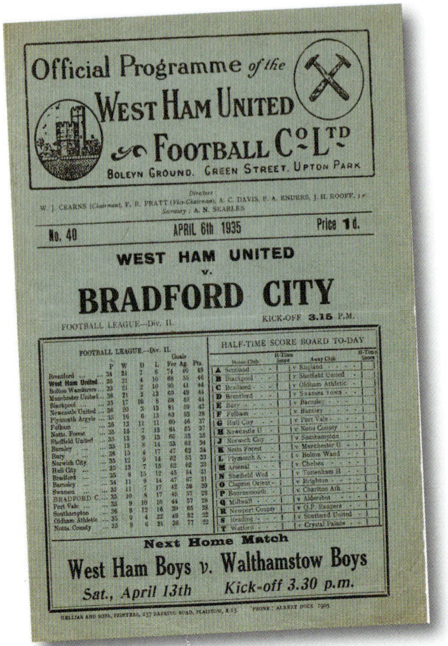

1934-35

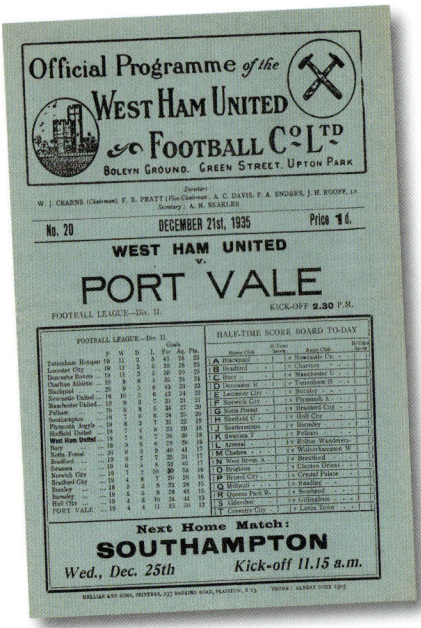

1935-36

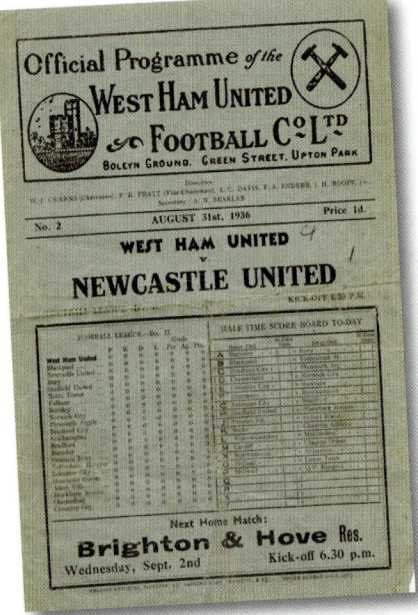

1936-37 (2)

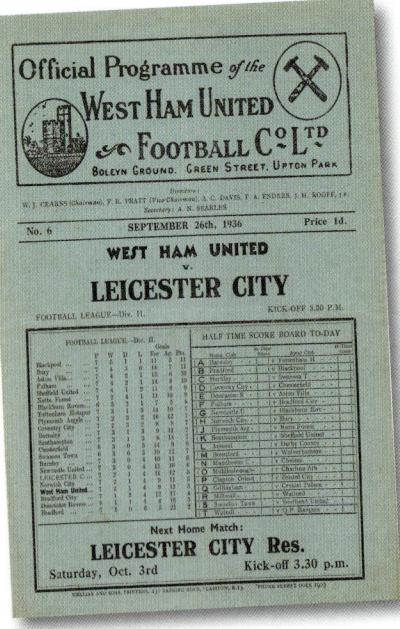

1936-37

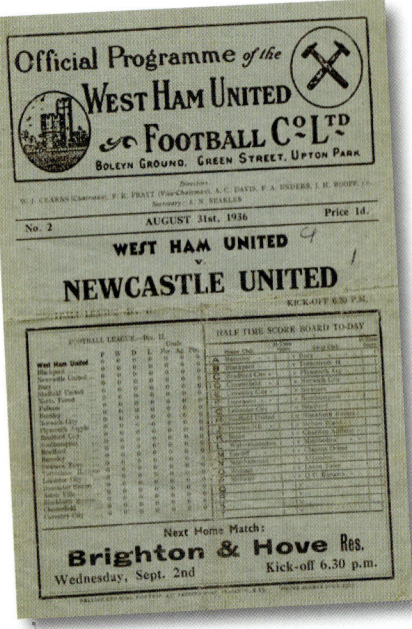

1936-37

UPTON PARK MEMORIES 237

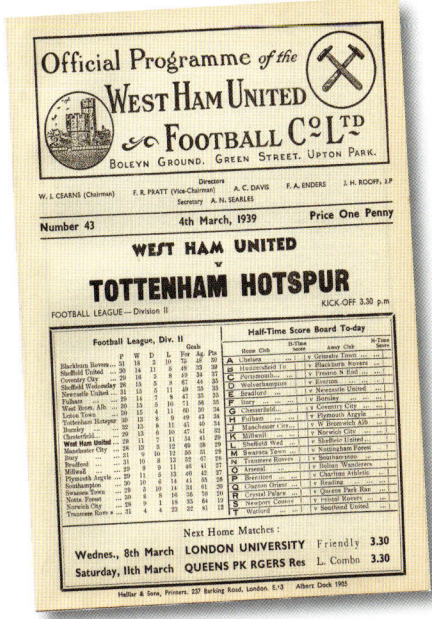

1938-39

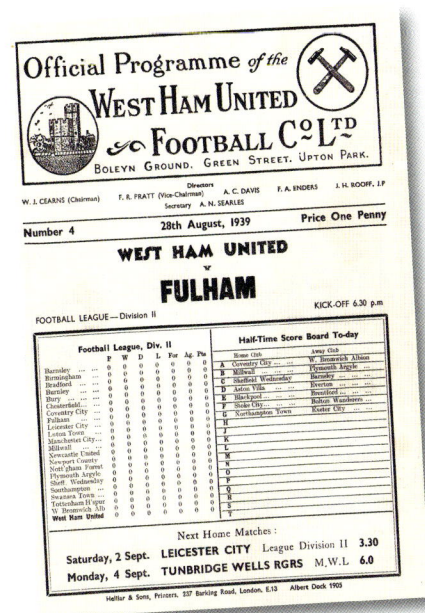

1939-40 (Expunged game)

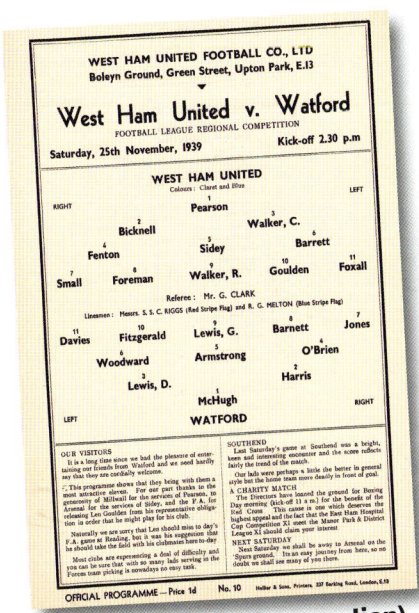

1939-40 (Regional competion)

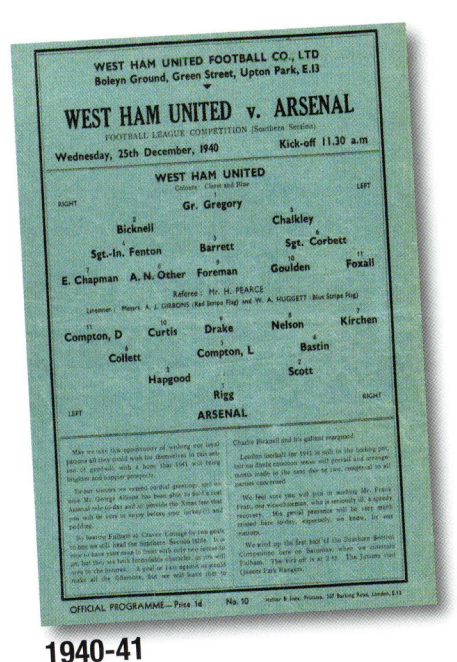

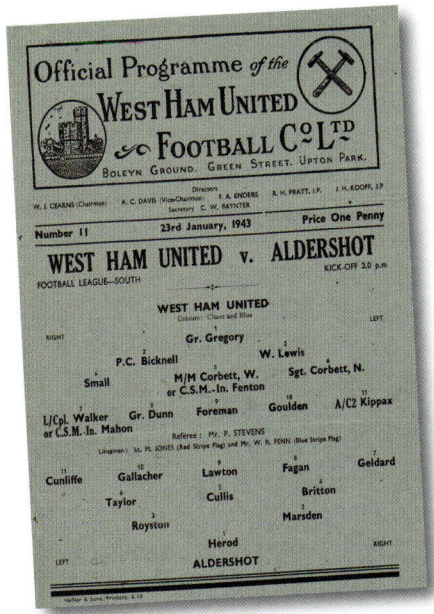

1940-41

1941-42

1942-43

238 UPTON PARK MEMORIES

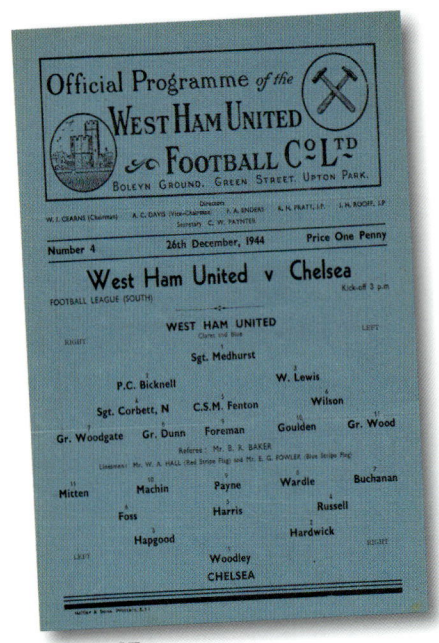

1944-45

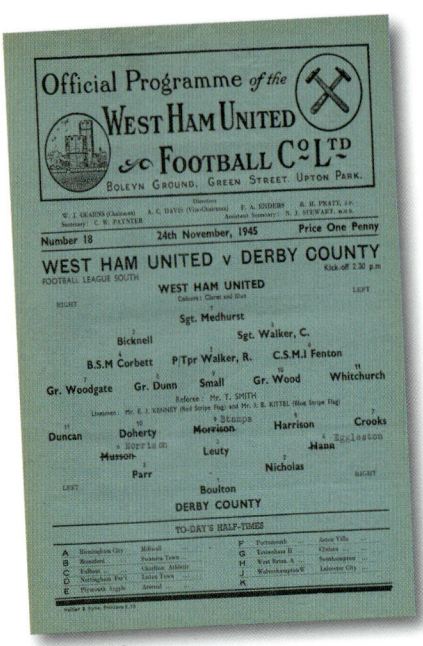

1945-46

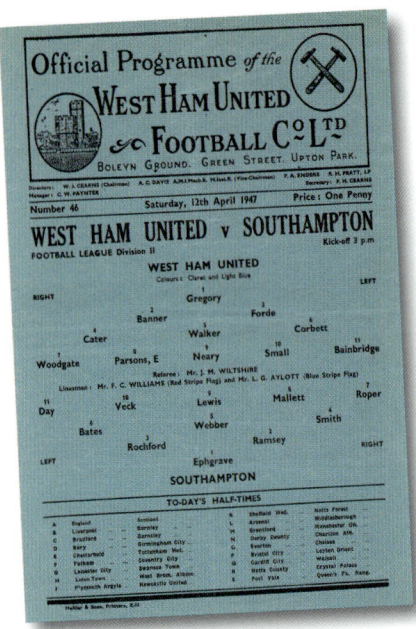

1946-47

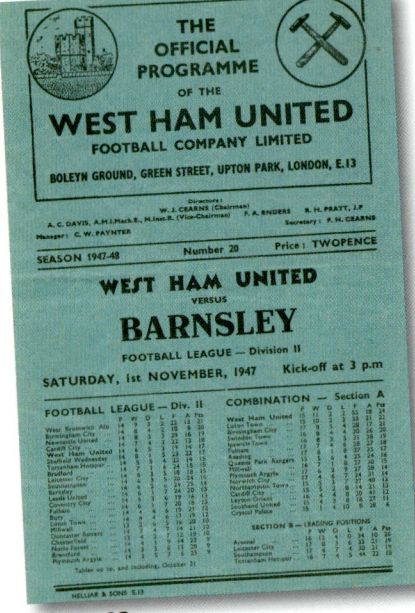

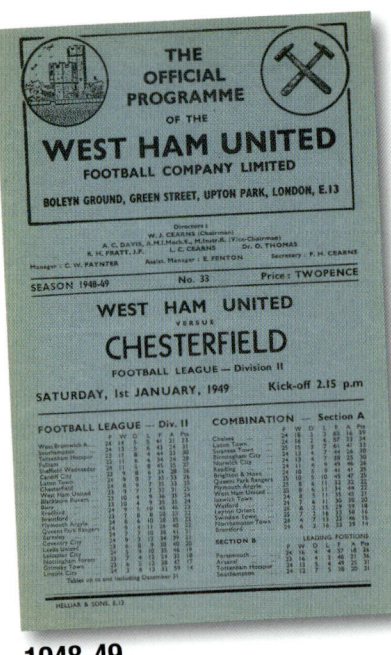

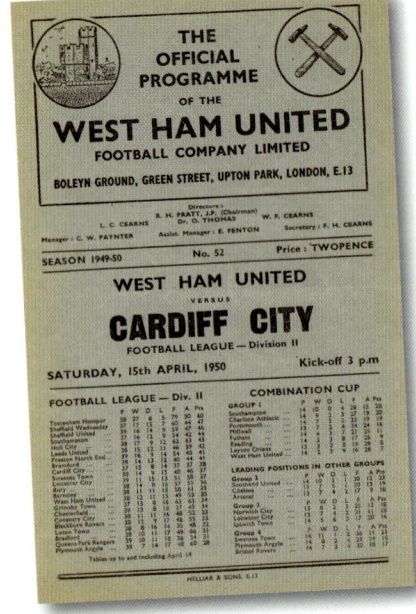

1947-48

1948-49

1949-50

UPTON PARK MEMORIES 239

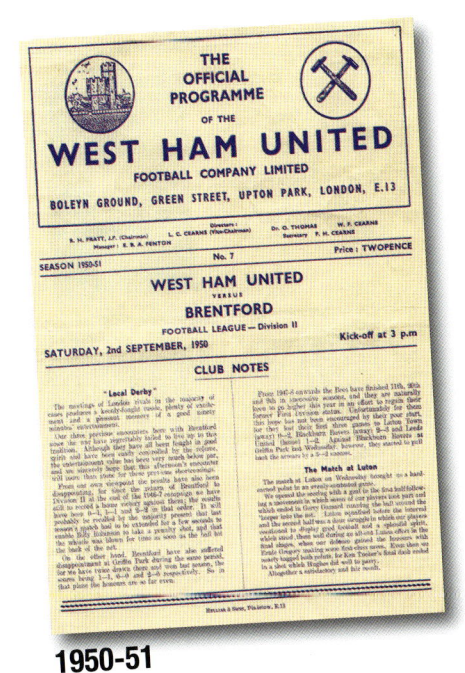

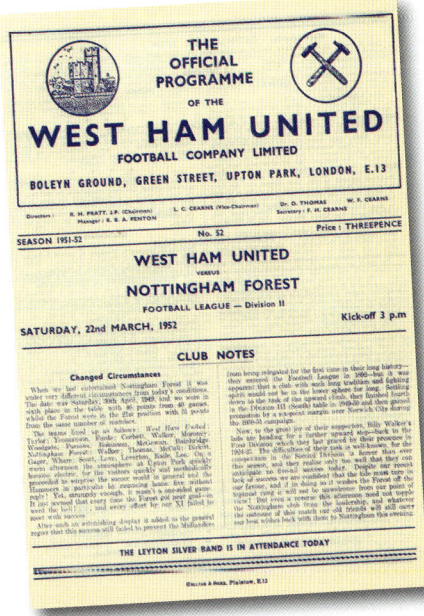

1950-51

1951-52

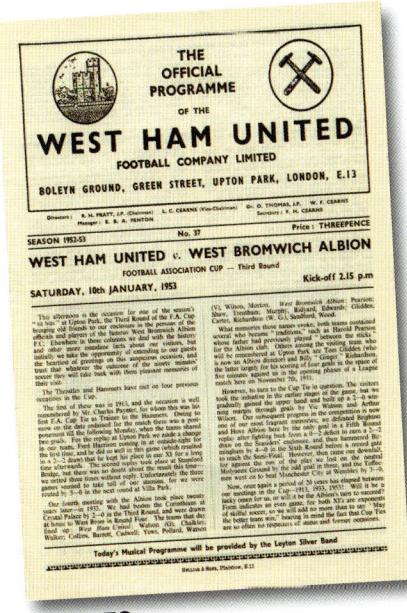

1952-53

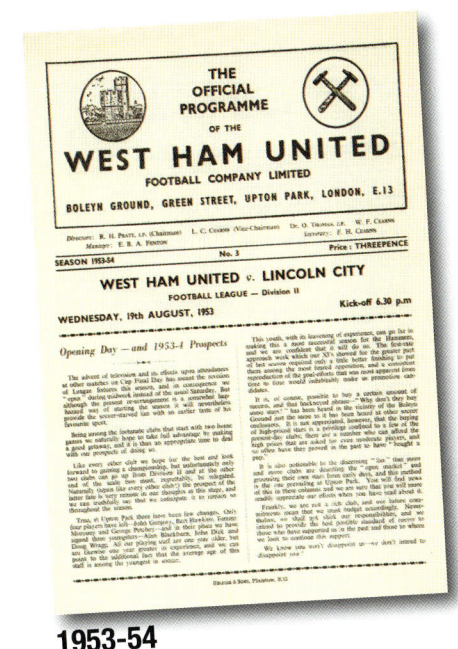

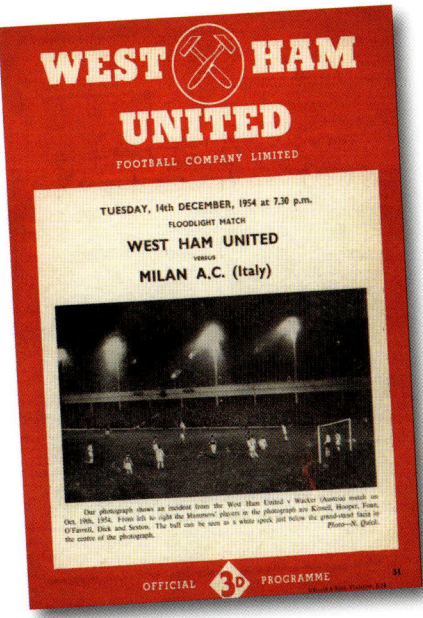

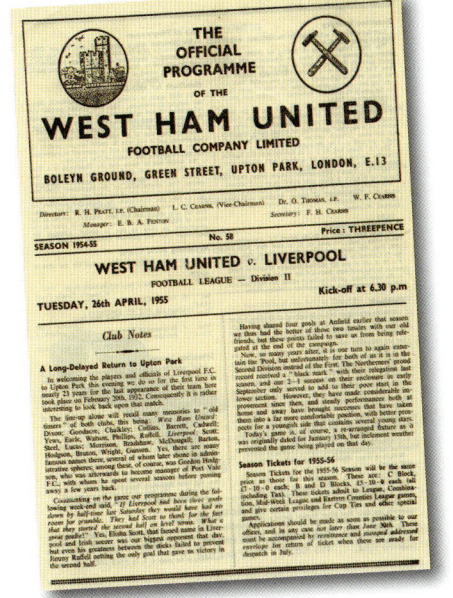

1953-54

1954-55

1954-55

UPTON PARK MEMORIES

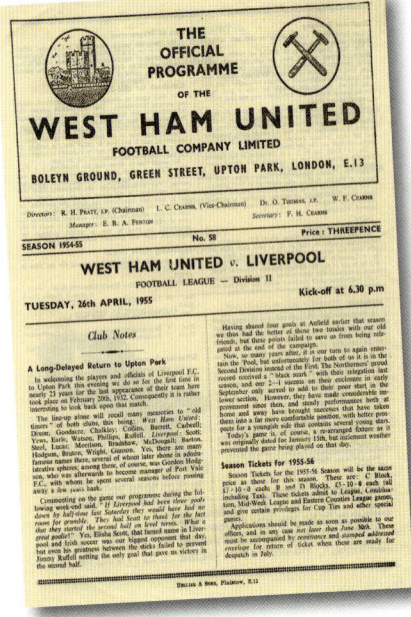

1954-55

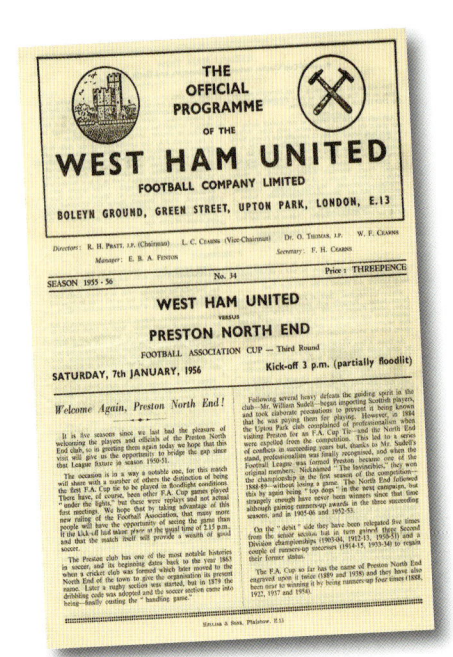

1955-56

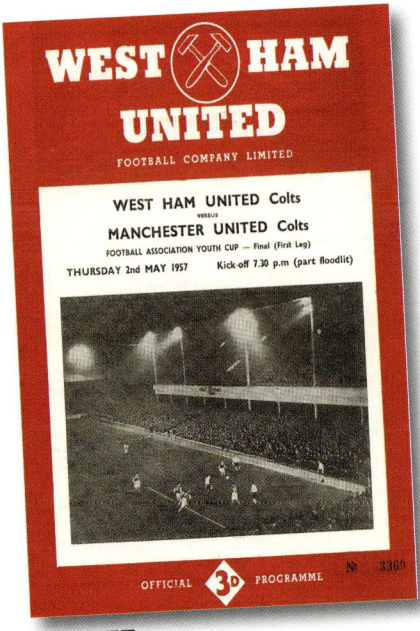

1956-57

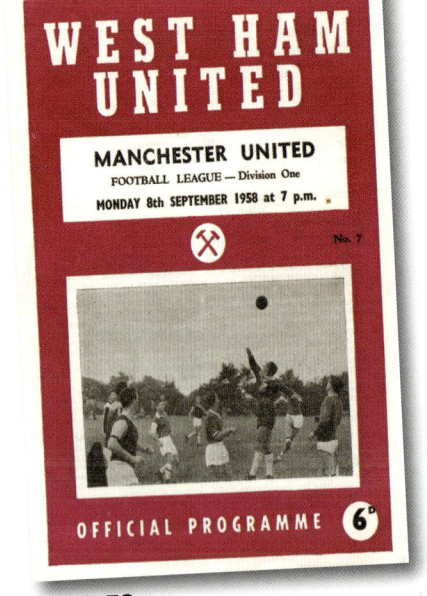

1957-58

1958-59

1959-60

UPTON PARK MEMORIES 241

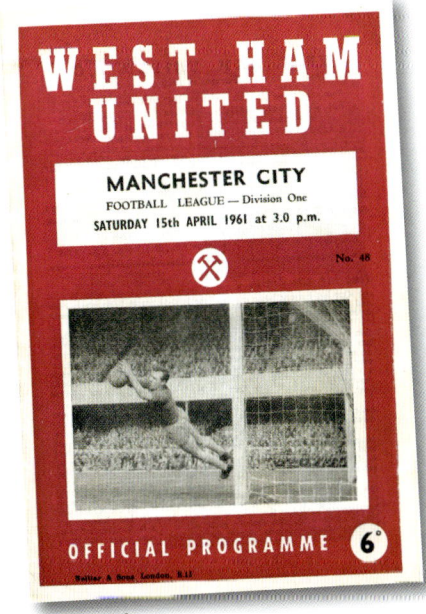

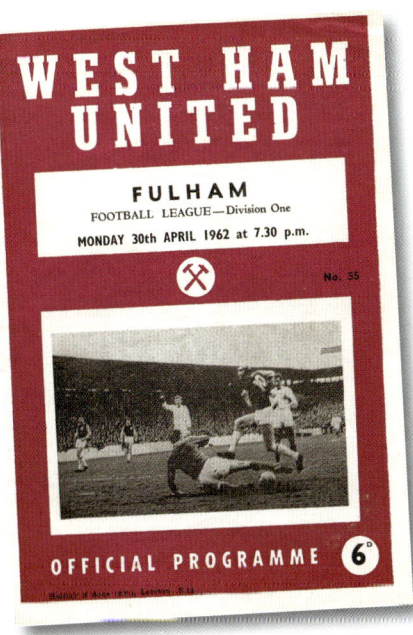

1960-61

1961-62

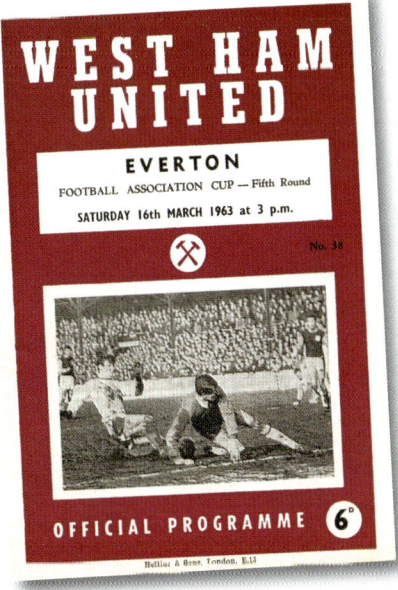

1962-63

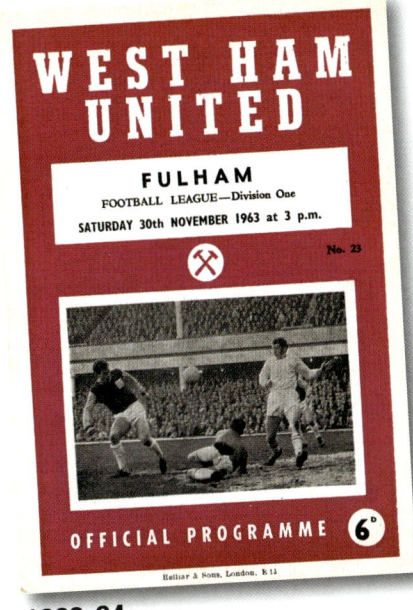

1963-64

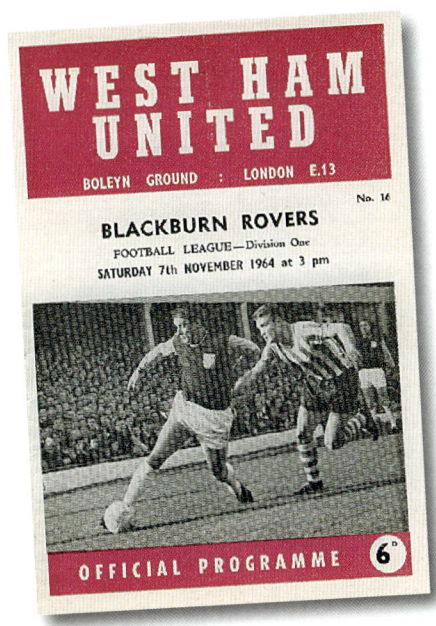

1964-65

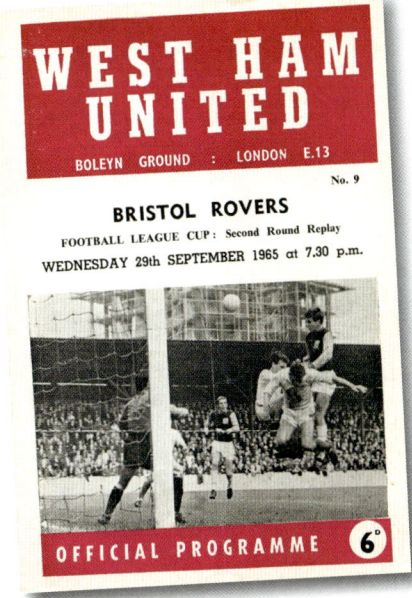

1965-66

UPTON PARK MEMORIES

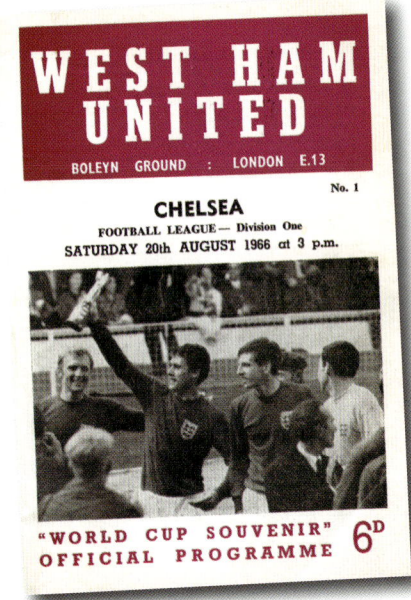

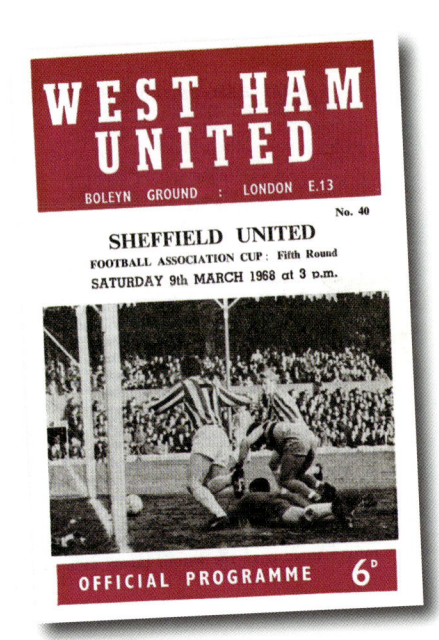

1966-67

1967-68

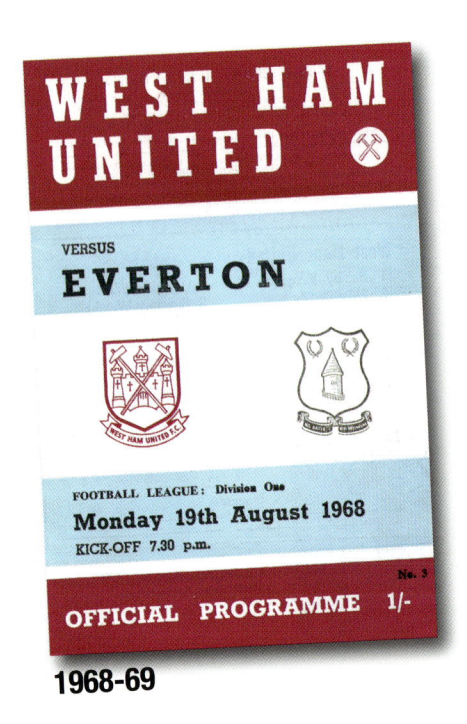

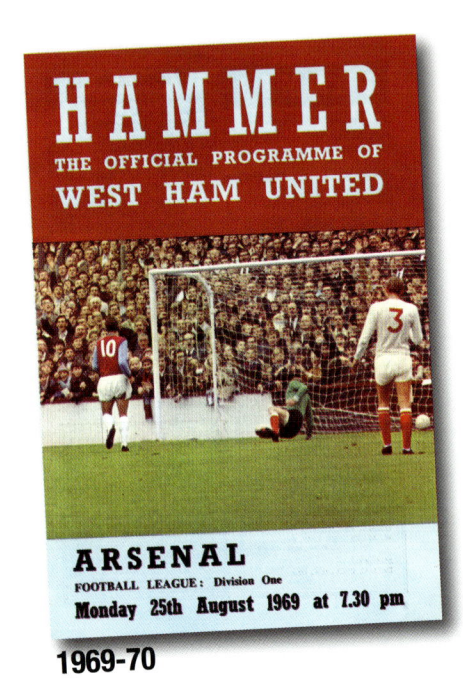

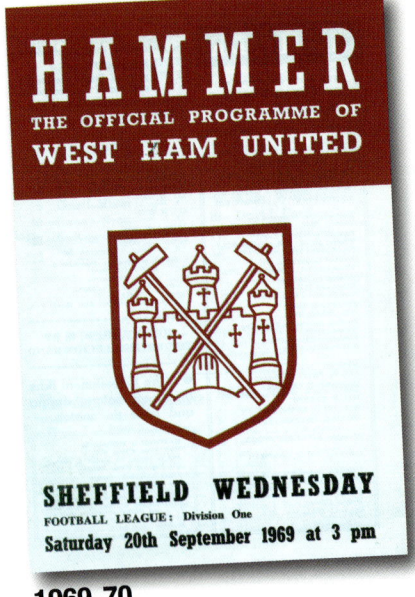

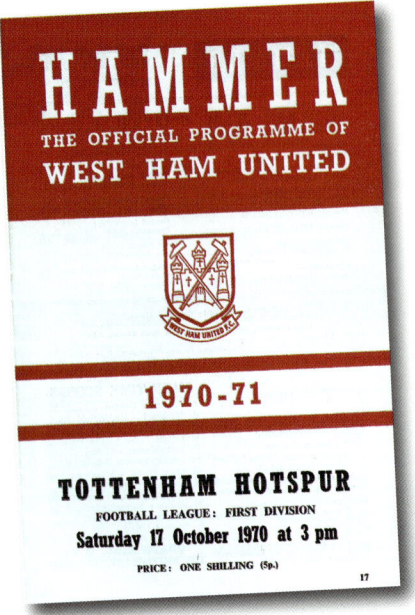

1968-69

1969-70

1969-70

1970-71

UPTON PARK MEMORIES 243

1971-72

1972-73

1973-74

1974-75

1975-76

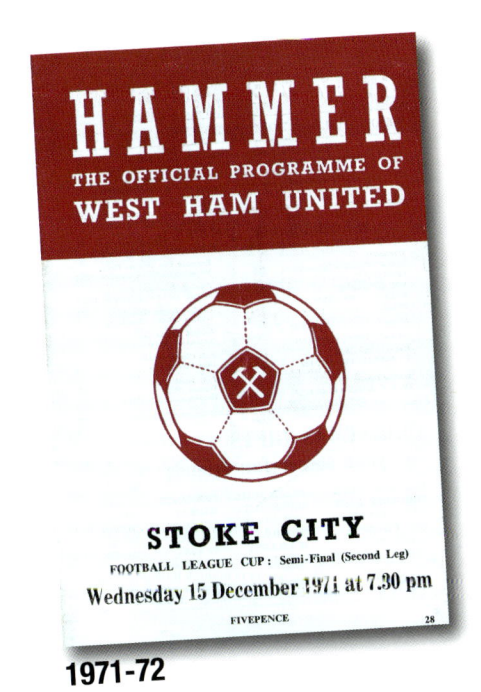

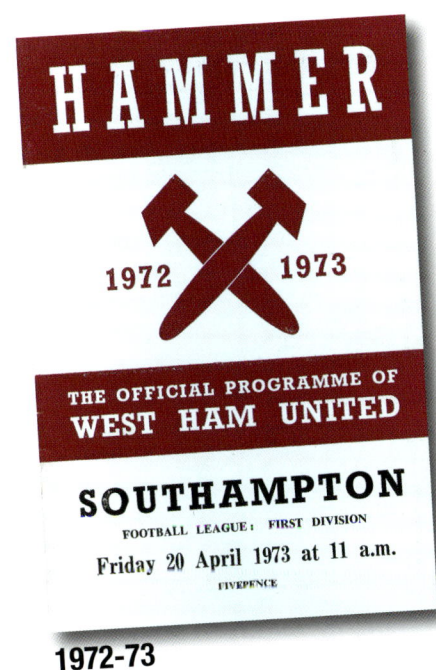

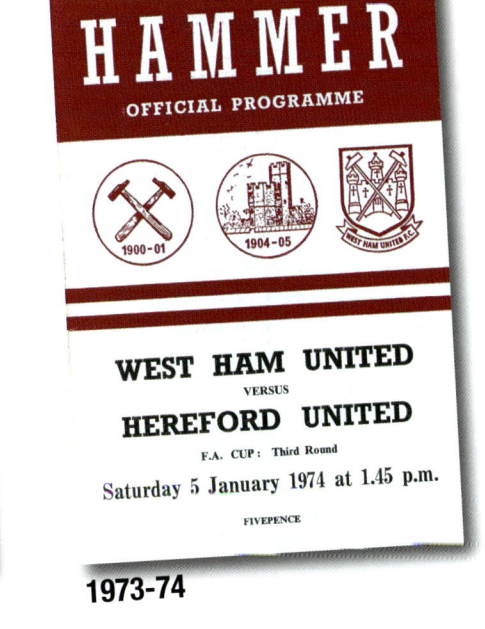

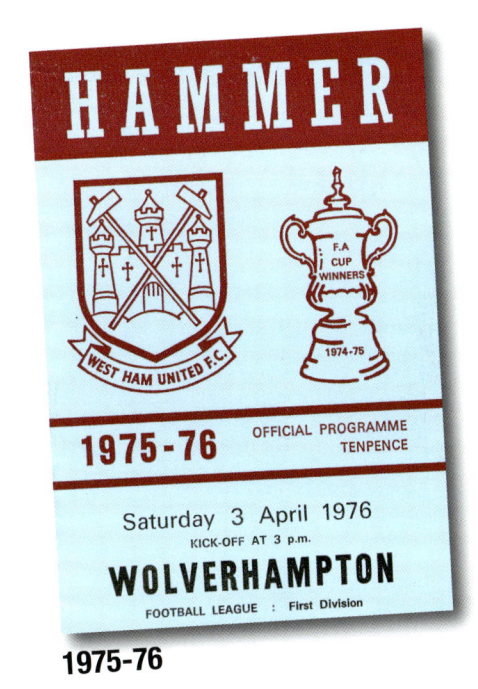

1976-77

244 UPTON PARK MEMORIES

1977-78

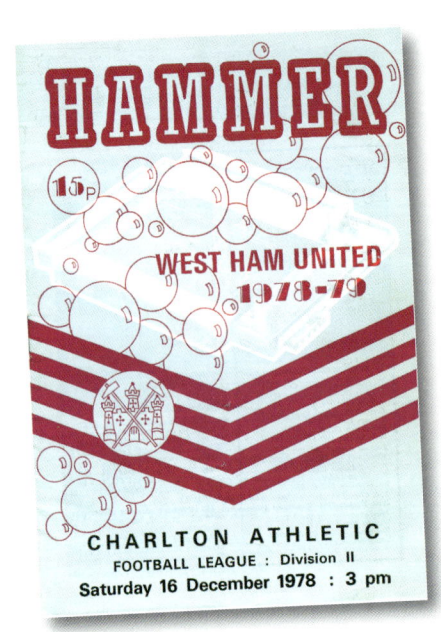

1978-79

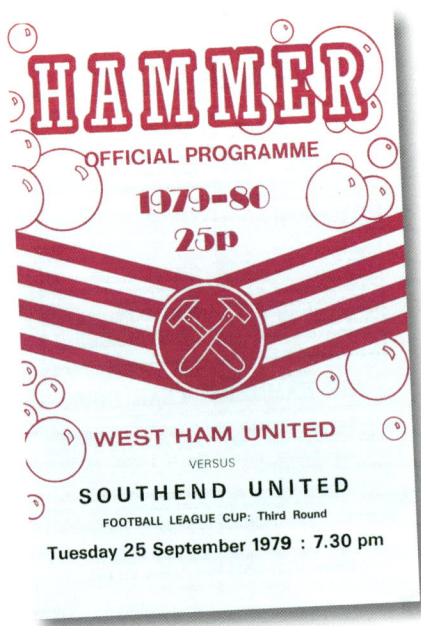

1979-80

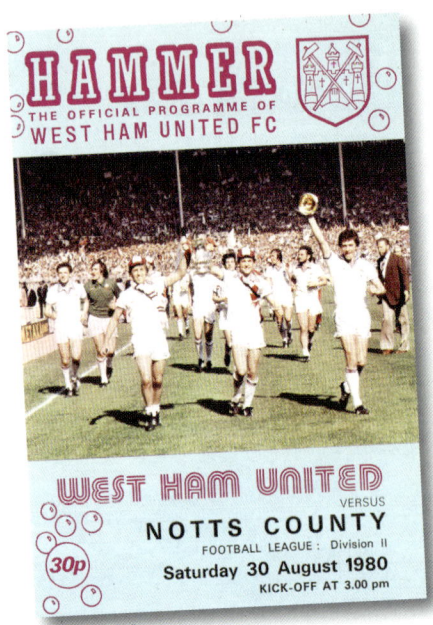

1980-81

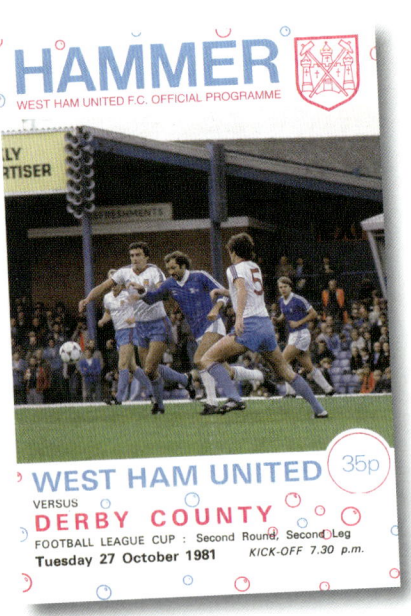

1981-82

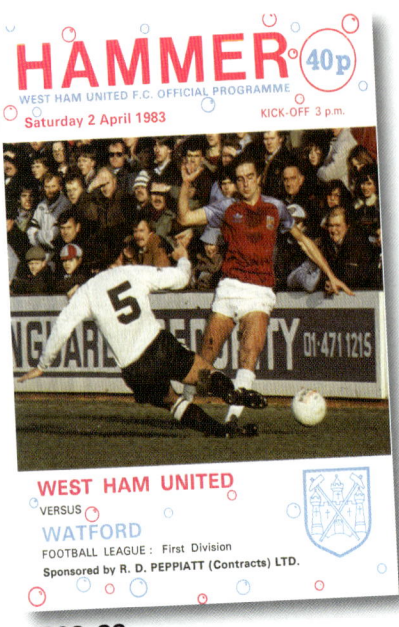

1982-83

UPTON PARK MEMORIES 245

1984-85

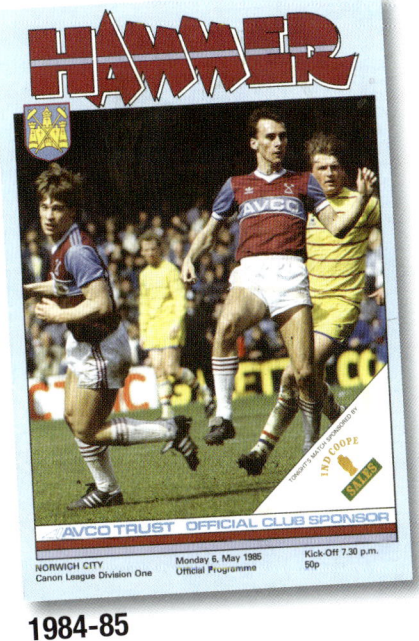

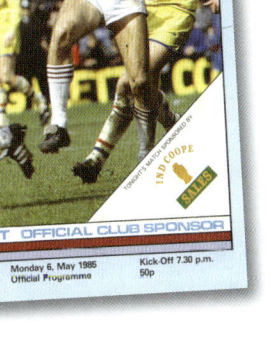

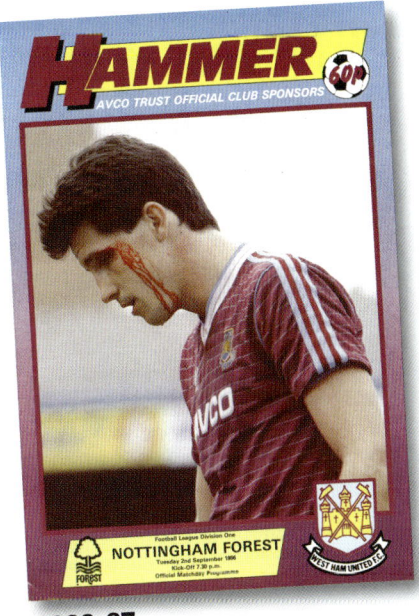

1985-86

1986-87

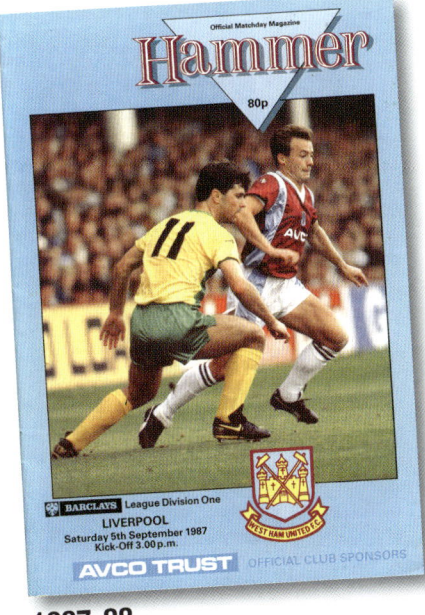

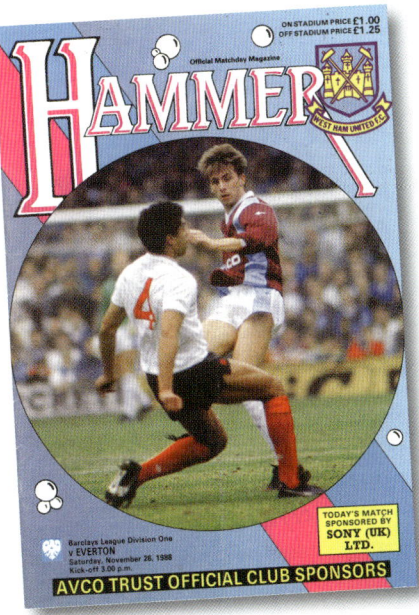

1987-88

1988-89

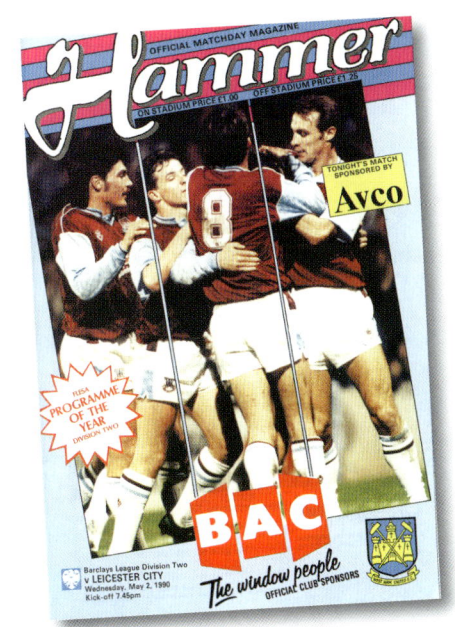

1989-90

246　UPTON PARK MEMORIES

1990-91

1991-92

1992-93

1993-94

1994-95

1995-96

1996-97

1997-98

UPTON PARK MEMORIES 247

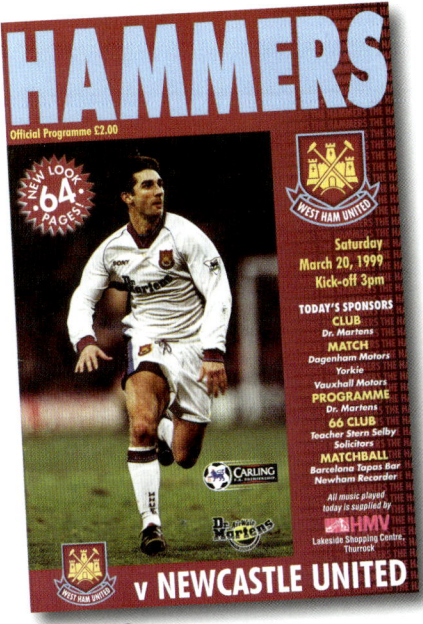

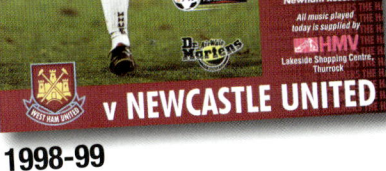

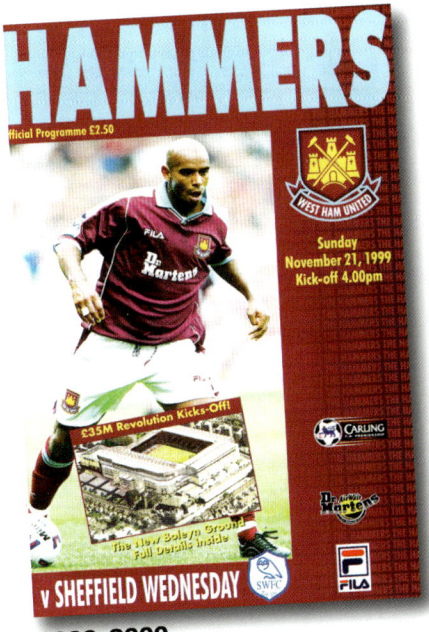

1998-99

1999-2000

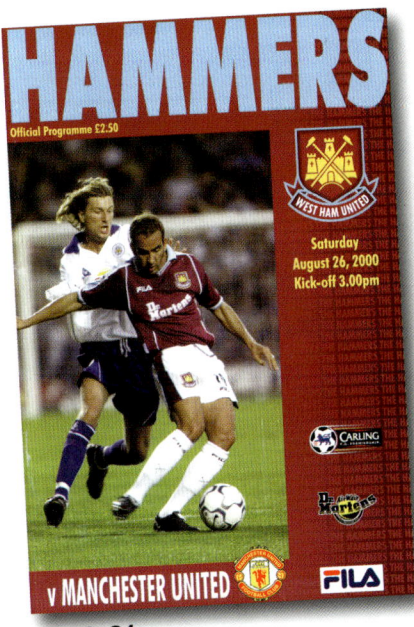

2000-01

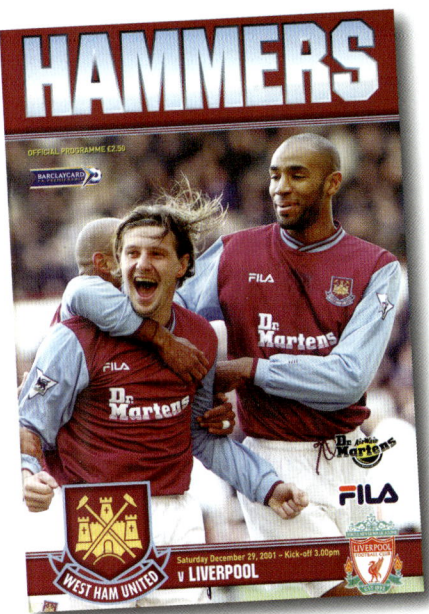

2001-02

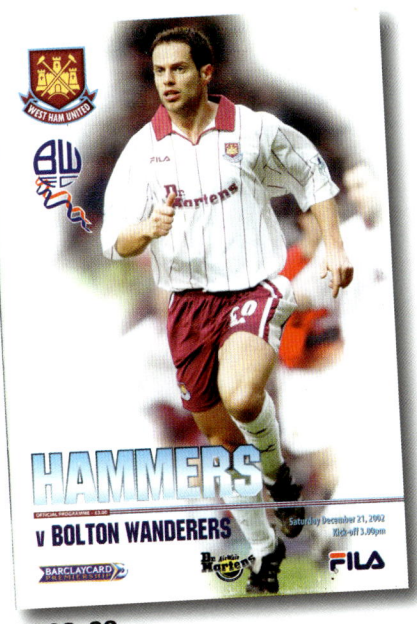

2002-03

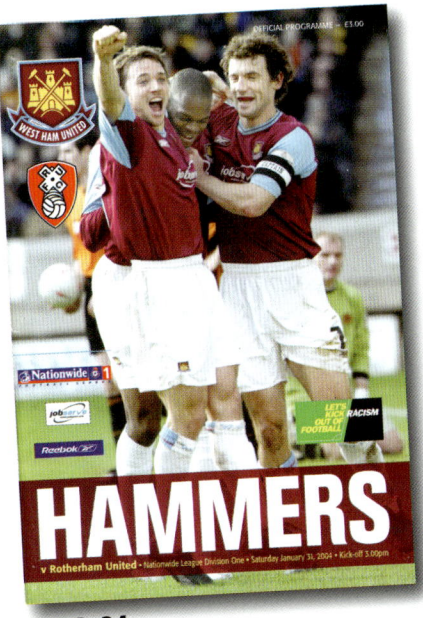

2003-04

248 UPTON PARK MEMORIES

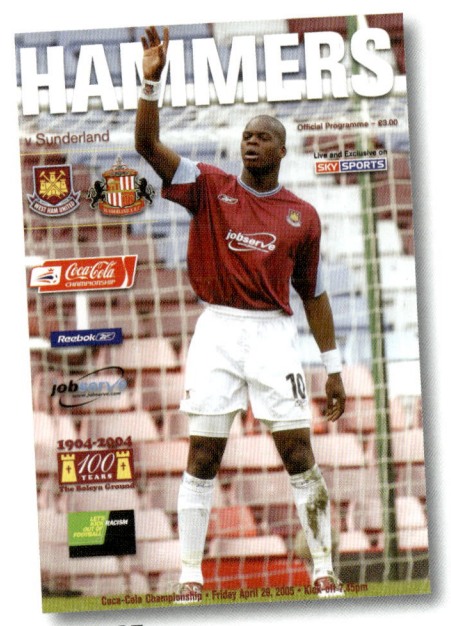

2004-05

2005-06

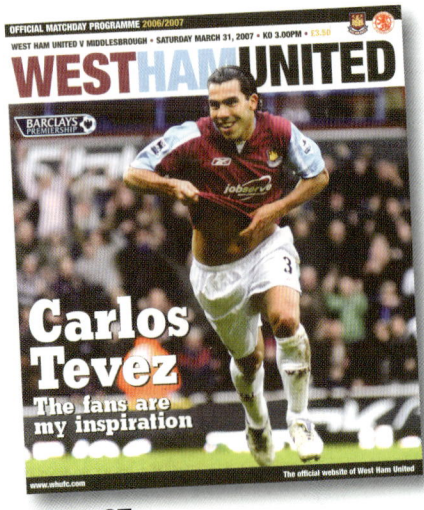

2006-07

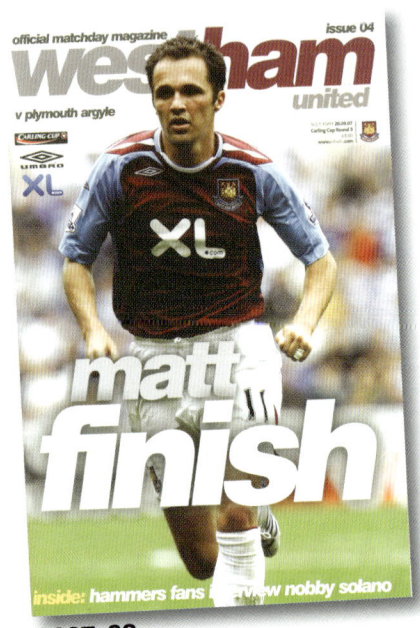

2007-08

2008-09

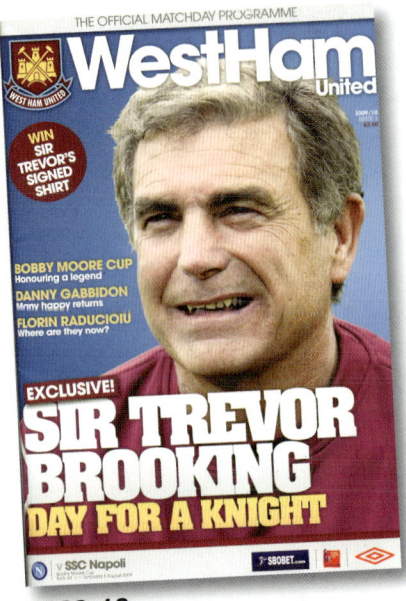

2009-10

UPTON PARK MEMORIES 249

2010-11

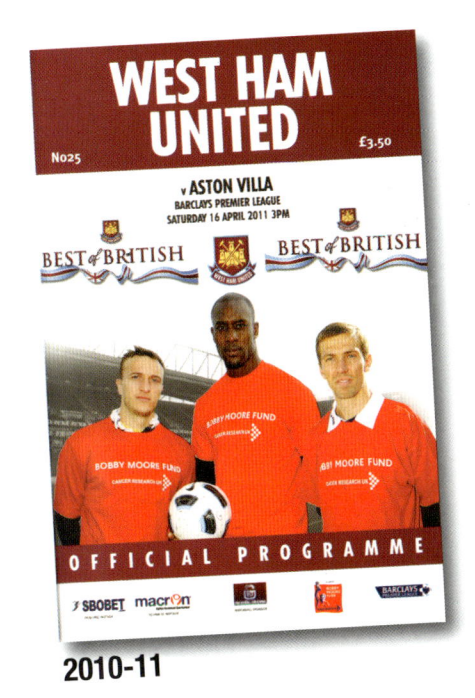

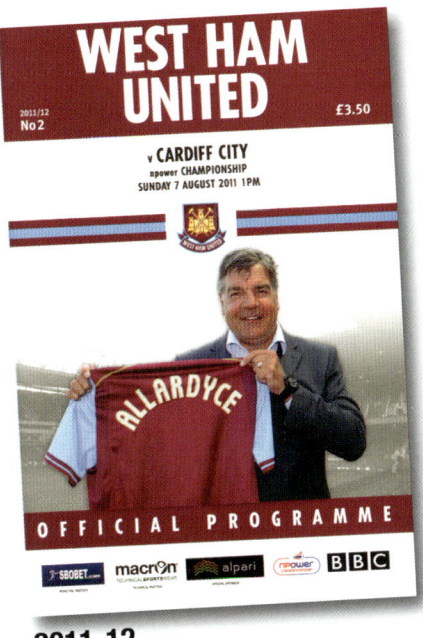

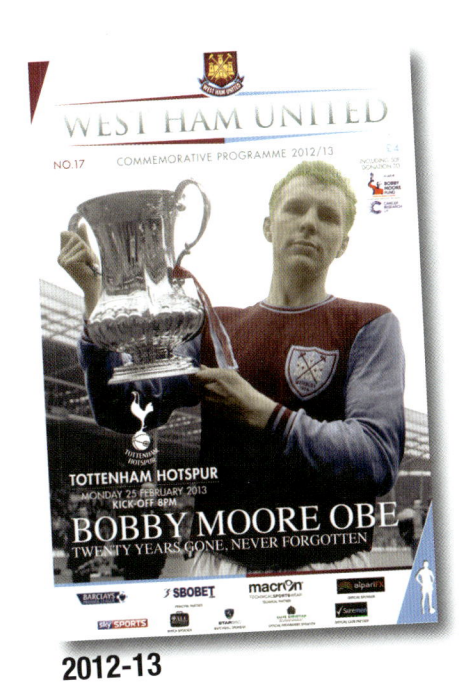

2011-12

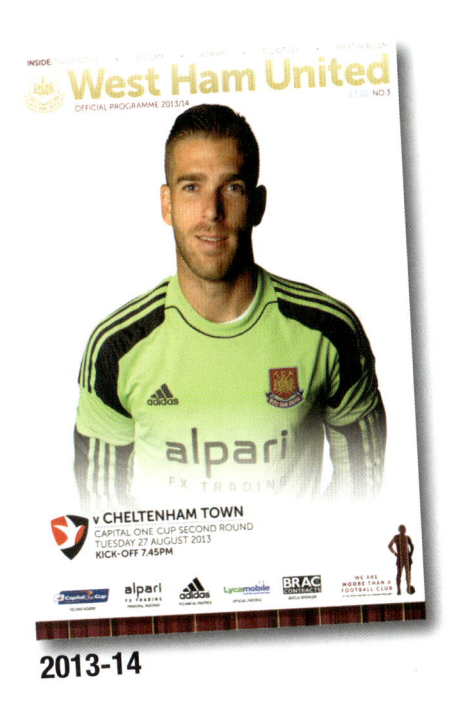

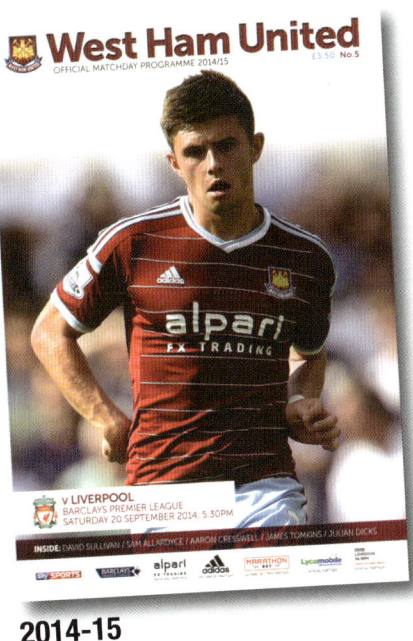

2012-13

2013-14

2014-15

2015-16

HOME FROM HOME

IN the early 90s West Ham produced two programmes for matches played at Upton Park . . . even though they were, technically, the away team against two sides from the county of Hampshire.

The draw for the third round of the FA Cup in 1991 and 1992 saw Hammers scheduled to visit fourth division Aldershot and non-league Farnborough Town, of the Conference, respectively.

But due to their limited stadium capacity and the need to comply with more stringent crowd and ground safety regulations in the post-Taylor era, both lower league clubs agreed to switch their original home ties to Upton Park. They were obviously compensated for any perceived loss of 'home advantage' by earning much more than they would otherwise have done from increased gate receipts.

Aldershot's Recreation Ground had a capacity of around 5,000, whereas 22,929 were at the Boleyn Ground to see the teams contest a 0-0 draw in January 1991. For this game, Hammers had to wear a change strip of all-white, so that The Shots could play in their usual home kit of red-and-blue, although West Ham did retain the home dressing room.

In the replay at The Boleyn under lights 11 days later, a crowd of 21,484 saw Billy Bonds' side – back in their familiar claret-and-blue – outclass the visitors with an exhilarating 6-1 win (who says home advantage counts for nothing!). It was an exciting time at West Ham, who were on course for promotion and an FA Cup semi-final.

A year later, it was Farnborough who seized the option to switch the third round tie from their Cherrywood Road ground (where 2,285 had watched them beat Torquay United 4-3 in the second round) to E13. And like Aldershot, the underdogs earned a lucrative replay with Bonzo's boys.

The first game ended 1-1 but Hammers were fortunate to scrape through to the fourth round, 1-0, in the replay 10 days later. Both matches, for which West Ham wore their home kit, attracted attendances of just under 24,000 but by now most fans had become angry and disenchanted by the bond scheme farce and Farnborough were not far from adding to the club's woes.

Prior to both 'away' games, those responsible for producing the West Ham programme liaised closely with their counterparts at Aldershot and Farnborough and, with the help of Leicester-based designers and printers ACL Polar, adapted the look of HAMMER to incorporate many regular features and content from both visiting clubs' usual home programmes, SHOTSCENE and BORO VIEW. A nice touch.

A rather crude looking unofficial four-page 'pirate' programme was produced for the club's first game back in the first division in 1958.

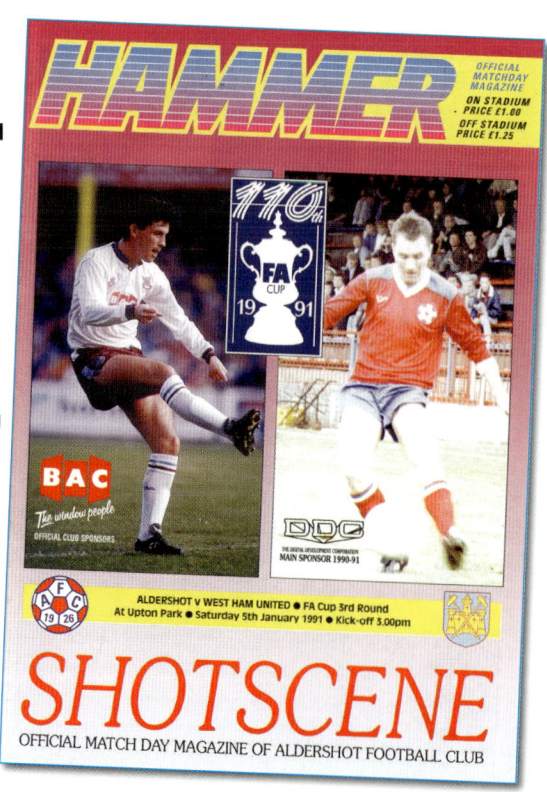

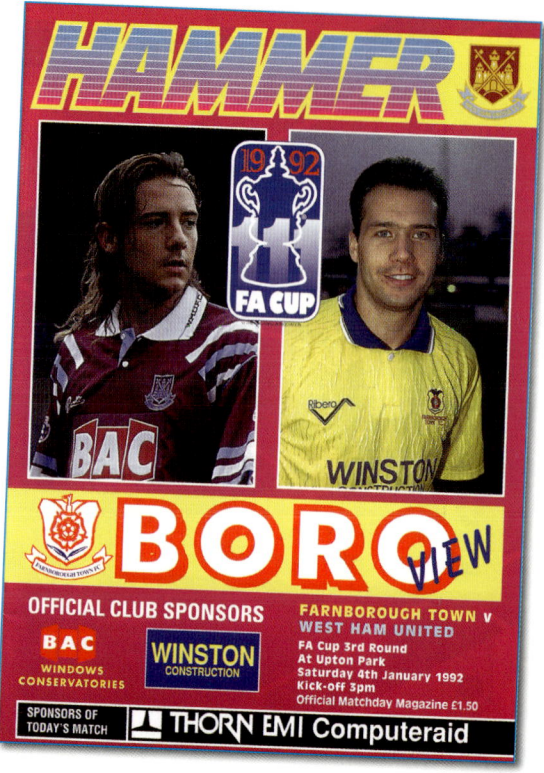

UPTON PARK MEMORIES 251

OFFICIAL PUBLICATIONS ● **OFFICIAL PUBLICATIONS** ● **OFFICIAL PUBLICATIONS** ● **OFFICIAL PUBLICA**

252 UPTON PARK MEMORIES

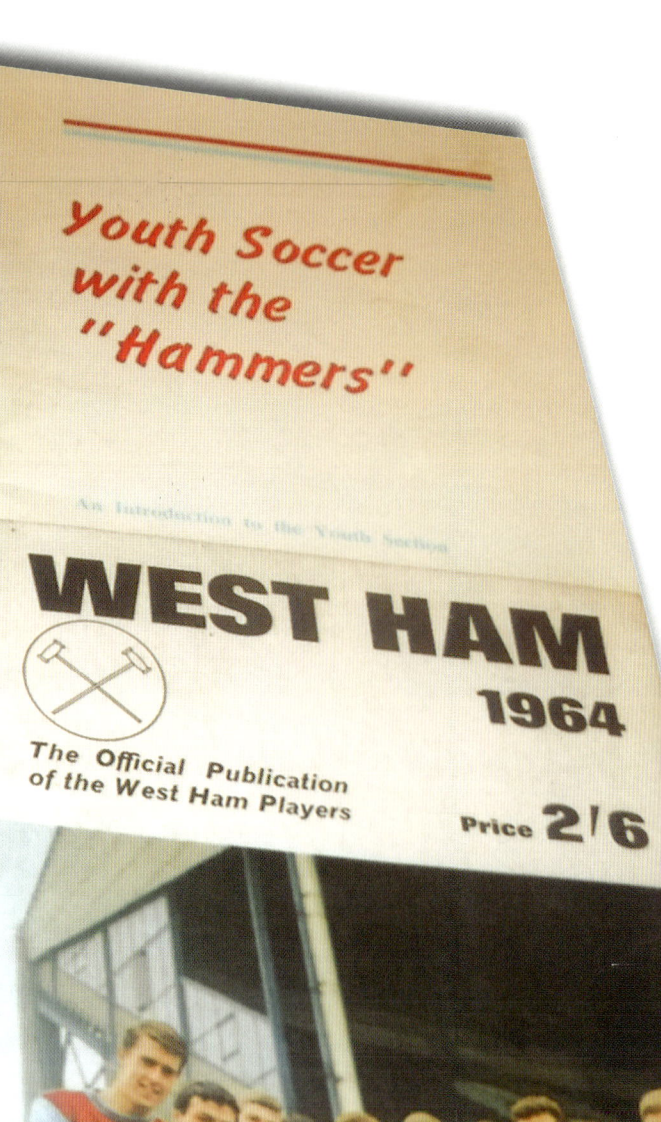

OFFICIAL PUBLICATIONS • OFFICIAL PUBLICATIONS • OFFICIAL PUBLICATIONS • OFFICIAL PUBLICATIONS

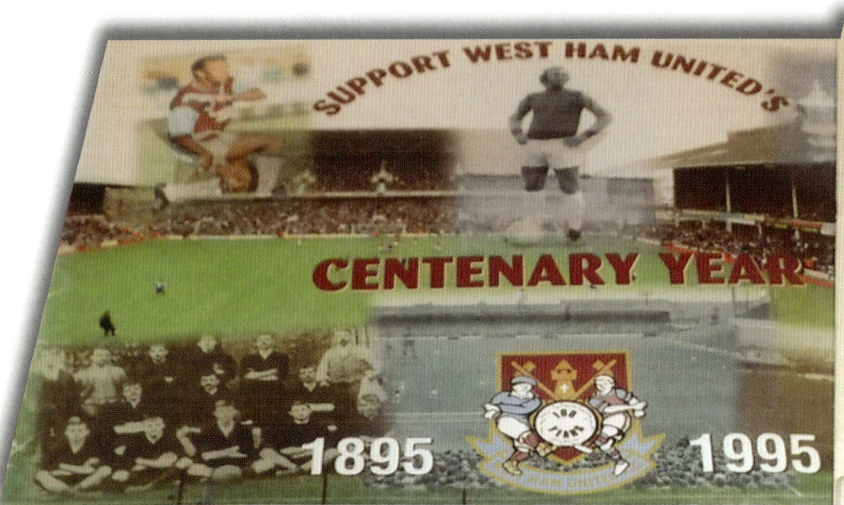

UPTON PARK MEMORIES 253

OFFICIAL PUBLICATIONS ● **OFFICIAL PUBLICATIONS** ● **OFFICIAL PUBLICATIONS** ● **OFFICIAL PUBLICATIONS**

Hammers' Annual 1990

West Ham United FA Premier Youth Academy
Building for a Better Future

WEST HAM UNITED FOOTBALL CLUB

A History of the Club
The Story of "Bubbles"
and : The Club Badge

WEST HAM UNITED OFFICIAL ANNUAL 1981
Edited by Harry Harris
The F.A. Cup story in glorious colour

254　UPTON PARK MEMORIES

OFFICIAL PUBLICATIONS ● **OFFICIAL PUBLICATIONS** ● **OFFICIAL PUBLICATIONS** ● **OFFICIAL PUBLICATIONS**

UPTON PARK MEMORIES 255

OFFICIAL PUBLICATIONS • OFFICIAL PUBLICATIONS • OFFICIAL PUBLICATIONS • OFFICIAL PUBLICATIONS

HANDBOOKS

ANOTHER tradition that has inevitably fallen by the wayside in the past decade has been the production of an official West Ham United Handbook. At the start of the season it provided a cheap and handy well illustrated reference for those interested in Hammers' history, as well as providing profiles and career statistics on current players at first team, reserves and youth level.

The club published its first handbook in its inaugural season, 1900-01, although not even one of the most fervent club historians, Steve Marsh, has ever seen a copy. He has, however, supplied us with an image of the second handbook, dated 1901-02, three years before the move to the Boleyn Ground.

With the exception of the 1914-18 First World War years, handbooks were produced every season up to, and including, the disrupted 1939-40 season that heralded the start of WW2.

Avid collectors will confirm that production since then has been sporadic. No handbooks were published in the 40s and the next one didn't appear until 1954-55. In the late 50s and for most of the 60s, the club took a break from putting out a handbook that fans could buy and, instead, issued an unusually thin-looking Press Handbook (see 1963-64 cover illustration) for visiting journalists, as well as an 'End of Season Summary' booklet.

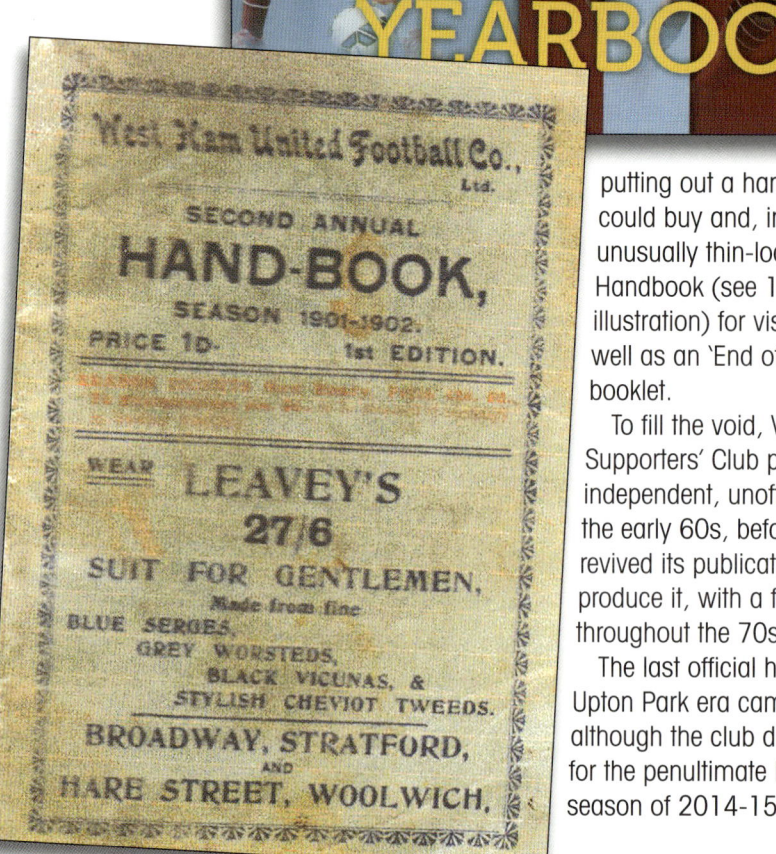

To fill the void, West Ham United Supporters' Club produced their own independent, unofficial handbook from the early 60s, before the football club revived its publication and continued to produce it, with a few exceptions, throughout the 70s, 80s and 90s.

The last official handbook of the Upton Park era came out in 2006-07, although the club did issue a Yearbook for the penultimate Boleyn Ground season of 2014-15.

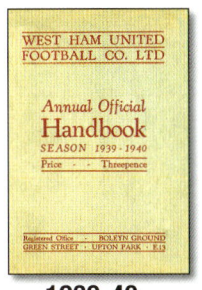

UPTON PARK MEMORIES 257

1939-40 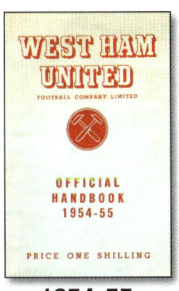　　1954-55 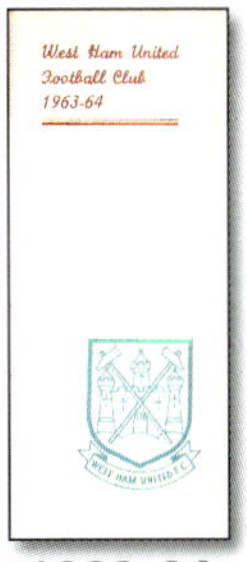　　1963-64 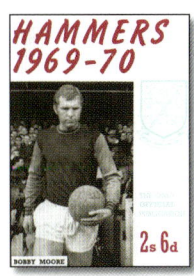　　1969-70 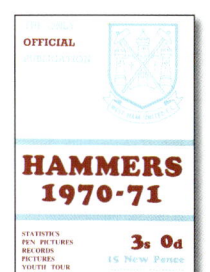　　1970-71

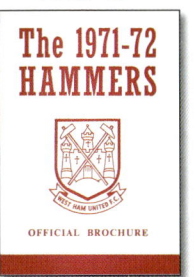

1971-72 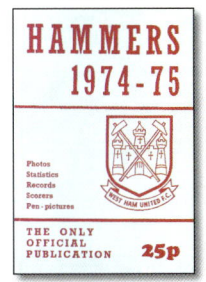　　1974-75 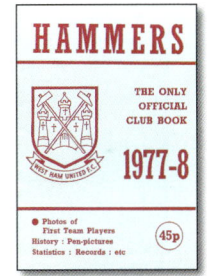　　1977-78 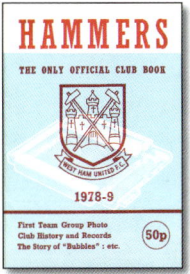　　1978-79 　　1981-82

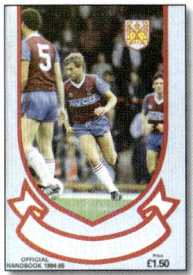

1984-85 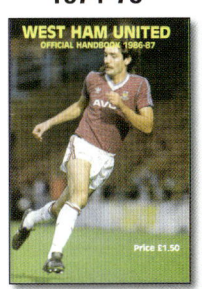　　1986-87 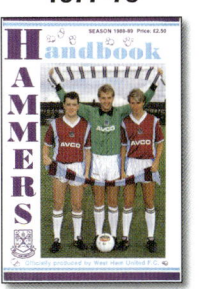　　1988-89 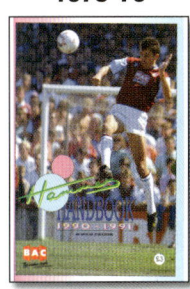　　1990-91 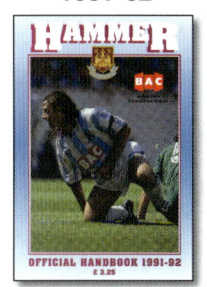　　1991-92

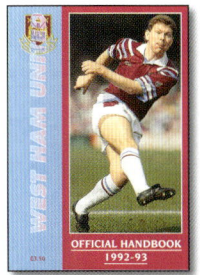

1992-93 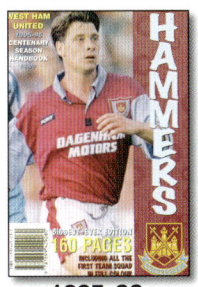　　1995-96 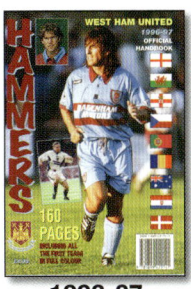　　1996-97 　　1999-00 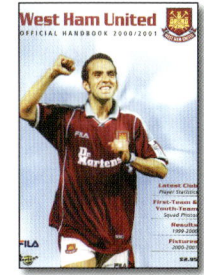　　2000-01

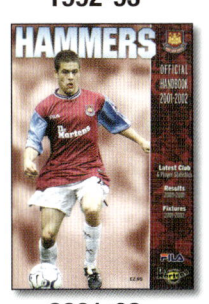

2001-02 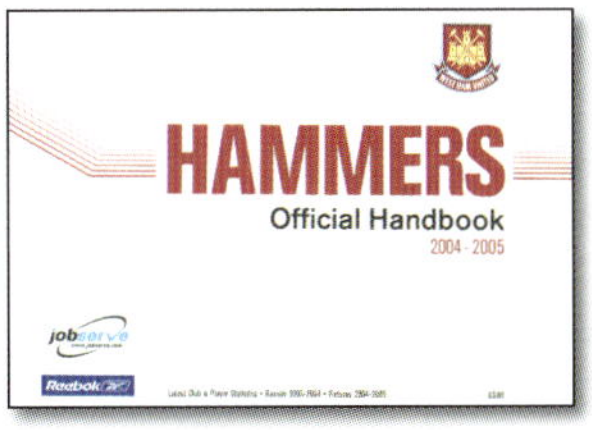　　2004-05 　　2005-06 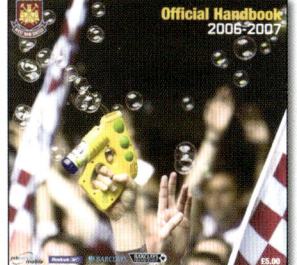 　　2006-07

UPTON PARK MEMORIES

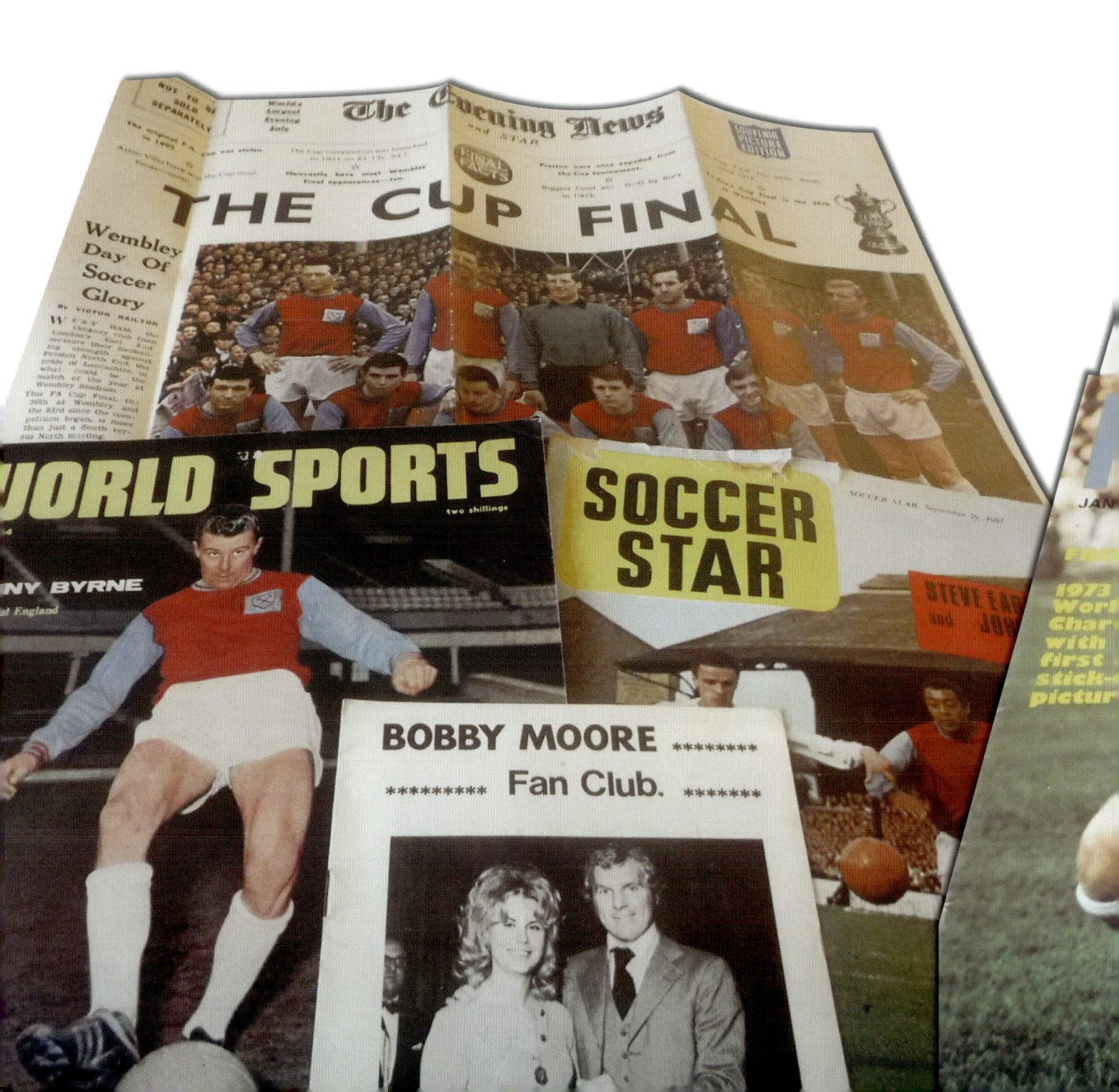

OTHER PUBLICATIONS ● OTHER PUBLICATIONS ● OTHER PUBLICATIONS ● OTHER PUBLICATIONS ● OTHER P

UPTON PARK MEMORIES 259

CATIONS ● **OTHER PUBLICATIONS** ● **OTHER PUBLICATIONS** ● **OTHER PUBLICATIONS** ● **OTHER PUBLICATIONS**

GENERAL BOOKS ● GENERAL BOOKS ● GENERAL BOOKS ● GENERAL BOOKS ● GENERAL BOOKS ● GENER

BOOKS ● **GENERAL BOOKS** ● **GENERAL BOOKS** ● **GENERAL BOOKS** ● **GENERAL BOOKS** ● **GENERAL BOOKS**

GENERAL BOOKS • GENERAL BOOKS • GENERAL BOOKS • GENERAL BOOKS • GENERAL BOOKS • GENER

FANZINES

FANZINES were a product of the late 80s, when disenfranchised, disgruntled fans finally found a voice and a platform to vent their spleens though the explosion of independent publications that probed, pilloried and poked fun at football clubs and their players, management and staff.

These often typically crude looking productions sprung up at just about every club in the land, announcing themselves with many weird and not so wonderful names. It didn't matter to those behind their launch that many of the writers were semi-literate and the pages were folded and stapled together in someone's back bedroom – that was all part of their charm and appeal.

Most importantly, they were relatively cheap to produce and buy and they offered an alternative view to the clubs' programmes and monthly magazines, or *Pravda* as the official editorial organs were called by the more cynical on the terraces.

To be fair, the club and its notoriously hamfisted handling of important and sensitive issues, gave the fanzines plenty to get their teeth into. Relegation in 1989 and 1992 and, in between, the bond scheme debacle inspired the keyboard warriors to get it all of their chest and offer their club some not very well chosen words of advice.

In fairness to the club, they tolerated these constant attacks in print without (as far as I know) calling up their lawyers to file libel suits. And when MD Peter Storrie was appointed the club's first executive director in 1991, West Ham started to engage with the most vocal fanzine editors.

Most fanzines soon fell by the wayside, in some cases after just a few editions, as editors and contributors ran out of steam, enthusiasm or became weary of a routine that involved standing on street corners peddling their wares in all weathers. By the late 90s, the Internet, with its myriad of online forums and, more recently, social networking sites such as Twitter and Facebook, have also driven more nails into the fanzine coffin.

Perhaps inevitably given their lack of silverware since 1980, West Ham spawned more fanzines than most clubs. Among those that came and went were: *The Water in Majorca*, *Who Ate All The Pies*, *The Boleyn Scorcher*, *The Ultimate Dream*, *Forever Blowing Bubbles*, *Never Mind The Boleyn*, *Ironworks Gazette*, *UTD-United* (a West Ham/Dundee Utd combo), *Cockney Pride*, *Bubbles*, *The East End Connection* and *The Ultimate Truth*.

Over Land and Sea (OLAS), *Fortune's Always Hiding* (edited by Steve Rapport – aka North Bank Norman), *On A Mission* (Shane Barber) and *On the Terraces* (Marc Williams) survived the longest and *OLAS* was still selling in the club's final season at Upton Park.

OLAS probably dented sales of the official programme when it increased frequency and published a new issue to coincide with every home game and by adding a middle section called *Home Alone* that contained in-depth match previews and team line-ups.

In the final season at Upton Park a new fanzine emerged in the form of *5Managers*, a reference to the first quintet who managed West Ham at Upton Park.

Last, but by no means least, the quarterly *Scandinavian Bubbles* (formerly *Norwegian Bubbles*), produced by Norway-based Gjermund Holt, has published more than 125 issues since its launch in 1988.

The man to look up to. Bobby Moore leads out his team as awestruck fans in the West Side gasp at the first glimpse of their blond hero in the number six shirt emerging from the players' tunnel.

7 FAVOURITE PLAYERS

OVER the course of 112 years at the Boleyn Ground, around 800 players have worn the claret-and-blue in competitive first team home matches. There have been some good. There have been some bad. And then there have been some greats.

Sadly, none of our contributors were around to witness the exploits of the original Upton Park heroes – the likes of Syd Puddefoot, Jimmy Ruffell, Len Goulden and the incomparable Vic Watson. But there have been plenty to follow that illustrious band over the years, men responsible for writing the history of our great club, and all of whom hold a special place in the hearts of Hammers fans.

Q: Name your three most favourite players and say what made each of them so special to you.

BOBBY MOORE

"Everything that epitomised the word legend"

Terry Connelly: Johnny Byrne was my personal favourite but Bobby Moore was undoubtedly the greatest player ever to pull on a claret-and-blue shirt. There is not much anyone can say that has not already been said. Cool, calm and collected is a typical cliche of which there are many more. There was no finer sight than to see Bobby catch a long ball from the opposing half on his chest, get it down and spread it wide.

Richard Miller: Simply the greatest defender in the history of the game. A national icon. I am privileged to have seen nearly 80 per cent of the 643 competitive first team games that Bobby played for Hammers. A true gentleman who was always willing to talk to supporters and sign autographs.

Rob Robinson: A classy, cultured and fantastic club man for West Ham. For a player who some of the press said was too slow, could not head a ball and could not tackle, he proved them all wrong with his stylish and superb positional play along with supreme tactical awareness.

Danny Cooper: Anyone old enough to have seen him play cannot fail to name Bobby Moore as number one. Imperious is a description I've stolen from somewhere – not just the way he played but the way he led the team out, a sight undoubtedly enhanced whenever the floodlights were on.

John Reynolds: My first hero was the great Bobby Moore. How we managed to keep him for the majority of his career is unbelievable really. I think he is best summed up by his manager Ron Greenwood, who said: "He was icily cold at moments of high stress and his positional sense was impeccable. He was at his best when his best was most needed."

Ted Pardoe: We've had great, class players but Bobby was the ultimate thoroughbred. His skill and timing just oozed class. A one-off.

Dennis Farrow: In my lifetime he would have to be the greatest. He wasn't the greatest header of a ball but he could read a game like nobody else.

Jimmy Ross: If you're asking me who the greatest West Ham player was, it can't be anybody else, can it? He's the best international we've produced, he was captain of England and he won the World Cup. What more do you want, for Christ's sake!

Tony Hoskins: He was everything that epitomised the word 'legend'. He was so calm and just exuded class.

Greg Faasen: I never actually saw him play but he was one of the reasons I supported West Ham in the beginning. He was my role-model growing up.

Dave Spurgeon: Do I have to find words to say why? He was a genius on the field of play and a great ambassador for the game off of it. He was a local hero, a national hero and he was a Hammer. Style, class, dignity in all he did on and off the pitch. Rightly revered throughout the whole world of football. We will never see his like again.

Eddie Parker: My first and ultimate hero.

Steve Burton: He is my all-time favourite for every reason under the sun.

Malcolm Downing: Because he was . . . Bobby Moore.

> **"Moore propped himself up on his elbow on the stretcher and watched the game like a Roman Emperor"**

Terry Roper: It is impossible to pick out three players who make up my 'top three.' I have had many favourites over the years but my all-time favourite is Bobby Moore. I first saw him play in West Ham's youth team. I saw his reserve team debut, plus his league debut and watched with awe as his career blossomed in the ensuing seasons.

He was captain of West Ham at 21; England captain at 22; Footballer of the Year at 23; he led his club to two momentous Wembley triumphs by the time he was 24; he was a World Champion as well as being named Player of the World Cup at 25. Six months later, he was voted BBC Sports Personality of the Year and, shortly thereafter, he was awarded an OBE. It was a progression so perfect that one could be forgiven for thinking that it had been ordained from above.

Apart from his jaw-dropping ability to judge situations with computer accuracy and then act upon them with complete technical skill, there was another trait in Moore's armoury that made him quite unique. Basically, he was immensely talented at being ice-cool on the field of play, even when the battle was at its fiercest.

If it is possible to capture Moore's mien in a single word, there is only one that will suffice and that word is 'imperious'.

He was not only football's greatest ever defender but also the finest, most inspirational England captain of all time.

So far as I am concerned, he will always remain the greatest Hammer of them all.

Tony Hogg: I have to pick Bobby Moore. Because, well, he was Bobby Moore. Imperious, impervious, unbeatable, unflappable and always capable of handling any situation, in any condition, at any time.

Be it the goal-saving tackle, the match-winning pass or his uncanny ability to be in the right place at precisely the right time, he always exuded sheer class as West Ham and England's captain of captains.

John Northcutt: A true footballing legend. He served his club and country with distinction and all Hammers supporters were proud when he held aloft the World Cup in 1966. The inscription on the statue outside Wembley Stadium says it all – 'Immaculate Footballer, Imperial Defender'.

Peter Thorne: Bobby was injured during one game (he was rarely injured) and had to be carried off. As the stretcher bearers carried him away to the tunnel, Moore propped himself up on his elbow on the stretcher and watched the game like a Roman Emperor.

The crowd cheered him around the touchline and the only thing missing as Bobby bestowed a wave to his adoring public was a bunch of grapes and a laurel wreath.

Tony McDonald: I don't 'do' celebrities as a rule but Bobby made such a huge impact upon us young Hammers fans in the 60s and early 70s that we had a lovely framed, signed photograph of him, looking relaxed in his favourite armchair and resplendent in green-and-white striped Ben Sherman shirt, hung on our living room wall for years.

As kids wanting to get his autograph at the training ground, Bobby would emerge, almost regal, from the old wooden cricket pavilion changing rooms and stroll to the car park. He'd make us form an orderly queue while he placed his holdall in the boot of his red Jaguar. Then he'd open his front driver's door, sit down and sign each of our books in turn. His signature must be the most iconic in football history. Even at eight, I knew I was in the presence of someone a bit special.

Trevor Brooking and Frank Lampard after the 1980 FA Cup Final victory against Arsenal.

TREVOR BROOKING

"A cockney Corinthian who belonged to a bygone age"

Peter Jones: In his early games he was always falling over but something clicked and he became the most elegant player, allowing the ball to run across his body and deceive opponents, then delivering a sublime pass.

John Reynolds: Trevor is a close second to Bobby Moore. I saw his entire career and not once did he let us down. Like Moore, he came up trumps in the big games. I was on the pitch when he did a lap of honour after his last game. He was a cockney Corinthian who belonged to a bygone age.

Andy Brooker: Trevor will always be my hero and all-time favourite player. From the first time I saw him in the 1975 FA Cup final until the last emotional moment, in May 1984, when he retired, he was the greatest player I witnessed live at Upton Park. I think the initial attraction was that our surnames were similar but then once I actually witnessed him in the flesh I realised how he graced our midfield and what vision, balance and control he had.

Ian Smith: His reading of the game was superb. He was never renowned for his pace, but he didn't need to be pacy. He could make a 30-yard pass land exactly on target and his creativity in midfield was second to none. The fact he scored the only goal in the 1980 FA Cup Final with his head always amuses me. He practically fell over to nod it past Pat Jennings and send the East End into raptures. His trademark tongue sticking out as he beat one after the other before setting somebody up to score, or maybe scoring himself. He (and John Lyall) went to my old school, Ilford County

Tony McDonald: My all-time favourite Hammer. Trevor embodied everything you could wish for in a top pro: supreme skill, silken first touch, two-footed (it's great credit to him that few could tell whether he was naturally right or left-footed), exquisite passer of the ball, and scorer of almost as many goals as he created for strikers in more advanced positions.

I had the pleasure of seeing his whole career develop – from a fringe player seemingly lacking confidence, unsure of his place and who always seemed to be falling over in the late 60s, to a supreme midfield maestro of the 70s, when he often carried a poor team single-handedly. Even on some of West Ham's darkest days scrapping against relegation, he would illuminate many a grey afternoon with his subtlety and vision, a shimmy here and a dummy there.

It still defies belief that when West Ham went down in 1978, just as he was reaching his peak at international level, he stayed to inspire his boyhood club's quest to get out of the second division. Trevor was at his cultured best in the John Lyall years but perhaps Ron Greenwood, who had left Upton Park to become England manager in 1977, didn't receive enough credit for offering Brooking the solid reassurance that second tier football wouldn't affect his England career. How Hammers benefited from that mutual trust and understanding between two fine gentlemen of the game, as the club embarked upon one of the greatest periods in its history, with Trevor at the heart of everything that was good about West Ham.

He would be the first to credit his great mate, Billy Bonds, for doing the 'dirty work' that enabled him to fully flourish in midfield and if he had a weakness, it was tackling. But with his height, strength and ability to shield the ball from opponents, he was much harder to dispossess than he was given credit for.

And for someone who supposedly 'couldn't head a ball' . . . well, his headed goals against Eintracht Frankfurt and Arsenal are enshrined in Hammers' history.

After he hung up his velvet boots and was trying to stay reasonably fit, he was persuaded to play for the same Havering Nalgo Sunday morning team I played for. Imagine that, playing in the same team as Trevor Brooking! Close-up views of him pulling off some trademark moves – a dip of the shoulder, inch-perfect curlers into the top corner of the net and pinpoint crosses on to the head of our centre-forward. He'd put on a few pounds, like the rest of us, but he hadn't lost his natural skill and that innate ability to bamboozle opponents. I swear he even passed to me once!

A great ambassador for club and country (I can't even recall him being booked, never mind sent-off, although it must have happened once or twice), my only regret concerning Trevor is that he was far too intelligent to accept the West Ham's manager's post on a full-time basis, when the job was there for the taking after Glenn Roeder was sacked in 2003.

Trevor Brooking enjoying the freedom of Upton Park in April 1974.

High, so I'm always going to put him on a pedestal but the reality is, he was one of the finest footballers to ever grace our team and the England team. Add to that he was a true gentleman – did he ever get booked in his career?

Norman Roberts: Trevor controlled the midfield and you didn't realise just how important this was until he missed a game. He also scored some vital goals, like the two against Eintracht Frankfurt in 1976 and his header at Wembley to beat Arsenal. What a great day that was!

Tony Hoskins: Just pure class and, of course, he scored THAT header in 1980.

Ian Crocker: A fantastic player, so very elegant. A lot of my school

> "At a time when mudbath pitches were frequent, Brooking floated around the park like he was playing on a carpet"

Urged on by Billy Jennings, Trevor Brooking leaves Bristol City defenders trailing in his wake during a match at Upton Park in February 1977.

mates in 1980 were Arsenal fans who thought they were going to cruise that FA Cup Final. Not with the King of Headers around they weren't!

Eddie Parker: Sublime skills.

Paul Clayden: A true gentleman and a fantastic player. And one of our best managers!

Alan Chapman: Sir Trevor was just different class. Elegance personified. The way he could glide over muddy pitches, effortlessly go past defenders and score tremendous goals.

> **Neil Humphreys:** I once queued for an hour to get my VHS copy of the Trevor Brooking Story signed. There he stood, a West Ham and England legend, in a crappy, freezing portacabin, scribbling his name on video cases. And he spoke to every one of us. He asked me if I played football, for which team and in what position. He was unfailingly polite.
>
> Twenty years later, I was a journalist and he was a West Ham director, but he was the same man.
>
> Thirty years later, I was covering the World Cup in Brazil and he was working for the English FA and holding a lift door open for me at our Manaus hotel, still polite, still amiable, still chatty, still thoroughly decent.
>
> It's no secret Bonds and Brooking are lifelong friends. They were cut from the same cloth.

The best manager West Ham never had. Trevor exuding the kind of calmness on the touchline during his first caretaker-manager stint in 2003 that became his trademark as a Hammers great.

Nick Morgan: I've never been shy and have no problem approaching celebs if I feel like it. But I worked at the BBC during the mid-90s and every Friday we'd go for fish, chips and mushy peas at the canteen. Sir Trev was always there but I was so in awe and overwhelmed, I never went up just to say hello. He wouldn't have minded . . . but he is a God! And I am not worthy!

Gary West: He was just a delight to watch. The way he could drop a shoulder and leave an opposing player dumped on his backside as he went past him was a joy, as was the perfect passing and crossing with both feet.

Greg Faasen: I remember in 1976, at school in Rhodesia, my school mates (many of them Leeds, Derby, Liverpool and Spurs supporters) and I decided to write to players and see who responded. Obviously, I chose Trevor Brooking and, obviously, only Trevor Brooking replied with a signed photo!

Mark Edwards: Class in every way. At a time when mudbath pitches were frequent, Brooking floated around the park like he was playing on a carpet. With a fantastic eye for a pass and a great goalscoring record, Brooking was and is the epitome of all that is great about West Ham United Football Club.

Liam Tyrell: It's hard enough picking an all-time

X1 line-up, with too many greats for one or two of the positions, so picking a top three is really tough. Trevor Brooking is the easiest call, being my first true hero and all-time favourite player. His classy skills, intelligence, scoring, dribbling, passing astuteness, and ability to use both feet equally well.

Dave Spurgeon: Another local hero. In some games his genius at creating space and getting in a cross, or creating a shooting chance with seemingly little physical effort or movement, was worth the entrance money alone. Like Billy Bonds, another whose loyalty and service to the club is immeasurable. On technical ability and tactical awareness, I would only put Martin Peters, Johnny Byrne and Paolo Di Canio in the same league as him as West Ham players in my lifetime. Only Byrne and Di Canio, like Trevor, had the ability to dominate and run games and generally win them single-handed but Trevor did it over a far longer Hammers career. Another gentleman of the beautiful game who played with style and grace that thrilled the fans.

Gary Bush: Trevor Brooking, Billy Bonds and Frank Lampard are my chosen favourites. I grew up with their pictures staring back at me from my bedroom walls and they all played together so many times it was like the team jigsaw was never complete when one was injured and missed a game. I recall having a toy cupboard as a kid and on the inside of the door I had a West Ham team group poster taken out of *Shoot!* magazine. My mum wasn't a football fan but she put up with my relentless passion for West Ham and I would show her the picture to see if she could remember the names. The three players she never failed to get wrong were Trevor, Billy and Frank. One of the best, my old Mum!

> **John Powles:** Such great flair in midfield. His flowing runs, baffling the opposition with a drop of the shoulder, or his 'dummy' of letting a pass run across his body, and a lay-off to a team-mate of the likes of Hurst and Peters, to finish off a move with the ball landing in the net.
>
> **Pete May:** For his body swerve and two-footed crossing ability.
>
> **Tim Crane:** He could put the ball anywhere with either foot.
>
> **John Northcutt:** Trevor had a unique talent to be able to beat a man just by his body movement. He had great passing skills and vision and for a midfielder he had an excellent scoring record.
>
> In a Hammers career spanning 17 seasons he scored a total of 102 league and cup goals and all West Ham fans will remember his winner v Arsenal in the 1980 FA Cup Final.

BILLY BONDS

"An inspiration to all around him"

Terry Connelly: In my opinion, Billy Bonds was second only to Moore in his greatness. It wasn't just the way he played the game, it was his whole manner and the way he conducted himself both off and on the pitch. He gave his all in every match, always urging and cajoling those around him to greater efforts even in a lost cause.

When he became our manager in 1990 I got to know him quite well and an example of what a great man he is came when we were playing away to Coventry (25/4/92), in a game that we had to win to have any chance of staying up. He had told me that Clyde Best was going to be at the game and agreed to get my *Who's Who of West Ham United* book signed by him. We lost the game and were relegated but on the following Monday he rang me to say the book was signed by Clyde and that I could collect it. A truly remarkable thing to have remembered given the situation.

Peter Jones: Billy epitomised the strong work ethic, tough tackling, sleeves-rolled-up approach that East Enders love and expect from their team. He was a leader supreme, setting a great example of commitment. I would have gone into battle for him and woe betide any player who shirked their duties.

> **Neil Humphreys:** Billy Bonds never forgot it was a job like any other, but only in a positive sense – i.e. give nothing less than your best, demand the same of your peers, but never take the cult of celebrity seriously or succumb to the leeches that surround the game. A role model, a man's man and, most of all, a family man. He adored the game and gave everything he had, but he loved his family more. As a father myself now, I respect his uncompromising attitude more than ever.
>
> The closest to Bonds in the modern era is Steven Gerrard. And even Gerrard won't be playing top-flight football when he's 42.
>
> **John Powles:** His never-say-die attitude was an example to others, even when he reached the age of 41. Despite his tough tackling, he was not the type to retaliate when tackled himself, and was the only player I can remember who would plead to the referee for an opponent not to be booked after he'd been clobbered himself.
>
> **Pete May:** For his commitment, beard and all round geezerness.
>
> **Steve Blowers:** Billy Bonds and Trevor Brooking are simply inseparable.
>
> A 'proper' bloke on and off the pitch, Bonzo was simply an inspiration to all around him, while that old terrace song said it all: "Trevor Brooking walks on water." Pure class the pair of them.

Inspirational leaders didn't come any better than Billy Bonds.

Tim Crane: He gave us steel and endeavour – a worthy successor as captain following Moore's departure.

John Northcutt: Our leader, our captain, and with him in the team anything was possible. He had spirit, aggression and boundless energy and was an inspiration to all around him.

I shall always remember his hat-trick v Chelsea (2/3/74) in a season when almost single-handedly he saved West Ham from relegation.

It was a shame that an injury prevented him gaining an England cap v Brazil in 1981.

Billy retired in 1988 and, aged 42, he was still the fittest player at the club.

Dan Francis: The man who represents everything that is good about West Ham United and, indeed, football itself. Honest, loyal, genuine and humble – and yes, he was the greatest player never to play for England. I, sadly, never got to see Bonzo in his prime, but then you could argue that his prime lasted throughout his entire career – at 41 he was still the fittest man on the pitch and refused to allow his standards to drop.

I recall watching him inspire us to a 3-2 win over Nottingham Forest (21/11/87), head bandaged, and my dad saying: "I can't believe he's a year older than me!"

I have clearer memories of Bonzo the manager and, personally, I don't think he has ever really been given the credit he deserves for his four years at the helm. Maybe it's because his playing career was so legendary, that anything that followed might be an anti-climax, but he led the club through one of the most turbulent and traumatic periods in its history – a challenge that would have been beyond most – managing to secure two promotions and reaching an FA Cup semi-final without sacrificing the standards and values he had shown as a player.

I honestly think that, without Billy Bonds steering the ship at that time, we might have had a very different football club to support in the years that have followed.

And as for Billy Bonds the man, there are simply no adjectives to do him justice. I've had the pleasure of his company on a few occasions in recent years, and I can't really describe the feeling that comes with chatting to him. It's almost as if the world becomes a better place. Decency and honesty just oozes out of the man, and he has a magical ability to make you feel like a personal friend of his, even if there are scores of people in the room jousting for his attention.

I just hope that, once they are in the Olympic Stadium, the club recognise his contribution to our history and ensure it doesn't become the after-thought that it was with Bobby Moore.

Norman Roberts: Billy always gave 100 per cent and was such a great tackler during an era when tackling was part and parcel of the game.

Ian Smith: I loved it when he would exact retribution on an opposition player and the way he let others know he was on the pitch. We've had other similar players, Julian Dicks and Tomas Repka spring to mind, but Bonzo was the first such player and the best at what he did. He was also a skilful player, more so than many give him credit for, and his surging runs through midfield would always get the crowd roaring. Our midfield always played better and looked more balanced when Bonzo was on the pitch and his leadership qualities and total commitment are what made him probably our best-ever captain behind Bobby Moore.

Dave Spurgeon: Could and should have been capped for England as a right-back, a midfield ball-winner who also knew how to pass it well, and as a central defender in the different stages of his illustrious career. A humble man and gentleman of the game. A role model off the pitch and one who demonstrated absolute loyalty to the club. If I were a soldier fighting in the trenches, I would want Bonzo at my side. An absolute hero.

Richard Miller: A true Hammers legend. Completely reliable, an inspirational leader, totally committed.

Spencer Dodd: Billy had claret-and-blue running through his veins. Had the ability to lift the team and the crowd with his commitment.

Alan Chapman: No-one has ever given more to the West Ham cause than Bonzo. What an inspirational player. How he never won an England cap is a mystery and a scandal.

Ian Crocker: Number one, Billy Bonds. My childhood hero lifting those FA Cups. What a player and what a servant to the club. What a man, too. I had the pleasure of working with him in the media. He was everything you would expect him to be. He'd have been embarrassed if I'd ever told him he was my childhood hero, although he might have sussed I quite liked him anyway!

Rob Robinson: Inspirational and a truly committed player who would never give up the fight. I remember being at Roker Park on the Monday evening after our momentous FA Cup victory over Arsenal. We needed to win to keep our promotion hopes alive. Sunderland went a goal in front. We then pressed very hard for an equaliser when one of our attacks broke down late in the second-half. Sunderland broke swiftly but it was Bonzo who ran back the whole length of the pitch to make a superbly-timed tackle and stop us going two down.

Gary West: Bonzo was just an unbelievable captain. When I first saw him with his socks rolled down, long hair and beard flowing in the wind, I had my first hero.

Liam Tyrell: Led by example on the pitch, perhaps the fittest ever

> **"If I were a soldier fighting in the trenches, I would want Bonzo at my side"**

Hammer who would run all day for the cause, brave and honest. Versatile too, when you think how he played at right-back and in central midfield, as well as establishing a superb pairing alongside Alvin Martin at the heart of the defence.

Gjermund Holt: I was lucky enough to see Billy play before he retired. What a player! What would he be worth today?

Danny Cooper: Did he ever stop running? The best buy West Ham ever made. Hard as nails and you just knew you wanted him on your side if it all kicked off on a Friday night.

Paul Clayden: Always a brilliantly inspirational player and managed us well at a very difficult time.

Greg Faasen: He just epitomised West Ham for me. I still have pictures of him, short sleeves rolled even shorter, fists clenched – giving it all for his team.

Steve Foster: Does he need any explaining? Just epitomised what West Ham fans love in a player. Amazing attitude and spirit, and of course he was a bloody decent player as well. Best player never to have played for England.

Andy Brooker: Strangely, I think I only came to appreciate what a player he was after Trevor Brooking retired. He was the player that you would want alongside you, socks rolled down throwing himself into one challenge after the other.

Eamonn McManus: Because of his loyalty to the club in many forms. To me it's a travesty the likes of him and others are not still involved in the club. Billy is 'Mr West Ham' to me, alongside 'Sir West Ham Bobby', of course.

Simon Hoppit: The man is a West Ham God. He gave everything and was our leader. Absolutely love the man!

Eddie Parker: A lion who never flinched.

Tony Hoskins: The ultimate warrior. His never-say-die attitude was an inspiration to all those who played alongside him, and he could certainly play.

ALAN DEVONSHIRE

"He epitomised the West Ham Way"

David Hughes: Probably because he cost us 'nothing' and was such a delightful, wonderfully gifted footballer who epitomised 'The West Ham Way'.

Peter Lush: He'd come from non-league football, was skinny but so skilful and quick. The night he and Trevor Brooking destroyed Bury in the 10–0 win was unforgettable.

Rob Robinson: I will always remember his dazzling performance in the 1980 FA Cup semi-final replay at Elland Road when we went on to beat Everton 2-1. He was a player who could ghost past defenders as if they were not there. His awareness, quick feet and change of direction fooled the best defenders in the league.

Nick Morgan: A brilliant winger whose performance in the 1980 FA Cup Final was jaw-dropping.

Norman Roberts: Alan was sublime. Watching him dashing down the pitch and taking on players with ease always gave me so much satisfaction.

Mark Matthews: He was an amazingly consistent player and his direct

Dev gliding across the Elland Road turf during the 1980 FA Cup semi-final replay in which he scored one of his greatest goals.

Robert Banks: The man just oozed class when he was on the ball.
Tim Crane: Dev was the lock-picker. Watching him gliding by the opposition with ease stands tall among my most enjoyable experiences from the Boleyn terraces.

running, clever passing and change of pace made him West Ham's main attacking threat week after week until his knee injury in 1984. I particularly remember his brilliant performances during my favourite season, the 1981 second division championship campaign, when some of his link play on the left with Trevor Brooking was a joy to behold. Even when he eventually returned from injury for the 1985-86 season, although he'd lost his pace, he was still a vital part of that great team.

"A real working class kind of guy the fans could relate to"

David Steadman: He remains my all-time Hammers hero, a real working class kind of guy the fans could relate to, who made it all look so easy.
Ian Crocker: Another who was a joy to watch. And to think he cost £5,000. That must rate as one of the greatest bargains of all-time. I met him a couple of years ago when he was Braintree Town boss. I was still in awe, although tried my best to hide it.
Simon Hoppit. Such a creative, brilliant player. Alongside Brooking, one of the best midfielders we ever had. Great to watch and so skilful.

PAOLO DI CANIO

"Inspirational, mad and brilliant"

Neil Roper: My favourite era as a West Ham fan was under Harry Redknapp. The football was exciting, we signed world class players (even if most of them were over the hill by the time we got them) and for a few seasons we were regulars in the top half of the Premier League, even finishing fifth in 1998-99. One of the main reasons for this was Paolo Di Canio. Aside from the Wimbledon volley and other audacious goals he scored with such regularity, his vision, his close control, his strength and, most of all, his skill on the ball made him the greatest West Ham player in the last 30 years.
David Steadman: The ultimate entertainer, probably the one player I would pay to see play above all else.
Mike Corbett: Pick any reason really but, ultimately, he was entertaining, and that's what we pay the money for. He was either scoring outrageous goals or generally having a proper meltdown. And you always had feeling that we might get something out of a game if he was on the pitch.
Jimmy Jacob: Passionate and played for the badge and the supporters, as well as providing brilliant skill and technique.
Mark Edwards: His outrageous skill and desire drove West Ham on many times. Stunning goals were frequent, as were the tantrums and histrionics, but Upton Park was never a dull place while the Italian was here.
Nick Morgan: Inspirational, mad and brilliant.
Ian Nunney: What an enigma, he could change a game in a moment. Looking rather out of sorts for most of the time, then win the match with a touch of brilliance.

Paolo Di Canio treated the pitch as his stage, the fans as the audience.

"A natural entertainer who put the drama of his individual performance above all else"

Steve Burton: For his technique and passion.

Jim Wilder: He brought a new dimension to West Ham's game and attitude.

Chris Ludlow: The guy was just a phenomenal talent. He played with his heart on his sleeve and scored some breathtaking goals.

Ian Smith: The circumstances in which he came to our club are well known and, as such, it was a massive gamble but once I saw what he could do I was mesmerised. His outrageous skill with the ball was amazing to see. He would just glide past the opposition with ease before scoring an amazing 20-yarder and jumping into the crowd, having ripped his shirt off in celebration. Who can ever forget his goal against Wimbledon? That day I was watching the game live on TV at home when the doorbell rang. It was the postman delivering a parcel just at the same time as Di Canio was putting the ball in the net. I heard the crowd roar from the TV and rushed into the lounge to see the players madly congratulating the maestro before the replay came up. I was gutted I never saw it in real time but I have watched it time and again since and it remains one of the all-time best Premier League goals to date. Also his 'Barthez goal' in the FA Cup, in front of 9,000 Hammers at Old Trafford, was such a tremendous feeling. But his grabbing of the ball when the Everton keeper was injured was, for me, really annoying. I am convinced we would have scored from that situation and it meant we missed out on three points. That was the thing with Di Canio - he could make you jump from your seat with excitement or really p*** you off with his falling about antics or picking up a 'niggling injury' before a Tuesday night match up north in January. But you cannot deny he was a true entertainer and his love of West Ham is now well documented, including his tattoo of our badge on his arm.

John Reynolds: It was certain events that brought Paolo and West Ham together, and I'm so glad they did. I doubt we will ever see a player like him again in a West Ham shirt. For pure skill, passion and commitment, he was worth every penny of the season ticket money.

Dan Francis: He may not have been everyone's cup of tea, and his aversion to stadiums north of Watford was an irritation at times, but Paolo provided one thing sadly lacking in today's game – showmanship.

It's rare now to witness those who treat the field of play as a theatre and the crowd as an audience. Di Canio, for all his crazy traits, was a natural entertainer who put the drama of his individual performance above all else, yet had the quality to ensure it contributed to the team's success at the same time.

And he was just as entertaining off the field as on it. Interviewing him for *Hammers News Magazine* was an adventure in itself. It would normally take at least four or five attempts to tie him down, at which point he would insist on giving no more than five minutes of his time as he was in a hurry. Two hours later, with both sides of the tape recorder almost full, it would be me desperately trying to wrap things up as Paolo passionately got his point across!

One afternoon after training, we arranged a photo shoot with him to model the club's new away kit. Looking around for a suitable backdrop and theme for the shoot, it was Paolo who suddenly decided to strip naked and wear the garment virtually as a loin cloth . . . telling anyone who would listen that he loved to feel the shirt on his skin. Never a dull moment.

Iain Dale: Paolo is the best player I have ever seen play for West Ham. He was a proven match-winner and would always entertain. You never knew what to expect from him but you knew that you'd go away talking about him. He was never boring.

I couldn't believe he was barely used in the run-in to our relegation season in 2002-03. He could have saved us single-handedly but wasn't given the chance. How different things might have been.

Frank McAvennie signals one of the 26 league goals he scored in the record-breaking 1985-86 season. This one was in a 2-1 win v Watford in November 1985, around the time the rest of the country was beginning to hear about the blond Scot who was taking the first division by storm.

FRANK McAVENNIE

Dan Francis: My first footballing hero and the man who I credit with instilling my belief that football is, most importantly, an entertainment industry. Frank stood out from the crowd the very first time I saw him play, and did the same for the rest of his career. The record books will, of course, show that he had one unforgettable season in the claret-and-blue but, for me, it goes far deeper than that with Frankie Mac.

He represented an ideal, the principle of the maverick – that the role of a top class professional footballer is to put a smile on the faces of the supporters, the majority of whom have worked hard all week and pay good money to be entertained.

From his little, wry half-smile when pulling off a moment of skill or clattering a defender into the advertising hoardings with a 'fair' challenge, to his ecstatic goal celebrations – punching the air in delight or simply raising both arms as high as possible as he strode towards the delirious fans, Frank just had the knack of bonding with those on the terraces and demonstrating the sense that he was one of them.

His lifestyle and charisma off the field obviously helped to embellish the reputation but his attraction to West Ham fans had nothing to do with that. He simply gave 100 per cent every week, played the game with skill, flair and imagination, and with a smile on his face.

I'll never forget the first time I met him. My Uncle Richard was a member in one of the executive lounges at Upton Park in the mid-80s and took me along to watch us play Aston Villa (22/11/86), which happened to be Frank's birthday. After the match, I was sat in the corner, reading my programme, when my uncle told me there was someone he wanted me to meet. I looked up and there was Frank, looking a million dollars with his beaming smile and stylish double-breasted grey suit. I remember standing in front of him, open-mouthed for what felt like hours, as he shook my hand.

All I could manage was a meek 'You're my favourite player'. On his arm was his then-fiancee, a glamorous blonde model (of course) named Anita Blue. She took a bit of a shine to the awestruck seven-year-old, and I sat next to her for the rest of the evening, wondering if I'd gone to heaven.

"We all wanted to be Frank"

Andy Brooker: A major player in us almost achieving the unthinkable. Frank scored goals for fun in 1985-86 and every time we played at Upton Park that season I just couldn't see anyone beating us. Although there were no televised games, I remember going to work and raving about our new blond striker to anyone who would listen to me.

Liam Tyrell: The 1985-86 campaign was my favourite ever season and he, as much as anyone, was responsible for that. I think at the time we all wanted to be Frank, with his blond locks, Page 3 girls and general lifestyle but, of course, most admired his scoring on the pitch and general application. He was never quite the same during his second spell but his first stint made it hard to criticise. The way he ended by scoring a hat-trick in his final game was truly fitting.

Fans' favourite Frank McAvennie in celebratory mood with Mark Ward.

JULIAN DICKS

Mark Edwards: All supporters want in a player is that they will play how you think you would play if given the chance. Simply put, Dicks gave everything. The fans adored him. Be it stopping a winger in full flight or hammering in a goal at the other end, Julian did it all with all he had. We will never see the like again.

David Steadman: Dicks carried the team a lot of the time. A fierce tackler who I believe even ended up top scorer one season . . . from left-back!

Iain Dale: I loved watching him. For someone who is so gentle off the pitch, it was as if he had a personality transplant once he crossed the white line. Even at the end of his career he gave his all and rarely had a bad game. How he didn't play for England when he was at the top of his career defies belief, when you look at some of the players who got the nod ahead of him.

His penalties were sublime and his marauding runs down the left wing will remain in my memory for a long time.

"He would run through a brick wall"

Gjermund Holt: I have to pick Julian. He made his home debut on my first visit to Upton Park. What a player and what a character. I have been so lucky to meet Julian a few times since and have interviewed him in front of crowds from our supporters' club. You'll never meet a more honest person. A fantastic player and a fantastic person.

Ian Nunney: Never knew when a game was lost, he would run through a brick wall to get a result. His tackling was ferocious and he had the shot of a mule.

Jimmy Jacob: My first Hammers hero. Passion, pride, determination, everything that epitomises the 'West Ham Way'.

Liam Corbett: He was everything you want in a hero.

Julian Dicks always gave his all and wore his heart on his sleeve. Tough, tenacious but also skilful with a cultured left foot.

Others to receive 'Favourite Player' nominations:

JOHNNY BYRNE

"England's Di Stefano, the complete player"

Terry Connelly: My all-time favourite Hammer was without doubt the mercurial 'Budgie' Byrne. The very fact that he arrived from Crystal Palace for a club record £65,000 fee in 1962 and that he was an England international was enough to excite any 15-year-old but it went way beyond that. Here was a player who could instantly control a ball with almost any part of his body, could beat an opponent with the merest shrug of his shoulder and could volley passes with unerring accuracy with either foot. Add to this the fact that he could score goals with both feet as well as his head, and to my mind he was the complete player.

Jim Wilder: He transformed West Ham and had a major part in the club winning the FA Cup for the first time in 1964.

Richard Miller: A tremendously gifted footballer who scored many magical goals. I still regard his effort in Lausanne in the 1965 European Cup Winners' Cup tie as the greatest goal I have seen scored by a West Ham player.

David Hughes: Sheer class and a talent that enabled him to 'murder' central defenders (the bigger the easier). Great goalscorer and so, so unlucky to be cut from Alf Ramsey's final squad in 1966.

> **Tony Hogg:** I have to include Budgie Byrne in my top three – if for no other reason than Bobby Moore himself held him in awe. The man who Greenwood claimed was 'England's Di Stefano', he was, in fact, more than that. His skill was such, he had no peers.
>
> They called Nat Lofthouse the 'Lion of Vienna' for his two goals against Austria in 1952 but there was no sobriquet for our Johnny when he scored a hat-trick to defeat Portugal 4-3 in Lisbon in 1964. So we'll bestow on him our very own: Johnny Byrne, 'The Iron of Lisbon'.

Johnny Byrne, the complete footballer. Tony Scott (right) watches the maestro at work.

Tony Cottee in the West Stand. As a boy he used to watch games from the West Enclosure terraces and dream of emulating his hero, Pop Robson.

TONY COTTEE

Paul Clayden: Part of our fantastic 80s side and made a big impact in his second spell at the club.

Eamonn McManus: From the moment he scored against Spurs on his debut at 17, it was TC for me. He seemed to score whenever he touched a ball and in the Boys of 86 season we were almost unbeatable. If he didn't score, Frankie did. Nuff said.

Mark Matthews: Tony was another great favourite of mine. A real natural goalscorer who scored over 100 goals for West Ham at almost a goal every other game.

Robert Banks: He is my age, a little bit older, so I saw him as a contemporary and was fortunate later on to get to know him for a short while. A very nice fella who bleeds claret-and-blue but never got the adoration he deserves despite the number of goals he scored, possibly because he was perceived as not always giving 100 per cent.
I can assure you he did.

BRYAN ROBSON

Peter Jones: He did not look like a footballer but he could certainly score goals. He worked his socks off to get alongside and feed off the centre-forward, whether it be Geoff Hurst, Clyde Best or Billy Jennings.

David Hughes: Mr Consistent, tireless worker, goalscorer and no mean football ability.

Peter Lush: A wonderful, underrated goal scorer who should have played for England.

Alan Chapman: Pop was a great player. He had all the attributes of an outstanding striker. Overhead kicks, volleys, shots from distance, tap-ins, headers – he scored them all.

GEOFF HURST

Graham Wright: What a fairytale story. He was an average wing-half who was converted by Ron Greenwood into a world class striker. He became just the kind of striker I loved to see – big and strong but agile, good with both feet and his head, and – most important of all – scored loads of goals every season. His striking partnership with Johnny Byrne was the best I've ever seen.

Pop Robson scored his goals every which way. This time a well-placed header finds the net in the 4-1 win v Southampton in April 1974.

Steve Blowers: A World Cup-winning hat-trick hero playing for West Ham United? Unbelievable, Geoff!

Geoff Hurst, Hammers' World Cup-winning hat-trick hero.

Alvin Martin, a strong central defender who was comfortable on the ball.

Phil Parkes, a goalkeeping giant in every sense.

ALVIN MARTIN

Gary West: I used to love watching him take a step back from the opposing centre-forward, control the ball with his chest and dribble out with it. He should have won a lot more than 17 England caps because he was different class to contemporaries like Terry Butcher, Steve Foster and Terry Fenwick.

Mike Corbett: He always looked calm, composed and in control, but could mix it up a bit if necessary. If there was a striker running toward our goal, but Alvin was in front of him, I would feel more confident they wouldn't score.

PHIL PARKES

Mark Matthews: Phil was the best goalkeeper I ever saw at Upton Park. Like Devonshire, he was incredibly consistent and made very few errors at the peak of his career. His calm presence was a major factor in

282 UPTON PARK MEMORIES

Innovator Malcolm Allison paved the way for the younger generation.

MALCOLM ALLISON

John Powles: The style of football he wanted to introduce, with the approval of manager Ted Fenton, went so much of the way towards that elusive promotion that came in 1957-58. Those ideas were initially greeted with much derision by some supporters, who were not used to the ball being played out of defence direct to feet and worked through midfield.

our defensive strength during the early 80s.

Simon Hoppit: When we used to stand behind the goal and watch him in his giant shorts, he oozed calmness. When a cross came in, he totally inspired confidence with his superb handling. A great goalkeeper.

KEN WRIGHT

Jim Wilder: An elegant centre-forward in the late 40s who scored some splendid goals. I was possibly influenced by the fact that he came to us in 1946, having been a bomber pilot in World War II and won the DFC. He did not stay long but rejoined the air force following a knee injury and became a flying instructor. Some years ago I read his obituary and learned that he and I had worked for the same company, Land Rover, in Solihull, but I never realised at the time.

KEN BROWN

Graham Wright: Ken was my first favourite player. He was a reliable and dependable centre-half, who was good enough to play for England on more than the one occasion he did. He always seemed to be happy and smiling, a very nice bloke. He once walked past my school when we were on the playing fields and one of the boys yelled out 'Kenny!' He responded with a laugh and a wave.

RONNIE BOYCE

Danny Cooper: His nickname said it all, the heartbeat of the side, but he didn't seem to get the plaudits given to lesser players. Tirelessly working up and down the pitch and, in my mind anyway, covered in mud.

Ron Boyce celebrating his 1964 FA Cup Final winner v Preston.

JACK BURKETT

Malcolm Downing: He made such spectacular saves and was as brave as a lion.

Graham Wright: He came into the side when he was about 19, via the youth team and reserves, and stayed there. He looked lightweight and I

LAWRIE LESLIE

Tony Hogg: They say the first cut is the deepest, so I make no apology for selecting my three favourite Hammers from my first decade supporting the club.

My first and absolute all-time favourite would have to be that courageous Scottish international goalkeeper, Lawrie Leslie, who was Greenwood's first signing. Us youngsters used to hero-worship him, not just for his tremendous goalkeeping skill, courage and passion, but for his friendliness to us young fans. He always made time to sign our autograph books no matter how many of us clamoured for his signature but, most importantly, he always gave the North Bank a wave as he ran down to take up his position before kick-off. That made us feel important and appreciated.

He was, and still is, the greatest.

wondered how he would manage the hurly-burly of defending in the first division. But he was a class left-back and made the position his own in the next few years, winning the FA Cup and European Cup Winners' Cup, and probably not being that far away from an England call-up.

GEOFF PIKE

Ian Nunney: His workload was second to none. He would be running up and down the pitch in the 90th minute with the same energy as he was in the first. He allowed the more talented players to display their silky skills. He would also weigh in with quite a few important goals.

DAVID CROSS

Danny Cooper: He wasn't a typical West Ham player but provided some much needed steel to the skill, and played a major part in our recovery from relegation in 1979 to win the FA Cup and second division.

RAY STEWART

Steve Foster: I could have easily gone for Dicks, Martin, McAvennie, Brooking, Brady or Devonshire. But I was a full-back as a player and used to watch 'Tonka' to pick up tips from the way he played. Plus I used to take penalties.

Hugo Porfirio could have become a big favourite.

IAN BISHOP

Neil Humphreys: He made the game look effortless, he could slow it down to his pace and ping a pass to anyone's bootlaces. He also looked and dressed like he should've been playing maracas with The Stone Roses. When you're an impressionable teenager, Bish ticked every box.

Unfortunately, he was often a Rolls-Royce surrounded by second-hand Ford Fiestas in those sides from the early 90s, but he still purred. Plonked on the centre circle pretty much for 90 minutes, he exuded class.

Steve Foster: Bish was very stylish with a great range of passing but had a tenacity about his game as well.

SLAVEN BILIC

Neil Roper: Given that I'm writing this just a week after Bilic has been named as the West Ham manager to take us into the Olympic Stadium, I realise this could be a dangerous nomination, but for the season-and-a-half that he played for us in the mid-90s, I thought he was imperious. A cultured centre-back who seemed just as much at home going steaming in for a full-blooded tackle as he was bringing the ball out from the back and setting up play with vision and calmness.

Slaven Bilic taking control of the situation against Coventry City.

HUGO PORFIRIO

Iain Dale: Hugo played only 27 games for West Ham, scoring four goals, and was only with us for one season, but he was some player. Skilful, tricky, knew where the goal was, he could have been a West Ham great.

But, sadly, his head was turned and he left at the end of his loan period, never to reach the heights his potential promised.

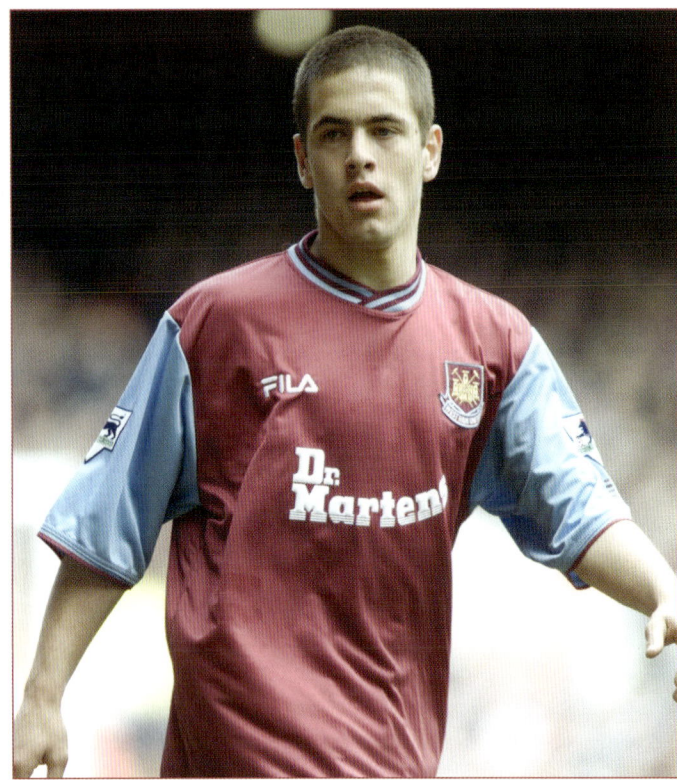

Talented Joe Cole, one of the greatest Academy products.

JOE COLE

George McDonald: One of the greatest West Ham Academy graduates of recent times. He had skill and flair, would try tricks and create chances out of nothing. He ran at defenders with the ball, he was an exciting young English midfielder. He ran his heart out for the club and carried the team at a very young age. I feel Joe has been wasted since leaving Hammers in 2003 and been discouraged from playing the same way. He would be stuck out wide-left for England and wide for Chelsea and yet he was much more effective behind the strikers. I genuinely believe that if he had played in this position for the majority of his career he could've been one of the best English players ever produced.

Jimmy Jacob: Joe came through the ranks, a player I idolised as a youngster and wanted to be. Clever, skilful and produced quality you would never have expected at such a young age.

RIO FERDINAND

Liam Corbett: He represented the best of the West Ham Academy and was just a hell of a player in any position he played.

EYAL BERKOVIC

Liam Corbett: A bit of an unlikely nomination but as I was too young for Sir Trevor's day, there's never been anyone close to him for the killer through-ball. Eyal was out on his own for weight of passing.

TREVOR SINCLAIR

Chris Ludlow: Work-rate was outstanding and he scored some brilliant goals.

Trevor Sinclair scored spectacular goals.

DEAN ASHTON

Robert Banks: He had everything. Power, pace, great header of the ball, powerful shot, tricky, acrobatic, agile. It is one of my greatest disappointments for West Ham in recent years that we lost 'Deano' to injury.

BOBBY ZAMORA

George Reynolds: Scorer of some absolutely crucial goals in my first season, in the 'Great Escape' of 2006-07 and, in my opinion, as important

Bobby Zamora after scoring the only goal of the 2005 play-off final against Preston at Cardiff's Millennium Stadium.

as Carlos Tevez in the final run-in (yet rarely gets acknowledged for it).

SCOTT PARKER

Neil Roper: If Di Canio was a match-winner in a successful period for the club, then Scott Parker was a one-man team as the club went into decline. One of Alan Curbishley's better signings, Parker simply gave everything he could for the club and was a very talented player to match his incredible work-rate. To be voted Hammer of the Year three years in a row shows just how reliant the club had become on his performances but it was the effort and desire that Parker put into those performances that will ensure he lives long in the hearts of the West Ham faithful.

CARLTON COLE

George Reynolds: I appreciate that he was never blessed with the skill of other players I've seen, such as Dean Ashton, Carlos Tevez or Dimitri Payet, but I have just always loved watching him. He scored instantly on his, and my, first game and other important ones, including the 2012 play-off final (which saw his induction into my family 'hall of fame', along with the commentary when he scored: "Target – 15. Achieved – 15"). Plus, having met him several times, he elevated himself to hero status in my eyes, as he was such a friendly man.

MARK NOBLE

George Reynolds: Coming through the Academy and then going on to play for West Ham was my dream growing up, so to watch him do it (and score an amazing goal against Bolton in the 'Great Escape' run) and finally become club captain in 2015, was amazing. He always gives 100 per cent and while he may not be the best midfielder I've watched play for us, he is certainly worthy of at least an England call-up.

Chris Ludlow: Claret-and-blue through and through. Just when people start to write him off, he always raises his game and proves all the doubters wrong.

Scott Parker was Hammer of the Year three seasons in succession.

Flying the flag for his local team, Mark Noble on the 2005 promotion celebration parade. Anton Ferdinand shows off the trophy, while Marlon Harewood and Elliott Ward capture the joyous scenes on film.

Autographs

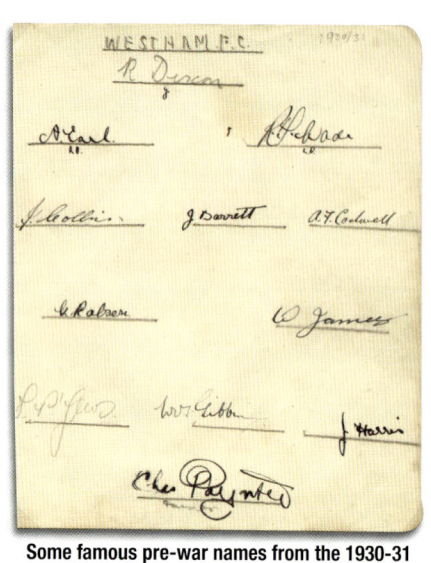

Some famous pre-war names from the 1930-31 season: Bob Dixon, Alf Earl, Reg Wade, Jimmy Collins, Jim Barrett, Albert Cadwell, Bill Robson, Wilf James, Tommy Yews, Viv Gibbins, Jimmy Harris and manager Charlie Paynter.

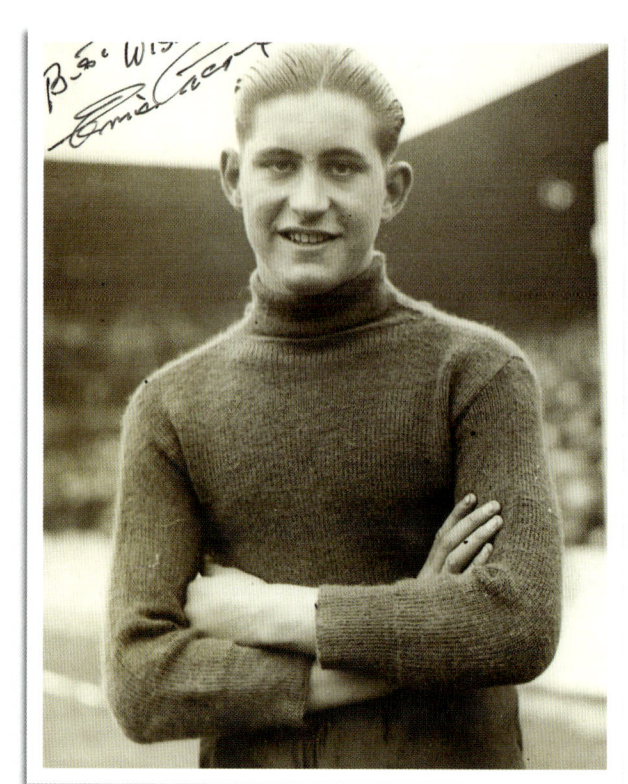

Goalkeeper Ernie Gregory aged 16 in 1937. He went on to serve the club for more than 50 years.

Phil Woosnam, classy signature by a classy player.

Signed by the 1956-57 squad, including (first page) Ken Tucker, John Bond, Eddie Lewis, Andy Malcolm, Ernie Gregory, Roy Smith, Bill Lansdowne, Dick Walker, Malcolm Musgrove, Harry Obeney, George Fenn. Second page: John Dick, Malcolm Allison, Terry McDonald, Malcolm Pyke, Albert Foan, Fred Cooper, Doug Wragg, George Wright, Billy Dare, Ken Brown.

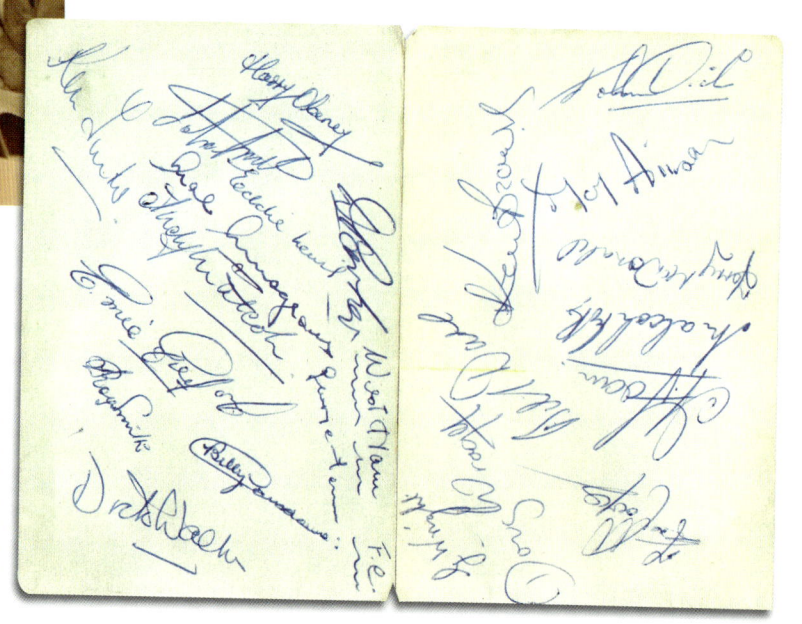

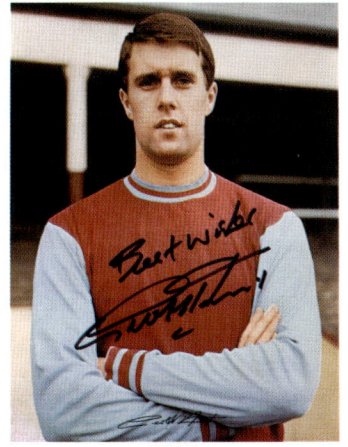

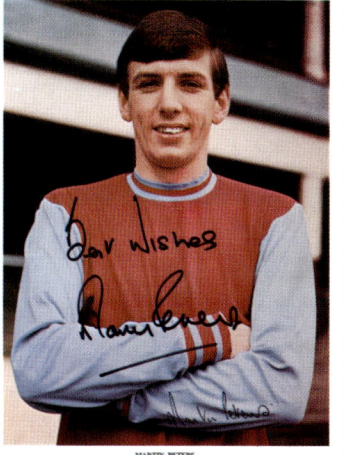

WEST HAM UNITED
Colours: Claret Jerseys with Light Blue Sleeves and Collars, White Shorts

1 GREGORY

2 BOND   3 CANTWELL

4 MALCOLM   5 BROWN   6 LANSDOWNE

7 GRICE   8 SMITH   9 KEEBLE   10 DICK   11 MUSGROVE

Referee: Mr. J. W. HUNT (Emsworth, Hants.)
Linesmen: Mr. A. L. MASON (Red Flag) and Mr. M. R. NESTER (Yellow Flag)

11 SCANLON   10 CHARLTON   9 VIOLLETT   8 TAYLOR   7 DAWSON

6 McGUINNESS   5 COPE   4 GOODWIN

3 GREAVES   2 FOULKES

1 GREGG

MANCHESTER UNITED

ANY ALTERATIONS IN PUBLISHED TEAMS WILL BE ANNOUNCED THROUGH THE PUBLIC ADDRESS SYSTEM

A rare, very early Bobby Moore autograph, as the then 17-year-old signed it in blue ink on the team line-ups page of the programme for his first team debut v Manchester United (8/9/58). Compare it to what became the conventional Moore autograph (below). The prog is signed by most players on both teams, plus United manager Matt Busby (top left).

Remember when packets of Typhoo Tea contained tokens you had to collect to then send away for cards of top players from various clubs? These two of Geoff Hurst and Martin Peters are both signed by the former greats. Typhoo also issued two cards of Bobby Moore, plus one depicting a 60s Hammers team group.

288   UPTON PARK MEMORIES

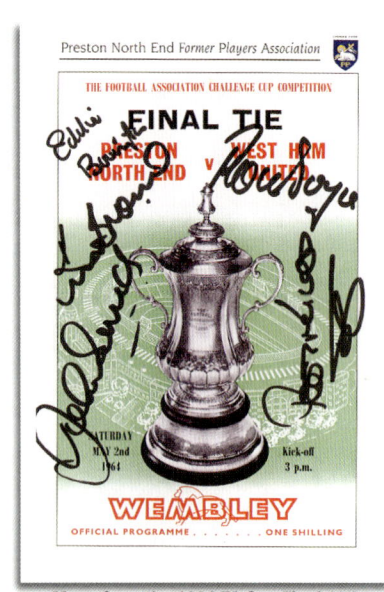

Menu from the 1964 FA Cup Final 40th anniversary reunion, hosted by Preston North End in Preston in 2004, signed by all five Hammers who attended: Eddie Bovington, Ron Boyce, Ken Brown, John Bond and Peter Brabrook.

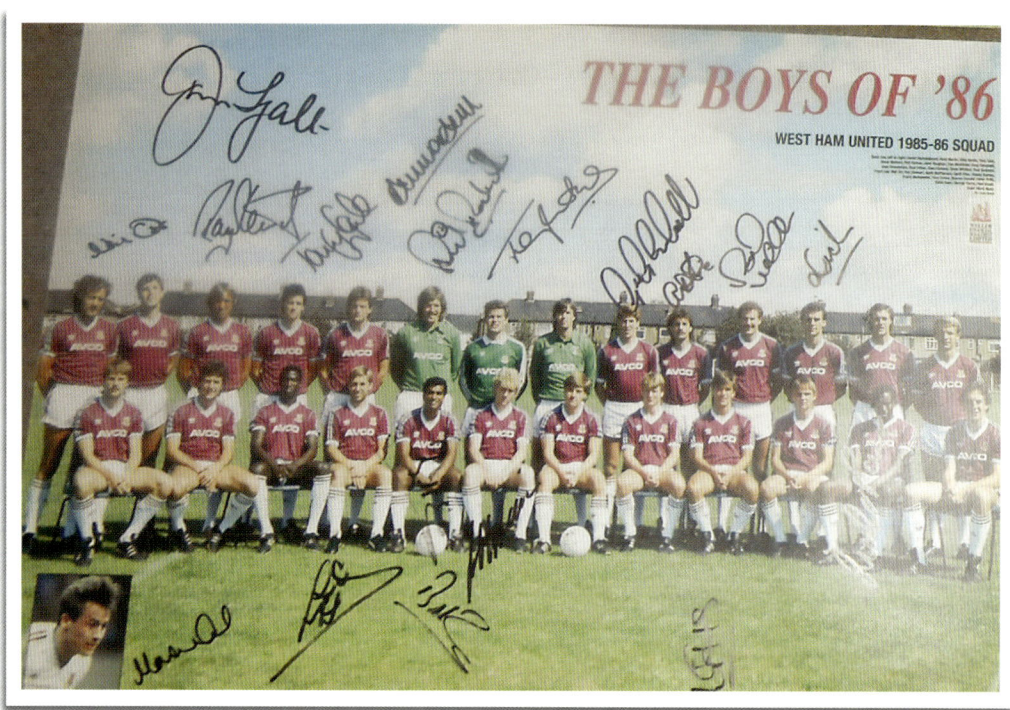

Poster of the record-breaking 1985-86 squad, signed by most of the players and manager John Lyall.

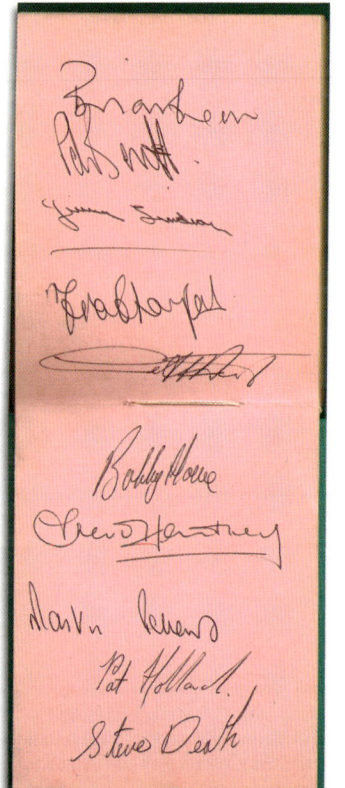

Four pages from a fan's book containing the signatures of the 1968-69 squad. Page 1: Brian Dear, Peter Bennett, Jimmy Lindsay, Frank Lampard, Geoff Hurst. Page 2: Bobby Howe, Trevor Hartley, Martin Peters, Pat Holland, Steve Death. Page 3: David Llewelyn, John Sissons, John Cushley, Ron Boyce, Alan Stephenson, Tim Clements. Page 4: Keith Miller, Billy Bonds, John Charles, Trevor Brooking, Harry Redknapp, Eddie Bovington, Roger Cross.

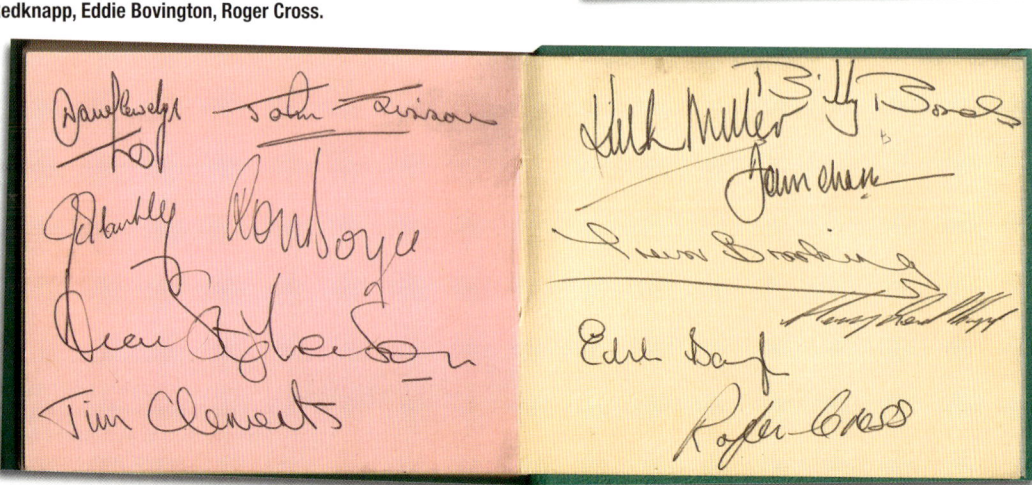

UPTON PARK MEMORIES 289

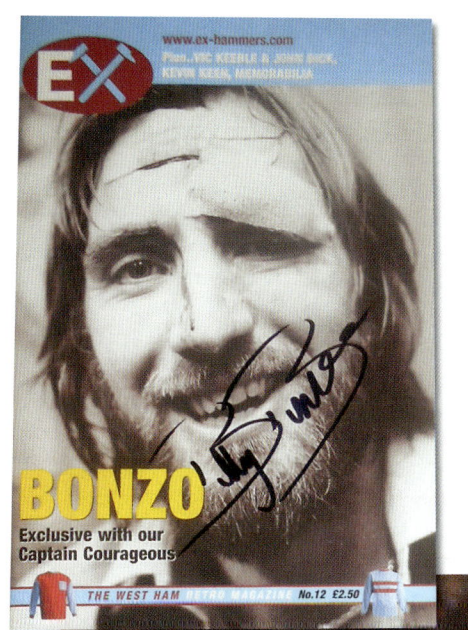

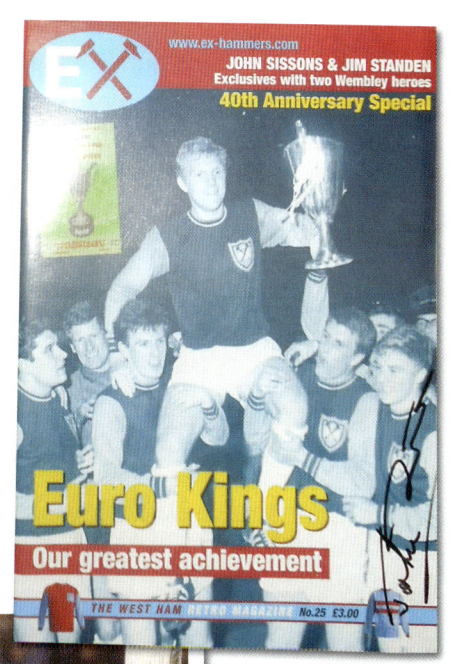

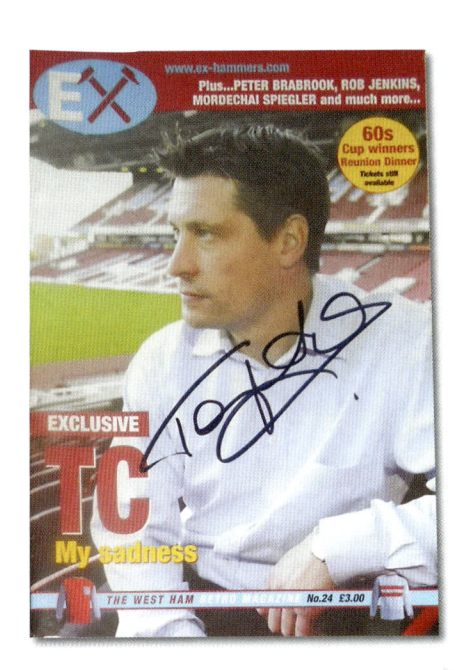

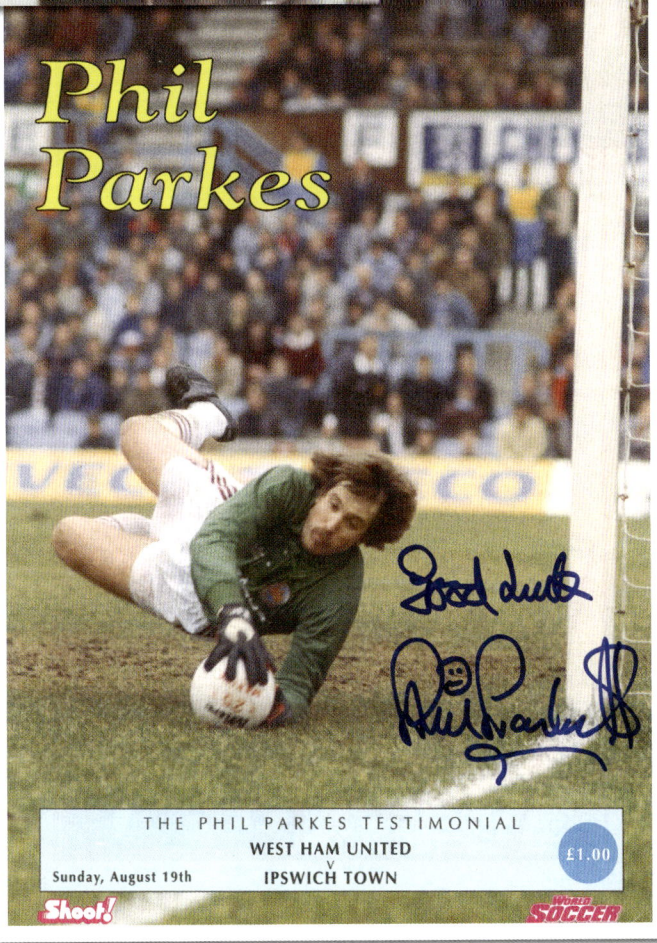

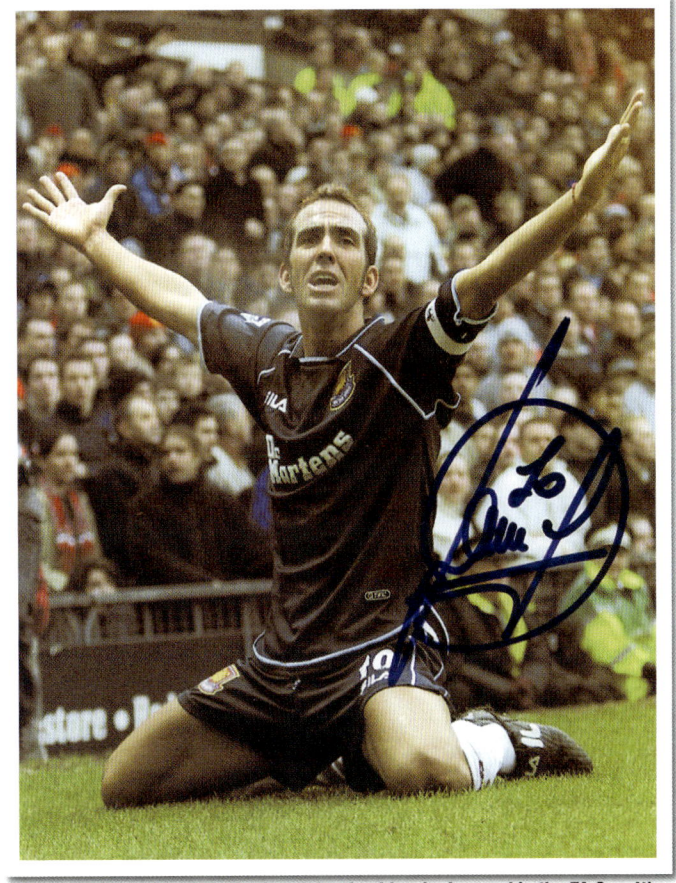

Famous photo of Paolo Di Canio celebrating his winning goal in the FA Cup 4th round at Manchester United (28/1/2001).

290 UPTON PARK MEMORIES

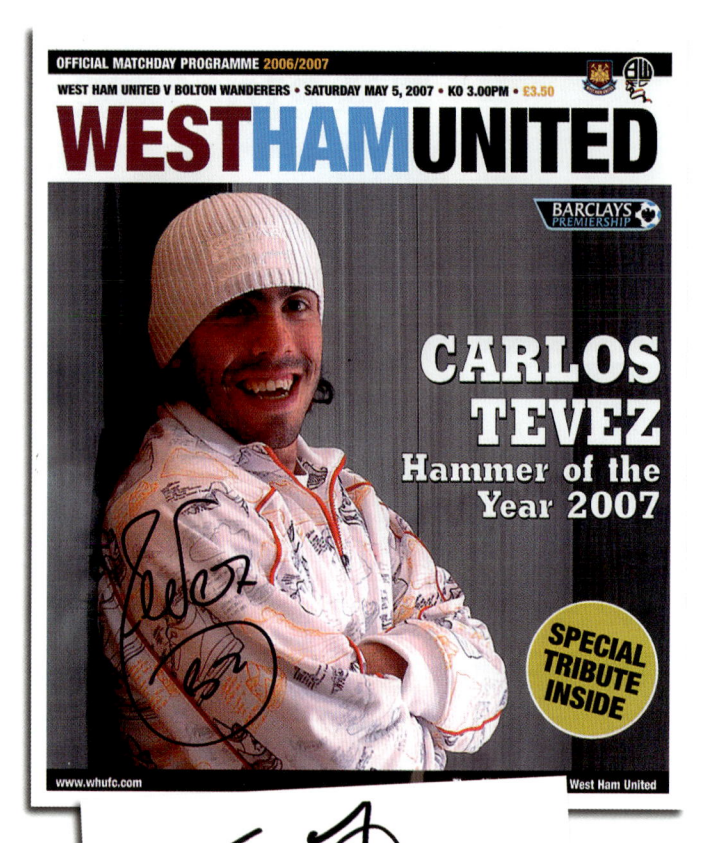

The signatures of many current players may be much more difficult to decipher but that doesn't stop youngsters from poking their programmes and books through the railings at the Boleyn Ground on match day.

Carlton Cole

Cheikhou Kouyaté

Even today legends Martin Peters and Sir Trevor Brooking still attract a lot of attention from autograph hunters.

Mark Noble

Aaron Cresswell

Andy Carroll

Adrian

Local lad made good, Ernie Gregory was a great East End character who had a special presence about him, on and off the field.

8 CULT HEROES

ANY debate about the greatest players in West Ham's history will generally throw up the same illustrious band of names. Moore, Hurst and Peters. Brooking, Bonds and Devonshire . . . their contribution is held in the highest regard by the vast majority of supporters.

But what about the players who didn't quite hit the heights of that sensational six in terms of ability, longevity and medals, yet still earned legendary status among sections of the Upton Park faithful? The players who can often be identified simply by a nickname or a memorable incident, who divided opinion on the terraces, or were famous more for style than substance?

Q: Your 'cult' favourite – not necessarily the best, but a player you admired or liked.

Steve Derby: Let me confess . . . my heart belongs to Ernie! Perhaps because he was the classic local boy makes good. I always saw big **ERNIE GREGORY** as special. Of course, we have been blessed with wonderful players down the years and putting one above another is an impossible task. But goalkeepers are special to me and I have so many memories of occasions when Ernie lit up many a jolly shooting match.

There was a time when goalkeepers enjoyed banter with the fans behind their goal. Step forward Ken Nethercott (Norwich) and Sam Bartram (Charlton). I heard Frank Swift (Man City) was not averse to signing autographs whilst play was going on! I recall the opening match of the 1957-58 season, when we struggled to get nothing more than a 2-2 draw out of Lincoln City. After the forwards had missed yet another simple chance, big Ern turned to look at the South Bank, raised his hands in the air, and delivered the immortal words: 'Gawd Almighty!'

A floodlit game against, I believe, Anderlecht in the late 50s saw our custodian take the field in a bright yellow jersey – a colour usually reserved for international matches. As he took his place for the warm-up, one wag from the terracing yelled: "What position are you playing tonight, Ern?" His grin was as wide as our laughter was loud.

Reuben Gane: ALBERT FOAN. I was a 14 year-old inside-right, the same as Albert, and he had a little feint where he would throw up one leg and switch to the other. I copied this and his little trap of the ball under his knee! A great player, Albert.

Another is **MALCOLM ALLISON** – I loved the way 'Big Mal' would play. He wasn't the most skilful of players but he wanted the game played the right way, with style and panache. He used to upset goalkeeper Ernie Gregory by asking for the ball to be thrown to his feet rather than the big boot downfield. Most of the crowd also wanted it kicked long. Malcolm LOOKED like an athlete, played with aplomb and always wanted to play the correct 'West Ham Way' – attractive with skill.

Peter Lush: A player I never saw play – **ROY STROUD**. He started his career in the Second World War as a 14-year-old with Hendon and, after doing very well as a striker in the amateur game, including winning nine England amateur caps, turned pro with West Ham when he was aged 23. When I was writing the history of Hendon Football Club I tracked him down and spoke to him on the phone but he was not well enough for me to interview him properly. A few other players played for both 'my' clubs but he was the best.

Ed Gillis: KEN TUCKER. It was always a moment to treasure when a bandsman would play the opening bars of *The Post Horn Gallop* to encourage the team and Ken would immediately set off down the left wing at a great rate of knots – with or without the ball!

Crispin Derby: JOHN BOND. Just the funniest, frighteningly casual, but most elegant full-back, who also managed to make defending attractive. It was certainly true that his suicidal forays into the opposition half created gaps in both defences. A lot of us played full-back, only because 'Muffin' made it glamorous and because he epitomised the West Ham 'cool' of that era.

Michael Harris: KEN BROWN. Solid and dependable, as a player and a man. He always played the game with a smile on his face. I have been privileged to have Ken and his wife Elaine as guests at my house. They are lovely people.

> **John Northcutt:** Centre-half **KEN BROWN**. He was strong, dependable, good in the air and was my favourite player when Hammers won trophies in the 60s. I have since met Ken at various functions and he is very approachable, always laughing and one of football's nicest characters.

Derek Price: The choice of a cult favourite is not as difficult for me as I first thought it might be. It has to be, of course, England's World Cup-winning captain, **BOBBY MOORE**, always elegant and always composed. A great leader of men. I must confess that I knew a lot about Bobby Moore before he had even left school, as my brother also played in the team for Tom Hood Technical School in Leyton, although he must have been two years under Bobby.

Graham Wright: It has to be **LAWRIE LESLIE**. Not as good as Phil Parkes or Ludo, or as safe as Jim Standen, but a very good goalkeeper nonetheless. He made fantastic saves and was the last word in bravery. However, this was his undoing, as he often got badly hurt diving at opponents' feet. He was another very nice bloke and a great, warm-hearted character.

Malcolm Downing: JOHNNY BYRNE, because whenever he received the ball the crowd seemed to stand on tip toes in anticipation of something happening.

Paul Walker: JOHN SISSONS would be my cult hero. I went to school with him at Mellow Lane Comprehensive in Hayes, Middlesex and was overjoyed when he joined my club. For a few years he was the best left-winger in the country, scoring some great goals in the FA Cup run and the final itself. I had watched him from the school field, to England boys at Wembley and then into a special part of West Ham history.

Jeff MacMahon: JACKIE BURKETT. Me and my mates all tried to walk like him.

Tony Hoskins: I have two cult heroes – **JULIAN DICKS** and **CLYDE BEST.** Julian was a very good footballer with the 'edge' that made him our hard man – The Terminator. Clyde Best was a striker who quickly became a North Bank hero.

Kevin Radley: It's hard to imagine what **CLYDE BEST** thought when he came from the sub-tropical climate of Bermuda to play for West Ham as a mere 18-year-old. It is incredibly uncomfortable to think back to the racist taunts from the terraces in the 70s and 80s, especially as many supporters, clubs and the authorities seemed to turn both a deaf ear and a blind eye to the problem. For my mates and me it was a matter of pride that we had black players in our team and it seemed quite exotic that Clyde

Lawrie Leslie at home with his son Grant and bearing his battle scars.

Tim Crane: BILLY BONDS. He played 793 league and cup games for the club in a career spanning 21 seasons. He was still playing first team football at the age of 41.

I always marvelled at him because he never gave less than 100 per cent in any match, presumably as he considered it a betrayal of himself, his team-mates and those of us who supported the club.

To play with the vigour and passion that Bonds displayed throughout his illustrious career – particularly in view of its longevity – was an astonishing achievement.

He showed indomitable courage, unyielding resolve and unquenchable willpower. It indicated an innate determination and hardness that allowed him to overcome the extreme demands of the professional game which are way beyond the comprehension of the ordinary man. Football is an unrelenting sport that repeatedly tests mind and body, nerve and sinew to their very limits and never once was Bonds left wanting.

I believe the whole-hearted attitude of Billy Bonds epitomises the reason why so many of us fell in love with the game from an early age and why we continue to maintain that enthusiasm into our adult lives. It is partly to do with excellence and endeavour but there is more to it than that. The game of football is one of the few professions that allows 'true character' to be portrayed during the heat of battle. It was this mightily impressive trait that the inspirational Bonds displayed so wondrously throughout more than two decades as a player at Upton Park and which set him apart from so many of his contemporaries.

Billy Bonds was a phenomenon and I regard him as the second greatest Hammer of all-time.

Clyde Best overcame prejudice on the terraces to become a big crowd favourite.

came all the way from Bermuda to play for us. But no-one believed he was only 18 – he was a big built lad and looked about 25!

There were tales that he lived in digs near the ground and embraced the cuisine of the East End with regular visits to the local pie and mash shop. And it was true that he would often be seen actually walking to the ground before a game – I witnessed it with my own eyes. This all endeared him to the core supporters and he quickly became a favourite with the crowd.

He came into a team that was past its best and in gradual decline and, although he didn't quite achieve greatness, he was a good player and, at times, very good. He was physically strong but displayed a lot of skill on the ball and was one of the first players that I remember who regularly passed the ball with the outside of the boot.

He formed a good partnership with Geoff Hurst and tended to play wide, which was unusual for a big fellow, but he had the skill and enough pace to get past defenders. He was one of the first black players to become established in top-flight English football and I believe he is regarded as a pioneer by some of the later black players.

I'd love to catch up with Clyde, buy him a beer and have a really good chat about his time at Upton Park. I can't say that about many players!

Roger Hillier: JOHNNY AYRIS. I had the pleasure of attending his debut game v Burnley (3/10/70), when Johnny supplied the crosses for two of Geoff Hurst's hat-trick goals. I thought it was incredible that a player just a couple of years older than me and about my size was playing in the West Ham first team, making a big impact in front of a 30,000 crowd. He was a very skilful player, great to watch but he suffered at the hands (or shoulder) of the likes of less skilful players such as Chelsea's Ron Harris.

Jeff Garner: A difficult one but **POP ROBSON** was great. I wish he had played for us more times than he did and it was such a shame he missed out on both cup finals in the mid-70s.

STUART PEARCE would have been an absolute legend if he had been with us longer. Looking back, I always had a soft spot for **CLYDE BEST** and also **PAT HOLLAND** who worked hard, was very underrated and provided some magical moments which made people realise that he was actually a better player than some gave him credit for.

Steve Wilks: In the 70s I loved **KEITH ROBSON.** He was a real battler. Never afraid of anybody and he would always give 100 per cent. I remember seeing him actually launch himself at a Spurs wall in one game. I think he fouled four of them at once! He was also a good footballer and no-one will forget his goal against Eintracht Frankfurt (14/4/76).

Dave Spurgeon: The unsung hero that was **PAT HOLLAND.** He always gave everything for the team's cause. I can remember some of the crowd getting on his back when he first broke into the team as an outright winger, probably because he did not measure up to the popularity of Peter Brabrook and Harry Redknapp. He took time and a lot of determination

Popular Pat Holland was never less than wholehearted.

to become a first team regular as a versatile midfield player and I admired that dedication. He became rightly popular with the West Ham faithful because he gave his all in every game and, technically, I thought he was very underrated, although I am sure his team-mates valued him much more highly than the fans.

Terry Connelly: PATSY HOLLAND had his critics and although he was certainly not the best player to represent the club, he gave his all in every game. No matter if he was playing badly, he would never hide and was always showing for the ball.

I saw him play his last game for the club, at Notts County, where in typical fashion he went in on goal, arriving a split-second before the onrushing keeper. He managed to push the ball into the net before being clattered and sustaining the knee ligament damage that finished his West Ham career. Billy Bonds said of Patsy: "He would run through a brick wall for you" – a fitting epitaph for a player who never gave less than 100 per cent for the cause.

Alan Byrne: PATSY HOLLAND. Unlucky with injuries but, like Bonzo, loyal to the core and always popped up with vital goals.

Gary Bush: A particular favourite of mine was **PAT HOLLAND**, a player who, when in full flow down our wing, was a great sight to see. He was so unlucky to miss out on a second Wembley appearance in the 1980 FA Cup Final to add to his memory of 1975. As a collector of all things claret-and-blue, I've often found Pat more than helpful to sign a few bits and pieces but more than that he always appreciates older fans like myself remembering him and taking the time to get in touch. A genuinely nice bloke and a very good player from my generation.

Joe Morris: GEOFF PIKE, a busy, bustling and tough-tackling midfielder who loved to make his presence felt at all times. Pike was the engine room of the team, a player of fire and brimstone, courage and bravery of the highest order.

I must also mention **PAT HOLLAND,** who would play the game as if his life depended on it, shirt flapping outside his shorts and ball magnetically glued to his feet. He was football's great adventurer, wandering and exploring new territories. He was like one of those mountaineers on an expedition who never give up on reaching the summit.

Paul Ford: My cult heroes are two players who were not skilful in a Dev/Brooking mode. Certainly not particularly quick and both predominately right-footed. Yet I was always happy to hear their names in the starting XI. I knew they would give 100 per cent, would never hide or shirk responsibility and were prepared to get hurt for the cause. They amassed 650-plus games and scored 70-plus goals between themselves and were an important part of success in the 70s and 80s.

What I would give for a **PAT HOLLAND** or **GEOFF PIKE** in our squad today. They never feature in West Ham folklore but without their graft, the likes of Brooking would not have had the chance to shine. The fact that Pat's career was ended by bravely scoring a goal at Notts County in our record-breaking 1980-81 promotion season really says it all.

Ian Smith: It has got to be **GEOFF PIKE**. The team of the late 70s and early 80s was one of West Ham's best-ever. It had players such as Lampard, Bonds, Brooking, Devonshire, Paul Allen and Ray Stewart but Pike was a regular too. He didn't have the creative skill of Brooking or the goal scoring capability of Stewart but he was vital in our midfield and acted as an anchor man to Trevor.

He did score the occasional goal but his work-rate was superb. He would dart all over the pitch and get the tackle in to break up an attack from the opposition . . . but he rarely got the kind of recognition more readily bestowed on other members of the team.

One of my most vivid memories of the 1980 FA Cup Final is him and Paul Allen parading the cup round Wembley, Geoff resplendent in a claret-and-blue hat!

Geoff Pike is mobbed by Mark Ward (right) and Tony Cottee (partly hidden), with George Parris about to join the celebrations, after 'Pikey' scored in the FA Cup at Manchester United in 1986.

I love the fact he played for us for 12 years (unheard of nowadays) but feel a little sad that his loyalty and contribution to West Ham is sometimes overlooked.

John Lawrence: A pick from two. **DAVID 'PSYCHO' CROSS** or **MARTIN 'MAD DOG' ALLEN.** I remember a lovely afternoon in Grimsby in 1981 watching us win 5-1 and clinching the second division title – Psycho scored four! He also scored all four goals at Spurs (2/9/81). I was in Malta on holiday at the time and in those pre-internet, pre-mobile days, probably got the news about two days later and thought it was a wind-up! That's it then. Four goals against Spurs . . . it's got to be Psycho!

Michael Oliver: DAVID CROSS was not much more than a target-man when he signed but became a genuinely good player and scored some great goals. Came across well when interviewed, with a dry sense of humour. How could anyone who scored four goals at White Hart Lane not be a cult hero!

Spencer Dodd: As a right-back myself growing up, I'd always watched out for the right-back and how he played the game. For me there were few better than **RAY STEWART.** Hard but fair, never shirked a tackle and with a hammer of a right foot. Whenever he stepped up to take a penalty there was no question of him placing it, he just thumped it as hard as he could and the ball was generally past the keeper before he'd had a chance to react.

Steve Foster: STEVE POTTS was a genuine one-club man and a solid defender. Harry Redknapp liked doing a transfer deal and players often came and went, but 'Pottsy' was always there to keep it together either at right-back or centre-half. Glad to see he's still involved with the club, running the Under-18s.

Ian Crocker: My cult favourite would probably be **GEORGE PARRIS.** He gave his all and a bit more besides. I remember some fan on the North Bank giving him serious stick whenever he was in earshot. George scored later in the game right in front of us and the same fan shouted: "Go on Georgie . . . I knew you had it in you!"

Phil Garner: GEORGE PARRIS – tough and genuine and, again, another great person.

Steve Smith: GEORGE PARRIS. Not the most skilful but one of the most committed. Liked the fact he'd walk into training after jumping off the 86 bus from Ilford. Favourite George memory? Giving it plenty to the obnoxious racists at Stamford

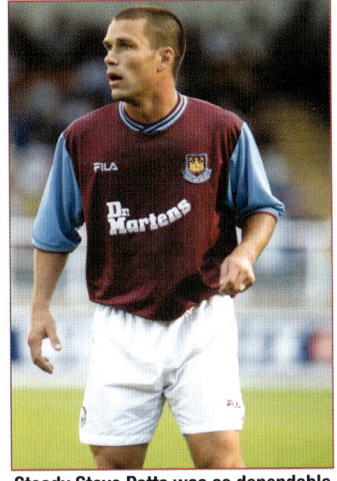

Steady Steve Potts was as dependable as they come.

Steve Blowers: ALAN DICKENS scored on his debut, aged 18, at Notts County (18/12/82) and the Barking-based, Boy of 86 was another key player in our greatest-ever league season.

For me, the mercurial midfielder came closest to replacing the irreplaceable Trevor Brooking but, sadly, a lack of self-belief saw him struggle to win over the Boleyn boo-boys, who just did not appreciate the local lad's talent. If only they'd got behind him.

Just how did such a talented Hammer end up swapping his black boots for a black cab?

Alan Dickens lacked only self-belief, not ability.

Bridge after setting up TC for a goal in the 4-0 win (29/3/86). Banging in a late goal at home to Watford (28/3/87) is also a great memory. George didn't do tap-ins.

David May: GEORGE PARRIS took no s***! Whatever position he found himself in, he performed well.

Ian McMaster: GEORGE PARRIS for his role in the historic 1985-86 season.

Mark Matthews: Although a relatively unsung player, **MARK WARD** was one that I particularly admired for his tremendous commitment and the effort he put in most weeks during his five years at the club. He arrived from Oldham Athletic in August 1985 as an unknown replacement for Paul Allen but made an instant impact. His performances during the 1985-86 season were outstanding – not only going forward, but also defensively, as he worked the right flank tirelessly in support of right-back Ray Stewart.

David Bernstein: MARK WARD. In my opinion, he gave 100 per cent all of the time. He would run the right wing tirelessly, make options for the rest of the team and was part of that magnificent 1985-86 squad.

Martin Scholar: LEROY ROSENIOR – scored loads of goals that kept us up and had a brilliant, positive attitude.

Gerard Daly: I always loved **IAN BISHOP.** Brilliant passer, had a great shot on him and lovely laid-back style. Rarely got his hair cut. He gave a goal away in a 3-2 win over Chelsea (12/3/97) and got terrible abuse. After the game he dropped his mate off at Upton Park tube and I got a chance to have a chat with him and apologise for the stick he got. Lovely bloke. I met him a few times and used to go to games with a pair of Adidas Gazelles with his autograph on the side on my feet.

Andy Brooker: Mine was **IAN BISHOP**. I loved watching 'Bish' play football, spreading passes from one side of Upton Park to the other, setting up chances and, something a few of our midfielders could do with today, a real eye for goal. I recently watched a compilation of Bish's goals on YouTube and I had forgotten what an accomplished finisher he actually was. I think Bish stood out in the team at that time because he tried to play football the right way and, with no disrespect to the players he played with during his spell with us, a bit more quality around him would arguably have seen the makings of another title-chasing team.

Ian Bishop oozed midfield style and tried to play football the right way.

David Steadman: **LUDEK 'LUDO' MIKLOSKO** – the best keeper I've seen at West Ham (including Parkes). I saw his debut up at Swindon (18/2/90), when the Macari scandal kicked off, and he just got better and better over time. One of the best keepers in the world at his peak. I recall a 1-1 draw at Sheffield Wednesday around 1991 and we should have been five down at half-time – he literally kept us in the game with save after save. We were 1-0 down at half-time and a 'Dicksy' free-kick in the second half got us a very lucky point.

Rob Robinson: Would have to be **JULIAN DICKS**, who was a

Ludek Miklosko arrived unknown from the old Czechoslovakia but became a star and the best of several very good Lou Macari signings.

Robert Banks: He had a lazy style but, boy, did **JIMMY QUINN** have an eye for goal too. I could not understand why manager Billy Bonds didn't seem to fancy him much and was disappointed he never got a crack at first division football with us.

Neil Humphreys: As an extraordinarily average teenage keeper with Barking Juniors, I loved **LUDEK MIKLOSKO**. He's still one of my favourite shot stoppers of all-time.

Leapt around like a cat on a hot tin roof, drove a Skoda around Chadwell Heath and his hair looked like it'd been cut by the council.

What more could you want?

Manager Harry Redknapp looks on as Julian Dicks receives the South African supporters' player of the year award from Greg Faasen in March 1997.

superbly committed left-back and played with a great deal of passion. In the mould of Billy Bonds, Julian was always up for the fight when the going got tough, as well as being an exceptionally skilful player who could turn defence into attack with one of his superb long passes.

Greg Faasen: It had to be **JULIAN DICKS**. I watched an away game v Wimbledon (18/3/97) at Selhurst Park and the day before, I handed Julian the Hammer of the Year trophy from the South African Hammers Supporters' Club, of which I am chairman. Before handing over the trophy, I had a cup of tea with Harry and watched the Hammers training – young Rio was just breaking into the squad. The players were not allowed to go for a shower after shooting practice until they had beaten Ludek. 'Dicksy' would score and then just go to the back of the queue until it was only him left in the queue. Legend!

Eamonn McManus: **JULIAN DICKS** gave everything for us and I think he played his football like we would have. A great club servant who came and went, and came again and is now part of the new era we're about to embark upon. I'd also nominate **CLYDE BEST,** such a lovely, huge man who always had time to say 'hello'.

Neil Roper: **MARTIN ALLEN**. 'Mad Dog' was a similar player to Scott Parker – good on the ball and tough in the tackle but it was his desire to chase back and win possession for the team that made me most fond of him. I was at Allen's debut when he scored v Plymouth

Martin Allen displayed aggression, eccentricity and good humour.

Argyle (26/8/89), which I'm sure helped his cause in becoming one of my favourite players. But I stayed true to him, even having his name and number on my back when this became a regular feature of football in the mid-90s. West Ham fans have always held dear those who gave their all for the cause and Martin Allen epitomised this, making him a hero in my eyes.

Gary West: For sheer exuberance, never-say-die attitude and basically being a mad dog, **MARTIN ALLEN** was pure entertainment. I remember an Anglo-Italian Cup match at Upton Park where the crowd was so small you could hear what the players were saying. It was hilarious listening to 'Mad Dog' shouting at his cousin, Clive: "Cuz, Cuz, give me the ball, Cuz."

Mike Corbett: JOHN MONCUR, if only for the 'Moncur turn', where he would switch the direction of play with a quick Cruyff manoeuvre. He did it so often in games that I started to assume he was on a 'turn bonus' or something. He'd often do it when there were no other players near him!

Arne Koellner: JOHN MONCUR. He didn't score many and wasn't the best player I saw, not even close. But he was always smiling and joking around on the pitch, taking the mickey at every opportunity. And he could cut an opponent in half with a tackle and still look totally innocent when getting his booking for it, like a kid who had just been caught with his hand in the cookie jar.

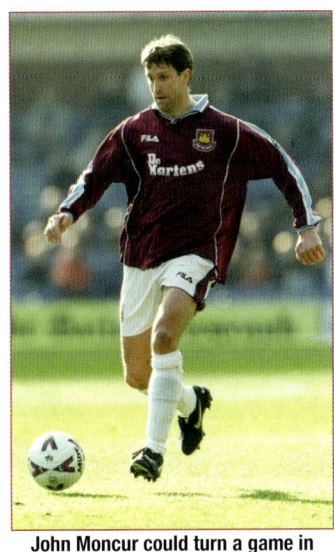

John Moncur could turn a game in more ways than one.

Liam Tyrell: The likes of **MATTY HOLMES** springs to mind, as he always gave his all but didn't have much luck with injuries. **GEOFF PIKE** and **GEORGE PARRIS** are other candidates, both better players than given credit for. I'll opt for **PETER BUTLER**, though. A hard Halifax man, tough in the tackle who ran all day and, like a lot of so-called ball winners, was actually better with the ball than often given credit for. He could certainly spread passes about, feeding the wingers Mark Robson and Kevin Keen, as well as make the odd forceful run at the opposition, too.

Matt Drury: I always had a soft spot for little **MATTY HOLMES**.

Jimmy Jacob: Cult hero for me is tricky **TREVOR SINCLAIR**. He produced top level performances, athleticism of a high level and a wand of a right foot! Scored some very good goals too.

Another one for me is **CARLTON COLE**, who gave his all for the team and the club, took a pay cut to show his loyalty to us. I feel he was

Dan Francis: I always had a soft spot for **STEVE JONES**. He had the look of a bloke who had won a raffle to become a professional footballer but he was a decent finisher and he ran his socks off for the team. I'll never forget his goal in the 4-1 win at White Hart Lane (4/4/94) – sliding on his knees in front of the Spurs fans was enough to earn cult hero status on its own!

Sadly, he never quite found the consistency to cut it in the top flight but I always got the impression that he was genuinely chuffed to be wearing a West Ham shirt and couldn't quite believe his luck.

I interviewed him years later when he was running a memorabilia shop in central London and he had the same bubbly, enthusiastic attitude. His is the kind of story that you just don't see in the modern game any longer.

I've also got to mention **PAULO FUTRE**, who spent a brief but unforgettable spell at the club at the beginning of the 1996-97 season.

From throwing a strop at

Steve Jones, chuffed to be a Hammer.

Highbury on the opening day of the season, when he discovered he hadn't been handed the No.10 shirt, to his stunning second-half display to inspire a comeback win over Southampton at Upton Park a few weeks later, there was never a dull moment.

It felt like he came and went in a flash but he was our very first foreign superstar and I don't think many of us realised just what a talent we had on our hands.

There haven't been too many European Cup winners arrive at Upton Park!

pounced on by the 'boo-boys' rather quickly and deserves more credit.

Marco Taviani: It has to be **PAOLO DI CANIO**. The passion he showed. The love he has for the club and fans. He is one of us. He was what each of us fans would be like given the chance to play for our club. He was a magician. He could create something from nothing.

Tony Cullen: PAOLO DI CANIO. I know he's a nutcase but his presence lifted matches. It was like theatre, he was on that football pitch stage to entertain. Where are these characters now?

David Meagher: PAOLO DI CANIO – ridiculously entertaining. The man simply did not do dull.

Danny Cooper: We've had our fair share of mavericks over the years, as well as players who weren't particularly good but did put a shift in. In any scientific assessment using strictly applied criteria, I think we're left

John Powles: PAOLO DI CANIO comes to mind, alternating between genius and madness, sometimes in the same match.

CARLOS TEVEZ for his undoubted skill, and his passion for the Hammers' fans when returning with the opposition.

And **DOUGIE WRAGG** (affectionately known to fans as 'Oily'), one of those players in the 50s who was on the fringes of the first team, sometimes fast and tricky on the wings to beat the full-back, and at other times tricking himself!

Iain Dale: SEBASTIEN SCHEMMEL became a cult hero for many of us sitting in the East Stand in the 2001-02 season, in which he deservedly became Hammer of the Year. But the Frenchman was never the same player again and only appeared 73 times, scoring once.

He was like a human dynamo down the right and he certainly knew how to both tackle and cross a ball. He now owns a bar in Luxembourg called 'Upton Park'. Legend.

Tony Hogg: This would have to be the great **SAMASSI ABOU**, the first name listed in the *Who's Who of West Ham United* and first on my short list of cult stars.

I don't think manager Harry Redknapp fully appreciated Samassi's worth to West Ham. His fleet-footed runs through opposition defences used to lift the Upton Park crowd and just his appearance in a claret-and-blue shirt caused a massive 'feelgood' factor.

Samassi and Hammers fans hit it off instantly, although opposing supporters were often confused by the chorus of 'boos' that seemed to accompany his every move.

But Samassi knew better – the Boleyn faithful were just making a play on his surname.

With a smile as wide as his native Ivory Coast, friendly disposition and genuine loyalty to West Ham, every man Jack of the West Ham support were sorry to see him given a free transfer in 2000.

No longer would Upton Park resemble scenes from *The Battle of Rorke's Drift* as fans chanted "Aboouu! Aboouu!" with Zulu-like intensity when they hailed their hero. His simple philosophy of "all I want to do is make or score goals for West Ham", was good enough for us but not the club and we lost a very loyal player.

Come back, Samassi!

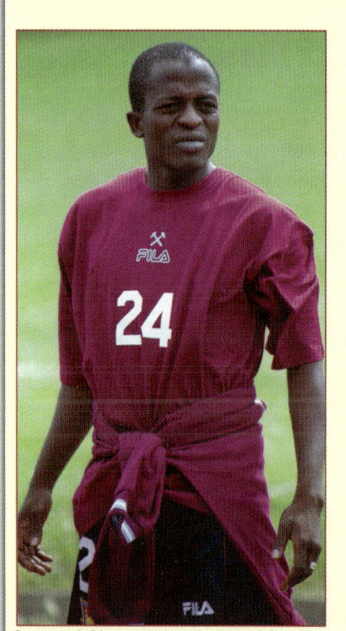

Samassi Abou was an instant hit with the 'boo boys'.

with just one name – **PAOLO DI CANIO**. Apart from the Chelsea goal – and I still get goosebumps just thinking about it – some great strikes mixed in with a sense of occasion, an inflated sense of worth and a tendency to sulk. What's not to like? I especially savour the assessment of Trapattoni, the Italian team manager, who apparently said: "There would have to be a bubonic plague for me to pick Di Canio." Anyone prompting that sort of comment will do for me.

Gjermund Holt: There have been a few cult heroes, like **SAMASSI ABOU**, **CHRISTIAN DAILLY**, **MARTIN ALLEN** and **GEORGE PARRIS**. Another player that maybe never was the best, but a true Hammer and a very nice bloke was **IAN BISHOP**. On his day, a fantastic player as well. I have been at a few training sessions at Chadwell Heath, and the first one to always come for a chat was 'Bish'. A West Ham great.

Jack McDonald: TOMAS REPKA. Not the best, but I loved him. A no-nonsense defender. If he didn't get the ball, he got his opponent's shin! A really passionate player who wore his heart on his sleeve, it's a shame he never scored for the club – in the opposing net anyway. He hit the post in the Play-off Final v Preston (30/5/2005) but, unfortunately, it didn't go in. Some didn't like him but I'd rather have him on my team than against it. Although he did give away a fair amount of free-kicks and penalties, he was a solid, hard player and every team needs one. Just think about Billy Bonds, Alvin Martin, Julian Dicks, etc, and what steel they brought to the team. Yes, they were far superior in ability to Repka but if you took those players out of their West Ham teams, we would have been a lot

Carlos Tevez was the catalyst for the Great Escape in 2007.

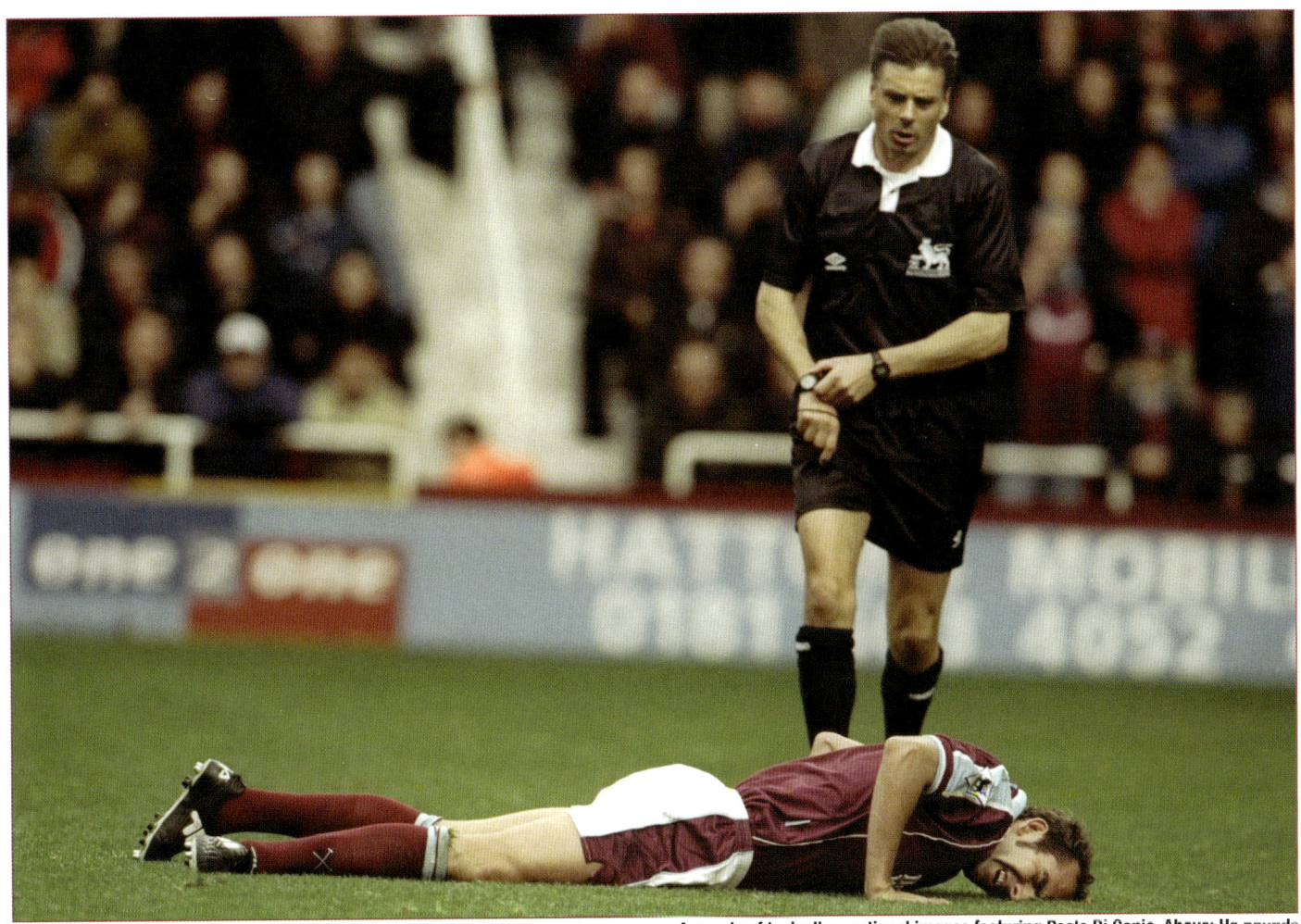

A couple of typically emotional images featuring Paolo Di Canio. Above: He pounds the turf in frustration at perceived injustice as yet another ref's decision goes against him. Below: Di Canio has just scored his last West Ham goal in his final home game. Seconds after the whistle blew on our 1-0 win v Chelsea (3/5/2003), a thrilling victory that ultimately didn't prevent relegation being confirmed at Birmingham a week later, the tearful Italian makes his slow walk towards the Bobby Moore Stand to engage with his adoring fans. Ciao, Paolo!

easier to play against. The same goes for Tomas. We needed at least one hard player, someone who wasn't afraid to put their boot in. He would get the crowd going and bring a bit of much needed fight to the team. 'Super Tommy Repka!'

Stephen George: CARLOS TEVEZ. Sidelined by Alan Curbishley for much of the infamous 'Great Escape' campaign but buoyed by a mixture of effervescence, tenacity and sheer willpower, he managed to galvanise a seemingly doomed team into believing it could survive the dreaded drop – which they did at Old Trafford.

Mark Edwards: My cult favourite is **CARLTON COLE.** No pace, not a great scoring record and not strong enough for his size. Not the greatest credentials but . . . I love him. He tries hard and given the amount of dross we have signed in the last 20 years, that, for me, is enough.

George Reynolds: While I was never fortunate to watch some of the true cult players like Paolo Di Canio, the closest I've seen would be **RICARDO VAZ TE**. Although he never quite got going in the Premier

Four Hammers of the 21st century try to re-create the scene from the 50s, when players congregated in Cassettari's Cafe to talk tactics. Seated for their fry-up are (clockwise, left to right) Junior Stanislas, Thomas Hitzlsperger (the first German to play for Hammers), Carlton Cole and Mark Noble.

League, watching him in the Championship, I always felt he would score, or might try something a little different, and added a bit of flair that we were sorely missing. His hat-trick v Brighton (14/4/2012) was superb – one long-range shot, a close-range effort and a bicycle kick showed that he had some technical ability, and he always seemed to score his goals in various ways.

Alan Porter: I'm going for a current player, **ADRIAN SAN MIGUEL DEL CASTILLO.** I am not for one minute suggesting that none of the players really care about us, but it seems some understand more than others that West Ham is a little more important to us than just being a customer.

There are some lovely quotes from this guy. "When we score I can't go up to the other end of the field to celebrate with the team, so I celebrate with the fans."

But it's more than that. He has gone out of his way to interact with the crowd. It doesn't take much effort to do this and I know that he is closer than anyone else, but can you think of any newcomer, particularly from overseas, who has achieved this? Yes, I know there is Paolo, Carlos and even Tomas Repka but they were cult heroes for different reasons.

And can you ever forget the final penalty in the FA Cup replay v Everton (13/1/2014). Just loved the way he threw his gloves away and the reason that he did it. Top guy.

One of the last great nights under the Upton Park lights. The FA Cup 4th round replay ended 2-2 but Hammers won the penalty shootout 9-8. Our hero was goalkeeper Adrian, the popular Spaniard who confidently struck the winning spot-kick himself to spark jubilant scenes.

COLLECTABLES

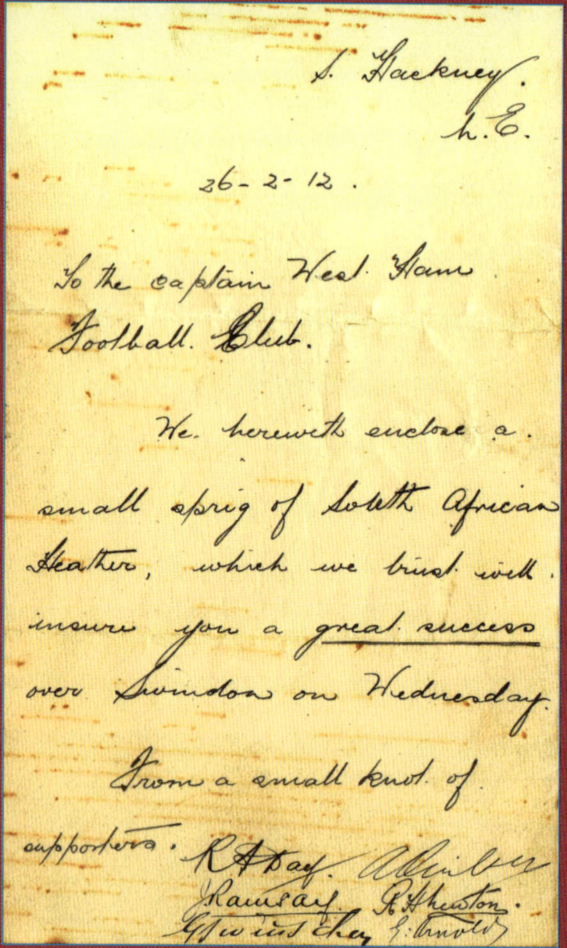

UPTON PARK MEMORIES

A job reference for Robert Fairman written by West Ham United manager Syd King in 1914.

A 'good luck' letter sent by a group of supporters to Hammers' centre-forward Robert Fairman in February 1912.

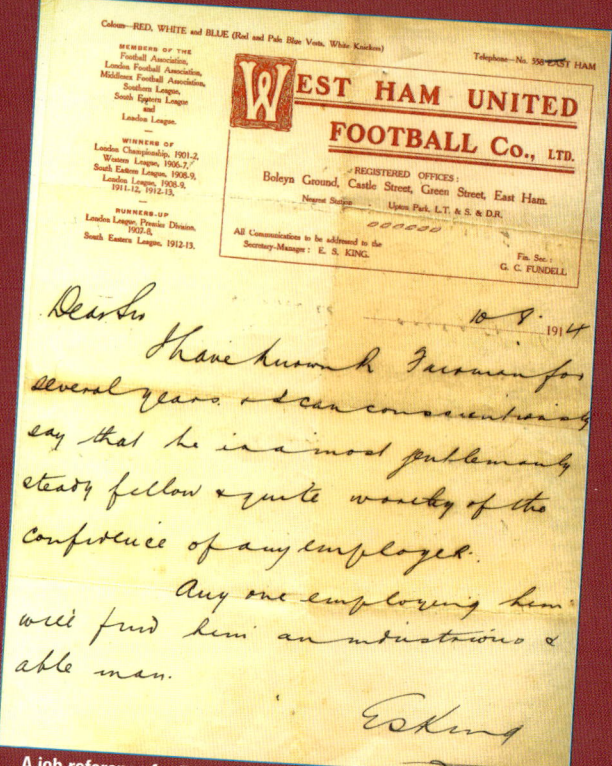

Brochure/Menu for the 1957-58 promotion-winning celebration dinner held at Cafe Royal, Regent Street, London on Saturday, July 12, 1958.

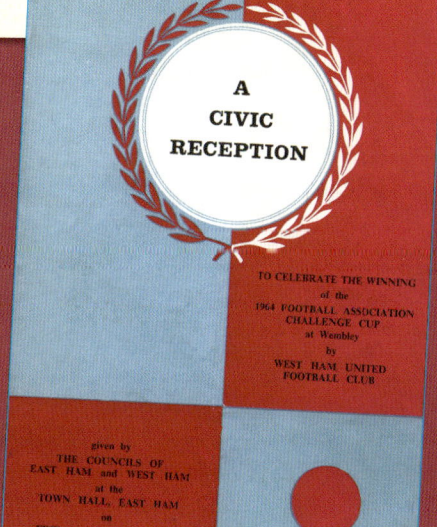

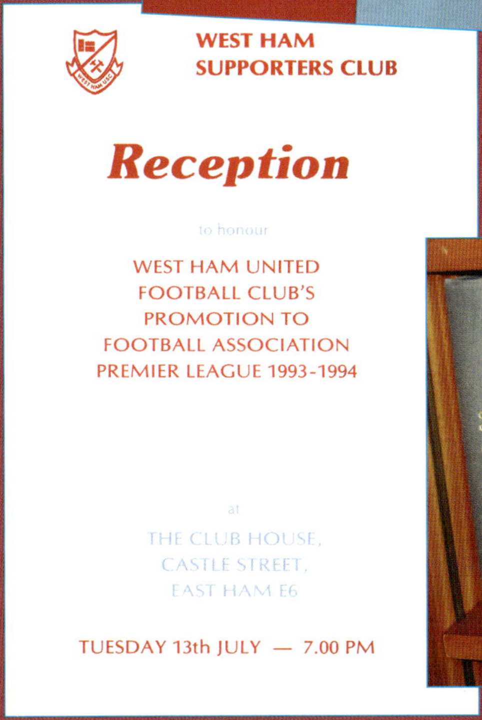

UPTON PARK MEMORIES 305

WEST HAM UNITED F.C.

BANQUET

at

The London Hilton

on

Saturday 2nd May 1964

to celebrate the appearance of
WEST HAM UNITED
in the Final of
The Football Association Challenge Cup

JOHN LYALL AND RON GREENWOOD

TRIBUTE DINNER

FRIDAY 9TH MAY 2008
AT UPTON PARK

A CIVIC RECEPTION

TO CELEBRATE THE WINNING
of the
1964 FOOTBALL ASSOCIATION
CHALLENGE CUP
at Wembley
by
WEST HAM UNITED
FOOTBALL CLUB

given by
THE COUNCILS OF
EAST HAM and WEST HAM
at the
TOWN HALL, EAST HAM
on
FRIDAY, 8th MAY, 1964

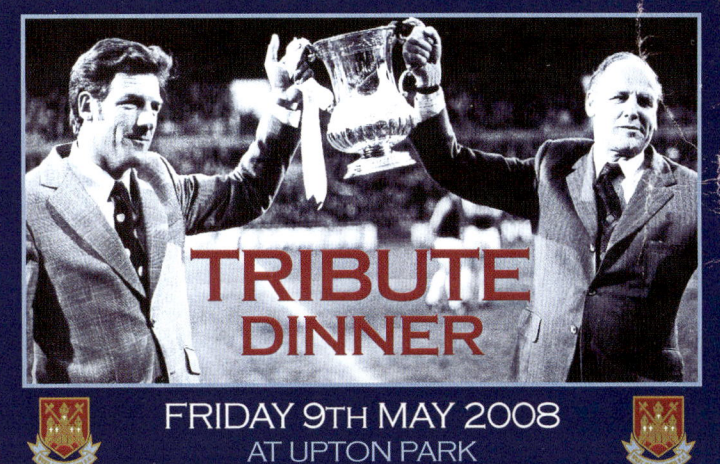

The **JOHN LYALL** and **RON GREENWOOD**
Tribute Dinner

At
WEST HAM UNITED FC
In the Castle, Premier & White Horse Lounges,
Boleyn Ground, Green Street, Upton Park,
London, E13

Friday, 9th May, 2008

To celebrate the achievements of two legendary
West Ham United managers

WEST HAM SUPPORTERS CLUB

Reception

to honour

**WEST HAM UNITED
FOOTBALL CLUB'S
PROMOTION TO
FOOTBALL ASSOCIATION
PREMIER LEAGUE 1993-1994**

at

THE CLUB HOUSE,
CASTLE STREET,
EAST HAM E6

TUESDAY 13th JULY — 7.00 PM

John Lyall's personal collection of bound home West Ham programmes, as presented to him by the club.

306 UPTON PARK MEMORIES

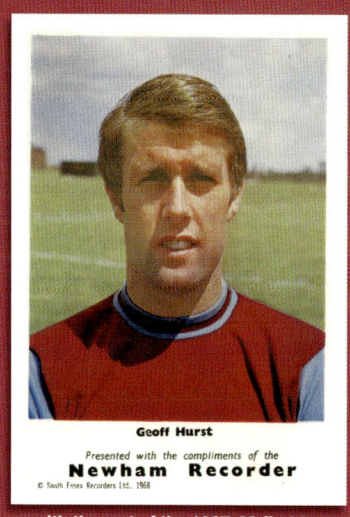

COLLECTABLES

Bobby Moore and Geoff Hurst as featured, along with the rest of the 1967-68 first team squad, in a series of prints given away by the Newham Recorder.

The Bobby Moore coin, part of the Esso coin collection featuring the England 1970 World Cup squad.

A seat from the original West Stand that was auctioned off by the club during the last redevelopment at the start of the millennium.

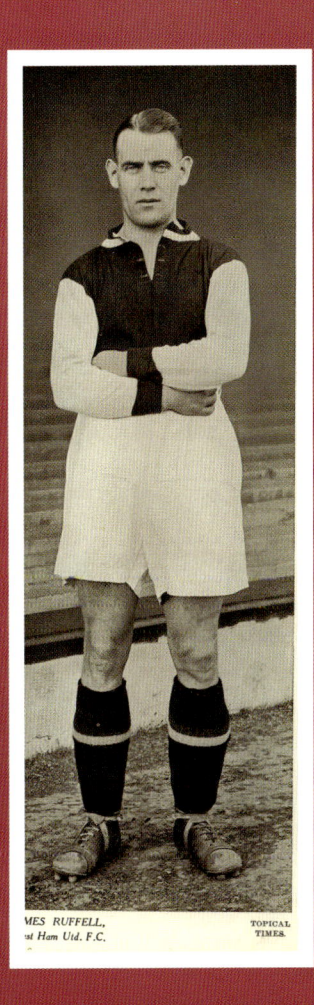

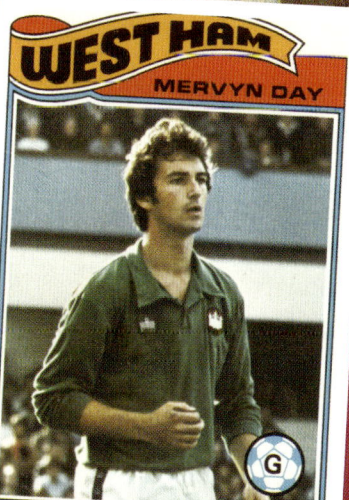

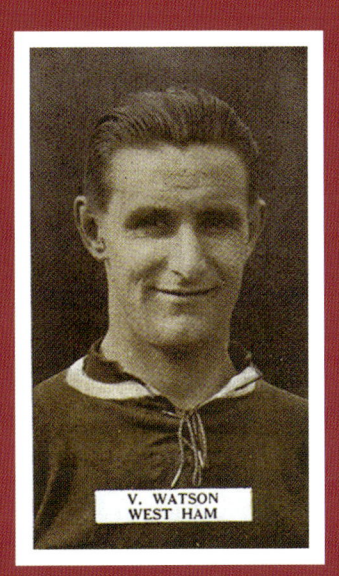

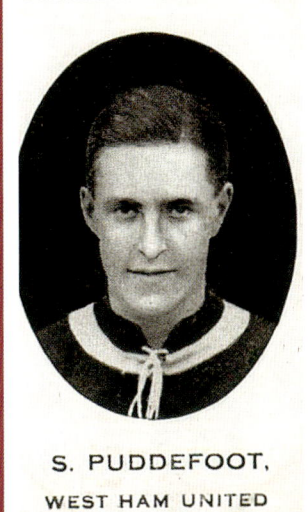

UPTON PARK MEMORIES 307

COLLECTABLES

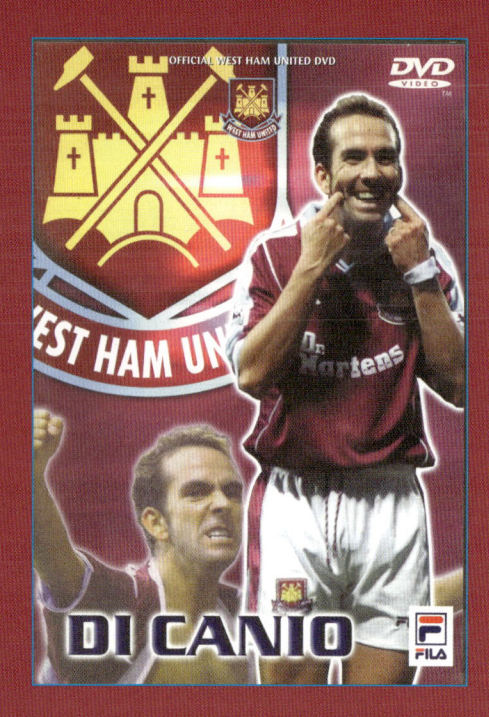

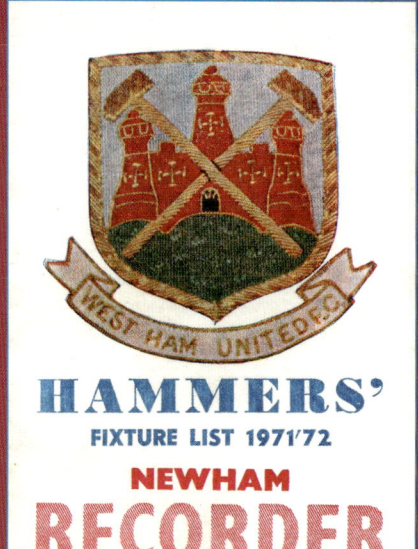

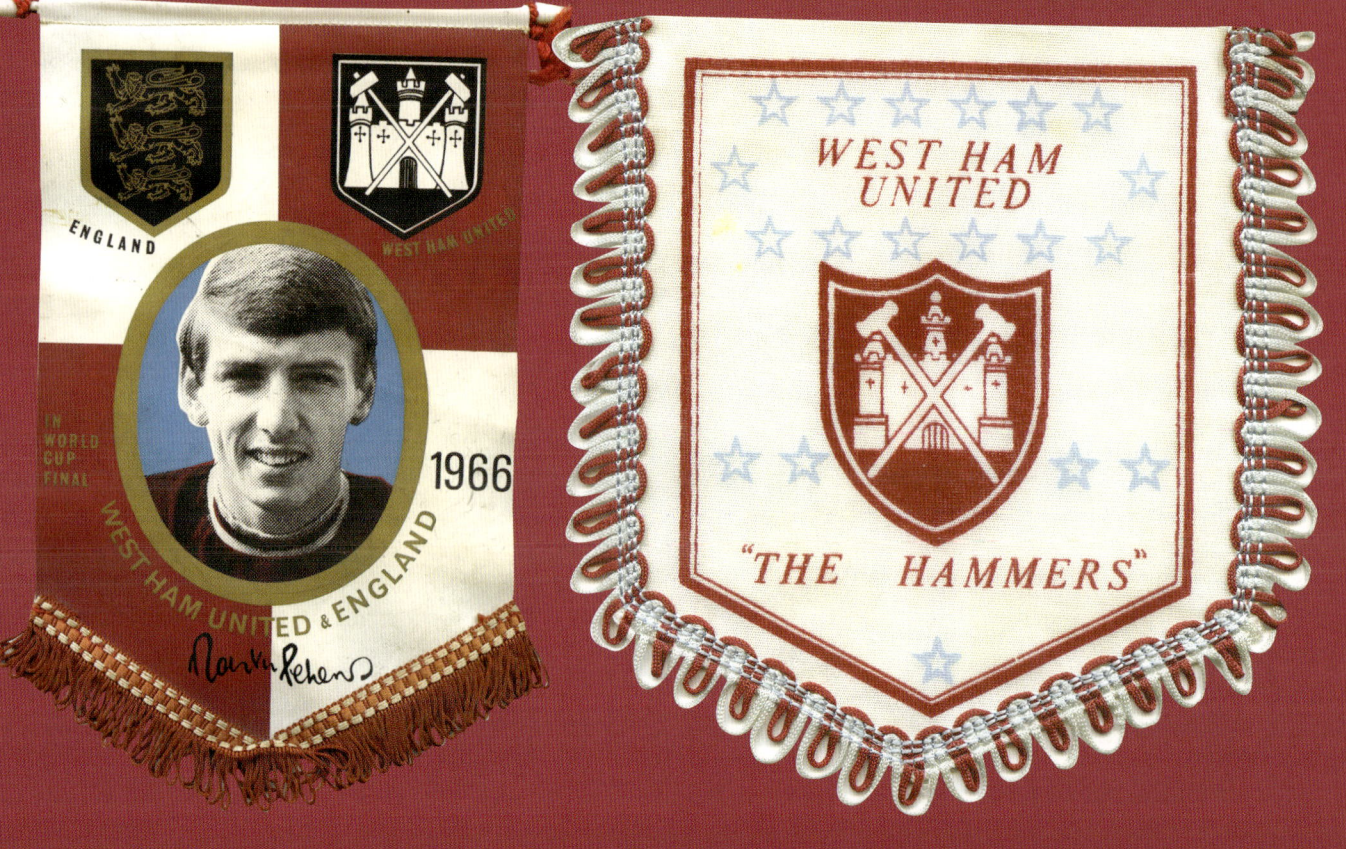

308 UPTON PARK MEMORIES

UPTON PARK MEMORIES 309

310 UPTON PARK MEMORIES

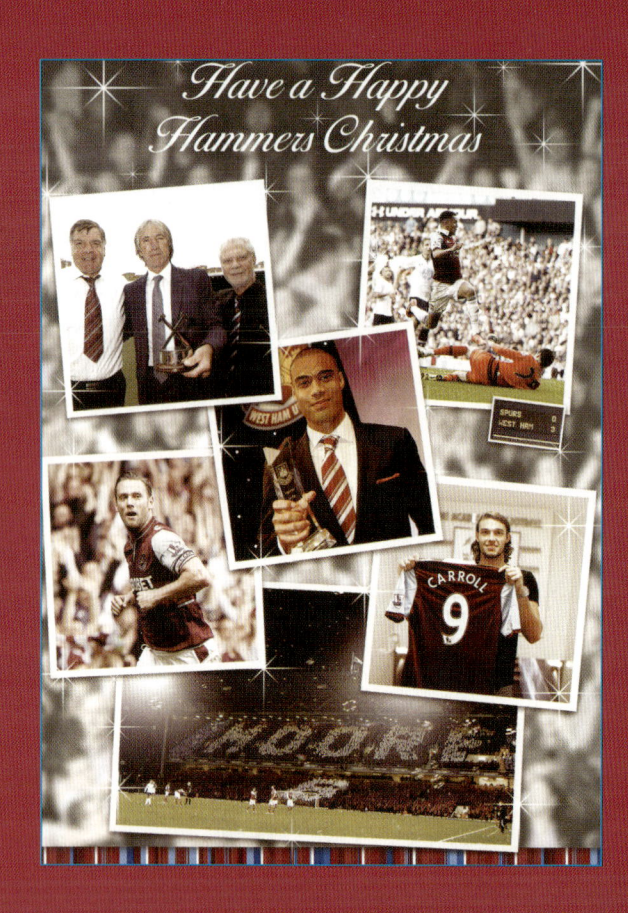

COLLECTABLES

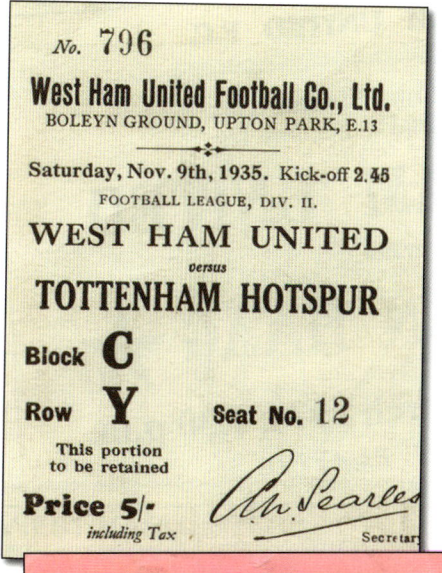

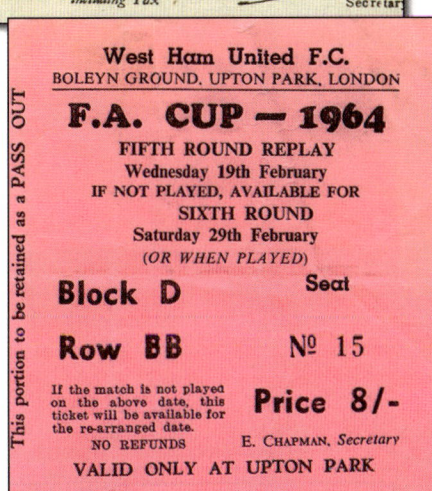

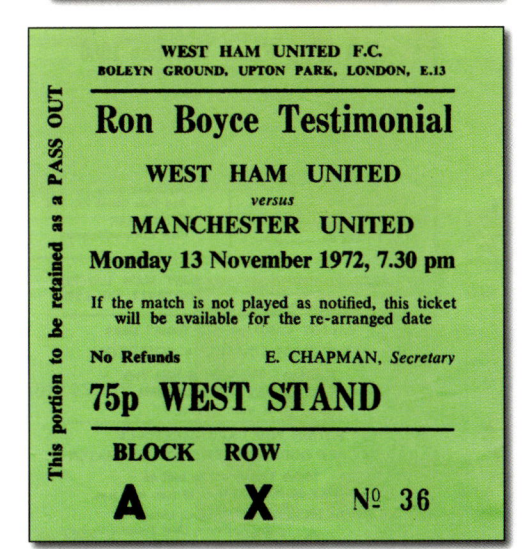

UPTON PARK MEMORIES 311

Mrs Jessie Gregg, West Ham's laundry lady, holding THAT shirt in August 1966.

9 KITS

REPLICA football kits are now firmly established as a key cog in a multi-billion pound global money-making machine, as fans all over the world rush out to buy their team's latest home, away and third strips and don't get change from £50 . . . for just a shirt.

It's far removed from the days when replica kits were not available to buy from club shops or retail outlets and teams stuck with the same shirt, shorts and socks year in, year out. Days when tradition counted and the loyalty of fans was not exploited anywhere near the extent it is today.

At the end of this section, you will see illustrations of every home kit worn by the club since it was founded as Thames Ironworks FC back in 1895. First, let's find out what supporters chose as their personal favourites . . .

Q: What is your all-time favourite Hammers home strip?

Ed Gillis: The one we wore in our first season back in Division One, 1958-59. V-neck claret shirt, with short sky blue sleeves and a silk badge, with white shorts and white socks. A class outfit for a class outfit.

Michael Harris: V-neck worn by Bobby Moore on his debut on September 8, 1958. No name on the back, just No.6.

Steve Derby: No hesitation – the 1958 outfit, advert free!

Rob Robinson: Has to be the 1958-59 strip my father, Bill, got for me (see picture). I've included a photo of me wearing it in the back garden of our home in Welling, Kent. I remember being so excited and couldn't wait to show my schoolmates.

Richard Miller: The iconic 60s plain claret shirt with blue sleeves and the square crossed hammers badge on the left-hand side.

Dave Spurgeon: The home strip of 1960-61. Crew neck shirts with the thin claret band on the sky blue collar, short sleeves and claret and blue hoops on the white socks. It was so stylish in comparison with the V-neck shirts and generally single colour or striped shirts all the other clubs wore that season.

Vic Lindsell: Classic 60s claret-and-blue round neck shirts with almost medicinal crisp white shorts and socks.

Norman Roberts: The 60s kit, in which we won the FA Cup and European Cup Winners' Cup, was our best.

Eamonn McManus: Got to be the 1964-65 strips, no others come anywhere near. The 80s and 90s brought us many awful shirts.

Alan Chapman: Has to be the classic 60s kit, especially from 1966-67 onwards when the badge was removed. The perfect claret and light blue shirt with no adornments; no badge, no manufacturer's logo, no sponsor's name and no competition badge. A football shirt as it should be.

Andrew Smith: The 60s home strip was the classic design and is still popular among fans today. It was worn by Moore, Hurst and Peters. Enough said!

UPTON PARK MEMORIES

Tony Hogg: Has to be the classic 60 style, surely? Nothing flash, just a clean, simple design – claret body to the shirt, light blue long or short sleeves with a double thin line claret trim on cuffs. As worn by Bobby Moore. Say no more.

Tony McDonald: Ron Greenwood famously said: "Simplicity is genius" and the kit Hammers wore from my first season attending as a fan, in 1968-69, lived up to the great coach's immortal words. The crossed hammers badge had been dropped in favour of an even simpler shirt design, with a plain white number on the back.

You knew who all the players were. They tended to keep the same numbers for several seasons – whole careers in many cases – and, of course, there was absolutely no need for some marketing bod with £££ signs in front of his eyes at Football League HQ to decide that players should have their names stitched on the back of their shirts.

Simply the best? Billy Bonds looking the business in 1968.

On rare occasions Hammers have worn their away kit, and different versions of the usual home strip, in official matches played at Upton Park. In this shot we see Geoff Hurst and John Sissons during the FA Cup tie with Sheffield United in 1966 in which Hammers played in the popular sky blue shirts with two claret hoops.

A rare full colour shot of the 1959-60 squad in the same kit Hammers wore on their return to the top flight in 1958, and in which Bobby Moore made his debut.

Paul Ford: I have to choose the one worn v Sheffield United in the FA Cup 5th round (9/3/68). For this home match we played in the classic AWAY kit of light blue shirts with two claret hoops, light blue shorts and socks. I have no idea why we did not wear our traditional home strip that day but as I love this kit and we wore it at home, I am making this my choice!

Kevin Pendegrass: Loved the Admiral shirt we wore between 1976 and 1980. First worn against Anderlecht in the 1976 ECWC final. Still wear a replica at matches now.

John Reynolds: The first classic Adidas strip worn in the 1980-81 season during our glorious, record-breaking, Second Division championship success. I was 19 when I bought it. I'm now 53. My 31-year-old daughter, Becky, still wears it to matches to this day (see picture).

Steve Smith: The Adidas kit from 1980-83. Simple, classic and cool.

Liam Tyrell: Adidas has always been my favourite kit manufacturer. The

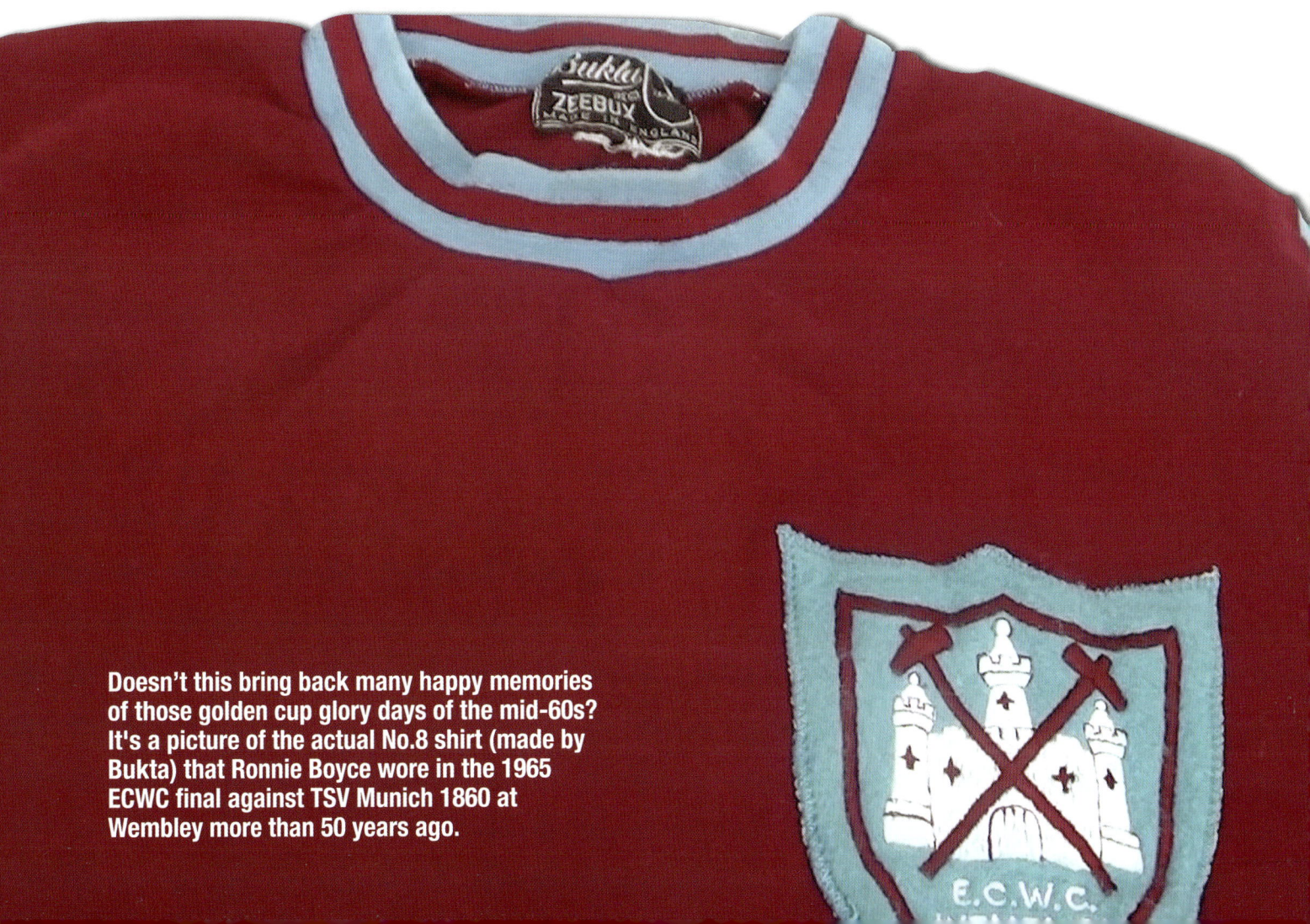

Doesn't this bring back many happy memories of those golden cup glory days of the mid-60s? It's a picture of the actual No.8 shirt (made by Bukta) that Ronnie Boyce wore in the 1965 ECWC final against TSV Munich 1860 at Wembley more than 50 years ago.

318 UPTON PARK MEMORIES

David Cross, pictured here against Brighton, looks the part in the popular first Adidas kit introduced in 1980.

Paul Goddard at home in 2007 with the tracksuit he wore for the 1981 League Cup final.

three stripes, the efficient modern German look. So it is fitting that my favourite Hammers home strip is the one from the 1980-81 season. I was at the opening home game v Luton when it was first aired. Another scorching day with the FA Cup paraded on the pitch, plus the introduction of record signing Paul Goddard. It felt like a smart modern strip for a club on the up. We've had some seriously dodgy kits since with a nice one every so often.

Andy Brooker: The new shirt for the 1980-81 season was our first supplied by Adidas. It was back to the classic claret with blue sleeves, the badge was yellow and it was just a quality shirt.

Ian Smith: Easy choice – the 1980-83 Adidas kit. The Admiral strip that this one replaced was good, with the chevron stripes on the front, but the Adidas top was smart with its trefoil design and traditional blue sleeves with a claret body. I still treasure my replica shirt from that time now but, unfortunately, there is no way on earth I will ever fit into it again!

Neil Roper: My favourite home strip has to be the 1985-86 Adidas kit. It

Tim Crane: My favourite strip was the first I received as a Christmas gift, in 1982. It was shiny and I actually believed I played like Francois Van der Elst when wearing it.

John Powles: The Adidas offering for the 1983-84 season. A claret shirt with a light blue band across the chest and a small crossed Hammers logo on the left side above the band.

Frank Lampard in the 1983-84 kit, shortly before the first shirt sponsor's name was added.

Worn by the club record-breaking Boys of '86.

was the first kit I owned and it symbolises our most successful league season in the club's history. It was also the season I first attended Upton Park, so it has special relevance for me. Looking back and seeing the goals of Cottee and McAvennie in the shirt makes me very proud of what that team achieved.

Gjermund Holt: I have worked as a salesman for Umbro in Norway for 18 years, so it was very special when Hammers finally played in Umbro in 2007-08. Apart from that my all-time favourite is the Admiral shirt from the late 70s.

Steve Blowers: Just loved that one-off kit for the Bobby Moore Memorial Match in March 1994.

Arne Koellner: I love the shirt I wore when I fell in love with West Ham – the 1995-96 centenary shirt with Dagenham Motors as sponsor. This was so fitting for West Ham as a club: no big corporate global brand but a local car dealer selling not overly glamorous cars, motors that did an OK and honest job, just like my West Ham.

This shirt incorporated the centenary theme, with its 'bubbles' and the number 100 woven into the fabric. Magic!

Jimmy Jacob: The centenary kit of 1995-96 – not only because it signified West Ham United's milestone, but I got to wear that strip as a match day mascot!

George McDonald: Fila's 1999-2000 kit was by far my favourite. It had a stylish European feel to it. We had some continental stars in the squad at the time and were producing players from our academy with flair and

Robert Banks: The home shirt for the Bobby Moore Memorial game in 1994. Traditional and unfussy. I was very disappointed when, instead of adopting that kit for the 1995-96 season, we had that awful shirt with the big flappy collars.

In Bobby Moore's honour and to mark the first anniversary of his death, West Ham hosted a unique memorial match. Hammers played against an FA Premier League representative side at Upton Park on Monday, March 7, 1994. This image shows a replica of the shirt worn by West Ham on the night, which went on sale in the club shop, and some supporters were disappointed it was not adopted as the first team's home kit the following season.

attacking prowess. Obviously, Di Canio was our top player and he made that kit iconic. The club website sells the replica version of the shirt and lists it as 'The Di Canio Shirt 99/00'.

Jack McDonald: The Fila kit worn by Paolo Di Canio, Joe Cole and co. in 2000-01. I also had the green Shaka Hislop goalkeeper shirt from that year.

Chris Ludlow: As worn for 2001-02 season – traditional claret shirt with blue sleeves. However, I do think the one worn in the last season at the Boleyn Ground is very good as well.

> **Dan Francis:** For both sentimental and style value, it would have to be the 1985-86 Adidas offering that so very nearly became the kit of the League Champions. I'll never forget opening the replica shirt on Christmas morning 1985 – I don't think I took it off for the next six months. It's an eternal regret that I didn't rescue it a few years later when my mum had one of her 'clear-outs' at home. That was in the days before the word 'retro' was back in vogue – if you were going to wear a football shirt it had to be a current version or you would be crucified in the playground. It probably ended up in a jumble sale and got snapped up for about 20p by an old lady who used it to clean her windows. Criminal.

SPONSORS

AVCO TRUST were the first commercial sponsor to have their name emblazoned across the front of Hammers' shirt.

The name of the financial services group was added midway through the 1983-84 season, although it was shortened to 'Avco' from the following campaign.

Since then, the club has promoted the name or brand of eight other companies on its shirt.

The only season in which the claret top has been sponsor-free was 1997-98, when West Ham failed to secure a commercial deal. For a while they had a proposed new South African airline lined up – but that company, literally, never got off the ground.

John Hartson wearing the sponsor-less Pony shirt.

A replica of the Fila shirt worn by Paolo Di Canio in his last two seasons at the club.

324 UPTON PARK MEMORIES

Mauro Zarate celebrates after scoring the first goal against Chelsea at the Boleyn Ground in October 2015. Hammers' well-earned 2-1 victory over the reigning champions was one of the last great memorable occasions at the old place.

For the final season at Upton Park, the home kit produced by Umbro was a nod to the strip Hammers wore in their first season at the Boleyn Ground, with the start and end years underlining the gold crest.

ILLUSTRATED HISTORY OF THAMES IRONWORKS AND WEST HAM UNITED HOME KITS 1895-2016

1895-96

1896-97

1899-00

1900-01

1901-03

1903-05

Illustrations supplied by David Moor at Historical Football Kits (www.historicalkits.co.uk)

326 UPTON PARK MEMORIES

1905-07

1907-22

1922-26

1923 FA Cup Final

1926-34

1934-49

UPTON PARK MEMORIES 327

1949-50

1950-52

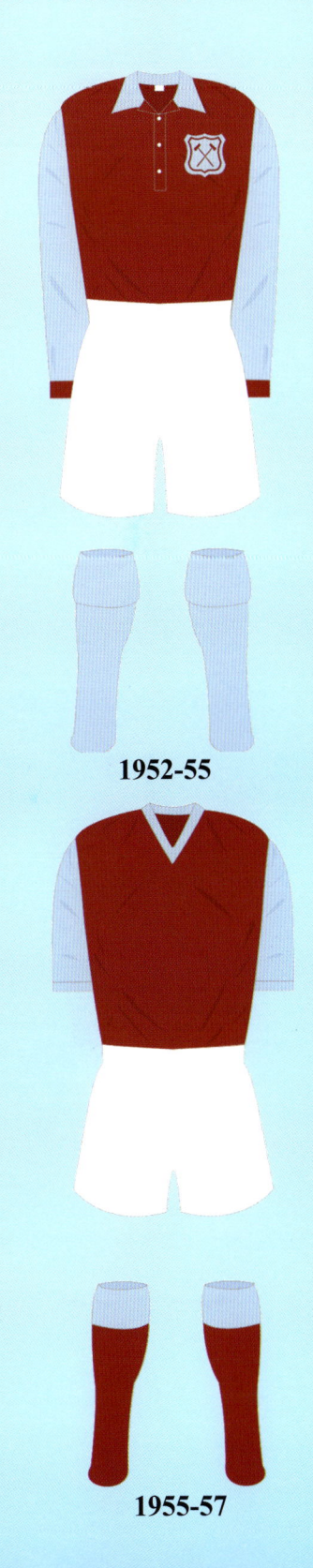

1952-55

1954-55 Euro Floodlit

1954-55

1955-57

328 UPTON PARK MEMORIES

1957-58

1958-60

1960-61

1961-63

1963-66

1964 FA Cup Final

UPTON PARK MEMORIES 329

1965 ECWC Final   **1966-67**   **1967 (August)**   **1967-73**

1973-74   **1974-75**   **1975-76**

330   UPTON PARK MEMORIES

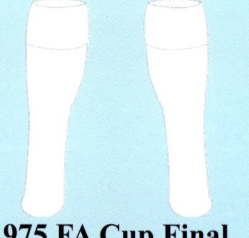

1975 FA Cup Final

1976 (August-December)

1976 ECWC Final

1976-77

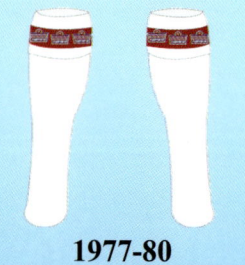

1977-80

1980-83

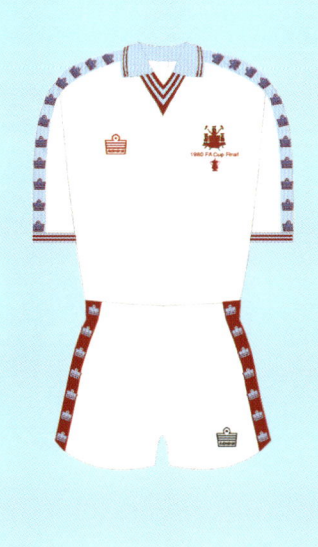

UPTON PARK MEMORIES 331

1980 FA Cup Final 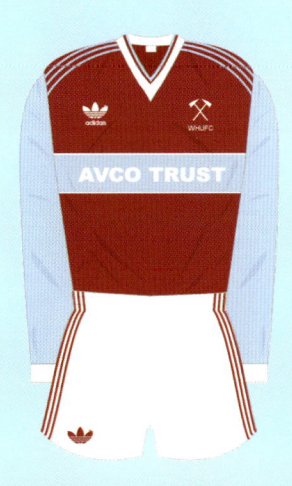 **1983-84**  **1984-85**

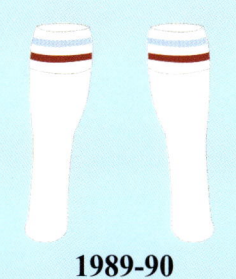

1985-87  **1987-89**  **1989-90**

332 UPTON PARK MEMORIES

1990-91

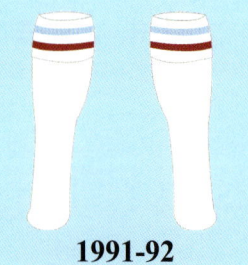

1991-92

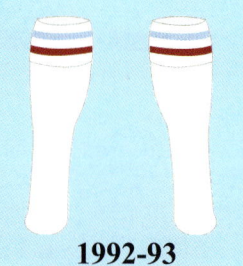

1992-93

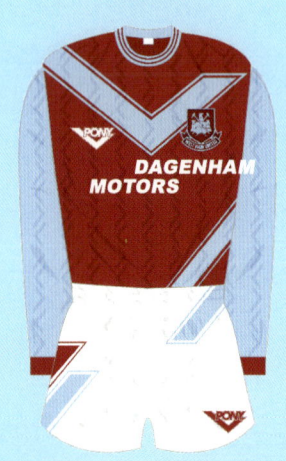

1993-95

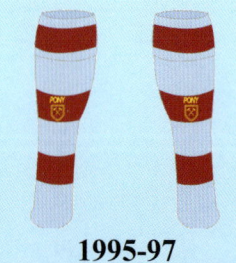

1995-97

1997-98

UPTON PARK MEMORIES 333

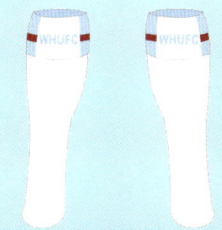

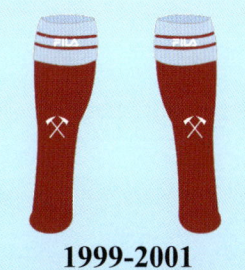

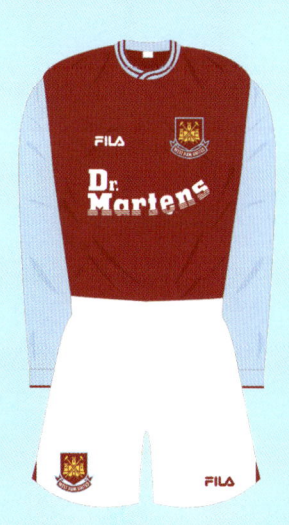

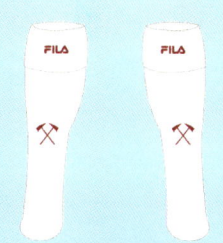

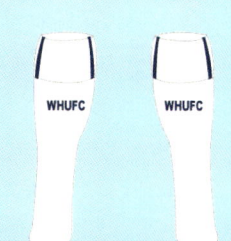

1998-99   **1999-2001**   **2001-03**

2003-05   **2005-07**   **2006 FA Cup Final**

334 UPTON PARK MEMORIES

2007-08

2008 (August-September)

2008 (September)

2008-(December)-09

2009-10

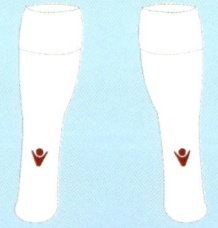

2010-11

UPTON PARK MEMORIES 335

2011-12

2012-13

2013-14

2014-15 (1)

2014-15 (2)

2015-16

TALKING SHOP

IT seems unbelievable now, but it was not until the late 60s and early 70s that West Ham United offered souvenirs and merchandise for sale to supporters. In those days football clubs regarded it more as a customer service, never a money-making exercise. They sold cheaper items, such as scarves, bobble hats, pennants, rosettes and photos. The progression to full replica kit and leisurewear didn't happen until the 80s.

If you were visiting the Boleyn Ground in the late 60s and wanted to buy a replica Hammers shirt, then the place to go was Bobby Moore Sports Wear at 542 Green Street – directly opposite the main entrance to the stadium (it's a washing machine repair shop now).

Although the shop was managed and run by members of Bobby's family, as these pictures confirm the great man did pay the occasional visit to help drum up trade.

BY the mid-80s, West Ham had become much more commercially-minded and under the management of Kate Bouchard, the range and quality of merchandise increased significantly, as did profits.

Not that they had ideal facilities to showcase all things claret-and-blue. For years a portakabin situated to the left of the main entrance as you approached the West Stand turnstiles was the club's main retail outlet, before the redevelopment at the start of the millennium led to the Stadium Store we know today.

For a brief time, the club also opened another shop just around the corner from the ground, in Barking Road, but that soon closed.

Today aside from the offical stadium store, there are club shops at Lakeside, Romford and Basildon.

OLD & NEW: The Boleyn Ground in the foreground and, in the distance, the Olympic Stadium at Stratford. The distance between them is 2.4 miles, as the crow flies, or 3.4 miles by road.

10 MOVING ON

SO here we are. The final chapter. Not only for this book but for West Ham United's home since 1904, the Boleyn Ground. On Saturday, May 7, 2016, Swansea City are due to be the visitors for the final competitive first team match at Upton Park.

Just a few months later, the club will take up residence at the Olympic Stadium in Stratford to begin a new chapter in their long and eventful history.

It is a move that has divided the claret-and-blue faithful, as the opinion of our contributors clearly proves . . .

Q: Your views on the club's move to the Olympic Stadium at Stratford and what you think the long-term future holds for West Ham United?

Ed Gillis: Very concerned. When I stood in the Chicken Run and delivered the odd critical barb to the likes of Tommy Docherty, Maurice Setters or Jimmy Scoular, there was a reasonable expectation that it might reach its target. At the Olympic Stadium? No chance!

Bobby George: I must confess I have mixed feelings concerning the move. Leaving the hotbed of an atmosphere at Upton Park is my main worry. Also the loss of custom for local pubs and shops would impact greatly, although I guess that's not the club's main concern.

The acceptance of change is always open to conflicting opinions but I believe the move to be the right one. It seems the obscene amount of money that pours into football now has changed the game that we once knew.

Kevin Mansell: I've not supported the move. Capacity could be increased to 45,000 at The Boleyn Ground if the East Stand was rebuilt and all the corners filled in. I fear the atmosphere at the Olympic Stadium won't match Upton Park. The only plus will be the chance of getting 15,000 children and young people in every game – there's no way we'll fill a 54,000 capacity ground without reduced prices. And it's every schoolchild's civil right to watch the local team every week without breaking the family bank.

Terry Connelly: Realistically, moving to the Olympic Stadium makes good commercial sense. Hopefully it will secure the long-term future for the club but, of course, this will naturally depend on the success of the team. If, for example, the team dropped down a couple of divisions, cheap prices would not fill the stadium against the likes of Shrewsbury or Peterborough.

Anyway, I am an idealist. All my memories of West Ham are at the Boleyn Ground and that's where they will remain, no matter how

Jim Wilder enjoying hospitality in one of the corporate lounges at Upton Park.

successful they might become (and I hope for future fans they are). I will not be darkening the doorstep of the Olympic Stadium.

Graham Wright: Whether it will be a success or not remains to be seen. With near-capacity crowds at Upton Park for some years, it seems wise to move to a stadium with a greater capacity. Whether we fill it or get anywhere near filling it will depend on how successful the team is. If the club can gear itself to being a regular top-eight outfit (or higher), there is no reason why the crowds won't come and the move will be a success. I certainly hope so. Regretfully, I'm now finding it difficult to get to the matches regularly, as I recently moved to Melbourne, Australia!

Jim Wilder: I've been going to West Ham for 79 years and I love the place. I have deep regrets about leaving. However, on the plus side, we will be moving to a worthy stadium with, due to its location, possibly the best access in the country, if not Europe.

Richard Miller: Being a traditionalist and having spent the last 59 years watching more than 1,250 games at Upton Park, I am rather disappointed that West Ham have decided to move to the Olympic Stadium. Many of my generation feel the same about the move and still need to be convinced that it will actually be in the best interests of the football club and its supporters. There has been a considerable capital outlay in recent years at the Boleyn Ground with excellent developments on three sides of the ground – the West, South and North. The East Stand could easily have been developed to increase the ground capacity.

Only time will tell but the move to the Olympic Stadium will not automatically and necessarily secure a better long-term future for West Ham United than remaining at the Boleyn Ground.

Michael Harris: When the move was announced, I hated the idea and still do. However, it is going to happen and we have to hope that, in these days of money ruling, the extra revenue might just turn us into a top four club. I am, along with my son, going to purchase a season ticket for our first season at the stadium.

Jeff MacMahon: Gone are the days when West Ham fans lived near the stadium, although, with the gentrification of inner-London, that may well be the case again. We need to move to progress and even though I would have preferred our own stadium, it is a great deal.

Football, like everything else, is changing. Fans are more fickle and need a better match day experience. I can visualise being one of the elite clubs in the future.

Although I don't know if I could cope with winning every week.

Steve Derby: The reality is that the game today is not what many of us fell in love with. As a result, survival is the name of the game and I suppose the decision to move to the Olympic Stadium is in keeping with what modern football is all about. Personally, it will break my heart to see the old ground removed from the map. Our souls are invested in the Boleyn Ground and I struggle to wonder if we will ever be able to say the same about the Olympic Stadium.

One thing's for sure, it is all about money, so I just hope that our directors have big enough pockets (or purses) to keep the dream alive. If they have, then we could be OK. If they haven't . . . well, you work it out.

Crispin Derby: It just all adds up. Bye-bye Boleyn, and so many great memories. It will spook the team for a season, I feel sure, but it had to be.

NOVEMBER 2007: In this handout illustration provided by the Olympic Delivery Authority (ODA), a CGI rendering of the 80,000-seater Olympic stadium is unveiled. Work on the London 2012 showpiece stadium began in April 2008.

Tony Hoskins with Sir Trevor Brooking.

Stratford isn't exactly the end of the world, my dear friends.

Tony Hoskins: Upton Park has been a huge part of my life since 1963, so leaving it behind will be a very sad day. However, in the money-driven Premier League, we need to maximise everything we can and that, like it or not, means a bigger stadium.

All I hope is that after the initial novelty of the first season, we are pushing forward to being a regular top six side. It will be a huge ask to sustain this but, surely, that is the reason for our move?

The time to reflect on this monumental move will be in five years' time. We can then look back and judge the merits of the move with the benefit of that wonderful thing – hindsight.

Rob Robinson: I have to say that Upton Park will ALWAYS be my spiritual home and no-one can take those memories away from me. Time moves on and if the current directors believe this to be best move to take the club forward, then I have to believe them. Only time will tell.

But one thing is for sure. We will definitely have to have a top six side in the Premier League so that the new stadium will be full enough to create an atmosphere.

As for the long-term future of the club, it comes down to money now. And plenty of it. Long gone are the days when we were allowed to develop future stars through our academy. Clubs now need instant success or they fail.

David Hughes: The move is the only way forward and I feel the fans will respond, particularly if the season prior to the move is fairly productive and the owners are able to continue financially supporting the club.

I am hopeful for the long-term because our West Ham is West Ham and until they fade and die, we'll always have our dreams.

Paul Walker: I understand the financial reasons and the need to expand and progress our club. We have the fan base to cope. But I will leave the Boleyn Ground with a heavy heart. It has been my second home for almost 60 years now. I know every inch of the place and standing on the old Chicken Run is an experience that can never be replicated. But it's onwards and, hopefully, upwards now.

Danny Cooper: It will be a great shame to leave but, as someone much wiser than me has pointed out, it isn't the same Upton Park we first went to 50 years ago. The move to Stratford should be good in the long-term, with easier access, bigger crowds and a potentially larger fan base. The

JANUARY 2011: Players James Tomkins, Scott Parker and Mark Noble pose outside the construction of the Olympic Stadium during a media event held jointly by West Ham United and Newham Council to promote Hammers' bid to move in after the 2012 Olympic Games.

Vic Lindsell secured a slice of Boleyn Ground history when he obtained a crash barrier from the old North Bank, which now stands in the back garden of his home at Loughton, Essex.

FEBRUARY 2011: West Ham United co-chairman David Gold (left) with (left to right) Sir Robin Wales (Mayor of Newham), David Sullivan (West Ham United co-chairman), Kim Bromley-Derry (Newham Council chief executive) and Karren Brady (West Ham United vice-chairman) in front of the Olympic Stadium after the club were officially named as the preferred bidder to take over the venue.

worry would be if we lost sight of our humble beginnings and the ethos which makes us West Ham.

Vic Lindsell: I am going to be in pieces when we sing *Bubbles* for the last time at The Boleyn. I've been very fortunate to see genuine world class players play in claret-and-blue. We've won trophies, played in Europe and if we are to get anywhere near repeating past glories, then I'm afraid we have to move, due to the game changing beyond all recognition.

My son, Robert, has already experienced two relegations and a lot of doom and gloom. Moving and the financial benefits that will provide, will hopefully raise the club back to somewhere near what my dad, Bill, introduced me to all those years ago.

Kevin Radley: Like most supporters, I think it is a huge wrench to leave the Boleyn Ground but I believe that moving to the Olympic Stadium presents a massive, one-off opportunity to transform West Ham into a bigger and much more successful club. I've been privileged to chair the Stadium Migration/Growing the Fanbase stream of the Supporters' Advisory Board and in the summer (2014) presented to the club the findings and recommendations from a supporters' questionnaire. We provided much input regarding affordable ticket pricing, reducing prices for under-25s and enhancing the value of the season ticket. So far, we have received a positive response from the club on some specific recommendations.

The board has demonstrated great ambition to secure the lease. If we can show the same level of ambition on the pitch, I believe the medium and long-term future looks very exciting.

Peter Jones: I am content with the move because Upton Park is not the ground that I knew and loved now that it has been modernised. I also think that the high-profile location will attract money to the club in the form of future owners, better players and more spectators. Any sports fan worldwide wants to visit an Olympic Stadium and to watch a football match in that stadium would be an ambition of many tourists. This would spread the name of West Ham United even further around the world.

Norman Roberts: I think they should have stayed at the Boleyn Ground but football is no longer a sport and has been ruined by the aspirations of big business. Prices are out of reach for the working class. It will be interesting to see what the attendances will be after the hype and hysteria of the first few seasons has died down.

Alan Porter: It's always going to be a wrench moving. Not many of us like such drastic changes but nothing lasts forever. I can recall when the Icelandics owned us, there was a plan to build a new purpose-built ground near to West Ham Underground station. I can't recall that there was a lot of opposition to that, even though it turned out to be a lot of nonsense.

The Olympic Stadium is modern and very convenient. Will we sell it out every week, will the 'Upton Park Roar' transfer with us? Who knows? It will be sad to leave The Boleyn but the future may well be brighter.

It's imperative that the heart remains in the club and we do not become

A computer-generated image distributed by West Ham United to the media in February 2011 showing how the Olympic Stadium would look if the club won the bid to be future residents of the site. At the same time, and just ahead of their victory over Tottenham to become the preferred bidder, the club released this artist impression of how the OS would look as a football stadium after the 2012 London Games.

another rich man's toy. I believe the current owners do care but I am more concerned about what happens to the ownership than moving to the new stadium.

Alan Chapman: I've seen 510 games at Upton Park over the last 49 years, a figure that would be much higher but for the steadily increasing ticket prices that has meant I have only gone to three or four games per season for the last 15 years. If the move to the Olympic Stadium will truly reduce the cost of tickets, then that will be worthwhile.

You can't help wondering whether the new ground will generate the right atmosphere. You can see the business case for it, with the increased capacity and improved transport links, but whether it will work in a football sense, only time will tell.

One thing I definitely won't miss is the interminable queue to get into Upton Park station after games. I seem to have spent several years standing in that queue!

Jeff Garner: I don't agree with the move. I see it as losing part of our identity and I have always described the fortnightly journey to Upton Park as a sort of pilgrimage. So many of us are proud of our East End roots and match day is when we go 'home'.

In my opinion we are also moving from a perfectly good football stadium to one that isn't and I feel it is a decision which has been based on business reasons rather than what fans really want. However, I fully accept that my reasons could well be more to do with my age.

It certainly seems as though the owners have got themselves the deal of the century but only time will tell. The pressure is on for them to fulfil their promises and make sure West Ham are one of the very top clubs in the country and regularly challenging for honours.

Doug Barrett: For me, one of the main benefits is the ease of reaching the Olympic Stadium by public transport. Also, I imagine there will be a reasonable amount of parking space available, unlike the area around The Boleyn where it is impossible to park within two miles of the ground (if that).

Doug Barrett (right) with Hammers' former long-serving kit manager Eddie Gillam.

Queuing for two hours to get into Upton Park tube station after an evening match makes it almost impossible to reach central London in time to make a connection to anywhere else. And how many supporters actually live within the vicinity of The Boleyn Ground? Very few, I would imagine. I suspect the majority of our fan base is out in Essex, for whom travel to Stratford will be much easier and quicker.

I was lucky enough to visit the Olympic Stadium during the 2012 Paralympics and was extremely impressed with what I saw. It can only be better by the time all the alterations have been made. Tickets will be much easier to obtain and, hopefully, cheaper than at present.

The traditionalists complain that we are moving from our 'spiritual' home but they forget that the original home of West Ham United was the Memorial Grounds in Canning Town – and the new stadium is actually closer to our original home than The Boleyn is.

Steve Wilks: Regrettably, I think the opportunity to move to the Olympic Stadium is too good to miss. Getting to and from Upton Park is an absolute nightmare and an increased capacity will give us the chance to move up another gear.

Ian Nunney: I look forward to our move with mixed feelings. Leaving Upton Park will be hard, because of all the history and memories, but to compete with the big boys we need the revenue that the move will generate. It is a fantastic ground but I am unsure about what the atmosphere will be like. That is where the fans will come into their own – it will be up to them to generate the volume of noise which will create a great atmosphere.

JULY 2012: Fireworks illuminate the stadium during the opening ceremony of the London 2012 Games on July 27.
Start of an athletic race during the 2012 Games. When it was first announced that West Ham had won the bid to become tenants at the OS, fans expressed their concerns that, even with retractable seating, the track would put too much distance between them and the playing area.

I remember the sound from the old Chicken Run and when that was demolished we thought it wouldn't be the same. But, if anything, it seemed better. The ground has been changed on several occasions but the atmosphere has always stayed. Now we have to transfer that to our new ground and this could be the start of something special.

Steve Perry: I have been a supporter of the move to the Olympic Stadium. I have longed for West Ham United to be up there challenging for all trophies and securing the types of revenues that are needed to invest in the club to allow us to compete.

I understand those that believe we may have sold our soul but football is a different business now and I want West Ham United to be able to compete in this new environment.

Marco Taviani: To be honest, I am so despondent at the moment that we could play at Wanstead Flats for all I care. I feel that the Boleyn

Ground is no longer the ground I grew up at during the 70s and 80s. It is just a shell – no longer the North Bank, the South Bank, or the West Side, even the Chicken Run is not the same. Just four characterless stands. People argue that there'll be no atmosphere over at the Olympic Stadium. Well, there's certainly no atmosphere at The Boleyn at the moment and hasn't been for many years, barring the odd game, and it's not even intimidating to the opposition anymore.

I know we may rarely fill a 54,000-seater stadium but at least we'll be able to go to the toilet and get a pie and a beer easily.

The crucial thing is that we make the stadium our own. We put our mark on it. We ensure it is not just another of these industrial park stadiums that have been built with no soul and no character. It should be decked out in claret-and-blue – inside and out.

In terms of the future, think about the potential influx of money from sponsorship deals and companies who want to be associated with the stadium (providing we are successful).

Pat Mahoney: Sad but inevitable. The club was in dire straits when Sullivan and Gold took over in 2010. At least they have given it a future.

Tony Cullen: I'm in favour and have been from the start. With our history and fantastic support, it's about time we were considered a big London club and I think the move will allow us to become that.

My only concern is the possible loss of identity, especially if big money came in. Would they want a name change? The club could become something along the lines of London United!

Michael Oliver: I'm positive about the move and cautiously optimistic about the future. I don't think lack of atmosphere will be an issue. There's not been the same atmosphere at Upton Park (or anywhere else) since terraces were abolished in the early 90s and the crowd will still get excited when we play well and beat good teams. Comfort and transport will be much better.

Long-term, we should have a higher turnover which, sadly, nowadays usually dictates one's league position. Not sure it will get us into the Champions League any time soon, though.

Mark Harknett: Not in favour of a move but it's obviously now inevitable. I think that Gold, Sullivan and Brady were disingenuous to say the least during the consultation process. Then again, the views of people like me probably shouldn't be taken into account, despite the fact that I voted against the move in various online polls. I gave up my season ticket at the end of the 1999-2000 season and have only been to a handful of games since. I don't really intend going to any more, either.

My wife, Jenny, summed it up perfectly. West Ham is like an old lover that you thought the world of and had a great time with for years but you then split up. You've tried getting back together but it just didn't work out, so it's time to say 'goodbye' forever!

John Reynolds: A move away from Upton Park has to be the way forward but it has got to be made to feel like our home. We must follow what Arsenal have done at The Emirates, where there are reminders of Highbury all around the new place.

We must also have a team worthy of watching. If we are continually struggling at the bottom of the Premier League or trying to make the play-

JULY 2013: General view of the stadium ahead of the Sainsbury's Anniversary Games – IAAF Diamond League.

offs every other year, it is not going to work.

Who knows, though, the Olympic Park is a big attraction and I just hope a mega-rich billionaire will one day turn us into a Manchester City.

Mark Edwards: I don't want to leave Upton Park. However, I understand that we have to give ourselves a chance to push forward. I am sure that Manchester City fans couldn't care less about Maine Road now they have success.

My main concern is that, once we are in the Olympic Stadium and Upton Park becomes flats, the current board will sell us to foreign investors who will bump up ticket prices. We will end up in a vastly expensive rented stadium with no progress made. I really hope I am wrong, only time will tell.

I just hope my young grandson, Theo, will have the same stories to tell when he gets to my age.

David Bernstein: I think it is a good move. Although Upton Park will hold great memories for me, it isn't the most pleasant of areas. Couple that with the limited access to the station and the parking problems around the area, the move can only be positive for us.

I feel the long-term future is bright. The co-chairmen are trying to steer us into the higher echelons of the Premier League and moving us to the Olympic Stadium will open up a more enjoyable match day experience.

David May: I'm 60/40 in favour of the move. Upton Park doesn't seem to have the same feel for me since the introduction of all-seater stadia. I used to love the way the crowd was so close to the pitch, it was a very intimidating place to come for opponents.

Hopefully we can progress as a club without losing too much of our identity. Most importantly, I would like it to be affordable to working class fans again, enabling the club to bring back all the people who have been priced out.

Gerard Daly: I'll be sad when the time to move comes. I've got hundreds of memories of E13 and decades worth of family connections with the area but, in all honesty, the true Boleyn Ground as we know it isn't there anymore, so I'm not heartbroken. If we can be a real force by moving then so be it.

I think the future holds frustration, heartbreak and despair, plus the occasional day or night that nobody who is there will ever forget. If we could just win the league or even just a cup again before I die, that would be a bonus.

Alan Byrne: The game has changed (not for the better) and I suppose the team has to evolve to survive within this money-obsessed Premier League. I think we will struggle in the Olympic Stadium, and for me, once no longer at Upton Park, a large part of the club I love will have died.

Stephen George: In our hearts we know that the atmosphere at Upton Park hasn't been the same since the terraces were pulled down and while, on its day, the old place is still capable of being a raucous and intimidating place for away fans to visit, those days are few and far between. I know many West Ham fans would disagree and see this as a simple choice between giving in to the rising tide of corporatism that has drank the soul of the people's game dry, or standing up for the principles on which we were founded where the values of community and tradition take precedence over profit and self-interest.

However, for West Ham to survive and compete at the upper echelons of the game – which I believe is something we can all agree on – it was a no-brainer. This couldn't happen at Upton Park.

West Ham can make this work but only if the board are true to their promise of 'affordable football', which is not 50 quid a ticket. It's not even 25 quid a ticket. I think if the board are serious about this, then the pricing strategy needs to be spot on. If the club further increase their ties to the local community (free tickets for schools, etc), then they can prevent the next generation of fans from being priced out and alienated from what has always been essentially a working class sport. If they stay true to their word and listen to the fans, then the future looks bright indeed.

Ian McMaster: Emotionally, I don't like the idea of the move away from Upton Park. But financially, it is probably essential. If we play badly or slip down a league, though, we are going to look very silly. We will need to spend a lot and wisely to put together a really good team.

Paul Clayden: Can't wait, if I'm honest. Fed up of Upton Park tube station, lack of decent pubs, most cafes closed down, queue for toilets, queue for tea.

Mark Edwards and grandson Theo.

NOVEMBER 2013: Joe Cole visits the Olympic Park's stadium to check on progress of construction to transform it into a year round multi-use venue, the permanent home of West Ham United and the new national competition stadium for UK Athletics.

I've been to the Olympic Park. It's superb. I'm sure the stadium will be great as well. One of the best in Europe.

Simon Hoppit: I have mixed feelings about the move to the Olympic Stadium. It is a fantastic stadium and will increase our capacity. However, like the last time I went to West Ham, up in the heavens, I fear it will be like watching ants. Not sure what the atmosphere will be like.

I am not anti-progress but would much rather stay put. All the history and tradition of Upton Park will be lost forever. I love walking along Green Street and am devastated to be leaving.

Steve Foster: I'm not too keen, to be honest. I love the club as it is. Success is all very well and good but I don't want the club to lose its identity with the fans, as has happened at Manchester City and Chelsea. I think Arsenal have the right balance, as the Emirates is a fantastic stadium, but those ticket prices!

John Ruane: Football has changed since my days as a season ticket holder in the Chicken Run. Clubs have to move with the times or they get left miles behind very quickly. I'm hoping this is our turn to move with the times and to become a bigger club than we are now.

We need to fill this stadium to create the atmosphere we all know and love. In order to do that we need to be successful on the pitch. When you dream big, you have to start somewhere, and I think the dream has started.

Andy Brooker: I really am split on the move. By the time we play our first game there in August 2016 I will have been attending Upton Park for 39 years. It is part of my life, the one constant when all around me has changed. The one place where, whatever was happening in your life, you could go to for a couple of hours every fortnight and forget about everything.

When I look out from the Bobby Moore lower, where I have my season ticket, in all reality the only part of the ground that is original to me is the Chicken Run – but it's still home. A home where we come every season on the off chance that we might win something. Of course, it rarely happens but you never know with West Ham . . . that's the beauty of this club.

On the flip side of all this is a move to a massive new ground with the

MARCH 2015: Hammers trio Diafra Sakho, Winston Reid and Mark Noble outside the OS during a Lycamobile/West Ham United partnership announcement.

AUGUST 2015: New signing Dimitri Payet shows off seat designs at the Olympic Stadium.

potential to attract better players, which we will be able afford due to regularly attracting 54,000 people to our home games. That I suppose is the blue sky vision, challenging for the top four, Europe and domestic cups on a regular basis. Winning cups and watching great players would be fantastic but for how long? How long before winning becomes boring? How long before there is no excitement in beating Manchester United, Arsenal, Liverpool on a regular basis? How long before fans start pining for Upton Park and a 1-1 draw against Middlesbrough? Do I want to turn into Chelsea with 20,000 fans who would not recognise David Speedie or Kerry Dixon if they passed them in the street? The answer is a resounding NO.

Perhaps in the last few sentences I have talked myself into a preference of staying at Upton Park. I will go to Stratford because I love my football club. I will dip my toes in and see how it feels. Beyond that first season, who knows?

Adrian White: I have mixed feelings. On the plus side, it should leave our club debt-free, the promise of cheaper tickets is attractive, too. And from a business point of view, I guess that is what's needed to push us to the next level and to be able to compete with the current top teams.

It will be very sad to leave the Boleyn Ground and all its history but I try to look at it as going home in a way, as Stratford is in the old borough of West Ham.

I just hope we don't lose the soul of our wonderful club in what has fast become Football PLC.

Kevin Pendegrass: I was totally against it at the start and still am now. In my opinion, Sullivan and Gold bought the club with the express desire to move to Stratford, making a profit from selling Upton Park in the process. Within two or three years, they will sell up to the highest bidder.

Even with the retractable seating, it's still an athletics stadium and the only reason the prices have been reduced for the first season there is because the club know the views in every part of the ground are vastly inferior to those currently at Upton Park. I reckon the £289 season tickets will come with a free telescope.

Gary Bush: I believe our move to the Olympic Stadium is one that no club in our present position would turn down and I dare say we will become the envy of a lot of clubs who would like to move but are faced with the prospect of either not gaining the required planning permission or simply can't afford to do so. For us to have the opportunity of playing in such a new arena which is on our doorstep wouldn't make sense to have snubbed, as hard as it will be to leave Upton Park behind.

I've been coming to watch my famous old club perform there since the 70s and it's always been such a special place to visit. What makes it so special are the fans within it and it's going to be those same fans who will make our new home a success. They will turn up and make some noise!

Ian Crocker: We've seen a lot of clubs move to new stadiums and it's mostly been for the better. Times change, needs must. Of course it's all right when it happens to other clubs but it's a bit different when it's your own. Some of the new arenas can appear soulless but not if the fans make a big noise and we have no problems on that front.

It's a new era for the club but I'm so going to miss Upton Park. I don't get to go there much these days unless I'm working for Sky but I'm going have to take in a game or two this season, to say goodbye to the old place. The memories are endless.

David Steadman: I would prefer to have stayed at Upton Park and increased capacity on the East Stand. I'll always support West Ham (it's in the blood) but feel football is so commercial nowadays that the game as it was pre-Premier League seems a lifetime away.

When we move to the Olympic Stadium, I can see us being sold to some rich Arab or Russian and some success would be nice.

Greg Faasen: Was totally against the move originally – I am a traditionalist at heart – but feel that I now need to go with the times. We are moving to the Olympic Stadium and that is that!

All I ask is for future owners and managers to understand the psyche of the West Ham fan. The passion, the dreams, the need for entertaining football. Please may I never again hear a Hammers manager who questions the West Ham way . . . that is pure ignorance.

I take my hat off to the loyal Hammers fans who follow this wonderful club, home and away and through thick and thin. May you be rewarded by a hierarchy who understands you fully.

Liam Tyrell: From day one I have always been open to the Olympic Stadium move and positive about the benefits. Crucially, any move had

Sean (left) and Liam Tyrell on the pitch celebrating promotion in 1993.

to be somewhere that felt like home and not out in the sticks towards Rainham Marshes, Lakeside or anywhere non-descript in the middle of Docklands. For me, Stratford will feel as close, possibly closer, to the club's Thames Ironworks origins.

I really do think that the move can lift us up a level in terms of attracting more corporate finance, a global audience and, in turn, the spending power which is sadly so crucial these days.

No-one knows what the atmosphere will be like at Stratford or how the sight lines will pan out. We must hope the retractable seating does a good job.

My real issue with the whole thing is how a succession of bureaucrats and politicians have made such a mess of the whole affair from day one. Had the stadium been built with a full conversion for football in the first place it would have saved a whole lot of money and legal wrangling. It's similar to the mess made with the Millennium Dome, and you'd think someone would have cited the success of the Manchester City situation at the Commonwealth Games Stadium and how that was successfully converted with the minimum of fuss.

I honestly don't think many clubs look back and long for the old grounds once they've settled into their new stadia. For me, it's all about how well our conversion is done.

The longer-term future would then more than likely depend on what type of owners we have. Certainly the wealthy ones at Manchester City seem to be going about things the right way in terms of further developing their stadium and the adjoining new training complex with its integrated learning facilities and much more.

So as much as leaving The Boleyn will hurt, I hope that our new home will generate the right kind of atmosphere and conditions to take the club forward.

Mike Corbett: I'd rather have stayed at the Boleyn Ground but I recognise that we need to advance and we can't do that there. That said, I think we'll struggle to fill the Olympic Stadium and the atmosphere will suffer as a result.

As for the future, I think that we'll have a couple of decent seasons and then get bought out by some oil-rich billionaire. We'll be the new Chelsea (having signed my son from a successful spell at Barcelona, at a cut price deal), and be accused of being glory-hunters when we reveal who we support. It'll certainly be nice to be successful for a bit.

But, at the risk of sounding ungrateful, I think the club will lose some of its charm. People like West Ham in the same way that misery loves company – and it makes the supporters of other clubs like us a bit too. Spurs and Millwall fans aside, I've found that any time I've been asked who I support, and have revealed I have claret-and-blue disease, people generally respond pretty well. Once we're successful, that will change. The English hate success.

AUGUST 2015: The first rugby match played at the Olympic Stadium, between The Barbarians and Samoa on August 29. The match, watched by 41,039, was delivered in partnership between The Barbarians, E20 Stadium LLP (a joint venture between the London Legacy Development Corporation and Newham Council) and England Rugby 2015, tournament organisers for Rugby World Cup 2015. The match (Baa-Baas won 27-24) was also a test event ahead of the venue hosting five RWC 2015 matches.

OCTOBER 2015: The real thing, as 52,187 fans watched Ireland beat Italy 16-9 in the Rugby World Cup Group D match at the OS.

Steve Smith: The move leaves me cold. Why couldn't we knock down the East Stand and fill in those corners at the ends? I guess we would have had a capacity of 40,000-odd, whereas 54,000 is too much for a club like us. I doubt we'll fill it and the distance between us and the pitch does disturb me.

What type of people will fill those seats? Part of our DNA will go, we'll become more of a corporate brand instead of what we were – a working class football club with values.

Quite honestly, the whole thing sickens me. I think we'll become a rich man's plaything and Gold, Sullivan and Brady will no doubt ride off into the sunset with suitcases full of dough.

Neil Roper: Looking back has made me realise how sad it will be to leave Upton Park. By the time we move I'll have been a season ticket holder for 20 years and I've got so many amazing memories from the stadium. I have to be honest, though, once we knew that it was viable for West Ham to move to the Olympic Stadium, I felt it was a great opportunity for us as a club and I think they've made the right decision.

It's impossible to know what the future holds for West Ham. We all hope that moving to a bigger stadium will improve the global image of the club, which should lead to them competing in the transfer market for better quality players. Given the money that's in the game now, though, we have to be realistic and moving stadium isn't an automatic entry into the Premier League's elite.

So long as we can continue to compete in the top half of the Premier League and improve the financial position of the club, then that's all we can hope for in the short-term. If we can achieve that, then let's see where it takes us.

Gjermund Holt: I was very nervous that the new Olympic Stadium would be a big white elephant with no West Ham identity. Now it looks from the drawings that the stadium will be a real West Ham home, and the distance from the seats will be OK. It will, of course, be very strange, and it will take time, but I am now getting used to the move.

The distance from the Black Lion will be almost the same!

Arne Koellner: My attachment to the Boleyn Ground can never be as strong as for people who have gone there with their grandfather, father and now their own children or grandchildren. I only went regularly for one-and-a-half seasons during my stay in East London, plus the occasional visit afterwards. But it was, and is still, a proper football ground, close to the pitch and especially under the lights it could be a cauldron full of passion, noise and emotion.

The Olympic Stadium, even after conversion, will never be a proper football ground but it should help us to compete with or even challenge the top clubs and give us the chance to field exciting teams year after year. We might even get to see European football again. Or Champions League football. Or win something.

Fortune's been hiding for far too long, it is time that the wonderful Hammers faithful all over the world finally got their reward for years of suffering and enduring the endless rollercoaster of emotions.

Jimmy Jacob: My view is that we do need to move to progress. As a club we need to be looking to the future. However, The Boleyn is our home, which holds so many memories – the heartache of losses, the elation of unexpected wins or wonderful goals, and the cheering of my idols and the club I love.

But more importantly for me, The Boleyn is a place which I visited with my family, including my great-grandad, father, nan, mother, aunties, uncles, brothers, cousins, girlfriend and friends, and made many more friends while being there.

The Boleyn Ground provided a feeling of warmth, a feeling of family, a feeling of belonging.

But the future is coming and it will hopefully bring us greater success.

Eamonn McManus: I did not like the idea of moving but football is now a big business, not a plaything of the Cearns and Pratt families. To move on we have to leave The Boleyn. It will be hard and I predict that after the final home game against Swansea, many grown men will be in tears.

The move to Stratford, like the switch from the Memorial Grounds to The Boleyn in 1904, will change our club for the better. I believe the two Daves will sell up. After all, they are businessmen and in it for money. I'm sure they do love the club but if an offer came in, I bet they would take it.

Whatever happens, we can rest assured that we have many fans who will keep following our great club long after we're long gone. Whoever has the privilege of owing the club, they must always remember our history, the players, the fans, the culture.

George Reynolds: Obviously I am sad to leave the Boleyn Ground. Even though I don't have many of the memories of it that my dad and others have told me about it; the terraces, the Chicken Run, or the small club shop cabin in the main forecourt of the West Stand (which I've only ever known as the Dr. Martens Stand!), I still have plenty of my own from the last nine years, which will mean it will be difficult to accept the Olympic Stadium and move away from our home.

Some elements of the move still worry me, though. Mainly the view and whether we can keep up a great atmosphere. But seeing some of the players that have joined us in the last two years and some of the football we have been capable of playing, it makes me think that the move is the chance for us to progress upwards and challenge for some trophies.

The long-term future could be very interesting if we can attract more players of the calibre of Kouyate, Song and Payet but, of course, knowing West Ham, it's never that easy, things are never logical, so who knows where we will end up!

Heroes in Bronze

George and Jack McDonald, the editor's sons, pictured in 2003 in front of 'The Champions' statue that was erected that same year at the junction of Barking Road and Green Street and unveiled by Prince Andrew, then president of the Football Association. Many were surprised that sculptor Philip Jackson – working from a photographic image and jointly commissioned by the club and Newham Council – decided to include Everton's Ray Wilson alongside Hammers' famous trio of Bobby Moore, Geoff Hurst and Martin Peters depicting a famous victory scene from the 1966 World Cup Final.

Jackson used as his subject material a series of photographs taken during a 12-second period after the game. In a scene described by the FA as "one of the enduring post-match images", Moore was pictured holding the Jules Rimet Trophy above his head, while he himself is being held shoulder-high by Hurst and Wilson, with Peters completing the scene. Jackson exercised some artistic license to not depict Wilson's expression entirely accurately, as he had been grimacing due to taking much of Moore's weight. "I didn't think he would mind," said Jackson.

The 'World Cup Sculpture', as it is also known, is a one-and-a-half times life-size bronze piece, 16 feet (4.9m) tall, weighing four tonnes. It was the brainchild of Newham councillor Graeme Cambage. After the unveiling, he said: "After Bobby Moore died, I thought there ought to be a statue of him but it's taken a long time to realise my dream."

A year in the making, the statue cost £725,000 in all, with £400,000 coming from a Government grant and the bulk of the remainder from the football club. The cost included associated street improvements. Contributions also came from the Green Street Single Regeneration Budget, the Arts Council for England, and Arts & Business.

Royal sculptor Jackson went on to also sculpt the statue of Bobby Moore unveiled at the new Wembley when it opened in 2007.

Jack McDonald: I will go to the Olympic Stadium once and if I enjoy it, I'll go again. My main concern is the running track and its possible impact on the atmosphere. I worry for fans sitting miles away from the pitch. People bang on about retractable seating but that's just for the lower tier closest to the pitch. What about the poor sods in row Z?

As a club, losing our biggest asset (our stadium) is a very risky and insecure position to be in. However, if we are to compete among the biggest teams in the country, I do believe we need a bigger ground.

It is such shame to see the Boleyn Ground demolished. Fans and ex-players have had their ashes scattered on the Upton Park turf, so it just doesn't feel right somehow. What makes us different from Arsenal, Chelsea, Manchester United and Liverpool (apart from the size of their trophy cabinets) is that those clubs and their fans expect success. They expect it so much that I doubt they even enjoy it anymore. I don't want to be like them. I want us to remain who we are, keep our identity, principles and heritage.

I also hope the club builds a new museum that fans can visit on a match day, so that even the new fans we hope to attract may take an interest in our history.

Ian Smith: The move to the Olympic Stadium is supposedly controversial – diehard old Hammers don't want to leave The Boleyn but other fans see the future potential of playing in an iconic stadium and the investment that will hopefully bring. It will always be an emotional subject and I will be really sad to leave Upton Park – it holds so many memories for me, both good and bad, but I really think this question should be answered with the head rather than the heart.

Football has changed dramatically since the Premier League started in 1992-93. Money is the operative word with TV and advertising cash being thrown at it from every direction. The days of the attendance money being the major earner are long gone and the game has moved into the modern media-driven world.

Personally, I want to see West Ham become successful and regularly challenge for silverware and play in Europe. We cannot do that if we stay at Upton Park with its awful travel infrastructure and general deterioration in the surrounding area. Stratford offers us a once-in-a-lifetime opportunity to realise those ambitions and we would have been mad, if not completely negligent, if we had not bid for the stadium. The rail and tube links are the best in the country and connections to Europe are superb. The stadium is much larger with 21st century facilities which will enable us to grow and attract the young, new supporter – a vital lifeblood for the club.

I am sure there are already potential investors waiting in the wings ready to build us a team to be proud of and get West Ham into the top five or six English clubs. We will then be able to compete at the very highest level and it will be a snowball effect seeing us grow, attract the best players and enjoy success a little more regularly than the odd cup win every 30 or so years.

We all love Upton Park/The Boleyn/The San Siro of the East End but things change and we have to move with the times.

Do I want to see us compete? Yes.

Do I want to see us play with the best players in a smart, new stadium? Yes.

Do I want to see my club grow and become successful? Yes.

Do I want to see Chelsea, Arsenal and Spurs looking East and seeing their greatest threat? Most definitely yes!

This can only be achieved by moving to the Olympic Stadium and as long as we remember our long and proud history in our new home and encourage fans to come and be part of the West Ham family, I am most definitely in favour of moving.

For me this subject is not controversial, it's a no-brainer unless we want to stagnate and maybe disappear.

The final match at The Boleyn is going to be emotional but so too is the first match in Stratford – and I intend to experience both. COYI!

Mark Matthews: From an emotional point of view I don't want us to leave Upton Park. But if the club is going to move forward, it's a no-brainer. The match day revenue and overall profile of the club can only be increased by the move.

Many fans of other clubs have said that the new stadium will only be half-full for most games but I think people will be surprised.

Martin Scholar: Not sure about the move to the Olympic Stadium. I am worried about being too far from the pitch and a lack of atmosphere – it's hard to imagine the stadium being full other than for the really big games. I think the East Stand could have been redeveloped.

A major part of our identity is Upton Park and there is no doubt that some of our character will disappear.

A familiar and friendly sight on match day at Upton Park. Former policeman Alan Deadman travelled over from the Isle of Wight to sell his vast range of excellent metal badges from his pitch outside the West Ham United Supporters' Club in Castle Street.

John Ledington: I am against the move. I'm a traditionalist and don't like change, I truly love the Upton Park experience - the pre-match ritual and the game, The Queens pub, giving *OLAS* owner Gary Firmager a hug when we meet and, above all, the experience and memories with my son, Andy, which I will treasure to the end of my days.

I hope Hammers' future is truly successful but I'm not sure if it will be. It depends on the custodians of the club – if they are ambitious and bring in top players and also, if they stay true to the academy and still nurture top talent from the local and surrounding area. To me, that is the absolute priority.

God bless, West Ham and thanks for the wonderful Upton Park memories.

Alan Deadman: I do not wish to move. Had the East Stand been developed we could have stayed put and held on to the unique atmosphere of Upton Park. I will certainly miss the Supporters' Club and the likes of Tony Hogg selling his "exclusive" *EX* magazines in Castle Street!

Derek Price: While I have always thought of myself as being a 'traditionalist', I do have very strong feelings that tradition has definitely held us back as a footballing nation, whereas other countries, such as Germany, have totally outstripped us by not being so hidebound by the conventional way of doing things. Look at The Allianz Arena where Bayern Munich play, it changes colour when TSV Munich play there. Other English clubs, such as Sunderland, Bolton Wanderers and Coventry City, have all left their traditional grounds to set up home anew somewhere else. Does anyone in their right minds now think that Arsenal did the wrong thing in leaving Highbury to play at The Emirates?

Where West Ham are concerned, leaving Upton Park will evoke great sadness for a lot of people but the club needs to look far ahead, which it hasn't done enough of for a very long time. Why did they have to sell an outstanding crop of young players, needing to pay for a new West Stand, which in a few short years will have become totally redundant.

I would feel far happier if it could have been a new beginning as well for Leyton Orient, with a ground-share arrangement. It has never ceased to amaze me that cities like Nottingham, Bristol and Sheffield have two separate grounds; why can't new grounds be built enabling clubs to share? I'm not suggesting that Arsenal and Tottenham should share, or Everton with Liverpool, for that matter, but lower down the leagues it could make a lot of sense, especially in west London where three clubs are so close together. Similarly with east London!

Richard Nott: The move to the Olympic Stadium is brilliant. It's much closer and I've always wanted to see us play in a big stadium like that. I think the long-term future is superb. I'm hoping we will get into the Champions League and win the League Cup.

Spencer Dodd: It's a step forwards and as much as I love Upton Park, it's essential to our future development and attracting the kind of players that we all want to see playing the type of football we appreciate. I'll certainly be taking my memories of Upton Park, my father and my grandfather with me to the new stadium.

Dave Spurgeon: I am generally cynical and saddened at how the once beautiful game has now turned ugly due to the obscene bankrolling of Murdoch's millions and the balance of power becoming boring and monotonous. The two Manchester clubs, plus those in London, financed by Arab sheiks, Russian oligarchs and American billionaires, let alone the mercenary attitude of most of the players, most of whom can never wear the local hero tag.

I have also become disillusioned and angered by the fact that, at 61, and very shortly to retire from work, I am of a generation of supporters who have been priced out of being a paying fan and, as a consequence, I have only gone to about 15 home games since the ill-fated bond scheme.

A trip to Upton Park from my home in Colchester, Essex is an expensive, frustrating and tiring experience whichever way I travel. And as for queuing half-an-hour at Upton Park station just to get into the station, let alone on a train to Stratford or Upminster . . . no thanks!

Great traditionalist that I am, I think it is myth about the Boleyn Ground atmosphere being lost when we move to Stratford. The current ground configuration is unrecognisable from the 60s, 70s and early 80s. As with all modernised grounds, the all-seater aspect has done way with the atmosphere we all knew in the days of standing on the terraces.

I was lucky enough to go to the Olympic Stadium in 2012 and it was incredible. Even towards the rear of the seating in that configuration, believe me, there are worse views at The Boleyn. I think the configuration, with the enclosed roof structure and retractable seating, is going to be great.

And, of course, affordable pricing and the fact I can travel from Colchester to Stratford in 45 minutes, means that the likes of me, who have moved away from the traditional Hammers' heartland, will be tempted to return to the fold. In fact, I have applied to join a Priority List for a 2016-17 season ticket, to at least give it a go, particularly as Bilic seems to want to build an entertaining, attacking team worth going to see.

I think we have to look at Arsenal as the benchmark here. Moving away from the tradition, history and splendour of Highbury must, initially, have seemed unthinkable but The Emirates speaks for itself.

If we stand still as a club, you can forget all the history and tradition quotes I keep hearing from cynics about the move. Our club history is something of which I am rightfully proud and pleased to have been a part of it in the halcyon years but it won't lead us to success tomorrow. Clubs like Leeds United, Wolves, Nottingham Forest, Derby County and Ipswich Town have had great history and tradition in my adult lifetime but look where they are now – and where they are destined to stay, because they cannot compete financially to get top players or hold on to ones they develop.

Chris Ludlow commissioned this painting of Stuart Slater scoring against Brighton in 1990 – the first game he attended at the Boleyn Ground.

Upton Park will always hold a place in my heart and the atmosphere will always give me goosebumps when I think about it.

Chris Ludlow: I have never been one that has backed the move to the Olympic Stadium and feel that redeveloping the East Stand would have given us a capacity of around 42,000, a nice tight stadium and, by moving the pitch closer to the stands, increased the atmosphere.

The main reservation I have about the move is that the OS was never built with its future use in mind and, therefore, is curved on the sides. I have been to the stadium to attend a rugby match and was surprised how good the views are from all parts of the stadium. However, there seems to be a lot of work to do to get the stadium ready for us, a feeling that was echoed by a vast number of people that were there who said it felt a bit like Wembley – a nice stadium to visit but not the kind of place where you would want to watch your team play every week.

Another worry is that the standard of football we have been playing over the last 12-18 months has not been of the level required to fill the 54,000 capacity of our new stadium. However, the introduction of Slaven Bilic has injected new life into us and the players brought in seem to be of the highest quality. While it is still early days this (2015-16) season, the signs are encouraging that we will be playing some very exciting, high-tempo football. We have a lot of options that can change a game this season, so, fingers crossed, the future is bright.

We can't do anything about the move now, so let's get behind the team and cheer them towards a new beginning. A new force in the East is rising. COYI!

Realistically, the so-called 'big four' of Arsenal, Chelsea and the two Manchester clubs will remain the top four for a while but it is nice to have a Hammers team that can give them a bloody nose now and then, so I am in favour of the move.

Charlie Beckwith: Although I don't like it, the move to the Olympic Stadium will make the club a force to be reckoned with, due to the financial boost it will give us.

Authors of books on West Ham United have their say

John Powles: If the seating arrangements are better than we think and there is an increase in attendances, the general atmosphere could make it an enjoyable experience. However, all this depends on Premier League survival and a team good enough to bring more fans in.

In terms of transport to the ground, it all depends on your location. Personally, that is a plus. However, selling your major asset (The Boleyn Ground) can be fraught with problems. A large annual rent, which is always likely to go up, will not be cheap. If the experience of Coventry City with the Ricoh Arena is anything to go by, it could be a disaster.

I believe that if the club remains in the Premier League the current owners will be looking for multi-million backing to keep it all afloat.

What will certainly not be afloat when we leave are the pubs and some businesses in the Upton Park area.

Neil Humphreys: Financially, it's a no-brainer. Whatever way you look at it, West Ham have had a result. The jaw-dropping arrogance and incompetence of the London 2012 committee with regards to the stadium and its legacy was hardly the fault of the Hammers. The white elephant was always going to fall into West Ham's lap.

Talk of Tottenham Hotspur and Leyton Orient becoming tenants was as shortsighted as the initial belief that the Olympic Stadium could survive on track and field meets and rock concerts. From the moment London was announced as the 2012 Games hosts back in 2005, the Olympic Stadium was going to end up being West Ham's home.

However, as a keen conservationist and student of social history, I am also aware of the crucial importance of cultural ties and local identity, particularly in sport. There is much more at stake than money here but, of course, these issues always take a back seat in the Premier League.

Every major cup fixture involving Manchester United could fill Wembley – but it doesn't mean it should. Some Premier League games could make more money being played in Dubai – but it doesn't mean they should.

West Ham will make more money in the Olympic Stadium but never

UPTON PARK MEMORIES

After his popular appointment as manager in the summer of 2015, former Hammers player Slaven Bilic got the team playing a more attacking, entertaining brand of football that has given fans new hope for a bright future in Stratford . . .

enough to truly compete with Manchester City and Chelsea – and they will lose their cultural heritage.

That's a hell of a price to pay when the potential rewards are by no means guaranteed.

Pete May: I will miss Upton Park but the Olympic Stadium does represent progress, if only for the sheer number of train lines at Stratford. And I think 54,000 gates will attract players and, ultimately, some mega-rich owners.

Robert Banks: I'm excited by the move. I will miss Upton Park, of course, but if we are to compete in the Premier League we need not just a stadium but an infrastructure and a global brand, and the OS will give us that. Whether you like it or not, if we are going to be a top side we have to have that in the 21st century game.

Iain Dale: My heart wants to stay at Upton Park but my head says that if we are to progress as a club, we have to go. Contrary to what most people think, I believe we will fill the Olympic Stadium for between a third and a half of our games in the first season, and by season five I suspect we'll fill it for all games . . . but it depends on the ticket pricing.

I was at the OS on the Saturday night when we won all those gold medals at the Olympics. I took the opportunity to go right to the top back row, and I'd have no problem in having a ticket there. I think it's a phenomenal stadium and while I will be sad to leave behind all that history, we need to look forward to a bright future.

Steve Blowers: With so many marvellous memories, I was initially dead against the move but there's no stopping the show now. Let's store those magic moments, embrace the change and just hope upon hope that OUR club can carry its coveted claret-and-blue legacy into the Olympic Stadium, where the bright new surroundings can, ultimately, propel the Hammers towards permanent top six status.

Terry Roper: We must embrace progress and having the Olympic Stadium, one of the greatest arenas in the world with its fantastic facilities and marvellous access, as our new home ground is something that cannot be denied or ignored.

However, I will be very sad to leave Upton Park. It has been a huge part of my life for almost 65 years and holds a million memories for me. Whatever happens in the future, it will forever remain West Ham's spiritual home.

John Northcutt: It will be a sad day when we leave the Boleyn Ground, there are so many

Robert Banks (far left) pictured in 2010 with his dad Bob, nephews Mark and Sam and great-nephew Jamie (10).

memories for us all, but for me the ground as I first knew it is no longer there. The North and South Banks, together with the dear old Chicken Run, have long since gone.

The change to an all-seater stadium was for the best and no doubt our forthcoming move to the Olympic Stadium will lift the club forward to a new level with bigger gates and better facilities in a magnificent stadium that will attract better players.

It will be the end of an era, 1904 to 2016, so let us all look forward to a new beginning.

Dan Francis: As depressing as it sounds, my over-riding emotion when it comes to the stadium move is one of indifference.

If we are talking about the atmosphere inside the stadium and the thrill of a match day then, for me, the magic of Upton Park disappeared a long time ago.

I was very fortunate and privileged to be able to watch West Ham from the press box for a number of years and always felt that meant I had no right to criticise or judge the mood and opinions of the crowd at the Boleyn Ground.

However, since becoming a paying supporter again in recent years, I've realised that it is a very, very different experience from the one that gave me so many happy and unforgettable memories during my childhood and teenage years.

Maybe it's just because I'm older and wiser, or maybe it's because there are so many elements of the modern game that I find unattractive, but – aside from the fact that the transport links are going to be far better for many people – I don't really see much of a change in the general match day experience.

As we hear Premier League managers insist so often now, football 'is a results business...'

And that sentiment has, I believe, created the most depressing aspect of modern-day top-flight football - that the supporters who spend the money to attend the stadium and follow the players in the flesh at every home game are actually no longer the lifeblood of the club.

Back at the start of West Ham's memorable 1985-86 campaign, when English football was in the gutter after a spate of stadium disasters and hooligan-related incidents, West Ham chairman Len Cearns made a personal plea to supporters in the match day programme after attendances had dropped to an all-time low. The crux of it was that the club itself was in grave danger if fans didn't dig deep to boost attendances and income.

Nowadays, that is simply no longer the case. Whether West Ham have capacity crowds of 54,000 every fortnight at the Olympic Stadium or float around the 30,000 mark they have been used to at Upton Park, it will make no difference to the financial well-being and growth of the club, as long as they stay in the Premier League.

The fact is that the latest TV rights deal is far more important to the owners, and gives the perverse impression that a Sky Sports or BT Sport subscriber can feel more valued and appreciated than the man who spends fortunes every season taking his family to 19 home matches.

I also think it is naïve to assume that moving to a bigger stadium is automatically going to catapult the club to a higher level on the pitch. You only have to look at the likes of Sunderland, Middlesbrough and Derby County to know that a shiny new stadium doesn't naturally lead to upward progression.

Which is why I'm slightly confused by the fears among many supporters that the current owners will offload it to the highest bidder as soon as they can.

Gold and Sullivan seem to be going to desperate lengths to stress that they won't be selling up and want to keep the club 'in the family', but why?

If an oil-rich sheikh offers to pay above and beyond the market value of the club and then promises to plough billions of pounds into developing it on and off the pitch, are they really going to turn it down, being the shrewd businessmen that they are?

And more to the point, will the majority of supporters want them to turn it down?

Surely the whole idea of a club the size of West Ham United moving to a bigger stadium is to increase the infrastructure and make it a more attractive proposition to the kind of investors who could actually turn us into challengers for the Premier League title?

Manchester City are only where they are today because of the funds poured in from Abu Dhabi but it is also fair to say that without the initial move from Maine Road to the new City of Manchester Stadium in 2003, those funds probably wouldn't have arrived.

So who knows what the future holds for West Ham? If there's one thing you can predict about this club, it's that we are unpredictable.

Looking ahead, it all comes down to personal choice and what your support means to you as an individual. I personally won't be rushing to the Olympic Stadium in August 2016 but, by the same token, leaving Upton Park won't cause me to turn my back on the club I have followed for more than 30 years.

My own son, Archie, is now 18-months-old and in five or six years' time, whatever West Ham's standing in the game, I will take him along to a match if he shows an interest.

And if he then falls in love with the claret-and-blue with his innocent eyes as I did at that age, I will continue to take him, because nothing would give me greater pleasure than sharing with him the memories and experiences that I shared with my dad.

And that is why, however you express your support for the club and wherever the football is played, it is tomorrow's generation who really matter.

Whoever is in charge simply has to fulfil the most basic duty of ensuring that there is a West Ham United FC to follow. The fans will do the rest . . .

Tony McDonald: To be honest, I fell out of love with Premier League football in general long before they will lock the Boleyn gates for the last time and throw away the keys. I stopped renewing my three £800-plus season tickets for me and my two sons in the summer of 2007, after Alan Curbishley – ironically, a once talented young player I'd championed in the late 70s – bored us senseless with his clueless tactics and inexplicable pursuit of 'nothing players' such as Nigel Quashie – most

Upton Park Memories editor Tony McDonald with John Lyall at the former manager's Suffolk home in 2005.

notable for having been relegated with four different clubs before Curbs deemed him worthy of a ludicrous 40 grand a week for doing absolutely nothing. After Roeder's folly and Pardew's smug, self-serving bullshit, it was the final straw. No wonder the naive Icelandics who fell for Curbs' insightful scouting genius – Freddie Ljungberg? – went into financial meltdown.

So I've not been back there too many times since and won't be too heartbroken to wave a very respectful goodbye to the Old Dear in May 2016. As other contributors have already rightly pointed out, the Boleyn Ground has long since ceased to be the cauldron of noise it was on those memorable electric nights under the lights, when you were so close you could smell the liniment oil on the legs of players who were just proud to wear the shirt and be paid 'just' twice as much as the average working class immortal image; a spontaneous gesture of mutual respect and admiration between two of the greatest players of all time – not a carefully orchestrated photo opportunity forming part of the relentless, gaudy caravan of celebrity projection.

Fame in the old-fashioned sense, particularly in Moore's era, was always acquired, whereas the tawdriness of modern day celebrity is gratuitously bestowed. Such an anomaly only exists these days because of the audience-jury syndrome that we supply and in which we sometimes compromise ourselves.

Conversely, Bobby Moore was not a 'celebrity' in the modern day sense of the word because he actually achieved something quite unique in his life, thus enabling him to earn his legendary status and the deserving world-wide fame that it brought him. The greatest irony is that it did not bring much comfort in the later years of his life, particularly in terms of monetary gain when our national game shamefully turned its back on him.

Moore retired from playing at the age of 36 – not necessarily 'midlife' for some of us, but certainly heading towards it. However, those of us of a certain age will know that, under normal circumstances, the usual clichés about reaching midlife usually turn out to have some semblance of truth. At the time, we kid ourselves that the best is yet to come and, once in a while, we might even believe it. Indeed, there are occasions when it might be true.

However, what if you are patently aware – just as Moore was – that you have already attained the ultimate pinnacle in the early part of your life? How do you get even close to replicating it in later years? It is what the great poets throughout history have sometimes described as "The melancholy of all things done."

Once you have captained your country to winning the World Cup – the crowning moment of any player's career – what can you possibly achieve as an encore? Anything else is surely anti-climatic, thus resulting in a yearning restlessness.

There is, of course, one notable exception – Beckenbauer – who went on to manage Germany's World Cup-winning team just 16 years after captaining them to victory. However, it is safe to assume that Beckenbauer was something of a 'one-off.'

Sadly, there was no 'second glory' for Bobby Moore. After lifting the World Cup in 1966, his career and, indeed parts of his private life, became a juxtaposition of pernicious disappointment and regret.

These included the infamous 'Blackpool affair' which resulted in him being dropped and suspended by West Ham; the lengthy and expensive legal battle to clear his name following the frame-up over the 'missing' bracelet in Bogota; kidnap threats to his wife and children; death threats to himself; being denied the opportunity to play under the legendary Brian Clough at Derby County; struggling in management at unfashionable and bankrupt Southend United; the excruciating break-up of his first marriage together with the ensuing divorce, plus several high-profile business ventures that failed spectacularly and resulted in considerable financial problems, endless worries and, at one time, mountainous debts.

In the absurd cliché-ridden world of professional football, it would no doubt be described as "a life of two halves." However, in a sense, those unfortunate episodes – all of which occurred during the second part of Moore's life – merely proved that he was fallible after all. Suffice to say, things were considerably different when he bestrode the great stadiums of the world like a colossus at the peak of his playing career.

Apart from his jaw-dropping ability to judge situations with computer accuracy and then act upon them with complete technical skill, there were other traits in Moore's armoury that made him quite unique. Basically, he was immensely talented at being ice-cool on the field of play – even when the battle was at its fiercest.

His apparent detachment often broke the hearts of both opposition players and fans alike. However, it should be stressed that Moore was not unemotional – rather, he was just a master at masking his own emotions.

He was almost Zen-like in moments of the most intense pressure. Though not a religious man, Moore could have almost been a Buddhist monk for the aura of calmness that enveloped him. He was the personification of the masculine ideal in Rudyard Kipling's immortal prose 'If' – majestically keeping his head while all those around him were losing theirs.

Also, another aspect that distinguishes a great footballer from merely a very good one is leadership. In every truly great player there is an ability to create a team around himself, one in which every member of that team is somehow forced to play way beyond their normal capabilities.

That is why West Ham won the FA Cup and European Cup Winners' Cup in successive seasons in the mid-60s and why, most importantly of all, England won the World Cup in 1966 with Moore as their inspirational leader and captain at the helm.

The captaincy of the national team represents the highest accolade any player in England can receive. It marks out the 'best of the best' – thus recognising an inextricable leader of men in the process. These days, we have become used to certain England captain's demeaning that exalted position with acts of mind-boggling tawdriness that has totally sickened those of us who retain even a modicum of national pride.

On the other hand, Moore treated the captaincy with immaculate good grace, honour and supreme dignity. Who can forget the way that he meticulously wiped his muddied hands on the blue velvet balustrade in the Royal Box at Wembley before meeting The Queen and collecting the Jules Rimet trophy?

He always admirably demonstrated that the captain of the England football team should occupy an estimable position in the life of the nation. It is a trait that some of the more recent incumbents – one of whom is a profane and serial lout who appears ambivalent towards even the most basic concept of common decency – could never hope to emulate, not even in their wildest dreams.

It should also be stressed that Moore showed great courage in his personal life. He was first diagnosed with cancer – the testicular variety – in 1964 when he was just 23-years-old. It is necessary to put Moore's diagnosis at the time into perspective. Thanks to the advances of modern day medicine, more men than ever are surviving testicular cancer and the current survival rate stands at 97 per cent.

However, when Moore was diagnosed with the disease in the mid-60s, the survival rate was less than 50 per cent. Amazingly, within six months of having a testicle removed and facing the ongoing debilitating treatment, he captained West Ham to victory in the greatest night in the club's history when they won the European Cup Winners' Cup at Wembley. Even more astonishingly, within another 14 months, he was leading England to victory in the 1966 World Cup final.

In a sense, he treated the disease with all the respect he would have given the most dangerous opponent on the field of play – intercepting at the first hint of danger, denying space and diverting it into areas where it could do least damage. Without question, Bobby Moore proved that he was made of the 'right stuff' long before the phrase had ever been invented.

Needless to say, England's historic victory propelled Moore to global fame but, despite his immense success, it is a strange anomaly that he never appeared particularly at ease in front of the television cameras or the occasions when he was required to carry out public speaking duties.

Indeed, Moore's responses during his television and radio interviews were generally stilted containing answers that, at times, did not go beyond the literal, superficial or blandly factual. He enunciated his words with extraordinary care, although the order in which they appeared was sometimes less than decisive.

At times, he attempted to speak with almost meticulous diction as though precision had its own set of rules and even a loose vowel might cause offence to those listening. Nevertheless, perhaps we should admire him for responding in what he considered was the most appropriate manner on such occasions.

It merely goes to prove that he was, basically, an intensely shy and private man who wore his special place in our mythology with an innate dignity. In doing so, he had the decency not to crowd our imaginations or diminish our fantasies about him as a person by fixing them with words that he could not find.

One of the most fascinating aspects of Moore's life was that it covered a revolution not only in football but also in social attitudes. The boy from Barking witnessed the end of the age of deference, the abolition of football's maximum wage, the rise of the superstar player, the demise of amateur administrators, the collapse of rigid class structures and the arrival of the permissive society.

As a result, Bobby Moore became synonymous with the glamorous 'Swinging 60s' lore and, in particular, the summer of 1966 when England's success created a carnival atmosphere across the entire country.

It was a time when the whole nation threw a gigantic party to simultaneously celebrate the abandonment of the starchy class-ridden values of the 50s and the fact that, incredibly, England had been crowned the new world champions.

It created a patriotic pride and euphoria that lifted our spirits in a glorious manner which remained unequalled in this country until the awe-inspiring 2012 Olympic and Paralympic Games exploded upon us and reignited our love of sport.

In 1966, mini-skirts were in, deference was out and 'golden boy' Bobby Moore – East End working class and immensely proud of it – had become one of the most iconic symbols of that exciting new age. In fact, he positively embraced the period, apparently mingling amongst the rich and famous almost as though he had been born into such a role.

Sadly and in all probability, we will never see his like again. Yet, in a strange way, such a thought inevitably precipitates a rarely found peacefulness within us because it means that our fondest memories of Bobby Moore cannot be transcended by the deeds of others.

Also, the fact that Moore died at a relatively young age means that we can remember him as he always was – handsome, blond-haired and imperious in the heat of battle for both club and country. If it is possible to capture Moore's mien in a single word, there is only one that will suffice – 'imperious'. Bobby Moore was, quite simply, imperious.

Such is the cynical nature of football that new 'heroes' will inevitably emerge with each passing decade. However, it is doubtful if any of them can ever match or, indeed, surpass the majesty of Moore in his prime.

Curiously and quite perversely, there is an aesthetic beauty about dying young. It allows us to remember the icons of the 20th century such as John F. Kennedy, Martin Luther King, Marilyn Monroe, James Dean, John Lennon et al in their prime before the ravages of time and old age took their inevitable toll.

Their untarnished images are frozen definitively in the deepest corners of our minds and will remain so throughout the mists of time. The world may have changed and so might we, but the pictures of these mesmeric figures remain ever present.

The same applies to Bobby Moore. Mention his name to any Englishman of almost any age and it will instantly generate the iconic picture of England's captain, resplendent in that famous red shirt, holding aloft the World Cup on that unforgettable July day in 1966.

More than two decades after his death, Moore remains a constant and integral part of our national consciousness. His story was, after all, an inextricable part of our story.

He was not only football's greatest ever defender but also the finest, most inspirational England captain of all time. Generous in defeat, magnanimous in victory – he stood for all that was good in the game. He was also a man of innate dignity, inspiring leadership and great personal courage.

There are certain individuals who command a special place in this nation's affections. Bobby Moore was such a person. Those of us who saw him in action and actually witnessed him at the height of his powers were indeed fortunate.

How could we not fail to accord him the status of a true English hero? May that noble distinction always serve as an enduring legacy to the greatest Hammer of them all.

Dignified exit

From a fan who saw Bobby Moore's final Hammers game

BOBBY was coming back from injury and the game was West Ham United Reserves against Plymouth Argyle Reserves at the Boleyn Ground on Saturday, March 9, 1974.

He had played his last first team game against Hereford United in the FA Cup 3rd round at Upton Park on January 5, when he limped off after 30 minutes.

From what I can remember, it was known that the Plymouth game would be Bobby's last prior to his transfer to Fulham. I believe the attendance was around 5,000.

The move must have been confirmed in the next week, because at the Coventry City game on the following Saturday Bobby waved farewell and shook hands with Ron Greenwood before kick-off.

I also went to see Bobby's first game for Fulham, v Middlesbrough. He was my hero (still is), as he was, of course, for thousands of others.

I cannot remember a great deal of his final match at Upton Park but Pop Robson, also returning from injury, scored with a header in a 1-1 draw (the first team drew by the same score at Derby County that day).

Hammers lined up as follows: Peter Grotier, Clive Charles, Alan Wooler, Bertie Lutton, Tony White, Bobby Moore, John Ayris, Ron Boyce, Bryan Robson, Geoff Pike, Yilmaz Orhan. Sub: Malcolm Hill.

Unfortunately, I wrote the team changes, etc, on the programme, which was a silly thing to do but I was young at the time. I even filled in the half-time scores!

I can still see in my mind Bobby running off the pitch at the end, no fuss, not milking the applause, just the embodiment of dignity and modesty.

Typical of the man.

Dave Purdom, Sandyford, Dublin 18, Ireland.

Fans holds up cards to mark the 20th anniversary of the death of Bobby Moore before the Premier League game v Tottenham Hotspur on February 25, 2013.

RON & JOHN

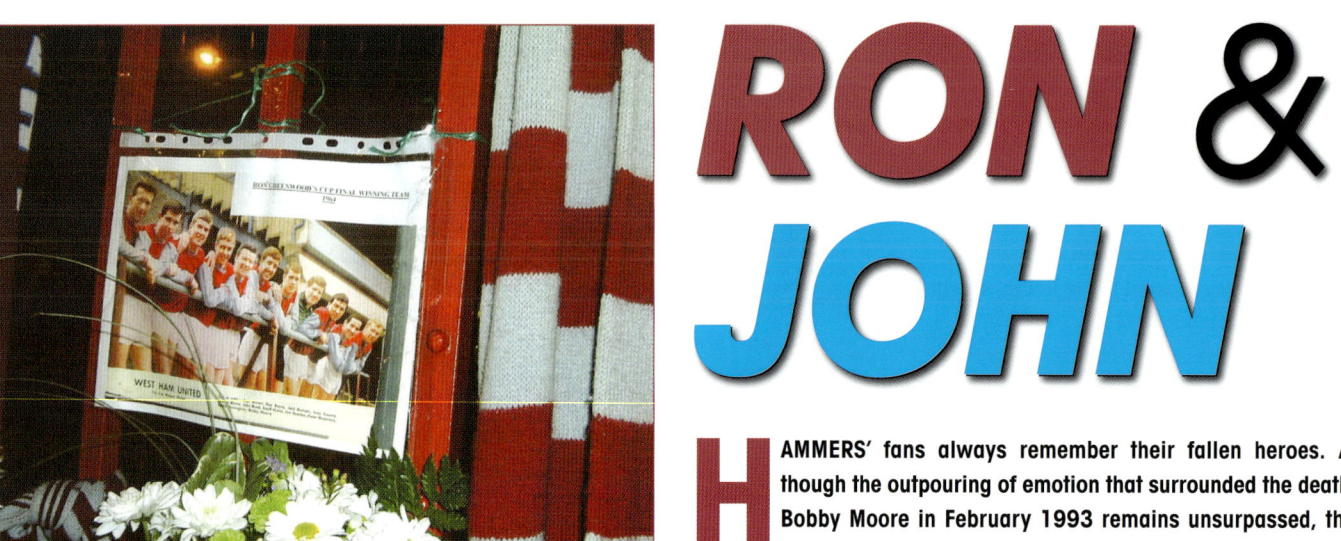

HAMMERS' fans always remember their fallen heroes. And though the outpouring of emotion that surrounded the death of Bobby Moore in February 1993 remains unsurpassed, there were still more tears shed 13 years later after West Ham lost its two greatest managers in the space of around nine weeks in 2006.

Ron Greenwood, the ultimate ideologist who brought the club its first major silverware since the 1940 War Cup when he led his team to glory in the 1964 FA Cup and the European Cup Winners' Cup a year later, died in a Sudbury care home on February 9, 2006. He was 84 and had fought a long battle against Alzheimer's disease.

Fans laid wreathes and left poignant, heartfelt messages at the main gates in memory of 'Reverand Ron', who built upon Ted Fenton's foundation-laying efforts in the late 50s and constructed a swashbuckling team that put the East Enders on the

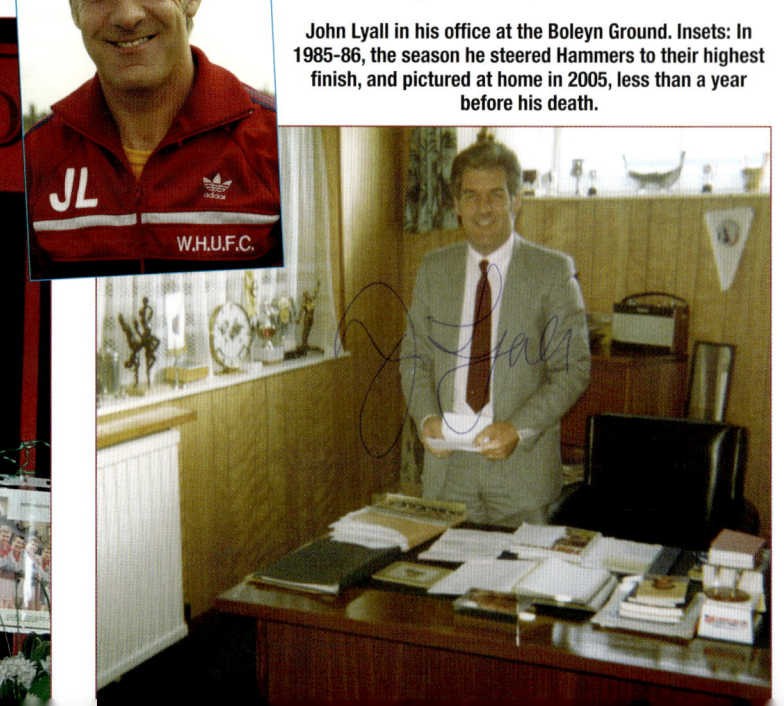

John Lyall in his office at the Boleyn Ground. Insets: In 1985-86, the season he steered Hammers to their highest finish, and pictured at home in 2005, less than a year before his death.

UPTON PARK MEMORIES 367

European football map – their finest achievement of the Boleyn years.

When he stood down as team manager in August 1974 to take more of a backseat role while scouting for new signings, he couldn't have left the club in safer hands than his protege John Lyall, who became a promising young coach under Greenwood after his playing days were finally ended in 1964 due to a recurring knee injury.

In 1975, Ron and John – master and pupil – walked side-by-side across the Wembley turf in celebration of Hammers' second FA Cup triumph, although Lyall was unable to emulate his mentor's European success a year later when his side lost to Anderlecht in the ECWC final.

By the time Greenwood left West Ham for good to become England manager in 1977, Lyall had begun rebuilding the team that would enjoy a prolonged spell of success . . . a third FA Cup victory in 1980, a record-breaking second division title win in 1981, a League Cup final appearance the same season and that 1985-86 campaign which so nearly ended in the club's first League championship.

Of these two great upstanding servants of West Ham, whose commitment and loyalty to the club spanned more than 50 years between them, it's fair to say that Lyall was more popular with supporters and players alike. But without Ron, there would more than likely have been no John – in terms of his immense contribution as coach and manager.

And it was typical of Lyall's self-effacing humility that he always credited Greenwood as the making of him both as a coach and manager. He led the eulogies to Ron and was still lavishing public praise upon his management predecessor in the days before being struck down by a fatal heart attack at his Suffolk farmhouse on April 18, 2006, aged 66.

When football romantics talk of the 'West Ham Way', you have to attribute that ideology, a slavish commitment to a stylish brand of attacking football, to these two great and much lamented gentleman of the game. Because they were the unwavering driving forces behind it.

Some of John Lyall's former team-mates and players on the pitch before the minute's applause in 2006. From left: Bobby Barnes, Ken Brown, Mervyn Day, Brian Dear, Alan Devonshire, Bobby Gould, Paul Goddard, Pat Holland, Kevin Keen.

DYLAN TOMBIDES could not possibly be remembered in the same reverential tones as legendary figures Bobby Moore, Ron Greenwood or John Lyall, but the Australian youngster still touched many people lives before his own was cruelly cut short.

Perth-born Tombides was just 20 when he died on April 18, 2014 after being diagnosed with testicular cancer in 2011.

He joined West Ham as a 15-year-old, playing as a striker for the youth team, and made his solitary senior appearance as a substitute in the 4-1 home League Cup defeat v Wigan Athletic (25/9/2012).

Tombides was 17 when he was first diagnosed after playing for Australia in the Under-17 World Cup in Mexico.

A random drugs test, taken after his team were beaten 4-0 by Uzbekistan, uncovered a tumour in one of his testicles.

Months of surgery and chemotherapy followed and Tombides worked hard to raise awareness of male cancer, supporting the One for the Boys campaign at a number of high-profile events with Hollywood star Samuel L Jackson, snooker player Jimmy White and Peter Andre.

1904-2016 THE BOLEYN GROUND

112 years and two World Wars
The final kick before closing the doors
Forever
Three FA Cups and European supremacy
Bobby Moore, Ron Greenwood and John Lyall's legacy
Layers of history laid to rest
A world of eyes saw worst and best

The small works team of Arnold Hills
Passionate, talented with ship building skills
Placed a small flame in East End hearts
While a King and a Paynter began forging the parts

George Kay's Boys of '23
The first to play at Wembley
The great White Horse for so many a saviour
But Billy's hooves were part of our failure

A modest castle with a scrap of land
The Pratts and Cearns building the stands
Attracting names like Goulden and Walker
And Malcolm Allison, the strategic talker

The pepper pots of Phil Cassettari
The betting slips of Lou Macari
This old place has seen it all
With entertaining football the clarion call

Brooking's right foot, Bonzo's heart
Brooking's left foot, Cottee's start
Endless chapters to chapter's end
No more the venue for family and friend

Hurst's half dozen and Watson's record
The stars remembered, the hopeless heckled
John Bond's hat-trick, Pottsy's goal
And the greatest judgement of captain Noel

Boy oh boy that Bobby Moore
Played football like never seen before
All our hearts hang on his name
The greatest defender of the beautiful game

The highest high from Alan Sealey
The fiasco surrounding Omoyinmi
But Boyce and Taylor and Brooking's head
Have ensured our immortality instead

A rabbit and stag have taken the field
A World Cup trio our Academy did yield
Mad Dogs and Psychos have raised the blood
A Terminator left many slain in the mud

Broken legs and punctured lungs
Fisticuffs and vile tongues
Careers shattered by one desperate lunge
Bill and Rob Jenkins' magic sponge

The best of Bonds
The worst of bonds
And alas the best of Banks
But what was best, the slaying of Leeds?
Or the humiliation of the Mancs?

Switch off the lights
Of those famous cup nights
But preserve Keith Robson's goal
File it next to Kenny Brown's and the mercurial Di Canio

Devonshire cream and Shea delight
Towering Parkes under towering floodlight
The valuable eye of Wally St Pier
The valuable high of a Black Lion beer

Charlo and Clyde and Coker too
Pioneering blacks who managed to cut through
All hold a special place in our hearts
But endured the bananas and racist chants

The Boys of 86 came close
But were pipped by the great King Kenny
We'll never forget the 4-0 at Chelsea
And a playboy called McAvennie

Fenton's Furies did the trick
With Muzzie, Keeble and the great Johnny Dick
Redknapp signed the United Nations
But still no trophy celebrations

Cole and Rio and young Lampard too
All signed for others but what can you do?
The game is bankrupt although worth a mint
The players all wealthy but loyally skint

GJERMUND HOLT captures the setting sun over the south-east corner of the Bobby Moore South Stand.

By TIM CRANE (Author of They Played with Bobby Moore – The West Ham Years)

To think they all cried when Hooper was sold
To Cullis' Wolves in the old black-and-gold
At least we still had our beloved ground
For our happy Hammers to run around

They'll tear up the turf, torn up by Ruffell
And viewed by kings and queens
Hitler failed to destroy the memory
So preserve what you have seen

We've had some keepers come and go
Gregory, Standen and the Czech Miklosko
Adrian thrilled with his penalty antics
But unhook the nets and take down the sticks
Forever

We've swayed and floated to the Bubbles song
And The Post Horn Gallop for which we still long
Surely these are the best in the land?
Especially when played by the Leyton Silver Band

The greatest opponents were probably Tbilisi
The top ticket tout was definitely Creasey!
But don't rule out Dortmund and Emmerich
Simply unplayable that son of a . . . . . !

Oh Charlie Paynter what would you say?
Is this really and truly the West Ham Way?
A wonderful old community club
Lost in the tumbleweed with no sign of a pub

The Chicken Run where dad and grandad watched
Their favourites in attack
Puddefoot, Watson, Hurst and Pop
No sign of a running track

It's all going, going and gone
They'll use a gavel to move it all on
Legends will grow while nostalgia soars
"I was there behind closed doors"

For crying out loud doesn't anyone care?
Hufton's and Budgie's ashes are there!
Along with so many claret-and-blue others
Dads and sons and uncles and brothers

It's gone, all gone and will never be back
Let it go or you'll never come back

But before it fades let the true fans sing
A song for the ages – We love the Boleyn…

We love the Boleyn, We love the Boleyn
Bobby Moore played there
We love the Boleyn…

FINAL WORDS

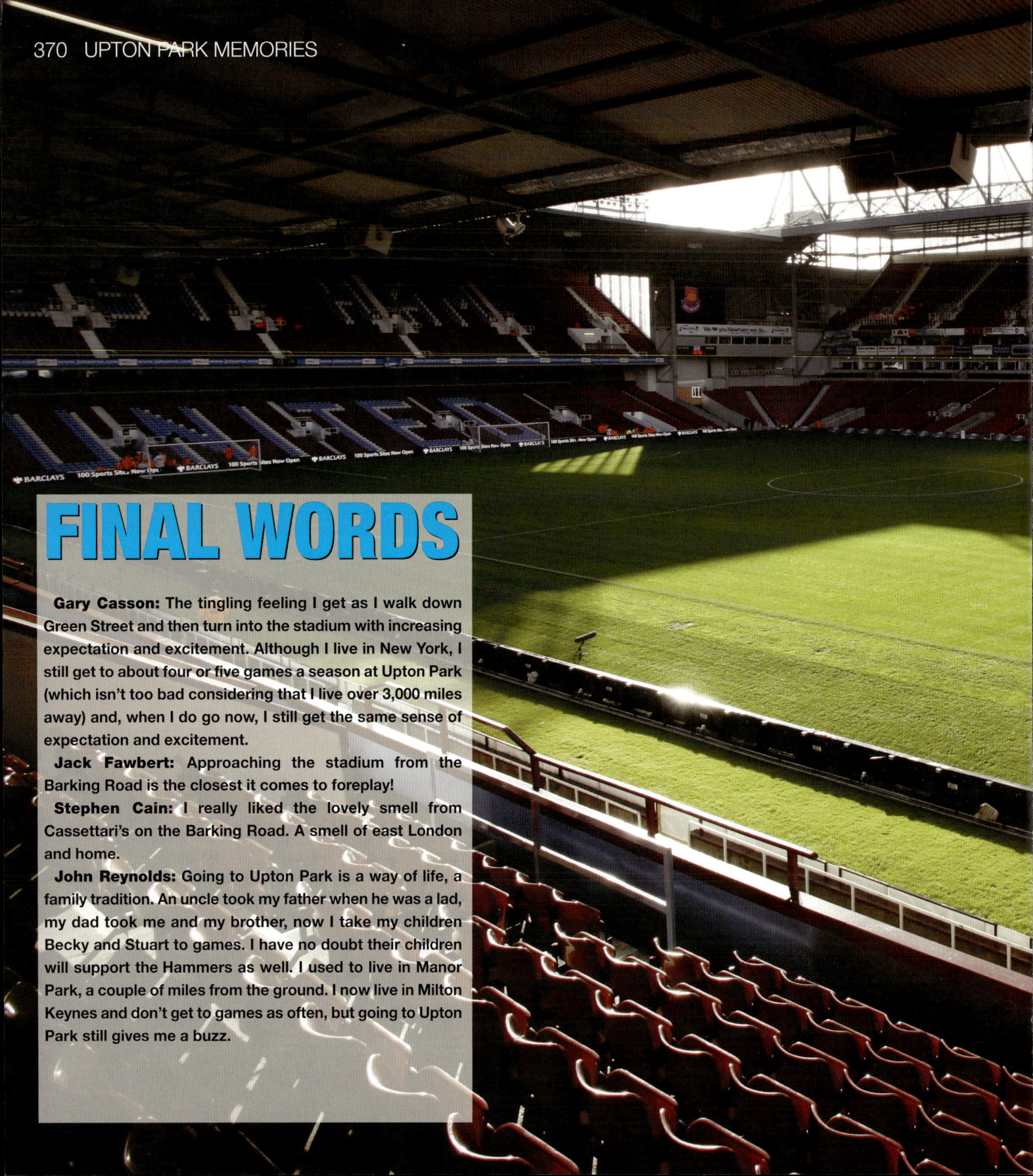

Gary Casson: The tingling feeling I get as I walk down Green Street and then turn into the stadium with increasing expectation and excitement. Although I live in New York, I still get to about four or five games a season at Upton Park (which isn't too bad considering that I live over 3,000 miles away) and, when I do go now, I still get the same sense of expectation and excitement.

Jack Fawbert: Approaching the stadium from the Barking Road is the closest it comes to foreplay!

Stephen Cain: I really liked the lovely smell from Cassettari's on the Barking Road. A smell of east London and home.

John Reynolds: Going to Upton Park is a way of life, a family tradition. An uncle took my father when he was a lad, my dad took me and my brother, now I take my children Becky and Stuart to games. I have no doubt their children will support the Hammers as well. I used to live in Manor Park, a couple of miles from the ground. I now live in Milton Keynes and don't get to games as often, but going to Upton Park still gives me a buzz.

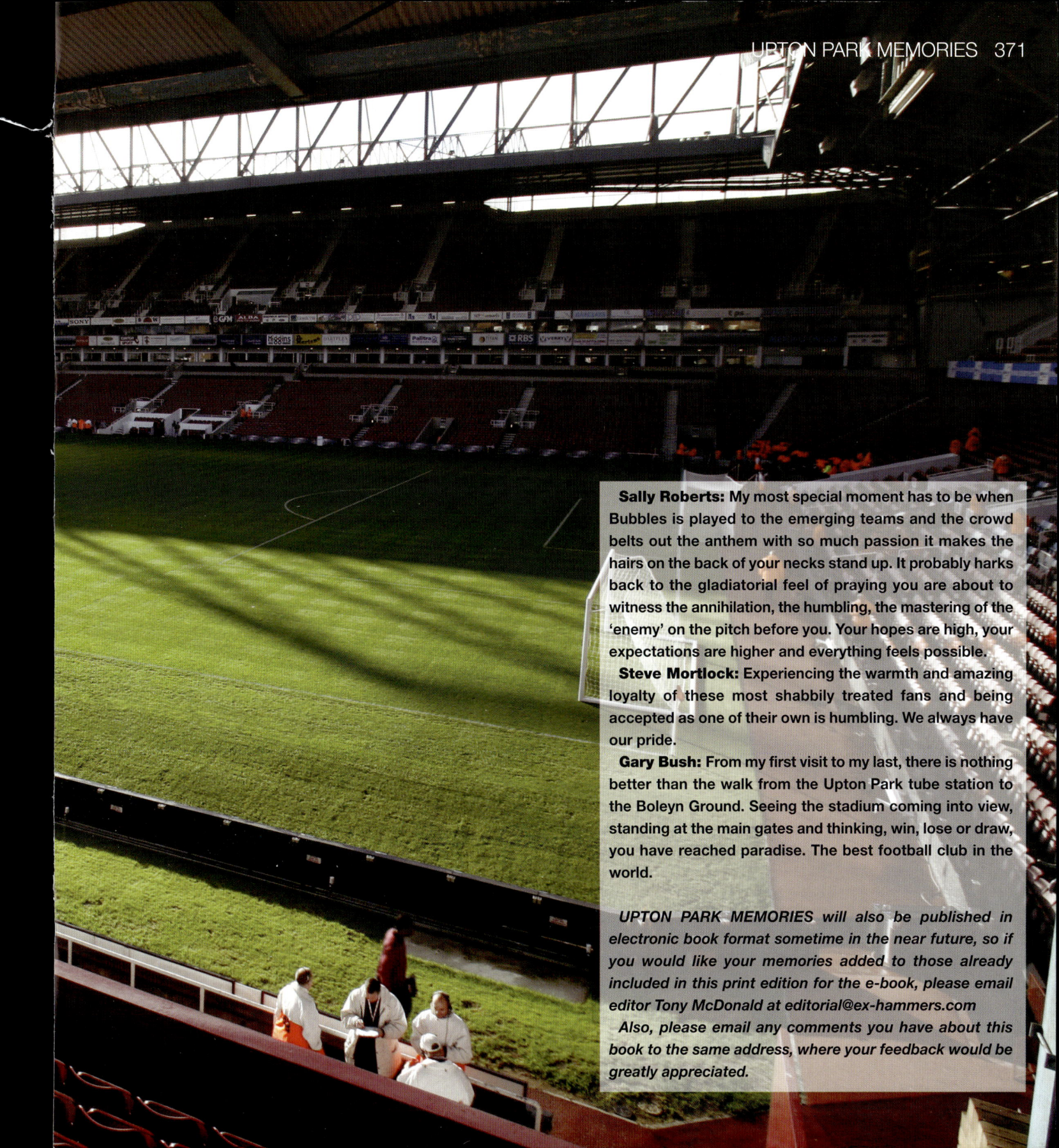

Sally Roberts: My most special moment has to be when Bubbles is played to the emerging teams and the crowd belts out the anthem with so much passion it makes the hairs on the back of your necks stand up. It probably harks back to the gladiatorial feel of praying you are about to witness the annihilation, the humbling, the mastering of the 'enemy' on the pitch before you. Your hopes are high, your expectations are higher and everything feels possible.

Steve Mortlock: Experiencing the warmth and amazing loyalty of these most shabbily treated fans and being accepted as one of their own is humbling. We always have our pride.

Gary Bush: From my first visit to my last, there is nothing better than the walk from the Upton Park tube station to the Boleyn Ground. Seeing the stadium coming into view, standing at the main gates and thinking, win, lose or draw, you have reached paradise. The best football club in the world.

UPTON PARK MEMORIES will also be published in electronic book format sometime in the near future, so if you would like your memories added to those already included in this print edition for the e-book, please email editor Tony McDonald at editorial@ex-hammers.com

Also, please email any comments you have about this book to the same address, where your feedback would be greatly appreciated.

CONTRIBUTORS

We thank the following supporters who took the time and trouble to respond to our questionnaire. There simply wasn't enough space to include every single response submitted by each contributor (which would have led to repetition in many cases) but you and your memories all played a big part in the making of *Upton Park Memories*:

A
Stuart Allen
Malcolm Allison
Graham Arnold
Robert Austen
David Axtell

B
Chris Ball
Robert Banks
David Barnard
Doug Barrett
Charlie Beckwith
Brian Belton
David Bernstein
Steve Blowers
Kirk Blows
Billy Bonds
Stanley Borgonha
Ronnie Boyce
Steve Brackley
Andy Brooker
Sir Trevor Brooking
Eric Brown
Ken Brown
Kenny Brown
Richard Bull
Lee Burch
John Burton
Steve Burton
Gary Bush
Alan Byrne

C
Stephen Cain
Mr P. Cappaert
Gary Casson
Martin Cearns
Alan Chapman
James Clark
Neal Clark
Paul Clayden
Tony Clement
Paul Cockerell
Terry Connelly
Danny Cooper
Liam Corbett
Mike Corbett
Tony Cottee
Kevin Courtney
Tim Crane
Ian Crocker
Colin Crowe
Tony Cullen
Alan Curbishley

D
Iain Dale
Gerard Daly
Alex Dawson
Howard Dawson
Alan Deadman
Brian Dear
Crispin Derby
Steve Derby
Paolo Di Canio
Julian Dicks
Spencer Dodd
Malcolm Downing
Bill Drury
Jim Drury
Matt Drury
Steven Duhig
Joe Durrell
Matt Dynan

E
Mark Edwards

F
Greg Faasen
Dennis Farrow
Jack Fawbert
Tom Fisk
Paul Ford
Steve Foster
Terry Foster
Dan Francis
Jason Fuller

G
Reuben Gane
Jeff Garner
Phil Garner
Bobby George
Steve George
Ed Gillis
Bob Godbolt
John Goff
Richard Goldby
Billy Green
Ernie Gregory
Pete Gumbrell
Peter Gurr

H
Gavin Hadland
Don Hanley
Kristian Hall
Mark Harknett
Michael Harris
Siobhan Hattersley
Ian Haywood
George Hibbins
G. E. Hill
Roger Hillier
Tony Hogg
Gjermund Holt
Simon Hoppit
Tony Hoskins
Alec Huett
David Hughes
Sir Geoff Hurst
Neil Humphreys
Barry Hutton

J
Jimmy Jacob
Roger Jacobsen
Peter Jones

K
Paul Kavanagh
Arne Koellner
Colin Kosky

L
Frank Lampard Snr
John Lawrence
John Ledington
Vic Lindsell
William Lloyd
Chris Ludlow
Peter Lush
John Lyall

M
Jeff MacMahon
Pat Mahoney
Martin McCormick
George McDonald
Jack McDonald
Terry McDonald
Tony McDonald
John McDowell
Eamonn McManus
Ian McMaster
Pat Mahoney
Kevin Mansell
Keith Martin
Mark Matthews
David May
Pete May
David Meagher
Mick Melbourne
Richard Miller
Steven Mitchell
Nick Morgan
Paul Morgan
Joe Morris
Peter Morris
Steve Mortlock
Richard Mumford

N
John Northcutt
Richard Nott
Ian Nunney

O
Jeff O'Brien
Michael Oliver
Gary Osborne

P
Ted Pardoe
Eddie Parker
Mick Pearcey
Kevin Pendegrass
Patrick John Perry
Steve Perry
Martin Peters
John Pocklington
G. Pope
Alan Porter
Syd Porter
John Powles
Derek Price
Gary Price
Dave Purdom
Ian Puxley

R
Kevin Radley
Harry Redknapp
George Reynolds
John Reynolds
Norman Roberts
Sally Roberts
Rob Robinson
Ivan Robeyns
Bryan 'Pop' Robson

Keith Robson
Neil Roper
Terry Roper
Richard Ross
John Ruane

S
Mark Sandell
Dave Satchell
Martin Scholar
Heikki Silvennoinen
Bjorn Arne Smestad
Andrew Smith
Ian Smith
Steve Smith
Dave Spurgeon
David Steadman
Ray Stewart
Jason Stone
Dean Sutherland

T
Marco Taviani
Roy Thomas
Peter Thorne
Trevor Treharne
Peter Tydeman
Liam Tyrell

W
Paul Walker
Colin Walkinshaw
Danny Waller
Peter Waller
John Walsh
Robert Wells
Gary West
Adrian White
Gary White
Graham Wright
Graham White
Jim Wilder
Steve Wilks

We would also like to thank the following supporters who sent in photographs or illustrations. It wasn't possible to use them all (mainly for space reasons but also because some were just not up to it, quality-wise) but, again, your thoughts and efforts were very much appreciated:
Robert Banks, Doug Barrett, Charlie Beckwith, Andrew Brooker, Liam Corbett, Tony Cullen, Mark Edwards, Greg Faasen, Roger Hillier, Chris Ludlow, Keith Martin, Mark Matthews, Ian McMaster, Rob Robinson, Andrew Smith, David Steadman, Liam Tyrell, Adrian White, Graham White.
We apologise if we have overlooked anyone in error.